"Composed in the style of the great medieval *catenae*, this new anthology of patristic commentary on Holy Scripture, conveniently arranged by chapter and verse, will be a valuable resource for prayer, study and proclamation. By calling attention to the rich Christian heritage preceding the separations between East and West and between Protestant and Catholic, this series will perform a major service to the cause of ecumenism."

AVERY CARDINAL DULLES, S.J.
Laurence J. McGinley Professor of Religion and Society
Fordham University

"The initial cry of the Reformation was *ad fontes*—back to the sources! The Ancient Christian Commentary on Scripture is a marvelous tool for the recovery of biblical wisdom in today's church. Not just another scholarly project, the ACCS is a major resource for the renewal of preaching, theology and Christian devotion."

TIMOTHY GEORGE
Dean, Beeson Divinity School, Samford University

"Modern church members often do not realize that they are participants in the vast company of the communion of saints that reaches far back into the past and that will continue into the future, until the kingdom comes. This Commentary should help them begin to see themselves as participants in that redeemed community."

ELIZABETH ACHTEMEIER
Union Professor Emerita of Bible and Homiletics
Union Theological Seminary in Virginia

"Contemporary pastors do not stand alone. We are not the first generation of preachers to wrestle with the challenges of communicating the gospel. The Ancient Christian Commentary on Scripture puts us in conversation with our colleagues from the past, that great cloud of witnesses who preceded us in this vocation. This Commentary enables us to receive their deep spiritual insights, their encouragement and guidance for present-day interpretation and preaching of the Word. What a wonderful addition to any pastor's library!"

WILLIAM H. WILLIMON
Dean of the Chapel and Professor of Christian Ministry
Duke University

"Here is a nonpareil series which reclaims the Bible as the book of the church by making accessible to earnest readers of the twenty-first century the classrooms of Clement of Alexandria and Didymus the Blind, the study and lecture hall of Origen, the cathedrae of Chrysostom and Augustine, the scriptorium of Jerome in his Bethlehem monastery."

GEORGE LAWLESS
Augustinian Patristic Institute and Gregorian University, Rome

"We are pleased to witness publication of the
Ancient Christian Commentary on Scripture. It is most beneficial for us to learn
how the ancient Christians, especially the saints of the church
who proved through their lives their devotion to God and his Word, interpreted
Scripture. Let us heed the witness of those who have gone before us in the faith."

Metropolitan Theodosius
Primate, Orthodox Church in America

"Across Christendom there has emerged a widespread interest
in early Christianity, both at the popular and scholarly level. . . .
Christians of all traditions stand to benefit from this project, especially clergy
and those who study the Bible. Moreover, it will allow us to see how our traditions are
both rooted in the scriptural interpretations of the church fathers while at
the same time seeing how we have developed new perspectives."

Alberto Ferreiro
Professor of History, Seattle Pacific University

"The Ancient Christian Commentary on Scripture fills a long overdue need for scholars and
students of the church fathers. . . . Such information will be of immeasurable
worth to those of us who have felt inundated by contemporary interpreters and novel theories
of the biblical text. We welcome some 'new' insight from the
ancient authors in the early centuries of the church."

H. Wayne House
Professor of Theology and Law
Trinity University School of Law

"Chronological snobbery—the assumption that our ancestors working without benefit of
computers have nothing to teach us—is exposed as nonsense by this magnificent
new series. Surfeited with knowledge but starved of wisdom, many of us are
more than ready to sit at table with our ancestors and listen to their holy
conversations on Scripture. I know I am."

Eugene H. Peterson
Professor Emeritus of Spiritual Theology
Regent College

ANCIENT CHRISTIAN
COMMENTARY on SCRIPTURE

OLD TESTAMENT
V

1-2 KINGS, 1-2 CHRONICLES, EZRA, NEHEMIAH, ESTHER

EDITED BY

MARCO CONTI

IN COLLABORATION WITH
GIANLUCA PILARA

GENERAL EDITOR
THOMAS C. ODEN

InterVarsity Press
Downers Grove, Illinois

InterVarsity Press
P.O. Box 1400, Downers Grove, IL 60515-1426
World Wide Web: www.ivpress.com
E-mail: mail@ivpress.com

InterVarsity Press® is the book-publishing division of InterVarsity Christian Fellowship/USA®, a student movement active on campus at hundreds of universities, colleges and schools of nursing in the United States of America, and a member movement of the International Fellowship of Evangelical Students. For information about local and regional activities, write Public Relations Dept., InterVarsity Christian Fellowship/USA, 6400 Schroeder Rd., P.O. Box 7895, Madison, WI 53707-7895, or visit the IVCF website at <www.intervarsity.org>.

Scripture quotations, unless otherwise noted, are from the Revised Standard Version of the Bible, copyright 1946, 1952, 1971 by the Division of Christian Education of the National Council of the Churches of Christ in the U.S.A., and are used by permission.

Selected excerpts from Fathers of the Church: A New Translation, ©1947-, used by permission of The Catholic University of America Press, Washington, D.C. Full bibliographic information on volumes of Fathers of the Church may be found in the Bibliography of Works in English Translation.

Selected excerpts from John Cassian, Conferences, translated and annotated by Boniface Ramsey, O.P., Ancient Christian Writers 57, ©1997 by Boniface Ramsey, O.P.; Cassiodorus, Explanation of the Psalms, translated and edited by P. G. Walsh, Ancient Christian Writers 51, 52 and 53, ©1990, 1991 by P. G. Walsh; Origen: An Exhortation to Martyrdom, Prayer and Selected Works, translation and introduction by Rowan A. Greer, The Classics of Western Spirituality, ©1979 by Paulist Press; Origen: Prayer, Exhortation to Martyrdom, translated and annotated by John J. O'Meara, Ancient Christian Writers 19, ©1954 by Rev. Johannes Quasten, S.T.D., and Joseph C. Plumpe, Ph.D; The Poems of St. Paulinus of Nola, translated and edited by P. G. Walsh, Ancient Christian Writers 40, ©1975 by Johannes Quasten, S.T.D., Rev. Walter J. Burghardt, S.J., and Thomas Comerford Lawler; The Sermons of St. Maximus of Turin, translated and annotated by Boniface Ramsey, O.P., Ancient Christian Writers 50, ©1989 by Boniface Ramsey, O.P. Reprinted by permission of Paulist Press, Inc. <www. paulistpress.com>.

Selected excerpts from Early Christian Fathers, translated by Cyril C. Richardson, The Library of Christian Classics 1, ©1953; Early Latin Theology, translated by S. L. Greenslade, The Library of Christian Classics 5, ©1956. Used by permission of SCM and Westminster John Knox Presses, London, England, and Louisville, Kentucky.

Selected excerpts from The Works of Saint Augustine: A Translation for the 21st Century, edited by John E. Rotelle, ©1990-. Used by permission of the Augustinian Heritage Institute.

Selected excerpts from Bede the Venerable, On the Temple, translated by Sean Connolly, Translated Texts for Historians 21, ©1995; On Ezra and Nehemiah, translated by Scott DeGregorio, Translated Texts for Historians 47, ©2006. Used by permission of Liverpool University Press, Liverpool, England.

Selected excerpts from Ephrem the Syrian, Commentary on Tatian's Diatessaron, translated and edited by C. McCarthy, Journal of Semitic Studies Supplement 2, ©1993. Used by permission of Oxford University Press for the University of Manchester.

Selected excerpts from Bede the Venerable, Commentary on the Acts of the Apostles, translated by Lawrence T. Martin, Cistercian Studies 117, ©1989; Homilies on the Gospels, translated by Lawrence T. Martin and David Hurst, Cistercian Studies 110 and 111, ©1991; The Syriac Fathers on Prayer and the Spiritual Life, translated by Sebastian Brock, Cistercian Studies 101, ©1987.

Every effort has been made to trace and contact copyright holders for additional materials quoted in this book. The authors will be pleased to rectify any omissions in future editions if notified by copyright holders.

Cover photograph: Scala/Art Resource, New York. View of the apse. S. Vitale, Ravenna, Italy.

Spine photograph: Byzantine Collection, Dumbarton Oaks, Washington D.C. Pendant cross (gold and enamel). Constantinople, late sixth century.

ISBN 978-0-8308-1475-6

Printed in the United States of America ∞

Library of Congress Cataloging-in-Publication Data

1-2 Kings, 1-2 Chronicles, Ezra, Nehemiah, Esther/edited by Marco
Conti.
    p. cm.—(Ancient Christian commentary on scripture. Old
    Testament; 5)
Includes bibliographical references and index.
ISBN 978-0-8308-1475-6 (cloth: alk. paper)
1. Bible. O.T. Kings—Commentaries. 2. Bible. O.T.
Chronicles—Commentaries. 3. Bible. O.T. Ezra—Commentaries. 4.
Bible. O.T. Nehemiah—Commentaries. 5. Bible. O.T.
Esther—Commentaries. I. Conti, Marco. II. Title: First-Second
Kings, First-Second Chronicles, Ezra, Nehemiah, Esther.
  BS1335.53.A13 2008
  222'.07709—dc22
            2008006460

P	25	24	23	22	21	20	19	18	17	16	15	14	13	12	11	10	9	8	7	6	5	4	3	2	1
Y	30	29	28	27	26	25	24	23	22	21	20	19	18	17	16	15	14	13	12	11	10	09	08		

CONTENTS

General Introduction

The Ancient Christian Commentary on Scripture has as its goal the revitalization of Christian teaching based on classical Christian exegesis, the intensified study of Scripture by lay persons who wish to think with the early church about the canonical text, and the stimulation of Christian historical, biblical, theological and pastoral scholars toward further inquiry into scriptural interpretation by ancient Christian writers.

The time frame of these documents spans seven centuries of exegesis, from Clement of Rome to John of Damascus, from the end of the New Testament era to A.D. 750, including the Venerable Bede.

Lay readers are asking how they might study sacred texts under the instruction of the great minds of the ancient church. This commentary has been intentionally prepared for a general lay audience of nonprofessionals who study the Bible regularly and who earnestly wish to have classic Christian observation on the text readily available to them. The series is targeted to anyone who wants to reflect and meditate with the early church about the plain sense, theological wisdom and moral meaning of particular Scripture texts.

A commentary dedicated to allowing ancient Christian exegetes to speak for themselves will refrain from the temptation to fixate endlessly upon contemporary criticism. Rather, it will stand ready to provide textual resources from a distinguished history of exegesis that has remained massively inaccessible and shockingly disregarded during the last century. We seek to make available to our present-day audiences the multicultural, multilingual, transgenerational resources of the early ecumenical Christian tradition.

Preaching at the end of the first millennium focused primarily on the text of Scripture as understood by the earlier esteemed tradition of comment, largely converging on those writers that best reflected classic Christian consensual thinking. Preaching at the end of the second millennium has reversed that pattern. It has so forgotten most of these classic comments that they are vexing to find anywhere, and even when located they are often available only in archaic editions and inadequate translations. The preached word in our time has remained largely bereft of previously influential patristic inspiration. Recent scholarship has so focused attention upon post-Enlightenment historical and literary methods that it has left this longing largely unattended and unserviced.

This series provides the pastor, exegete, student and lay reader with convenient means to see what Athanasius or John Chrysostom or the desert fathers and mothers had to say about a particular text for preaching, for study and for meditation. There is an emerging awareness among Catholic, Protestant and Orthodox laity that vital biblical preaching and spiritual formation need deeper grounding beyond the scope of the historical-critical orientations that have governed biblical studies in our day.

Hence this work is directed toward a much broader audience than the highly technical and specialized scholarly field of patristic studies. The audience is not limited to the university scholar concentrating on the study of the history of the transmission of the text or to those with highly focused philological interests in textual morphology or historical-critical issues. Though these are crucial concerns for specialists, they are not the paramount interests of this series.

This work is a Christian Talmud. The Talmud is a Jewish collection of rabbinic arguments and comments on the Mishnah, which epitomized the laws of the Torah. The Talmud originated in approximately the same period that the patristic writers were commenting on texts of the Christian tradition. Christians from the late patristic age through the medieval period had documents analogous to the Jewish Talmud and Midrash (Jewish commentaries) available to them in the *glossa ordinaria* and catena traditions, two forms of compiling extracts of patristic exegesis. In Talmudic fashion the sacred text of Christian Scripture was thus clarified and interpreted by the classic commentators.

The Ancient Christian Commentary on Scripture has venerable antecedents in medieval exegesis of both eastern and western traditions, as well as in the Reformation tradition. It offers for the first time in this century the earliest Christian comments and reflections on the Old and New Testaments to a modern audience. Intrinsically an ecumenical project, this series is designed to serve Protestant, Catholic and Orthodox lay, pastoral and scholarly audiences.

In cases where Greek, Latin, Syriac and Coptic texts have remained untranslated into English, we provide new translations. Wherever current English translations are already well rendered, they will be utilized, but if necessary their language will be brought up to date. We seek to present fresh dynamic equivalency translations of long-neglected texts which historically have been regarded as authoritative models of biblical interpretation.

These foundational sources are finding their way into many public libraries and into the core book collections of many pastors and lay persons. It is our intent and the publisher's commitment to keep the whole series in print for many years to come.

Thomas C. Oden
General Editor

A Guide to Using This Commentary

Several features have been incorporated into the design of this commentary. The following comments are intended to assist readers in making full use of this volume.

Pericopes of Scripture

The scriptural text has been divided into pericopes, or passages, usually several verses in length. Each of these pericopes is given a heading, which appears at the beginning of the pericope. For example, the first pericope in the commentary on 1 Kings is "1:1-4 David's Old Age." This heading is followed by the Scripture passage quoted in the Revised Standard Version (RSV) across the full width of the page. The Scripture passage is provided for the convenience of readers, but it is also in keeping with medieval patristic commentaries, in which the citations of the Fathers were arranged around the text of Scripture.

Overviews

Following each pericope of text is an overview of the patristic comments on that pericope. The format of this overview varies within the volumes of this series, depending on the requirements of the specific book of Scripture. The function of the overview is to provide a brief summary of all the comments to follow. It tracks a reasonably cohesive thread of argument among patristic comments, even though they are derived from diverse sources and generations. Thus the summaries do not proceed chronologically or by verse sequence. Rather they seek to rehearse the overall course of the patristic comment on that pericope.

We do not assume that the commentators themselves anticipated or expressed a formally received cohesive argument but rather that the various arguments tend to flow in a plausible, recognizable pattern. Modern readers can thus glimpse aspects of continuity in the flow of diverse exegetical traditions representing various generations and geographical locations.

Topical Headings

An abundance of varied patristic comment is available for each pericope of these letters. For this reason we have broken the pericopes into two levels. First is the verse with its topical heading. The patristic comments are then focused on aspects of each verse, with topical headings summarizing the essence of the patristic comment by evoking a key phrase, metaphor or idea. This feature provides a bridge by which modern readers can enter into the heart of the patristic comment.

Identifying the Patristic Texts

Following the topical heading of each section of comment, the name of the patristic commentator is given. An English translation of the patristic comment is then provided. This is immediately followed by the title of the patristic work and the textual reference—either by book, section and subsection or by book-and-verse references.

The Footnotes

Readers who wish to pursue a deeper investigation of the patristic works cited in this commentary will find the footnotes especially valuable. A footnote number directs the reader to the notes at the bottom of the right-hand column, where in addition to other notations (clarifications or biblical cross references) one will find information on English translations (where available) and standard original-language editions of the work cited. An abbreviated citation (normally citing the book, volume and page number) of the work is provided. A key to the abbreviations is provided on page xv. Where there is any serious ambiguity or textual problem in the selection, we have tried to reflect the best available textual tradition.

Where original language texts have remained untranslated into English, we provide new translations. Wherever current English translations are already well rendered, they are utilized, but where necessary they are stylistically updated. A single asterisk (*) indicates that a previous English translation has been updated to modern English or amended for easier reading. The double asterisk (**) indicates either that a new translation has been provided or that some extant translation has been significantly amended. We have standardized spellings and made grammatical variables uniform so that our English references will not reflect the odd spelling variables of the older English translations. For ease of reading we have in some cases edited out superfluous conjunctions.

For the convenience of computer database users the digital database references are provided to either the Thesaurus Linguae Graecae (Greek texts) or to the Cetedoc (Latin texts) in the appendix found on pages 400-405 and in the bibliography found on pages 427-32.

Abbreviations

ACW	Ancient Christian Writers: The Works of the Fathers in Translation. Mahwah, N.J.: Paulist Press, 1946-.
AHSIS	*The Ascetical Homilies of Saint Isaac the Syrian.* Boston, Mass.: Holy Transfiguration Monastery, 1984.
ANF	A. Roberts and J. Donaldson, eds. Ante-Nicene Fathers. 10 vols. Buffalo, N.Y.: Christian Literature, 1885-1896. Reprint, Grand Rapids, Mich.: Eerdmans, 1951-1956; Reprint, Peabody, Mass.: Hendrickson, 1994.
ARL	St. Athanasius. *The Resurrection Letters.* Paraphrased and introduced by Jack N. Sparks. Nashville: Thomas Nelson, 1979.
CCL	Corpus Christianorum. Series Latina. Turnhout, Belgium: Brepols, 1953-.
Cetedoc	Centre de Traitement Electronique des Documents.
CS	Cistercian Studies. Kalamazoo, Mich.: Cistercian Publications, 1973-.
CSCO	Corpus Scriptorum Christianorum Orientalium. Louvain, Belgium, 1903-.
CSEL	Corpus Scriptorum Ecclesiasticorum Latinorum. Vienna, 1866-.
ECTD	C. McCarthy, trans. and ed. *Saint Ephrem's Commentary on Tatian's Diatessaron: An English Translation of Chester Beatty Syriac MS 709. Journal of Semitic Studies* Supplement 2. Oxford: Oxford University Press for the University of Manchester, 1993.
ECS	Pauline Allen, et al., eds. Early Christian Studies. Strathfield, Australia: St. Paul's Publications, 2001-.
ESOO	J. A. Assemani, ed. *Sancti Patris nostri Ephraem Syri Opera omnia.* Rome, 1737.
FC	Fathers of the Church: A New Translation. Washington, D.C.: Catholic University of America Press, 1947-.
GCS	Die griechischen christlichen Schriftsteller der ersten Jahrhunderte. Berlin: Akademie-Verlag, 1897-.
HOP	Ephrem the Syrian. *Hymns on Paradise.* Translated by S. Brock. Crestwood, N.Y.: St. Vladimir's Seminary Press, 1990.
JDDI	St. John of Damascus. *On the Divine Images.* Translated by David Anderson. Crestwood, N.Y.: St. Vladimir's Seminary Press, 1980.
LCC	J. Baillie et al., eds. The Library of Christian Classics. 26 vols. Philadelphia: Westminster, 1953-1966.
LF	A Library of Fathers of the Holy Catholic Church Anterior to the Division of the East and West. Translated by members of the English Church. 44 vols. Oxford: John Henry Parker, 1800-1881.
MFC	Message of the Fathers of the Church. Edited by Thomas Halton. Collegeville, Minn.: The Liturgical Press, 1983-.
NPNF	P. Schaff et al., eds. A Select Library of the Nicene and Post-Nicene Fathers of the Christian Church. 2 series (14 vols. each). Buffalo, N.Y.: Christian Literature, 1887-1894; Reprint, Grand Rapids, Mich.: Eerdmans, 1952-1956; Reprint, Peabody, Mass.: Hendrickson, 1994.
OSW	*Origen: An Exhortation to Martyrdom, Prayer and Selected Writings.* Translated by Rowan A. Greer with Preface by Hans Urs von Balthasar. The Classics of Western Spirituality. New York: Paulist Press, 1979.
PDCW	*Pseudo-Dionysius: The Complete Works.* Translated by Colm Luibheid. The Classics of Western Spirituality. New York: Paulist Press, 1987.

PG   J.-P. Migne, ed. Patrologiae cursus completus. Series graeca. 166 vols. Paris: Migne, 1857-1886.

PL   J.-P. Migne, ed. Patrologiae cursus completus. Series latina. 221 vols. Paris: Migne, 1844-1864.

POG   Eusebius. *The Proof of the Gospel.* 2 vols. Translated by W. J. Ferrar. London: SPCK, 1920; Reprint, Grand Rapids, Mich.: Baker, 1981.

PS   R. Graffin, ed. Patrologia cursus completus. Series syriaca. 3 vols. Paris: Firmin-Didot et socii, 1894-1926.

PSt   Patristic Studies. Washington, D.C.: Catholic University of America Press, 1922-.

PTS   Patristische Texte und Studien. New York: de Gruyter, 1964-.

RTAM   *Recherches de Théologie ancienne et médiévale.* Louvain, Belgium: Abbaye Du Mont César, 1929-1996.

SC   H. de Lubac, J. Daniélou et al., eds. Sources Chrétiennes. Paris: Editions du Cerf, 1941-.

TLG   L. Berkowitz and K. Squiter, eds. *Thesaurus Linguae Graecae: Canon of Greek Authors and Works.* 2nd ed. Oxford: Oxford University Press, 1986.

TTH   G. Clark, M. Gibson and M. Whitby, eds. Translated Texts for Historians. Liverpool: Liverpool University Press, 1985-.

WSA   J. E. Rotelle, ed. *Works of St. Augustine: A Translation for the Twenty-First Century.* Hyde Park, N.Y.: New City Press, 1995.

Introduction to 1-2 Kings, 1-2 Chronicles, Ezra, Nehemiah and Esther

The commentaries included in this volume cover the second part of the so-called historical books of the Bible.[1] What is immediately evident to the reader is that the narrative materials and topics that form these books are extremely varied and complicated, as they concern an extended period of the ancient history of Israel and different crucial events that follow each other at a fast pace. Modern scholarship, through its mainly historical and philological approach, has been able to ascertain that while these books are linked by a shared historical focus, they may be distinguished by their ideological points of view.

The Deuteronomic and Chronicler's Outlooks

In the books of Samuel and Kings, modern scholars have noticed and emphasized how the covenant, which God has made with the people of Israel, is clearly regarded as a reciprocal engagement, and any infringement of this covenant is necessarily and severely punished by God while obedience is rewarded with blessings. In this regard, contemporary biblical scholarship has recognized that Kings conforms to the theology and ideology of Deuteronomy, where these terms of covenant are plainly expressed for the first time. This is confirmed by the fact that our historical books appear to follow consistently the Deuteronomic Code[2] when they express their judgment on each king or character described in the biblical narrative. Therefore those characters who conform to the Deuteronomic Code are praised, and those who disobey it are inevitably condemned. Besides this general outlook, the book of Deuteronomy has a central role in 2 Kings, where the biblical narrative describes its discovery in the temple during the reign of Josiah.[3]

Chronicles, Ezra and Nehemiah, on the other hand, share a perspective that differs from the Deuteronomistic vision, one that has been labeled the Chronicler's History. This has been observed in a common vocabulary and ideas, such as the building and worship of the temple, priestly service and the restoration of Israel. Whether this perspective was originally due to a common author or editor, or to a later editor, is a matter of debate.

---

[1]The first part is constituted by the books of Joshua, Judges, Ruth and 1-2 Samuel: see the commentary in this series by J. R. Franke (ACCS OT 4; Downers Grove, IL: InterVarsity Press, 2005).

[2]The so-called Deuteronomic Code envisions a complete devotion to Yahweh as Israel's only God and views the obligation to perform all sacrifices in the temple of Jerusalem as the most important and essential terms in the covenant between God and the people. All the individuals who receive praise in 1-2 King are people who comply with these terms.

[3]See 2 Kings 22:8-20; 2 Chron 34:15-28; P. R. Ackroyd and C. F. Evans, eds., *The Cambridge History of the Bible* (Cambridge: Cambridge University Press, 1970), 120-21.

Patristic Exegesis

The fathers of the church were not interested in a philological and historical reading of the Bible, so their exegesis did not take into consideration the Deuteronomic or Chronicler's outlook, which link or separate the historical books included in the present volume, but moved along different lines of interpretation. Their exegesis, as has been amply discussed in many volumes of this series,[4] was mostly based on a typological-allegorical[5] and/or moral interpretation. Consequently their reading of the historical books was not comprehensive and systematic but concentrated on those single episodes, where a typological or moral interpretation was possible, while those other events described in the biblical narrative which did not fit in with their exegetical principles were neglected. This interpretative approach, as we will see, is present not only in the incidental comments on the historical books made by the Fathers in their homilies or doctrinal works but also in the exegetical commentaries on single books.

1-2 Kings

Certain narratives included in 1-2 Kings offered the Fathers abundant material for a typological or moral interpretation. As a consequence, their discussion and analysis constantly concentrate on these passages, while other large sections of the biblical text, as we have already hinted above, were mostly neglected.

The episodes of 1-2 Kings that the Fathers considered to be the most suitable to a typological interpretation were those concerning King Solomon (his election,[6] his famous judgments,[7] his construction of the temple and the royal palace[8]), the prophet Elijah[9] and the prophet Elisha.[10] The episodes that offered the most apt materials for moral meditation were those concerning the fate of kings and powerful people, such as Ahab,[11] the man of God,[12] Jehu[13] and Josiah.[14]

Greek Fathers

All the passages from the Greek Fathers that are included in our commentary on 1-2 Kings are taken from exegetical works on other books of the Bible, or from doctrinal and critical works, because no standard Greek commentary on 1-2 Kings survives. The only work that comprehensively comments on 1-2 Kings and 1-2 Chronicles is *De Quaestionibus Ambiguis in Libros Regnorum et Paralipomenon*[15] by Theodoret of Cyr, to which we can only add two very similar catenae, the one by Procopius of Gaza, which has been only partly

---

[4]See, for instance, Franke (ACCS OT 4; Downers Grove, Ill.: InterVarsity Press, 2005), xvii-xxix; J. T. Lienhard (ACCS OT 3; Downers Grove, Ill.: InterVarsity Press, 2001), xv-xxxii.

[5]By "typological" we indicate a kind of interpretation that sees in the events described in the Old Testament a foreshadowing of those of the New Testament, that is, a foreshadowing of the advent of Christ and the salvation of humankind through him.

[6]1 Kings 2:1-46.

[7]1 Kings 3:1-28.

[8]1 Kings 5:1—7:51.

[9]1 Kings 17:1—21:29; 2 Kings 1:1—2:13.

[10]2 Kings 2:14—8:15; 13:14-21.

[11]1 Kings 16:29—22:40.

[12]1 Kings 13:1-34.

[13]2 Kings 9:1—10:35.

[14]2 Kings 22:1—23:30.

[15]"On the uncertain questions in the Books of the Kings (that is, 1-2 Samuel and 1-2 Kings) and the Chronicles," see *Clavis Patrum Graecorum* 3:201 n. 6201; PG 80:527-858.

published and is mostly available in a Latin translation and not in its original Greek text,[16] and the one edited in the eighteenth century[17] by Nikephoros Hieromonachos Theotokis. The work by Theodoret, however, cannot be considered to be an organic and systematic commentary, as it only discusses and tries to explain those passages that are more difficult or uncertain for the reader. By contrast, the catenae gather together passages from many different authors (in our case from twenty-seven authors) and inevitably appear to be patchy and often arbitrary in their selections, even though they are precious in preserving passages from important patristic commentators that otherwise would have been completely lost.

Justin Martyr (c. 110-165). The only comment by Justin on the book of Kings[18] that we have been able to trace is from his *Dialogue with Trypho*. In it the great Christian philosopher demonstrates once more how his exegesis of the Old Testament is mostly typological. The piece of wood thrown by Elisha into the river typifies the cross, while the water foreshadows salvation through baptism.

Clement of Alexandria (c. 150-215). In Clement we see a further development of the typological vision of Justin. He not only considers the Old Testament as a preparation and foreshadowing of the truths of the New Testament but also notices in all the Scriptures two levels of comprehension: the first is immediate and open to all; the second is more profound and reserved only for the perfect Christian. As a consequence, his interpretation of the events described in 1-2 Kings is always attentive to these two levels of comprehension. On the one hand, there is an immediate message to all Christians, which is mostly moral and typological; on the other, there is a more profound message that unveils the secrets of the divine wisdom of Christ.

Origen (c. 185-253). As far as we know, Origen never wrote any specific homily or commentary on 1-2 Kings (3-4 Kings or Kingdoms according to the Septuagint).[19] All the passages by Origen included in this volume are taken from his doctrinal works (*On Prayer, Against Celsus, On First Principles*) or from exegetical commentaries on other books of the Bible (*Homilies on Genesis, Leviticus, John*). The interpretation appears to be substantially allegorical, according to the critical trend[20] that was brought to perfection by Origen. The events reported in the biblical narrative are therefore seen as a foreshadowing of the advent of Christ and the doctrine of the New Testament (typological interpretation); symbols of truths that are not immediately visible; and figurative messages and admonitions to Christians. Inside this allegorical vision Origen is constantly able to develop a consistent moral reflection which makes the biblical text of the Old Testament a topical instrument of meditation for the Christian.

Methodius (c. 250-311). Methodius, who criticized Origen for his theory on the pre-existence of the soul and his mostly spiritualizing notion of the resurrection of the body, appears to follow Origen's allegorical method in his exegesis of the Bible. In 2 Kings 20:7-11 he sees the fig tree and its fruits as symbols of the Holy Spirit and its love for humankind, and therefore he interprets the healing of King Hezekiah as a result of the love of the Holy Spirit.

---

[16]See *Clavis Patrum Graecorum* 3:388 n. 7430; PG 87:1147-220.

[17]Nikephoros Hieromonachos Theotokis, *Catenae in Octateucum et Libros Regnorum*, 2 vols. (Leipzig, 1772-1773). In this edition all the available Greek fragments of the catena compiled by Procopius of Gaza are also included.

[18]2 Kings 6:4-7.

[19]Origen wrote homilies on 1 Kings or Kingdoms (= 1 Samuel), of which only those on 1 Samuel 1-2 and 1 Samuel 28 are extant; see *Clavis Patrum Graecorum* 1:148 n. 1423.

[20]The so-called Alexandrian school of exegesis.

Athanasius (c. 295-373). Following the typical allegorical and typological trend of Alexandrian exegesis, Athanasius sees that the unity of Scripture is founded on the figure of Christ. Therefore he follows this principle in his interpretation of the narrative of 1-2 Kings. This is particularly evident in his comment on 1 Kings 1:19-26, in which he compares the figures and roles of Solomon and Christ.

Cyril of Jerusalem (c. 315-387). The most important work of Cyril, the Catechetical Lectures, is concerned with the preparation of the faithful for the sacraments of baptism, confirmation and Eucharist. Consequently, Cyril's meditations on 1-2 Kings have both a typological approach, as he sees in the biblical narrative a foreshadowing of the salvation in Christ (e.g., in 1 Kings 8:27) which the neophytes are about to receive, and a moral approach, as he finds in the events related in the Scripture examples of conduct for new Christians (e.g., in 2 Kings 25:1-11).

Basil the Great (c. 330-379). Even though clear traces of allegorical exegesis in the style of Origen are obvious in the work of Basil,[21] with this author we notice a shift to a more literal interpretation of the Scripture in which the moral aspect becomes essential. In his comment on 1 Kings 12:14, Basil sees the biblical narrative as a direct admonition to all rulers, who should avoid exalting themselves with secular honors.

Gregory of Nazianzus (c. 330-390). Gregory was a close friend of Basil for most of his life and shared his views about exegesis, even though he never wrote any systematic commentary on any section of the Bible. In his examination of Solomon's wisdom (1 Kings 3:12; 4:29-34) he shows a deeply philosophical approach in which he stresses the limitations of human nature in the comprehension of God and the universe and asserts that meekness and humility are the principles on which human wisdom must be founded.

Apostolic Constitutions (c. end of the fourth century). The Apostolic Constitutions is an anonymous work that reached its present form at the end of the fourth century but reworks materials and writings that date from the first century, such as the *Didache,* to the early fourth, such as the *Didascalia Apostolorum.* Due to the character of this work, which is mostly liturgical, the exegetical approach is substantially moral: the examples of punished wickedness in 1-2 Kings serve as an admonition to the faithful as do the examples of repentance (2 Kings 21:1-17, 19-24).

John Chrysostom (c. 344-407). Considering the extent of his literary output and the complexity of his works, Chrysostom is undoubtedly the most important representative of the Antiochian school of exegesis. This school can be defined, in a very simple way, as the main opponent to the Alexandrian school which had in Origen its most typical exponent and utilized allegory and typology in its exegetical principles. In contrast, Chrysostom used in his comments a mostly literal interpretation of the Scripture, where typological hints are obvious but always quite concise, while the moral and pastoral contents amply prevail. These are evident in all his comments on 1-2 Kings, where he sometimes recognizes how episodes of the biblical narrative foreshadow the advent of Christ, but where he mostly concentrates on those episodes that can be useful to edify the faithful and especially to awaken moral potentials through powerful examples.

Cyril of Alexandria (c. 370-444). A complete commentary on 1-4 Kings or Kingdoms[22] (i.e., 1-2 Samuel and 1-2 Kings) is attributed by manuscript tradition to Cyril of Alexandria. However, R. Devreesse has

---

[21]See especially his *Philocalia.*
[22]PG 69:679-98.

demonstrated that these are extracts from other exegetical and doctrinal works by Cyril, which were gathered by a medieval compiler under the title of *In Regum Libri I-IV*.[23] The exegesis of Cyril represents a late example of the Alexandrian tradition, so that the allegorical and typological interpretations prevail, even though he introduces some limitations and does not accept as a whole Origen's spiritual and christological interpretation of the Old Testament.

Theodoret of Cyr (c. 393-466). As we have mentioned, Theodoret is the author of the only extant Greek commentary covering 1-2 Kings and 1-2 Chronicles: the *De Quaestionibus Ambiguis in Libros Regnorum et Paralipomenon*. However, this is by no means a systematic commentary, as it concentrates on those passages that are confusing or difficult for the reader and tries to clarify and explain them. The exegetical approach of Theodoret is that typical of the Antiochian school, so that in his comments a literal interpretation prevails. However, Theodoret often tends to expand the typological components concerning Christ, which are present in a concise and sparse form in the traditional Antiochian exegesis, and by developing them, he introduces certain innovations in his commentaries.

John the Monk (c. the eighth century). This author, who is otherwise unknown, has been identified with the great theologian and poet John of Damascus (c. 670-749).[24] In his hymn he emphasizes how Christ causes the conversion of Elisha in 1 Kings 19:19-20, so that Elisha does not appear to be a type of Christ but a mere instrument of Christ's power.

Latin Fathers

In the context of Latin patristic exegesis we find a situation that does not significantly differ from that concerning the Greek fathers. No standard complete commentary on 1-2 Kings written in the patristic age (c. second through eighth centuries) survives, so that the majority of the patristic passages that we have selected come from doctrinal treatises or exegetical works on other books of the Bible. However, the material on 1-2 Kings available from the Latin fathers is in general much larger than that available in Greek. To these abundant incidental comments we can add a partial but extremely detailed commentary by Bede on the temple (1 Kings 5:1–7:51) and two early medieval complete commentaries by Rabanus and Walafridius, which do not differ substantially in their style and purpose from Bede's work. Therefore, we can assert with certainty that interest in our historical books was higher among the Latin fathers than the Greek. Many possible reasons can be brought forward to explain this greater interest. I believe that it is due to the situation of the Western empire in the fifth and sixth centuries. When the traditional Roman administrative and political organization of the state collapsed, many Latin authors living in the failing Western empire were led by the historical events of their age to meditate on the destruction and reconstruction of the reigns of Israel and Judah which are described in detail in Kings, Chronicles, Ezra and Nehemiah. Most of the comments are not from the early Latin patristic age (the second through fourth centuries) but from the later one (fifth and sixth centuries), which coincides with the end of the Roman Empire and a period of extreme political and social turmoil.

Tertullian (c. 155-220). Tertullian's interpretation of the Scripture wavers between a typological vision, in

---

[23]R. Devreesse, *Les Anciens Commentateurs Grecs de l'Octateuque et des Rois* (Studi e Testi 201; Rome: Città del Vaticano, 1959), 179.
[24]See *Analecta Hymnica Graeca* 10 (1972), 65.

which Christ is the center and the reason of the unity of the two Testaments, and a more literal approach, in which he emphasizes the moral contents of the biblical narrative. Both these trends are evident in his comments on 2 Kings 6:4-7 (typological) and 1 Kings 13:19 (moral).

Cyprian (c. 200-258). The comments by Cyprian on 1-2 Kings (1 Kings 11:14; 11:31-32; 2 Kings 17:20-28; 24:1-3) appear to be mostly literal. His main interest is not to interpret the biblical narrative in an allegorical sense but to read in it examples for the moral conduct of the Christian community.

Novatian (c. 210-260). Novatian, in his polemic against the Jews, is mostly concerned with the letter of the biblical text which cannot be taken at face value but should be analyzed also for its possible symbolism. Therefore he emphasizes how the words of God, who in 2 Kings 19:20-31 speaks about his ears, symbolically mean that God is able to hear all things.

Lactantius (c. 260-330). In his comment on 1 Kings 9:7-9, Lactantius gives us a typical example of typological exegesis, as he reads the words of God to Solomon as a prediction of the destruction of Israel after the passion of Christ.

Ambrose (c. 337-397). A large number of passages by Ambrose have been included in our commentary. Ambrose's exegesis makes use, according to his own definition, of a "moral" and "mystical" interpretation. Therefore he is constantly attentive to both the moral and social import of the biblical text, as is evident from his comments on Elijah's fasting (1 Kings 17:1-6) and Naboth's execution (1 Kings 21:1-29), and to the Bible's allegorical value, as he shows in his comments on Elisha's miracles in the war against the Arameans (2 Kings 6:16-23).

Jerome (347-420). At the beginning of his activity as an exegete, Jerome was an enthusiastic follower of Origen and his allegorical method of biblical interpretation. Later, after the polemics about Origen's doctrinal errors, Jerome became more cautious in following his exegetical approach and added to his comments clear literal and moral elements derived from the Antiochian school of exegesis. This is evident from his comments on 1-2 Kings, where we find typical allegorical interpretations (1 Kings 1:3), together with others where the moral sense strongly prevails (1 Kings 19:4; 21:7).

Prudentius (c. 348-410). We cannot speak of a precise exegetical orientation in Prudentius's works, as he exclusively wrote poetry in which he expresses his religious passion through feelings and emotions more than through a systematic discussion of the Scripture. In his comment on 1 Kings 5:4-5 concerning the building of the temple, he uses a typical typological interpretation in which Solomon's temple is naturally compared with the church of Christ.

Augustine (354-430). Augustine's exegesis of the Old Testament in general, and of 1-2 Kings in particular, reflects the extreme complexity of his thought and personality. Obviously it is not possible, in this concise introduction to the exegesis of the Fathers, to describe the details and nuances of Augustine's interpretation. We can assert with certainty that he was always deeply concerned with the problem that a concrete and a figurative language are both used in the Bible. As a consequence, an allegorical interpretation is necessary in the figurative passages, whereas a literal and moral one is necessary in the concrete ones. This exegetical method is particularly evident in Augustine's comments on the case of the two mothers (1 Kings 3:16-28), where he applies a typical allegorical interpretation, and in his discussion on the reign of Jehu (2 Kings 10:18-24), where the cruelty of the king is considered in its historical context but is ultimately condemned and used as a moral admonition to the faithful.[25]

Paulinus of Nola (355-431). Paulinus was influenced in his exegetical method by the allegorical works of Rufinus, who translated Origen and wrote an allegorical comment on Genesis 49 at his explicit request.[26] However, in his comment on 2 Kings 19:1-7, he shows a typical literal approach and examines the biblical text especially in its historical reality.

John Cassian (360-432). John Cassian's work is centered on monastic life, his rules and inspirational models. Therefore his exegetical method is substantially moral, as he finds in the Scripture models of conduct to be proposed to the monks. This is amply demonstrated by his comments on 1 Kings 8:58, 1 Kings 13:24-28 and 2 Kings 24:8-16.

Peter Chrysologus (c. 380-450). Peter Chrysologus, in his activity as a bishop, was mostly concerned with the moral and pastoral import of the biblical text. This is evident in his moral interpretation of 1 Kings 12:28, in which he condemns the idolatry of Jeroboam and shows how similar kinds of errors are still possible among Christians.

Maximus of Turin (c. end of the fourth century-423). Maximus appears to depend on Ambrose in his literary style as well as in his exegetical method. Therefore he makes use of "moral interpretation," as in 1 Kings 20:11, and of an extremely clear and effective form of "mystical exegesis," as in 2 Kings 2:19-22, where he reads the miracle of the water purified by Elisha as a foreshadowing of the church which was to be cleansed by Christ.

Salvian the Presbyter (c. 400-480). Salvian's interpretation of 1 Kings 20:20-30 is both literal, as he examines the war of Israel against the Arameans in its historical reality, and allegorical, as he sees in the victory of the Israelites an open manifestation of God's providence and power.

Fulgentius of Ruspe (c. 467-532). In his doctrinal works and his letters to friends and collaborators, Fulgentius concentrates on his trinitarian polemic against the Arians[27] and his opposition to the Pelagians.[28] In his comment on 1 Kings 1:8-27, he gives a doctrinally correct description of the Trinity against any possible error.

Caesarius of Arles (c. 470-543). Caesarius's most important work, the sermons, is a summary of his long and passionate pastoral activity as the bishop of Arles (c. 500-543). As a consequence, his exegetical orientation is mostly attuned to a moral interpretation to support his pastoral preaching (see especially 1 Kings 1:21-22; 2 Kings 1:9-14). To this substantially moral exegesis Caesarius often adds a typological interpretation that appears to be mostly christological, that is, entirely centered on the figure of Christ (see 2 Kings 2:19-22).

Gregory the Great (c. 540-604). As in the case of Augustine, it is impossible to summarize in a few lines the complex exegetical personality of Gregory, who wrote a large number of works of different kinds and

---

[25]Augustine's comments on 1 Kings 3:16-28, as well as some on 1 Kings 17 and 18, were originally attributed to Caesarius of Arles, which is noted by means of including Caesarius of Arles within parentheses following the name of Augustine. This is meant to clarify for readers that these texts are usually found within collections of sermons by Caesarius of Arles.

[26]Rufinus Presbyter *De Benedictionibus Patriarcharum* (CCL 20:183-228).

[27]The Arians maintained that Christ was not generated but created by the Father; therefore, even though the Son was a divine being, his divinity was somehow inferior to that of the Father, and his substance was only similar (and, according to some extreme forms of Arianism, different) to that of the Father.

[28]The Pelagians, whose religious movement is extremely complex and concerns Christian anthropology as a whole, was characterized by a commitment to imitate Christ and by hostility toward the concept of divine grace in favor of human liberty and free will.

purpose. In his comments on 1 Kings 13:24-28 and 2 Kings 4:30-37 the moral and pastoral tone and intent prevail, while a strong typological approach is evident in the parallel between the miracle of Elisha and Christ's passion and resurrection.

The Venerable Bede (c. 672-735). As the most significant representative of the Anglo-Latin tradition which contributed to producing the Carolingian renaissance, Bede receives in his exegetical works the tradition of the great Latin fathers: Ambrose, Jerome, Augustine and Gregory the Great. As a consequence, his exegetical method emulates theirs and makes ample use of allegorical and typological interpretations as well as moral and edifying ones. In his commentary on the temple of Solomon,[29] which covers in detail 1 Kings 5:1–7:51, his typological approach is particularly evident, as he constantly sees in the different parts of the temple a foreshadowing of the truths of the doctrine of Christ and the entire New Testament.

Rabanus Maurus (780-856) and his pupil *Walafridius (Walahfrid) Strabo* (c. 808-849). Both writers are representative of the second phase of the Carolingian renaissance, so that their works do not belong to the patristic age but to the early Middle Ages. They are both more renowned for their poetical production than their exegetical works which cover most of the Scripture, including 1-2 Kings. There is no doubt about Rabanus's authorship of his commentary,[30] whereas many reservations have been raised about that by Walafridius,[31] where large sections appear to be abbreviations and summaries of passages taken from Rabanus's commentary. Their exegesis is very close to that of Bede, whose work they continue in many respects, so that in their comments both the moral and typological interpretations characteristic of Bede's works are largely employed.

Syriac Fathers

Only in the works of the Syriac fathers do we find two commentaries belonging to the patristic age that cover all of 1-2 Kings; the most ancient is that attributed to Ephrem, while the most recent was composed by Isho'dad of Merv in the mid-ninth century. According to Western chronology, Isho'dad should belong to the early Middle Ages, as do Rabanus and Walafridius, but according to the chronology of Syriac patrology, he is still considered to be a father of the church.

Even though we have no difficulty defining these two commentaries as complete, Ephrem and Isho'dad, like the Greek and Latin fathers, tend to concentrate their attention on particular aspects and sections of the biblical text that are suitable to their literal, typological or moral exegesis, so that they neglect large portions of the narrative of 1-2 Kings. The reason why we have two complete commentaries only in Syriac might be due to the fact that Syriac exegesis, even though it does not differ from that of the Greek and Latin fathers in preferring certain biblical books to others, was in a sense more attentive to a global vision of the Scripture, as is confirmed by the fact that both Ephrem and Isho'dad wrote commentaries covering more or less the entire Old and New Testaments.

Together with the passages from Ephrem's and Isho'dad's complete commentaries, we have included a

---

[29]*De Templo Salomonis Libri II* = PL 91:737-808; English translation: Bede, *On the Temple*, trans. with notes by S. Connolly (Translated Texts for Historians 21; Liverpool: Liverpool University Press, 1995).

[30]See F. Stegmüller, *Repertorium Biblicum Medii Aevi*, 7 vols. (Madrid: Consejo superior de investigaciones cientificas, Instituto Francisco Suárez, 1940-1980), nn. 7033-36.

[31]See J. de Blic, "L'œuvre Exégétique de Walafrid Strabon et la Glossa Ordinaria," *RTAM* 16 (1949): 5-28; Stegmüller, *Repertorium Biblicum Medii Aevi*, nn. 8322-23.

few incidental comments on 1-2 Kings taken from other Syriac fathers.

Aphrahat (c. 270-345). In his comments, Aphrahat shows all the characteristics of the early stage of Syriac exegesis to which his works belong. He is not interested in any trinitarian discussion and appears to ignore the Nicene Creed, while he concentrates his attention on a substantially literal interpretation of the Scripture, where ample space is given to moral meditation and to the crucial importance of charity in Christian faith. In his comment on 1 Kings 15:9-13, he emphasizes the role of the devil as the constant enemy of humankind.

Ephrem (c. 306-373). The complete commentary on 1-2 Kings traditionally ascribed to Ephrem is preserved in only two manuscripts: the first from the Vatican Library[32] and the second from the British Library.[33] The printed edition of this text[34] makes use only of the Vatican manuscript, while the manuscript of the British Library remains unpublished. Even though both manuscripts attribute the authorship of the work to Ephrem, scholars[35] had no difficulties in excluding the genuineness of this text. There is no doubt that it dates from a later age than that of Ephrem, although it is not possible to establish a precise date. In my opinion, the clear references to Nestorian doctrines and the ample use of allegorical and typological interpretations suggest a period between the end of the fifth century and the sixth century, when Syriac exegesis was influenced by Greek models. Even though it concentrates mostly on certain sections of the biblical narrative, the commentary is extremely interesting for its ample discussion on the figures of Elijah and Elisha, its profound moral reflection and its intriguing allegorical and typological interpretations.

In addition to the passages from the complete commentary on 1-2 Kings, we have employed a few incidental comments taken from the genuine works of Ephrem (*Hymns on Faith, Commentary on the Diatessaron*). In them all the characteristic aspects of Ephrem's exegetical style are evident: his literalism and closeness to Jewish exegesis, his openness to Greek patristic tradition revealed by a frequent use of allegory and typology and finally his lyricism and poetical vision of Scripture.

Sahdona (Martyrius) (first half of the seventh century). The entire literary work of Sahdona (Martyrius) is centered on his principles of ascetical spirituality, which lead him to privilege the moral aspects of the Scripture instead of its possible mystical interpretations. As a consequence, he concentrates on those episodes that favor a moral meditation. This is evident in his comment on 2 Kings 19:15-18, where he emphasizes the power of prayer.

Isaac of Nineveh (second half of the seventh century). Asceticism and spiritual meditation characterize the works of Isaac, a monk who devoted much of his attention to the spiritual instruction of his brothers. In his comment on 2 Kings 13:21, he shows how a holy life gives human beings a complete power over all bodily afflictions, even death itself.

Isho'dad of Merv (mid-ninth century). The second complete commentary on 1-2 Kings is that by Isho'dad of Merv, who was ordained bishop of Hedatta, near Mossoul in Mesopotamia, around 850. Isho'dad's commentary appears to be much more concise than that by Ephrem. The author follows a critical criterion

---

[32]Vaticanus Syriacus 103.

[33]British Library Add. 12144.

[34]*In Primum et Secundum Librum Regnorum*, in J. S. Assemani, ed., *Sancti Patris nostri Ephraem Syri Opera omnia quae exstant Graece, Syriace, Latine*, vol. 1 (Syriace et Latine; Rome, 1737), 439-567.

[35]Cf. B. Outtier in *Le Saint Prophète Élie d'apres les Peres de l'Eglise* (Spiritualité Orientale 53; Abbaye de Bellefontaine, 1992), 384-85.

which seems to have many similarities to that used by Theodoret of Cyr: he concentrates on those passages that seem to be more obscure or even simply grammatically difficult for the reader. In general, Isho'dad favors a literal approach to the biblical text, according to the prevailing trend in Syriac exegesis, but he also uses frequent typological and allegorical interpretations which are often quite original and demonstrate the enduring vitality of Syriac patristic literature in its later phase.

1-2 Chronicles

Through a rapid survey of the available patristic comments on 1-2 Chronicles, it is immediately evident that the Fathers' attention toward these biblical books was more rare than that toward 1-2 Kings. This is due to two main reasons: the nature of the narrative of 1-2 Chronicles, which includes extremely long genealogies and lists of characters which give no room to any kind of exegetical interpretation; and the nearly identical repetition in the text of Chronicles of episodes already reported in 1-2 Samuel and 1-2 Kings, of which Chronicles represent an often prolix complement. As a result, the Fathers concentrated their attention on 1-2 Samuel and 1-2 Kings and neglected extremely large sections of the text of Chronicles. Their criterion in choosing passages to comment is the same used for 1-2 Kings: they privilege those episodes from Chronicles where a typological and allegorical or literal and moral interpretation is possible, while they tend to neglect all those that are not suitable for their kind of exegesis. Therefore particular attention is paid to David and his role as king and holy man,[36] because his deeds provide ample material for moral meditation, as well as for allegorical and typological interpretations. The same can be said about the figure of Solomon, both in his role as the wisest man and the builder of the temple.[37]

Greek Fathers

The exegesis of the Greek Fathers on 1-2 Chronicles does not differ from that on 1-2 Kings. All their comments are incidental and taken from doctrinal or exegetical works on other books of the Bible, because there is no extant complete commentary on 1-2 Chronicles, except for that by Theodoret, and the catena by Procopius, which is a patchy collection of passages from other authors. In general, the amount of this patristic exegetical material is significantly scarcer than that on 1-2 Kings. The Greek authors who have commented on Chronicles are substantially the same as those who commented on 1-2 Kings. For a profile of Basil, the Apostolic Constitutions, Gregory of Nazianzus, Justin Martyr, Origen and Theodoret of Cyr, we refer the reader to the introduction to 1-2 Kings. Here we will discuss only those authors who have not been mentioned already.

Eusebius of Caesarea (c. 263-340). The exegesis of Eusebius is indissolubly linked to his polemical activity against the pagans, who accused Christian interpreters of the Scripture as indiscriminately using allegory. As a consequence, Eusebius analyzes the biblical text by always considering attentively its historical context, and he draws his typological conclusions after selecting those passages that are less exposed to possible criticism. This is particularly evident in his comment on 2 Chronicles 26:16-23.

Procopius of Gaza (c. 465-530). As we have already hinted above and in the introduction to 1-2 Kings,

---

[36]1 Chron 11:1—14:17; 16:1-43.
[37]2 Chron 1:1—9:31.

Procopius is the author of a catena on the Octateuch and Kings. However, what has been transmitted to us is not a full and complete catena but Procopius's summary of it, that is, a collection of summarized exegetical comments.[38] The text of the summarized catena has been published only in part, and large sections of it are available only in a later Latin translation.[39] In his selection, Procopius, being a dedicated follower of Origen, privileges passages with a clear allegorical approach, while he mostly neglects the literal exegesis of the Antochian school and of his near contemporary Theodoret of Cyr.

Pseudo-Dionysus the Areopagite (early sixth century). The work of Pseudo-Dionysus is by now considered to be a perfect synthesis of the neo-Platonism of Proclus and the theology of the Cappadocian fathers (Basil, Gregory of Nazianzus and Gregory of Nyssa). In this intensely philosophical context, Pseudo-Dionysus's exegetical approach appears to be substantially literal, that is, in accordance with that of the Cappadocians, as is confirmed by his comment on 2 Chronicles 26:16-23.

John of Damascus (c. 670-749). In the ample literary and polemical activity of John of Damascus, exegesis does not occupy a central position. Being involved in the iconoclast crisis, he often uses Scripture to support his defense of the cult of images. We may say that his use of exegesis is mostly apologetic. In addition, he pays great attention to the moral content of the biblical message, as is amply demonstrated by his comment on 1 Chronicles 28:3, because many of his works are addressed to a monastic audience and contain practical suggestions for a pious and ascetical life.

Latin Fathers

There is no significant difference with 1-2 Kings in the Latin fathers' exegetical treatment of 1-2 Chronicles, except for the fact that the amount of their comments on these two biblical books is much scarcer than that on 1-2 Kings. The only two available complete commentaries, which also cover 1-2 Kings, are both from the Middle Ages,[40] while Bede's commentary on the temple,[41] which treats in detail 1 Kings 5:1–7:51, discusses only those few passages in 2 Chronicles that differ from 1 Kings in their description of the temple. Again, the Latin fathers who comment on 1-2 Chronicles are substantially the same as those who comment on 1-2 Kings. Here we add only a profile of Cassiodorus, who was not included in the list of the Latin commentators of 1-2 Kings.

Cassiodorus (c. 485-580). In his exegetical orientation and the choice of the subject of his main biblical commentary, namely, the Psalms, Cassiodorus appears to be influenced by Augustine, whose profound and complex thought he simplifies for his audience at the monastery of Vivarium. In his comments on 1 Chronicles 16:22 and 1 Chronicles 25:1, he appears to make use of a typical typological interpretation.

Syriac Fathers

In general, the attention of the Syriac fathers toward 1-2 Chronicles is extremely scarce. Only a few incidental comments by Aphrahat and Ephrem[42] are available on these two large biblical books.

---

[38]See A. Di Berardino, ed., *Patrologia—I Padri Orientali (secoli V-V3)* (Rome: Marietti, 2000), 621-22.

[39]See *Clavis Patrum Graecorum* 3:388 n. 7430; PG 87:1147-220.

[40]See above "Introduction to 1-2 Kings."

[41]*De Templo Salomonis Libri II* = PL 91:737-808; English translation: Bede, *On the Temple.*

[42]For a profile of these two Syriac authors, see the introduction on 1-2 Kings.

Ezra and Nehemiah

In the introduction to 1-2 Kings and 1-2 Chronicles I have emphasized the fact that there is no extant complete and systematic patristic commentary on these books of the Bible, so that most of the exegetical passages from the Fathers used in this volume were taken from patristic doctrinal works or commentaries on other books of the Bible.

In the case of Ezra and Nehemiah, the situation is reversed: incidental comments from the Fathers are quite scanty,[43] while an extremely detailed and systematic commentary by Bede[44] is available. We have already mentioned[45] that Bede is a typical representative of the Anglo-Latin tradition, who received in his exegetical works the heritage of the great Latin fathers, Ambrose, Jerome, Augustine and Gregory the Great, whose exegetical method and orientation he followed. In his desire to revaluate and continue the exegetical heritage of the great Western fathers, he also covered those sections of the Bible that were neglected by his predecessors. From this point of view Bede's exegetical activity is extremely precious, even in view of the fact that his discussion of biblical books that had never been covered before gave him the possibility to express new and original interpretations of the Scripture, though he is constantly and soundly anchored to the typological, moral and allegorical exegesis of the Latin fathers.[46]

In accordance with the main trend in patristic exegesis, Bede privileges in his commentary on Ezra and Nehemiah those sections that were more suitable to an allegorical, moral or typological interpretation. However, in an admirable effort to analyze the text in its entirety, Bede tries to extend his interpretation to nearly all the verses, so that he neglects only a small portion of the biblical text.

The reason why the books of Ezra and Nehemiah were entirely neglected by the Fathers until the time of Bede, who ends the patristic age, is not easily explicable. In fact, they do not substantially differ from those of Kings and Chronicles, towards which, as we have already seen, there was a certain attention. Probably the fact that they were placed at the end of a long series of historical books caused the Fathers to dismiss them as mere appendixes to 1-2 Kings and 1-2 Chronicles.

Esther

The attention of the Fathers, Latin, Greek and Syriac, toward the book of Esther was extremely scarce. After examining a large amount of patristic doctrinal and exegetical works, I have been able to find and include in this commentary a few passages by Clement of Rome, Origen, Clement of Alexandria and Athanasius, among the Greek fathers;[47] Ambrose, Jerome, Augustine and John Cassian, among the Latin;[48] and Aphrahat among the Syriac.[49]

With regard to the comment by Clement of Rome (fl. c. 92-101), who is one of the apostolic fathers and

---

[43]We have been able to locate four passages from Origen, Athanasius, Basil and Cassiodorus. For a profile of these authors, see "Introduction to 1-2 Kings."

[44]*In Esdram et Nehemiam Prophetas Allegorica Expositio* (CCL 119A:235-392; PL 91:807-924); Bede, *On Ezra and Nehemiah,* trans. with notes by S. DeGregorio (Translated Texts for Historians 47; Liverpool: Liverpool University Press, 2006).

[45]See "Introduction to 1-2 Kings."

[46]See *In Esdram et Nehemiam,* xxii-xxv.

[47]For a profile of Origen, Clement of Alexandria and Athanasius, see "Introduction to 1-2 Kings."

[48]For a profile of Ambrose, Jerome, Augustine and John Cassian, see "Introduction to 1-2 Kings."

[49]For a profile of Aphrahat, see "Introduction to 1-2 Kings."

one of the first Christian writers, we notice that he makes use of an extreme form of literal and moral interpretation, typical of this early phase of Christianity, in his description of Esther's heroism (Esth 4:5-17). All the other Greek, Latin and Syriac fathers employ a more allegorical and typological approach.

However, if we had to rely on these passages only, it would have been impossible to provide the reader with a proper commentary on Esther. Therefore, I have employed the commentary by Rabanus Maurus, which is the only one available on Esther. As I have already mentioned above, it is a medieval commentary. It nonetheless appears to be close to the exegetical works of Bede, as Rabanus closely follows Bede's exegetical style in many respects by making large use of the moral and typological interpretations characteristic of his exegesis.

Rabanus's analysis of Esther is extremely interesting, especially because it is possible to notice in his interpretations a certain exaggeration of some of the features of Bede's exegesis. In a sense, the literal and historical dimension of the biblical book almost disappears in Rabanus's analysis, while it was still firmly present in Bede. Rabanus makes use of a form of extreme allegorism, which sees symbols and types in almost all the details of the biblical narrative. From this point of view Rabanus clearly belongs to a new historical phase which partially departs from the typical tradition of Western patristic exegesis.

With regard to the reason for the lack of attention toward the book of Esther, I think again that its place at the end of a long series of historical books caused the Fathers to dismiss it as a mere appendix to 1-2 Kings and 1-2 Chronicles. In addition, we must consider the character of the book, which has many typical features of a work of fiction, so that it might have appeared to be less suitable for a profound exegetical analysis.

Biblical Text

The English text used as the basis for the pericopes of our commentary is that of the Revised Standard Version. Like all modern translations of the Old Testament,[50] it employs the Hebrew Masoretic Text, which was fixed in its present form after the death of Rabbi Akiba (c. 50-132). The Fathers of the church, who were Greek, Latin and Syriac, employed translations of the Old Testament into their own languages instead of the Hebrew Masoretic Text. The Greek fathers used the so-called Septuagint version (LXX), which dates from the third century B.C. and used a more ancient and ampler Hebrew text than the Masoretic. Until the seventh century A.D., the Latin fathers used the Vetus Latina (VL), which was a Latin translation of the Septuagint. From the eighth century they adopted the Vulgate (Vg), a translation that Jerome had made from the Masoretic Text by also employing other texts slightly different from the Masoretic and by including many readings from the Septuagint. The Syriac fathers employed the Peshitta, that is, the simple Syriac version of the Bible. It was mostly based on the Masoretic Text but also presented certain variants, because the Syriac translators also used the Targum,[51] the Septuagint and other Hebrew texts different from the Masoretic. As a consequence, it is inevitable that there are differences between the Masoretic Text that is translated into English in the Revised Standard Version and the Greek, Latin and Syriac versions, namely, the Septuagint, the Vetus Latina, the Vulgate and the Peshitta. However, the dif-

---

[50]For a discussion on the text of the New Testament, see A. Louth, in collaboration with Marco Conti, *Genesis 1-11* (ACCS OT 1; Downers Grove, IL: InterVarsity Press, 2001), xl; M. Simonetti and M. Conti, *Job* (ACCS OT 6; Downers Grove, IL: InterVarsity Press, 2006), xxvi.

[51]Explanatory translations in Aramaic of the Old Testament.

ferences between these versions and the Masoretic Text are not quantitatively constant in all the books of the Bible but are more significant and frequent in some of them. In the case of 1-2 Kings, 1-2 Chronicles, Ezra and Nehemiah, the differences are in general quite sporadic. When they are of certain significance, we have always recorded them at the end of each pericope, so that the reader can immediately locate them and make a comparison between the two texts.

The case of Esther is different, as two versions of this biblical book exist, a Hebrew and a Greek one. The Hebrew version is that of the Masoretic Text, while the Greek one is that contained in the Septuagint, which was also translated into Latin in the Vetus Latina. The Greek text appears to be much larger than the Hebrew, as it includes many episodes omitted in the Hebrew: a dream of Mordecai, prayers of Mordecai and Esther, a decree of Artaxerxes for the Jews and the interpretation of the dream of Mordecai. There is much debate about the relationship of the two versions, as some scholars think that the Greek version expanded the Hebrew, while others believe that the original Greek text was abridged in the Hebrew Masoretic Text. We can only say that the text used by Rabanus, who is our main source for our patristic commentary, is that of the Vulgate, which faithfully follows the Masoretic Text. As a consequence there are no significant variants between the text he uses and that of the RSV, that is, the Masoretic.

Marco Conti
Rome

1 KINGS

1:1-4 DAVID'S OLD AGE

¹*Now King David was old and advanced in years; and although they covered him with clothes, he could not get warm.* ²*Therefore his servants said to him, "Let a young maiden be sought for my lord the king, and let her wait upon the king, and be his nurse; let her lie in your bosom, that my lord the king may be warm."* ³*So they sought for a beautiful maiden throughout all the territory of Israel, and found Abishag the Shunammite, and brought her to the king.* ⁴*The maiden was very beautiful; and she became the king's nurse and ministered to him; but the king knew her not.*

OVERVIEW: David was cold not because of old age but as a consequence of his fear after the apparition of the angel, who entered Jerusalem to destroy it, as is confirmed in 1 Chronicles 21:16. David suffered not only from coldness but from dryness as well (ISHO'DAD). Abishag the Shunammite is not a girl who gives David the warmth his body needs but is rather a symbol of the wisdom of old age, which warms the heart of human beings (JEROME). David reveals his temperance and self-control in avoiding any intercourse with the girl (ISHO'DAD).

1:1 David Could Not Get Warm

THE REASON FOR THE COLDNESS IN DAVID'S BODY. ISHO'DAD OF MERV: There are different opinions about this coldness in David's body. Some say, "[That was] due to the fact that he was a child of old age, [who was born] after all his brothers, so that, as the body of his father had already become cold with age, so he also, while getting old, grew weak and cold." But we actually see that in all generations the children born from old parents are often stronger than those who were generated in youth. Others say, "[That coldness] derived from his extremely old age, and from his prolonged fast and the mortifying of the flesh and the abstinence that he had imposed on himself as a penitence for his sin." However, "Caleb was eighty-five years old and still possessed the vigor of youth,"[1] as he himself declared. And, among other things, David was not so old, as at that time he was only seventy.[2] Others say, "He had become cold as a consequence of his numerous toils and wars." But the true reason is that taught by the School:[3] "It was because of the fright [caused by] the vision of the angel, who appeared to him in a terrifying manner, that his

---

[1]Cf. Josh 14:10. [2]See 2 Sam 5:4. [3]Isho'dad is referring to the Nestorian exegetical school, which prevailed in Syriac biblical exegesis from the fifth and sixth centuries and was mostly based on the biblical commentaries by Theodore of Mopsuestia (c. 350-428).

body withered and grew cold as a consequence of his fear, as is attested in the book of the Chronicles as well."[4] And this is what Daniel says too: "At the sight of you my bowels were turned within me, and so how could I continue to live?"[5] Therefore the same happens to David: after he saw the angel holding his sword, who entered Jerusalem to destroy it,[6] the warmth fled and the coldness reigned over his body. BOOKS OF SESSIONS 1 KINGS 1.1.[7]

1:2 So That You May Be Warm

DAVID SUFFERED FROM COLDNESS AND DRYNESS. ISHO'DAD OF MERV: [The king] could get no warmth from blankets, because blankets cannot provide warmth by themselves; if you put them on stones or corpses, they certainly cannot warm them; but when there is heat emanating from the inside of our body, then they are useful and are an aid for us, because they imprison the heat, which comes from the inside of our bodies and warms us up again. Therefore blankets were useless for David, so that it was prescribed by the wise men and the physicians that a young virgin was brought to him—and that was a real novelty—because heat and humidity are prevalent in the female sex, and especially in virgins. Indeed, she refreshed him through the humidity of her body and warmed him up with the heat of her blood, since it was evident that he suffered from both these distresses: coldness and dryness. BOOKS OF SESSIONS 1 KINGS 1.2.[8]

1:3 Abishag Brought to the King

ABISHAG SYMBOLIZES THE PROFOUND WISDOM OF OLD AGE. JEROME: Once David had been a man of war, but at seventy, age had chilled him so that nothing would make him warm. A girl is accordingly sought from the coasts of Israel—Abishag the Shunammite—to sleep with the king and warm his aged frame. Does it not seem to you—if you keep to the letter that kills[9]—like some farcical story or some broad

jest from an Atellan play?[10] A chilly old man is wrapped up in blankets and only grows warm in a girl's embrace. Bathsheba was still living, Abigail was still left, and the remainder of those wives and concubines whose names the Scripture mentions. Yet they are all rejected as cold, and only in the one young girl's embrace does the old man become warm. Abraham was far older than David; still, so long as Sarah lived, he sought no other wife. Isaac counted twice the years of David yet never felt cold with Rebekah, old though she was. I say nothing of the antediluvians, who, although after nine hundred years their limbs must have been not old merely, but decayed with age, had no recourse to girls' embraces. Moses, the leader of the Israelites, counted one hundred and twenty years, yet sought no change from Zipporah.

Who, then, is this Shunammite, this wife and maid, so glowing as to warm the cold, yet so holy as not to arouse passion in him whom she warmed? Let Solomon, wisest of men, tell us of his father's favorite; let the man of peace recount to us the embraces of the man of war. "Get wisdom," he writes, "get understanding: forget it not; neither decline from the words of my mouth. Forsake her not, and she shall preserve you: love her, and she shall keep you. Wisdom is the principal thing; therefore, get wisdom, and with all your getting get understanding. Exalt her, and she shall promote you. She shall bring you to honor, when you do embrace her. She shall give to your head an ornament of grace; a crown of glory shall she deliver to you."[11]

Almost all bodily excellences alter with age, and while wisdom alone increases, all things else decay.... So even the very name Abishag, in its mystic meaning, points to the greater wisdom of old men. For the translation of it is, "My father is over and above," or, "my father's roaring." The term "over and above" is obscure, but in this pas-

---

[4]See 1 Chron 21:16. [5]Dan 10:16 (quoted with variants). [6]See 1 Chron 21:16. [7]CSCO 229:97-98. [8]CSCO 229:98. [9]See 2 Cor 3:6. [10]A traditional form of Roman comedy, which originated from the Oscan town of Atella. [11]Prov 4:5-9.

sage is indicative of excellence and implies that the old have a larger stock of wisdom and that it even overflows by reason of its abundance. LETTER 52 (TO NEPOTIAN) 2-3.[12]

1:4 The King Did Not Know Her

THE TEMPERANCE OF DAVID. ISHO'DAD OF MERV: But he "did not know her," that is, he did not get close to her, not because he was by now devoid of concupiscence but because he restrained the movements of concupiscence, fearing that it might be believed that he, who had many women, had asked for that girl out of lust. He paid for his inordinate desire for Bathsheba through his restraint toward this girl and inflicted this punishment on himself: indeed, the sin with Bathsheba[13] remained fixed in his memory until his death. BOOKS OF SESSIONS 1 KINGS 1.4.[14]

---

[12]NPNF 2 6:89-90. [13]See 2 Sam 12:1–13:31. [14]CSCO 229:98-99.

1:5-27 ADONIJAH'S STRUGGLE TO TAKE POWER

[5]Now Adonijah the son of Haggith exalted himself, saying, "I will be king"; and he prepared for himself chariots and horsemen, and fifty men to run before him. [6]His father had never at any time displeased him by asking, "Why have you done thus and so?" He was also a very handsome man; and he was born next after Absalom. [7]He conferred with Joab the son of Zeruiah and with Abiathar the priest; and they followed Adonijah and helped him. [8]But Zadok the priest, and Benaiah the son of Jehoiada, and Nathan the prophet, and Shime-i, and Rei, and David's mighty men were not with Adonijah.

[9]Adonijah sacrificed sheep, oxen, and fatlings by the Serpent's Stone, which is beside En-rogel, and he invited all his brothers, the king's sons, and all the royal officials of Judah, [10]but he did not invite Nathan the prophet or Benaiah or the mighty men or Solomon his brother.

[11]Then Nathan said to Bathsheba the mother of Solomon, "Have you not heard that Adonijah the son of Haggith has become king and David our lord does not know it? [12]Now therefore come, let me give you counsel, that you may save your own life and the life of your son Solomon. [13]Go in at once to King David, and say to him, 'Did you not, my lord the king, swear to your maidservant, saying, "Solomon your son shall reign after me, and he shall sit upon my throne"? Why then is Adonijah king?' [14]Then while you are still speaking with the king, I also will come in after you and confirm your words."

[15]So Bathsheba went to the king into his chamber (now the king was very old, and Abishag the Shunammite was ministering to the king). [16]Bathsheba bowed and did obeisance to the king, and the king said, "What do you desire?" [17]She said to him, "My lord, you swore to your maidservant by the LORD your God, saying, 'Solomon your son shall reign after me, and he shall sit upon my throne.' [18]And now, behold, Adonijah is king, although you, my lord the king, do not know it. [19]He

has sacrificed oxen, fatlings, and sheep in abundance, and has invited all the sons of the king, Abiathar the priest, and Joab the commander of the army; but Solomon your servant he has not invited. ²⁰And now, my lord the king, the eyes of all Israel are upon you, to tell them who shall sit on the throne of my lord the king after him. ²¹Otherwise it will come to pass, when my lord the king sleeps with his fathers, that I and my son Solomon will be counted offenders."

²²While she was still speaking with the king, Nathan the prophet came in. ²³And they told the king, "Here is Nathan the prophet." And when he came in before the king, he bowed before the king, with his face to the ground. ²⁴And Nathan said, "My lord the king, have you said, 'Adonijah shall reign after me, and he shall sit upon my throne'? ²⁵For he has gone down this day, and has sacrificed oxen, fatlings, and sheep in abundance, and has invited all the king's sons, Joab the commander^a of the army, and Abiathar the priest; and behold, they are eating and drinking before him, and saying, 'Long live King Adonijah!' ²⁶But me, your servant, and Zadok the priest, and Benaiah the son of Jehoiada, and your servant Solomon, he has not invited. ²⁷Has this thing been brought about by my lord the king and you have not told your servants who should sit on the throne of my lord the king after him?"

a Gk: Heb *commanders*

OVERVIEW: Solomon is called a servant according to the style of the Old Testament, but his nature and rights as a son are not inferior to those of David's other children (ATHANASIUS).

1:19-26 *Your Servant Solomon*

MEANING OF THE TERM SERVANT. ATHANASIUS: Thus fathers often call their sons their servants, yet without denying the genuineness of their nature. In fact, they often affectionately call their own servants children, yet without losing sight of the fact they did purchase them originally. For they use the one appellation from their authority as fathers, but in the other they speak from affection. Thus Sara called Abraham lord, although she was not a servant but a wife. And while the Apostle joined Onesimus the servant to Philemon the master as a brother, Bathsheba called her son a servant even though she was his mother when she said to his father, "Your servant Solomon." Afterwards also Nathan the Prophet came in and repeated her words to David, "Solomon your servant." Nor did they mind calling the son a servant, for while David heard it, he rec-ognized the nature of what they were referring to, and even while they said it, they did not forget genuineness [of his sonship], praying that the one they called a "servant" might be made his father's heir; for to David he was his son by nature.

So then, when we read this we interpret it fairly without considering Solomon a servant because we hear him called this. Instead we understand him to be a natural and genuine son. In the same way, if the saints, when referring to the Savior who is confessed to be in truth the Son and the Word by nature, say, "Who was faithful to him that made him," or if he says of himself, "The Lord created me," and, "I am your servant and the Son of your handmaid,"[1] and the like, no one should on this account deny that he is proper to the father and from him. Rather, as in the case of Solomon and David, let them think properly about the Father and the Son. For if, though they hear Solomon called a servant, they acknowledge him to be a son, are they not deserving of many deaths, who, instead of preserving the same explanation in the instance of the Lord, whenever

---

[1]Ps 116:16 (115:7 LXX).

they hear "Offspring," and "Word," and "Wisdom," forcibly misinterpret and deny the generation, natural and genuine, of the Son from the Father; but on hearing words and terms proper to a work, immediately condescend to the notion of his being by nature a work and deny the Word—doing this even though it is possible, from his having been made man, to refer all these terms to his humanity?[2] And are they not also proven to be "an abomination to the Lord," when they use "differing weights"[3] with them, using one set of measurements here and another there in order to blaspheme the Lord? But perhaps they grant that the word "servant" is to be understood in a certain way, but lay stress upon the phrase "who made" as some great support of their heresy. But

this argument of theirs also is but a broken reed. For if they are aware of the style of Scripture, they must at once condemn themselves. For as Solomon, though a son, is called a servant, so, to repeat what was said above, although parents refer to the sons springing from themselves as "made" and "created" and "becoming"—in none of these do they deny their nature. DISCOURSES AGAINST THE ARIANS 2.3-4.[4]

---

[2]Here Athanasius is confuting the theories of the Arians, who maintained that Christ was not generated, but created by the Father; therefore, even though the Son was a divine being, his divinity was somehow inferior to that of the Father, and his substance was only similar (and, according to some extreme forms of Arianism, different) to that of the Father. [3]Prov 20:23. [4]NPNF 2 4:349-50**.

1:28-53 SOLOMON IS ANOINTED AS THE NEW KING

[28]*Then King David answered, "Call Bathsheba to me." So she came into the king's presence, and stood before the king.* [29]*And the king swore, saying, "As the LORD lives, who has redeemed my soul out of every adversity,* [30]*as I swore to you by the LORD, the God of Israel, saying, 'Solomon your son shall reign after me, and he shall sit upon my throne in my stead'; even so will I do this day."* [31]*Then Bathsheba bowed with her face to the ground, and did obeisance to the king, and said, "May my lord King David live for ever!"*

[32]*King David said, "Call to me Zadok the priest, Nathan the prophet, and Benaiah the son of Jehoiada." So they came before the king.* [33]*And the king said to them, "Take with you the servants of your lord, and cause Solomon my son to ride on my own mule, and bring him down to Gihon*;* [34]*and let Zadok the priest and Nathan the prophet there anoint him king over Israel; then blow the trumpet, and say, 'Long live King Solomon!'* [35]*You shall then come up after him, and he shall come and sit upon my throne; for he shall be king in my stead; and I have appointed him to be ruler over Israel and over Judah."* [36]*And Benaiah the son of Jehoiada answered the king, "Amen! May the LORD, the God of my lord the king, say so.* [37]*As the LORD has been with my lord the king, even so may he be with Solomon, and make his throne greater than the throne of my lord King David."*

[38]*So Zadok the priest, Nathan the prophet, and Benaiah the son of Jehoiada, and the Chere-*

5

thites and the Pelethites, went down and caused Solomon to ride on King David's mule, and brought him to Gihon. [39]There Zadok the priest took the horn of oil from the tent, and anointed Solomon. Then they blew the trumpet; and all the people said, "Long live King Solomon!" [40]And all the people went up after him, playing on pipes, and rejoicing with great joy, so that the earth was split by their noise.

[41]Adonijah and all the guests who were with him heard it as they finished feasting. And when Joab heard the sound of the trumpet, he said, "What does this uproar in the city mean?" [42]While he was still speaking, behold, Jonathan the son of Abiathar the priest came; and Adonijah said, "Come in, for you are a worthy man and bring good news." [43]Jonathan answered Adonijah, "No, for our lord King David has made Solomon king; [44]and the king has sent with him Zadok the priest, Nathan the prophet, and Benaiah the son of Jehoiada, and the Cherethites and the Pelethites; and they have caused him to ride on the king's mule; [45]and Zadok the priest and Nathan the prophet have anointed him king at Gihon; and they have gone up from there rejoicing, so that the city is in an uproar. This is the noise that you have heard. [46]Solomon sits upon the royal throne. [47]Moreover the king's servants came to congratulate our lord King David, saying, 'Your God make the name of Solomon more famous than yours, and make his throne greater than your throne.' And the king bowed himself upon the bed. [48]And the king also said, 'Blessed be the LORD, the God of Israel, who has granted one of my offspring[b] to sit on my throne this day, my own eyes seeing it.'"

[49]Then all the guests of Adonijah trembled, and rose, and each went his own way [50]And Adonijah feared Solomon; and he arose, and went, and caught hold of the horns of the altar. [51]And it was told Solomon, "Behold, Adonijah fears King Solomon; for lo, he has laid hold of the horns of the altar, saying, 'Let King Solomon swear to me first that he will not slay his servant with the sword.'" [52]And Solomon said, "If he prove to be a worthy man, not one of his hairs shall fall to the earth; but if wickedness is found in him, he shall die." [53]So King Solomon sent, and they brought him down from the altar. And he came and did obeisance to King Solomon; and Solomon said to him, "Go to your house."

b Gk: Heb one   * Heb: Syr *Šiloha*

OVERVIEW: David appoints Solomon as the new king in order to protect him and his mother and to assert his equal rights in spite of his birth outside marriage. David makes Solomon ride his mule because it was considered at that time a royal animal, which was bought from the Gentiles at a high price. The fountain of Šiloha takes its name from the fact that it emits water straight up at intervals (ISHO'DAD). Solomon is not the promised messiah but only foreshadows the advent of the true King (AUGUSTINE). The anointing of Solomon is a figure of our true chrism (CYRIL OF JERUSALEM). All fathers want their children to become more illustrious than themselves, just like God the Father with his Son (THEODORET). Solomon gives Adonijah the chance to demonstrate his innocence and obedience (EPHREM).

1:30 Solomon to Succeed David as King

DAVID, IN HIS RIGHTEOUSNESS, PROTECTS BATHSHEBA AND SOLOMON. ISHO'DAD OF

Merv: In the first place, he appoints Solomon as king, even though he had many sons, in order to confound the fools, who believed that nature is more valuable than a virtuous spirit before God. In the second place, he did this because he feared that he, a just man, might be mocked after his death, and Solomon and his mother might be treated with contempt—he as a bastard and she as an adulteress. This is what Bathsheba meant when she said, "My son Solomon and I will be counted offenders,"[1] that is, "If my son is not appointed as king, it will be believed that we are excluded from the kingdom, because we have sinned in this affair of the adultery, and consequently we will be condemned to contempt and cursing as impure persons for the rest of our lives." Books of Sessions 1 Kings 1.30.[2]

1:33 Solomon Rides on David's Mule

THE MULE IS A ROYAL ANIMAL. Isho'dad of Merv: [David] orders [Zadok, Nathan and Benaiah] to make "Solomon ride [his] mule," because this animal was highly valued among the Hebrews, just like the white donkey among the Romans. The Jews, in fact, did not possess mules, since they were not allowed to "breed their animals with another kind,"[3] but mules were bought at very high prices from the Gentiles. Books of Sessions 1 Kings 1.33.[4]

THE SPRING AT ŠILOHA. Isho'dad of Merv: [David] orders them to bring [Solomon] down to Šiloha, where the tabernacle was, not far from the spring of water, which is called Šiloha. Šiloha is a Hebrew name, which is given because the water of the spring gushes out straight up and on and off; indeed, it does not gush out regularly and all the time. And the same can be said about the Nile: since, at different intervals, it suddenly becomes full and then overflows, it is called Gihon, because its waters spread out. Books of Sessions 1 Kings 1.33.[5]

1:35 Appointed to Be Ruler

A TYPE OF THE KINGDOM OF CHRIST. Augustine: Solomon, it will be remembered, succeeded to the throne during his father David's lifetime—a kind of succession unique among Jewish kings—for no other reason save to furnish further clear evidence that Solomon is not the man our prophecy proclaims. Nathan says to David, "And when your days shall be fulfilled and you shall sleep with your fathers, I will raise up your seed after you, which shall proceed out of your bowels, and I will establish his kingdom."[6] In view of these words, how can anyone think that, because of the later verse, "He shall build a house to my name,"[7] Solomon is the subject of the prophecy and fail to realize that in view of the earlier words, "And when your days shall be fulfilled and you shall sleep with your fathers, I will raise up your seed after you," a different Peacemaker is promised—one to be raised up not before David's demise as Solomon was but afterwards? It makes no difference how long was the lapse of time before the destined coming of Jesus Christ. The thing that is beyond question is that he who was promised in such terms to king David was destined to come after his death, the very same who was to build a house for God such as we rejoice to see rising up today, a house not fashioned of timbers and stones but of human beings. It is these people, believers in Christ, whom Saint Paul addresses in these words: "Holy is the temple of God, and this temple you are."[8] City of God 17.8.[9]

1:39 Zadok Anointed Solomon

DONE TO YOU IN TRUTH. Cyril of Jerusalem: You must know that this chrism is prefigured in the Old Testament. When Moses, conferring on his brother the divine appointment, was ordering him high priest, he anointed him after he had bathed in water, and thenceforward he was called

---

[1]1 Kings 1:21. [2]CSCO 229:99. [3]Lev 19:19. [4]CSCO 229:99. [5]CSCO 229:100. [6]2 Sam 7:12. [7]2 Sam 7:13. [8]1 Cor 3:17. [9]FC 24:50.

"christ" [anointed], clearly after the figurative chrism. Again, the high priest, when installing Solomon as king, anointed him after he had bathed in Gihon. But what was done to them in figure was done to you, not in figure but in truth, because your salvation began from him who was anointed by the Holy Spirit in truth. Christ is the beginning of your salvation, since he is truly the "first handful" of dough and you "the whole lump."[10] And if the first handful is holy, plainly its holiness will permeate the lump. MYSTAGOGICAL LECTURES 3.6.[11]

1:47-48 The Fame of Solomon

ALL FATHERS WISH THEIR SONS TO GAIN THE HIGHEST GLORY. THEODORET OF CYR: In blessing David, why did the leaders who were next to the king want the young king to become more illustrious and glorious than his father? They said, "May God make the name of Solomon more famous than yours, and make his throne greater than your throne."

They knew that no one who has a true paternal love could be jealous of his sons. The wish to see their sons more illustrious than them is characteristic of fathers. Only Arius and his sons oppose this truth with their madness.[12] Therefore David was pleased with what was said by the leaders since it enabled him to worship God even when his old age prevented him from getting to his feet. Indeed he had announced the fulfillment of the promise: "Blessed be the Lord, the God of Israel, who today has granted one of my offspring to sit on my throne and permitted me to witness it." QUESTION 3, ON 1 KINGS.[13]

1:52 No Hair of His Shall Fall to the Ground

NO PUNISHMENT FOR THE INNOCENT. EPHREM THE SYRIAN: "Not one of his hairs shall fall to the ground," that is, he shall not undergo any punishment of the guilty, if he proves to be innocent; but he will deserve capital punishment, if he is found to conspire against my sovereignty. Indeed, if he still aspires to take hold of the kingdom, he will be executed: punishment restrains that ambition that discipline could not bring under control. ON THE FIRST BOOK OF KINGS 1.52.[14]

---

[10]Rom 11:16. [11]FC 64:172-73. [12]Theodoret alludes here to the Arians, who maintained that the Son was inferior to the Father, and made of a similar or even different substance. [13]PG 80:669 A-C [14]ESOO 1:444.

2:1-10 DAVID'S LAST INSTRUCTIONS TO SOLOMON

[1]When David's time to die drew near, he charged Solomon his son, saying, [2]"I am about to go the way of all the earth. Be strong, and show yourself a man, [3]and keep the charge of the LORD your God, walking in his ways and keeping his statutes, his commandments, his ordinances, and his testimonies, as it is written in the law of Moses, that you may prosper in all that you do and wherever you turn; [4]that the LORD may establish his word which he spoke concerning me, saying, 'If your sons take heed to their way, to walk before me in faithfulness with all their heart and with

all their soul, there shall not fail you a man on the throne of Israel.'

⁵*"Moreover you know also what Joab the son of Zeruiah did to me, how he dealt with the two commanders of the armies of Israel, Abner the son of Ner, and Amasa the son of Jether, whom he murdered, avenging^c in time of peace blood which had been shed in war, and putting innocent blood^d upon the girdle about my^e loins, and upon the sandals on my^e feet. ⁶Act therefore according to your wisdom, but do not let his gray head go down to Sheol in peace. ⁷But deal loyally with the sons of Barzillai the Gileadite, and let them be among those who eat at your table, for with such loyalty they met me when I fled from Absalom your brother. ⁸And there is also with you Shime-i the son of Gera, the Benjaminite from Bahurim, who cursed me with a grievous curse on the day when I went to Mahanaim; but when he came down to meet me at the Jordan, I swore to him by the LORD, saying, 'I will not put you to death with the sword.' ⁹Now therefore hold him not guiltless, for you are a wise man; you will know what you ought to do to him, and you shall bring his gray head down with blood to Sheol."*

¹⁰*Then David slept with his fathers, and was buried in the city of David.*

c Gk: Heb *placing*   Gk: Heb *blood of war*   e Gk: Heb *his*

OVERVIEW: Joab's punishment is a necessary action to make the kingdom stable and safe from any danger (ISHO'DAD). David's decision to entrust Solomon with the punishment of Joab and Shimei reveals his absolute trust in his son's wisdom (EPHREM). David, like Abel, foreshadows the figure of the Christian who embraces and cleaves to the doctrine of Christ (AMBROSE).

2:5-6 Do Not Let Joab Go to Sheol in Peace!

A NECESSARY PUNISHMENT. ISHO'DAD OF MERV: [David] orders Solomon to punish [Joab], not out of viciousness or hatred for him but because he knew that he was wicked and that, if he had acted with hostility against him who was a mature man, he would act even worse against a young man, so that the kingdom would become unstable, and the house would not be firmly established. Therefore he entrusts his son with the revenge against him who had offended him, in order that, after the killing of that evil man by the hand of the new king, he might be feared by everyone, and no revolt might ever occur. BOOKS OF SESSIONS 1 KINGS 2.5-6.[1]

2:9 A Wise Man

DAVID CONFIDENT IN SOLOMON'S WISDOM. EPHREM THE SYRIAN: After expounding the crimes of Joab and Shimei, David entrusts Solomon with their punishment, but only gives him few details about the manner and quality of the punishment: "You will do," he says, "according to your wisdom."[2] It is as if he said, Since both Joab and Shimei committed such [terrible] actions, it is unlawful that they are left unpunished. Therefore, solve this matter with the help of your wisdom so that your equity may catch them in their iniquity: may your severity, with the revelation of new crimes, find out the sins that your father's indulgence had hidden. ON THE FIRST BOOK OF KINGS 2.8-9.[3]

2:10 David Dies

THE CHRISTIAN WHO CLEAVES TO GOD. AMBROSE: By Abel we understand the Christian

---

[1]CSCO 229:100.   [2]This reading does not belong to the Peshitta (the standard Syriac Bible) but to an unknown version used by Ephrem.   [3]ESOO 1:445.

who cleaves to God, as David says: "It is good for me to adhere to my God,"[4] that is, to attach oneself to heavenly things and to shun the earthly. Elsewhere he says, "My soul has fainted in your word,"[5] thus indicating his rule of life was directed toward reflections on the Word and not on the pleasures of this world. Wherefore we realize that what we read concerning David in the book of Kings is not an idle statement but is said

with due weight and reflection: "And he was laid with his fathers." We are given to understand that his faith was like that of his father's. It is clear, then, that there is reference here to participation in life and not to the burial of a body. CAIN AND ABEL 1.5.[6]

---

[4]Ps 73:28 (72:28 LXX, Vg). [5]Cf. Ps 119:81 (118:81 LXX, Vg). [6]FC 42:362.

2:11-46 SOLOMON'S BATTLES TO PACIFY HIS NEW KINGDOM

[13]Then Adonijah the son of Haggith came to Bathsheba the mother of Solomon. . . . [17]And he said, "Pray ask King Solomon—he will not refuse you—to give me Abishag the Shunammite as my wife." [18]Bathsheba said, "Very well; I will speak for you to the king."

[19]So Bathsheba went to King Solomon, to speak to him on behalf of Adonijah. . . . [21]She said, "Let Abishag the Shunammite be given to Adonijah your brother as his wife." [22]King Solomon answered his mother, "And why do you ask Abishag the Shunammite for Adonijah? Ask for him the kingdom also; for he is my elder brother, and on his side are Abiathar[f] the priest and Joab the son of Zeruiah." [23]Then King Solomon swore by the LORD, saying, "God do so to me and more also if this word does not cost Adonijah his life! [24]Now therefore as the LORD lives, who has established me, and placed me on the throne of David my father, and who has made me a house, as he promised, Adonijah shall be put to death this day." [25]So King Solomon sent Benaiah the son of Jehoiada; and he struck him down, and he died.

[26]And to Abiathar the priest the king said, "Go to Anathoth, to your estate; for you deserve death. But I will not at this time put you to death, because you bore the ark of the Lord GOD before David my father. . . ."

[28]When the news came to Joab—for Joab had supported Adonijah although he had not supported Absalom—Joab fled to the tent of the LORD and caught hold of the horns of the altar. [29]And when it was told King Solomon, "Joab has fled to the tent of the LORD, and behold, he is beside the altar," Solomon sent Benaiah the son of Jehoiada, saying, "Go, strike him down." [30]So Benaiah came to the tent of the LORD, and said to him, "The king commands, 'Come forth.'" But he said, "No, I will die here." Then Benaiah brought the king word again, saying, "Thus said Joab, and thus he answered me." [31]The king replied to him, "Do as he has said, strike him down and bury

him; and thus take away from me and from my father's house the guilt for the blood which Joab shed without cause. . . . [34]*Then Benaiah the son of Jehoiada went up, and struck him down and killed him. . . .*

[36]*Then the king sent and summoned Shime-i, and said to him, "Build yourself a house in Jerusalem, and dwell there, and do not go forth from there to any place whatever.* [37]*For on the day you go forth, and cross the brook Kidron, know for certain that you shall die. . . ."*

[39]*But it happened at the end of three years that two of Shime-i's slaves ran away to Achish, son of Maacah, king of Gath. And when it was told Shime-i, "Behold, your slaves are in Gath,"* [40]*Shime-i arose and saddled an ass, and went to Gath to Achish, to seek his slaves; Shime-i went and brought his slaves from Gath. . . .* [46]*Then the king commanded Benaiah the son of Jehoiada; and he went out and struck him down, and he died.*

So the kingdom was established in the hand of Solomon.

f Gk Syr Vg: Heb *and for him and for Abiathar*

OVERVIEW: Solomon cannot be blamed for the killing of his brother Adonijah, because he behaved according to the political rules followed by kings (THEODORET). Joab's behavior may be compared with that of the demons exorcised by Jesus, because he tried to cause Solomon's death; so too the demons, who entered into the pigs and made them fall into the sea, tried to cause the rage of the owner of the herd, so that he might kill our Lord (ISHO'DAD). Ephrem sees a parallel between the punishment and killing of Adonijah, Joab and Shimei and the ruin that befell Jerusalem for not recognizing the power of Christ (EPHREM).

2:25 Adonijah Dies

SOLOMON CANNOT BE BLAMED. THEODORET OF CYR: Some people blame Solomon because he killed his brother. Now the ways of life of people are different. Some of them certainly practice the highest form of philosophy; others pursue that virtue which is called political or civil; others manage the kingdom or hold power militarily. It is necessary to judge each of them according to the way of life that they follow. Therefore an apostolic or prophetic perfection cannot be expected from Solomon, but only those actions that are appropri-

ate to kings. He knew that Adonijah desired to gain supreme command. In fact, he had tried to take hold of the kingdom. When he attacked him the first time openly, he still forgave him and promised him that he would be safe if he behaved with modesty. But after he asked for the partner of his father, he did not grant this to him because Adonijah was opening the way to tyranny. Therefore Solomon ordered him to be killed, as he was concerned for the tranquility of his kingdom. QUESTIONS 7, ON 1 KINGS.[1]

2:28 Joab Fled

JOAB COMPARED WITH THE DEMONS EXORCISED BY CHRIST. ISHO'DAD OF MERV: Joab runs to the tent for two reasons: first of all, in order to escape his death, if possible; second, because he imagined that, if he were killed in that place, the tent of God would become polluted as a consequence of his death, and the people would rise up against Solomon, so that, since he had not been able to harm him during his life, he conspired to cause a rebellion at his death. This can be compared with what the demons who entered the swine did in order that the owners of the herd

---

[1]PG 80:673.

might become enraged and might kill our Lord; but it did not happen as they had planned.[2] That is why Solomon, in the same manner, acting in accordance with the commandment of the law, "Take him, who has sinned, from my altar for execution,"[3] forcing Joab to get out so that the innocent blood which he had shed without reason was avenged. BOOKS OF SESSIONS 1 KINGS 2.28.[4]

2:44 Your Evil Be on Your Own Head

A FORESHADOWING OF RUIN. EPHREM THE SYRIAN: You can see here four people who were condemned by Solomon because they were guilty of treason: they all foreshadowed the Jewish nation's ruin, which would derive from Christ's unjust killing. Adonijah, who was appointed as king and was killed shortly later, was the first to presage the fall of the Jewish kingdom; then, after the abrogation of the priesthood of Aaron, Abiathar was expelled from his office; and Joab, who had the dignity of captain of the army, was deprived of his life by the leaders of the people and all his military force was destroyed. Finally, Shimei expressed in an even more evident and definitive manner the sin and punishment of the Jews, especially of the inhabitants of Jerusalem who blasphemed Christ and demanded his crucifixion. And that last prayer of Christ, like a supreme commandment, was postponed for four more decades[5] and was not inflicted until the Jews were caught in a new crime when they persecuted the apostles and the other disciples of Christ. ON THE FIRST BOOK OF KINGS 2.39.[6]

---

[2]See Mt 8:30-34; Mk 5:11-17; Lk 8:32-37. [3]Exod 21:14. [4]CSCO 229:101. [5]Ephrem is referring to the destruction of Jerusalem by the army of Titus during the reign of Vespasian. [6]ESOO 1:449-50.

3:1-15 THE DIVINE WISDOM OF SOLOMON

[1]Solomon made a marriage alliance with Pharaoh king of Egypt; he took Pharaoh's daughter, and brought her into the city of David, until he had finished building his own house and the house of the LORD and the wall around Jerusalem. [2]The people were sacrificing at the high places, however, because no house had yet been built for the name of the LORD.

[3]Solomon loved the LORD, walking in the statutes of David his father; only, he sacrificed and burnt incense at the high places. [4]And the king went to Gibeon to sacrifice there, for that was the great high place; Solomon used to offer a thousand burnt offerings upon that altar. [5]At Gibeon the LORD appeared to Solomon in a dream by night; and God said, "Ask what I shall give you." [6]And Solomon said, "Thou hast shown great and steadfast love to thy servant David my father, because he walked before thee in faithfulness, in righteousness, and in uprightness of heart toward thee; and thou hast kept for him this great and steadfast love, and hast given him a son to sit on his throne this day. [7]And now, O LORD my God, thou hast made thy servant king in place of David my father, although I am but a little child; I do not know how to go out or come in. [8]And thy servant is in the midst of thy people whom thou hast chosen, a great people, that cannot be numbered

or counted for multitude. ⁹Give thy servant therefore an understanding mind to govern thy people, that I may discern between good and evil; for who is able to govern this thy great people?"

¹⁰It pleased the Lord that Solomon had asked this. ¹¹And God said to him, "Because you have asked this, and have not asked for yourself long life or riches or the life of your enemies, but have asked for yourself understanding to discern what is right, ¹²behold, I now do according to your word. Behold, I give you a wise and discerning mind, so that none like you has been before you and none like you shall arise after you. ¹³I give you also what you have not asked, both riches and honor, so that no other king shall compare with you, all your days. ¹⁴And if you will walk in my ways, keeping my statutes and my commandments, as your father David walked, then I will lengthen your days."

¹⁵And Solomon awoke, and behold, it was a dream. Then he came to Jerusalem, and stood before the ark of the covenant of the LORD, and offered up burnt offerings and peace offerings, and made a feast for all his servants.

OVERVIEW: Solomon is led by political opportunity in his choice of marrying Pharaoh's daughter, and therefore cannot be blamed for this action. Solomon made sacrifices in Gibeon, that is, outside Jerusalem, because the tabernacle was there at that time (ISHO‛DAD). Solomon knew how to ask wisely of the heavenly king (ISAAC OF NINEVEH). The description of Solomon's qualities in the holy Scripture is a way to foreshadow the qualities of Christ, to whom real wisdom and sovereignty belong (EPHREM). Solomon received this wisdom from him and passed this along to us in authoring the book of Proverbs (HIPPOLYTUS).

3:1 Solomon's Alliance with Pharaoh

SOLOMON'S INTENTION TO AVOID THE DANGER OF WARS. ISHO‛DAD OF MERV: Some wonder why Solomon made alliances with the Gentiles through marriages without being blamed, even though [the Law] forbade [the Hebrews] mixing with them. The reason for that prohibition was "lest" [the Scripture says], "[their daughters] might make your sons also prostitute themselves to their gods."[1] And this is what happened to Solomon[2] as well. However, we also see others who married daughters of the Gen-

tiles, but since they were not seduced to follow their paganism, they were filled with praises: for instance, Mahlon, Chilion and Boaz.[3] With regard to Solomon, since he thought he would avert his people from war and establish a house for the Lord through his connections with the foreign kings, for this reason he married their daughters, and not out of lust; therefore he was not blamed for this. But after he fell into the error of their idolatry—that is, he did not correct [his women] from their error[4]—he was blamed by God. BOOKS OF SESSIONS 1 KINGS 3.1.[5]

3:4 Solomon Sacrifices at Gibeon

WHY DID SOLOMON SACRIFICE IN GIBEON?
ISHO‛DAD OF MERV: Since the Law forbade praying or sacrificing outside Jerusalem,[6] why did Solomon offer one thousand whole burnt offerings on the altar of Gibeon? Because the tabernacle was in Gibeon, as is attested in the book of Chronicles,[7] and therefore, out of veneration for

---

[1]Exod 34:16. [2]See 1 Kings 11:4-8. [3]See Ruth 1:2-4; 4:1-22. [4]Here Isho‛dad presents Solomon's sin under a favorable and benevolent light. [5]CSCO 229:101. [6]See Deut 12:1-32. [7]See 1 Chron 16:39; 21:29.

the ancient residence, [Solomon] went there every year to offer his burnt offerings. BOOKS OF SESSIONS 1 KINGS 3.4.[8]

3:9 Solomon's Request

ASK FOR WHAT IS IMPORTANT. ISAAC OF NINEVEH: Do not be foolish in the request you make to God, otherwise you will insult God through your ignorance. Act wisely in prayer so that you may become worthy of glorious things. Ask for things that are honorable from him who will not hold back so that you may receive honor from him as a result of the wise choice your free will has made. Solomon asked for wisdom—and along with it he also received the earthly kingdom, for he knew how to ask wisely of the heavenly King, that is, for things that are important. DISCOURSE 3.[9]

3:12 No One Like You

THE QUALITIES OF SOLOMON MOSTLY BELONG TO CHRIST. EPHREM THE SYRIAN: Since the narrative [of the book of Kings] is accurate in the facts, nobody can have any doubt that Solomon received his noble sovereignty, his elevated thought and extraordinary power as a gift from God, thus it is evident that no one among those kings who were dead, nor among those who would succeed him, could be compared with him. It is certain, nevertheless, that these qualities, and others, which are described in the psalms about Solomon, mostly are to be transferred to Christ; otherwise the words [of these biblical passages] would not be in absolute and complete agreement with their meaning and truth. Therefore Christ is that prince of peace whose wisdom

and royal power were never preceded in time or overcome in greatness. And before him no Son was born of an eternal nature or equal to the Father, nor after him will there ever be someone similar to him, as the Word, God says through another prophet: "Before me no god was formed, nor will be after me."[10] ON THE FIRST BOOK OF KINGS 3.12.[11]

THE AUTHOR OF PROVERBS. HIPPOLYTUS: Proverbs are words of exhortation that serve the whole path of life. They serve as guides and signs for those who are seeking their way to God by reviving them when they become tired by the length of the road. These, moreover, are the proverbs of "Solomon," that is to say, the "peacemaker," who, in truth, is Christ the Savior. And since we understand the words of the Lord without offence as being the words of the Lord, that no one may mislead us by likeness of name, he tells us who wrote them and of what people he was king in order that the credit of the speaker may make the discourse acceptable and the hearers attentive. For these proverbs are the words of that Solomon to whom the Lord said, "I will give you a wise and understanding heart; so that there has been no one like you upon the earth, and after you there shall not arise any one like you." . . . Now he was the wise son of a wise father. This is why David's name, by whom Solomon was begotten, was added. From a child he was instructed in the sacred Scriptures and obtained his dominion not by lot, nor by force, but by the judgment of the Spirit and the decree of God. FRAGMENT ON PROVERBS.[12]

---

[8]CSCO 229:102. [9]CS 101:246. [10]Is 43:13 (Peshitta). [11]ESOO 1:451. [12]ANF 5:172**.

3:16-28 THE CASE OF THE TWO MOTHERS

[16]*Then two harlots came to the king, and stood before him.* [17]*The one woman said, "Oh, my lord, this woman and I dwell in the same house; and I gave birth to a child while she was in the house.* [18]*Then on the third day after I was delivered, this woman also gave birth; and we were alone; there was no one else with us in the house, only we two were in the house.* [19]*And this woman's son died in the night, because she lay on it.* [20]*And she arose at midnight, and took my son from beside me, while your maidservant slept, and laid it in her bosom, and laid her dead son in my bosom.* [21]*When I rose in the morning to nurse my child, behold, it was dead; but when I looked at it closely in the morning, behold, it was not the child that I had borne."* [22]*But the other woman said, "No, the living child is mine, and the dead child is yours." The first said, "No, the dead child is yours, and the living child is mine." Thus they spoke before the king.*

[23]*Then the king said, "The one says, 'This is my son that is alive, and your son is dead'; and the other says, 'No; but your son is dead, and my son is the living one.'"* [24]*And the king said, "Bring me a sword." So a sword was brought before the king.* [25]*And the king said, "Divide the living child in two, and give half to the one, and half to the other."* [26]*Then the woman whose son was alive said to the king, because her heart yearned for her son, "Oh, my lord, give her the living child, and by no means slay it." But the other said, "It shall be neither mine nor yours; divide it."* [27]*Then the king answered and said, "Give the living child to the first woman, and by no means slay it; she is its mother."* [28]*And all Israel heard of the judgment which the king had rendered; and they stood in awe of the king, because they perceived that the wisdom of God was in him, to render justice.*

OVERVIEW: In solving the case of the two mothers, Solomon demonstrated that the mind of God was in him (AMBROSE). The mother who killed her child represents the synagogue, whereas the other, who is falsely accused, is a figure of the church (EPHREM, AUGUSTINE). The murderous mother can also symbolize false Christians who are still slaves to the law and only pretend to be true followers of Jesus. The solution of the case of the two mothers exhorts us to fight always for the truth until the end (AUGUSTINE). The judgment of Solomon demonstrates that sometimes the use of a lie reveals the truth (CASSIAN). The two mothers can also symbolize two different people inside the same church: the first dominated by insincerity, the latter by the love of truth (AUGUSTINE). The innocent mother is also a symbol of

excellence (AMBROSE) that distinguishes the true church from any Arian heresy (AUGUSTINE). She also shows how true charity is the only aim that the faithful and righteous members of the church of God must pursue (AUGUSTINE).

3:16-28 Two Women Came Before the King

THE MIND OF GOD WAS IN SOLOMON.

AMBROSE: Is not that noble judgment of Solomon full of wisdom and justice? Let us see whether it is so. "Two women," it says, "stood before King Solomon, and the one said to him, 'Hear me, my lord, I and this woman dwell in one house, and before the third day we gave birth and bore a son apiece and were together; there was no witness in the house, nor any other woman with us, only we two alone. And her son died this night, because she laid on him, and she arose at midnight, and took my son from my breast and laid him in her bosom, and her dead child she laid at my breast. And I arose in the morning to nurse my child and found him dead. And I examined him at dawn, and behold, it was not my son.' And the other woman said, 'No, but the living is my son, and the dead is your son.'" This was their dispute, in which either tried to claim the living child for herself and denied that the dead one was hers. Then the king commanded a sword to be brought and the infant to be cut in half, and either piece to be given to one, one half to the one, and one half to the other. Then the woman whose the child really was, moved by her feelings, cried out, "Do not divide the child, my lord; rather, let it be given to her and live, and do not kill it." But the other answered: "Let it be neither mine nor hers; divide it." Then the king ordered that the infant should be given to the woman who had said "do not kill it," for, as it says, "her compassion earned over her son."

It is not wrong to suppose that the mind of God was in him; for what is hidden from God? What can be more hidden than the witness that lies deep within; into which the mind of the wise king as though to judge a mother's feelings and elicited as it were the voice of a mother's heart? For a mother's feelings were laid bare when she chose that her son should live with another, rather than that he should be killed in his mother's sight. It was therefore a sign of wisdom to distinguish between secret heart thoughts, to draw the truth from hidden springs and to pierce as it were with the sword of the Spirit not only the inward parts of the body but even of the mind and soul. It was the part of justice also that she who had killed her own child should not take away another's but that the real mother should have her own back again. Indeed the Scriptures have declared this. "All Israel," it says, "heard of the judgment that the king had judged, and they feared the king, for they saw that the wisdom of God was present in judgment." Solomon also

himself had asked for wisdom, so that a prudent heart might be given him to hear and to judge with justice.[1] DUTIES OF THE CLERGY 2.8.44-47.[2]

AN ALLEGORY OF THE CHURCH AND THE SYN-AGOGUE. EPHREM THE SYRIAN: The two women indicate to us the church and the synagogue. The latter, after it tried to suppress the sacrament of human redemption and persecuted and killed the Redeemer through false accusations, claims, nevertheless, that its child should still be alive, that is, that the Jewish people should still be pleasing and acceptable to God and that he should give eternal life to the Mosaic law, which is dead. Since the [synagogue] is soaked in these errors, it perpetually quarrels with the church, which is represented by the other woman. However, the peaceful king settled the argument not by dividing but by gathering the children of both mothers, so that a single body might be created from the Jews and the Gentiles, whose head is Christ. And both mothers assert that they live under the same roof, because the church and the synagogue inhabit this world in dwellings, where they are mixed. ON THE FIRST BOOK OF KINGS 3.16.[3]

THE DEAD CHILD BELONGS TO THE JERUSA-LEM BELOW, THE LIVING TO THAT ABOVE. AUGUSTINE: The first idea that occurs to me on consideration is that the two women are the synagogue and the church. For the synagogue is convicted of having killed Christ her son, born of the Jews according to the flesh, in her sleep; that is, by following the light of this present life and not perceiving the revelation of trust in the sayings of the Lord. That is why it is written, "Rise, sleeper, and arise from the dead, and Christ will enlighten you."[4] That they were two and that they were alone, living in one house, may be taken to mean, without being far-fetched, that besides the circumcision and the uncircumcision there is no other kind of religion to be found in this world. So under the person of one woman you can

---

[1]See 1 Kings 3:9. [2]NPNF 2 10:50-51*. [3]ESOO 1:452. [4]Eph 5:14.

include the race of circumcised men bound by the worship and the law of one God, while under the person of the other woman you can comprehend all the uncircumcised Gentiles given over to the worship of idols.

But they were both harlots. Well, the apostles say that Jews and Greeks are all under sin. Every soul that forsakes eternal truth for base earthly pleasures is whoring away from the Lord. Now about the church that comes from the whoredom of the Gentiles, it is clear that it did not kill Christ.... Pay attention to the Gospel and listen to what the Lord says: "Whoever does the will of my Father, this is my mother and brother and sister."[5] So when did this one sleep, not indeed to smother her child in sleep but at least so that the dead one could be substituted and the living one taken away from her? Does it perhaps mean this, that the very sacrament of circumcision which had remained dead among the Jews because their view of it was wholly carnal and literal—that this lifeless sacrament of circumcision some Jews wished to foist like a lifeless body on the Gentiles who had believed in Christ, as it says in the Acts of the Apostles, telling them that they could not be saved unless they had themselves circumcised?[6] They were foisting this on those ignorant of the law, as though they were substituting the dead child in the darkness of the night. But that argument would have no chance of success except where the sleep of folly had stolen over some part of the church of the Gentiles. From this sleep the apostle seems to be shaking her when he exclaims, "O foolish Galatians, who has bewitched you?" And a little later: "Are you such fools," he says, "that after beginning with the spirit you now end with the flesh?"[7] as though he were saying, "Are you such fools, that after first having a living spiritual work, you lose it and go on to accept someone else's dead one?"

Indeed, the same apostle says elsewhere, "The spirit is life because of justice."[8] And in another place, "To be wise according to the flesh is death."[9] At these and similar words, then, that mother wakes up, and early morning dawns on her when the obscurity of the law is lit up by the word of God, that is, by Christ who was rising like the sun,[10] that is, was speaking in Paul. He lit up this darkness when he said, "Tell me, you who wish to be under the law, have you not heard the law? For it is written that Abraham had two sons, one by a slave woman and one by a free woman. But the one by the slave woman was born according to the flesh, the one by the free woman through a promise; which is all an allegory. For these are the two Testaments, one from Mount Sinai, bringing forth into slavery, which is Hagar (for Sinai is a mountain in Arabia), and she corresponds to the present Jerusalem, because she is in slavery with her children. But the Jerusalem above is free."[11] No wonder, then, if on account of dead works the dead child belongs to the Jerusalem below, while on account of spiritual ones the living child belongs to the Jerusalem above. After all, hell is sown below, where the dead belong; and heaven above, where the living belong. Enlightened in this way, as by the coming of daybreak, the church has an understanding of spiritual grace and thrusts away from it the carnal accomplishments of the law, like the other woman's dead child. Instead [the church] claims for itself a living faith—since "the just person lives by faith"[12]—which it has acquired in the name of the Father and the Son and the Holy Spirit; that is why it recognizes with certainty the son as three days old and does not allow him to be snatched away. SERMON 10.2.[13]

A TYPE OF FALSE CHRISTIANS. AUGUSTINE: Now let the other one claim that the gospel is hers, as being owed to her and produced through her. For that is what they were saying to the Gentiles in this dispute, those of the Jews who, while clinging to the letter of the law, dared to call themselves Christians. They were saying that the gospel had come as something owed to them for their justice. But it was not theirs, because they

---

[5]Mt 12:50. [6]See Acts 15:1. [7]Gal 3:1-3. [8]Rom 8:10. [9]Rom 8:6. [10]See Lk 1:78. [11]Gal 4:21-26. [12]Rom 1:17. [13]*WSA* 3 1:283-84.

did not know how to grasp its spirit. So they even had the audacity to contend that they were to be called Christians, boasting in someone else's name like that woman claiming a son she had not borne; and this though by excluding a spiritual understanding from the works of the law they had as it were drained the soul out of the body of their works, and while smothering the live spirit of prophecy had remained attached to their material keeping of the law, which lacked all life, that is to say, spiritual understanding. They wanted to foist all this on the Gentiles too, and take from them, like the living child, the name of Christian. In refuting them, the apostle went so far as to say that the more they claim Christian grace as their due and boast that it is theirs as though by right of the works of the law, the less it really belongs to them. "For to one who works," he says, "his wages are not reckoned as a grace or favor but as his due. But to one who does not work but believes in him who justifies the wicked, it is faith that is reckoned as justice."[14] And therefore he does not count among their number those of the Jews who had believed rightly and were holding fast to a living spiritual grace. He says this remnant of the Jewish people were saved, when the majority of them had gone to perdition. "So therefore at the present time also," he says, "a remnant has been saved, chosen by grace. But if it is by grace, it is no longer as a result of works; otherwise grace would no longer be grace."[15] So those are excluded from grace who claim the prize of the gospel is theirs by right, owed and given them for their works. This is like the synagogue claiming, "It is my son." But [the synagogue] was lying. It too, you see, had received him, but by sleeping on him, that is, by being proud in its own conceits, it had killed him. But now this other mother was awake and understood that it was not through her own merits, since she is a harlot, but through God's grace that she had been granted a son, namely, the work of evangelical faith, which she longed to nurse in the bosom of her heart. So that while one was using another person's son to acquire human respectability, this one was preserving a true love for her own. Sermon 10.3.[16]

Fight for the Truth. Augustine: As for the royal judgment between the two of them, it simply admonishes us to fight for the truth and to drive hypocrisy away from the spiritual gift of the church like a spurious mother from another woman's living son and not to let her control the grace granted to others when she could not take care of her own. But let us do this, defending and fighting for the truth without running the risk of division. That decision of the judge, when he ordered the baby to be cut in two, is not meant as a breach of unity but as a test of charity. The name Solomon means peaceable. So a peaceable king does not tear limbs apart that contain the spirit of life in unity and concord. But his threat discovers the true mother, and his judgment sets aside the spurious one. So then, if it comes to this sort of crisis and trial, to prevent the unity of Christian grace from being torn apart, we are taught to say, "Give her the child, only let him live." The true mother, you see, is not concerned about the honor of motherhood but about the well-being of her son. Wherever he may be, his mother's true love will make him more her possession than that of the false claimant. Sermon 10.4.[17]

A Wise Judgment. John Cassian: What about Solomon, who received the gift of wisdom from God and who made his first judgment with the help of a lie? For, in order to elicit the truth that was hidden by a woman's lie, he himself also made use of a very cleverly thought-out lie when he said, "Bring me a sword, and cut the living infant in two pieces, and give half to one and half to the other." When this semblance of cruelty profoundly shook the real mother but was praised by the one who was not the mother, he at once, as a result of this most astute discovery of

---

[14]Rom 4:4-5. [15]Rom 11:5-6. [16]WSA 3 1:284-85*. [17]WSA 3 1:285-86*.

the truth, handed down the sentence that everyone believes was inspired by God: "Give the living infant to this woman," he said, "and do not let it be slain. This is its mother." CONFERENCE 17.25.4.[18]

THE HARLOT'S SON SYMBOLIZES THE SINNER'S GRACE. AUGUSTINE: Again, I see these two women in one house as representing two kinds of people in one church: one of them dominated by insincerity, the other ruled by charity. So we may regard these two kinds of people simply like two women, called love and insincerity. Insincerity, of course, deceitfully imitates love. That is why the apostle warns us against her when he says, "Let love be without insincerity."[19] Although the two live in one house as long as that gospel net is in the sea, enclosing good and bad fish together until it is brought ashore, yet each is doing her own thing. They were both harlots, though, because everyone is converted to the grace of God from worldly desires, and nobody can properly boast about any prior justice and its merits. A harlot's committing fornication is her own doing; her having a son is God's. All human beings, after all, are fashioned by the one creator God. Nor it is surprising that God works well even in the sins of men and women. After all, even the crime of Judas the traitor was used by our Lord to achieve the salvation of the human race. But the difference is that when God brings something good out of anyone's sin, it is not usually something that the sinner wants. It is not only that when he sins he does not sin with the same intention as God's providence turning his sin to a just end—Judas, you see, did not betray Christ with the same intention as Christ had in allowing himself to be betrayed; it is also that when he realizes his sin has produced a better result that he never wanted to happen, it gives him more pain than pleasure. Suppose, for example, someone wants to give his enemy poison while he is sick, but he makes a mistake about the kind of medicine and gives him something beneficial instead, so that the sick person gets better

through the kindness of God, who decided to turn his enemy's villainy to his advantage. But when the wicked person realizes that his own hand has restored the other to health, he suffers torments and frustration. But if a harlot is willing to have the child she has conceived and is not driven by lust or avaricious concern for her shameful earnings to take an abortifacient and eliminate what she has conceived from her womb, in case her fertility should interfere with her sinning, then the appetite that had been dissipated among a great many is now concentrated on the one gift of God and will no longer be called greed, but love. So the harlot's son is rightly understood as representing the sinner's grace; the new creature born of the old shame is the forgiveness of sins. SERMON 10.5.[20]

THE REAL MOTHER IS A TYPE OF THE CHURCH. AMBROSE: Such a Shechem[21] is the church; for Solomon chose her whose hidden love he had discerned. Such a Shechem is Mary, whose soul God's sword pierces and divides.[22] Such a Shechem is a "coming up," even as it appears in the meaning of the word. As to what the "coming up" is, hear Solomon speaking in reference to the church, "Who is she that comes up clothed in white, leaning on her brother?"[23] She is radiant, a word expressed in Greek as *aktinodes*, because she is resplendent in faith and in works. To her children it is said, "Let your works shine before my Father, who is in heaven."[24] THE PRAYER OF JOB AND DAVID 4.4.16.[25]

FIGURES OF THE CATHOLIC CHURCH AND THE ARIAN HERESY. AUGUSTINE (CAESARIUS OF ARLES): The lesson to be read at Vespers, dearly beloved, concerns the two harlots who came for the decision of Solomon; one of them, who was not only dissolute but also cruel and wicked,

---

[18]ACW 57:605-6. [19]Rom 12:9. [20]WSA 3 1:286*. [21]See Gen 48:22. Shechem is a symbol of excellence: it is that splendid portion that Jacob allotted to his son Joseph. [22]See Lk 2:35. [23]Song 8:5 (LXX). [24]Mt 5:16. [25]FC 65:401*.

shouted to the king that he should command the infant to be cut in two. Now, if you willingly listen, we would like to mention to the ears of your charity what the holy Fathers have explained about the matter. The woman who cried out that the boy should be kept whole represented a type of the Catholic church; the other cruel and impious woman who shouted that the boy should be divided signified the Arian heresy. The Catholic church like a most devoted mother exclaims to all heretics: Do not make Christ less than the Father; do not divide his unity; do not divide the one God in various degrees and fashion, as it were, idols of the pagans in your hearts. Keep him with you entirely; if you want to have peace, do not divide his unity. Indeed, if you have the whole, everything remains yours. So great is the omnipotence of God that all possess him entire, and each one possesses all of him. However, the impious, cruel heresy exclaims, "No, but divide him." What does this mean, divide him, except that the Son is not equal to the Father? If a person takes equality from the Son, he denies that the Father is good and omnipotent. If God the Father could beget a Son like himself but would not, he is not good; if he would but could not, he is not almighty. Be assured, brothers, that none of the Arians can answer this statement; but whenever they are limited by the truest reason, like a slippery snake they take refuge in some sort of clever and involved inquiries. SERMON 123.1.[26]

TRUE CHARITY WILL BE THE AIM OF THE CHURCH OF CHRIST. AUGUSTINE: But there is no greater proof of charity in Christ's church than when the very honor that seems so important among people is despised, in order to prevent the limbs of the infant being cut in two and Christian infirmity being torn to shreds by the break of unity. The apostle says that he had shown himself like a mother to the little ones among whom he had done the good work of the gospel, not he but the grace of God in him.[27] That harlot could call nothing her own except her sins, whereas the gift of fertility she had

from God. And the Lord says beautifully about a harlot, "She to whom much is forgiven loves much."[28] So the apostle Paul says, "I became a little one among you, like a wet-nurse fondling her children."[29] But when it comes to the danger of the little one being cut in two, when Insincerity claims for herself a spurious dignity of motherhood and is prepared to break up unity, the mother despises her proper dignity provided she may see her son whole and preserve him alive; she is afraid that if she insists too obstinately on the dignity due to her motherhood, she may give Insincerity a chance to divide the feeble limbs with the sword of schism. So indeed let mother Charity say, "Give her the boy." "Whether in pretense or in truth, let Christ be preached."[30] In Moses Charity exclaims, "Lord, either pardon them or blot me out of your book."[31] But in the Pharisees Insincerity speaks: "If we let him go, the Romans will come and take away our nation and place."[32] It was not the reality of justice that they wished to have but its name, and they desired to hold on dishonestly to the honor owed to just men and women. And yet Insincerity reigning in them was permitted to sit in Moses' seat, and so the Lord could say, "Do what they say, but do not do what they do;"[33] and so while enjoying a spurious honor they would still nurture the little ones and the weak on the truth of the Scriptures. Insincerity, you see, has her own proper crime—smothering with the weight of her slumbers the new creature she had received through the grace of God pardoning her, but the milk of faith which she has is not hers. Because even after the death of the child, who represents the new life of being born again, Insincerity now set in her bad ways still retains in her memory, as in her breasts, Christian doctrine and the words of faith, which are handed on to all who come to the church. From this milk even the spurious mother could give suck of the true faith to the infant being

---

[26]FC 47:206-7*. [27]See 1 Thess 2:7. [28]Lk 7:47. [29]1 Thess 2:7. [30]Phil 1:18. [31]Exod 32:32. [32]Jn 11:48. [33]Mt 23:2-3.

suckled. For that reason the true mother is without anxiety when her baby is being nurtured even by the insincere on the milk of the divine Scriptures of the Catholic faith, when unity is saved and division prevented, and Charity is approved by the judge's final sentence, which represents Christ's last judgment. Since, in order to save her baby and uphold unity, she was prepared to concede the dignity of motherhood even to Insincerity, for holding on to love and embracing the grace of life she will enjoy the everlasting reward of a devoted mother. SERMON 10.8.[34]

---

[34]*WSA* 3 1:288-89*.

4:1-34 SOLOMON'S RULE
WAS MAGNIFICENT AND WISE

[7]Solomon had twelve officers over all Israel, who provided food for the king and his household; each man had to make provision for one month in the year. [8]These were their names: Ben-hur, in the hill country of Ephraim; [9]Ben-deker, in Makaz, Sha-albim, Beth-shemesh, and Elon-beth-hanan; [10]Ben-hesed, in Arubboth (to him belonged Socoh and all the land of Hepher); [11]Ben-abinadab, in all Naphath-dor (he had Taphath the daughter of Solomon as his wife); [12]Baana the son of Ahilud, in Taanach, Megiddo, and all Beth-shean which is beside Zarethan below Jezreel, and from Beth-shean to Abel-meholah, as far as the other side of Jokmeam; [13]Ben-geber, in Ramoth-gilead (he had the villages of Jair the son of Manasseh, which are in Gilead, and he had the region of Argob, which is in Bashan, sixty great cities with walls and bronze bars); [14]Ahinadab the son of Iddo, in Mahanaim; [15]Ahima-az, in Naphtali (he had taken Basemath the daughter of Solomon as his wife); [16]Baana the son of Hushai, in Asher and Bealoth; [17]Jehoshaphat the son of Paruah, in Issachar; [18]Shime-i the son of Ela, in Benjamin; [19]Geber the son of Uri, in the land of Gilead, the country of Sihon king of the Amorites and of Og king of Bashan. And there was one officer in the land of Judah.

[20]Judah and Israel were as many as the sand by the sea; they ate and drank and were happy. [21g]Solomon ruled over all the kingdoms from the Euphrates to the land of the Philistines and to the border of Egypt; they brought tribute and served Solomon all the days of his life.

[22]Solomon's provision for one day was thirty cors of fine flour, and sixty cors of meal, [23]ten fat oxen, and twenty pasture-fed cattle, a hundred sheep, besides harts, gazelles, roebucks, and fatted fowl. [24]For he had dominion over all the region west of the Euphrates from Tiphsah to Gaza, over all the kings west of the Euphrates; and he had peace on all sides round about him. [25]And Judah and Israel dwelt in safety, from Dan even to Beer-sheba, every man under his vine and under his fig tree, all the days of Solomon. [26]Solomon also had forty thousand stalls of horses for his chariots,

and twelve thousand horsemen. *²⁷And those officers supplied provisions for King Solomon, and for all who came to King Solomon's table, each one in his month; they let nothing be lacking. ²⁸Barley also and straw for the horses and swift steeds they brought to the place where it was required, each according to his charge.*

²⁹And God gave Solomon wisdom and understanding beyond measure, and largeness of mind like the sand on the seashore, ³⁰so that Solomon's wisdom surpassed the wisdom of all the people of the east, and all the wisdom of Egypt. ³¹For he was wiser than all other men, wiser than Ethan the Ezrahite, and Heman, Calcol, and Darda, the sons of Mahol; and his fame was in all the nations round about. ³²He also uttered three thousand proverbs; and his songs were a thousand and five. ³³He spoke of trees, from the cedar that is in Lebanon to the hyssop that grows out of the wall; he spoke also of beasts, and of birds, and of reptiles, and of fish. ³⁴And men came from all peoples to hear the wisdom of Solomon, and from all the kings of the earth, who had heard of his wisdom.

g Ch 5.1 in Heb

OVERVIEW: The twelve prefects appointed by Solomon to administer his kingdom foreshadow the twelve apostles chosen by Christ (EPHREM). The testimonies concerning David and especially Solomon in the Old Testament demonstrate how all Christians have the duty to become wise. The passages in the Scripture concerning Solomon's wisdom prove that all pagan philosophers were influenced by him, and what can be considered wise in their reflections undoubtedly derives from him, who was divinely inspired (ORIGEN). Only a small part of Solomon's writings is extant, while a large number were lost (ISHO'DAD).

4:1-19 Solomon's Officials

THE APOSTLES FORESHADOWED IN SOL-OMON'S OFFICIALS. EPHREM THE SYRIAN: The officials elected by Solomon designate the order of the chosen ones whom Christ affirmed in his grace and appointed as rulers of his people. Indeed, twelve prefects were selected to administer the incomes of this king and his house, because just as many apostles had to be distributed over the entire world and had to be appointed as treasures of the divine mysteries, so that they might nourish with living and immortal food the Israel of God and might administer the incomes of the house of the peaceful king. Therefore, also the limits of each prefecture were clearly denoted, because, in a similar way, each apostle received a certain province: Simon preached in Rome, John in Ephesus, Matthew in Palestine and Thomas in the region of India. ON THE FIRST BOOK OF KINGS 4.1.[1]

4:29-34 God Gave Solomon Great Wisdom

THE OBJECT OF A CHRISTIAN IS TO BECOME WISE. ORIGEN: But that the object of Christianity is that we should become wise can be proved from the ancient Jewish writings, which we also use, as well as from those that were composed after the time of Jesus and that are believed among the churches to be divine. Now, in the fiftieth psalm, David is described as saying in his prayer to God these words: "The unseen and secret things of your wisdom you have manifested to me."[2] Solomon, too, because he asked for wisdom, received it; and if anyone were to peruse the Psalms, he would find the book filled with many maxims of wisdom; and the evidences of Solomon's wisdom may be seen in his treatises, which contain a great amount of wisdom expressed in few words, and in which

---

[1]ESOO 1:453. [2]Ps 51:6 (50:8 LXX).

you will find many praises of wisdom and encouragements towards obtaining it. So wise, moreover, was Solomon, that the queen of Sheba,[3] having heard his name and the name of the Lord, came to try him with difficult questions and spoke to him all things, whatsoever were in her heart; and Solomon answered her all her questions. There was no question omitted by the king that he did not answer her. And the queen of Sheba saw all the wisdom of Solomon and the possessions that he had, and there was no more spirit in her. And she said to the king, "The report is true that I heard in my own land regarding you and your wisdom; and I did not believe them who told me, until I had come, and my eyes have seen it. And, lo, they did not tell me the half. You have added wisdom and possessions above all the report that I heard."[4] It is also recorded of him that "God gave Solomon very great wisdom, discernment and breadth of understanding as vast as the sand on the seashore, so that Solomon's wisdom surpassed the wisdom of all the people of the east and all the wisdom of Egypt. He was wiser than anyone else, wiser than Ethan the Ezrahite, and Heman, Calcol and Darda, children of Mahol; his fame spread throughout all the surrounding nations. He composed three thousand proverbs, and his songs numbered a thousand and five. He would speak of trees, from the cedar that is in Lebanon to the hyssop that grows in the wall; he would speak of animals, and birds, and reptiles and fish. People came from all the nations to hear the wisdom of Solomon; they came from all the kings of the earth who had heard of his wisdom." AGAINST CELSUS 3.45.[5]

SOLOMON WAS THE FIRST AND ONLY DIVINE PHILOSOPHER. ORIGEN: [Greek philosophers] took these ideas from Solomon, since it was long before them in age and time that he first gave these teachings through the Spirit of God. The Greeks have brought them forth as their own discoveries, and they have also included them in their books of instructions and left them to be handed down to their successors. But, as we have said, Solomon discovered them before all the rest and taught them through the wisdom he received from God, as it is written, "And God gave Solomon understanding and wisdom beyond measure, and largeness of heart like the sand on the seashore. And his wisdom was made greater than that of all the ancient sons of humankind and all the wise men of Egypt." Thus, Solomon, since he wished to distinguish from one another and to separate what we have called earlier the three general disciplines, that is, moral, natural and contemplative, set them forth in three books, each one in its own logical order. Thus, he first taught in Proverbs the subject of morals, setting regulations for life together, as was fitting, in concise and brief maxims. And he included the second subject, which is called the natural discipline, in Ecclesiastes, in which he discusses many natural things. And by distinguishing them as empty and vain from what is useful and necessary, he warns that vanity must be abandoned and what is useful and right must be pursued. He also handed down the subject of contemplation in the book we have in hand, that is, Song of Songs, in which he urges on the soul the love of the heavenly and the divine under the figure of the bride and the bridegroom, teaching us that we must attain fellowship with God by the paths of loving affection and of love. Indeed, he was not unaware that he was laying the foundations of the true philosophy and founding the order of its disciplines and principles. COMMENTARY ON THE SONG OF SONGS PROLOGUE 3.[6]

THE LOSS OF SOLOMON'S WORKS. ISHO'DAD OF MERV: Of his three thousand proverbs a single book is left, while all the others perished during the captivity. And of his one thousand and five songs we still possess a single one, that is the Song of Songs. BOOKS OF SESSIONS 1 KINGS 4.32.[7]

---

[3]See 1 Kings 10:1-13. [4]1 Kings 10:6-7. [5]ANF 4:482*. [6]OSW 231-32. [7]CSCO 229:102.

5:1-12 SOLOMON PREPARES TO BUILD THE TEMPLE

¹ᵇNow Hiram king of Tyre sent his servants to Solomon, when he heard that they had anointed him king in place of his father; for Hiram always loved David. ²And Solomon sent word to Hiram, ³"You know that David my father could not build a house for the name of the Lord his God because of the warfare with which his enemies surrounded him, until the Lord put them under the soles of his feet. ⁴But now the Lord my God has given me rest on every side; there is neither adversary nor misfortune. ⁵And so I purpose to build a house for the name of the Lord my God, as the Lord said to David my father, 'Your son, whom I will set upon your throne in your place, shall build the house for my name.' ⁶Now therefore command that cedars of Lebanon be cut for me; and my servants will join your servants, and I will pay you for your servants such wages as you set; for you know that there is no one among us who knows how to cut timber like the Sidonians."

⁷When Hiram heard the words of Solomon, he rejoiced greatly, and said, "Blessed be the Lord this day, who has given to David a wise son to be over this great people." ⁸And Hiram sent to Solomon, saying, "I have heard the message which you have sent to me; I am ready to do all you desire in the matter of cedar and cypress timber. ⁹My servants shall bring it down to the sea from Lebanon; and I will make it into rafts to go by sea to the place you direct, and I will have them broken up there, and you shall receive it; and you shall meet my wishes by providing food for my household." ¹⁰So Hiram supplied Solomon with all the timber of cedar and cypress that he desired, ¹¹while Solomon gave Hiram twenty thousand cors of wheat as food for his household, and twenty thousandⁱ cors of beaten oil. Solomon gave this to Hiram year by year. ¹²And the Lord gave Solomon wisdom, as he promised him; and there was peace between Hiram and Solomon; and the two of them made a treaty.

h Ch 5.15 in Heb   i Gk: Heb *twenty*

OVERVIEW: The temple was built by Solomon after the destruction of his enemies, when peace had been restored in Israel, and in the same way the church was built in the peace following the victory against earthly vices (PRUDENTIUS). The servants of Hiram, who cut the wood of Lebanon, represent the teachers chosen among the Gentiles in order to correct and convert the nations to the obedience and doctrine of Christ (BEDE). Hiram did not hesitate to help Solomon, because he had been previously converted to the religion of God by David (ISHO'DAD). Solomon foreshadows, in his act of building the temple, the spiritual construction of the church accomplished by Jesus

through his saving actions (EPHREM).

5:4-5 Building a House for God

THE CHURCH IS BUILT IN TIMES OF PEACE.
PRUDENTIUS:

After this war one work remains for us,
O leaders, that which Solomon achieved,
The peaceful scion and the unarmed heir
Of a warlike realm, whose father's weary hand
Was sullied by the ardent blood of kings.
The blood effaced, a temple is upraised
And golden altar, house sublime of Christ.
Jerusalem then by its temple crowned,

Received its God, now that the wandering ark
On the marble altar found repose.
In our camp let a sacred temple rise,
that God may in its sanctuary dwell.
What profits it to have repelled the hosts
Of earth-born vices, if the Son of man
From heaven descending, enter the body
  cleansed,
But unadorned and not a temple fair?
Thus far we have engaged in fierce conflict:
Now let white-vestured Peace perform its
  tasks,
And youth unarmed build up a sacred house.
THE SPIRITUAL COMBAT 804-22.[1]

5:6 The Servants of Solomon and Hiram

TYPES OF THE TEACHERS CHOSEN AMONG
THE GENTILES. BEDE: For the servants of Hiram
who cut down cedars from Lebanon for Solomon
are the teachers chosen from among the Gentiles
whose task is to fell those who enjoy the goods
and glory of this world by correcting their pride
and arrogance and convert their ambition into
obedience to their Redeemer. Now with these
servants were also the servants of Solomon, and
together they set about the work referred to
because the first teachers from among the Gentiles needed the apostles, who had received training by being instructed in the word of faith, lest,
were they to begin to teach without masters, they
might turn out to be teachers of error. For the
reason why Solomon wanted the servants of
Hiram to hew timber from Lebanon for him was
that they were more experienced than his own
servants in felling, but the reason why he also
wanted his own servants to be there with them
was that they might show the lumbermen what
length the planks ought to be. What this symbolizes is plain, namely, that the apostles had a surer
knowledge of how to preach to others the word of
the gospel that they were privileged to hear from
the Lord, but the Gentiles, converted from error
and brought into conformity with the truth of the
gospel, had a better knowledge of the actual

errors of the Gentiles, and the surer their knowledge the more skillfully they learned to counter-
act and refute them. Paul indeed had a better
knowledge of the mystery of the gospel, which he
had learned through revelation, but Dionysus
was better able to refute the false teachings of
Athens, whose syllogisms as well as errors and all
of whose arguments he knew since a boy. With
this explanation the statement that follows is
fully in keeping: "For you know that there is not a
man among my people who has the skill to hew
wood like the Sidonians." For when the Lord was
bodily present teaching, there was not one among
the Jewish people who knew so well how to refute
the errors of the Gentiles as the actual Gentile
converts to the faith and those of the Gentiles
who had become Christians. For the Sidonians
and Tyrians are rightly taken as a type of the
Gentiles because they were Gentile peoples. ON
THE TEMPLE 1.2.4-5.[2]

5:7 Hiram Heard and Rejoiced

HIRAM HAD BEEN CONVERTED BY DAVID.
ISHO'DAD OF MERV: This Hiram had been converted to [the worship of] God through his rela-
tionships with David, and "he rejoiced greatly,
when he heard" that a house would be built for
the Lord. He asks to be supplied with bread and
oil in exchange for the wood that he delivers
because the Tyrians and the Sidonians, as it
appears, did not sow or harvest since their commerce was exclusively maritime. BOOKS OF SES-
SIONS 1 KINGS 5.7.[3]

5:10 Hiram Supplied Timbers of Cedar

A PARALLEL BETWEEN SOLOMON AND
CHRIST. EPHREM THE SYRIAN: Here we do not
need to work around any concealed meaning;
indeed, in this event there is a clear analogy with
Christ and the actions he undertook for the
building of the church. As Solomon ordered tim-

---

[1]FC 52:106-7. [2]TTH 21:8-9. [3]CSCO 229:102-3.

bers to be cut from the mountains of Lebanon and stones to be shipped by sea, and employed them after they had been brought to the builder's yard of the temple, so Christ, after receiving the Jews and the Gentiles from the timbers of infidel-

ity, transported them to the builder's yard of the temple which is not made by human hands. On the First Book of Kings 5.10.[4]

---

[4]*ESOO* 1:456.

5:13-18 WORKERS ARE CONSCRIPTED FROM ISRAEL

[13]*King Solomon raised a levy of forced labor out of all Israel; and the levy numbered thirty thousand men.* [14]*And he sent them to Lebanon, ten thousand a month in relays; they would be a month in Lebanon and two months at home; Adoniram was in charge of the levy.* [15]*Solomon also had seventy thousand burden-bearers and eighty thousand hewers of stone in the hill country,* [16]*besides Solomon's three thousand three hundred chief officers who were over the work, who had charge of the people who carried on the work.* [17]*At the king's command, they quarried out great, costly stones in order to lay the foundation of the house with dressed stones.* [18]*So Solomon's builders and Hiram's builders and the men of Gebal did the hewing and prepared the timber and the stone to build the house.*

OVERVIEW: The fact that Solomon summoned people from all districts of Israel demonstrates that priests must be chosen from the entire community of the Christians, and not only from certain specific groups (BEDE). The number of the stonecutters and laborers symbolizes the host of angels sent by God to help us in our Christian battles (EPHREM), as well as apostolic preaching, the Gospels and the Trinity (JEROME). The costly and square stones used to make the foundations of the temple are figures of the teachers of the church, who built the spiritual church through their holy preaching (BEDE).

5:13-14 Solomon Conscripted Labor from All Israel

CHRISTIAN PRIESTS MUST BE CHOSEN FROM THE WHOLE CHURCH. BEDE: The first thing to

note here is that it was not for nothing that Solomon chose workmen from all Israel, nor was there any section of the people from which men fit for such a great task were not taken, because, of course, priests nowadays are not to be chosen from the stock of Aaron alone; rather, people are to be sought from the whole church who, whether by example or word, are competent to build the house of the Lord, and wherever they are found they are to be promoted to the office of teachers without any exception of persons. And when such people are ordained to instruct the infidel and those who are to be called into the joint pastorate of the church, they are sent as energetic and picked men, as it were, to hew in Lebanon the materials for the temple. And indeed the number of thirty thousand, which was the tally of the hewers of wood, can be aptly applied figuratively to those who are perfect in the faith of the holy Trinity, because it is most appropriate for teachers. ON THE TEMPLE 1.3.1.[1]

5:15-16 Laborers and Stonecutters

THE SYMBOLISM OF THE LABORERS AND THE STONECUTTERS. EPHREM THE SYRIAN: These thousands of men employed in the cutting and transportation of the wooden beams and the stones signify the thousands of thousands of assistant spirits sent for our salvation. In the first place, [we see that] God ordered his angels to cut from the rock of the world and to polish and direct accurately the souls of the saints. . . . Second, in this same symbol, we can observe the toils of the saints for the conversion and salvation of souls, either when they endeavor to drive human beings away from the love of the world or when, after they have accomplished that, they begin to polish the stones cut from the rock until they provide them with luster by a thorough polishing and make them worthy of the heavenly building. Then they are taken and employed by the supreme builder. . . . Finally we can interpret the workers of Solomon to be the angels sent to accomplish their ministry, as well as the prophets and the apostles chosen from the old people to build the church. . . . The builders sent by the king of Tyre symbolize those strong in doctrine and holiness, whom the nation of the Gentiles abundantly supplied for the same purpose. ON THE FIRST BOOK OF KINGS 5.10.[2]

FIGURES OF GREAT MYSTERIES. JEROME: Listen to even greater mysteries. At the time when Solomon built the temple, it was our peacemaker who says, "Peace I leave with you, my peace I give to you,"[3] "for he himself is our peace,"[4] "the peace of God that surpasses all understanding,"[5] who himself built the temple for God. Observe what Scripture says about the building of the temple by Solomon: "And there were seventy thousand quarrymen and eighty thousand carriers." Mark the number. The masons who were cutting stones, who were preparing, as it were, the foundations of the buildings, who were taking up stones from the ground to build the temple of God, are reckoned in the number seven, in the prophets, in the patriarchs, for while they seemingly were driving the human race from off the earth, they were making preparations for the temple of the Lord. The latter, the eighty thousand, symbolize the apostolic preaching and the Gospels; these are they who with the Lord Savior and Solomon were carrying the heavy burden of the nations. This surely is the height of mystery, but hear of even deeper mysteries! "And the overseers over the works and the temple were three thousand." They cannot be greater, not even the overseers in charge of the work, except that they proclaim the Trinity. HOMILIES ON THE PSALMS 19 (Ps 89 [90]).[6]

5:17 Quarrying Stones for the Foundation of the House

A TYPE OF THE TEACHERS OF THE HOLY CHURCH. BEDE: But it seems to be in accord with the solemn celebration that we are observing to recall something about the building of the temple and to search out how appropriately its adornment suits the significance of the church. Scripture tells how Solomon ordered that "they should take very great costly stones for the foundation of the temple and should square them off." These great and costly stones that were laid as a foundation and that supported the entire bulk of the temple built on them suggest the extraordinary teachers of the holy church: "great" because of the outstanding quality of their merits; "costly" because of the splendor of the signs that those who heard the word from the Lord himself produced by their preaching as the fabric of the growing church. HOMILIES ON THE GOSPELS 2.25.[7]

---

[1]TTH 21:9-10. [2]ESOO 1:456. [3]Jn 14:27. [4]Eph 2:14. [5]Phil 4:7. [6]FC 48:152-53*. [7]CS 111:262.

5:18 *The Giblites[8] Prepared Timber and Stone*

THOSE WHO PREPARE PEOPLE'S HEARTS.
BEDE: "Furthermore the men of Biblos [i.e., the Giblites] prepared wood and stones to build the house." Biblos is a city in Phoenicia[9] that Ezekiel mentions: "Your skilled men, Tyre, were your pilots. The elders of Biblos and its skilled men,"[10] for which [city] in Hebrew is written Gobel or Gebal, which means "defining" or "limiting." This word is very appropriate to those who prepare people's hearts for the spiritual edifice that is built of the virtues of the soul. For they are only equal to the task of teaching their hearers faith and the works of righteousness when they themselves have first been instructed by the sacred page and thoroughly learned from a clear definition of the truth what belief one must hold and on what path of virtue one must walk. For one who does not know what is definitely catholic faith is wasting his time assuming the office of teacher, and those who try to teach others the norm that they themselves have not learned do not build a sanctuary for the Lord but ruin for themselves. ON THE TEMPLE 1.4.3.[11]

---

[8]This is the Hebrew name of the inhabitants of Biblos, a city in Lebanon. [9]This is the ancient name of Lebanon. [10]Ezek 27:8-9. [11]TTH 21:15-16*.

6:1-22 SOLOMON COMPLETES THE TEMPLE

[1]In the four hundred and eightieth year after the people of Israel came out of the land of Egypt, in the fourth year of Solomon's reign over Israel, in the month of Ziv, which is the second month, he began to build the house of the LORD. [2]The house which King Solomon built for the LORD was sixty cubits long, twenty cubits wide, and thirty cubits high. [3]The vestibule in front of the nave of the house was twenty cubits long, equal to the width of the house, and ten cubits deep in front of the house. [4]And he made for the house windows with recessed frames. [5]He also built a structure against the wall of the house, running round the walls of the house, both the nave and the inner sanctuary; and he made side chambers all around. [6]The lowest story[j] was five cubits broad, the middle one was six cubits broad, and the third was seven cubits broad; for around the outside of the house he made offsets on the wall in order that the supporting beams should not be inserted into the walls of the house.

[7]When the house was built, it was with stone prepared at the quarry; so that neither hammer nor axe nor any tool of iron was heard in the temple, while it was being built.

[8]The entrance for the lowest[k] story was on the south side of the house; and one went up by stairs to the middle story, and from the middle story to the third. [9]So he built the house, and finished it; and he made the ceiling of the house of beams and planks of cedar. [10]He built the structure against the whole house, each story[l] five cubits high, and it was joined to the house with timbers of cedar.

[11]Now the word of the LORD came to Solomon, [12]"Concerning this house which you are building,

if you will walk in my statutes and obey my ordinances and keep all my commandments and walk in them, then I will establish my word with you, which I spoke to David your father. [13]*And I will dwell among the children of Israel, and will not forsake my people Israel."*

[14]*So Solomon built the house, and finished it.* [15]*He lined the walls of the house on the inside with boards of cedar; from the floor of the house to the rafters[m] of the ceiling, he covered them on the inside with wood; and he covered the floor of the house with boards of cypress.* [16]*He built twenty cubits of the rear of the house with boards of cedar from the floor to the rafters,[m] and he built this within as an inner sanctuary, as the most holy place.* [17]*The house, that is, the nave in front of the inner sanctuary, was forty cubits long.* [18]*The cedar within the house was carved in the form of gourds and open flowers; all was cedar, no stone was seen.* [19]*The inner sanctuary he prepared in the innermost part of the house, to set there the ark of the covenant of the* LORD. [20]*The inner sanctuary[n] was twenty cubits long, twenty cubits wide, and twenty cubits high; and he overlaid it with pure gold. He also made[o] an altar of cedar.* [21]*And Solomon overlaid the inside of the house with pure gold, and he drew chains of gold across, in front of the inner sanctuary, and overlaid it with gold.* [22]*And he overlaid the whole house with gold, until all the house was finished. Also the whole altar that belonged to the inner sanctuary he overlaid with gold.*

j Gk: Heb *structure*   k Gk Tg: Heb *middle*   l Heb lacks *each story*   m Gk: Heb *walls*   n Vg: Heb *and before the inner sanctuary*   o Gk: Heb *covered*

OVERVIEW: The numbers in the chronology of the construction of the temple symbolize evangelical perfection and the grace of the Holy Spirit (BEDE). David had already prepared the materials for the construction of the temple (ISHO'DAD). The measures of the house of God are symbolic figures of the virtues of the Christian church. The porch represents the people belonging to the holy church, who precede the time of our Lord's incarnation. The windows of the temple are the holy teachers to whom when in divine ecstasy it is granted to see the hidden mysteries of heaven. The side chambers or porticoes were built to support the house (ISHO'DAD). The three floors denote the levels of the faithful, namely, married people, those who practice continence and virgins (BEDE). Hammers, axes and tools of iron symbolize the devil and his instruments (ORIGEN, AMBROSE). The entrance of the house is a type of our ascension from the present life of the church, in its pilgrimage on earth, to the life of heavenly blessedness. The ceilings signify the just people of most exalted virtue, who are an example for all the faithful in the church. The structure denotes

the divine protection that helps us not to give up while still struggling in this world. In the mystical sense, the temple walls are the nations of believers of whom the holy universal church consists. The inner house that was built at the rear of the temple is the promised life in heaven that precedes this life of our exile. Different mystical meanings are symbolized by the number forty. The entire house is covered inside with cedar wood when the hearts of the righteous begin to shine with the love of good works. The ark of the covenant prefigures our Savior in whom alone we have a covenant of peace with the Father. The altar signifies typically the life of the perfectly righteous who concentrate all their attention on entering the kingdom of heaven. The gold leaf represents the manifold works of piety that pure love exhibits in the service either of its Creator or of a brother's need (BEDE).

6:1 480 Years from the Exodus

THE TIME OF CONSTRUCTION AND ITS SYMBOLISM. BEDE: Where it says, "in the fourth

year in the month of Zio,[1] which is the second month of the reign of Solomon over Israel," the intended order is, in the fourth year of the reign of Solomon in the month of Zio, that is, the second month. He calls the second month May, for April, in which the Pasch, the principal feast among the Hebrews, is held, was the first month of the year.[2] From this it is quite clear that later when the Pasch was over, he began to build a house for the Lord, and after they had been consecrated by the mystical solemnity, the people set their hands to the mystical task. A commemoration is made of the exodus from Egypt when work began on the building of the tabernacle so that the reader may be made aware what a period of time had passed between the building of both houses and learn the spiritual mystery attaching to this period of time. For four times 120 make 480; now four is very appropriate to evangelical perfection on account of the actual number of the Evangelists; 120 is appropriate to the teaching of the law on account of the same number of years of the legislator.[3] It was also in this number of men that the primitive church received the grace of the Holy Spirit,[4] clearly showing that those who use the law legitimately, that is, those who recognize and embrace the grace of Christ in it, are deservedly filled with the grace of his Spirit so that they may become more ardent in his love. On the Temple 1.5.1.[5]

6:2 The House's Dimensions

David Had Prepared Materials for the House. Isho'dad of Merv: The house that Solomon built for the [Lord] was sixty cubits long," that is, the double of the tabernacle. It is extremely likely that it included two rooms, an interior and an exterior. The interior was twenty cubits long, while the exterior was forty cubits. [The house] was built on the threshing floor of Ornan the Jebusite,[6] which David had bought together with the garden.[7] David had prepared the materials for the construction of the house, as

the book of Chronicles reports.[8] Books of Sessions 1 Kings 6.2.[9]

Figures of Faith, Charity and Hope. Bede: The temple was built of Parian marble, a white stone, to represent the brilliance of chastity in the church, concerning which the Lord says in the canticle of love: "Like a lily among thorns, so is my love among maidens."[10] [The temple] "was sixty cubits long, twenty cubits wide and thirty cubits high." The length of the temple designates the faith of the holy church, through which it bears with long-suffering patience, in the midst of its good works, the adversities brought against it by the wicked. The width designates the charity by which [the church] expands inwardly through the essential working of piety. The height designates the hope with which it awaits the rewards of the heavenly life, [which it will receive] as a result of the good deeds it performs through charity. Homilies on the Gospels 2.25.[11]

6:3 The Vestibule

The People Who Preceded the Time of the Savior. Bede: "There was also a porch in front of the temple, twenty cubits in length to correspond with the width of the temple."[12] It had a door opposite the door of the temple and was ten cubits deep, facing the east. This porch represents the people belonging to holy church who precede the time of our Lord's incarnation, yet were not empty of faith in his incarnation. This is [the meaning of] the door of the porch opposite the door of the temple, facing the east—that the faith of the people in Christ before his coming was the same as that of those who came after his arrival and that the hearts of all the faithful are illumined by the same light of the grace of the Orient. Homilies on the Gospels 2.25.[13]

---

[1]In the Hebrew text, Ziv. [2]See Exod 12:2. [3]See Deut 34:7. [4]See Acts 1:16. [5]TTH 21:17-18. [6]See 2 Chron 3:1. [7]This mention of the garden is only in the text of the Peshitta. [8]See 1 Chron 22:2-14. [9]CSCO 229:103. [10]Song 2:2. [11]CS 111:263. [12]1 Kings 6:3 (Vg). [13]CS 111:266.

6:4 Windows with Recessed Frames

A TYPE OF THOSE WHO SEE THE MYSTERIES OF HEAVEN. BEDE: The windows of the temple are the holy teachers and all the spiritual people in the church to whom when in divine ecstasy it is granted more specially than to the others to see the hidden mysteries of heaven. And when they reveal publicly to the faithful what they have seen in private, they fill all the inner recesses of the temple as windows do with the sunlight they let in. Hence these windows are appropriately said to have been slanting, that is, wider on the inside, because, of course, whoever receives a ray of heavenly contemplation even for a moment must expand the bosom of his heart more fully by mortification and prepare it by resourceful asceticism to strive for greater things. ON THE TEMPLE 1.7.1.[14]

6:5 Side Chambers All Around

THE USE OF THE SIDE CHAMBERS. ISHO'DAD OF MERV: Against the sides of the house he made side chambers, that is, some porticos like those built around a basilica, one on the other, in three levels. He did this, in the first place, because the portico was narrow and could not been divided into separate parts; secondly, in order that they might work as a support to the house so that it did not collapse. BOOKS OF SESSIONS 1 KINGS 6.5.[15]

6:6 The Dimensions of the Lowest Story

THE THREE FLOORS DENOTE THE LEVELS OF THE FAITHFUL. BEDE: In the Gospel where the Lord is tempted by the devil these floors are called the pinnacles of the temple.[16] But we also read that the apostle James, the brother of the Lord, was lifted to the pinnacle of the temple from which to address the people. Whether it was the practice of teachers to deliver their address to the people standing around below them while they sat on these floors is something

we find nowhere in the Scriptures. So what the mystery obviously means is that these three floors denote the corresponding number of levels of the faithful, namely, married people, those who practice continence and virgins, levels distinguished according to the loftiness of their profession but all of them belonging to the house of the Lord and intently clinging to him by reason of their fellowship in the same faith and truth. ON THE TEMPLE 1.7.2.[17]

6:7 No Tool of Iron Was Used

AN ALLEGORICAL FIGURE OF THE DEVIL. ORIGEN: How, he says, "was the hammer of the whole earth broken and crushed? How was Babylon brought to destruction?"[18] One needs to enquire here who is the "hammer of all the earth" or in what way its brokenness is prophesied, since it was "broken" before it was "crushed," so that after bringing together what has been written elsewhere about the "hammer," when we find its name, we will also investigate the meaning of the name from these examples that we have brought forth.

At one time there was constructed a "house of God," according to the third book of Kings,[19] and it was Solomon who built and erected it; and it was said here, as if in praise, about the "house of God," that "hammer and axe were not heard in the house of God." Therefore as the "hammer is not heard in the house of God," since the "house of God" is the church, so the "hammer is not heard" in the church. Who is this "hammer" who wants to obstruct, insofar as he can, the stones for building the temple, so that, "broken," they are not suited for its foundations? See with me if the devil is not the "hammer of the whole earth." HOMILIES ON JEREMIAH 27(50).1-2.[20]

---

[14]TTH 21:25. [15]CSCO 229:104. [16]Mt 4:5. [17]TTH 21:25. [18]Jer 50:23. [19]In LXX, VL and Jerome's Vg, 1-2 Samuel and 1-2 Kings are entitled 1-4 Kings (literally *Libri Regnorum* = Books of Kingdoms). [20]FC 97:245*.

The Tools of the Devil. Ambrose: Christ knocks with his hand that you may open, whereas the adversary cuts the door down with axes; and therefore it is written that hammer and axe should not enter into the house of God. Pride and deceit ought to be outdoors, not inside; conflicts indeed ought to be outside;[21] but within, the peace that surpasses all understanding.[22] Let not your soul be cut with the iron, but even as Joseph's soul, so may your soul pass by the iron.[23] Otherwise, your ruling part, which is like a kind of tabernacle of the Word, may be destroyed at the very beginning of faith and the entrance into spiritual learning. The Prayer of Job and David 4.7.28.[24]

6:8 The Entrance for the Middle Story

Symbolism of the Entrance and the Different Stories. Bede: The way to the upper and third [parts of the] building was made through the innermost part of the southern wall, as if by an invisible entrance, so that only its beginning might be evident from the eastern corner of the before-mentioned [southern] wall. Only he who could climb [it] knew the progress of this ascent, of which Scripture recalls: "The door in the center of the side was on the right [i.e., southern] part of the house, and they ascended by a circular stairway to the middle room and from the middle room to the third." When our Lord was suffering on the cross, "one of the soldiers opened his side with a lance, and immediately there came forth blood and water."[25] This [prefigured] the water of baptism by which we are cleansed [from sin] and the blood of the Lord's chalice by which we are sanctified. Through these holy mysteries of his side, as a consequence of our invisible faith, we ascend from the present life of the church, in its pilgrimage on earth, to the life of heavenly blessedness that the souls of the righteous enjoy once they have laid aside their bodies. When we have recovered our [earthly] bodies at the [general] resurrection, we will pass over from that life even to the supreme glory of eternal bliss, with our faith

in our Lord's passion leading the way. It is undoubtedly of this glory that Isaiah says, "In their own land they will come into possession of a double portion, undying happiness will be theirs,"[26] that is, they will receive the eternal joys of an immortal body and a happy soul together in the land of the living, which is the only land of the saints. The lowest [part of the] building signifies the present way of life of the saints; the middle [part signifies] the repose of souls that is acquired after this life; and the top [part signifies] the glory of the [final] resurrection, which will never be changed and will last forever. The door in the center of the side, which was situated in the right [i.e., southern] part of the building, and which opened up the way to the upper parts, [represents] our faith in the passion of Christ, from whose pierced right side, [while he was hanging] on the cross, there flowed forth the sacraments, by receiving which we will be able to ascend to the joys of heavenly life. Homilies on the Gospels 2.1.[27]

6:9 Roofed with Beams and Planks of Cedar

The Ceilings Signify Just People in the Church. Bede: Ceilings are boardwork constructed and adorned with great beauty and fixed to the beams on the lower side, and because the house of the Lord had been built three times the double height, naturally it had three ceilings. What is more fitting for us to believe than these ceilings signify all the just people of most exalted virtue in the holy church? And their work and teaching is held up as an example to all as being much loftier than any other, and by their intercessions and exhortations they keep the spirits of the weak from failing in temptation. These ceilings are indeed rightly described as being of cedarwood. For cedar is by nature a completely incorruptible tree, of pleasant fragrance and luxuriant appearance, and when it is set on fire it

---

[21]See 1 Cor 6:1-11. [22]See Phil 4:7. [23]See Ps 105:17-18 (104:17-18 LXX, Vg). [24]FC 65:412-13. [25]Jn 19:34. [26]Is 61:7. [27]CS 111:10-11.

drives away and destroys serpents by its dazzling brightness. These things are an apt figure of all the perfect whose patience is indomitable, whose outstanding reputation for virtue is far more pleasing to the good than that of anyone else, whose powers of refuting and proving wrong those who resist the truth are utterly unshakable, and who, both in this life and the life to come, shine with a resplendence that outshines the rest of the saints. ON THE TEMPLE 1.8.3.[28]

6:10 Each Story Five Cubits High

DIVINE PROTECTION HELPS US IN THIS WORLD. BEDE: This means the breastworks that were constructed on top of the roof of the house all around in case anyone who came up to the upper parts of the building should suddenly fall to the bottom. And in every house that anyone built, Moses ordered this to be done, saying, "When you build a new house, you shall make a parapet for your roof all the way around, lest blood be shed in your house and you be to blame should anyone slip and fall down headlong."[29] Now these structures or breastworks are called sides above,[30] where, after the words "and on the wall of the temple he built structures all around, running around the walls of the house, both the temple and the oracle," the following is immediately added: "and he made side chambers all around." These side chambers, of course, we have understood as denoting the divine protection that helps us not to give up while still struggling in this world and daily striving after higher things according to our capacity. We ought to understand this passage also in the same sense, but with this distinction that in this life, whether amid the frequent temptations of our implacable enemy or the obstacles of our frailty, we are often, indeed constantly, protected by heavenly compassion, but in the life which, as we have stated above, the top of the roof of the temple suggests, we are protected by so great a grace of God who is with us, that we neither want nor are able to sin, nor are we affected by fear of either death or pain or the adversary who tempts us. The Lord speaks of the helps he gives us in the present life, as if they were the sides of the structures, when he says of his people, "They will call on me, and I shall hear them; I am with them in their tribulation, and I shall rescue them and glorify them."[31] Of his grace to come whereby that heavenly city is illumined, the prophet says to the same city, "Praise the Lord, Jerusalem,"[32] and so forth as far as "peace in your borders." Now this structure on the roof of the house of the Lord is rightly said to be five cubits high because, of course, the presence of God's glory in that homeland [of ours] fills us in such a way that nothing else is sweet to our sight, our hearing, our sense of smell or taste or touch except to love the Lord our God with our whole heart, our whole soul, our whole mind, and to love our neighbor as ourselves. ON THE TEMPLE 1.8.4.[33]

6:15 The Walls Lined Inside with Boards of Cedar

THE TEMPLE WALLS SYMBOLIZE THE NATIONS OF BELIEVERS. BEDE: On the inside, indeed, the house was lined with cedar, for on the outside, the actual stone it was built of glinted with as much brilliance as if it had been covered with glowing white marble. Taken in the mystical sense, however, the temple walls are the nations of believers of whom the holy universal church consists and whose widespread distribution throughout the whole world is denoted by the width of the walls, whereas the height denotes the hope and whole upward thrust of the church toward heavenly things, or at any rate the height of the wall, which consists of courses of stones laid one on top of the other, denotes the state of the present church where the elect are all built on the foundation of Christ and follow each other in succession through the course of the ages and, by supporting each other, fulfill the law of Christ,[34] which is charity. ON THE TEMPLE 1.8.6.[35]

---

[28]TTH 21:32. [29]Deut 22:8. [30]See TTH 21:25. [31]Ps 91:15 (90:15 Vg). [32]Ps 147:12 (147:1 Vg). [33]TTH 21:32-33. [34]See Gal 6:2. [35]TTH 21:34.

6:16 The East Side of the Temple

A TYPE OF THE PROMISED LIFE IN HEAVEN.
BEDE: He calls the east side of the temple the
rear; for the temple had its entrance on the east
and its inner house, that is, the Holy of Holies,
on the west. The fact that he says that the board
partitions that separated the inner house from
the outer one were erected from the floor to the
top does not mean they were built to the ceiling,
which was at the height of thirty cubits from the
floor, as has already been said above,[36] but only
up to a height of twenty cubits, as one can clearly
read in what follows. But the portion above these
partitions up as far as the ceiling was left open
and empty to a height of ten cubits and a length
of twenty cubits across the width of the house,
and, of course, through this aperture the smoke
of the burnt offerings from the altar of sacrifice
used to ascend and penetrate all the way in to
cover the ark of the Lord. This division of the
Lord's house is a clear figure of a mystery and,
thanks to the explanation of the apostle, is clearer
than daylight because the first house into which
"the priests" continually "go performing their ritual duties"[37] is the present church, where, intent
on works of piety, we daily offer sacrifices of
praise to the Lord, but the inner house, which
was built at the rear of the temple,[38] is the promised life in heaven, which indeed precedes this life
of our exile, which is celebrated there in the presence of the supreme king as a perpetual solemnity
of the blessed, both angels and humankind.
Hence it is with reference to it that the servant is
quite deservedly told, "Enter into the joy of your
Lord"[39] but is later in time because it is after the
labors of this world that we succeed in entering it.
ON THE TEMPLE 1.9.2.[40]

6:17 The Nave

**THE MYSTICAL MEANING OF THE NUMBER
FORTY.** BEDE: We have said that the temple itself
before the doors of the oracle was a type of the
present church. Hence it was rightly forty cubits

long, for this number is often used to signify the
present labor of the faithful, just as the number
fifty stands for the rest and peace to come. For
the number ten contains the precepts, the observance of which leads to life. Likewise the number
ten signifies that very eternal life that we desire
and for which we live. But the world in which we
strive to attain that life is a square. Hence too the
psalmist, foreseeing the church that was to be
assembled from the nations said, "He has gathered them out of the countries from the rising
and from the setting of the sun, from the north
and from the sea."[41] Now ten multiplied by four
makes forty. Hence the people liberated from
Egypt as a figure of the present church were subjected to many hardships for forty years in the
desert,[42] but at the same time they were also
regaled with heavenly bread,[43] and in this way
they finally reached the land promised them of
old. They were subjected to trials for forty years
in order to draw attention to the hardships with
which the church contends throughout the whole
world in observing the law of God; they were fed
on manna from heaven for those forty years to
demonstrate that the very sufferings that the
church endures in the hope of the heavenly
denarius, that is, of eternal happiness, are to be
alleviated when those "who now hunger and
thirst for righteousness will have their fill,"[44] and
as the same church sings to its Redeemer, "But as
for me, I will appear before your sight in righteousness; I shall be satisfied when your glory
shall appear."[45] In the same way then the people
of God is both subjected to adversities and
regaled with manna to confirm the saying of the
apostle: "Rejoicing in hope, patient in tribulation."[46] In this figure too our Lord fasted forty
days before his bodily death and feasted forty
more with his disciples after his bodily resurrection "appearing to them by many proofs and
speaking of the kingdom of God, and eating

---

[36]See TTH 21:22-23, 30-31. [37]Heb 9:1-9. [38]See TTH 21:43. [39]Mt
25:21. [40]TTH 21:36-37. [41]Ps 107:3 (106:2 Vg). [42]See Deut 2:7.
[43]See Exod 16:35. [44]Mt 5:6. [45]Ps 17:15 (16:15 Vg). [46]Rom 12:12.

together with them."[47] For by fasting he showed in himself our toil, but by eating and drinking with his disciples he showed his consolation in our midst. While he was fasting he was crying out, as it were, "Take heed lest perhaps your hearts be weighed down with dissipation and drunkenness and the cares of this life,"[48] whereas while he was eating and drinking he was crying out, as it were, "Behold, I am with you all days even to the consummation of the world";[49] and "But I will see you again, and your heart shall rejoice, and your joy no one shall take from you."[50] For as soon as we set our feet on the way of the Lord we both fast from the vanity of the present world and are cheered with the promise of the world to come, not setting our heart on the life here below but feeding our heart on the life up there. ON THE TEMPLE 1.10.[51]

6:18 Carvings of Gourds and Flowers

THE SYMBOLISM OF THE CEDAR AND ITS CARVINGS. BEDE: We have said of cedarwood that it betokened the unsurpassable beauty of the virtues. Now the entire house is covered inside with this wood when the hearts of the righteous begin to shine with nothing but the love of good works, and the house has its turnings made of cedar boards and its joints skillfully wrought when these elect are joined to each other by the most beautiful bond of charity so that, though the multitude of the faithful is innumerable, they can nevertheless, with good reason, be said to have one heart and one soul on account of the community of the faith and love they share.[52] For the turnings that were attached to the joints of the planks in order that they might all make one partition are the very services of charity by which the holy brotherhood is bound together and formed into one house of Christ all over the world. Moreover, this house has carvings standing in relief when, far from covering and hiding their works of virtue, the saints, by a clear outward expression, show forth to all, as an example for living, what they themselves are like and what

they do, as did the apostle Paul who not only by preaching Christ to the Gentiles and by personally suffering for Christ showed how outstanding he was, but also in his letters addressed to the churches declared how many perils he underwent for Christ and by what great revelations he was raised aloft in a blessed glorification.[53] And when he said to his listeners without any hesitation, "Be imitators of me, just as I am of Christ,"[54] what did he show them but the carvings standing in relief in the house of the Lord, which by the exceptional eminence of his virtue showed itself to be within the power of all to imitate? ON THE TEMPLE 1.11.1.[55]

6:19 The Ark of the Covenant

THE ARK OF THE COVENANT IS CHRIST. BEDE: The exposition of this has been anticipated to the effect, namely, that the secret inner house of our heavenly homeland designated the ark of the covenant, the Lord our Savior in whom alone we have a covenant of peace with the Father, [our Savior] who ascending into heaven after his resurrection placed at the right hand of his Father the flesh that he had taken from the Virgin. ON THE TEMPLE 1.12.1.[56]

6:20 The Inner Sanctuary

THE ALTAR SIGNIFIES THE LIFE OF THE PERFECTLY RIGHTEOUS. BEDE: "And the altar he also covered with cedar." He means the altar of incense which was in front of the oracle [i.e., the inner sanctuary], about which a little further down are added the words "also the whole altar, which belonged to the oracle, he covered with gold." From this we are given to understand that the same altar was indeed made of stone and overlaid with cedar and then covered with gold. It signifies typically the life of the perfectly right-

---

[47]Acts 1:3. [48]Lk 21:34. [49]Mt 28:20. [50]Jn 16:22. [51]TTH 21:38-40. [52]See Acts 4:32. [53]See 2 Cor 11:26. [54]1 Cor 11:1. [55]TTH 21:40. [56]TTH 21:43.

eous who are, as it were, placed near the oracle and giving up the basest pleasures concentrate all their attention merely on entering the kingdom of heaven. Hence quite appropriately it was not the flesh of victims that was burned on this altar but only incense, because such people no longer need to sacrifice in themselves carnal sins or seductive thoughts but only offer up the fragrance of spiritual prayers and heavenly desires through the fire of eternal love in the sight of their Creator. Now what the stone, cedar and gold represent in this kind of altar can be easily understood from what has been said above. ON THE TEMPLE 1.12.3.[57]

6:21 The Inside of the House Overlaid with Pure Gold

THE MANIFOLD WORKS OF PIETY. BEDE: The gold leaf with which the house was covered is the manifold works of piety that pure love exhibits in the service either of its Creator or of a brother's need. The gold nails[58] with which the gold leaf was attached are the very precepts of charity or promises of eternal glory through which by the gift of the grace of Christ we are kept constant in the exercise and pursuit of virtue in case we should fail. ON THE TEMPLE 1.12.4.[59]

---

[57]TTH 21:44. [58]The text of Jerome's Vulgate, which was used by Bede for his commentary, reads, "He fastened the plates with nails of gold," whereas the Hebrew Masoretic Text reads, "He drew chains of gold across, in front of the inner sanctuary." [59]TTH 21:45.

6:23-38 THE HOLY ORNAMENTS
OF THE HOUSE OF THE LORD

[23]In the inner sanctuary he made two cherubim of olivewood, each ten cubits high. [24]Five cubits was the length of one wing of the cherub, and five cubits the length of the other wing the cherub; it was ten cubits from the tip of one wing to the tip of the other. [25]The other cherub also measured ten cubits; both cherubim had the same measure and the same form. [26]The height of one cherub was ten cubits, and so was that of the other cherub. [27]He put the cherubim in the innermost part of the house; and the wings of the cherubim were spread out so that a wing of one touched the one wall, and a wing of the other cherub touched the other wall; their other wings touched each other in the middle of the house. [28]And he overlaid the cherubim with gold.

[29]He carved all the walls of the house round about with carved figures of cherubim and palm trees and open flowers, in the inner and outer rooms. [30]The floor of the house he overlaid with gold in the inner and outer rooms.

[31]For the entrance to the inner sanctuary he made doors of olivewood; the lintel and the doorposts formed a pentagon.[p] [32]He covered the two doors of olivewood with carvings of cherubim, palm trees, and open flowers; he overlaid them with gold, and spread gold upon the cherubim and upon the palm trees.

[33]So also he made for the entrance to the nave doorposts of olivewood, in the form of a square,

³⁴*and two doors of cypress wood; the two leaves of the one door were folding, and the two leaves of the other door were folding.* ³⁵*On them he carved cherubim and palm trees and open flowers; and he overlaid them with gold evenly applied upon the carved work.* ³⁶*He built the inner court with three courses of hewn stone and one course of cedar beams.*

³⁷*In the fourth year the foundation of the house of the Lord was laid, in the month of Ziv.* ³⁸*And in the eleventh year, in the month of Bul, which is the eighth month, the house was finished in all its parts, and according to all its specifications. He was seven years in building it.*

p Heb obscure

Overview: The cherubim are properly said to have been made of olive wood, because they represent the angelic retinues that are anointed with the grace of the Holy Spirit. Wings signify the grace of perpetual and unfailing happiness of those who persevere continually in heavenly things. Two cherubim were made in order to signify a sharing in the same love, because love cannot exist between fewer than two. The cherubim stretch out their wings as if to fly because angelic spirits always have their mind in readiness to comply with the divine will. The two cherubim also symbolize the completeness and complementarity of the two Testaments (Bede). The engravings on the walls represent either a type of the saints praying in the temple of God (Ephrem) or the manifold functions of the virtues. The floor of the house was overlaid with gold inside and outside to signify that our Lord has filled the angels and the souls of the righteous in heaven with the perfect gift of love. There was one entrance to the oracle, which symbolizes the one entrance to the church and to the kingdom of heaven. The engraved images of the cherubim and palm trees and the carvings in bold relief are all types of the works of virtue. The posts were foursquare because of the four books of the holy gospel by whose teaching we are instructed in the true faith. The three courses of polished stones, with which the inner court was built, are faith, hope and charity. The fact that the house of the Lord was built in seven years prefigures the fact that the holy church is being built of the souls of the elect for the entire duration of this world, which

is also completed in a period of six days, and it too brings its growth to an end with the end of the world (Bede).

6:23 Two Cherubim

The Cherubim Represent the Angelic Retinues. Bede: "Cherubim," as the prophet Ezekiel explicitly declares, is a title of dignity, and in the singular number the form cherub is used, but cherubim in the plural. Hence the figures of the cherubim that were made in the oracle can be appropriately taken to mean the angelic retinues that always wait on their Creator in heaven. And they are properly said to have been made of olive wood because, of course, angelic virtues are anointed with the grace of the Holy Spirit lest they should ever grow arid in the love of God. For they are those fellow companions of ours of whom the prophet speaks in his praise of Christ: "God your God has anointed you with the oil of gladness above your fellows."[1] In figurative terms it was quite right that those whom their Creator later filled with the light of heavenly wisdom were made of olive wood. That is why he wanted them called cherub, which means in Latin "a great store of knowledge." And they are ten cubits high because they enjoy the denarius of eternal life having preserved ever untarnished in themselves the image of their Creator by the sanctity and uprightness and truth that they received in the first creation. For a denarius is worth ten

---

[1]Ps 45:7 (44:8 Vg).

obols and customarily bore the name and likeness of the king. Consequently, it also makes a very fitting metaphor for the kingdom of heaven where, on the one hand, the holy angels ever remain in their Creator's likeness according to which they were made, and on the other hand, the human elect receive his image that they had lost by sinning. For "we know," he says, "that when he appears we shall be like him [and] see him as he is."[2] ON THE TEMPLE 1.13.1.[3]

6:24 Each Wing Was Five Cubits Long

DIFFERENT INTERPRETATIONS OF THE CHERUBIM'S WINGS. BEDE: Wings when used as a figure of holy people signify their virtues whereby they delight in always flying to heavenly things and passing their lives in preoccupation with these things. But when wings are used to signify angels, what do they more aptly demonstrate than the grace of perpetual and unfailing happiness of those who persevere continually in heavenly things in the service of their Creator? Or at all events because they are endowed with the lightness of spiritual nature so that they can get to wherever they want, as it were, by flying, they are here both figuratively represented with wings and actually shown with wings. Now it has been well said: "One wing of the cherub was five cubits, and the other wing of the cherub five cubits," since the angelic powers keep with untiring devotion the law of God which is written in five books, that is, by loving the Lord their God with all their strength and by loving their neighbors as themselves.[4] "For love is the fulfilling of the law."[5] Now "their neighbors" includes both the angelic spirits themselves reciprocally and elect human beings who are equally their fellow citizens. So the reason each wing is said to be of the same dimensions is that with the same devotion as they love each other in God they also long for our company as we ascend to them, and so two wings together take up ten cubits when, in a twofold demonstration of love, the angels rejoice in the presence of their Maker. ON THE TEMPLE 1.13.2.[6]

6:25 The Same Measure and Form

LOVE CANNOT EXIST BETWEEN FEWER THAN TWO. BEDE: Two cherubim were made in order to signify a sharing in the same love of which we speak, because love cannot exist between fewer than two. Moreover, the reason why the Savior took care to send the disciples in twos[7] to preach was that he might tacitly teach that those who were to preach the word of faith must before all works possess the virtue of love. And the two cherubim were of the same dimensions and shape because there is no difference of will or thought in the heavenly homeland where all are illumined by one and the same vision and glory of God present there. ON THE TEMPLE 1.13.3.[8]

6:27 In the Innermost Part of the House

ALWAYS READY TO COMPLY WITH THE DIVINE WILL. BEDE: From what has been said already it is clear why the cherubim, whose abode is always in heaven, were placed in the middle of the interior of the temple. The cherubim, moreover, stretch out their wings as if to fly because angelic spirits always have their mind in readiness to comply with the divine will. But the fact that one cherub's wing was touching one wall and the second cherub's wing the other wall has to do with that ministry of love that the angels perform for us. The fact that the other wings in the middle of the temple touched each other expresses that grace of love with which they embrace each other. ON THE TEMPLE 1.13.4.[9]

6:28 The Cherubim Overlaid with Gold

THE TWO CHERUBIM AS THE TWO TESTAMENTS. BEDE: The two cherubim can also stand for the two Testaments. These cherubim, no doubt, were made in the oracle[10] because in the

---

[2]1 Jn 3:2. [3]TTH 21:47. [4]See Lk 10:27. [5]Rom 13:10. [6]TTH 21:47-48. [7]See Lk 10:1. [8]TTH 21:48. [9]TTH 21:48-49. [10]The inner sanctuary.

design of God's providence, which is, of course, inaccessible and incomprehensible to us, it was arranged before the world began, when and how and by what authors sacred Scripture was to be written. They were made of olive wood because the divine books were composed by men "of mercy, whose godly deeds have not failed,"[11] men who were enlightened by the unction of the Holy Spirit. They were made of olive wood because they afford us the light of knowledge with the help of the flame of God's love that is poured forth in our hearts by the Holy Spirit. They are ten cubits high because by the observance of the Decalogue of the law they preach that God is to be served since they show that those who serve God faithfully are to be rewarded with the denarius of an everlasting kingdom. They have twin sets of wings because they proclaim that the Testaments have always, both in adversity and prosperity, pursued heavenly things with tireless resolve and attained to them, because they point out to their listeners that they must do exactly the same. Five cubits is the length of one cherub's wing and five the length of the other's since in all the fluctuations of transient things the saints lay all the senses of their eyes ever on the Lord. They desire to hear the sound of his praise and to recount all his wonderful works, considering his words are sweeter to their throats than honey and the honeycomb to their mouths. Running after the odor of his ointments and while there is breath left in them and the spirit of God in their nostrils, they do not speak evil with their lips or utter folly with their tongue. Thus going on their way "with the armor of righteousness on the right hand and on the left,"[12] they succeed in receiving the heavenly denarius that the supreme master of the household has promised to the workers in his vineyard.[13]

And the two cherubim formed one work because the writers of both documents served God with one and the same purity of work and devotedness of love and proclaim God with one harmonious voice and belief. What the New Testament relates as accomplished facts regarding

the Lord's incarnation, passion, resurrection and ascension, the calling of the Gentiles, the expulsion of the Jews and the manifold affliction of the church, these same facts the Old Testament, rightly understood, truthfully foretold as events that were to happen. ON THE TEMPLE 1.13.7-8.[14]

6:29 The Walls of the House

THE SAINTS PRAYING IN THE TEMPLE.
EPHREM THE SYRIAN: Here it is indicated that there were four symbols of cherubim, palm trees, narcissus and lilies, which we said represent the saints praying in the temple and contemplating divine things. And these same saints were foreshadowed with a similar sense by Moses, even though he used different symbols, when he distributed the tribes of his people in four groups to the four regions of the world, so that they might all live around the tabernacle. Indeed, the tabernacle represented the person of God, whom he wanted them to contemplate and to observe constantly.[15] ON THE FIRST BOOK OF KINGS 6.29.[16]

THE SYMBOLISM OF THE ENGRAVINGS. BEDE: Solomon makes cherubim in the temple walls when the Lord grants to his elect to guide their lives according to the rule of the holy Scriptures, which contain a great store of knowledge. He makes cherubim when he teaches them to imitate in this world, according to their limited capacity, the chastity of the life of angels, and this is done particularly by vigils and the divine praises, by sincere love of the Creator and the neighbor. He makes palm trees when he fixes in their minds the thought of their eternal reward so that the more they have the reward of righteousness ever before the eyes of their hearts, the less likely are they to fall from the pinnacle of uprightness. He makes several representations, as it were, standing out in relief from the wall when he assigns to the faithful the manifold functions of the virtues,

---

[11]2 Chron 3:13. [12]2 Cor 6:7. [13]See Mt 20:1-2. [14]TTH 21:50-52*. [15]See Num 2. [16]ESOO 1:459.

for instance, "compassion, kindness, lowliness, patience and self-restraint, to show forbearance toward one another and forgive one another and above all these things" to have "love, which is the bond of perfection."[17] That is to say, these virtues, when they become such a habit with the elect that they seem, as it were, to be naturally ingrained in them, what else are they than the pictures of the Lord's house done in relief as if they were coming out of the wall, because they no longer learn the words and works of truth extrinsically from others but have them deeply rooted within themselves. Holding them in constant readiness, they can bring forth from their inmost hearts what ought to be done and taught. ON THE TEMPLE 1.14.2.[18]

6:30 The Floor Overlaid with Gold

ALL BROTHERS IN CHRIST. BEDE: Inside and outside[19] mean in the oracle and in the temple itself. Now we have said above[20] that the evenness of the floor denoted the humble harmony of the holy brotherhood where, though there are Jews and Gentiles, barbarians and Scythians, freeborn and slaves, highborn and lowborn,[21] they all boast of being brothers in Christ, all boast of having the same Father who is in heaven, for no one may doubt the perfectly harmonious humility of the heavenly citizens. The reason why Solomon overlaid the floor of the house with gold inside and outside is that our king of peace[22] has filled the angels and the souls of the righteous in heaven perfectly and fully with the gift of love and has set apart the citizens of the same heavenly homeland who are in pilgrimage in this world from the baseness of the rest of mortals by the hallmark of love, saying, "By this shall all know that you are my disciples, if you have love one for another."[23] ON THE TEMPLE 1.14.3.[24]

6:31 Doors of Olivewood for the Inner Sanctuary

ONE ENTRANCE. BEDE: As regards the first part of his statement, namely, "he made little doors of olive wood," he seems to have wanted to explain this more clearly when he added "and two doors of olive wood."[25] For there was one entrance to the oracle. But this entrance was closed by two doors and was opened again when they were unlocked, just as the temple and the portico before the temple no longer had an entrance. They give rise to a certain mystery because [since there is] "one Lord, one faith, one baptism, one God,"[26] we must hope for one entrance into the present church after baptism and one entrance into the heavenly kingdom through works of faith. ON THE TEMPLE 1.15.[27]

6:32 The Doors Covered with Carvings

TYPES OF THE WORKS OF VIRTUE. BEDE: Now all these items, that is, cherubim and palm trees and carvings in the adornment of the temple walls, have been set forth and explained above[28] according to our ability. There is no need to go to the trouble of adding anything further. For the works of virtue that the church performs throughout the world in its holy and perfect members should be pursued with all diligence by those especially to whom the care of the faithful has been committed and the keys of the kingdom of heaven granted, so that to the extent that they rank higher than the rest, they should also excel them in merit of good actions. For they have the image of the cherubim engraved on them when they imitate, both in thought and action, the life of angels on earth insofar as mortals can. They resemble palm trees when they keep their minds ever steadfastly intent on the gifts of their heavenly reward. For it is with the palm that the hand

---

[17]Col 3:12-14. [18]TTH 21:54*. [19]Bede follows the text of Vg, which reads, "The floor of the house he overlaid with gold, both inside and outside." [20]See TTH 21:35-36. [21]See Col 3:11. [22]See 1 Chron 22:9. [23]Jn 13:35. [24]TTH 21:55. [25]Bede follows the text of Vg, which reads, "And in the entrance to the oracle he made little doors of olive wood and five-cornered posts and two doors of olive wood." [26]Eph 4:5-6. [27]TTH 21:55. [28]See the passage at 6:29 entitled "The Symbolism of the Engravings."

of a victor is adorned. They have carvings in bold relief when they show to all who observe them the clearest proofs of good works, proofs that no one can misconstrue. And all these works are covered with sheets of gold when, as has often been said and must always be said, the brightness of love outshines the rest of the flowers of virtue, especially in the eminent members of the church. ON THE TEMPLE 1.16.1.[29]

6:33-34 Doorposts of Olivewood and Two Doors of Cypress Wood

AN ALLEGORY OF THE BEGINNING OF CHRISTIAN LIFE. BEDE: Just as the entrance to the inner sanctuary by which one reached the ark of the Lord and the cherubim signifies the entrance to the kingdom of heaven whereby we hope and desire to be introduced to the vision of our Creator and the heavenly citizens, so the entrance into the temple shows in type the beginnings of our life oriented on God when we enter the church of this present time. The latter entrance denotes our entry into the faith, the former our entry into vision. Hence the posts of this entrance were foursquare because of the four books of the holy gospel by whose teaching we are instructed in the true faith, or because of the four cardinal virtues of prudence, fortitude, temperance and justice, on whose most firm foundation, as it were, every edifice of good actions rests; prudence, by which we learn what we ought to do and how we ought to live; fortitude, through which we carry out what we have learned must be done; and the prophet briefly sums up these virtues in one verse, saying, "The Lord is my light and my salvation";[30] light, that is, to teach us the things we ought to do, salvation to strengthen us to do them; temperance by which we have discretion so as not to find ourselves giving more or less than the right amount of attention to prudence or fortitude; and since anyone who exercises prudence, fortitude and temperance will be proved beyond dispute to be just, the fourth virtue that follows after prudence, fortitude and temperance

is justice. ON THE TEMPLE 1.16.4.[31]

6:35 Cherubim, Palm Trees and Open Flowers

SYMBOLS OF CHRISTIAN DOCTRINE AND FAITH. BEDE: [These symbols] have already been expounded above, because the same representations or carvings were wrought on the walls of the house and on the inner doors, and the meaning of the figures is obviously that the first door of the temple actually received the same representations and carvings and the same cherubim as the inner parts. The reason for this is that the same mysteries of faith, hope and charity, which the sublime and the perfect each grasp in a sublime manner and that all the elect in heaven fully understand in the divine vision, are handed on also in the instruction of the unlettered for each one to learn and confess, in as much as those who have been initiated into the mysteries sometimes also succeed in understanding what they have devoutly believed. ON THE TEMPLE 1.16.8.[32]

6:36 The Inner Court[33] Built with Three Courses of Dressed Stone

FAITH, HOPE, CHARITY AND GOOD WORKS. BEDE: Hence it is aptly noted that the priests' court was constructed of three courses of polished stones and one course of cedar beams. For the three courses of polished stones are faith, hope and charity, and the expression "of polished stones" is appropriate because each one needs a certain amount of intelligence to discern how he ought to believe and what he ought to hope for as well as love. But the one course of cedar beams is good works performed without being vitiated by outward show, since, if this condition is lacking, faith, hope and charity cannot be genuine. For it has often been said that on account of their pleasant fragrance and naturally incorruptible quality,

---

[29]TTH 21:57*. [30]Ps 27:1 (26:1 Vg). [31]TTH 21:59-60*. [32]TTH 21:63. [33]That is, the court reserved to the priests.

cedar beams symbolize the enduring character and good repute of works of piety. All the elect who aim at pleasing God by faith, hope, love and action get as far as this court. Beyond it climb the perfect by the exalted grace of their merits since they reach such a peak of virtue that they can say to their hearers, "Be imitators of us as we also are of Christ,"[34] and boast and say, "Do you not know that we shall judge the angels? How much more the things of this world?"[35] ON THE TEMPLE 2.17.8.[36]

6:37-38 Seven Years in Building It

THE TEMPLE WAS COMPLETED IN SEVEN YEARS AND SEVEN MONTHS. BEDE: The allegorical meaning of the fact that the house of the Lord was built in seven years is plain, because, of course, the holy church is being built of the souls of the elect for the entire duration of this world, which is also completed in a period of six days, and it too brings its growth to an end with the end of the world. Or, at all events, it is built in seven years on account of the import of the grace of the Spirit through which the church alone gets the authority to be the church. For Isaiah enumerates the seven gifts of the Holy Spirit without which no one can either become a believer or keep the faith or by the merit of faith attain the crown.[37] On the other hand, the fact that it was in the eighth year and in the eighth month of that year that the house was completed in all its parts and all its specifications has to do with the world to come and the day of judgment when the holy church will already have reached such a degree of perfection that it will not be possible to find anything to add to it. For it will then have what that dutiful devotee suppliantly asked of the Lord, saying, "Lord, show us the Father, and it is enough for us."[38] For it is well known that the day of judgment is often represented typologically in the Scriptures by the number eight from the fact

that it follows this world, which lasts for seven days. This is also why the prophet gave the title "For the eighth" to the psalm he used to sing through fear of this severe judge, beginning with the words "Lord, rebuke me not in your indignation, nor chastise me in your wrath,"[39] and so forth.

But there arises the rather important question as to how the house of the Lord is said to have been completed in all its parts in the eighth month and in all its specifications, whereas in what follows one reads that its dedication was completed in the seventh month.[40] On the other hand, it is not credible that Solomon, though he built the temple in seven years and completed it in the eighth month of the eighth year, nevertheless deferred the dedication of the completed building until the seventh month of the ninth year. Hence it seems more likely that the house was built in seven years and seven months so that the solemn ceremony of dedication might be celebrated in the same seventh month, and, as the Chronicles relate,[41] on the twenty-third day of that month Solomon sent the people away to their tents, and thus after one week when the eighth month had come around, the house of the Lord was found to be complete and already finished, that is to say, both in all its parts and in its actual dedication. Unless perhaps one should think that after the dedication of the temple some extra features were added for its services up to the beginning of the eighth month, the king speeding up the work so that the temple would be dedicated in the seventh month, . . . and that in this way the two things might turn out to be true, namely, both that the temple had been completed in the eighth month in all its parts and specifications and that it had been dedicated in the seventh month. ON THE TEMPLE 2.18.1-2.[42]

---

[34]1 Cor 11:1. [35]1 Cor 6:3. [36]TTH 21:71. [37]See Is 11:2-3. [38]Jn 14:8. [39]Ps 6:1-2. [40]See 1 Kings 8:2. [41]2 Chron 7:10. [42]TTH 21:71-73.

7:1-51 THE FURNISHINGS OF SOLOMON'S
ROYAL PALACE

^{1}Solomon was building his own house thirteen years, and he finished his entire house.

^{2}He built the House of the Forest of Lebanon; its length was a hundred cubits, and its breadth fifty cubits, and its height thirty cubits, and it was built upon three^q rows of cedar pillars, with cedar beams upon the pillars. ^{3}And it was covered with cedar above the chambers that were upon the forty-five pillars, fifteen in each row. ^{4}There were window frames in three rows, and window opposite window in three tiers. ^{5}All the doorways and windows^r had square frames, and window was opposite window in three tiers.

^{6}And he made the Hall of Pillars; its length was fifty cubits, and its breadth thirty cubits; there was a porch in front with pillars, and a canopy before them.

^{7}And he made the Hall of the Throne where he was to pronounce judgment, even the Hall of Judgment; it was finished with cedar from floor to rafters.^{s}

^{8}His own house where he was to dwell, in the other court back of the hall, was of like workmanship. Solomon also made a house like this hall for Pharaoh's daughter whom he had taken in marriage.

^{9}All these were made of costly stones, hewn according to measure, sawed with saws, back and front, even from the foundation to the coping, and from the court of the house of the LORD^t to the great court. ^{10}The foundation was of costly stones, huge stones, stones of eight and ten cubits. ^{11}And above were costly stones, hewn according to measurement, and cedar. ^{12}The great court had three courses of hewn stone round about, and a course of cedar beams; so had the inner court of the house of the LORD, and the vestibule of the house.

^{13}And King Solomon sent and brought Hiram from Tyre. ^{14}He was the son of a widow of the tribe of Naphtali, and his father was a man of Tyre, a worker in bronze; and he was full of wisdom, understanding, and skill, for making any work in bronze. He came to King Solomon, and did all his work.

^{15}He cast two pillars of bronze. Eighteen cubits was the height of one pillar, and a line of twelve cubits measured its circumference; it was hollow, and its thickness was four fingers; the second pillar was the same.^{u} ^{16}He also made two capitals of molten bronze, to set upon the tops of the pillars; the height of the one capital was five cubits, and the height of the other capital was five cubits. ^{17}Then he made two^v nets of checker work with wreaths of chain work for the capitals upon the tops of the pillars; a net^w for the one capital, and a net^w for the other capital. ^{18}Likewise he made pomegranates;^{x} in two rows round about upon the one network, to cover the capital that was upon the top of the pillar; and he did the same with the other capital. ^{19}Now the capitals that were upon the tops of the pillars in the vestibule were of lily-work, four cubits. ^{20}The capitals were upon the two pillars and also above the rounded projection which was beside the network; there were two hundred pomegranates, in two rows round about; and so with the other capital. [21]He set up the pillars at the vestibule of the temple; he set up the pillar on the south and called its name Jachin; and he set up the pillar on the north and called its name Boaz. [22]And upon the tops of the pillars was lily-work. Thus the work of the pillars was finished.

[23]Then he made the molten sea; it was round, ten cubits from brim to brim, and five cubits high, and a line of thirty cubits measured its circumference. [24]Under its brim were gourds, for thirty[y] cubits, compassing the sea round about; the gourds were in two rows, cast with it when it was cast. [25]It stood upon twelve oxen, three facing north, three facing west, three facing south, and three facing east; the sea was set upon them, and all their hinder parts were inward. [26]Its thickness was a handbreadth; and its brim was made like the brim of a cup, like the flower of a lily; it held two thousand baths.

[27]He also made the ten stands of bronze; each stand was four cubits long, four cubits wide, and three cubits high. [28]This was the construction of the stands: they had panels, and the panels were set in the frames [29]and on the panels that were set in the frames were lions, oxen, and cherubim. Upon the frames, both above and below the lions and oxen, there were wreaths of beveled work. [30]Moreover each stand had four bronze wheels and axles of bronze; and at the four corners were supports for a laver. The supports were cast, with wreaths at the side of each. [31]Its opening was within a crown which projected upward one cubit; its opening was round, as a pedestal is made, a cubit and a half deep. At its opening there were carvings; and its panels were square, not round. [32]And the four wheels were underneath the panels; the axles of the wheels were of one piece with the stands; and the height of a wheel was a cubit and a half. [33]The wheels were made like a chariot wheel; their axles, their rims, their spokes, and their hubs, were all cast. [34]There were four supports at the four corners of each stand; the supports were of one piece with the stands. [35]And on the top of the stand there was a round band half a cubit high; and on the top of the stand its stays and its panels were of one piece with it. [36]And on the surfaces of its stays and on its panels, he carved cherubim, lions, and palm trees, according to the space of each, with wreaths round about. [37]After this manner he made the ten stands; all of them were cast alike, of the same measure and the same form.

[38]And he made ten lavers of bronze; each laver held forty baths, each laver measured four cubits, and there was a laver for each of the ten stands. [39]And he set the stands, five on the south side of the house, and five on the north side of the house; and he set the sea at the southeast corner of the house.

[40]Hiram also made the pots, the shovels, and the basins. So Hiram finished all the work that he did for King Solomon on the house of the LORD: [41]the two pillars, the two bowls of the capitals that were on the tops of the pillars, and the two networks to cover the two bowls of the capitals that were on the tops of the pillars; [42]and the four hundred pomegranates for the two networks, two rows of pomegranates for each network, to cover the two bowls of the capitals that were upon the pillars; [43]the ten stands, and the ten lavers upon the stands; [44]and the one sea, and the twelve oxen underneath the sea.

⁴⁵*Now the pots, the shovels, and the basins, all these vessels in the house of the LORD, which Hiram made for King Solomon, were of burnished bronze.* ⁴⁶*In the plain of the Jordan the king cast them, in the clay ground between Succoth and Zarethan.* ⁴⁷*And Solomon left all the vessels unweighed, because there were so many of them; the weight of the bronze was not found out.*

⁴⁸*So Solomon made all the vessels that were in the house of the LORD: the golden altar, the golden table for the bread of the Presence,* ⁴⁹*the lampstands of pure gold, five on the south side and five on the north, before the inner sanctuary; the flowers, the lamps, and the tongs, of gold;* ⁵⁰*the cups, snuffers, basins, dishes for incense, and firepans, of pure gold; and the sockets of gold, for the doors of the innermost part of the house, the most holy place, and for the doors of the nave of the temple.*

⁵¹*Thus all the work that King Solomon did on the house of the LORD was finished. And Solomon brought in the things which David his father had dedicated, the silver, the gold, and the vessels, and stored them in the treasuries of the house of the LORD.*

q Gk: Heb *four*   r Gk: Heb *posts*   s Syr Vg: Heb *floor*   t With 7.12: Heb *from the outside*   u Tg Syr Compare Gk and Jer 52.21: Heb *and a line of twelve cubits measured the circumference of the second pillar*   v Gk: Heb lacks *he made two*   w Gk: Heb *seven*   x With 2 Mss Compare Gk: Heb *pillars*   y Heb *ten*

OVERVIEW: The House of the Forest of Lebanon took its name from the fact that weapons abounded there, just as trees abound in the forests of Lebanon (ISHO'DAD). The Tyrian craftsman whom Solomon employed to help in his work stands for the ministers of the word chosen from the Gentiles. The pillars symbolize James, Cephas and John, who preceded the coming of our Redeemer, to bear testimony to his coming. The two capitals, which were placed on these pillar tops, are the two Testaments, which holy teachers are bound both in mind and body to meditate on and observe. The reason why there were seven rows of nets in both capitals is that it was through the grace of the Holy Spirit, symbolized by the number seven, that the fathers of both Testaments received the privilege of election. Both the rows have seven rows of nets in order to show that without the grace of the Holy Spirit neither God nor the neighbor can be loved. The lilies signify the glory of the heavenly homeland and the beauty of immortality fragrant with the flowers of paradise. The two hundred pomegranates around the second capital suggests mystically that the people of both Testaments, who were to be unified in Christ, were to be brought in to re-ceive the crown of eternal life (BEDE). "Jachin" indicates the humility of priesthood, while "Boaz" signifies the power of kingship (ISHO'DAD).

The molten sea was made as a figure of the laver of salvation in which we are cleansed for the remission of our sins. The beveled sculptures surrounding the sea rightly denote examples of former times that we must judiciously ponder to see by what works the saints have pleased God (BEDE). The oxen allude to the perfect structure of the created world (ISHO'DAD). By the brim of a cup is expressed the taste of the Lord's passion, and by the leaf of a crisped lily the glory of his resurrection. The length of four cubits of the bases refers to the patience of long endurance, the width to the expansiveness of love, the height to the hope of heavenly reward. The surface of the bases was carved with mystical figures on every side because the minds of the saints display the charm of the virtues in everything. The four wheels are the four books of the Gospels, which are aptly compared with wheels because, just as the wheel can travel with the greatest rapidity wherever it is steered, so with the Lord's help the word of the gospel filled all the regions of the world. The whole cubit in the laver denotes the perfection of good works. The number forty conventionally typifies great perfection. The fact that the sea was placed at the right side of the temple signifies that it is through the bath of baptism that we must reach the kingdom of heaven. It is appropriate that the vessels of the Lord's house were cast in the region of the Jordan, namely, in the river in which our Lord deigned to be baptized, because every baptism of the faithful in which they are consecrated to the Lord is celebrated on the model of his baptism. The table of gold is the sacred Scripture that is rich in the light of spiritual understanding. The lampstands symbolize the words of God, because they give the light of wisdom to the erring. The hinges represent the angels and the holy people who are made of gold because of the merit of their own glory or because of the love they have for God. The reason why Solomon made one house of the Lord but furnished it with many treasuries was that there is one house of the Father not made with hands that will last eternally in heaven, but many mansions in it will receive all who fear him (BEDE).

7:2 The House of the Forest of the Lebanon

THE MEANING OF THE "HOUSE OF THE FOREST OF THE LEBANON." ISHO'DAD OF MERV: "The House of the Forest of the Lebanon" does not mean that this house was built in a forest or in Lebanon, as is sometimes asserted, but that [Solomon] built a huge house where weapons were gathered in large quantity, just as the Forest of Lebanon [abounds] in trees. BOOKS OF SESSIONS I KINGS 7.2.[1]

7:13-14 Solomon Invited Hiram, an Artisan in Working Bronze

A TYPE OF THE MINISTERS CHOSEN FROM THE GENTILES. BEDE: And this was done on account of the mystery. For the Tyrian craftsman whom Solomon employed to help in his work stands for the ministers of the word chosen from

the Gentiles. The allusion to this man as a craftsman is a beautiful touch because he was the son of a widow of Israel, a person who is sometimes wont to be taken as prefiguring the church of the present day from whom her husband, namely, Christ, after having tasted death, rose and ascended into heaven, leaving her meanwhile to sojourn on the earth. However, there is no need to labor the explanation of how the sons of this widow are preachers since all the elect individually profess themselves children of the church. Also since in regard to these preachers of the New Testament a special promise is made in the words of the prophet: "Instead of your fathers, sons are born to you; you shall make them princes over all the earth."[2] Now Hiram did all Solomon's work, that is to say, because the holy teachers, while they devote themselves faithfully to the ministry of the word, do indeed do the work of God, since by speaking outwardly they open the way of truth to those whom he himself has predestined to eternal life by enlightening them inwardly. "I," he says, "planted, Apollo watered; but God gave the increase."[3] Moreover, he made the work of bronze because the energetic teacher seeks to entrust the word to those who . . . desire to receive it with reverence and keep it to the end, and who also by preaching to others do their utmost to spread more widely whatever right doctrine they have learned themselves; for it is common knowledge that bronze is a metal which is very durable and produces all kinds of sounds. ON THE TEMPLE 2.18.3.[4]

7:15 Two Pillars of Bronze

ILLUSTRIOUS TEACHERS BORE TESTIMONY TO THE COMING OF OUR REDEEMER. BEDE: Hence it is good that we are told that two bronze pillars of excellent and marvelous work were set up in this porch[5] and that capitals worked to resemble lilies were placed on top of them. The

---

[1]CSCO 229:105. [2]Ps 45:16 (44:17 Vg). [3]1 Cor 3:6. [4]TTH 21:73-74*. [5]See 1 Kings 6:3 and notes.

pillars stood in front of the door of the temple because illustrious teachers, concerning whom the apostle says, "James and Cephas and John, who were reputed to be pillars,"[6] precede the coming of our Redeemer, to bear testimony to the coming of the one who said, "I am the door; if anyone enters through me, he will be saved."[7] One of these [pillars] stood at the right of the door and the other at the left, because they foretold to the people of Israel, then fervent with divine faith and charity, the future incarnation of their Redeemer; and they proclaimed to the Gentiles, still as it were facing north, numb with the cold of unbelief, that this [door] was to be opened to make way for the entry of the Redeemer. That the capitals of the pillars were made by a workman to resemble lilies signifies that the entire import of the preaching [of James, Cephas and John] resounded with the clarity of everlasting happiness and promised that his glory would be seen by their hearers. He who existed as God before the ages became a human being at the end of the ages, so that like the flower of the lily he might have a golden color within and be white on the outside. For what is the significance of the glow of gold surrounded by whiteness except the brilliance of divinity in a human being? He first revealed this human being as brilliant because of his virtues, and after his death he clothed him in the snowy white splendor of incorruptibility. Homilies on the Gospels 2.25.[8]

7:16 Two Capitals of Molten Bronze

The Two Capitals as the Two Testaments. Bede: The tops of the pillars, that is, their highest part, are the hearts of faithful teachers whose God-centered thoughts guide all their actions and words as the head guides the members of the body. On the other hand, the two capitals that were placed on these pillar tops are the two Testaments, which holy teachers are totally bound both in mind and body to meditate and observe. It is appropriate, then, that both capitals were five cubits high because the Scripture of the Mosaic law comprises five books, and furthermore the entire collection of Old Testament writings embraces the five ages of the world. But the New Testament does not proclaim to us something different from what Moses and the prophets had said should be proclaimed: "If you believed Moses you would believe me, for he wrote of me."[9] For Moses wrote much about the Lord not only in figure but also quite plainly as when he relates what had been promised to Abraham in the Lord's words: "In your seed shall the families of the earth bless themselves,"[10] and when in his own words he says to the Israelites, "The Lord will raise up for you among your brothers a prophet like me; him you shall hear according to all things whatsoever he shall speak to you."[11] Of this prophecy the voice of the Father from heaven reminded the disciples when, as the Lord appeared to them in glory between Moses himself and Elijah on the holy mountain, it rang out, saying, "This is my beloved Son in whom I am well pleased; listen to him."[12] Therefore, with the admirable harmony of divine activity, the grace of the New Testament was hidden under the veil of the Old at first, but now the mysteries of the Old Testament are revealed by the light of the New, as if the reason why the capital of each of the two pillars was five cubits high was that it is manifest that the grace of the perfection of the gospel too is innate in the Old Testament whose mysteries are noted beforehand in the five books of the Law or are all comprised more fully in the five ages of the world; and so it happens that each eminent preacher, whether destined to be sent to the Jews or to the Gentiles, fortified with the harmonious testimony of the word of God, keeps the sure and correct rule of faith and conduct free from error, and in the course of his teaching he knows how to draw forth "out of his treasure house new things and old."[13] Not only do the Testaments harmonize with each other in their account of the divine mysteries, but also all the

---

[6]Gal 2:9. [7]Jn 10:9. [8]CS 111:266-67. [9]Jn 5:46. [10]Acts 3:25. [11]Acts 3:22. [12]Mt 17:5. [13]Mt 13:52.

elect who are written about in the books of these Testaments are endowed with the one faith and are bound to each other by the same charity. ON THE TEMPLE 2.18.8.[14]

7:17 Seven Nets for Each Capital

SEVEN DENOTES THE GRACE OF THE HOLY SPIRIT. BEDE: For the number seven is conventionally used to denote the grace of the Holy Spirit, as attested in the Apocalypse by John, who, after saying that he had seen "the lamb with seven horns and seven eyes," went on to add, by way of explanation, "which are the seven spirits of God sent into the whole world."[15] This the prophet Isaiah more clearly explains when, speaking of the Lord who was to be born in the flesh, he says, "And the spirit of the Lord shall rest on him, the spirit of wisdom and of understanding, the spirit of counsel and of fortitude, the spirit of knowledge and of godliness. And he shall be filled with the spirit of the fear of the Lord."[16] The reason why there were seven rows of net in both capitals is that it was through the grace of one and the same septiform Spirit that the Fathers of both Testaments received the privilege of election. ON THE TEMPLE 2.18.10.[17]

7:18 Columns with Two Rows

THE VIRTUE OF LOVE AND THE GRACE OF THE HOLY SPIRIT. BEDE: True, there were two rows of networks right around the capital, but both rows were repeated seven times over until the capital was encircled and the row rejoined itself after going full circle. Nor is the figure of the mystery obscured by the fact that there are two rows of network since it is well known that the virtue of love consists of two distinct aspects, namely, when we are bidden to love God with our whole heart, our whole mind and our whole strength and our neighbor as ourselves.[18] But both of those rows have seven rows of nets because without the grace of the Holy Spirit neither God nor the neighbor can be loved. For the statement "because the love of God has been poured into our hearts through the Holy Spirit who has been given to us"[19] remains true. But where the love of God is, there, assuredly, the love of the neighbor also is poured into the hearts of the faithful because, of course, the one cannot be had without the other. Furthermore, these networks were made to cover the capitals, that is, to encircle them completely, because, rightly understood, every page of holy Scripture echoes throughout with the sound of the grace of love and peace. For the capitals are indeed the volumes of the divine Word, the networks are the bonds of mutual love, and the capitals are covered with networks when the sacred words, if I may say so, are shown on all sides to be clothed with the gift of love. For even in the things that we do not understand in the Scriptures, love is abundantly in evidence. ON THE TEMPLE 2.18.11.[20]

7:19 Capitals of Lily Work

THE GLORY AND BEAUTY OF IMMORTALITY. BEDE: What else can the lilies mean but the glory of the heavenly homeland and the beauty of immortality fragrant with the flowers of paradise? What else can the four cubits mean but the word of the gospel, which promises us entry into eternal happiness and shows us the road by which we may reach it? Therefore, when holy teachers show us the promised threshold of the heavenly kingdom in the four books of the holy gospel, it is as if the tops of the pillars display the lily work of four cubits that is on them. Taking this text literally, it should be noted that when the lily work on the capitals is recorded as having been of four cubits and the words "in height" or "in width" are not added, it is, of course, left to the reader's judgment whether this ought to be understood as referring to height or to width. It is agreed beyond the slightest doubt that a pillar that a

---

[14]TTH 21:76-77*. [15]Rev 5:6. [16]Is 11:2-3. [17]TTH 21:78. [18]See Mk 12:30-31. [19]Rom 5:5. [20]TTH 21:78-79*.

rope of twelve cubits spanned would be four cubits thick. For the circumference of every circle is three times the length of its diameter. Finally because the bronze sea was ten cubits in diameter, as we read in what follows, it was thirty cubits in circumference. But because the lily work is said to have been four cubits, whether this means in width or height, at all events, the meaning of the figure is clear, because it is only through the gospel that the voice most ardently longed for has sounded: "Do penance, for the kingdom of heaven is at hand."[21] ON THE TEMPLE 2.18.13.[22]

7:20 Two Hundred Pomegranates

RECEIVING THE CROWN OF ETERNAL LIFE. BEDE: We have said that the pomegranates were a type of either the whole church or of each individual believer,[23] but the number one hundred that was originally applied to the right hand was sometimes apt to be used as a figure of eternal beatitude. There were twice this number of pomegranates around the second capital to suggest mystically that the people of both Testaments who were to be unified in Christ were to be brought in to receive the crown of eternal life. In keeping with this figure are the words written about the apostles fishing after the Lord's resurrection when they saw him standing on the shore: "For they were not far from the land, but, as it were, two hundred cubits, dragging the net with the fish."[24] For the disciples indeed drag the net full of large fish for two hundred cubits to the Lord who is already on the shore showing the effects of his resurrection when holy preachers entrust the word of faith to both Jews and Gentiles and drag the elect of both peoples from the waves of this present world and lead them to the glory of the peace and immortality to come. The circumference, therefore, of the second capital has two rows of pomegranates when the sublimity of the heavenly kingdom assembles the elect of both peoples in one citadel of peace. ON THE TEMPLE 2.18.15.[25]

7:21 Jachin and Boaz

JACHIN AND BOAZ. ISHOʿDAD OF MERV: [The Scripture] calls the [pillar] on the south "Jachin," indicating through it the humility of the priesthood; while the one on the north, called "Boaz," signifies the power of kingship. It is possible that in Hebrew the two pillars indicate the two powers. The capitals at their top symbolize the power that is due to priests and kings and the weights of government, which are imposed on them. The sculptures, the lily work and the garlands of flowers[26] signify the brightness and dignity of priesthood and kingship. BOOKS OF SESSIONS 1 KINGS 7.21.[27]

7:23 The Molten Sea

SYMBOLS OF PURIFICATION, BAPTISM AND SALVATION. BEDE: "He also made a molten sea of ten cubits from brim to brim, completely round." This molten sea was made as a figure of the laver of salvation in which we are cleansed for the remission of our sins. For priests were washed in it, as the Chronicles assure us;[28] but it is agreed that all the elect are called priests in a typological sense in the Scriptures since they are members of the high priest Jesus Christ. And rightly has Scripture given the name of sea to this vessel, in memory, that is, of the Red Sea in which once, through the destruction of the Egyptians and the deliverance of the people of God, the form of baptism was anticipated, as the apostle explains when he says, "that our fathers were all under the cloud and all passed through the sea, and all in Moses were baptized in the cloud and in the sea."[29] Now the sacrament of baptism both requires of us purity of life and promises us the glory of eternal life in the world to come, both of which things are denoted in this bronze sea in one sentence where it is said to be ten cubits from

---

[21]Mt 4:17. [22]TTH 21:81. [23]See TTH 21:79-81. [24]Jn 21:8. [25]TTH 21:83. [26]See 1 Kings 5:16-18. [27]CSCO 229:106. [28]See 2 Chron 4:6 [29]1 Cor 10:1-2.

brim to brim. For by the Ten Commandments in the law the Lord expressed all that we must do. Likewise by the denarius he indicated the reward of good deeds when he foretold that it was to be given to those working in the vineyard.[30] The reason why the sea was ten cubits from brim to brim was that the whole choir of the faithful from the first one baptized in the name of Jesus Christ to the last to believe and be baptized at the end of the world must enter on one and the same way of truth and hope for a common crown of righteousness from the Lord. It was completely circular in order to signify that the whole universe all the way around was to be cleansed in the laver of life from the filth of its sins.

In this regard the remark is well made that "its height was five cubits," because, of course, whatever fault we have committed with the sense of sight or hearing or smell or taste or touch, all this the grace of God washes away from us through the ablution of the life-giving font. But the remission of past sins is not enough if one does not thereafter devote oneself to good works; otherwise, if the devil, after leaving a person, sees such a one to be lacking in good actions, he comes back in greater numbers and makes "the last state of that person worse than the first."[31]

Hence it is fittingly added, "And a line of thirty cubits compassed it all the way around." For by the line can fittingly be meant the discipline of the heavenly precepts with which we are restrained from the indulgence of our passions since Scripture says that "a threefold cord is not easily broken."[32] [This is] because, of course, the observance of the commandments of God, which is established in the hearts of the elect by faith, hope and the love of an eternal reward, cannot be frustrated by any obstacle of temporal things. And the line encircles the sea when by works of piety we strive to enhance the sacrament of baptism that we have received. Now this line is aptly said to be three cubits long. For five times six make thirty. By the number six in which the Lord both made humankind when it did not exist and remade it when it had perished, our good actions

are also rightly represented, and six is multiplied by five to make thirty, when we humbly subject all our bodily senses to divine things. However, there is also another sense in which we can quite appropriately take this number thirty as applying mystically to the sea. For three tens make thirty. And after the flood, from the issue of Noah's three sons, the human race filled the whole expanse of the universe;[33] for the tribe of Shem occupied Asia, Ham's descendants occupied Africa, and the progeny of Japheth occupied Europe and the islands of the sea. And because, together with the performance of good works and the hope of heavenly rewards, the sacrament of baptism was to be administered to all the nations, it was fitting that a line of thirty cubits should encircle the sea, in which the water of baptism was prefigured. But it must also be said that the Lord at the age of thirty years came to the Jordan to be baptized by John.[34] For since by his baptism that he received at the age of thirty he consecrated for us the water of the laver of salvation, it is right that a line should encircle the sea, which is a figure of our baptism, so that, by the gift of him who underwent baptism without sin, it might be signified that baptism was specifically given to all of us who believe in him for the remission of our sins. ON THE TEMPLE 2.19.1-3.[35]

7:24 Two Rows of Panels

EXAMPLES FOR THE EDIFICATION OF THE FAITHFUL. BEDE: "And a carved work under its brim surrounded it, encircling the sea for ten cubits. There were two rows cast of chamfered sculptures."[36] Since it has been said above that a line of thirty cubits encircled the sea and it is now added that this carved work under the brim went around it for ten cubits, it is obvious from both accounts that the vessel was bent backwards and

---

[30]See Mt 20:2. [31]Lk 11:24-26. [32]Eccles 4:12. [33]See Gen 9:18-19. [34]See Lk 3:23. [35]TTH 21:84-86*. [36]The text of Vg (used by Bede) differs here from the Hebrew text, which reads, "There were two rows of panels, cast when it was cast."

spread out like a bowl, because from a circumference of thirty cubits, which it measured at the brim, it narrowed to ten cubits. The chamfered sculpture is one that represents some historical events. Hence also the chamfered sculptures surrounding the sea rightly denote examples of former times that we must judiciously ponder to see by what works the saints have pleased God from the beginning and with what obstinacy the reprobate persisted in crimes and with what wickedness they perished because of their crimes; how in the beginning of the nascent world Cain was condemned for the malice of envy and Abel crowned for the merit of his uprightness;[37] how Lamech was cursed for his adultery and murder[38] and Enoch brought back to paradise for the grace of his piety;[39] how after the flood Ham was detested by his father for his lack of filial piety and the peoples of Shem and Japheth were granted a perpetual blessing for their reverential obedience;[40] how Abraham was made the heir of the divine promise in recognition of his faith[41] while the numerous other nations were left in their ancestral unbelief; how when the Lord came in the flesh, Judea was rejected for the offense of unbelief and the Gentiles brought back to salvation by the grace of faith, and other things of the kind in both Testaments, which, when judiciously and devoutly contemplated, are of great profit to all earnest-minded people. And that perhaps is the reason why two orders of chamfered sculptures were made in the bronze sea, namely, that those who were immersed in the font of baptism may listen carefully to the stories of both Testaments; and the reason why they were ten cubits in circumference was that they might strive to imitate whomsoever they perceived in these stories to have been committed to carrying out the heavenly commands and totally rapt in the pursuit of heavenly rewards. ON THE TEMPLE 2.19.4.[42]

7:25 The Sea Was Set on Twelve Oxen

THE SEA AND THE OXEN. ISHO'DAD OF MERV: [The sea] is set on the oxen in order not to be defiled by the ground. The oxen allude to the perfect structure of the created world, because it was prescribed in the Law that this animal should be offered in sacrifice;[43] at the same time, the nourishment of human beings reaches its maturity through the strength of the ox. Their number of twelve refers to the constant revolution of an entire year which is accomplished in twelve months. Through their division into groups of three, which are set toward each cardinal point, [the Scripture] alludes to the four seasons. Finally, "the interior of the house" is called "the space under the sea." The water contained in the sea was used for the washing of the victims. It is possible that small ships and other objects, which are connected to the sea, were on it, and for this reason it was called "the sea." BOOKS OF SESSIONS 1 KINGS 7.25.[44]

7:26 Its Brim Was Like the Brim of a Cup

THE PASSION OF THE LORD AND THE GLORY OF HIS RESURRECTION. BEDE: For by the brim of a cup is expressed the taste of the Lord's passion, and by the leaf of a crisped lily the glory of his resurrection is openly revealed. For that the chalice of his passion is indicated in the cup is attested by the Lord, who on approaching his passion prayed to his Father, saying, "Father, if you are willing, remove this chalice from me";[45] but the lily, which, in addition to the grace of a most pleasant fragrance, displayed a white color on the outside and a golden color on the inside, appositely suggests the glory of the resurrection of him who showed the disciples the immortality of his body externally and at the same time taught that there was within him a soul shining with divine light. One can also fittingly take the crisped lily as the "mediator of God and humankind"[46] himself crowned with glory and honor on account of the suffering of his death, who prior to his passion was still, as it were, a closed lily and

---

[37]See Gen 4:3-16. [38]See Gen 4:19-24. [39]See Gen 5:24. [40]See Gen 9:20-27. [41]See Gen 15:4-6. [42]TTH 21:86-87*. [43]See Lev 1:3. [44]CSCO 229:106-7. [45]Lk 22:42. [46]1 Tim 2:5.

shone forth as an illustrious human being by reason of his signs and wonders, but after his resurrection and ascension showed himself to the citizens of the heavenly homeland a crisped lily because he showed forth in his assumed humanity the power of the divine glory that he had with the Father before the world was.[47] ON THE TEMPLE 2.19.8.[48]

7:27 The Measurements of Each Stand

FIGURES OF CHRISTIAN VIRTUES. BEDE: However, that each of the bases was four cubits long and four cubits high is easy to understand. For the length refers to the patience of long endurance, the width to the expansiveness of love, the height to the hope of heavenly reward. Moreover, there are four principal virtues on which the rest of the structure of the virtues depends, namely, prudence, fortitude, temperance and justice, and the reason why the length and width of the bases was four cubits was that holy preachers, whether they endure outwardly the adversities of the world, the lengthy exile and present labors, or expand their heart in the love of their Creator and of their neighbors with inward joy, always pay attention to the virtues, that is, by prudently distinguishing between good things and evil, courageously bearing adversity, restraining their heart from its desire of pleasures and maintaining uprightness in their manner of acting. But the height of the bases is three cubits when, through the exercise of the virtues that they practice by the endurance of evils and the love of what is good, they strive with sustained resolve to attain the vision of the holy Trinity. ON THE TEMPLE 2.20.3.[49]

7:28-29 Borders Within the Frames

THE SAINTS ARE TIRELESS IN PERFORMING GOOD WORKS. BEDE: Hence the surface of the bases was not level at any point, but whichever side one turned, it was carved with mystical figures because the minds of the saints, indeed their whole way of life, displays the charm of the virtues in everything, and not an empty or idle hour passes them by that they fail to have time for good works or words or, at all events, thoughts. They have little crowns carved on them when they yearn with untiring longing for entry into eternal life; they have ledges when, amid their longing for the life of heaven that is above, they never undo the bonds of fraternal intercourse that is at hand; they have lions between the little crowns and ledges when they so raise their minds to hope for heavenly things and so open them out to the love of their neighbor that they do not shirk the zealous exercise of stern denunciation on any sinners entrusted to their charge. In addition to lions, they have oxen when they employ even the invective of correction in a spirit of meekness, when, in the heat of rebuking, they never cease to have the cloven hoof of prudent action and word or to roll the words of divine reading around in the mouth as if ruminating on them. Finally, blessed Stephen, the one who was the pillar of excellence of the Lord's temple, seemed to show the fierce teeth and claws of a lion when he said to his persecutors, "You stiffnecked people, uncircumcised in heart and ears, you always resist the Holy Spirit; which of the prophets did your fathers not persecute?" and so forth;[50] but in saying this he showed how much of the compassion of bovine meekness he nurtured in his heart within, when, for these same persecutors raging to kill him, he knelt and said, "Lord, lay not this sin to their charge."[51] But because we can have neither hope of things eternal in heaven, nor love of neighbor on earth, nor the fervor of trenchant zeal nor the gentleness of compassionate restraint, without knowledge of the holy Scriptures, it is aptly remarked that after crown and ledges, after lions and oxen, cherubim too were carved. For it is generally accepted that cherubim are a type of sacred scripture, whether because the two cherubim on the propitiatory of

---

[47]Jn 17:5. [48]TTH 21:89. [49]TTH 21:94-95. [50]Acts 7:51-52. [51]Acts 7:60.

the ark were fashioned as a figure of the two Testaments that sing in harmony of Christ or because the name itself means "much knowledge."[52] ON THE TEMPLE 2.20.5.[53]

7:30 Four Bronze Wheels and Axles of Bronze

THE FOUR WHEELS ARE THE FOUR BOOKS OF THE GOSPELS. BEDE: The four wheels are the four books of the Gospels, which are very aptly compared with wheels because, just as the wheel's whirling motion can travel with the greatest rapidity wherever it is steered, so with the Lord's help through the instrumentality of the apostles the word of the gospel filled all the regions of the world in a short space; as the wheel raises from the earth the chariot laid on it, and when raised carries it where the driver steers it, so the preaching of the gospel lifts up the minds of the elect from earthly cravings to heavenly desires and, having lifted them up, guides them to progress in good works or to the ministry of preaching, in whichever direction the helping grace of the Spirit wills. For since, in the text that follows, it says that "they were the kind of wheels usually designed for a chariot," and moreover, we read of the saints, "The chariot of God is attended by ten thousands; thousands of them that rejoice,"[54] why, then, is it that the wheels of the bases are compared with the wheels of chariots, unless it is that one and the same word of the gospel makes some of those whom it teaches chariots of God and others pillars of God's temple? ON THE TEMPLE 2.20.7.[55]

7:31-32 An Opening Within the Crown

UNITY IN BAPTISM AND PERFECTION OF GOOD WORKS. BEDE: The mouth of the laver was one cubit on account of the unity of confession and faith because we are all baptized in the confession of the Father and the Son and the Holy Spirit, as the apostle says: "One Lord, one faith, one baptism, one God and Father of all."[56]

And the mouth itself was at the top of the capital[57] to teach that the way to the heavenly kingdom had been opened to us through baptism. But the actual laver was a cubit and a half in size, in view, no doubt, of the perfection of good works and the beginning of contemplation. For the whole cubit in the laver denotes the perfection of good works. ON THE TEMPLE 2.20.9.[58]

7:38 Each Basin Held Forty Baths

THE NUMBER OF PERFECTION. BEDE: The number forty conventionally typifies great perfection because, of course, four tens make forty; now there are ten precepts whereby our whole code of conduct is laid down in the divine law, but four books of the Gospels in which entry into our heavenly homeland was opened to us through the plan of the Lord's incarnation. And because all who are involved in the ministry of sacred baptism must, together with the faith and mysteries of the gospel, show the fruits of upright conduct, it is fitting that each of the lavers in which the whole burnt offerings were washed should hold forty baths. ON THE TEMPLE 2.20.12.[59]

7:39 The Sea Set on the Southeast Corner of the House

THE BATH OF BAPTISM. BEDE: "And the sea he set on the right side of the temple facing the east southwards."[60] And this was placed in the same court to the east. His words, "on the right side of the temple," he repeats when he says "southwards." For those who entered the court from the east had first to turn southwards, where the sea stood in the very corner ready for the priests to

[52]See Jerome Nom. Hebr. (CCL 72.4[line 11]). [53]TTH 21:95-96. [54]Ps 68:17 (67:18 Vg). [55]TTH 21:97. [56]Eph 4:5-6. [57]This is the reading of 1 Kings 7:31 in Vg, whose text is employed by Bede throughout his commentary. [58]TTH 21:99. [59]TTH 21:101*. [60]Instead of "he set the sea on the southeast corner of the house," which is the reading of the Hebrew Bible, the text of Vg, which is employed by Bede, reads, "And the sea he set on the right side of the temple facing the east southwards."

wash; then, as they proceeded inside, they were met by lavers placed on either side for washing the victims; inside these was a bronze dais five cubits long and five cubits wide and three cubits high, on which Solomon stood when dedicating the temple;[61] then as they proceeded further they came to the altar of burnt offering facing the south side of the court, then the temple porticoes or vestibule in which were bronze pillars around the door of the temple. Therefore, the fact that he placed the sea at the right side of the temple signifies that it is through the bath of baptism we must reach the kingdom of heaven, which is properly represented by the term "right hand." For "he who believes and is baptized shall be saved."[62] For where right as well as left hand are taken in the positive sense, they indicate either Judea and the Gentiles, as we have said above in the explanation of the bases, or the present and future life of the church, or the happy and sad things of the world, or something of the sort, but where the right hand by itself is used in the positive sense, it more frequently stands for eternal joys. But the fact that he made the sea face eastwards has virtually the same significance, namely, that the splendor of eternal glory is revealed to us through the bath of the holy font; the fact that it was at the south side of the court signifies that the faithful are apt to be kindled into a blazing fire of genuine love through the reception of the Holy Spirit, for in the Scriptures the heat of the noonday sun customarily meant the ardor of love and the light of the Holy Spirit, through whom this love is poured forth in the hearts of the elect. On the Temple 2.20.15.[63]

7:45-46 All the Vessels Were Cast in the Plain of the Jordan

Why Were All the Vessels Cast in the Region of the Jordan? Bede: It is appropriate that the vessels of the Lord's house were cast in the region of the Jordan, namely, in the river in which our Lord deigned to be baptized and by his immersion in the waves of its waters changed the

element for us into a bath for sins. For every baptism of the faithful in which they are consecrated to the Lord is celebrated on the model of his baptism whereby he himself sanctified the waters. It is proper that the vessels of the Lord's house should have been made in the country of the Jordan, for there is no other way for us to become vessels of election and mercy than by looking to his baptism that he underwent in that river and making sure that we too are washed in that life-giving river. However, it must be noted that he says these vessels were made not only in the country around the Jordan but also in its plains to signify the multiplication of the faithful that was to take place not only in Judea but also in the wide world of all the nations in fulfillment of the prophecy that says, "The plains and everything in them will rejoice."[64] On the Temple 2.21.1.[65]

7:48 A Golden Table for the Bread of the Presence[66]

The Golden Table Is the Sacred Scripture. Bede: The table of gold is the sacred Scripture, rich in the light of spiritual understanding of which the psalmist says to the Lord, "You have prepared a table before me in the presence of those who afflict me."[67] For lest our enemies who afflict us should divert us into the path of error, our Creator has prepared for us a table of knowledge to strengthen us in the true faith. For the loaves of proposition are the holy teachers whose salutary words or works, anyone who searches in the divine pages will find proposed to us as a model for living. Hence it was prescribed in Exodus that twelve of these loaves be made,[68] that is, on account of the twelve apostles through whose ministry both the New Testament Scripture was written and the mysteries of the Old Testament revealed by the condescension of the Lord. That is to say, this number designates not

---

[61]See 1 Kings 8:63-64. [62]Mk 16:16. [63]TTH 21:102-3*. [64]Ps 96:12 (95:12 Vg). [65]TTH 21:103-4*. [66]Or proposition. [67]Ps 23:5 (22:5 Vg). [68]See Exod 25:30; Lev 24:5-6.

only these apostles but also all who, by proclaiming the word, administer the nourishment of life to the faithful, because, of course, all follow the same norm of teaching as the apostles received from the Lord. ON THE TEMPLE 2.22.4.[69]

7:49 Lampstands of Gold, Five on the South Side and Five on the North[70]

A TYPE OF THE WORDS OF GOD. BEDE: For just as the tables are rightly used as a type of holy Scripture because they both minister righteousness to those hungering for the bread of the word and bear the vessels of the heavenly ministry, that is, they propose for our imitation the actions of the righteous, so also by these lampstands the words of God are symbolized, that is, because they give the light of wisdom to the erring. That is why the psalmist says, "A lamp to my feet," and so forth;[71] that, too, is why Solomon says, "Because the commandment is a lamp, and the law a light."[72] Moreover, the reason why five lampstands were placed on the right and five on the left is quite easy to see from our discussion of the tables. But when he said five on the right and five on the left, he added fittingly: "over against the oracle." For the oracle, where the ark was, as has often been said, stands for the way to the heavenly homeland: "where Christ is seated at the right hand of God,"[73] privy, that is, to his Father's secrets. And the temple lampstands of gold were placed opposite the oracle because the words of God always have in view the abode of the heavenly city that they may instill into our hearts the knowledge and desire of it and inflame those who take their fleshy origin from the earth to long for and to merit a place of everlasting abode in heaven. ON THE TEMPLE 2.24.1.[74]

7:50 The Sockets[75] Were of Gold

THE MINDS AND HEARTS OF ANGELS OR SAINTS. BEDE: If the doors of the inner house of the Holy of Holies are the ministries of angels that unlock the entrance to celestial life for us

when we have left the body, and [if] the doors of the house of the temple are the holy teachers and priests who throw open to us the first thresholds of the present church by teaching, baptizing and communicating to us the mysteries of the Lord's body and blood, what are the hinges of both doors? They are the minds and hearts of these angels or saints by which they cleave fixedly to the contemplation and love of their Creator so that those who never turn their gaze from the will of him whom they serve may thereby properly fulfill the ministry entrusted to them. For the gates are opened and closed at the appropriate time, but at no time do they leave their hinges, because both angels and holy people, whether they receive the faithful and the elect in this life of faith or in the other life of vision, keep their minds ever firmly rooted in love. These hinges are well said to have been made of gold for this reason, namely, either because of the merit of their own glory or because of the love they have for God. ON THE TEMPLE 2.25.1.[76]

7:51 The Things That David Had Dedicated

THE SYMBOLISM OF THE SACRED OFFERINGS OF DAVID. BEDE: Silver applies to the clarity of eloquence, gold to the brilliance of wisdom and vessels generally to rational creatures; and David, Solomon's father, sanctifies the silver when God the Father strengthens speakers with the grace of the Holy Spirit to speak the word of the gospel; he sanctifies the gold when he enlightens those endowed with natural ability by filling them with his Spirit in order to contemplate the wonders in his law; he sanctifies the vessels too when, having bestowed the grace of this Spirit on all the church's children in general that they may love the gifts of eternal salvation, he inflames them with a desire for them. This silver, this gold,

---

[69]TTH 21:109-10. [70]The text of Vg, used by Bede, reads, "five on the right hand, and five on the left." [71]Ps 119:105 (118:105 Vg). [72]Prov 6:23. [73]Col 3:1. [74]TTH 21:112-13. [75]"Hinges" in the text of Vg. [76]TTH 21:116*.

these consecrated vessels Solomon brings into the temple, when, after the universal judgment is over, our Lord brings into the joy of his heavenly kingdom all the elect. These are the company both of teachers and the rest of the faithful, and he lays up the various kinds of vessels, silver or gold, in the treasuries of the Lord's house when he hides in the covert of his countenance away from the bustle of human beings those who have merited to enjoy the abundance of his sweetness. It is fitting that the treasuries in which the vessels of election should be hidden are many, whereas the house of the Lord in which these treasuries are is one; for on the one hand, the church in which all the elect are contained is one, however much they may differ in merits, and on the other hand, the heavenly homeland promised to all the elect is one and not of different kinds, even though, just as "star differs from star in glory, so also is the resurrection of the dead."[77] Both of these things the Lord, the very judge and distributor of rewards, has shown in one sentence when he says, "In my Father's house there are many mansions."[78] The reason why Solomon made one house of the Lord but furnished it with many treasuries to accommodate the vessels of various kinds, though it was sanctified with only one blessing, was that there is one house of the Father not made with hands that will last eternally in heaven but many mansions in it to receive all who fear him. ON THE TEMPLE 2.25.3.[79]

---

[77]1 Cor 15:41-42. [78]Jn 14:2. [79]TTH 21:116*.

8:1-21 THE INAUGURATION OF THE TEMPLE

[1]*Then Solomon assembled the elders of Israel and all the heads of the tribes, the leaders of the fathers' houses of the people of Israel, before King Solomon in Jerusalem, to bring up the ark of the covenant of the LORD out of the city of David, which is Zion.* [2]*And all the men of Israel assembled to King Solomon at the feast in the month Ethanim, which is the seventh month.* [3]*And all the elders of Israel came, and the priests took up the ark.* [4]*And they brought up the ark of the LORD, the tent of meeting, and all the holy vessels that were in the tent; the priests and the Levites brought them up.* [5]*And King Solomon and all the congregation of Israel, who had assembled before him, were with him before the ark, sacrificing so many sheep and oxen that they could not be counted or numbered.* [6]*Then the priests brought the ark of the covenant of the LORD to its place, in the inner sanctuary of the house, in the most holy place, underneath the wings of the cherubim.* [7]*For the cherubim spread out their wings over the place of the ark, so that the cherubim made a covering above the ark and its poles.* [8]*And the poles were so long that the ends of the poles were seen from the holy place before the inner sanctuary; but they could not be seen from outside; and they are there to this day.* [9]*There was nothing in the ark except the two tables of stone which Moses put there at Horeb, where the LORD made a covenant with the people of Israel, when they came out of the land of Egypt.* [10]*And when the priests came out of the holy place, a cloud filled the*

house of the Lord, [11]so that the priests could not stand to minister because of the cloud; for the glory of the Lord filled the house of the Lord.

[12]Then Solomon said,

"The Lord has set the sun in the heavens,
　but[z] has said that he would dwell in thick darkness.
[13]I have built thee an exalted house,
　a place for thee to dwell in for ever."

[14]Then the king faced about, and blessed all the assembly of Israel, while all the assembly of Israel stood. [15]And he said, "Blessed be the Lord, the God of Israel, who with his hand has fulfilled what he promised with his mouth to David my father, saying, [16]'Since the day that I brought my people Israel out of Egypt, I chose no city in all the tribes of Israel in which to build a house, that my name might be there; but I chose David to be over my people Israel.' [17]Now it was in the heart of David my father to build a house for the name of the Lord, the God of Israel. [18]But the Lord said to David my father, 'Whereas it was in your heart to build a house for my name, you did well that it was in your heart; [19]nevertheless you shall not build the house, but your son who shall be born to you shall build the house for my name.' [20]Now the Lord has fulfilled his promise which he made; for I have risen in the place of David my father, and sit on the throne of Israel, as the Lord promised, and I have built the house for the name of the Lord, the God of Israel. [21]And there I have provided a place for the ark, in which is the covenant of the Lord which he made with our fathers, when he brought them out of the land of Egypt."

z Gk: Heb lacks *has set the sun in the heavens, but*

Overview: The two weeks of festivity prefigure the festivals of the Christian church and the day of the last judgment (Ephrem). The biblical writer indicates only the most important object preserved in the ark, namely, the two tablets of stone. Solomon blessed his people while standing on a bronze pillar according to the custom of kings (Isho'dad).

8:1-2 At the Festival in the Seventh Month

Symbols of Christ and the Last Judgment. Ephrem the Syrian: The two weeks [of festivity] and the two solemn celebrations were accomplished by the people of the Lord with the greatest joy. The former prefigured the festivals of our church, which Christ began with the mystical dedication of his temple and the transferring of the flesh which he had assumed, to heaven; the latter foreshadowed the last day, the greatest of all solemn days, that will dawn for all saints after the resurrection of the flesh. And the distribution of the ministries and offices in the heavenly and everlasting temple will follow that day. On the First Book of Kings 8.1.[1]

8:9 The Two Tablets of Stone

The Biblical Author Makes No Omissions. Isho'dad of Merv: The words "there was nothing in the ark except the two tablets of stone" does not mean that the author did not know that there were also the jar [containing the manna], the staff [of Aaron], and so forth. He simply wants to signify all the rest by mentioning the most important part, because he writes for

---

[1]ESOO 1:463.

the Jews who already knew the other objects. BOOKS OF SESSIONS 1 KINGS 8.9.[2]

8:14 *The King Blessed the Assembly*

BLESSING FROM THE PILLAR. ISHO'DAD OF MERV: While the king prayed and blessed the people, he stood on a pillar of bronze whose height was five cubits and whose width was two cubits.[3] He climbed it by means of a flight of steps. All the kings stood on it when they needed to speak to the people. This is why [the Scripture] says, "And when she looked up, Jehoash stood on the pillar, according to the royal custom."[4] BOOKS OF SESSIONS 1 KINGS 8.14.[5]

---

[2]CSCO 229:107-8. [3]See 2 Chron 6:13. [4]2 Kings 11:14. [5]CSCO 229:108.

8:22-53 SOLOMON PRAYS BEFORE THE ALTAR OF THE LORD

[22]*Then Solomon stood before the altar of the LORD in the presence of all the assembly of Israel, and spread forth his hands toward heaven;* [23]*and said, "O LORD, God of Israel, there is no God like thee, in heaven above or on earth beneath, keeping covenant and showing steadfast love to thy servants who walk before thee with all their heart;* [24]*who hast kept with thy servant David my father what thou didst declare to him; yea, thou didst speak with thy mouth, and with thy hand hast fulfilled it this day.* [25]*Now therefore, O LORD, God of Israel, keep with thy servant David my father what thou hast promised him, saying, 'There shall never fail you a man before me to sit upon the throne of Israel, if only your sons take heed to their way, to walk before me as you have walked before me.'* [26]*Now therefore, O God of Israel, let thy word be confirmed, which thou hast spoken to thy servant David my father.*

[27]*"But will God indeed dwell on the earth? Behold, heaven and the highest heaven cannot contain thee; how much less this house which I have built!* [28]*Yet have regard to the prayer of thy servant and to his supplication, O LORD my God, hearkening to the cry and to the prayer which thy servant prays before thee this day;* [29]*that thy eyes may be open night and day toward this house, the place of which thou hast said, 'My name shall be there,' that thou mayest hearken to the prayer which thy servant offers toward this place.* [30]*And hearken thou to the supplication of thy servant and of thy people Israel, when they pray toward this place; yea, hear thou in heaven thy dwelling place; and when thou hearest, forgive.*

[31]*"If a man sins against his neighbor and is made to take an oath, and comes and swears his oath before thine altar in this house,* [32]*then hear thou in heaven, and act, and judge thy servants, condemning the guilty by bringing his conduct upon his own head, and vindicating the righteous by rewarding him according to his righteousness.*

[33]"When thy people Israel are defeated before the enemy because they have sinned against thee, if they turn again to thee, and acknowledge thy name, and pray and make supplication to thee in this house; [34]then hear thou in heaven, and forgive the sin of thy people Israel, and bring them again to the land which thou gavest to their fathers.

[35]"When heaven is shut up and there is no rain because they have sinned against thee, if they pray toward this place, and acknowledge thy name, and turn from their sin, when thou dost afflict them, [36]then hear thou in heaven, and forgive the sin of thy servants, thy people Israel, when thou dost teach them the good way in which they should walk; and grant rain upon thy land, which thou hast given to thy people as an inheritance.

[37]"If there is famine in the land, if there is pestilence or blight or mildew or locust or caterpillar; if their enemy besieges them in any[a] of their cities; whatever plague, whatever sickness there is; [38]whatever prayer, whatever supplication is made by any man or by all thy people Israel, each knowing the affliction* of his own heart and stretching out his hands toward this house; [39]then hear thou in heaven thy dwelling place, and forgive, and act, and render to each whose heart thou knowest, according to all his ways (for thou, thou only, knowest the hearts of all the children of men); [40]that they may fear thee all the days that they live in the land which thou gavest to our fathers.

[41]"Likewise when a foreigner, who is not of thy people Israel, comes from a far country for thy name's sake [42](for they shall hear of thy great name, and thy mighty hand, and of thy outstretched arm), when he comes and prays toward this house, [43]hear thou in heaven thy dwelling place, and do according to all for which the foreigner calls to thee; in order that all the peoples of the earth may know thy name and fear thee, as do thy people Israel, and that they may know that this house which I have built is called by thy name.

[44]"If thy people go out to battle against their enemy, by whatever way thou shalt send them, and they pray to the LORD toward the city which thou hast chosen and the house which I have built for thy name, [45]then hear thou in heaven their prayer and their supplication, and maintain their cause.

[46]"If they sin against thee—for there is no man who does not sin—and thou art angry with them, and dost give them to an enemy, so that they are carried away captive to the land of the enemy, far off or near; [47]yet if they lay it to heart in the land to which they have been carried captive, and repent, and make supplication to thee in the land of their captors, saying, 'We have sinned, and have acted perversely and wickedly'; [48]if they repent with all their mind and with all their heart in the land of their enemies, who carried them captive, and pray to thee toward their land, which thou gavest to their fathers, the city which thou hast chosen, and the house which I have built for thy name; [49]then hear thou in heaven thy dwelling place their prayer and their supplication, and maintain their cause [50]and forgive thy people who have sinned against thee, and all their transgressions which they have committed against thee; and grant them compassion in the sight of those who carried them captive, that they may have compassion on them [51](for they are thy people, and thy heritage, which thou didst bring out of Egypt, from the midst of the iron furnace).

^{52}Let thy eyes be open to the supplication of thy servant, and to the supplication of thy people Israel, giving ear to them whenever they call to thee. ^{53}For thou didst separate them from among all the peoples of the earth, to be thy heritage, as thou didst declare through Moses, thy servant, when thou didst bring our fathers out of Egypt, O Lord God."

a Gk Syr: Heb *the land*   * Heb *knowing the afflictions* Syr *knowing the rebellion*

OVERVIEW: Solomon prayed not only for his people but also for the foreigners and the strangers who distrusted the nation of Israel and were often hostile to it (EPHREM). The incarnation of the Lord is foreshadowed in the words pronounced by Solomon: "Will God in very deed dwell with men on the earth?" (CLEMENT OF ALEXANDRIA, CYRIL OF JERUSALEM). In Solomon's words, "Even heaven and the highest cannot contain you, much less this house that I have built," we have a further proof that God cannot be contained in any material space (FULGENTIUS). In Solomon's words, "Only you know what is in every human heart," there is also a foreshadowing of Christ's omniscience during his life on earth (CHRYSOSTOM).

8:22-23 Solomon Stood Before the Altar

SOLOMON'S PRAYER WAS FOR ALL. EPHREM THE SYRIAN: Now notice that Solomon did not only pray for his people but also for the foreigners and the strangers who distrusted the nation of Israel and were often hostile to it, so that the son of David might show the God of David to everyone in general, by praying for his enemies and by speaking ahead of time for us those future words: "But I say to you, Love your enemies and pray for those who persecute you."[1] ON THE FIRST BOOK OF KINGS 8.21.[2]

8:27 Will God Dwell on Earth?

A FORESHADOWING OF THE LORD'S INCARNATION. CLEMENT OF ALEXANDRIA: Solomon the son of David, in the books styled The Reigns of the Kings, comprehending not only that the structure of the true temple was celestial and spiritual but had also a reference to the flesh, which he who was both the son and the Lord of David was to build up, both for his own presence, where, as a living image, he resolved to make his shrine, and for the church that was to rise up through the union of faith, says expressly, "Will God in very deed dwell with humans on the earth?" He dwells on the earth clothed in flesh, and his abode with humans is effected by the conjunction and harmony that obtain among the righteous and that build ... a new temple. For the righteous are the earth, being still encompassed with the earth; and earth, too, in comparison with the greatness of the Lord. Thus also the blessed Peter does not hesitate to say, "You also, as living stones, are built up, a spiritual house, a holy temple, to offer up spiritual sacrifices, acceptable to God by Jesus Christ."[3] And with reference to the body, which by circumscription he consecrated as a hallowed place for himself on earth, he said, "Destroy this temple, and in three days I will raise it up again." The Jews therefore said, "In forty-six years was this temple built, and will you raise it up in three days?" "But he spoke of the temple of his body."[4] FRAGMENT 12.3.[5]

SOLOMON'S WORDS ANNOUNCE THE COMING OF CHRIST. CYRIL OF JERUSALEM: Afterwards Solomon, hearing his father David say these things, and having built a wondrous house and foreseeing him who would come to it, says in astonishment, "Is it then to be thought that God should indeed dwell on earth?" Yes, says David in anticipation in the psalm inscribed "For Solomon," wherein it is said, "He shall be like

---

[1]Mt 5:44. [2]ESOO 1:463. [3]1 Pet 2:5. [4]Jn 2:19-21. [5]ANF 2:584-85*, referred to as *Fragment* 36 in TLG.

rain coming down on the fleece";[6] "rain" because of his heavenly origin but "on the fleece" because of his humanity. For rain, falling on fleece, falls noiselessly; so that, the mystery of his birth being unknown, the wise men said, "Where is he that is born king of the Jews?" And Herod, being troubled, inquired concerning him who had been born, and said, "Where is the Christ born?"[7] CATECHETICAL LECTURES 12.9.[8]

GOD CANNOT BE CONTAINED BY ANY MATERIAL SPACE. FULGENTIUS OF RUSPE: Therefore, the one God, the Father and the Son and the Holy Spirit, fills up the whole, contains the whole; as the whole is in each thing, so the whole is in everything; as the whole is in small things, so the whole is in the largest creatures. This is true of nature but not of grace. When it creates human beings, it does not by the same act save them. While it makes them, it does not by the same act remake them. While it makes that sun to rise over the good and the evil, it does not do the same when the sun of justice rises on those on whom the light, not of the flesh but of the heart, is poured by the gift of prevenient mercy. As it belongs to all to be born through nature, it does not in the same way belong to all to be reborn through grace. Since the Father and the Son and the Holy Spirit by nature are one God, eternal and infinite, there is nothing in heaven, nothing on earth, nothing above the heavens, nothing in any nature that he made that has not been made, where the same one God, Father, Son and Holy Spirit, could be missing. In God, just as there is no mutability of times, so there is no spatial capacity. As Solomon truly said at the dedication of the temple in these words: "Even heaven and the highest cannot contain you, much less this house that I have built." LETTER (FULGENTIUS TO SCARILA) 10.7.[9]

8:37 Blight, Mildew, Other Plagues

BLIGHT AND MILDEW. ISHO'DAD OF MERV: [The Scripture] defines them as diseases deriving from changes in the weather. Blight [occurs when] wheat does not grow. Therefore [we read] these words: "Pharaoh saw ears blighted by a burning wind."[10] Mildew derives from excessive heat and constant bad weather and descends on wheat in the form of drops like rain. One who ignores it calls it "dew," but it burns and dries up wheat when it falls on it. BOOKS OF SESSIONS 1 KINGS 8.37.[11]

8:38 The Afflictions of Their Hearts

GUILT WILL BE ACKNOWLEDGED. ISHO'DAD OF MERV: The words "knowing the rebellion of their own heart," mean that, when they are saved, they will know that God had previously turned away from them and had crushed them by misfortunes because they had sinned and acted rebelliously. BOOKS OF SESSIONS 1 KINGS 8.38.[12]

8:39 God Knows What Is in Every Human Heart

A PREDICTION OF JESUS' OMNISCIENCE. JOHN CHRYSOSTOM: "When he was in Jerusalem for the feast of the Passover, many believed in his name, seeing the signs that he was working. But Jesus himself did not trust himself to them."[13] For those disciples were more dependable who came to him not only by reason of miracles but also because of his teaching. Miracles, indeed, attracted the more slow-witted, but prophecies and teaching, the more intelligent. And those who were won over by teaching were, in truth, more steadfast than those won by miracles. Christ has even called them blessed, saying, "Blessed are they who have not seen and yet have believed."[14] That the others were not of his true disciples the next words show, for the Evangelist added, "Jesus did not trust himself to them."[15] Why? In that he knew all people and because he

---

[6]Ps 72:6 (71:6 Vg). [7]Mt 2:2, 4. [8]FC 61:232*. [9]FC 95:430-31. [10]Gen 41:6. [11]CSCO 229:108. [12]CSCO 229:108. [13]Jn 2:23-24. [14]Jn 20:29. [15]Jn 20:24.

had no need that anyone should bear witness concerning humankind, for he himself knew what was in humanity. What this means is as follows: He who dwells in the very hearts of people and enters into their minds did not give heed to outward words. Knowing clearly that the fervor of these people was transient, he did not feel confidence in them as full-fledged disciples, nor did he entrust all his teachings to them as if they were already firm believers. Now to know what is in the hearts of people belongs to him who "has fashioned the heart of each of them,"[16] that is, to God, for "you only," Scripture says, "know what is in every human heart." He did not, then, need witness in order to know the minds of his own creatures; therefore, he did not have confidence in them by reason of their inconstant faith. People who know neither the present nor the future often both say and confide everything without hesitation to those who treacherously approach them and who will presently forsake them, but not so Christ, for he clearly knows all secrets. HOMILIES ON THE GOSPEL OF JOHN 24.1.[17]

---

[16]Ps 33:5 (32:15 LXX). [17]FC 33:232-33.

8:54-66 SOLOMON'S BLESSING AND SACRIFICE

[54]*Now as Solomon finished offering all this prayer and supplication to the LORD, he arose from before the altar of the LORD, where he had knelt with hands outstretched toward heaven;* [55]*and he stood, and blessed all the assembly of Israel with a loud voice, saying,* [56]*"Blessed be the LORD who has given rest to his people Israel, according to all that he promised; not one word has failed of all his good promise, which he uttered by Moses his servant.* [57]*The LORD our God be with us, as he was with our fathers; may he not leave us or forsake us;* [58]*that he may incline our hearts to him, to walk in all his ways, and to keep his commandments, his statutes, and his ordinances, which he commanded our fathers.* [59]*Let these words of mine, wherewith I have made supplication before the LORD, be near to the LORD our God day and night, and may he maintain the cause of his servant, and the cause of his people Israel, as each day requires;* [60]*that all the peoples of the earth may know that the LORD is God; there is no other.* [61]*Let your heart therefore be wholly true to the LORD our God, walking in his statutes and keeping his commandments, as at this day."*

[62]*Then the king, and all Israel with him, offered sacrifice before the LORD.* [63]*Solomon offered as peace offerings to the LORD twenty-two thousand oxen and a hundred and twenty thousand sheep. So the king and all the people of Israel dedicated the house of the LORD.* [64]*The same day the king consecrated the middle of the court that was before the house of the LORD; for there he offered the burnt offering and the cereal offering and the fat pieces of the peace offerings, because the bronze altar that was before the LORD was too small to receive the burnt offering and the cereal offering and the fat pieces of the peace offerings.*

[65]*So Solomon held the feast at that time, and all Israel with him, a great assembly, from the*

entrance of Hamath to the Brook of Egypt, before the LORD our God, seven days.[b] [66]*On the eighth day he sent the people away; and they blessed the king, and went to their homes joyful and glad of heart for all the goodness that the LORD had shown to David his servant and to Israel his people.*

b Gk: Heb *seven days and seven days, fourteen days*

OVERVIEW: Solomon also demonstrates in his speech that every human being is endowed with free will (CASSIAN). The two altars set by Solomon in the temple of God symbolize the altar of our body and the altar of our heart (CAESARIUS). Solomon, in dismissing the people, who blessed the king and set out for their own dwellings joyfully, foreshadows Christ, who, after bringing to completion the gift of resurrection, dismisses his elect joyfully to their eternal dwelling places (BEDE).

8:58 Walk in God's Ways and Keep His Commandments

BIBLICAL EVIDENCE OF OUR FREE WILL. JOHN CASSIAN: Divine Scripture corroborates the freedom of our will when it says, "Guard your heart with all care."[1] But the apostle lays bare its weakness when he says, "May the Lord guard your hearts and your understanding in Christ Jesus."[2] David proclaims the power of free will when he says, "I have inclined my heart to do your righteous deeds."[3] But he also teaches its weakness when he prays and says, "Incline my heart to your testimonies and not to avarice."[4] Solomon says as well, "May the Lord incline our hearts to himself, so that we may walk in all his ways and keep his commands and his ceremonies and his judgments." CONFERENCE 13.10.1.[5]

8:64 Consecrating the Court in Front of the Temple

THE ALTAR OF THE BODY AND THE ALTAR OF THE HEART. CAESARIUS OF ARLES: We read that two altars were set up in the temple built by Solomon, one outside and one within. On the one that was outside, the sacrifice of animals took place, while on the one inside, the burning of incense was offered. Let us see, brothers, whether there are two altars set up in ourselves, the one that is of the body and the other that is of the heart. God, finally, asks a twofold sacrifice of us: the one, that we be chaste in body; the other, that we should be pure of heart. For this reason good works are offered on the exterior altar, that is, in our body. May holy thoughts emit a sweet fragrance in our hearts, and let us continually do what is pleasing to God on the altar or our heart. We celebrate the consecration of an altar with joy and in right order of things at the time when we offer the altars of our heart and body purified in the sight of the divine majesty and with a good conscience. SERMON 228.2.[6]

8:66 The People Blessed the King

A SYMBOL OF THE JOY OF ETERNAL LIFE. BEDE: But we should note this too: having explained the dedication and subsequent festival, Scripture concludes, "And Solomon dismissed the people, who blessed the king and set out for their own dwellings joyfully and glad of heart for all the goodness the Lord had done for David his servant and for his people Israel." When he has brought to completion the gift of resurrection, our Lord dismisses his elect joyfully to their eternal dwelling places. Surely he does not move them further away from his presence but lets them pass into the dwelling place of the heavenly fatherland after the division at the final judgment (which, according to the saying of the apostle, we know will take place in the air),[7] so that each may receive his promised seat in the kingdom in pro-

---

[1]Prov 4:23. [2]Phil 4:7. [3]Ps 119:112 (118:12 LXX). [4]Ps 119:36 (118:36 LXX). [5]ACW 57:475-76. [6]FC 66:169. [7]See 1 Thess 4:17.

portion to his deserts. What is said here, that the people set out for their own dwellings, refers to the setting-out of which our Lord speaks in the Gospel: "In my Father's house are many mansions."[8] And it is well said that the people set out for their own dwellings while blessing the king, because this is the single supremely tranquil and joyful action of the heavenly citizens, singing hymns of thanksgiving to their Maker. Thus is it written, "Happy are they who dwell in your house; they will praise you forever."[9] Thus the same prophet [David] has filled the final seven psalms[10] with the sweetness of the divine praises; moreover, in the eighth psalm before the end of the psalter,[11] he commemorates by blessing the Lord for his victory in the fight in which he killed the giant [Goliath]. In this he clearly indicates that all who triumph in their contests against the malignant enemy here below will sing the praises of their Maker and Helper there, where they will have true rest. "They blessed the king and set out

for their own dwellings joyfully and glad of heart for all the goodness the Lord had done for David his servant and for his people Israel." The just do indeed go into the dwellings of the heavenly mansions joyfully because of the goodness they have received from the Lord. Although the labors of this age are burdensome and prolonged, whatever ends in eternal blessedness seems short-lived and trifling. Hence each one of us, dearly loved, must press on with his devout actions by exerting himself to the extent of his ability by encouraging, entreating and rebuking in the building up of the house of God, lest, if the heavenly King catches sight of anyone slothful now in the work [of building] his temple, he may make him an outcast from his great solemn celebration at the time of the dedication. HOMILIES ON THE GOSPELS 2.24.[12]

---

[8]Jn 14:2. [9]Ps 84:4 (83:5 Vg). [10]Ps 145:1–147:11; 147:12–150:6 (144–150 LXX). [11]Ps 144 (143 Vg). [12]CS 111:252-53.

9:1-25 THE LORD APPEARS TO SOLOMON A SECOND TIME

[1]When Solomon had finished building the house of the LORD and the king's house and all that Solomon desired to build, [2]the LORD appeared to Solomon a second time, as he had appeared to him at Gibeon. [3]And the LORD said to him, "I have heard your prayer and your supplication, which you have made before me; I have consecrated this house which you have built, and put my name there for ever; my eyes and my heart will be there for all time. [4]And as for you, if you will walk before me, as David your father walked, with integrity of heart and uprightness, doing according to all that I have commanded you, and keeping my statutes and my ordinances, [5]then I will establish your royal throne over Israel for ever, as I promised David your father, saying, 'There shall not fail you a man upon the throne of Israel.' [6]But if you turn aside from following me, you or your children, and do not keep my commandments and my statutes which I have set before you, but go and serve other gods and worship them, [7]then I will cut off Israel from the land which I have given them; and the house which I have consecrated for my name I will cast out of my sight;

and Israel will become a proverb and a byword among all peoples. ⁸And this house will become a heap of ruins;ᶜ everyone passing by it will be astonished, and will hiss; and they will say, 'Why has the LORD done thus to this land and to this house?' ⁹Then they will say, 'Because they forsook the LORD their God who brought their fathers out of the land of Egypt, and laid hold on other gods, and worshiped them and served them; therefore the LORD has brought all this evil upon them.'"

¹⁰At the end of twenty years, in which Solomon had built the two houses, the house of the LORD and the king's house, ¹¹and Hiram king of Tyre had supplied Solomon with cedar and cypress timber and gold, as much as he desired, King Solomon gave to Hiram twenty cities in the land of Galilee. ¹²But when Hiram came from Tyre to see the cities which Solomon had given him, they did not please him. ¹³Therefore he said, "What kind of cities are these which you have given me, my brother?" So they are called the land of Cabul to this day. ¹⁴Hiram had sent to the king one hundred and twenty talents of gold.

¹⁵And this is the account of the forced labor which King Solomon levied to build the house of the LORD and his own house and the Millo and the wall of Jerusalem and Hazor and Megiddo and Gezer ¹⁶(Pharaoh king of Egypt had gone up and captured Gezer and burnt it with fire, and had slain the Canaanites who dwelt in the city, and had given it as dowry to his daughter, Solomon's wife; ¹⁷so Solomon rebuilt Gezer) and Lower Beth-horon ¹⁸and Baalath and Tamar in the wilderness, in the land of Judah,ᵈ ¹⁹and all the store-cities that Solomon had, and the cities for his chariots, and the cities for his horsemen, and whatever Solomon desired to build in Jerusalem, in Lebanon, and in all the land of his dominion. ²⁰All the people who were left of the Amorites, the Hittites, the Perizzites, the Hivites, and the Jebusites, who were not of the people of Israel— ²¹their descendants who were left after them in the land, whom the people of Israel were unable to destroy utterly—these Solomon made a forced levy of slaves, and so they are to this day. ²²But of the people of Israel Solomon made no slaves; they were the soldiers, they were his officials, his commanders, his captains, his chariot commanders and his horsemen.

²³These were the chief officers who were over Solomon's work: five hundred and fifty, who had charge of the people who carried on the work.

²⁴But Pharaoh's daughter went up from the city of David to her own house which Solomon had built for her; then he built the Millo.

²⁵Three times a year Solomon used to offer up burnt offerings and peace offerings upon the altar which he built to the LORD, burning incense before the LORD. So he finished the house.

c Syr Old Latin: Heb *high*   d Heb lacks *of Judah*   e Gk: Heb *burning incense with it which*

OVERVIEW: Only our wickedness can turn God's gifts away from us (ISHO'DAD). In God's words, "Israel shall be for perdition and a reproach to the people, and this house shall be desolate," there is a foreshadowing of the ruin of Israel after the killing of Jesus (LACTANTIUS).

9:3 There for All Time

OUR WICKEDNESS TURNS GOD'S GIFTS AWAY. ISHO'DAD OF MERV: How can God say that he will always be in this temple when he threatens to destroy the house? The gifts of God

are without second thoughts, as far as it depends on him, but our wickedness turns them away from us. In fact, he does not simply give gifts but gives them in order that we may repent. That is why he says in Jeremiah, "And if I shall pronounce a decree on a nation and kingdom, to rebuild and to plant it, and they do evil before me, so as not to listen to my voice, then I will repent of the good that I spoke of, to do it to them."[1] BOOKS OF SESSIONS 1 KINGS 9.3.[2]

9:7-9 *This House Will Become a Heap of Ruins*

PREDICTION OF THE DESTRUCTION OF ISRAEL. LACTANTIUS: After a short time the emperor Vespasian subdued the Jews and laid waste their lands with the sword and fire, besieged and reduced them by famine, overthrew Jerusalem, led the captives in triumph and prohibited the others who were left from ever returning to their native land. And these things were done by God on account of that crucifixion of Christ, as he before declared this to Solomon in their Scriptures, saying, "And Israel shall be for perdition and a reproach to the people, and this house shall be desolate; and every one that shall pass by shall be astonished, and shall say, 'Why has God done these evils to this land, and to this house?' And they shall say, 'Because they forsook the Lord their God and persecuted their King, who was dearly beloved by God, and crucified him with great degradation; therefore has God brought on them these evils.'" For what would they not deserve who put to death their Lord, who had come for their salvation? EPITOME OF THE DIVINE INSTITUTES 46.[3]

---

[1]Jer 18:9-10; here Isho'dad quotes the LXX instead of the Syriac Peshitta. [2]CSCO 229:108-9. [3]ANF 7:241. See CSEL 19:719 where the reference is to *Epitome of the Divine Institutes* 41.7.

9:26–10:29 POLITICAL AND ECONOMIC POWER OF ISRAEL

26King Solomon built a fleet of ships at Ezion-geber, which is near Eloth on the shore of the Red Sea, in the land of Edom. 27And Hiram sent with the fleet his servants, seamen who were familiar with the sea, together with the servants of Solomon; 28and they went to Ophir, and brought from there gold, to the amount of four hundred and twenty talents; and they brought it to King Solomon. 10 Now when the queen of Sheba heard of the fame of Solomon concerning the name of the LORD, she came to test him with hard questions. 2She came to Jerusalem with a very great retinue, with camels bearing spices, and very much gold, and precious stones; and when she came to Solomon, she told him all that was on her mind. 3And Solomon answered all her questions; there was nothing hidden from the king which he could not explain to her. 4And when the queen of Sheba had seen all the wisdom of Solomon, the house that he had built, 5the food of his table, the seating of his officials, and the attendance of his servants, their clothing, his cupbearers, and his burnt offerings which he offered at the house of the LORD, there was no more spirit in her.

⁶And she said to the king, "The report was true which I heard in my own land of your affairs and of your wisdom, ⁷but I did not believe the reports until I came and my own eyes had seen it; and behold, the half was not told me; your wisdom and prosperity surpass the report which I heard. ⁸Happy are your wives!ᶠ Happy are these your servants, who continually stand before you and hear your wisdom! ⁹Blessed be the LORD your God, who has delighted in you and set you on the throne of Israel! Because the LORD loved Israel for ever, he has made you king, that you may execute justice and righteousness." ¹⁰Then she gave the king a hundred and twenty talents of gold, and a very great quantity of spices, and precious stones; never again came such an abundance of spices as these which the queen of Sheba gave to King Solomon.

¹¹Moreover the fleet of Hiram, which brought gold from Ophir, brought from Ophir a very great amount of almug wood and precious stones. ¹²And the king made of the almug wood supports for the house of the LORD, and for the king's house, lyres also and harps for the singers; no such almug wood has come or been seen, to this day.

¹³And King Solomon gave to the queen of Sheba all that she desired, whatever she asked besides what was given her by the bounty of King Solomon. So she turned and went back to her own land, with her servants.

¹⁴Now the weight of gold that came to Solomon in one year was six hundred and sixty-six talents of gold, ¹⁵besides that which came from the traders and from the traffic of the merchants, and from all the kings of Arabia and from the governors of the land. ¹⁶King Solomon made two hundred large shields of beaten gold; six hundred shekels of gold went into each shield. ¹⁷And he made three hundred shields of beaten gold; three minas of gold went into each shield; and the king put them in the House of the Forest of Lebanon. ¹⁸The king also made a great ivory throne, and overlaid it with the finest gold. ¹⁹The throne had six steps, and at the back of the throne was a calf's head, and on each side of the seat were arm rests and two lions standing beside the arm rests, ²⁰while twelve lions stood there, one on each end of a step on the six steps. The like of it was never made in any kingdom. ²¹All King Solomon's drinking vessels were of gold, and all the vessels of the House of the Forest of Lebanon were of pure gold; none were of silver, it was not considered as anything in the days of Solomon. ²²For the king had a fleet of ships of Tarshish at sea with the fleet of Hiram. Once every three years the fleet of ships of Tarshish used to come bringing gold, silver, ivory, apes, and peacocks.ᵍ

²³Thus King Solomon excelled all the kings of the earth in riches and in wisdom. ²⁴And the whole earth sought the presence of Solomon to hear his wisdom, which God had put into his mind. ²⁵Every one of them brought his present, articles of silver and gold, garments, myrrh, spices, horses, and mules, so much year by year.

²⁶And Solomon gathered together chariots and horsemen; he had fourteen hundred chariots and twelve thousand horsemen, whom he stationed in the chariot cities and with the king in Jerusalem. ²⁷And the king made silver as common in Jerusalem as stone, and he made cedar as plentiful as the sycamore of the Shephelah. ²⁸And Solomon's import of horses was from Egypt and Kue, and the king's traders received them from Kue at a price. ²⁹A chariot could be imported from Egypt for six

hundred shekels of silver, and a horse for a hundred and fifty; and so through the king's traders they were exported to all the kings of the Hittites and the kings of Syria.

f Gk Syr: Heb *men* g Or *baboons*

OVERVIEW: The queen of Sheba came to visit Solomon in order to be enlightened by him (EPHREM). The sending by the Ethiopian queen of the treasures of the nations to Jerusalem signifies that the church would bring gifts of the virtue and faith to the Lord (BEDE). Like the queen of Sheba, we must admire God's riches and embrace his treasures of wisdom (ORIGEN). Solomon divided his servants into classes, which were recognizable according to the uniform they wore (ISHO'DAD). Solomon is a type of Christ, while the queen of Sheba foreshadows the faithful women who will listen to the word of Jesus (AMBROSE). Solomon is also a figure of the church of the saints, who are the living temples of Christ (CAESARIUS). As the queen of Sheba came from her distant land to Solomon, so the church came together from the four regions of the world to Christ (SEVERUS). Silver signifies the holy doctrine (of Christ), which must be spread all over the world (EPHREM).

10:1 The Queen of Sheba Came to Test Solomon

ENLIGHTENED BY SOLOMON'S WISDOM.
EPHREM THE SYRIAN: The queen of Sheba was a sheep that had come into the place of wolves. The lamp of truth did Solomon give her who also married[1] her when he fell away. She was enlightened and went away, but they[2] were dark as their manner was. THE PEARL, HYMN 3.3.[3]

10:2 Gold and Precious Stones

THE CHURCH WILL BRING GIFTS OF FAITH TO THE LORD. BEDE: We read also in the book of Kings that the queen of the South[4] came from the end of the earth to listen to the wisdom of Solomon. Actually, it was customary for that nation to be always ruled by women, whom they called Kandakes.[5]

The sending by the Ethiopian queen of the treasures of the nations to Jerusalem signifies that the church would bring gifts of the virtue and of faith to the Lord. The etymology of her name is also appropriate, for in Hebrew Candace [Kandake] means "exchanged."[6] In the Scriptures (in the psalm "For those who will be exchanged") it is she to whom it was said, "Hear, daughter, and see, and incline your ear. Forget your people and your father's home,"[7] and so forth. COMMENTARY ON THE ACTS OF THE APOSTLES 8.27.[8]

10:4 She Observed All the Wisdom of Solomon

WE MUST EMBRACE THE RICHES OF OUR LORD. ORIGEN: The Scriptures express astonishment that the queen of Sheba came from "the end of the earth to hear Solomon's wisdom." When she saw his dinner, his furnishings and the attendants in his place, she was astounded and wholly in a state of wonder. If we do not embrace the great riches of our Lord, the great furnishings of his Word and the wealth of his teachings; if we do not eat the "bread of life";[9] if we are not fed with the flesh of Jesus and do not drink his blood; if we disdain the banquet of our Savior, we should realize that God has both "kindness and severity."[10] Of these, we should pray more for his kindness on us, in Christ Jesus our Lord. HOMILIES ON THE GOSPEL OF LUKE 38.6.[11]

---

[1]This is a Jewish tradition (partly based on Song 1:5), which was commonly accepted by Syriac writers. [2]The Jews. [3]NPNF 2 13:295. [4]Of Sheba; the LXX, Vg and VL read "of Saba." [5]See Pliny *Natural History* 6.35, 186. [6]Jerome *Nom. Hebr.* (CCL 72.144.3). [7]Ps 45:10 (44:11 Vg). [8]CS 117:82. [9]Jn 6:35. [10]Rom 11:22. [11]FC 94:158.

10:5 Solomon's Servants and Their Clothing

DIVIDED INTO CLASSES. ISHO'DAD OF MERV: The words "the attendance of the servants [and their clothing]." It seems that Solomon, in his wisdom, had divided into classes all his servants, that is, all the craftsmen that did their duty, so that they might be identifiable from their clothing and uniforms which [indicated] the different classes of the bakers, the cooks, the cupbearers. Everyone was recognizable from his gear. BOOKS OF SESSIONS 1 KINGS 10.5.[12]

10:6-8 The Report Was True

SOLOMON COMBINES IN HIMSELF JUSTICE AND PRUDENCE. AMBROSE: We entrust our case to the most prudent person we can find and ask advice from him more readily than we do from others. However, the faithful counsel of a just person stands first and often has more weight than the great abilities of the wisest of people: "For better are the wounds of a friend than the kisses of others."[13] And just because it is the judgment of a just person, it is also the conclusion of a wise one: in the one lies the result of the matter in dispute, in the other readiness of invention. And if one connects the two, there will be great soundness in the advice given, which is regarded by all with admiration for the wisdom shown and with love for its justice. And so all will desire to hear the wisdom of that person in whom those two virtues are found together, as all the kings of the earth desired to see the face of Solomon and to hear his wisdom. No, even the queen of Sheba came to him and tried him with questions. She came and spoke of all the things that were in her heart and heard all the wisdom of Solomon, nor did any word escape her. Who she was whom nothing escaped, and that there was nothing which the truth-loving Solomon did not tell her, learn, O man, from this which you hear her saying, "It was a true report that I heard in my own land of your words and of your prudence, yet I did not believe those that told it me until I came

and my eyes had seen it; and behold, the half was not told me. You have added good things over and above all that I heard in my own land. Blessed are your women and blessed your servants, who stand before you and hear all your prudence." Recognize the feast of the true Solomon and those who are set down at that feast; recognize it wisely and think in what land all the nations shall hear the fame of true wisdom and justice and with what eyes they shall see him, beholding those things that are not seen. "For the things that are seen are temporal, but the things that are not seen are eternal."

What women are blessed but those of whom it is said "that many hear the word of God and bring forth fruit"?[14] And again: "Whosoever does the will of my Father in heaven is my brother and sister and mother."[15] And who are those blessed servants, who stand before him, but Paul, who said, "Even to this day I stand witnessing both to great and small";[16] or Simeon, who was waiting in the temple to see the consolation of Israel?[17] How could he have asked to be allowed to depart, except that in standing before the Lord he had not the power of departing, but only according to the will of God? Solomon is put before us simply for the sake of example, of whom it was eagerly expected that his wisdom should be heard. DUTIES OF THE CLERGY 2.10.50-53.[18]

SOLOMON IS A TYPE OF THE CHURCH OF THE SAINTS. CAESARIUS OF ARLES: In almost all places from the east to the west where the Christian religion is practiced, your manner of life[19] for the glory of God is preached with most illustrious fame. It is rightly required of you that what is believed in your case should also be proved. With the Lord's help, then, do what you have always done, and preserve charity, humility, meekness and obedience in such a way that what is believed about you in the whole world may be augmented

---

[12]CSCO 229:109. [13]Prov 27:6. [14]Lk 11:28. [15]Mt 12:50. [16]Acts 26:22. [17]See Lk 2:25. [18]NPNF 2 10:51-52*. [19]Caesarius is referring to holy men who have the reputation of saints.

by the deeds of an ever spotless life. Then whoever has merited to see you will be able to give verbal utterance to the sentence uttered by that queen who wanted to seek out Solomon as a type of the church. When each one of you like living temples of Christ, adorned with the pearls of good works, filled with the burnt offerings of prayers and fragrant with the spices of virtues has merited to be contemplated, then immediately breaking forth with the voice of exultation, may he exclaim and say with that queen, "The report I heard in my country" about the life of this saintly community "is true." Behold, now in truth "I have discovered that they were hardly telling me the half"; for I have merited to see with my eyes much greater things than I first heard with my ears. When anyone merited to seek and behold you like angels placed on earth, he rejoiced at such things and uttered words with his own lips. Then he happily announced throughout the whole world: Consider and see how much glory is added to you and how precious and holy a joy is produced for the universal church throughout the entire world. Sermon 236.3.[20]

10:10 A Great Quantity of Gifts

The Queen of Sheba as a Type of the Church. Ephrem the Syrian: The queen of Sheba was a type of our church. She came from her distant land to king Solomon, the church came together from the four regions of the world to Christ. What [the queen] ignored, she learned from Solomon, and she went back to her land with many gifts. Here the mystery which had remained hidden for centuries and generations was finally revealed: after she had been taught to despise earthly possessions, she was made a participant and dispenser of the heavenly treasure. Why do not we imitate the queen of the South, whom our mother [the church] emulated, by offering gold, precious stones and spices to Christ? The transaction is that we lose worthless things, so that we may get great ones, which we search for and lack in the highest degree. Syriac Fragment on 1 Kings 10.10.[21]

10:27 Silver as Common in Jerusalem as Stones

Silver Signifies the Holy Doctrine of Christ. Ephrem the Syrian: This means that the knowledge of divine things must be imparted to all nations everywhere through the advent and manifestation of Christ; and Isaiah predicted the coming of Christ in the clearest way by saying, "The earth will be full of the knowledge of the Lord as the waters cover the sea."[22] The Scripture usually employs the symbol of silver to signify the holy doctrine [of Christ]. Indeed it is a pure, bright and sonorous metal, and its qualities are extraordinarily appropriate to Christ's gospel. Haggai predicted that the temple of the Lord, which is the church of Christ, must be filled with this kind of silver.[23] On the First Book of Kings 10.27.[24]

---

[20]FC 66:212-13*. [21]ESOO 1:466. This passage is attributed by the editor Assemani to Severus of Antioch (ninth century), who is the medieval compiler of the catena including Ephrem's commentary. [22]Is 11:9. [23]See Hag 2:8. [24]ESOO 1:467.

11:1-13 SOLOMON'S LAPSE INTO IDOLATRY

¹Now King Solomon loved many foreign women: the daughter of Pharaoh, and Moabite, Ammonite, Edomite, Sidonian, and Hittite women, ²from the nations concerning which the LORD had said to the people of Israel, "You shall not enter into marriage with them, neither shall they with you, for surely they will turn away your heart after their gods"; Solomon clung to these in love. ³He had seven hundred wives, princesses, and three hundred concubines; and his wives turned away his heart. ⁴For when Solomon was old his wives turned away his heart after other gods; and his heart was not wholly true to the LORD his God, as was the heart of David his father. ⁵For Solomon went after Ashtoreth the goddess of the Sidonians, and after Milcom the abomination of the Ammonites. ⁶So Solomon did what was evil in the sight of the LORD, and did not wholly follow the LORD, as David his father had done. ⁷Then Solomon built a high place for Chemosh the abomination of Moab, and for Molech the abomination of the Ammonites, on the mountain east of Jerusalem. ⁸And so he did for all his foreign wives, who burned incense and sacrificed to their gods.

⁹And the LORD was angry with Solomon, because his heart had turned away from the LORD, the God of Israel, who had appeared to him twice, ¹⁰and had commanded him concerning this thing, that he should not go after other gods; but he did not keep what the LORD commanded. ¹¹Therefore the LORD said to Solomon, "Since this has been your mind and you have not kept my covenant and my statutes which I have commanded you, I will surely tear the kingdom from you and will give it to your servant. ¹²Yet for the sake of David your father I will not do it in your days, but I will tear it out of the hand of your son. ¹³However I will not tear away all the kingdom; but I will give one tribe to your son, for the sake of David my servant and for the sake of Jerusalem which I have chosen."

OVERVIEW: Solomon was not blamed for marrying the Gentile daughter of Pharaoh, but later he took other wives and was led to idolatry by them (EPHREM). Solomon obtained wisdom through spiritual love but lost it through carnal love (AUGUSTINE). Solomon was not the Messiah promised by God, because God knew that Solomon would fall (AUGUSTINE). Solomon allowed his wives to practice idolatry instead of opposing them (ISHO'DAD). The Gentile wives of Solomon turned Solomon aside from the fear of God to their idols by means of their allurements (EPHREM). Solomon's apostasy and idolatry teach us that no hope must be placed in any human being (AUGUSTINE). Solomon was not punished by God for his idolatry thanks to the merits of his father, David (CHRYSOSTOM).

11:1-2 Solomon Loved Many Foreign Women

SOLOMON'S CRIME IS A CONSEQUENCE OF HIS MARRIAGES. EPHREM THE SYRIAN: In the previous chapters the Scripture related the marriage of Solomon with the daughter of Pharaoh and did not rebuke him because she was the one wife only who did not secretly practice the religion of her homeland and was no reason of offense for him. But later he took other wives, so that the holy Scripture justly condemned both the previous marriage and these new ones. And there were four reasons for this: the first was his open transgression against religion because he had brought back [Israel's] ancient idolatry which he had previously rejected; the second was that he took many wives against the clear precept of the Law; the third was that he loved these wives to distraction; the fourth was his apostasy from the worship of the true God which derived, as the Law had predicted, from such marriages. Therefore, with good reason the Scripture emphasizes many times, with very severe words, that the crime of Solomon was a consequence of his familiarity with these women. A further detail, which increases Solomon's guilt, is that he did not only cause harm with his actions but also with his example. He was harmful not only because he was corrupted but also because he corrupted the kings that followed him, with the exception of one or two. Solomon was certainly the first among the leaders and kings of Israel who established public ceremonies and sacrifices of idolatry through the authority of magistrates. On the First Book of Kings 11.1.[1]

Solomon Ruled by Carnal Passions.
Augustine: However, in [David's] son Solomon libido was not a passing guest; it reigned as a king. Scripture does not pass this over in silence but blames him as a lover of women. His beginnings were redolent with the desire for wisdom; when he had obtained it through spiritual love, he lost it through carnal love. Christian Instruction 3.21.31.[2]

Solomon Was Not the Messiah Promised by God. Augustine: [God] promised that something everlasting would spring from David's seed. Then Solomon was born, and he became a man of such profound wisdom that everyone supposed God's promise concerning David's offspring had been fulfilled in him. But no, Solomon fell and so made room for people to stretch their hope toward Christ. God can neither be deceived nor deceive us, so we can be certain that he did

not ground his promise in Solomon, for he knew Solomon would fall. The divine purpose was that after Solomon's fall you would look to God and earnestly press him for what he had promised.

Did you lie, then, Lord? Do you go back on your promises? Do you fail to deliver what you swore to give? Perhaps God will counter you by saying, "I did swear, and I did promise, but that man did not persevere." But how can that be the answer? Did you not foresee, O Lord God, that he would not persevere? Of course you foresaw it. Why, then, did you promise me something that would last forever and attach that promise to someone who would not persevere? You said to me, "'If his children forsake my law and do not walk according to my ordinances, if they break my commandments and violate my covenant,'[3] nevertheless my promise shall endure, and my oath shall be fulfilled.'Once I have sworn in my holiness,'[4] within myself." In that most secret place you swore it, in the fountain from which the prophets drank, those prophets who belched out for us the words, "Once have I sworn in my holiness, and I will not lie to David."[5] Make good your oath then, and deliver what you promised. I was stripped away from David of old, lest in that David we should hope for its fulfillment, and so that you can say to us, "Keep hoping for what I promised."

Even David himself was aware of this. Consider what he says: "Yet you, you yourself, have rejected him to nothing."[6] So what has become of your promise? "You have put off your Anointed."[7] The speaker has doleful things to relate, but by these very words he cheers us, because he is implying, "What you promised stands absolutely firm, O God, for you have not taken your Anointed right away from us, but only put him off." Exposition 2 of Psalm 88.6-7.[8]

---

[1]ESOO 1:468. [2]FC 2:142. [3]Ps 89:30 (88:31 LXX, Vg). [4]Ps 89:34-35 (88:35-36 LXX, Vg). [5]Ps 89:35 (88:36 LXX, Vg). [6]Ps 89:38 (88:39 LXX, Vg). [7]Ps 89:38 (88:39 LXX, Vg) (LXX; the Hebrew text reads, "you are full of wrath against your anointed"). [8]WSA 3 18:295-96*.

11:3 Solomon's Wives Turned Away His Heart

SOLOMON ALLOWED HIS WIVES TO WORSHIP IDOLS. ISHO'DAD OF MERV: The words "the wives turned away his heart" do not mean that Solomon himself apostatized and worshiped the idols but that he gave [his wives] freedom to worship their idols without preventing them or converting them, as his father David [had done]. Therefore, since "man and wife become one flesh,"[9] and the Scripture usually attributes to them both the action of one because of their union . . . this is why [Solomon] is justly rebuked for allowing his wives to adore [the idols]. Silence, as they say, expresses consent. Other commentators[10] assert that [Solomon] worships the idols but is not punished, even though he deserved it, thanks to his father and all his merits and toil in building the house. BOOKS OF SESSIONS 1 KINGS 11.3.[11]

GENTILE WOMEN TURNED SOLOMON ASIDE FROM THE FEAR OF GOD. EPHREM THE SYRIAN: The hands of the sinful woman were stretched out over his feet, that they might receive a gift from his divinity.[12] Our Lord, therefore, showed his humanity so that the sinful woman might approach him. He also revealed his divinity in order that the Pharisee might be found guilty by him. Consequently, the sinful woman could scoff at the cunning thoughts of him who had been scoffing at her tears. She, through her love, brought into the open the tears that were hidden in the depths of her eyes, and [the Lord], because of her courage, brought into the open the thoughts that were hidden in the Pharisee. The sinful woman thought he was like God. Her faith was witness to this. Simon thought he was [merely] like a man. What he had worked out in his mind showed this. Our Lord, therefore, standing in the middle, worked out a parable between the two of them, so that the sinful woman might be encouraged through his pronouncing the parable and the Pharisee might be denounced through the explanation of the parable.

But now, likewise, we are in the middle; and like Solomon we have fallen between women. But, even if we, like Solomon, have fallen between women, we are not, like Solomon, wounded by women. For these Gentile women were turning Solomon aside from the fear of God to their idols by means of their allurements. We place the faith of the Gentile women above the heroic exploits of the Hebrew women. For the latter, through the wholeness of their bodies, rendered Solomon's healthy faith sick, while the former, through their being healed, restore our ailing faith to health. Who therefore would not [wish] to be healed [by such faith]? COMMENTARY ON TATIAN'S DIATESSARON 7.18.[13]

11:7-8 Solomon Built a Place for Chemosh and Molech

NO HOPE MUST BE PLACED IN ANY HUMAN BEING. AUGUSTINE: Solomon was in his time David's son, a great man, through whom many holy precepts and healthful admonitions and divine mysteries have been wrought by the Holy Spirit in the Scriptures. Solomon himself was a lover of women and was rejected by God: and this lust was so great a snare to him that he was induced by women even to sacrifice to idols, as Scripture witnesses concerning him. But if, by his fall, what was delivered through him were blotted out, it would be judged that he had himself delivered these precepts and not that they were delivered through him. The mercy of God, therefore, and his Spirit, excellently wrought that whatever of good was declared through Solomon, might be attributed to God; and the man's sin, to the man. What marvel that Solomon fell among God's people? Did not Adam fall in paradise? Did not an angel fall from heaven and become the devil? We are thereby taught that no hope must be placed in any human being. EXPOSITIONS OF THE PSALMS 127.1.[14]

---

[9]Gen 2:24. [10]Isho'dad refers to unknown sources. [11]CSCO 229:110-11. [12]See Lk 7:38, 44-46. [13]ECTD 137-38. [14]NPNF 1 8:606*.

11:13 God Will Not Tear Away the Entire Kingdom

GOD'S CLEMENCY TOWARD SOLOMON ON ACCOUNT OF DAVID. JOHN CHRYSOSTOM: The son of this David, Solomon by name, was caught by the same snare as his father, and out of complacence to women fell away from the God of his fathers. You see how great an evil it is not to master pleasure, not to upset the ruling principle in nature and for a man to be slave of women. This same Solomon, then, who was formerly righteous and wise but who ran a risk of being deprived of all the kingdom on account of his sin, God permitted to keep the sixth part of the government on account of the renown of his father. LETTER TO THE FALLEN THEODORE 2.2.[15]

---

[15]NPNF 1 9:112.

11:14-43 A REBELLION AT THE END OF SOLOMON'S REIGN

[14]And the LORD raised up an adversary against Solomon, Hadad the Edomite; he was of the royal house in Edom. [15]For when David was in Edom, and Joab the commander of the army went up to bury the slain, he slew every male in Edom [16](for Joab and all Israel remained there six months, until he had cut off every male in Edom); [17]but Hadad fled to Egypt, together with certain Edomites of his father's servants, Hadad being yet a little child. [18]They set out from Midian and came to Paran, and took men with them from Paran and came to Egypt, to Pharaoh king of Egypt, who gave him a house, and assigned him an allowance of food, and gave him land. [19]And Hadad found great favor in the sight of Pharaoh, so that he gave him in marriage the sister of his own wife, the sister of Tahpenes the queen. [20]And the sister of Tahpenes bore him Genubath his son, whom Tahpenes weaned in Pharaoh's house; and Genubath was in Pharaoh's house among the sons of Pharaoh. [21]But when Hadad heard in Egypt that David slept with his fathers and that Joab the commander of the army was dead, Hadad said to Pharaoh, "Let me depart, that I may go to my own country." [22]But Pharaoh said to him, "What have you lacked with me that you are now seeking to go to your own country?" And he said to him, "Only let me go."

[23]God also raised up as an adversary to him, Rezon the son of Eliada, who had fled from his master Hadad-ezer king of Zobah. [24]And he gathered men about him and became leader of a marauding band, after the slaughter by David; and they went to Damascus, and dwelt there, and made him king in Damascus. [25]He was an adversary of Israel all the days of Solomon, doing mischief as Hadad did; and he abhorred Israel, and reigned over Syria.

[26]Jeroboam the son of Nebat, an Ephraimite of Zeredah, a servant of Solomon, whose mother's name was Zeruah, a widow, also lifted up his hand against the king. [27]And this was the reason

why he lifted up his hand against the king. Solomon built the Millo, and closed up the breach of the city of David his father. ²⁸The man Jeroboam was very able, and when Solomon saw that the young man was industrious he gave him charge over all the forced labor of the house of Joseph. ²⁹And at that time, when Jeroboam went out of Jerusalem, the prophet Ahijah the Shilonite found him on the road. Now Ahijah had clad himself with a new garment; and the two of them were alone in the open country. ³⁰Then Ahijah laid hold of the new garment that was on him, and tore it into twelve pieces. ³¹And he said to Jeroboam, "Take for yourself ten pieces; for thus says the Lord, the God of Israel, 'Behold, I am about to tear the kingdom from the hand of Solomon, and will give you ten tribes ³²(but he shall have one tribe, for the sake of my servant David and for the sake of Jerusalem, the city which I have chosen out of all the tribes of Israel), ³³because he has^b forsaken me, and worshiped Ashtoreth the goddess of the Sidonians, Chemosh the god of Moab, and Milcom the god of the Ammonites, and has^b not walked in my ways, doing what is right in my sight and keeping my statutes and my ordinances, as David his father did. ³⁴Nevertheless I will not take the whole kingdom out of his hand; but I will make him ruler all the days of his life, for the sake of David my servant whom I chose, who kept my commandments and my statutes; ³⁵but I will take the kingdom out of his son's hand, and will give it to you, ten tribes. ³⁶Yet to his son I will give one tribe, that David my servant may always have a lamp before me in Jerusalem, the city where I have chosen to put my name. ³⁷And I will take you, and you shall reign over all that your soul desires, and you shall be king over Israel. ³⁸And if you will hearken to all that I command you, and will walk in my ways, and do what is right in my eyes by keeping my statutes and my commandments, as David my servant did, I will be with you, and will build you a sure house, as I built for David, and I will give Israel to you. ³⁹And I will for this afflict the descendants of David, but not for ever.'" ⁴⁰Solomon sought therefore to kill Jeroboam; but Jeroboam arose, and fled into Egypt, to Shishak king of Egypt, and was in Egypt until the death of Solomon.

⁴¹Now the rest of the acts of Solomon, and all that he did, and his wisdom, are they not written in the book of the acts of Solomon? ⁴²And the time that Solomon reigned in Jerusalem over all Israel was forty years. ⁴³And Solomon slept with his fathers, and was buried in the city of David his father; and Rehoboam his son reigned in his stead.

b Gk Syr Vg: Heb *they have*

OVERVIEW: When Solomon sinned and departed from the ways of the Lord, "the Lord stirred up the adversary," namely, the devil, "against Solomon" (CYPRIAN). God's gifts are showered on everyone, but humans refuse them deliberately (ISHO'DAD). When the twelve tribes of Israel were being rent, the prophet Ahijah rent his garment, but since Christ's people cannot be rent, his coat, woven throughout as a single whole, was not rent by its owners (CYPRIAN). The words of the prophet Ahijah announce the line of kings descending from David, which will lead to Jesus (ISHO'DAD).

11:14 The Lord Raised an Adversary Against Solomon

POWER IS GIVEN TO EVIL AGAINST US ACCORDING TO OUR SINS. CYPRIAN: The adversary has no power against us unless God has previously permitted it, in order that all our fear and devotion and obedience may be turned to God, since in temptations nothing is permitted evil, unless the power is granted by God. . . . Moreover, power is given to evil against us according to our sins, as it is written: "Who has given Jacob for spoil and Israel to those who despoiled him? Has not God, against whom they have sinned and were unwilling to walk in his ways and to hear his law, even poured out upon them the indignation of his fury?"[1] And again when Solomon sinned and departed from the precepts and the ways of the Lord, it is set down: "And the Lord stirred up the adversary[2] against Solomon himself." THE LORD'S PRAYER 25.[3]

11:31-32 Take Ten Pieces

GOD'S ABSOLUTE GENEROSITY. ISHO'DAD OF MERV: Here God's mercy is absolutely evident. Even though he knew how wicked Jeroboam was, [God] appoints him king in order to show that, as far as it depends on him, his gifts are never denied but showered on everyone. Humans themselves, however, refuse them deliberately. BOOKS OF SESSIONS 1 KINGS 11.31.[4]

THE NATION OF CHRIST WILL NEVER BE DIVIDED. CYPRIAN: In the Gospel there is a proof of this mystery of unity, this inseparable bond of harmony, when the coat of the Lord Jesus Christ is not cut or rent at all. The garment is received whole and the coat taken into possession unspoiled and undivided by those who cast lots for Christ's garment, asking who should put on Christ. Holy Scripture says of this, "But for the coat, because it was not sewn but woven from the top throughout, they said to each other: Let us not rend it but casts lots for it, whose it shall be."[5] He showed a unity that came from the top, that is, from heaven and the Father, a unity that could

by no means be rent by one who received and possessed it. Its wholeness and unity remained solid and unbreakable forever. He who rends and divides the church cannot possess the garment of Christ. In contrast, when at Solomon's death his kingdom and people were being rent, the prophet Ahijah, meeting King Jeroboam in the field, rent his garment into twelve pieces, saying, "Take for yourself ten pieces, for thus says the Lord: Behold, I rend the kingdom out of the hand of Solomon and will give ten scepters to you; but he shall have two scepters for my servant David's sake, and for Jerusalem's sake, the city that I have chosen, to put my name there." When the twelve tribes of Israel were being rent, the prophet Ahijah rent his garment. But since Christ's people cannot be rent, his coat, woven throughout as a single whole, was not rent by its owners. Undivided, conjoined, coherent, it proves the unbroken harmony of our people who have put on Christ. By the type and symbol of his garment he has manifested the unity of the church. THE UNITY OF THE CHURCH 7.[6]

11:36 One Tribe for David's Son

CHRIST, THE KING DESCENDING FROM DAVID. ISHO'DAD OF MERV: The words "so that David may always have a lamp" refer to that small part of the kingdom which was like the sun in the abundance of its light: "Your throne will be like the sun before me."[7] Moreover, as we light many firebrands from a lamp, so a large number [of kings] will descend from the royal lineage of David "until he, to whom kingship belongs, comes."[8] BOOKS OF SESSIONS 1 KINGS 11.36.[9]

---

[1]Is 42:24-25. [2]Cyprian interprets Solomon's adversary Hadad, the Edomite, as a symbol of Satan. [3]FC 36:149*. [4]CSCO 229:112. [5]Jn 19:23-24. [6]LCC 5:128-29*. [7]Ps 89:36 (Peshitta). [8]Adapted quotation from Gen 49:10. [9]CSCO 229:111.

12:1-25 JEROBOAM LEADS THE TEN TRIBES TO SECESSION

¹Rehoboam went to Shechem, for all Israel had come to Shechem to make him king. ²And when Jeroboam the son of Nebat heard of it (for he was still in Egypt, whither he had fled from King Solomon), then Jeroboam returned from¹ Egypt. ³And they sent and called him; and Jeroboam and all the assembly of Israel came and said to Rehoboam, ⁴"Your father made our yoke heavy. Now therefore lighten the hard service of your father and his heavy yoke upon us, and we will serve you." ⁵He said to them, "Depart for three days, then come again to me." So the people went away.

⁶Then King Rehoboam took counsel with the old men, who had stood before Solomon his father while he was yet alive, saying, "How do you advise me to answer this people?" ⁷And they said to him, "If you will be a servant to this people today and serve them, and speak good words to them when you answer them, then they will be your servants for ever." ⁸But he forsook the counsel which the old men gave him, and took counsel with the young men who had grown up with him and stood before him. ⁹And he said to them, "What do you advise that we answer this people who have said to me, 'Lighten the yoke that your father put upon us'?" ¹⁰And the young men who had grown up with him said to him, "Thus shall you speak to this people who said to you, 'Your father made our yoke heavy, but do you lighten it for us'; thus shall you say to them, 'My little finger is thicker than my father's loins. ¹¹And now, whereas my father laid upon you a heavy yoke, I will add to your yoke. My father chastised you with whips, but I will chastise you with scorpions.'"

¹²So Jeroboam and all the people came to Rehoboam the third day, as the king said, "Come to me again the third day." ¹³And the king answered the people harshly, and forsaking the counsel which the old men had given him, ¹⁴he spoke to them according to the counsel of the young men, saying, "My father made your yoke heavy, but I will add to your yoke; my father chastised you with whips, but I will chastise you with scorpions." ¹⁵So the king did not hearken to the people; for it was a turn of affairs brought about by the LORD that he might fulfil his word, which the LORD spoke by Ahijah the Shilonite to Jeroboam the son of Nebat.

¹⁶And when all Israel saw that the king did not hearken to them, the people answered the king,

"What portion have we in David?

We have no inheritance in the son of Jesse.

To your tents, O Israel!

Look now to your own house, David."

So Israel departed to their tents. ¹⁷But Rehoboam reigned over the people of Israel who dwelt in the cities of Judah. ¹⁸Then King Rehoboam sent Adoram, who was taskmaster over the forced labor, and all Israel stoned him to death with stones. And King Rehoboam made haste to mount his chariot, to flee to Jerusalem. ¹⁹So Israel has been in rebellion against the house of David to this day. ²⁰And when all Israel heard that Jeroboam had returned, they sent and called him to the assembly *and made him king over all Israel. There was none that followed the house of David, but the tribe of Judah only.*

²¹When Rehoboam came to Jerusalem, he assembled all the house of Judah, and the tribe of Benjamin, a hundred and eighty thousand chosen warriors, to fight against the house of Israel, to restore the kingdom to Rehoboam the son of Solomon. ²²But the word of God came to Shemaiah the man of God: ²³"Say to Rehoboam the son of Solomon, king of Judah, and to all the house of Judah and Benjamin, and to the rest of the people, ²⁴'Thus says the LORD, You shall not go up or fight against your kinsmen the people of Israel. Return every man to his home, for this thing is from me.'" So they hearkened to the word of the LORD, and went home again, according to the word of the LORD.

²⁵Then Jeroboam built Shechem in the hill country of Ephraim, and dwelt there; and he went out from there and built Penuel.

i Gk Vg Compare 2 Chron 10.2: Heb *dwelt in*

OVERVIEW: Rehoboam demonstrates through his foolish behavior that an excess of honors and power lead people to insane arrogance (BASIL). Rehoboam rejected the salutary counsel of the elders and yielded to the words of men of his age by his own will (AUGUSTINE). The people, however, reject his leadership (AMBROSE). The tribes that moved into Samaria had a king from the tribe of Ephraim (JEROME). The people were divided into the kingdom of ten tribes under Jeroboam and the kingdom of two tribes under Rehoboam, and those under Jeroboam were called Israel, and those under Rehoboam Judah. There is another Israel, which is not according to the flesh but according to the Spirit (ORIGEN).

12:14 I Will Add to Your Yoke

POLITICAL HONORS CAUSE INSANE ARROGANCE. BASIL THE GREAT: [Not only by reason of wealth] but also because of political honors do people exalt themselves beyond what is due their nature. . . . The position they occupy is entirely out of keeping with reason, for they possess a glory more unsubstantial than a dream. They are surrounded with a splendor more unreal than the phantoms of the night, since it comes into being or is swept away at the nod of the populace. A fool of this sort was that famous son of Solomon, youthful in years and younger still in wisdom, who threatened his people desiring a milder rule with an even harsher one and thereby destroyed his kingdom. By his threat, the very expedient whereby he hoped to be elevated to a more royal state, he was bereft of the dignity already his. Strength of arm, swiftness of foot and comeliness of body—the spoils of sickness and the plunder of time—also awaken pride in people, unaware as they are that "all flesh is grass and all the glory of humankind as the flower of the field. The grass is withered, and the flower is fallen."[1] ON HUMILITY.[2]

12:15 Rehoboam Did Not Listen to the People

REHOBOAM ACTED ACCORDING TO HIS OWN WILL. AUGUSTINE: Who can help but tremble at the thought of these judgments of God whereby he accomplishes whatever he pleases even in the hearts of wicked people, while yet rendering to each according to his merits? Solomon's son, Rehoboam, rejected the salutary counsel of the elders, not to deal harshly with the people, and yielded to

---

[1]Is 40:6-7. [2]FC 9:476-77*.

the words of men of his own age by replying with threats to those who should have been given a gentle reply. And how did this come about, except by his own will? But as a result of it, the ten tribes of Israel withdrew from him and set up for themselves another king, Jeroboam, that the will of God, who had been angered, might be accomplished, as he had also foretold that it would come to pass. For what does the Scripture say? "And the king condescended not to the people, for the Lord was turned away from him to make good his word, which he had spoken though Ahias, the Silonite, to Jeroboam the son of Nabat." All this was certainly done by human will, but in such a way that the "turning way" came from the Lord. ON GRACE AND FREE WILL 21.42.[3]

12:16 What Share Do We Have in David?

REHOBOAM'S INJUSTICE IN RULING HIS PEOPLE. AMBROSE: Justice, then, especially graces people who are set over any office; on the other hand, injustice fails them and fights against them. Scripture itself gives us an example, where it says that when the people of Israel, after the death of Solomon, had asked his son Rehoboam to free their neck from their cruel yoke and to lighten the harshness of his father's rule, he, despising the counsel of the old men, gave the following answer at the suggestion of the young men: "He would add a burden to the yoke of his father and change their lighter toils for harder." Angered by this answer, the people said, "We have no portion in David or inheritance in the son of Jesse. Return to your tents, O Israel. For we will not have this man for a prince or a leader over us." So, forsaken and deserted by the people, he could keep with him scarcely two of the ten tribes for David's sake. DUTIES OF THE CLERGY 2.18.93-94.[4]

12:25 Jeroboam Built Shechem

A KING FROM THE TRIBE OF EPHRAIM. JEROME: We have learned in the books of Kings that under Rehoboam, the son of Solomon, Jero-

boam, the son of Nabat, made a division among the people and led ten tribes into Samaria. The tribes of Judah and Benjamin, however, remained under the rule of Rehoboam; and many likewise from the tribe of Levi who were dwelling in Jerusalem as priests and Levites—as it is written in Paralipomenon[5]—returned to the temple of God, that is, to Jerusalem. Thus, there were three tribes in Judea: Judah itself the royal tribe, and Benjamin, and later the Levites from the various tribes, when they had come to the temple. They who were in Samaria had a king from the tribe of Ephraim. Just as they who held sway in Judea had a king from the tribe of Judah and from the family of David, so they who prevailed in Samaria had a king from the tribe of Ephraim, and their kings were called Ephraim. HOMILIES ON THE PSALMS 11 (Ps 77 [78]).[6]

THE CONSTANT DIVISION OF THE JEWISH PEOPLE. ORIGEN: The people were divided in those times into the kingdom of ten tribes under Jeroboam and the kingdom of two tribes under Rehoboam. And those under Jeroboam were called Israel, and those under Rehoboam Judah. And the division of the people persisted, according to the history, until today. For we know of nothing in the history that united Israel and Judah "into the same nation."[7] Then Israel first, under Jeroboam and under his successors, sinned excessively, and Israel sinned so much beyond Judah that they were sentenced by Providence to become captives "to the Assyrians until the sign,"[8] as the Scripture says. After this, the sons of Judah also sinned, and as captives they were sentenced to Babylon, not until a sign, as Israel, but for "seventy years," which Jeremiah prophesied[9] and Daniel also mentioned.[10] HOMILIES ON JEREMIAH 4.2.[11]

ISRAEL ACCORDING TO THE FLESH AND THE SPIRIT. ORIGEN: The divine writings proclaim

---

[3]FC 59:300-301. [4]NPNF 2 10:58. [5]2 Chron 11–

that a certain nation on earth was elected by God. And they give this nation a number of different names, for sometimes the entire nation is called Israel, sometimes Jacob; and in particular, when the nation was divided by Jeroboam the son of Nebat into two parts, the ten tribes constituted under him were called Israel, while the other two, with which was also the tribe of Levi and which included the tribe from which the royal family of David descended, were named Judah. Moreover, all those places which that nation held and which it had received from God were called Judea, in which Jerusalem was the metropolis; it is called a metropolis as a kind of mother of a great many cities. You will find the names of these cities men- tioned frequently in passages scattered in the other divine books, but they are included woven together in one place in the book of Joshua, son of Nun. Therefore, although all these facts are the case, the holy apostle, wishing us to lift our understanding and raise it somehow from earth, says in one place, "Consider Israel according to the flesh."[12] By this he means that there is another Israel, which is not according to the flesh but according to the Spirit. And in another place he says, "For not all who are from Israel are Israel."[13] ON FIRST PRINCIPLES 4.3.6.[14]

---

[12]1 Cor 10:18. [13]Rom 9:6. [14]*OSW* 194.

12:26-33 THE REVIVAL OF THE CULT OF THE GOLDEN CALVES

[26]*And Jeroboam said in his heart, "Now the kingdom will turn back to the house of David; [27]if this people go up to offer sacrifices in the house of the* LORD *at Jerusalem, then the heart of this people will turn again to their lord, to Rehoboam king of Judah, and they will kill me and return to Rehoboam king of Judah." [28]So the king took counsel, and made two calves of gold. And he said to the people, "You have gone up to Jerusalem long enough. Behold your gods, O Israel, who brought you up out of the land of Egypt." [29]And he set one in Bethel, and the other he put in Dan. [30]And this thing became a sin, for the people went to the one at Bethel and to the other as far as Dan.[j] [31]He also made houses on high places, and appointed priests from among all the people, who were not of the Levites. [32]And Jeroboam appointed a feast on the fifteenth day of the eighth month like the feast that was in Judah, and he offered sacrifices upon the altar; so he did in Bethel, sacrificing to the calves that he made. And he placed in Bethel the priests of the high places that he had made. [33]He went up to the altar which he had made in Bethel on the fifteenth day in the eighth month, in the month which he had devised of his own heart; and he ordained a feast for the people of Israel, and went up to the altar to burn incense.*

j Gk: Heb *went to the one as far as Dan*

OVERVIEW: Jeroboam introduced again the cult of the golden calves in order to cause political dis- sension, which might be useful to him in his fight for kingship (EPHREM). Jeroboam feared that if he came to God's temple in Jerusalem, his subjects might be alienated from his allegiance and reattached to David's blood successors as the royal dynasty so that, with this in mind, he established idolatry in his own kingdom (AUGUSTINE). Jeroboam set up golden calves as gods for the people to keep them from seeking the living God (CHRYSOLOGUS).

12:28 Jeroboam Made Two Golden Calves

WHY DID JEROBOAM MAKE TWO CALVES OF GOLD? EPHREM THE SYRIAN: While he prepared to establish the reign which was reserved to him by God according to the predictions of the prophets Shemaiah and Ahijah, Jeroboam thought that nothing could be more useful for his purpose than kindling the hatred of the two opposite parties to the highest possible degree, so that he might preclude any chance of reconciliation and peace. Therefore, in order that those who already distrusted each other might be removed from each other even further, he introduced a new reason for dissension concerning the worship of God. He persuaded his party to leave behind their Jewish rites and to take up the religion of the Egyptians which was superior to all other religions, just as Egyptian wisdom and power were greater that those of the Canaanites and the Jews. Since the majority of the tribes agreed, he proposed to worship the ancient idols of the Hebrews, namely, two calves of gold, and dedicated them by using, according to the old custom, the formula "These are your gods, O Israel, who brought you up out of the land of Egypt."[1] ON THE FIRST BOOK OF KINGS 12.18.[2]

JEROBOAM'S FEAR OF LOSING POWER. AUGUSTINE: For all that, King Jeroboam of Israel, who had proof that God was true, when he got the kingdom God had promised, was so warped in mind as not to believe in him. Actually, he feared that if he came to God's temple in Jerusalem (as all Jews without exception were bound by divine ordinance to do for the offering of sacrifices), his

subjects might be alienated from his allegiance and reattached to David's blood successors as the royal dynasty. With this in mind, he established idolatry in his own kingdom and, with shocking impiety, tricked God's people into joining him in the worship of idols. Even so, God did not entirely give up sending prophets to reprimand the king, and his successors who continued his idolatry and the people themselves. For it was in Israel that there appeared Elijah and his disciple, Elisha, both magnificent prophets and wonder workers as well. CITY OF GOD 17.22.[3]

12:30 The People Went to Worship the Calf

THE CITY OF DAN. ISHO'DAD OF MERV: "The people went before the other [god] as far as Dan." In order to worship the calf, the crowd walks in procession before it. Dan is the city that is now called Panias. When Israel took possession of the promised land, the children of Dan moved to take hold of that town and called it Dan. Two springs originated from there: Yor and Dan. BOOKS OF SESSIONS 1 KINGS 12.30.[4]

THE SCANDAL CAUSED BY JEROBOAM'S IDOLATRY. PETER CHRYSOLOGUS: Now let us talk also about the second kind of scandal, which, we said, arises from human cleverness. . . . Jeroboam raised up a scandal. He set up as gods for the people, golden calves—pitiful images—to keep them from seeking the living God, the true temple, God's law, the rightly appointed kings and their ancestral rites. Consequently, the whole people thus delivered over to error became a source of scandal like that given, according to the apostle,[5] when a person eats, as harmless to his own conscience, the flesh of animals that were sacrificed to idols. He thinks that through such conduct he may well bring contempt on the inanimate stones and wooden gods that can neither sanctify nor profane anything. But what he thinks is an exam-

---

[1]Exod 32:4. [2]ESOO 1:473. [3]FC 24:79*. [4]CSCO 229:112-13. [5]See 1 Cor 8:7-8; 10:23-30.

ple of his faith becomes an occasion of error for uninstructed people, for it leads them not to contempt but to worship, and it causes the meal to appear to be a banquet of religious honor to those very inanimate gods that he is intentionally diminishing by this ridicule. Consequently, the apostle wisely concludes and explains, "And through your 'knowledge' the weak one will perish, the brother for whom Christ died."[6] SERMON 27.[7]

[6]1 Cor 8:11. [7]FC 17:72-73.

13:1-32 THE MAN OF GOD FROM JUDAH

[1]*And behold, a man of God came out of Judah by the word of the* LORD *to Bethel. Jeroboam was standing by the altar to burn incense.* [2]*And the man cried against the altar by the word of the* LORD, *and said, "O altar, altar, thus says the* LORD: *'Behold, a son shall be born to the house of David, Josiah by name; and he shall sacrifice upon you the priests of the high places who burn incense upon you, and men's bones shall be burned upon you.'"* [3]*And he gave a sign the same day, saying, "This is the sign that the* LORD *has spoken: 'Behold, the altar shall be torn down, and the ashes that are upon it shall be poured out.'"* [4]*And when the king heard the saying of the man of God, which he cried against the altar at Bethel, Jeroboam stretched out his hand from the altar, saying, "Lay hold of him." And his hand, which he stretched out against him, dried up, so that he could not draw it back to himself.* [5]*The altar also was torn down, and the ashes poured out from the altar, according to the sign which the man of God had given by the word of the* LORD. [6]*And the king said to the man of God, "Entreat now the favor of the* LORD *your God, and pray for me, that my hand may be restored to me." And the man of God entreated the* LORD; *and the king's hand was restored to him, and became as it was before.* [7]*And the king said to the man of God, "Come home with me, and refresh yourself, and I will give you a reward."* [8]*And the man of God said to the king, "If you give me half your house, I will not go in with you. And I will not eat bread or drink water in this place;* [9]*for so was it commanded me by the word of the* LORD, *saying, 'You shall neither eat bread, nor drink water, nor return by the way that you came.'"* [10]*So he went another way, and did not return by the way that he came to Bethel.*

[11]*Now there dwelt an old prophet in Bethel. And his sons[k] came and told him all that the man of God had done that day in Bethel; the words also which he had spoken to the king, they told to their father.* [12]*And their father said to them, "Which way did he go?" And his sons showed him the way which the man of God who came from Judah had gone.* [13]*And he said to his sons, "Saddle the ass for me." So they saddled the ass for him and he mounted it.* [14]*And he went after the man of God, and found him sitting under an oak; and he said to him, "Are you the man of God who came from Judah?" And he said, "I am."* [15]*Then he said to him, "Come home with me and eat bread."*

¹⁶And he said, "I may not return with you, or go in with you; neither will I eat bread nor drink water with you in this place; ¹⁷for it was said to me by the word of the LORD, 'You shall neither eat bread nor drink water there, nor return by the way that you came.'" ¹⁸And he said to him, "I also am a prophet as you are, and an angel spoke to me by the word of the LORD, saying, 'Bring him back with you into your house that he may eat bread and drink water.'" But he lied to him. ¹⁹So he went back with him, and ate bread in his house, and drank water.

²⁰And as they sat at the table, the word of the LORD came to the prophet who had brought him back; ²¹and he cried to the man of God who came from Judah, "Thus says the LORD, 'Because you have disobeyed the word of the LORD, and have not kept the commandment which the LORD your God commanded you, ²²but have come back, and have eaten bread and drunk water in the place of which he said to you, "Eat no bread, and drink no water"; your body shall not come to the tomb of your fathers.'" ²³And after he had eaten bread and drunk, he saddled the ass for the prophet whom he had brought back. ²⁴And as he went away a lion met him on the road and killed him. And his body was thrown in the road, and the ass stood beside it; the lion also stood beside the body. ²⁵And behold, men passed by, and saw the body thrown in the road, and the lion standing by the body. And they came and told it in the city where the old prophet dwelt.

²⁶And when the prophet who had brought him back from the way heard of it, he said, "It is the man of God, who disobeyed the word of the LORD; therefore the LORD has given him to the lion, which has torn him and slain him, according to the word which the LORD spoke to him." ²⁷And he said to his sons, "Saddle the ass for me." And they saddled it. ²⁸And he went and found his body thrown in the road, and the ass and the lion standing beside the body. The lion had not eaten the body or torn the ass. ²⁹And the prophet took up the body of the man of God and laid it upon the ass, and brought it back to the city,ˡ to mourn and to bury him. ³⁰And he laid the body in his own grave; and they mourned over him, saying, "Alas, my brother!" ³¹And after he had buried him, he said to his sons, "When I die, bury me in the grave in which the man of God is buried; lay my bones beside his bones. ³²For the saying which he cried by the word of the LORD against the altar in Bethel, and against all the houses of the high places which are in the cities of Samaria, shall surely come to pass."

k Gk Syr Vg: Heb *son*   l Gk: Heb *he came to the city of the old prophet*

OVERVIEW: Jeroboam's hand, which had withered by sacrilege, was healed by true religion (AMBROSE). The old prophet may either be a sincere man who invited the true prophet out of human sympathy or a false prophet who tried to seduce him (ISHO'DAD). The prophet paid the severe penalty of his breach of fast (TERTULLIAN). The Lord punished the prophet mildly, for it was not from his own obstinacy that he refused to carry out the command but because of the deceit of another person (AUGUSTINE). The lion was not urged by hunger but acted in compliance with God's order (ISHO'DAD). The man of God was corrected temporarily even at the point of death rather than being punished after death (AUGUSTINE). The prophet's disobedience was atoned for by his death, because the lion attacked the living prophet and killed him, yet did not dare touch him once he was dead (GREGORY THE GREAT). Even holy people have been given over to great sufferings on account of some slight sins, because the divine clemency does not permit the least blemish or stain to be found in them on the day of judgment (CASSIAN). When the old prophet insists in saying that he wants to be buried in the grave of the prophet, he foreshadows baptism, which is the grave of the Emmanuel (EPHREM). The old prophet insists on being buried besides the true prophet, because he knows that the tomb of the true prophet will never be violated (AUGUSTINE).

13:4-6 Jeroboam's Hand Withered

THE MERCY OF GOD AND THE POWER OF REPENTANCE. AMBROSE: But when in the temple of our God, that wicked king Jeroboam took away the gifts that his father had laid up and offered them to idols on the holy altar, did not his right hand, which he stretched, wither, and his idols, which he called on, were not able to help him? Then, turning to the Lord, he asked for pardon, and at once his hand, which had withered by sacrilege, was healed by true religion. So complete an example was there set forth in one person, both of divine mercy and wrath, when he who was sacrificing suddenly lost his right hand but when penitent received forgiveness. CONCERNING VIRGINS 2.5.38.[1]

13:11 An Old Prophet in Bethel

WHICH WAS THE OLD PROPHET'S REAL INTENTION? ISHO'DAD OF MERV: Some authors[2] assert that [the old prophet] was not an impostor but invited [the true prophet] to eat out of human sympathy in order to refresh and thank him for admonishing Jeroboam. And that is why God did not harm him as a consequence of this. According to others, he was a false prophet because, if he had been a true prophet, as others maintained, he would have not seduced a true prophet, and his children would not have served in a house of idols;[3] therefore it was in order to seduce him that he went to meet the prophet. BOOKS OF SESSIONS 1 KINGS 13.11.[4]

13:19 The Man of God Ate with Him

A PUNISHMENT FOR BREAKING THE FAST. TERTULLIAN: For even if God does prefer the works of righteousness, still, these works are not without sacrifice, which represents a soul afflicted with fasts. He, at all events, is the God to whom neither a people incontinent of appetite nor a priest nor a prophet was pleasing. To this day the "monuments of concupiscence" remain, where the people, greedy of "flesh"—until, by devouring without digesting the quails, they brought on cholera—were buried. Eli breaks his neck before the temple doors,[5] his sons fall in battle, his daughter-in-law expires in childbirth.[6] For such was the blow that had been deserved at the hand of God by the shameless house, the defrauder of the fleshy sacrifices.[7] Sameas,[8] a man of God, after prophesying the issue of the idolatry introduced by king Jeroboam (the drying up and immediate restoration of that king's hand; after the rending in two of the sacrificial altar), being on account of these signs invited [home] by the king by way of reward, plainly declined [for he had been prohibited by God] to touch food at all in that place. However, having presently afterwards rashly taken food from another old man who deceitfully professed himself a prophet, he was deprived of burial in his fathers' sepulchers, in accordance with the word of God then and there uttered over the table. For he was felled by the rushing of a lion on him along the way and was buried among strangers; and thus he paid the penalty of his breach of fast. These will be warnings both to people and to bishops, even spiritual ones, in case they may ever have been guilty of not controlling their appetite. ON FASTING 16.[9]

---

[1]NPNF 2 10:379-80. [2]Isho'dad refers to unknown sources. [3]The unknown source quoted by Isho'dad supposes that the children of the false prophet were servants in the sanctuary of Bethel. [4]CSCO 229:113. [5]See 1 Sam 4:13-18. [6]See 1 Sam 4:17-21. [7]See 1 Sam 2:12-17, 22-25. [8]The name Sameas (Shemaiah) is not mentioned in the Hebrew text, where the prophet remains anonymous, but only in the LXX and VL. Probably there is a confusion with the prophet Shemaiah (1 Kings 12:22). [9]ANF 4:112-13*.

13:21-22 His Body Not Returned to the Ancestral Tomb

A MILD PUNISHMENT. AUGUSTINE: Yet from that love of the human heart, because of which "no one ever hated his own flesh,"[10] if people believe that anything would be lacking to their bodies after death that in their own people or country the solemnity of burial demands, they become sad . . . , and before death they fear for their bodies that which has no effect on them after death. Thus we read in the book of Kings that God through a prophet threatens another prophet who transgressed his word, that his body should not be returned to the sepulcher of his ancestors. Scripture records it in these words: "Thus says the Lord: Because you have not been obedient to the Lord and have not kept the commandment that the Lord your God commanded you, and [you] have returned and eaten bread and drunk water in the place where he commanded you that you should not eat bread or drink water, your dead shall not be brought in the sepulcher of your ancestors." If we consider the extent of this punishment according to the Evangelist, where we learn that after the body has been slain there is no occasion to fear that the lifeless members will suffer, it should not be called punishment. But, if we consider it in relation to the love of a person for his own flesh, then he might have been frightened and saddened while living at what he was not to feel when dead. This, then, was the nature of the punishment: The soul grieved that something would happen to its body, although, when it did happen, the soul did not grieve. Only to this extent did the Lord wish to punish his servant, for it was not from his own obstinacy that he refused to carry out the command, but, because of the deceit of another person who was deceiving him, he thought he obeyed when he did not obey. THE CARE TO BE TAKEN FOR THE DEAD 7.9.[11]

13:24-28 A Lion Killed Him

THE LION ACTED ACCORDING TO GOD'S COM- MAND. ISHO'DAD OF MERV: Through the words "a lion killed him" [the Scripture] shows that [the lion] strangled and killed him according to God's command. And through the sentence "it did not eat him," it shows that [the animal] was not urged by hunger but acted in compliance with God's order. And this was done in order that Jeroboam and his priests might understand that, if this had happened to the prophet just because he had eaten, something extremely more serious would happen to those who made offerings to the idols. BOOKS OF SESSIONS 1 KINGS 13.24-28.[12]

THE MAN OF GOD WAS CORRECTED TEMPORARILY. AUGUSTINE: It is not to be imagined that one has been so annihilated by the teeth of a beast that his soul has then been snatched away to infernal punishment, since the same lion who killed his very body guarded it. Even the beast of burden on which the man had been riding was unhurt and with great courage stood in the presence of the wild beast at the destruction of his master. By this miraculous sign it is made clear that the man of God was corrected temporarily even at the point of death rather than that he was punished after death. On this subject the apostle Paul, when he had made mention of certain unpleasant infirmities and death experienced by many, said, "But if we judged ourselves, we should not thus be judged by the Lord. But when we are judged, we are being chastised by the Lord, that we may not be condemned with the world."[13] THE CARE TO BE TAKEN FOR THE DEAD 7.9.[14]

SANCTIFIED IN THE DEATH HE SUFFERED. GREGORY THE GREAT: It is written in the Scriptures, "But the just man, though he die early, shall be at rest."[15] What, then, does it matter to the just if they undergo harsh treatment at death, since they are on their way to eternal life? Sometimes, perhaps, it is a fault of theirs, slight though

---

[10]Eph 5:29. [11]FC 27:362-63. [12]CSCO 229:113. [13]1 Cor 11:31-32. [14]FC 27:363. [15]Wis 4:7.

it be, that has to be expiated by such a death. For this reason the reprobate are given power over the just while they are still alive. But, once the just have died, the wicked are punished all the more severely because of the cruel power they exercised against holy people. This is demonstrated in the case of the barbarian who was permitted by God to strike down the deacon but was not allowed to rejoice over his death. It is also verified in holy Scripture. The man of God, for instance, who was sent to Samaria stopped on the way for a meal, contrary to God's command. For this disobedience he was killed by a lion. But Scripture at once adds that the donkey and the lion were standing by the dead prophet, and "the lion had not eaten of the dead body." From this passage we see that the sin of disobedience was atoned for by his death, because the lion attacked the living prophet and killed him, yet did not dare touch him once he was dead. God allowed the beast to kill, but not to eat of its kill, because the prophet, though blameworthy in life, was sanctified in the death he suffered as a punishment for his disobedience. In the first instance the lion took away the life of a sinner; in the second he stood guard over the body of a just man. Dialogue 4.24-25.[16]

Divine Clemency Does Not Permit the Least Stain. John Cassian: Moreover, we know that even holy men have been given over bodily to Satan or to great sufferings on account of some slight sins. For the divine clemency does not permit the least blemish or stain to be found in them on the day of judgment. According to the words of the prophet, which are in fact God's, he purges away all the dross of their uncleanness in the present so that he may bring them to eternity like fire-tried gold or silver, in need of no penal cleansing. "And I will," he says, "utterly purge away your dross, and I will remove all your alloy. And after this you shall be called the city of the righteous, the faithful city."[17] And again: "Just as silver and gold are tried in a furnace, so the Lord chooses hearts."[18] And again: "Fire tries gold and silver, but a man is tried in the furnace of humiliation."[19] And this also: "The Lord chastises the one whom he loves, and he scourges every son whom he receives."[20] In the Third Book of Kings we see this clearly exemplified in the case of that prophet and man of God who was immediately destroyed by a lion because of a single sin of disobedience that he contracted not even out of the workings or the viciousness of his own will but through another's deceptive behavior. Scripture says of him, "That is the man of God who was disobedient to the word of the Lord, and the Lord delivered him over to a lion, and it destroyed him, according to the word of the Lord which he spoke." When this happened, the very sparingness and abstinence of the predator (for the voracious beast did not dare to eat anything at all of the corpse that had fallen to him) appeared as not only the punishment for his present offense and heedless error but also as the deserts of his righteousness, on account of which the Lord delivered over his prophet for a time to the tormenter. Conference 7.25.2-26.1.[21]

13:31 The Grave of the Man of God

An Allegory of Future Salvation Through Baptism. Ephrem the Syrian: While this old man insists in saying to his sons that he wants them to bury him, their father, in the grave of the prophet Shemaiah[22] and hopes that his bones will find peace, he represents the allegorical type of an ancient Adam who exhorts and even urges his sons to lower him into baptism, which is the grave of the Emmanuel. Through him all those who have been buried with him through baptism certainly hope for peace and life.[23] On the other hand, when this same old man lies and deceives the other prophet, he represents the Jewish people, about whom we

---

[16]FC 39:216-17. [17]Is 1:25-26. [18]Prov 17:3 (LXX). [19]Sir 2:5. [20]Heb 12:6. [21]ACW 57:264-65. [22]The anonymous prophet, simply defined as "a man of God" at the beginning of the chapter (1 Kings 13:1), is identified by Ephrem with the prophet Shemaiah (cf. 1 Kings 12:22-24). [23]Rom 6:4.

read in the psalm: "But they flattered him with their mouths; they lied to him with their tongues."[24] ON THE FIRST BOOK OF KINGS 13.20.[25]

NO ONE WILL VIOLATE THE TOMB OF THE MAN OF GOD. AUGUSTINE: Well did the man who had deceived the man of God bury him with honor in his own tomb and give orders that he himself should be buried next to his bones, hoping thus to spare his own bones. He knew that the time would come according to the prophecy of that man of God when Josiah, king of the Jews, would dig up in the land the bones of many dead and with them defile the sacrilegious altars that had been set up for graven images. He spared that tomb where the prophet lay who more than three hundred years before had predicted these things. And because of him the burying place of the man who deceived him was not violated.[26] By that love because of which no one ever hated his own flesh, he provided for his own corpse, while he had slain his soul by deceit. From this fact, then, because each one naturally loves his own flesh, it was punishment for him to learn that he would not be in the tomb of his fathers. So he took care that his bones be spared by burying them next to him whose tomb no one would violate. THE CARE TO BE TAKEN FOR THE DEAD 7.9.[27]

---

[24]Ps 78:36 (77:36 LXX). [25]ESOO 1:479. [26]See 1 Kings 13:24-32; 2 Kings 23:16-18. [27]FC 27:363-64.

13:33–14:20 THE REIGN OF JEROBOAM

[33]After this thing Jeroboam did not turn from his evil way, but made priests for the high places again from among all the people; any who would, he consecrated to be priests of the high places. [34]And this thing became sin to the house of Jeroboam, so as to cut it off and to destroy it from the face of the earth.

14 At that time Abijah the son of Jeroboam fell sick. [2]And Jeroboam said to his wife, "Arise, and disguise yourself, that it be not known that you are the wife of Jeroboam, and go to Shiloh; behold, Ahijah the prophet is there, who said of me that I should be king over this people. [3]Take with you ten loaves, some cakes, and a jar of honey, and go to him; he will tell you what shall happen to the child."

[4]Jeroboam's wife did so; she arose, and went to Shiloh, and came to the house of Ahijah. Now Ahijah could not see, for his eyes were dim because of his age. [5]And the LORD said to Ahijah, "Behold, the wife of Jeroboam is coming to inquire of you concerning her son; for he is sick. Thus and thus shall you say to her."

When she came, she pretended to be another woman. [6]But when Ahijah heard the sound of her feet, as she came in at the door, he said, "Come in, wife of Jeroboam; why do you pretend to be another? For I am charged with heavy tidings for you. [7]Go, tell Jeroboam, 'Thus says the LORD, the God of Israel: "Because I exalted you from among the people, and made you leader over my people

Israel, ⁸*and tore the kingdom away from the house of David and gave it to you; and yet you have not been like my servant David, who kept my commandments, and followed me with all his heart, doing only that which was right in my eyes, ⁹but you have done evil above all that were before you and have gone and made for yourself other gods, and molten images, provoking me to anger, and have cast me behind your back; ¹⁰therefore behold, I will bring evil upon the house of Jeroboam, and will cut off from Jeroboam every male, both bond and free in Israel, and will utterly consume the house of Jeroboam, as a man burns up dung until it is all gone. ¹¹Any one belonging to Jeroboam who dies in the city the dogs shall eat; and any one who dies in the open country the birds of the air shall eat; for the Lord has spoken it.'" ¹²Arise therefore, go to your house. When your feet enter the city, the child shall die. ¹³And all Israel shall mourn for him, and bury him; for he only of Jeroboam shall come to the grave, because in him there is found something pleasing to the Lord, the God of Israel, in the house of Jeroboam. ¹⁴Moreover the Lord will raise up for himself a king over Israel, who shall cut off the house of Jeroboam today. And henceforth^m ¹⁵the Lord will smite Israel, as a reed is shaken in the water, and root up Israel out of this good land which he gave to their fathers, and scatter them beyond the Euphrates, because they have made their Asherim, provoking the Lord to anger. ¹⁶And he will give Israel up because of the sins of Jeroboam, which he sinned and which he made Israel to sin."*

¹⁷*Then Jeroboam's wife arose, and departed, and came to Tirzah. And as she came to the threshold of the house, the child died. ¹⁸And all Israel buried him and mourned for him, according to the word of the Lord, which he spoke by his servant Ahijah the prophet. ¹⁹Now the rest of the acts of Jeroboam, how he warred and how he reigned, behold, they are written in the Book of the Chronicles of the Kings of Israel. ²⁰And the time that Jeroboam reigned was twenty-two years; and he slept with his fathers, and Nadab his son reigned in his stead.*

m Heb obscure

Overview: Jeroboam tries to cheat the prophet Ahijah in order to get the cure for his ill son from God whom he has abandoned. Through divine revelation Ahijah immediately discloses Jeroboam's deceit (Ephrem). Jeroboam neglected those commandments that David had kept (Jerome). Only true prophets must be consulted for any kind of prediction (Origen). In his attitude toward Jeroboam, God shows again his infinite mercy (Isho'dad).

14:1-3 Jeroboam Sends His Wife to See the Prophet Ahijah

Jeroboam's Hopeless Attempt at Obtain-

ing His Son's Cure. Ephrem the Syrian: "At that time Abijah son of Jeroboam fell sick," and [the king], being worried for the health of his son, sent his wife to the prophet Ahijah because he was confident that through the prayers of that holy man he would obtain from God, whom he had repudiated, the healing of his son. And he did not want the queen to appear [before the prophet] without a present against the custom of the ancestors. Therefore "she took ten loaves of bread," that is, ten soldiers' biscuits, "a jar of honey and dry fruits"¹: the Greek text has *staphylas*, that is, grapes,

---

¹The text of the Peshitta reads "dry fruits" instead of "cakes."

instead of dry fruits. He did not want her to offer a regal present, lest she might appear in her real nature. On the First Book of Kings 14.1.[2]

14:6 Why Do You Pretend to Be Another?

Nobody Can Deceive God. Ephrem the Syrian: But when Ahijah heard the sound of her feet as she came in at the door, he said, "Come in, wife of Jeroboam; why do you pretend to be another?" He heard her coming in, [the text] says, because he could not see anymore after his eyes had become dim from his old age. Yet through divine revelation he understood that she was Jeroboam's wife, even though she wanted to hide this from the prophet, whom she knew to be justifiably enraged [with her husband]. Therefore the prophet, beginning his speech, harshly attacked Jeroboam and condemned with very severe words his violation of pacts and piety and his oblivion to all the benefits that he had received from the generous hand of God, so that [the prophet] finally predicted huge calamities, the destruction of the kingdom and the complete ruin of [Jeroboam's] entire family. On the First Book of Kings 14.6.[3]

14:8 You Have Not Kept God's Commandments

God's Commandments Can Be Observed by Everybody. Jerome: "The Lord is compassionate and merciful, long-suffering and plenteous in mercy."[4] "The Lord is sweet to all, and his tender mercies are over all his works."[5] You hear that his mercies are so great, and do you dare to put your trust in your own virtue? "Let all your works, O Lord, confess to you."[6] If people are also part of his works, then all people should confess their sins. We read it said in Samuel about Solomon: "He shall build a house to my name, and I shall establish the throne of his kingdom forever. I will be to him a father, and he shall be to me a son."[7] And again: "If he commits any iniquity, I will correct him with the rod of people, but my mercy I will not take away from him."[8] After

giving thanks to God, David said in conclusion, "And this is the law of humankind."[9] Have recourse, O Lord, always to your mercy, and sustain the weakness of my flesh by your divine assistance. "What have I to do," he says, "with you also, you sons of Sarvia? Let Shimei curse. The Lord had bid him curse David. And who shall say to him, why have you done so?"[10] For the will of God is not to be discussed but kindly accepted. And in another place: "The Lord commanded that the profitable counsel of Ahitophel be defeated that he might bring evil on Absalom,"[11] whose counsel was certainly the counsel of God. And for what reason was the power of the free will subverted by a greater power? Jeroboam, who caused Israel to sin, is reproved for having neglected the commandment of the Lord, and it is said to him, "I gave you the kingdom of the house of David, and you have not been as my servant David, who kept my commandments and followed me with all his heart, doing that which was well pleasing in my sight." Therefore, the commandments of God are possible, which we know David had kept; and yet, we find holy people growing weary in maintaining justice forever. Against the Pelagians 2.20.[12]

14:12 When Your Feet Enter the City, the Child Shall Die

Only the Prophets Must Be Consulted. Origen: There is therefore no absurdity in the prophets [of the Jews] having uttered predictions even about events of no importance, to soothe those who desire such things, as when Samuel prophesies regarding three donkeys that were lost,[13] or when mention is made in the third book of Kings respecting the sickness of a king's son. And why should not those who desired to obtain auguries from idols be severely rebuked by the

---

[2]ESOO 1:480. [3]ESOO 1:480. [4]Ps 103:8 (102:8 LXX, Vg). [5]Ps 145:9 (144:9 LXX, Vg). [6]Ps 145:10 (144:10 LXX, Vg). [7]2 Sam 7:13-14. [8]2 Sam 7:14-15. [9]2 Sam 7:19. [10]2 Sam 16:10. [11]2 Sam 17:14. [12]FC 53:327-28. [13]See 1 Sam 9:20.

administrators of the law among the Jews, as Elijah is found rebuking Ahaziah and saying, "Is it because there is not a God in Israel that you go to inquire of Baalzebub, god of Ekron?"[14] AGAINST CELSUS 1.36.[15]

14:13 Something Pleasing to the Lord

GOD IS ALWAYS MERCIFUL TOWARD SINNERS. ISHO'DAD OF MERV: [The Scripture] calls "something pleasing" the fact that [Jeroboam] sent his wife to the prophet of God and not to the impostors and diviners. We must constantly admire the mercy of God, who increases many times over every good [action] performed by mortals and then returns it to them. This is quite evident from what he did for that father of the error of the calves and protector of the iniquity of Baal, namely, Ahab.[16] Because of his fast of one day, and the night in which he slept in sackcloth, punishment was averted from his house and his kingdom for three years in order to show [God's] mercy and exhort sinners to repentance. BOOKS OF SESSIONS 1 KINGS 14.13.[17]

---

[14]2 Kings 1:3. [15]ANF 4:412. [16]See 1 Kings 16:30-33. [17]CSCO 229:114.

14:21–15:8 THE IMPIETY OF REHOBOAM AND ABIJAM

[21]Now Rehoboam the son of Solomon reigned in Judah. Rehoboam was forty-one years old when he began to reign, and he reigned seventeen years in Jerusalem, the city which the LORD had chosen out of all the tribes of Israel, to put his name there. His mother's name was Naamah the Ammonitess. [22]And Judah did what was evil in the sight of the LORD, and they provoked him to jealousy with their sins which they committed, more than all that their fathers had done. [23]For they also built for themselves high places, and pillars, and Asherim on every high hill and under every green tree; [24]and there were also male cult prostitutes* in the land. They did according to all the abominations of the nation which the LORD drove out before the people of Israel.

[25]In the fifth year of King Rehoboam, Shishak king of Egypt came up against Jerusalem; [26]he took away the treasures of the house of the LORD and the treasures of the king's house; he took away everything. He also took away all the shields of gold which Solomon had made; [27]and King Rehoboam made in their stead shields of bronze, and committed them to the hands of the officers of the guard, who kept the door of the king's house. [28]And as often as the king went into the house of the LORD, the guard bore them and brought them back to the guardroom.

[29]Now the rest of the acts of Rehoboam, and all that he did, are they not written in the Book of the Chronicles of the Kings of Judah? [30]And there was war between Rehoboam and Jeroboam continually. [31]And Rehoboam slept with his fathers and was buried with his fathers in the city of David.

His mother's name was Naamah the Ammonitess. And Abijam his son reigned in his stead.

15

Now in the eighteenth year of King Jeroboam the son of Nebat, Abijam began to reign over Judah. [2]He reigned for three years in Jerusalem. His mother's name was Maacah the daughter of Abishalom. [3]And he walked in all the sins which his father did before him; and his heart was not wholly true to the LORD his God, as the heart of David his father. [4]Nevertheless for David's sake the LORD his God gave him a lamp in Jerusalem, setting up his son after him, and establishing Jerusalem; [5]because David did what was right in the eyes of the LORD, and did not turn aside from anything that he commanded him all the days of his life, except in the matter of Uriah the Hittite. [6]Now there was war between Rehoboam and Jeroboam all the days of his life. [7]The rest of the acts of Abijam, and all that he did, are they not written in the Book of the Chronicles of the Kings of Judah? And there was war between Abijam and Jeroboam. [8]And Abijam slept with his fathers; and they buried him in the city of David. And Asa his son reigned in his stead.

* Heb *male cult prostitutes* Syr *prostitution*

OVERVIEW: The Lord willed to be born from the sinful stock of Rehoboam in order to take on him all the sins of humankind (ORIGEN). The prostitution practiced at the time of Rehoboam was spread by demons who wanted to corrupt God's creatures (ISHO'DAD). Rehoboam increased the worship of idols and was supported in this by his impious mother. Abijam reigns in Judah after Rehoboam and is able to defeat in battle the superior forces of the Israelites (EPHREM).

14:21-23 Rehoboam Sinned More Than All His Ancestors

BORN OF SIN TO SAVE US FROM SIN. ORIGEN: Our Lord and Savior had come for this end, to take on himself humanity's sins. God "made him who had committed no sin to be sin for our sake."[1] For this reason, he came down into the world and took on the person of sinners and depraved people. He willed to be born from the stock of Solomon, whose sins have been recorded,[2] and from Rehoboam, whose transgressions are reported, and from the rest of them, many of whom "did evil in the sight of the Lord."[3] HOMILIES ON THE GOSPEL OF LUKE 28.2.[4]

14:24 Male Temple Prostitutes

PROSTITUTION SPREAD BY DEMONS. ISHO'DAD OF MERV: "There was also prostitution in the land." [The Scripture] does not refer to the mere [prostitution] of bodies, nor to that of the soul, which is idolatry, but to that [prostitution] spread by demons among the Gentiles in order to corrupt God's creature and work, namely, humanity. And this [form of prostitution] did not exist among the people. It is in this regard that the Fathers warned the children of the church, "[to abstain] from prostitution, from anything that has been strangled and from blood."[5] This is a first form of that prostitution: before being united in marriage according to the law,[6] the virgins had intercourse with the priests of the demons. A second form took place when in the course of one or two years the virgins devoted themselves to prostitution for the satisfaction of Satan and later became property of men, that is, they sat along the roads and sold their bodies. BOOKS OF SESSIONS 1 KINGS 14.24.[7]

14:25 Shishak Attacks Jerusalem

---

[1]2 Cor 5:21. [2]See 1 Kings 11:6-8. [3]1 Kings 15:26, 34. [4]FC 94:116. [5]Acts 15:20. [6]That is, in the ancient time of paganism. [7]CSCO 229:114-15.

A PUNISHMENT OF IDOLATRY. EPHREM THE
SYRIAN: Rehoboam spread and increased the idolatry introduced by Solomon after being instigated
in this sin by his Gentile mother Naamah. And
this seems to be hinted at in the Scripture which
reports Rehoboam's apostasy just after mentioning
his impious mother. Many examples that occur in
this book, such as those of Maacah,[8] Jezebel[9] and
Athaliah,[10] amply demonstrate how the marriages
made with foreign women had the power to corrupt the customs of the Israelites in this regard.
Therefore, since God wanted to punish the offense
caused by the violation of piety, he allowed
Shishak, the king of Egypt, to enter Judea with a
huge army, to conquer Jerusalem, to plunder the
temple and the royal house and to destroy everything. ON THE FIRST BOOK OF KINGS 14.25.[11]

15:1-7 Abijam Began to Reign

ABIJAM DEFEATED JEROBOAM. EPHREM THE
SYRIAN: "Now in the eighteenth year of King Jeroboam son of Nebat, Abijam began to reign over
Judah," and under his rule the Jews obtained a
magnificent victory over the Israelites in a battle,
which was greater than all those fought before in
their civil wars. It is said that after the two multitudes of soldiers were drawn up in fighting order,
Abijam appeared to have four hundred thousand
men, and Jeroboam eight hundred thousand. The
Jews won, while the number of the Israelites who
fell in action was larger than five hundred thousand, which is an extremely rare occurrence in
history. ON THE FIRST BOOK OF KINGS 15.1.[12]

---

[8]See 1 Kings 15:13. [9]See 1 Kings 16:31. [10]See 2 Kings 11:1. [11]ESOO
1:481. [12]ESOO 1:482.

15:9-24 ASA RESTORES THE WORSHIP
OF GOD IN JUDAH

[9]In the twentieth year of Jeroboam king of Israel, Asa began to reign over Judah, [10]and he
reigned forty-one years in Jerusalem. His mother's name was Maacah the daughter of Abishalom.
[11]And Asa did what was right in the eyes of the LORD, as David his father had done. [12]He put
away the male cult prostitutes out of the land, and removed all the idols that his fathers had made.
[13]He also removed Maacah his mother from being queen mother because she had an abominable
image made for Asherah; and Asa cut down her image and burned it at the brook Kidron. [14]But
the high places were not taken away. Nevertheless the heart of Asa was wholly true to the LORD
all his days. [15]And he brought into the house of the LORD the votive gifts of his father and his own
votive gifts, silver, and gold, and vessels.

[16]And there was war between Asa and Baasha king of Israel all their days. [17]Baasha king of
Israel went up against Judah, and built Ramah, that he might permit no one to go out or come in to
Asa king of Judah. [18]Then Asa took all the silver and the gold that were left in the treasures of the
house of the LORD and the treasures of the king's house, and gave them into the hands of his ser-

vants; and King Asa sent them to Ben-hadad the son of Tabrimmon, the son of Hezion, king of Syria, who dwelt in Damascus, saying, [19] "Let there be a league between me and you, as between my father and your father: behold, I am sending to you a present of silver and gold; go, break your league with Baasha king of Israel, that he may withdraw from me." [20]And Ben-hadad hearkened to King Asa, and sent the commanders of his armies against the cities of Israel, and conquered Ijon, Dan, Abel-beth-maacah, and all Chinneroth, with all the land of Naphtali. [21]And when Baasha heard of it, he stopped building Ramah, and he dwelt in Tirzah. [22]Then King Asa made a proclamation to all Judah, none was exempt, and they carried away the stones of Ramah and its timber, with which Baasha had been building; and with them King Asa built Geba of Benjamin and Mizpah. [23]Now the rest of all the acts of Asa, all his might, and all that he did, and the cities which he built, are they not written in the Book of the Chronicles of the Kings of Judah? But in his old age he was diseased in his feet. [24]And Asa slept with his fathers, and was buried with his fathers in the city of David his father; and Jehoshaphat his son reigned in his stead.

OVERVIEW: Asa restores the cult of the Lord in Judah and banishes the impious Maacah, mother of his father, Abijam (EPHREM). God has foretold that the images of the many false gods would be overturned and has commanded them to be overturned (AUGUSTINE). The devil tried to tempt Asa through his mother but was defeated (APHRAHAT). Asa erred in not removing the high places, which were places of worship consecrated to idols, and was saved only through the merits of his ancestor David (JEROME) The high places were not altars dedicated to idols, but to God, even though they were built against the command of the Law, which prescribed to worship God in Jerusalem only (ISHO'DAD). In his old age, Asa was diseased in his feet as a punishment for his sins (CHRYSOSTOM).

15:9-13 Asa Removed All the Idols

ASA RESTORES THE WORSHIP OF THE TRUE GOD. EPHREM THE SYRIAN: In the meantime, Asa devoted himself to the reconstruction of the ruins of religion. He destroyed the temples of the idols, smashed the statues, set the sacred woods on fire and removed the ignominy of the effeminate priests. He also drove away Maacah, the mother of his father, Abijam. [She] was the high priestess of that abomination, and he chased her off from that place of honor that she was holding and broke her idols and burned them. Therefore, after removing the worship of the idols in this manner, he restored the holy rites of true religion and constantly protected all the sacred institutions for the forty-one years in which he ruled over the state. ON THE FIRST BOOK OF KINGS 15.1.[1]

GOD HAS COMMANDED THAT IDOLS BE OVERTURNED. AUGUSTINE: Look for a little at those books on the Republic[2] from which you drew that ideal of the most devoted citizen: that there should be no limit or legitimate restriction on his service. Look, I beg you, and notice with what high praise frugality and temperance are there spoken of, as well as fidelity to the marriage bond, and chaste, honorable and upright conduct. When a state excels in these, it can truly be said to bloom. But in churches in growing numbers all over the world, as in holy gatherings of peoples, these principles are taught and learned; above all, the devotion by which the true and truth-giving God is worshiped, who not only commands these principles to be kept

---

[1]ESOO 1:482. [2]See Cicero *De Republica* fragment 4.7.7.

but also gives them fulfillment. It is by these that the human mind is prepared and made fit for the divine society and for its habitation in the eternal heavenly country. Hence he has foretold that the images of the many false gods would be overturned and has commanded them to be overturned. LETTER 91.[3]

ASA DEFEATED THE DEVIL. APHRAHAT: Furthermore, the adversary tempted Job through his children and his possessions, and when he could not prevail over him, he went and brought against him his armor, and he came, bringing with him a daughter of Eve, who had caused Adam to sink, and through her mouth he said to Job, her righteous husband, "Curse God."[4] But Job rejected her counsel. King Asa also conquered the Accursed-of-life, when he wished to come in against him, through his mother. For Asa knew his craftiness and removed his mother from her high estate and cut in pieces her idol and cast it down. DEMONSTRATION 6.3.[5]

15:14 The High Places Not Taken Away

ASA IS SAVED THROUGH THE MERIT OF DAVID. JEROME: Regarding many kings of the line of David, we read that they were saved not through their own merit but through the virtues of their father, David, who did that which was pleasing in the sight of God. And we come to Asa, the king of Judah, of whom it is written: "Asa did that which was right in the sight of the Lord, as did David, his father." And after a lengthy account of his many virtues, the story is concluded with these words: "But the high places he did not take away. Nevertheless, the heart of Asa was perfect with God all the days of his life." You see that he, too, is referred to as just, and his heart, indeed, was perfect with God, and yet he erred in that he did not take

away the high places, as, we read, Hezekiah and Josiah had done. AGAINST THE PELAGIANS 2.21.[6]

MANY ALTARS DEDICATED TO GOD. ISHO'DAD OF MERV: "High places" refers to the altars that had been erected for the true God. This means that sacrifices were offered to God in any place, just like Solomon offered a thousand holocausts to God in Gibeon.[7] Therefore the words "the high places were not taken away [by Asa]" mean that they did not worship or sacrifice before a single altar according to the commandment of God, that is, in Jerusalem, as is prescribed by the Law.[8] [The Scripture] does not speak here about the altars [consecrated] to idols but about those consecrated to the true God. BOOKS OF SESSIONS 1 KINGS 15.14.[9]

15:23 Asa Was Diseased in His Feet

EVERY BLOW MUST BE ENDURED WITH GRATITUDE. JOHN CHRYSOSTOM: "What, then," you will say, "do all illnesses come in punishment for sin?" No, not all, but many do; some spring from laxity. I say this because gluttony and drunkenness and sloth give rise to sicknesses of this kind. Accordingly, we must be watchful for one thing only: that we bear every blow with gratitude. At times the blow comes to chastise sin, as in the book of Kings we see a man [i.e., King Asa] seized with a foot disease for this reason. On the other hand, the blow might be inflicted to increase righteousness still further, as God says to Job, "Do you think that I have had dealings with you for any other reason than 'that you might be justified?' "[10] HOMILIES ON THE GOSPEL OF JOHN 38.1.[11]

---

[3]FC 18:43. [4]Job 2:9. [5]NPNF 2 13:365-66. [6]FC 53:328*. [7]See 1 Kings 3:4. [8]See Deut 12:13. [9]CSCO 229:115. [10]Job 40:8. [11]FC 33:369-70.

15:25–16:28 THE FOUR KINGS OF ISRAEL

²⁵*Nadab the son of Jeroboam began to reign over Israel in the second year of Asa king of Judah; and he reigned over Israel two years.* ²⁶*He did what was evil in the sight of the* Lord, *and walked in the way of his father, and in his sin which he made Israel to sin.*

²⁷*Baasha the son of Ahijah, of the house of Issachar, conspired against him; and Baasha struck him down at Gibbethon, which belonged to the Philistines; for Nadab and all Israel were laying siege to Gibbethon.* ²⁸*So Baasha killed him in the third year of Asa king of Judah, and reigned in his stead.* ²⁹*And as soon as he was king, he killed all the house of Jeroboam; he left to the house of Jeroboam not one that breathed, until he had destroyed it, according to the word of the* Lord *which he spoke by his servant Ahijah the Shilonite;* ³⁰*it was for the sins of Jeroboam which he sinned and which he made Israel to sin, and because of the anger to which he provoked the* Lord, *the God of Israel.*

³¹*Now the rest of the acts of Nadab, and all that he did, are they not written in the Book of the Chronicles of the Kings of Israel?* ³²*And there was war between Asa and Baasha king of Israel all their days.*

³³*In the third year of Asa king of Judah, Baasha the son of Ahijah began to reign over all Israel at Tirzah, and he reigned twenty-four years.* ³⁴*He did what was evil in the sight of the* Lord, *and walked in the way of Jeroboam and in his sin which he made Israel to sin.*

16 *And the word of the* Lord *came to Jehu the son of Hanani against Baasha, saying,* ²*"Since I exalted you out of the dust and made you leader over my people Israel, and you have walked in the way of Jeroboam, and have made my people Israel to sin, provoking me to anger with their sins,* ³*behold, I will utterly sweep away Baasha and his house, and I will make your house like the house of Jeroboam the son of Nebat.* ⁴*Any one belonging to Baasha who dies in the city the dogs shall eat; and any one of his who dies in the field the birds of the air shall eat."*

⁵*Now the rest of the acts of Baasha, and what he did, and his might, are they not written in the Book of the Chronicles of the Kings of Israel?* ⁶*And Baasha slept with his fathers, and was buried at Tirzah; and Elah his son reigned in his stead.* ⁷*Moreover the word of the* Lord *came by the prophet Jehu the son of Hanani against Baasha and his house, both because of all the evil that he did in the sight of the* Lord, *provoking him to anger with the work of his hands, in being like the house of Jeroboam, and also because he destroyed it.*

⁸*In the twenty-sixth year of Asa king of Judah, Elah the son of Baasha began to reign over Israel in Tirzah, and he reigned two years.* ⁹*But his servant Zimri, commander of half his chariots, conspired against him. When he was at Tirzah, drinking himself drunk in the house of Arza, who was over the household in Tirzah,* ¹⁰*Zimri came in and struck him down and killed him, in the twenty-seventh year of Asa king of Judah, and reigned in his stead.*

¹¹*When he began to reign, as soon as he had seated himself on his throne, he killed all the house of Baasha; he did not leave him a single male of his kinsmen or his friends.* ¹²*Thus Zimri destroyed all the house of Baasha, according to the word of the LORD, which he spoke against Baasha by Jehu the prophet,* ¹³*for all the sins of Baasha and the sins of Elah his son which they sinned, and which they made Israel to sin, provoking the LORD God of Israel to anger with their idols.* ¹⁴*Now the rest of the acts of Elah, and all that he did, are they not written in the Book of the Chronicles of the Kings of Israel?*

¹⁵*In the twenty-seventh year of Asa king of Judah, Zimri reigned seven days in Tirzah. Now the troops were encamped against Gibbethon, which belonged to the Philistines,* ¹⁶*and the troops who were encamped heard it said, "Zimri has conspired, and he has killed the king"; therefore all Israel made Omri, the commander of the army, king over Israel that day in the camp.* ¹⁷*So Omri went up from Gibbethon, and all Israel with him, and they besieged Tirzah.* ¹⁸*And when Zimri saw that the city was taken, he went into the citadel of the king's house, and burned the king's house over him with fire, and died,* ¹⁹*because of his sins which he committed, doing evil in the sight of the LORD, walking in the way of Jeroboam, and for his sin which he committed, making Israel to sin.* ²⁰*Now the rest of the acts of Zimri, and the conspiracy which he made, are they not written in the Book of the Chronicles of the Kings of Israel?*

²¹*Then the people of Israel were divided into two parts; half of the people followed Tibni the son of Ginath, to make him king, and half followed Omri.* ²²*But the people who followed Omri overcame the people who followed Tibni the son of Ginath; so Tibni died, and Omri became king.* ²³*In the thirty-first year of Asa king of Judah, Omri began to reign over Israel and he reigned for twelve years; six years he reigned in Tirzah.* ²⁴*He bought the hill of Samaria from Shemer for two talents of silver; and he fortified the hill, and called the name of the city which he built, Samaria, after the name of Shemer, the owner of the hill.*

²⁵*Omri did what was evil in the sight of the LORD, and did more evil than all who were before him.* ²⁶*For he walked in all the way of Jeroboam the son of Nebat, and in the sins which he made Israel to sin, provoking the LORD, the God of Israel, to anger by their idols.* ²⁷*Now the rest of the acts of Omri which he did, and the might that he showed, are they not written in the Book of the Chronicles of the Kings of Israel?* ²⁸*And Omri slept with his fathers, and was buried in Samaria; and Ahab his son reigned in his stead.*

OVERVIEW: God had entrusted Baasha with the task of restoring the true religion, but he and his successors persevered in their idolatry and impiety (EPHREM). God's words against Baasha and his house were pronounced against all sinners, and especially against the pagans and the heretics (RABANUS MAURUS). Baasha was allowed to punish Nadab's impiety with death, but since he did not fear such punishment and behaved impiously as well, he was condemned to suffer the same punishment (ISHO'DAD).

16:1 The Word of the Lord

THE EVIL OF THE KINGS OF ISRAEL. EPHREM THE SYRIAN: [Baasha] was appointed king by God and was sent to restore the true religion which had been destroyed by Jeroboam and his successor Nadab, and to take revenge on the evil that was committed as well as impiety. He was certainly able to accomplish in the best possible way his first task, as he completely erased the progeny of both Jeroboam and Nadab. However, with regard to his second task, he promoted their impiety by perversely and foolishly worshiping the idols of both [his predecessors] and did not destroy at all the calves made by Jeroboam but incited his own subjects to adore them. Therefore the prophet Jehu harshly condemns the crime of Baasha's ungrateful soul in this passage and proclaims the revenge which will strike him shortly. So Baasha was deprived of his kingdom and life for this reason, and after the killing of Elah, his son and successor, in the second year of his reign, Zimri took hold of the power and kept it for seven days, as is written. Then he was put under siege by Omri in Tirzah, and after the city had been conquered, [Zimri] took refuge in the palace and set himself on fire together with the royal house. Omri, the founder of Samaria, succeeded him. He died after twelve years and left his reign to his son. ON THE FIRST BOOK OF KINGS 16.1.[1]

16:2-4 God Will Consume Baasha and His House

WORDS ADDRESSED TO ALL SINNERS.

RABANUS MAURUS: "Since I exalted you out of the dust and made you leader over my people Israel, and you have walked in the way of Jeroboam and have caused my people Israel to sin, provoking me to anger with their sins, therefore, I will consume the past actions[2] of Baasha and the past actions of his house, and I will make your house like the house of Jeroboam son of Nebat. Anyone belonging to Baasha who dies in the city the dogs shall eat; and anyone of his who dies in the field the birds of the air shall eat." These words were pronounced against all sinners, and especially against the pagans and the heretics. Indeed, those who always add new sins to their old sins and are depraved by the examples of evil

become the greatest in their crimes. "I will cut off the past actions of Baasha," [the Lord] says, "and the past actions of his house, and I will make your house like the house of Jeroboam son of Nebat." The Lord cuts off the past actions of Baasha when he takes revenge on the sin of the wicked after the end of life. And he cuts off the past actions of his house when he condemns the inhabitants of that house to eternal torments. And he will make the house of Baasha like the house of Jeroboam son of Nabat when he gives the sinners who persevere in their iniquity to the torments of hell together with the devil and his angels. In fact, Baasha, as we have already said, is interpreted as "confusion" or "dryness," Jeroboam as "he who divides the people," and Nabat as "spontaneous." Therefore, when one follows the confusions of errors and sinners and neglects the possibility of having a wife of spiritual grace, then his past actions will be cut off as those of the devil. COMMENTARY ON THE THIRD BOOK OF KINGS 15.[3]

16:7 Like the House of Jeroboam

BAASHA WILL BE PUNISHED. ISHO'DAD OF

MERV: " . . . In being like the house of Jeroboam, and also because he destroyed it." This does not mean that Elah killed Jeroboam, but that Baasha, father of Elah, killed the son of Jeroboam. And he is not threatened with evils by the prophet because he killed him but because he does not fear the punishment which was performed by his hands as a consequence of Nadab's sins.[4] And since he is at the moment imitating the evil actions of that one, he will undergo the same punishment as well. BOOKS OF SESSIONS 1 KINGS 16.7.[5]

---

[1]ESOO 1:486. [2]Rabanus is quoting from Vg, which reads "the past actions of Baasha and the past actions of his house." [3]PL 109:203-4. [4]Nadab was Jeroboam's son and was killed by Baasha (1 Kings 15:25). [5]CSCO 229:116.

16:29–17:7 THE BEGINNING OF AHAB'S REIGN AND THE PROPHECY OF ELIJAH

²⁹*In the thirty-eighth year of Asa king of Judah, Ahab the son of Omri began to reign over Israel, and Ahab the son of Omri reigned over Israel in Samaria twenty-two years.* ³⁰*And Ahab the son of Omri did evil in the sight of the* LORD *more than all that were before him.* ³¹*And as if it had been a light thing for him to walk in the sins of Jeroboam the son of Nebat, he took for wife Jezebel the daughter of Ethbaal king of the Sidonians, and went and served Baal, and worshiped him.* ³²*He erected an altar for Baal in the house of Baal, which he built in Samaria.* ³³*And Ahab made an Asherah. Ahab did more to provoke the* LORD, *the God of Israel, to anger than all the kings of Israel who were before him.* ³⁴*In his days Hiel of Bethel built Jericho; he laid its foundation at the cost of Abiram his first-born, and set up its gates at the cost of his youngest son Segub, according to the word of the* LORD, *which he spoke by Joshua the son of Nun.*

17 *Now Elijah the Tishbite, of Tishbe*ⁿ *in Gilead, said to Ahab, "As the* LORD *the God of Israel lives, before whom I stand, there shall be neither dew nor rain these years, except by my word."* ²*And the word of the* LORD *came to him,* ³*"Depart from here and turn eastward, and hide yourself by the brook Cherith, that is east of the Jordan.* ⁴*You shall drink from the brook, and I have commanded the ravens to feed you there."* ⁵*So he went and did according to the word of the* LORD; *he went and dwelt by the brook Cherith that is east of the Jordan.* ⁶*And the ravens brought him bread and meat in the morning, and bread and meat in the evening; and he drank from the brook.* ⁷*And after a while the brook dried up, because there was no rain in the land.*

n Gk: Heb *of the settlers*

OVERVIEW: Ahab increased the idolatry introduced by Jeroboam by establishing more pagan cults and by building new altars (EPHREM). Ahab demonstrated all his insolence and impiety in refuting the words of Joshua and in rebuilding the city of Jericho (ISHO'DAD). Elijah appeared when Ahab's arrogance was at its climax, so that the impious king not only practiced idolatry but also persecuted the prophets and saints. Elijah was sent to show with words and actions of power the truth of the curses, which the fathers had proclaimed against the transgressors of the Law (EPHREM). So great is the power of fasting that a word sent from the fasting mouth of Elijah closed heaven to the sacrilegious (AMBROSE). The wadi signifies both the stream coming out of the sanctuary, where the sick are healed, and the baptism of the Lord. The Scripture shows that animals of an evil nature, such as the raven, performed what was ordered to them by God and provided for the necessities of the prophet, whereas the children of Israel, even though they were endowed with reason, did not want to observe the law of God (ISHO'DAD). The ravens that took care of blessed Elijah at the Lord's bidding prefigured the Gentiles and their church (AUGUSTINE). Bread represents perfection and justice accomplished together, while meat refers to the mortification of flesh (EPHREM). Elijah was fasting while he was alone at the Wadi Cherith and never boasted about his fasting (AMBROSE).

16:29-30 *Ahab Did Evil in God's Sight*

AHAB'S IMPIOUSNESS. EPHREM THE SYRIAN: This is that Ahab who thought that he would make little progress in the new religion [i.e., idolatry] if he worshiped only the gods introduced by Jeroboam. Therefore he established rites for Baal, the god of the Sidonians, built his temple in the royal city, erected altars and planted sacred groves. And these actions bitterly enraged the prophets and the other worshipers of the true God. ON THE FIRST BOOK OF KINGS 16.29.[1]

16:34 Hiel of Bethel Built Jericho

AHAB'S INSOLENCE IN REBUILDING JERICHO. ISHO'DAD OF MERV: Jericho remained in ruins as a sign and memory of the power of God and the victory of the people of Israel. But the insolent Ahab decided to refute the words of Joshua[2] and said, "As the words of his master Moses, who said, 'The sky over your head shall be bronze and the earth under you iron'[3] did not happen, so the words of his disciple will not happen." However, when [the city] was re-established at the cost of Abiram's death, his firstborn, the people feared God and showed him that he was not allowed to rebuild the city, so he stopped. But, a bit later, he attributed all these events to chance and resumed his work by setting the gates of the city. Then Segub, his youngest son, died. For this reason Elijah burned with zeal and stopped heaven for three and a half years. BOOKS OF SESSIONS 1 KINGS 16.7.[4]

17:1 Elijah Spoke to Ahab

AT THE CLIMAX OF AHAB'S REBELLION. EPHREM THE SYRIAN: Exactly at the time when the prophet and father of the prophets Elijah appeared, the rebellion of Ahab and his wife Jezebel had increased to such an extent that they not only trampled the law and fear of God underfoot, nor were content to promote the worship of idols, but even persecuted and killed the prophets and the saints. ON THE FIRST BOOK OF KINGS 17.1.[5]

WHY WAS ELIJAH SENT? EPHREM THE SYRIAN: Elijah was sent to prevent Ahab's insane rage and to show with words and actions of power and vigor the truth of the curses that the fathers had proclaimed against the transgressors of the law of God, as they were not vain threats.... Moses wrote a large book of curses and ordered Joshua to proclaim them before the assembly of all the tribes of Israel with great clamor and loudly. He especially mentions the harsh famine and the other evils that follow it, the deprivation of the rain, the aridity and infertility of the land. Ahab despised and laughed at them, because he saw how abundant his supplies were, thanks to his father who was an impious king like him. Therefore, that arrogant king necessarily had to be punished for his arrogance.

But the main reason why Elijah was sent was Jezebel, whose pride the Lord wanted to humiliate and whose falsehood he wanted to disclose. She had actually appointed herself as minister of Baal and had entrusted herself with the religious service for this god. She also proclaimed that Baal was the supreme god who ruled over those living in heaven and on earth and sent rain, watered the skies and gave fertility to the ground. She took as witnesses her fellow citizens, the Sidonians and the Tyrians and the other peoples of Phoenicia who were prosperous in those days in wealth and possessions more than any other of the neighboring nations and were also the most fervent worshipers of Baal. It was with good reason and according to justice that Elijah rose and came at that time of distress, and finally issued a stern rebuke against Ahab and his leaders and threatened to bring on them a sky of iron, as Moses had predicted, and a land of bronze.[6] ON THE FIRST BOOK OF KINGS 17.1.[7]

THE POWER OF FASTING. AMBROSE: Great is the virtue of fasting; in short so splendid is the

---

[1]ESOO 1:486. [2]See Josh 6:26. [3]Deut 28:23. [4]CSCO 229:116-17. [5]ESOO 1:487. [6]See Deut 28:23. [7]ESOO 1:487-88.

warfare that it delighted even Christ to fast; and so mighty that it raised people to heaven. And, that we may use human rather than divine examples, a word sent from the fasting mouth of Elijah closed heaven to the sacrilegious people of the Jews. For when an altar had been set up to an idol by Ahab, at the word of the prophet for three years and six months dewy rain did not fall on the earth. A worthy punishment fittingly to check insolence, that heaven should be closed to the impious who had polluted the things of earth! It was also right that a prophet, for the condemnation of a sacrilegious king, was sent to a widow in Zarephath of Sidonia, who, since she preferred piety to food, merited that she alone should not feel the distress of the general drought. And so the "urn of barley meal did not fail"[8] when the water of the torrent failed. Why should I present the rest of this history? While fasting he raised the widow's son from the dead,[9] while fasting he brought down rain at his word,[10] while fasting he drew down fire from heaven, while fasting he was snatched in a chariot to heaven,[11] and by a fast of forty days he gained the presence of God.[12] Then finally, he deserved more when he fasted more. With fasting mouth he caused the waters of the Jordan to stand, and with dusty footsteps he passed over the channel of the overflowing stream suddenly become dry.[13] The divine will judged him to be just and worthy of heaven, so that with his very body he was snatched up, since he lived the heavenly life in the body and exemplified on earth the manner of living above. ON ELIJAH AND FASTING 2.2-3.[14]

17:3 Hiding by the Wadi Cherith

TYPOLOGICAL MEANING OF THE WADI. EPHREM THE SYRIAN: From the typological point of view this symbol has two meanings. The stream [wadi] of Elijah prefigures that, at the fullness of time, the Messiah will come and will send the sinners to the stream that comes out of the sanctuary, just like the one that Ezekiel saw.[15]

That is the stream that gives healing to the sick when its waters are applied. The [second meaning is that] the stream is the baptism of the Messiah. ON THE FIRST BOOK OF KINGS 17.2.[16]

17:6 The Ravens Brought Bread and Meat

WHY WAS ELIJAH NOURISHED WITH THE HELP OF RAVENS? ISHO'DAD OF MERV: It is taught: When the priests, his brothers, saw that he had escaped the anger of Ahab, they saved for him a part of the food and bread reserved [to them], and a raven brought it to him through divine intervention.

The Schools say,[17] A raven stole the [food] from houses, inns, markets and peasants, since it is an impudent, wild and merciless bird by nature. It has no natural love for its young and does not feed them, but another bird adopts them and feeds them. Through this [the Scripture] shows that animals of such a nature performed what God ordered them to do and provided for the necessities of the prophet, whereas the children of Israel, even though they were endowed with reason, did not want to observe the law of God.

At the same time, the fact that [Elijah] was nourished by ravens, and then that the "wadi dried up," occurred through the mercy of God in order to induce the prophet to pity and compassion toward the people, so that his spirit might relent and he might pray God to send rain. But when, in spite of this, his anger against the people was not appeased, [God] ordered him to go among the nations, in order to show him that the plague of famine has spread among them as well, and that he had at least to show compassion for the nations, if he could show any for the people; but [this happened] also because there was

---

[8]1 Kings 17:22. [9]See 1 Kings 17:16. [10]See 1 Kings 18:45. [11]See 2 Kings 2:11. [12]See 1 Kings 19:8. [13]See 2 Kings 2:8. [14]PSt 19:45. [15]See Ezek 47. [16]ESOO 1:489. [17]Isho'dad is referring to the Nestorian exegetical school, which prevailed in Syriac biblical exegesis from the fifth to the sixth centuries and was mostly based on the biblical commentaries by Theodore of Mopsuestia (c. 350-428).

nobody among the people who was worthy of receiving Elijah.

Other [authors][18] say, The bread and the food were made from the elements every day through an angelic operation, just like the manna had been made from air and the quails from the sea, and just like the half cake was brought to Paul the anchorite,[19] and the bunch of dates was brought by a lion to the anchorite of the desert of Sodom.[20] But [the food was not brought to Elijah] by an angel, as it was to John,[21] nor by a man, as Daniel received it by Habakkuk,[22] but by a raven, in order to show that there is nothing impure in the creation of God—just as God gave to Samson water to drink from the jaw of a donkey[23]—and in order to signify, at the same time, the abrogation of the prescriptions of the Law. According to other authors, the angels were disguised as ravens. BOOKS OF SESSIONS 1 KINGS 17.6.[24]

THE SYMBOLIC MEANING OF BREAD AND MEAT. EPHREM THE SYRIAN: "The ravens brought him bread in the morning and meat in the evening."[25] The bread represents perfection and justice accomplished together. This is the bread about which Isaiah says that it is given to those "who will live on the heights, and whose refuge will be the fortress of the rocks, and whose eyes will see the king in his beauty."[26] Indeed, bread, which is the principal nourishment of human beings, indicates quite appropriately their main good. With regard to meat, the fact that it was brought in the evening shows two things: the first is the mourning of penitence, as the psalmist says: "Weeping may linger for the night,"[27] and the mortification of flesh and the hard toils, which the penitents marching toward perfection suffer. But their grief will become joy in the morning when the sun of justice, which dispels the darkness of sin, rises.

And these words have an even higher meaning, because they are also referred to God the Word, who clothed himself with the flesh of our humanity and came to us in the evening, that is, at the consummation of times, and "filled with

good things the hungry"[28] through the Holy Spirit, which "God poured out on them richly through the Messiah, our Savior."[29] ON THE FIRST BOOK OF KINGS 17.2.[30]

A FIGURE OF THE CHURCH OF THE GENTILES.
AUGUSTINE (CAESARIUS OF ARLES): Blessed Elijah typified our Lord and Savior. Just as Elijah suffered persecution by the Jews, so our Lord, the true Elijah, was condemned and despised by the Jews. Elijah left his own people, and Christ deserted the synagogue; Elijah departed into the wilderness, and Christ came into the world. Elijah was fed in the desert by ministering ravens, while Christ was refreshed in the desert of this world by the faith of the Gentiles. Truly, those ravens that took care of blessed Elijah at the Lord's bidding prefigured the Gentiles, for on this account it is said concerning the church of the Gentiles, "I am dark and beautiful, O daughter of Jerusalem."[31] Why is the church dark and beautiful? It is dark by nature, beautiful by grace. Why dark? "Indeed, in guilt I was born, and in sin my mother conceived me."[32] Why beautiful? "Cleanse me of sin with hyssop, that I may be purified; wash me, and I shall be whiter than snow."[33] Why dark? The apostle says, "I see another law in my members, warring against the law of my mind and making me prisoner to the law of sin."[34] Why beautiful? "Who will deliver me from the body of this death? The grace of God through Jesus Christ our Lord."[35] Truly, the church of the Gentiles was like a raven, when it despised the living and before receiving grace served idols as dead bodies. SERMON 124.1.[36]

---

[18]Isho'dad refers to unknown sources. [19]See Jerome Vita Pauli 10 (PL 23.24). [20]See Theodoret of Cyr Religiosa Historia (PG 82:1361-64). [21]Maybe an allusion to John the Baptist, but there is no trace of this episode in any extant commentary. [22]See Dan 14:33-38 (Vg). [23]See Judg 15:19. [24]CSCO 229:117-18. [25]The Peshitta version employed by Ephrem reads, "The ravens brought him bread in the morning and meat in the evening" instead of "The ravens brought him bread and meat in the morning, and bread and meat in the evening." [26]Is 33:16-17. [27]Ps 30:5 (29:6 LXX). [28]Lk 1:53. [29]Tit 3:6. [30]ESOO 1:490. [31]Song 1:4. [32]Ps 50:7. [33]Ps 50:9. [34]Rom 7:23. [35]Rom 7:24, 25. [36]FC 47:209-10*.

ELIJAH PRACTICED FASTING AT THE WADI CHERITH. AMBROSE: Therefore do not boast when you fast, do not glory lest fasting profit you nothing; for those things that are done for ostentation will not prolong their fruit into the future, but they consume the reward for present deeds. Elijah was in the desert that no one might see him fast except the ravens alone, when they supplied him with food. Elisha was in the desert where no food except poisonous wild gourds could be found.[37] John was in the desert, where he could find only locusts and wild honey.[38] Feasts were served to those fasting by the holy ministry of angels. Daniel dined among fasting lions. He dined on the dinner of another; the wild beasts did not taste theirs.[39] Feasts fly to those who fast, the feet stagger of those who dine: manna descended from heaven to those who were fasting,[40] the sin of prevarication ascended from those who were banqueting. ON ELIJAH AND FASTING 11.40.[41]

---

[37]See 2 Kings 4:39. [38]See Mt 3:4. [39]See Dan 14:32. [40]See Exod 16:13-15; 32:6. [41]PSt 19:73*.

17:8-24 A MIRACLE OF RESURRECTION IN ZAREPHATH

[8]*Then the word of the LORD came to him,* [9]*"Arise, go to Zarephath, which belongs to Sidon, and dwell there. Behold, I have commanded a widow there to feed you."* [10]*So he arose and went to Zarephath; and when he came to the gate of the city, behold, a widow was there gathering sticks; and he called to her and said, "Bring me a little water in a vessel, that I may drink."* [11]*And as she was going to bring it, he called to her and said, "Bring me a morsel of bread in your hand."* [12]*And she said, "As the LORD your God lives, I have nothing baked, only a handful of meal in a jar, and a little oil in a cruse; and now, I am gathering a couple of sticks, that I may go in and prepare it for myself and my son, that we may eat it, and die."* [13]*And Elijah said to her, "Fear not; go and do as you have said; but first make me a little cake of it and bring it to me, and afterward make for yourself and your son.* [14]*For thus says the LORD the God of Israel, 'The jar of meal shall not be spent, and the cruse of oil shall not fail, until the day that the LORD sends rain upon the earth.'"* [15]*And she went and did as Elijah said; and she, and he, and her household ate for many days.* [16]*The jar of meal was not spent, neither did the cruse of oil fail, according to the word of the LORD which he spoke by Elijah.*

[17]*After this the son of the woman, the mistress of the house, became ill; and his illness was so severe that there was no breath left in him.* [18]*And she said to Elijah, "What have you against me, O man of God? You have come to me to bring my sin to remembrance, and to cause the death of my son!"* [19]*And he said to her, "Give me your son." And he took him from her bosom, and carried him up into the upper chamber, where he lodged, and laid him upon his own bed.* [20]*And he cried to the*

Lord, "O Lord my God, hast thou brought calamity even upon the widow with whom I sojourn, by slaying her son?" [21]Then he stretched himself upon the child three times, and cried to the Lord, "O Lord my God, let this child's soul come into him again." [22]And the Lord hearkened to the voice of Elijah; and the soul of the child came into him again, and he revived. [23]And Elijah took the child, and brought him down from the upper chamber into the house, and delivered him to his mother; and Elijah said, "See, your son lives." [24]And the woman said to Elijah, "Now I know that you are a man of God, and that the word of the Lord in your mouth is truth."

Overview: God sends Elijah to the city of Zarephath, so that he may see the distress of its inhabitants and change his hardness into mercy (Ephrem). The widow, whom Elijah meets on arriving at Zarephath, symbolizes the future church of Christ (Augustine). When Elijah sees her dressed in rags and miserably thin, he is moved to compassion for the first time (Ephrem). The widow is gathering sticks, which signify the mystery of the cross, and Elijah asks her for water, which foreshadows baptism in Christ (Augustine). By asking for a cake, Elijah teaches the widow that some of the first fruits of her crops have to be offered to God (Isho'dad). The widow receives a great reward for her faith and devotion. The widow does not blame the judgment of God for the death of her child but recognizes that she is struck because of her sins (Ephrem). In his action of stretching himself on the child three times and crying out to the Lord, Elijah foreshadows the mysteries of baptism and the resurrection in Christ (Ephrem, Augustine).

17:9 Go to Zarephath

God Sends Elijah to Zarephath. Ephrem the Syrian: God sends Elijah to a city of [Gentile] people in order to change his hardness into mercy. He who had given him power over rain and dew did not want to withdraw by force what he had granted him. He wanted, nevertheless, to help the world which was tormented by starvation, but only with the consent of his servant. That is why he sends to the big city of Zarephath Elijah, who had stayed hidden to that time in the valley of Cherith, so that he may see with his own eyes the distress of its inhabitants, even though they had given no cause for that suffering, as they had not participated in the rebellion of Ahab. And even if they did not observe the law of Moses, they did not ridicule it, because they did not know it. On the First Book of Kings 17.2.[1]

The Widow Symbolizes the Future Church of Christ. Augustine (Caesarius of Arles): After this, Elijah was commanded to set out for Zarephath of the Sidonians, in order that he might be fed there by a widow. Thus, the Lord spoke to him, "Go to Zarephath of the Sidonians: I have commanded a widow there to feed you." How and by whom did God command the widow, since there was almost no other prophet at that time except blessed Elijah, with whom God spoke quite plainly? Although the sons of some of the prophets lived at that time, they feared the persecution of Jezebel so much that they could scarcely escape even when hidden. "I have commanded a widow," said the Lord. How does the Lord command, except by inspiring what is good through his grace within a soul? Thus, God speaks within every person who performs a good work, and for this reason no one should glory in himself but in the Lord. Were there not many widows in Judea at that time? Why was it that no Jewish widow merited to offer food to blessed Elijah, and he was sent to a Gentile woman to be fed? That widow to whom the prophet was sent typified the church, just as the ravens that ministered

---

[1]ESOO 1:490.

to Elijah prefigured the Gentiles. Thus, Elijah came to the widow because Christ was to come to the church. Sermon 124.2.[2]

17:10-12 A Widow Gathering Sticks

ELIJAH IS MOVED TO COMPASSION. EPHREM THE SYRIAN: When Elijah reached the gate of Zarephath, he met a woman and immediately realized, through the Holy Spirit, that she was the widow about whom God had talked to him. She was there and looked at him. It seems to me that Elijah had asked his Lord whether she was the one, as he was afraid that his severity would be weakened if he began to make inquiries about the widows of Zarephath. And, at the same time, the woman had received the order to feed the prophet through revelation, dream or another means. This is, in fact, what the words of God to Elijah indicate: "I have commanded a widow there to feed you."

When he found her barefoot and dressed in rags in the act of gathering some wood, wasted by starvation and made miserably thin, he had the impression of seeing a burned stick, and he himself was ashamed of asking her for bread so that he first asked her for water. Later he added the request of bread. He knew for sure that a jug of flour would not have been lacking thanks to the promise of his Lord. ON THE FIRST BOOK OF KINGS 17.2.[3]

SYMBOLS OF THE CROSS AND BAPTISM. AUGUSTINE (CAESARIUS OF ARLES): Let us further see where blessed Elijah found that widow, dearly beloved. She had gone out to get water and to pick up sticks of wood. Let us now consider what the water and the wood signify. We know that both are very pleasing and necessary for the church, as it is written: "He is like a tree planted near running water."[4] In the wood is shown the mystery of the cross, in the water the sacrament of baptism. Therefore, she had gone out to gather two sticks of wood, for thus she replied to blessed Elijah when he asked her for food: "As the Lord

lives, I have nothing but a handful of meal and a little oil in a cruse; and behold, I am going out to gather two sticks that I may make food for me and my son . . . and we will eat it and die." The widow typified the church, as I said above; the widow's son prefigured the Christian people. Thus, when Elijah came, the widow went out to gather two sticks of wood. Notice, brothers, that she did not say three or four, nor only one stick; but she wanted to gather two sticks. She was gathering two sticks of wood because she received Christ in the type of Elijah; she wanted to pick up those two pieces because she desired to recognize the mystery of the cross. Truly, the cross of our Lord and Savior was prepared from two pieces of wood, and so that widow was gathering two sticks because the church would believe in him who hung on two pieces of wood. For this reason that widow said, "I am gathering two sticks that I may make food for me and my son, and we will eat it and die." It is true, beloved; no one will merit to believe in Christ crucified unless he dies to this world. For if a person wishes to eat the body of Christ worthily, he must die to the past and live for the future. SERMON 124.3.[5]

17:13 First Make Me a Little Cake

AN OFFERING TO GOD IS NECESSARY. ISHO'DAD OF MERV: "[First] make me a [little] cake." He certainly did not make this request because he was hungry but to teach the widow that, through the mediation of the priests, some of the first fruits of her crops had to be offered to God. In the same manner Elijah said to the wife of the prophet, "Bring me a full vessel."[6] BOOKS OF SESSIONS 1 KINGS 17.13.[7]

17:15-16 She Did as Elijah Said

GREATNESS OF GOD'S REWARD. EPHREM THE SYRIAN: "She went and did as Elijah said." Con-

---

[2]FC 47:210*. [3]ESOO 1:490-91. [4]Ps 1:3. [5]FC 47:210-11*. [6]2 Kings 4:4 (Peshitta). [7]CSCO 229:118.

sider the faith of the widow, her obedience and charity, and then meditate on the greatness of the reward that he granted her. Indeed it is written, "The jar of meal was not emptied, neither did the jug of oil fail, according to the word of the Lord that he spoke by Elijah," nor did the number of her family members diminish, because, in exchange for the nourishment given to the prophet, her dead child was resurrected. ON THE FIRST BOOK OF KINGS 17.2.[8]

17:17-18 The Son of the Widow Became Ill

THE HUMILITY OF THE WOMAN. EPHREM THE SYRIAN: Observe carefully the tears of that woman, and see her humility in her grief, because she does not at all blame the judgment of God or rise against the prophet. In the humility of her intellect, she recognizes that that sentence struck her because of her guilt, and she says to the prophet, "You have come to me to bring my sin to remembrance." ON THE FIRST BOOK OF KINGS 17.2.[9]

17:19-22 Elijah Stretches Himself on the Child Three Times

SYMBOLS OF RESURRECTION AND BAPTISM. EPHREM THE SYRIAN: "He stretched himself on the child three times and cried out to the Lord, 'O Lord my God, let this child's life come into him again.'" These words contain many symbols. [The Scripture] shows us immediately that through the invocation of the three names[10] a human being will come back to life. If he kills the ancient Adam with the help of the Messiah in the holy baptism. The divine Paul says, "If we have died with the Messiah, we believe that we will also live with him."[11] And what follows agrees precisely with this meaning: "He stretched himself on the child," because in this life, which he will give us after we are dead to that ancient Adam, "he will transform the body of our humiliation that it may be conformed to the body of his

glory."[12] And here you can also see a symbol of the triple descent of the Son of God to the dead: the first symbol consists here in the fact that he was made flesh and included his infinite nature into the womb of the Virgin; the second, that he stretched his body on the wood and was crucified; the third, that whoever accepts death lies in the grave and goes down to Sheol, so that, in order to vivify humankind, God consented to stretch his majesty on our smallness. "O ineffable miracle," which Isaiah calls "wonder,"[13] "his Lord has come down to the man and has assumed the likeness of a slave."[14] ON THE FIRST BOOK OF KINGS 17.2.[15]

THE RESURRECTION OF CHRISTIAN PEOPLE. AUGUSTINE (CAESARIUS OF ARLES): As we mentioned, that widow prefigured the church, and her son was a type of the Gentiles. The son of the widow lay dead because the son of the church, that is, the Gentiles, was dead because of many sins and offenses. At the prayer of Elijah, the widow's son was revived; at the coming of Christ, the church's son or the Christian people were brought back from the prison of death. Elijah bent down in prayer, and the widow's son was revived; Christ sank down in his passion, and the Christian people were brought back to life. Why blessed Elijah bent down three times to arouse the boy I believe that the understanding of your charity has grasped even before I say it. In the fact that he bowed three times is shown the mystery of the Trinity. Not only the Father without the Son, nor the Father and Son without the Holy Spirit, but the whole Trinity restored the widow's son or the Gentiles to life. Moreover, this is further demonstrated in the sacrament of baptism, for the old person is plunged in the water three times, in order that the new person may merit to rise. SERMON 124.4.[16]

---

[8]ESOO 1:491. [9]ESOO 1:491-92. [10]That is, the names of the divine persons of the Trinity. [11]Rom 6:8. [12]Phil 3:21. [13]See Is 9:6. [14]Phil 2:7. [15]ESOO 1:492-93. [16]FC 47:211-12*.

18:1-18 ELIJAH PRESENTS HIMSELF TO AHAB

¹After many days the word of the LORD came to Elijah, in the third year, saying, "Go, show yourself to Ahab; and I will send rain upon the earth." ²So Elijah went to show himself to Ahab. Now the famine was severe in Samaria. ³And Ahab called Obadiah, who was over the household. (Now Obadiah revered the LORD greatly; ⁴and when Jezebel cut off the prophets of the LORD, Obadiah took a hundred prophets and hid them by fifties in a cave, and fed them with bread and water.) ⁵And Ahab said to Obadiah, "Go through the land to all the springs of water and to all the valleys; perhaps we may find grass and save the horses and mules alive, and not lose some of the animals." ⁶So they divided the land between them to pass through it; Ahab went in one direction by himself, and Obadiah went in another direction by himself.

⁷And as Obadiah was on the way, behold, Elijah met him; and Obadiah recognized him, and fell on his face, and said, "Is it you, my lord Elijah?" ⁸And he answered him, "It is I. Go, tell your lord, 'Behold, Elijah is here.' " ⁹And he said, "Wherein have I sinned, that you would give your servant into the hand of Ahab, to kill me? ¹⁰As the LORD your God lives, there is no nation or kingdom whither my lord has not sent to seek you; and when they would say, 'He is not here,' he would take an oath of the kingdom or nation, that they had not found you. ¹¹And now you say, 'Go, tell your lord, "Behold, Elijah is here."' ¹²And as soon as I have gone from you, the Spirit of the LORD will carry you whither I know not; and so, when I come and tell Ahab and he cannot find you, he will kill me, although I your servant have revered the LORD from my youth. ¹³Has it not been told my lord what I did when Jezebel killed the prophets of the LORD, how I hid a hundred men of the LORD's prophets by fifties in a cave, and fed them with bread and water? ¹⁴And now you say, 'Go, tell your lord, "Behold, Elijah is here"' ; and he will kill me." ¹⁵And Elijah said, "As the LORD of hosts lives, before whom I stand, I will surely show myself to him today." ¹⁶So Obadiah went to meet Ahab, and told him; and Ahab went to meet Elijah.

¹⁷When Ahab saw Elijah, Ahab said to him, "Is it you, you troubler of Israel?" ¹⁸And he answered, "I have not troubled Israel; but you have, and your father's house, because you have forsaken the commandments of the LORD and followed the Baals."

OVERVIEW: God teaches Elijah, through the affliction of the child who had died, that he also is grieved for his creatures tormented by starvation and thirst. The Lord orders Elijah to appear before Ahab exactly on the day when the king was searching for food to feed the horses and mules of his house, in order that the impious king may come to know the providence of God toward all creatures (EPHREM). While a rich person is a slave subject to his properties, one who has nothing fears no confiscation or loss of riches (CHRYSOSTOM). God gives Elijah authority over the spirit of the king (EPHREM).

18:1 God Will Send Rain

GOD INTENDS TO MOVE ELIJAH TO COMPASSION. EPHREM THE SYRIAN: "After many days the word of the Lord came to Elijah, in the third year of the drought, saying, 'Go, present yourself to Ahab; I will send rain on the earth.'" The Lord, by giving life back to the child, granted grace to Elijah. He had taught him through the affliction of the child, who had died, that his Lord was also grieved for his creatures tormented by starvation and thirst, even though he did not want to destroy or sever the link of the word of his servant against his will. After preparing the spirit of Elijah through this thought, he calls him and says to him, "Go, present yourself to Ahab; I will send rain on the earth." ON THE FIRST BOOK OF KINGS 18.1.[1]

18:5 Grass to Keep the Horses and Mules Alive

A WAY TO SHOW GOD'S MERCY TO THE IMPIOUS KING. EPHREM THE SYRIAN: Observe again and see how the Lord orders Elijah to appear before Ahab exactly on the day when [the king] had taken up the heavy burden of searching for food to feed the horses and the mules of his house. This was part of the divine plan, so that the impious king might come to know the providence of God toward all creatures, even toward horses and mules, and to realize how much more the Creator would be ready to make up the indigence of the king if he had not been ungrateful to God and had not lightheartedly taken advantage of his favors. And God showed this same benevolence of his good will and indulgence toward animals when he said to Jonah, "And should I not be concerned about Nineveh, that great city, in which there are more than a hundred and twenty thousand persons, who do not know their right hand from their left, and also many animals?"[2] ON THE FIRST BOOK OF KINGS 18.1.[3]

18:17-18 I Have Not Troubled Israel, but You Have

POVERTY PRODUCES BOLDNESS. JOHN CHRYSOSTOM: Were Elijah and John then lacking in boldness? Did not the one reprove Ahab, and the other Herod? The latter said, "It is not lawful for you to have your brother Philip's wife."[4] And Elijah said to Ahab with boldness: "It is not I that trouble Israel, but you and your father's house." You see that this poverty especially produces boldness? For while the rich person is a slave, being subject and in the power of every one wishing to do him hurt, one who has nothing fears no confiscation or fine. So, if poverty had made people to lack in boldness, Christ would not have sent his disciples with poverty to a work requiring great boldness. ON THE EPISTLE TO THE HEBREWS 18.4.[5]

ELIJAH'S REPROACH. EPHREM THE SYRIAN: "When Ahab saw Elijah, Ahab said to him, "Is it you, you troubler of Israel?" He answered, "I have not troubled Israel; but you have, and your father's house." "It is you and your father Omri who ruined this people, because through your abominable customs and your evil commandments you corrupted their spirit and their worship and ridiculed the holy law that God had given them, and for that reason rain and dew stopped falling from heaven, and people were overwhelmed by starvation. Therefore it is not my words, which are good, but it is your actions, which are disgusting and trouble Israel." And this freedom of speech torments Ahab greatly, but he does not fight back or rebuke Elijah about anything, as is related in the two histories of the kings, so that you may know the authority that the Lord had given Elijah over the spirit of the king and the fear toward his prophet that he had put in [Ahab's] heart. This is what [God] had done in the ancient times to Pharaoh through Moses and Aaron, when they spoke with harshness and afflicted him [with their actions] even more than with their words. ON THE FIRST BOOK OF KINGS 18.8.[6]

---

[1]ESOO 1:494. [2]Jon 4:11. [3]ESOO 1:494. [4]Mk 6:18. [5]NPNF 1 14:453*. [6]ESOO 1:495-96.

18:19-40 THE DEFEAT OF THE PRIESTS OF BAAL

[19]"Now therefore send and gather all Israel to me at Mount Carmel, and the four hundred and fifty prophets of Baal and the four hundred prophets of Asherah, who eat at Jezebel's table."

[20]So Ahab sent to all the people of Israel, and gathered the prophets together at Mount Carmel. [21]And Elijah came near to all the people, and said, "How long will you go limping with two different opinions? If the LORD is God, follow him; but if Baal, then follow him." And the people did not answer him a word. [22]Then Elijah said to the people, "I, even I only, am left a prophet of the LORD; but Baal's prophets are four hundred and fifty men. [23]Let two bulls be given to us; and let them choose one bull for themselves, and cut it in pieces and lay it on the wood, but put no fire to it; and I will prepare the other bull and lay it on the wood, and put no fire to it. [24]And you call on the name of your god and I will call on the name of the LORD; and the God who answers by fire, he is God." And all the people answered, "It is well spoken." [25]Then Elijah said to the prophets of Baal, "Choose for yourselves one bull and prepare it first, for you are many; and call on the name of your god, but put no fire to it." [26]And they took the bull which was given them, and they prepared it, and called on the name of Baal from morning until noon, saying, "O Baal, answer us!" But there was no voice, and no one answered. And they limped about the altar which they had made. [27]And at noon Elijah mocked them, saying, "Cry aloud, for he is a god; either he is musing, or he has gone aside, or he is on a journey, or perhaps he is asleep and must be awakened." [28]And they cried aloud, and cut themselves after their custom with swords and lances, until the blood gushed out upon them. [29]And as midday passed, they raved on until the time of the offering of the oblation, but there was no voice; no one answered, no one heeded.

[30]Then Elijah said to all the people, "Come near to me"; and all the people came near to him. And he repaired the altar of the LORD that had been thrown down; [31]Elijah took twelve stones, according to the number of the tribes of the sons of Jacob, to whom the word of the LORD came, saying, "Israel shall be your name"; [32]and with the stones he built an altar in the name of the LORD. And he made a trench about the altar, as great as would contain two measures of seed. [33]And he put the wood in order, and cut the bull in pieces and laid it on the wood. And he said, "Fill four jars with water, and pour it on the burnt offering, and on the wood." [34]And he said, "Do it a second time"; and they did it a second time. And he said, "Do it a third time"; and they did it a third time. [35]And the water ran round about the altar, and filled the trench also with water.

[36]And at the time of the offering of the oblation, Elijah the prophet came near and said, "O LORD, God of Abraham, Isaac, and Israel, let it be known this day that thou art God in Israel, and that I am thy servant, and that I have done all these things at thy word. [37]Answer me, O LORD, answer me, that this people may know that thou, O LORD, art God, and that thou hast turned their hearts back." [38]Then the fire of the LORD fell, and consumed the burnt offering, and the wood, and the stones, and the dust, and licked up the water that was in the trench. [39]And when all

the people saw it, they fell on their faces; and they said, "The LORD, he is God; the LORD, he is God." ⁴⁰And Elijah said to them, "Seize the prophets of Baal; let not one of them escape." And they seized them; and Elijah brought them down to the brook Kishon, and killed them there.

OVERVIEW: The priests of Baal rely on their slyness in order to defeat the authority of Elijah, but to no avail. With the words "I alone am left as a prophet to the Lord," Elijah did not calumniate the just, because they were no longer to be found, but rather he was denouncing sinners (EPHREM). Elijah orders the priests of Baal to sacrifice first, in order to show that he is not trying to take any advantage over them (ISHO'DAD). In passing among the pieces of the victim lying on the altar, the priests of Baal make use of a typical pagan practice (EPHREM). Elijah and the priests of Baal had fixed a deadline for the fire, which had to burn the bull, in order that nobody might find any excuse about the failure of his sacrifice (ISHO'DAD). In pouring water on the wood and in calling the fire on it, Elijah foreshadows the baptism in Christ and in the fire of the Holy Spirit (AMBROSE, ORIGEN). Elijah, who abolished the sacrifices of the pagan priests through the burnt offering, gives us a living image of the whole burnt offering, which the Emmanuel made on the mount Golgotha (EPHREM). The fire that burns the victim on the wood symbolizes the breath of the Holy Spirit, which consumes every sin (AMBROSE). Elijah, who was concerned for the safety of the assembly, killed the priests of Baal in order to be the only one who could be accused of their murder (EPHREM).

18:19 Israel and the Prophets of Baal Assemble at Mount Carmel

ANY HOPE IN THE SLYNESS OF BAAL'S PROPHETS IS VAIN. EPHREM THE SYRIAN: "Have all Israel assemble for me at Mount Carmel." Now, it is amazing how the king obeyed Elijah, who asked him for a general gathering of the people; and how also the people obeyed him humbly, even though he bitterly reproached them

for their evil actions. It is also amazing how his request was granted, when he asked to be allowed to fight against the prophets of Baal. It is certain that they could not find a way to avoid meeting him, and they even looked for him, if it is true what some of the doctors[1] say. And we also know that in our days false and deceiving people do the same. Therefore they thought that the prophets of Baal would make an altar in which they would have someone, who, at their sign, would set the fire and destroy the wood and the bull that were on the altar. And since they were confident in this scheme, they came to the fight, confident of the expected victory and in order to provoke Elijah. ON THE FIRST BOOK OF KINGS 18.8.[2]

18:22 The Only Prophet of the Lord Left

AN ACCUSATION AGAINST SINNERS. EPHREM THE SYRIAN: When Elijah said, "I alone am left as a prophet to the Lord," he was not speaking against the just, because they were no [longer] to be found. Rather he was denouncing sinners, because they had done away with [the just]. He did not wish it to be, therefore, that he alone be found just, and for this reason, he could not be found by them for three years,[3] for he had discovered that they were not worthy of being visited by God. COMMENTARY ON TATIAN'S DIATESSARON 7.14.[4]

18:25 Choose One Bull and Prepare It First

NO EXCUSE FOR THE PRIESTS OF BAAL. ISHO'DAD OF MERV: [Elijah] ordered [the prophets of Baal] to sacrifice first, in order that they might not have any excuse [by saying], "If we had

---

[1]Ephrem alludes to unknown authors who commented or preached on Kings. [2]ESOO 1:496-97. [3]See 1 Kings 18:1. [4]ECTD 135*.

sacrificed first, [Baal] would have accepted our sacrifice, but now he is angry with us, because we have sacrificed last." They planned to set the fire secretly, according to their custom, but were prevented by divine power at this time. BOOKS OF SESSIONS 1 KINGS 18.25.[5]

18:26 They Limped Around the Altar

THE DANCE OF THE PROPHETS OF BAAL. EPHREM THE SYRIAN: "They limped about the altar that they had made." This means they had cut the bull in pieces and passed among the pieces lying on the altar by going from side to side. The Scripture shows us another image of this in the sacrifice of Abraham. He divided the animals and saw a torch of fire passing among the pieces.[6] And Jeremiah mentions something similar when he reproaches the Jews because they had become similar to the pagan people and passed among the pieces of their sacrifices: "I will make [those who transgressed my covenant] like the calf which they cut in two and passed between its parts—the officials of Judah, the officials of Jerusalem, the eunuchs, the priests and all the people of the land who passed between the parts of the calf shall be handed over to their enemies."[7] ON THE FIRST BOOK OF KINGS 18.26.[8]

18:29 Until the Time of the Offering

A TIME FIXED FOR THE SACRIFICE. ISHO'DAD OF MERV: [Elijah and the prophets of Baal] had agreed to fix a specific time and deadline [by saying], "We will stay until this hour, and he whose sacrifice is not accepted will die." Otherwise they might have said, "Today [our sacrifice] was not accepted, but it will be accepted tomorrow." BOOKS OF SESSIONS 1 KINGS 18.29.[9]

18:33-34 Elijah Prepares a Sacrifice

A TYPE OF THE BAPTISM IN CHRIST. AMBROSE: Moreover, if anyone has not been baptized, let him be converted all the more securely by receiving the remission of his sins, [so that baptism] as a kind of fire may consume his sins, because Christ baptizes in fire and spirit. Hence, you read of this type in the books of Kings, where Elijah placed wood upon the altar and told them to pour water on it from urns. "And he said, 'Do the same the second time.' And they did it the second time. And he said, 'Do the same also the third time,'" and when the water dripped about, Elijah prayed, and fire descended from heaven. You, O mortal, are on an altar, you who are purified by water and whose sin is burned out that life may be renewed; for fire consumes wood and stubble. Do not fear the fire through which you are enlightened. Therefore it is said to you, "Come to him to be enlightened."[10] Take up the yoke of Christ; do not fear because it is a yoke; hasten because it is light. It does not bruise the neck but adorns it. Why do you hesitate, why do you delay? It does not bind the neck with chains but unites the mind by grace. ON ELIJAH AND FASTING 22.83.[11]

CHRIST BAPTIZES WITH THE HOLY SPIRIT AND FIRE. ORIGEN: And what is the source of your belief that Elijah who is to come will baptize? Did he not even baptize the wood on the altar in the times of Ahab, when it required a bath that it might be burned up when the Lord appeared in fire? He commanded the priests to do this, and not only once, for he says, "Do it a second time, when also they did it a second time," and "Do it a third time, when also they did it a third time." How, then, will he who did not himself baptize at that time, but gave the task to others, baptize when he has come in fulfillment of the things said by Malachi?[12] Christ, therefore, does not baptize in water, but his disciples.[13] He reserves for himself the act of baptizing with the Holy Spirit and fire.[14] COMMENTARY ON THE GOSPEL OF JOHN 6.125.[15]

---

[5]CSCO 229:120. [6]See Gen 15:10, 17. [7]Jer 34:18-20. [8]ESOO 1:497. [9]CSCO 229:120. [10]Ps 34:5 (33:6 LXX, Vg). [11]PSt 19:107. [12]See Mal 4:5-6. [13]See Jn 4:2. [14]See Mt 3:11; Lk 3:16. [15]FC 80:204*.

18:38 *The Fire of the Lord Consumed the Offering*

A LIVING IMAGE OF THE EMMANUEL. EPHREM THE SYRIAN: Elijah, who on mount Carmel abolished the sacrifices of the pagan priests, ministers of vanity, through the burnt offering which he offered to the living God, gives us a living image of the burnt offering that the Emmanuel made on Mount Golgotha, bringing to an end through his own sacrifice which was offered only once,[16] all the sacrifices prescribed by Moses, as well as the burnt offerings which the pagans offered to their infamous gods. "Then the fire of the Lord fell and consumed the burnt offering, the wood, the stones and the dust, and even licked up the water that was in the trench." You acted justly, Elijah, and quite wisely! Your fire will consume the stones, and the worshipers of the stones[17] will blush for their shame. It will consume the wood, and those who make their gods out of carved wood will be upset and will turn away from their madness. It will consume the bull, so that nobody may ever worship the bull. ON THE FIRST BOOK OF KINGS 18.26-38.[18]

THE BREATH OF THE HOLY SPIRIT CONSUMES EVERY SIN. AMBROSE: In the time of Elijah, also, fire came down when he challenged the prophets of the heathen to light up the altar without fire. When they could not do so, he poured water three times over his victim, so that the water ran around about the altar; then he cried out, and the fire fell from the Lord from heaven and consumed the burnt offering. You are that victim. Contemplate in silence each single point. The breath of the Holy Spirit descends on you; he seems to burn you when he consumes your sins. The sacri-

fice that was consumed in the time of Moses was a sacrifice for sin, wherefore Moses said, as is written in the book of the Maccabees: "Because the sacrifice for sin was not to be eaten, it was consumed."[19] Does it not seem to be consumed for you when in the sacrament of baptism the whole outer person perishes? "Our old self is crucified,"[20] the apostle exclaims. Herein, as the example of the Fathers teaches us, the Egyptian is swallowed up—the Hebrew arises renewed by the Holy Spirit, as he also crossed the Red Sea dry shod—where our fathers were baptized in the cloud and in the sea.[21] DUTIES OF THE CLERGY 3.18.106-7.[22]

18:40 *Elijah Killed the Priests of Baal*

ELIJAH'S CONCERN FOR THE SAFETY OF THE ASSEMBLY. EPHREM THE SYRIAN: "Elijah brought them down to the Wadi Kishon, and cut their throats[23] there." There is no doubt that the people rose against the prophets of shame and brought them before Elijah. But it is not entirely clear who killed them. The Scripture says that Elijah cut their throats. And this is in perfect agreement with the true spirit of Elijah, who was concerned for the safety of the assembly: he tried to be the only one who could be accused of the murder of the prophets. Indeed, he knew that Jezebel would have claimed vengeance for the shed blood of her priests. ON THE FIRST BOOK OF KINGS 18.40.[24]

---

[16]See Heb 7:27. [17]Ephrem refers here to the marble statues of the pagans. [18]ESOO 1:497. [19]2 Macc 2:11. [20]Rom 6:6. [21]See 1 Cor 10:1-2. [22]NPNF 2 10:85. [23]This is the reading in the Syriac Bible employed by Ephrem. [24]ESOO 1:497.

18:41-46 ELIJAH PUTS AN END TO THE DROUGHT

> [41]And Elijah said to Ahab, "Go up, eat and drink; for there is a sound of the rushing of rain." [42]So Ahab went up to eat and to drink. And Elijah went up to the top of Carmel; and he bowed himself down upon the earth, and put his face between his knees. [43]And he said to his servant, "Go up now, look toward the sea." And he went up and looked, and said, "There is nothing." And he said, "Go again seven times." [44]And at the seventh time he said, "Behold, a little cloud like a man's hand is rising out of the sea." And he said, "Go up, say to Ahab, 'Prepare your chariot and go down, lest the rain stop you.'" [45]And in a little while the heavens grew black with clouds and wind, and there was a great rain. And Ahab rode and went to Jezreel. [46]And the hand of the LORD was on Elijah; and he girded up his loins and ran before Ahab to the entrance of Jezreel.

OVERVIEW: Elijah, seeing that the people had turned away from their evil thoughts and that the priests of Baal had received a just sentence, announces the rain to the king. In order to show clearly that Elijah had bound the heavens and now opened them, it was necessary that the people see the prophet in the act of causing the rain to come down through the power of his prayer (EPHREM). Elijah prayed for rain to come on the earth, while Christ prayed that divine grace might come down into human hearts (AUGUSTINE). Elijah ran to Ahab to comfort him in his distress and fear for the sudden weather changes, but the king was unworthy of the honor accorded to him by the prophet (EPHREM).

18:41 A Sound of Rushing Rain

A REWARD FOR THE REPENTANCE OF THE PEOPLE. EPHREM THE SYRIAN: "Elijah said to Ahab, 'Go up, eat and drink; for there is a sound of rushing rain.'" Elijah, after acknowledging that the people, thanks to the miracle that he had showed them, had turned away from their evil thoughts, and that the priests of Baal, their deceivers, had received a just sentence, wisely prophesies and announces the rain to the king. And he asks his Lord for a new miracle, in order to confirm his first miracle and accomplish his

promise. Indeed, he had promised his people to give them rain if they repented of their iniquity. Therefore he prophesies [the coming of the rain], because he is certain that God is reconciled with his people in consequence of their repentance and the killing of the prophets who had misled them. ON THE FIRST BOOK OF KINGS 18.40.[1]

18:42 Elijah Went to the Top of Carmel

ELIJAH MUST SHOW THE POWER OF HIS PRAYER. EPHREM THE SYRIAN: "And Elijah went up to the top of Carmel." He does not go to Jerusalem in order to offer a sacrifice to the Lord, even though he knows the commandment of the law, which prevents the Jews from sacrificing outside the place that God had appointed as holy for them. He goes up to top of the Carmel in order to ask for rain, even though he knows that Solomon had mentioned the rain in his prayer for the people[2] and the Lord had promised him that he would have given rain to those who prayed to him inside the temple of Jerusalem. Therefore Elijah prayed, so that they might see the miracle, because many of them still had not realized that the famine that overwhelmed them had been sent by the Lord through Elijah, who had prayed to

---

[1]ESOO 1:498. [2]See 1 Kings 8:35-36.

him. In order that the word might confirm that Elijah had bound the heavens and now opened them, it was necessary that the people saw the prophet kneeling down in prayer, in the act of causing the rain to come down through his prayer. ON THE FIRST BOOK OF KINGS 18.42.[3]

18:44 A Little Cloud Rose from the Sea

ELIJAH PRAYED SEVEN TIMES. EPHREM THE SYRIAN: "Look, a little cloud no bigger than a person's hand is rising out of the sea." Before going up, Elijah prayed seven times. He did this, in the first place, in order to invite the people who were waiting for the rain, to meditate on the greatness of the grace that they received from their Lord; second, in order to teach them that even if their prayers were not fulfilled [immediately], they should not cease from multiplying their prayers until they were fulfilled at the time appointed by God. And at the seventh time a cloud bringing rain appeared, so that they might know that God had released [them] from the bondage of the famine into the abundance of his mercy in the fourth year, even though he had originally fixed the term to the seventh. ON THE FIRST BOOK OF KINGS 18.44.[4]

ELIJAH AS A TYPE OF CHRIST. AUGUSTINE (CAESARIUS OF ARLES): After this blessed Elijah presented himself to the king, "went up to Mount Carmel and put his head between his knees," praying the Lord to send rain on the earth. "And he said to his servant, 'Look toward the sea.'" When the boy reported that he saw nothing at all, he told him, "Go and look seven times." The seventh time he returned and said, "'I see a little cloud rising out of the sea like a person's foot.' And suddenly the heavens grew dark, and there fell a great rain." For this reason, as we said, Elijah prefigured our Lord and Savior. Elijah prayed and offered sacrifice; Christ offered himself as a spotless sacrifice for the whole world. Elijah prayed for rain to come on the earth; Christ prayed that divine grace might come down into

the hearts of humankind. When Elijah told his servant, "Go and look seven times," he signified the sevenfold grace of the Holy Spirit that was to be given to the church. When he declared that he saw a little cloud rising out of the sea, it prefigured the body of Christ, which was to be born in the sea of this world. Therefore, lest anyone doubt, he said that the cloud had the foot of a person who said, "Who do people say the Son of man is?"[5] After three years and six months, rain came down from heaven at the prayer of Elijah, because at the coming of our Lord and Savior the rain of the word of God happily watered the whole world during the three years and six months in which he deigned to preach. Just as at the coming of Elijah all the priests of the idols were killed and destroyed, so at the advent of the true Elijah, our Lord Jesus Christ, the wicked observances of the pagans were destroyed. SERMON 124.5.[6]

18:45-46 Elijah Ran in Front of Ahab

AHAB IS UNWORTHY OF THE HONOR ACCORDED HIM. EPHREM THE SYRIAN: In my opinion Elijah accorded a great honor to Ahab, of which he was unworthy, when he ran in front of him like a servant. And there are two reasons for this. In the first place, [the prophet intended] to comfort with his company the terrified and trembling king who was troubled in his spirit by the sudden weather changes that had occurred. It seems that he was taken by a great fear when, in a second, the sun had veiled its light and a heavy darkness had spread over all the land. And in that obscure and thick darkness he saw lightning and heard terrifying peals of thunder and a storm of violent winds and the rain falling like a cataract. Indeed, it was necessary that the atmosphere was clothed with such a dress in order to show the greatness of the sign that God had accomplished before his prophet. But the main reason for this action was that the king, who saw the honor that

---

[3]ESOO 1:498. [4]ESOO 1:498. [5]Mt 16:13. [6]FC 47:212-13*.

the prophets, messengers of the Highest, accorded to him, might learn that he had to honor God, his Creator, over all things, might be converted, might fulfill his commandments, observe his laws and obey the prophets sent to him.

See the humility of Elijah, and admire his wisdom before the pride, insanity and foolishness of Ahab. I certainly call mad and senseless one who, after seeing the wind, the water, the fire and the weather subjected to the power of Elijah, and hearing the entire people proclaim his power sim-

ilar to that of God, did not recognize the excellence of his dignity, did not admire his action or honor his person, but in the excess of his pride, let him march before him, as a servant precedes one who is superior to him many times over. Indeed, the king should have let the prophet climb up and sit with him on his chariot. On THE FIRST BOOK OF KINGS 18.46.[7]

---

[7]ESOO 1:498-99.

19:1-8 ELIJAH'S FLIGHT FROM JEZEBEL

[1]*Ahab told Jezebel all that Elijah had done, and how he had slain all the prophets with the sword.* [2]*Then Jezebel sent a messenger to Elijah, saying, "So may the gods do to me and more also, if I do not make your life as the life of one of them by this time tomorrow."* [3]*Then he was afraid, and he arose and went for his life, and came to Beer-sheba, which belongs to Judah, and left his servant there.*

[4]*But he himself went a day's journey into the wilderness, and came and sat down under a broom tree; and he asked that he might die, saying, "It is enough; now, O Lord, take away my life; for I am no better than my fathers."* [5]*And he lay down and slept under a broom tree; and behold, an angel touched him, and said to him, "Arise and eat."* [6]*And he looked, and behold, there was at his head a cake baked on hot stones and a jar of water. And he ate and drank, and lay down again.* [7]*And the angel of the Lord came again a second time, and touched him, and said, "Arise and eat, else the journey will be too great for you."* [8]*And he arose, and ate and drank, and went in the strength of that food forty days and forty nights to Horeb the mount of God.*

OVERVIEW: Jezebel decides to postpone her revenge against Elijah because she fears to infuriate the people and to be stoned (EPHREM). The providence of God caused the fear in Elijah's soul, because he had slightly turned away from him (ISHO'DAD). Elijah's flight was merely inspired by wisdom, as he had to protect his life and soul from any danger. The death Elijah is asking for is not the one with which Jezebel had threatened

him but a different kind of death (EPHREM). Fear proceeds from a disturbance of the soul, which cannot be faultless (JEROME). A great prophet like Elijah was not fleeing a woman but this world (AMBROSE). The bread baked in the ashes, which the angel offers to Elijah, signifies the toils of penitence (EPHREM).

19:2 Elijah's Oath

Jezebel Did Not Take Her Revenge Immediately. Ephrem the Syrian: "Then Jezebel sent a messenger to Elijah, saying, 'So may the gods do to me, and more also, if I do not make your life like the life of one of them by this time tomorrow.'" The insane woman contemplated that after learning from the king what Elijah had done to the prophets of Baal. However, she postponed the revenge that she desired, until the people, who were around [the prophet], were dispersed. In fact, in spite of her madness, she feared to be stoned if the people discovered her scheme to kill the prophet, who was well-known for the justice of his customs and had been seen in the act of releasing the clouds and making rain and fire, through which he had benefited his people by humiliating the arrogance of the friends of Baal and by defeating completely the famine. On the First Book of Kings 19.2.[1]

19:3 Elijah Fled for His Life

God's Providence Benefits and Corrects. Isho'dad of Merv: Somebody may ask why Elijah, who did not fear Ahab's authority, was frightened and fled when Jezebel sent him the message. We answer: The providence of God is directed by him and proceeds toward us in two different ways: either by means of benefits or corrections. This is evident from many events. When [Elijah] stopped the heavens,[2] and tortured the Jews through a famine,[3] and killed the prophets of Baal[4] and made the fire come down on the fifty and fifty,[5] he did not tremble before the king because [God's] providence assisted him. But when he slightly turned away from him, he could not resist before Jezebel's threats. The same thing happened to David. He was brave and warlike when the army of Israel was frightened by Goliath, and he killed Goliath, because he was supported by divine providence.[6] But when he was tested through divine desertion, even though the generals of his army surrounded him, he was afraid of the other Philistine.[7] Books of Sessions 1 Kings 19.2.[8]

A Flight Inspired by Wisdom. Ephrem the Syrian: "Then he was afraid; he got up and fled for his life." It was out of wisdom that he turned away from danger, because it was absolutely wrong that he disposed of his soul, since he had no reason to give it to death, but, on the contrary, he had every reason to keep it alive. And that was done so that the prophets of falsehood might not say that the god—whose worship he had disrupted, whose sacrifices he had despised and whose prophets he had killed—had handed him over to the power of the queen. On the First Book of Kings 19.3.[9]

19:4 Elijah Asked to Die

What Kind of Death Does Elijah Request? Ephrem the Syrian: "He came and sat down under a solitary broom tree. He asked that he might die." He hopes for death, but not for the one with which Jezebel had threatened him, that is, the one that would have given the prophets of Baal the pretext to say that Baal had defeated the God of Israel, otherwise he would have never abandoned his servant in such a danger: therefore he had forsaken him by force. On the First Book of Kings 19.4.[10]

Fear Cannot Be Faultless. Jerome: Elijah, whom John the Baptist followed in spirit and virtue and who caused fire to fall from heaven and the waters of the Jordan to part by his prayers, was afraid of Jezebel and fled, and, exhausted, he sat down in the wilderness under a tree, and, wearied from walking, he prayed for death, saying, "It is enough for me, Lord, take away my soul, for I am no better than my ancestors." Who can deny that he was a just man? And yet fear, not to mention of a woman, but of a human being, proceeds from a disturbance of the soul, which cannot be faultless, as David says: "The Lord is my helper; I

---

[1]ESOO 1:500. [2]See 1 Kings 17:1. [3]See 1 Kings 18:2. [4]See 1 Kings 18:40. [5]See 2 Kings 1:10-12. [6]See 1 Sam 17. [7]See 2 Sam 21:15-17. [8]CSCO 229:122. [9]ESOO 1:500. [10]ESOO 1:501.

will not fear what people can do to me."[11] AGAINST THE PELAGIANS 2.21.[12]

FLEEING THE IMPIETY OF THE WORLD.
AMBROSE: To be sure, it was not a woman that such a great prophet was fleeing, but it was this world. And it was not death that he feared, for he offered himself to the one that searched for him and said to the Lord, "Take my soul." He endured a weariness of this life, not a desire for it, but he was fleeing worldly enticement and the contagion of filthy conduct and the impious acts of an unholy and sinful generation. FLIGHT FROM THE WORLD 6.34.[13]

19:5-8 A Cake and a Jar of Water

THE SYMBOLISM OF ELIJAH'S MEAL. EPHREM THE SYRIAN: "The angel of the Lord came a second time, touched him and said, 'Get up and eat, otherwise the journey will be too much for you.'" Elijah was sleeping under a tree. Now an angel came to him and woke him up (sleep was weighing him down because of his fatigue, affliction and discouragement) and provided him with strength and comfort through the meal that he prepared for him. The nourishment of the prophet consisted of bread baked in the ashes and his drink of water. "And he said, 'The journey will be too much for you,'" that is, "you will not escape the affliction which you fear, through your death, as you believe, but through your flight. Therefore the journey is too long for you, and it is not like going to Cherith, a place close by. Rather, you are leaving for a distant location among foreign people where you will get peace and prosperity. That is why, until you are allowed to do so, you must eat and drink and prepare yourself to be strong enough for a long journey, because in a barren and desert land, you will not find any food."

Allegorically the bread baked in the ashes, which the vigilant [the angel] offers to Elijah, has two different meanings: on the one side, it immediately shows the toils of penitence which the ashes symbolize perfectly, since they are a figure of mourning and of a contrite heart; the unleavened bread soaked in ashes and the water are also the food of the poor and the miserable. But we can say, with greater accuracy, that they are figures of all the righteous, for whom the providence of the Creator has established a course of life in the paths of privation. Therefore he leads them through much suffering, privation of food and a severe fast in order to purify them completely from all the filth of earthly things. Then he guides them to the mountain, which is the perfection and the accomplishment of the saints. ON THE FIRST BOOK OF KINGS 19.4.[14]

---

[11]Ps 118:6 (117:6 LXX, Vg). [12]FC 53:328-29*. [13]FC 65:307-8. [14]ESOO 1:501-2.

19:9-18 THE LORD SPEAKS TO ELIJAH AT HOREB

[9]*And there he came to a cave, and lodged there; and behold, the word of the LORD came to him, and he said to him, "What are you doing here, Elijah?"* [10]*He said, "I have been very jealous for the LORD, the God of hosts; for the people of Israel have forsaken thy covenant, thrown down thy altars, and slain thy prophets with the sword; and I, even I only, am left; and they seek my life, to*

take it away." [11]*And he said, "Go forth, and stand upon the mount before the Lord. "And behold, the Lord passed by, and a great and strong wind rent the mountains, and broke in pieces the rocks before the Lord, but the Lord was not in the wind; and after the wind an earthquake, but the Lord was not in the earthquake;* [12]*and after the earthquake a fire, but the Lord was not in the fire; and after the fire a still small voice.* [13]*And when Elijah heard it, he wrapped his face in his mantle and went out and stood at the entrance of the cave. And behold, there came a voice to him, and said, "What are you doing here, Elijah?"* [14]*He said, "I have been very jealous for the Lord, the God of hosts; for the people of Israel have forsaken thy covenant, thrown down thy altars, and slain thy prophets with the sword; and I, even I only, am left; and they seek my life, to take it away."* [15]*And the Lord said to him, "Go, return on your way to the wilderness of Damascus; and when you arrive, you shall anoint Hazael to be king over Syria;* [16]*and Jehu the son of Nimshi you shall anoint to be king over Israel; and Elisha the son of Shaphat of Abel-meholah you shall anoint to be prophet in your place.* [17]*And him who escapes from the sword of Hazael shall Jehu slay; and him who escapes from the sword of Jehu shall Elisha slay.* [18]*Yet I will leave seven thousand in Israel, all the knees that have not bowed to Baal, and every mouth that has not kissed him."*

Overview: Elijah confirms again before God his zeal in condemning and fighting any form of idolatry and impiety. The earthquake and the fire kindled by the strong winds prefigure the type of the dreadful signs that will precede the final day of judgment. Elijah did not move from his original severity, even when he saw the image of the benevolence of his Lord. Elijah anoints Hazael, Jehu and Elisha, who will become the avengers of the iniquity of Ahab, Jezebel and the people. Only seven thousand people remained faithful to the true religion of God and gave victory to Israel (Ephrem). The words "I have left me seven thousand men who have not bowed the knee to Baal" mean that not only the Gentiles have been called to salvation, but the Jews as well (Origen).

19:9-10 *What Are You Doing Here, Elijah?*

Elijah's Severity in Condemning Sin and Idolatry. Ephrem the Syrian: Then the word of the Lord came to him, saying, "What are you doing here, Elijah?" After reaching Horeb, the mountain of God, Elijah spent the night in a cave, and on the next day, when he heard the noise of God coming to him, he went out to the entrance of the cave where he heard him saying, "What are you doing?" And he answered, "I have been very zealous for the Lord, the God of hosts. That is why I have stopped the heavens, so that it might no longer rain on the sinners, or on the earth either so that it might not give them any food, even though this seems to be a mild punishment for those who deserve a harsh and cruel torture. Should I have been quiet and kept silent while I was seeing the apostasy of an impious people that despised your commandments, abandoned your covenant made on this mountain, and exchanged you for Baal, the idol of the Sidonians, and for the vain cults of the pagans? Or should I have endured the insanity of Jezebel, who persecuted and killed your prophets? But I stood, thanks to the abundance of your mercy, because your powerful hand protected me at the Wadi Cherith and in Zarephath of Sidon. And now you have led me to your sacred mountain, even though the mad queen does not cease from setting up ambushes to destroy my soul." On the First Book of Kings 19.9.[1]

---

[1]ESOO 1:502.

19:11-12 A Great Wind, an Earthquake and a Fire

FIGURES ANNOUNCING JUDGMENT DAY.
EPHREM THE SYRIAN: "Now there was a great wind, so strong that it was splitting mountains and breaking rocks in pieces before the Lord, but the Lord was not in the wind." Now, after the wind, the earthquake came, and after the earthquake the fire, and [Elijah] noticed that the Lord was not in the earthquake or in the fire. This was the purpose of such a revelation: the Lord wanted to instruct the prophet through various figures in order to correct his excessive zeal and to lead him to imitate, according to righteousness, the providence of the most High who regulates the judgments of his justice through the abundant mercy of his grace. From the allegorical point of view this is the meaning of the frightening signs that precede the coming of the Lord: the earthquake and the fire kindled by the strong winds prefigure the type of the dreadful signs that will precede the final day of judgment. ON THE FIRST BOOK OF KINGS 19.11.[2]

19:13-14 What Are You Doing Here, Elijah?

ELIJAH DOES NOT RECEDE FROM HIS SEVERITY. EPHREM THE SYRIAN: "When Elijah heard it, he wrapped his face in his mantle and went out and stood at the entrance of the cave. Then there came a voice to him that said, 'What are you doing here, Elijah?' He answered, 'I have been very zealous for the Lord, the God of hosts; for the Israelites have forsaken your covenant.'" He stayed at the entrance of the cave because he did not dare approach the Lord who was coming to him. He wrapped his face, saying, "The creature is not worthy of seeing his Creator." But he did not move from his first thought, even though he saw the image of the benevolence of his Lord in the symbol that was presented to him, and in addition he experienced his admirable mercy and ineffable love for human beings. Who would not have been astonished by the word of the divine majesty who asked him with love, "What are you doing here, Elijah?" But Elijah did not change his mind or shut his mouth. Instead he rose against the sinners once again and complained about the sons of his people before the Lord who asked him the reason for his flight. ON THE FIRST BOOK OF KINGS 19.13.[3]

19:15-17 Anoint Hazael and Jehu as Kings and Elisha as Prophet

THE THREE ANOINTINGS. EPHREM THE SYRIAN: "Go, return on your way to the wilderness of Damascus; when you arrive, you shall anoint Hazael as king over Aram." As I have already said, "the sound of a sweet word"[4] which comes after the storm and the fire divulged this good news. And what follows this manifestation fits perfectly with this context: Elijah, who had so far fled from Jezebel the queen, is now sent to anoint the kings and to hallow the prophets. And he anoints Hazael as king of Aram with his word; Jehu, son of Namsi, as king of Israel, judge of Ahab and avenger of innocent blood with oil; and Elisha [as prophet] with his mantle. Now, since the Lord had decided that those who had been condemned by Elijah because of their rebellion should receive the just retribution for their iniquity, their condemnation was prepared in this way: a part of the people would be punished by Hazael, king of Aram, whereas Ahab and Jezebel would receive their condemnation from Jehu; finally, if anything had been overlooked by them, Elisha would accomplish the task through the authority that the Lord had given him. And the people truly deserved punishment for not turning from their error. Even after learning the truth through the great and obvious signs that Elijah had performed, they did not abandon the worship of Baal. Also the sins of Ahab and Jezebel were great, well known and evident, and both of them had to be harshly punished for that reason. And since Jezebel had appointed new priests of

---

[2]ESOO 1:502-3. [3]ESOO 1:503-4. [4]1 Kings 19:13 (Peshitta).

Baal, her god, in order to replace those who had been killed by Elijah, it was necessary that they received the same punishment as their predecessors.

In addition, other reasons obliged Elijah to raise Elisha to the dignity of prophet exactly at that time when he was about to leave this world: first, in order to assist him in the time of affliction; second, in order to confirm through his word the event of the kidnapping of his master and his ascension to heaven because nobody had ever heard anything like that before. Therefore [Elijah elevated Elisha to the dignity of prophet] in order to cut short the lies of the priests of Baal who could not commend the works of Elijah, their persecutor, and tried with all their might to persuade the people with false words that the disciples of Elijah had entirely invented the kidnapping of their master and pretended that God had raised him to heaven. ON THE FIRST BOOK OF KINGS 19.13.[5]

19:18 Seven Thousand in Israel

THE RIGHTEOUS WILL GIVE VICTORY TO ISRAEL. EPHREM THE SYRIAN: Through these words it is clear that seven thousand people remained faithful to the true religion of the ancestors, while the others had turned away from it, even though at the time of Jeroboam, king of the ten tribes, it is written that 800,000 men came out with him to fight.[6] But it is wonderful how this small troop was precious in the eyes of the Lord, and how, because of it, he gave a double victory to the sons of their people and to Ahab, their king, who were absolutely unworthy of it.

The Scripture says that in those days Ben-hadad, king of Aram, came against Samaria with thirty-two kings.[7] Now 7,000 men with 232 youths, who preceded the troop, came out of the city,[8] and fought against the Arameans, and killed them[9] and defeated that great army. ON THE FIRST BOOK OF KINGS 19.18.[10]

CALLED TO SALVATION. ORIGEN: [The apostle Paul], treating of those who belong to the circumcision, says, "Those who serve to the example and shadow of heavenly things."[11] Now perhaps, through these illustrations, no doubt will be entertained regarding the five books of Moses by those who hold the writings of the apostle as divinely inspired. And if they require, with respect to the rest of the history, that those events that are contained in it should be considered as having happened for an example to those of whom they are written, we have observed that this also has been stated in the epistle to the Romans, where the apostle adduces an instance from the third book of Kings, saying, "I have left me seven thousand who have not bowed the knee to Baal";[12] which expression Paul understood as figuratively spoken of those who are called Israelites according to the election, in order to show that the advent of Christ had not only now been of advantage to the Gentiles but that very many even of the race of Israel had been called to salvation. ON FIRST PRINCIPLES 4.1.13.[13]

---

[5]ESOO 1:504-5. [6]See 2 Chron 13:3. [7]See 1 Kings 20:1. [8]See 1 Kings 20:15, 19. [9]See 1 Kings 20:20. [10]ESOO 1:505. [11]Heb 8:5. [12]See also Rom 11:4. [13]ANF 4:362 (TLG reference is *On First Principles* 4.2.6).

19:19-21 THE CALL OF ELISHA

[19]*So he departed from there, and found Elisha the son of Shaphat, who was plowing, with twelve yoke of oxen before him, and he was with the twelfth. Elijah passed by him and cast his mantle upon him.* [20]*And he left the oxen, and ran after Elijah, and said, "Let me kiss my father and my mother, and then I will follow you." And he said to him, "Go back again; for what have I done to you?"* [21]*And he returned from following him, and took the yoke of oxen, and slew them, and boiled their flesh with the yokes of the oxen, and gave it to the people, and they ate. Then he arose and went after Elijah, and ministered to him.*

OVERVIEW: Elisha is a type of the apostles, and the mantle of Elijah signifies the gifts of the Spirit, which the apostles received (EPHREM). The call of Elisha came directly from Christ, who understood his natural inclination to goodness (JOHN THE MONK). Elisha killed the oxen to offer a banquet to his friends, after leaving behind any earthly possession (ISHO'DAD).

19:19-20 The Passing of the Mantle

ELISHA IS A TYPE OF THE APOSTLES. EPHREM THE SYRIAN: "So he set out from there and found Elisha son of Shaphat. He passed by him and threw his mantle over him." With his mantle Elijah took Elisha from farming to prophesying. From the symbolic point of view, Elisha represents the type of the apostles to whom our Lord said in the Gospel, "So stay here in the city of Jerusalem until you have been clothed with power from high."[1] Therefore the mantle of Elijah signified the gifts of the Spirit which the apostles would receive. ON THE FIRST BOOK OF KINGS 19.19.[2]

THE CALL OF ELISHA CAME FROM CHRIST.

JOHN THE MONK:[3]

> After receiving the garment from the prophetical hand,

> at the same time you have received the privilege,
> when you were transformed from worker into a prophet
> through the radiance of the Spirit that was glorified.
> Since you foreknew, O Christ, the inclination to goodness
> Of the heart of Elisha, he has understood with no doubt
> The glorious call that you had established and followed it.

CANON 6, ON ELISHA THE PROPHET, ODE 1.[4]

19:21 Elisha Prepares a Banquet

ELISHA LEAVES BEHIND ALL WORLDLY GOODS. ISHO'DAD OF MERV: "He slaughtered the oxen." He did that not [as a sacrifice] to God, because Elisha was not a priest, but he killed them for a banquet which he offered to his people. From now on, he was lifted above earthly things and did not make use of anything that belonged to this world. BOOKS OF SESSIONS 1 KINGS 19.21.[5]

---

[1]Lk 24:49. [2]ESOO 1:505. [3]John the Monk, author of a series of odes in honor of Elisha, has been identified by scholars with John of Damascus (c. 660-750). See *Analecta Hymnica Graeca* 10 (1972), 63-64. [4]*Analecta Hymnica Graeca* 10 (1972), 65. [5]CSCO 229:124.

20:1-43 THE WARS AGAINST THE ARAMEANS*

¹Ben-hadad the king of Syria gathered all his army together; thirty-two kings were with him, and horses and chariots; and he went up and besieged Samaria, and fought against it. ²And he sent messengers into the city to Ahab king of Israel, and said to him, "Thus says Ben-hadad: ³'Your silver and your gold are mine; your fairest wives and children also are mine.'" ⁴And the king of Israel answered, "As you say, my lord, O king, I am yours, and all that I have." ⁵The messengers came again, and said, "Thus says Ben-hadad: 'I sent to you, saying, "Deliver to me your silver and your gold, your wives and your children"; ⁶nevertheless I will send my servants to you tomorrow about this time, and they shall search your house and the houses of your servants, and lay hands on whatever pleases them,° and take it away.'"

⁷Then the king of Israel called all the elders of the land, and said, "Mark, now, and see how this man is seeking trouble; for he sent to me for my wives and my children, and for my silver and my gold, and I did not refuse him." ⁸And all the elders and all the people said to him, "Do not heed or consent." ⁹So he said to the messengers of Ben-hadad, "Tell my lord the king, 'All that you first demanded of your servant I will do; but this thing I cannot do.'" And the messengers departed and brought him word again. ¹⁰Ben-hadad sent to him and said, "The gods do so to me and more also, if the dust of Samaria shall suffice for handfuls for all the people who follow me." ¹¹And the king of Israel answered, "Tell him, 'Let not him that girds on his armor boast himself as he that puts it off.'"† ¹²When Ben-hadad heard this message as he was drinking with the kings in the booths, he said to his men, "Take your positions." And they took their positions against the city.

¹³And behold, a prophet came near to Ahab king of Israel and said, "Thus says the LORD, Have you seen all this great multitude? Behold, I will give it into your hand this day; and you shall know that I am the LORD." ¹⁴And Ahab said, "By whom?" He said, "Thus says the LORD, By the servants of the governors of the districts." Then he said, "Who shall begin the battle?" He answered, "You." ¹⁵Then he mustered the servants of the governors of the districts, and they were two hundred and thirty-two; and after them he mustered all the people of Israel, seven thousand.

¹⁶And they went out at noon, while Ben-hadad was drinking himself drunk in the booths, he and the thirty-two kings who helped him. ¹⁷The servants of the governors of the districts went out first. And Ben-hadad sent out scouts, and they reported to him, "Men are coming out from Samaria." ¹⁸He said, "If they have come out for peace, take them alive; or if they have come out for war, take them alive."

¹⁹So these went out of the city, the servants of the governors of the districts, and the army which followed them. ²⁰And each killed his man; the Syrians fled and Israel pursued them, but Ben-hadad king of Syria escaped on a horse with horsemen. ²¹And the king of Israel went out, and captured ᵖ the horses and chariots, and killed the Syrians with a great slaughter.

²²Then the prophet came near to the king of Israel, and said to him, "Come, strengthen yourself,

and consider well what you have to do; for in the spring the king of Syria will come up against you."

²³*And the servants of the king of Syria said to him, "Their gods are gods of the hills, and so they were stronger than we; but let us fight against them in the plain, and surely we shall be stronger than they.* ²⁴*And do this: remove the kings, each from his post, and put commanders in their places;* ²⁵*and muster an army like the army that you have lost, horse for horse, and chariot for chariot; then we will fight against them in the plain, and surely we shall be stronger than they." And he hearkened to their voice, and did so.*

²⁶*In the spring Ben-hadad mustered the Syrians, and went up to Aphek, to fight against Israel.* ²⁷*And the people of Israel were mustered, and were provisioned, and went against them; the people of Israel encamped before them like two little flocks of goats, but the Syrians filled the country.* ²⁸*And a man of God came near and said to the king of Israel, "Thus says the* Lord, '*Because the Syrians have said, "The* Lord *is a god of the hills but he is not a god of the valleys," therefore I will give all this great multitude into your hand, and you shall know that I am the* Lord.' " ²⁹*And they encamped opposite one another seven days. Then on the seventh day the battle was joined; and the people of Israel smote of the Syrians a hundred thousand foot soldiers in one day.* ³⁰*And the rest fled into the city of Aphek; and the wall fell upon twenty-seven thousand men that were left.*

Ben-hadad also fled, and entered an inner chamber in the city. ³¹*And his servants said to him, "Behold now, we have heard that the kings of the house of Israel are merciful kings; let us put sackcloth on our loins and ropes upon our heads, and go out to the king of Israel; perhaps he will spare your life."* ³²*So they girded sackcloth on their loins, and put ropes on their heads, and went to the king of Israel and said, "Your servant Ben-hadad says, 'Pray, let me live.' " And he said, "Does he still live? He is my brother."* ³³*Now the men were watching for an omen, and they quickly took it up from him and said, "Yes, your brother Ben-hadad." Then he said, "Go and bring him." Then Ben-hadad came forth to him; and he caused him to come up into the chariot.* ³⁴*And Ben-hadad said to him, "The cities which my father took from your father I will restore; and you may establish bazaars for yourself in Damascus, as my father did in Samaria." And Ahab said, "I will let you go on these terms." So he made a covenant with him and let him go.*

³⁵*And a certain man of the sons of the prophets said to his fellow at the command of the* Lord, "*Strike me, I pray." But the man refused to strike him.* ³⁶*Then he said to him, "Because you have not obeyed the voice of the* Lord, *behold, as soon as you have gone from me, a lion shall kill you." And as soon as he had departed from him, a lion met him and killed him.* ³⁷*Then he found another man, and said, "Strike me, I pray." And the man struck him, smiting and wounding him.* ³⁸*So the prophet departed, and waited for the king by the way, disguising himself with a bandage over his eyes.* ³⁹*And as the king passed, he cried to the king and said, "Your servant went out into the midst of the battle; and behold, a soldier turned and brought a man to me, and said, 'Keep this man; if by any means he be missing, your life shall be for his life, or else you shall pay a talent of silver.'* ⁴⁰*And as your servant was busy here and there, he was gone." The king of Israel said to him, "So shall your judgment be; you yourself have decided it."* ⁴¹*Then he made haste to take the bandage away*

from his eyes; and the king of Israel recognized him as one of the prophets. [42]*And he said to him, "Thus says the LORD, 'Because you have let go out of your hand the man whom I had devoted to destruction, therefore your life shall go for his life, and your people for his people.' "* [43]*And the king of Israel went to his house resentful and sullen, and came to Samaria.*

o Gk Syr Vg: Heb *you*   p Gk: Heb *smote*   *In the LXX the order of the chapters 20 and 21 is reversed, so that chapter 20 corresponds to chapter 21 of the Hebrew Bible and chapter 21 to chapter 20.   † LXX and Vg *Let no one who is humpbacked boast as if he were upright*

OVERVIEW: The words "let no one who is crooked boast as if he were upright" refer to no bodily deformity but to moral deformity (MAXIMUS). The disastrous defeat of the Arameans was caused by God, who pronounced judgment on their impiety (EPHREM, SALVIAN). The saints are on the mountains, the fallen are in the valleys, because the Lord "is the God of the mountains and not the God of the valleys" (AMBROSE). Ahab makes a treaty with Ben-hadad and allows him to leave, as he thinks that his mercy is better than God's command (CASSIAN). The man who struck the prophet was saved, whereas the one who spared the prophet was punished: this demonstrates that when God commands, one must not question deeply the nature of the action but only obey. We must always examine the decrees of God before considering the nature of our actions, and whenever we find something that accords with his decree, we must approve that, and only that (CHRYSOSTOM). Ben-hadad, who was notoriously impious and an open and arrogant despiser of divine majesty, fully deserved to be condemned (EPHREM).

20:11 One Who Puts on Armor

THE HUMP SYMBOLIZES A SOUL DEFORMED BY EVIL WAYS OF LIFE. MAXIMUS OF TURIN:
For a hump is, as it were, to think or to do something base of soul, and it is a kind of twisted deformity of mind always to incline toward unclean things and to be withdrawn from the holy threshold of the church by worldly concerns. Hence it seems to me that the prophet, when he spoke spiritually of this bodily deformity, alluded instead to a moral hideousness

when he said, "Let no one who is crooked boast as if he were upright."[1] It is as if he were saying, "Let not the sinner boast who is distorted by the wickedness of his vices, as the righteous boasts who is made upright by the sincerity of a good conscience." For although, O sinner, you rejoice in your tall stature, although you are glad because of the straightness of your shoulders, nonetheless your soul is deformed by your evil way of life. Rightly, then, is a rich person compared with a camel, since bodily ungainliness prevents the one from passing through a needle, while concern for his property hinders the other from entering the church. And just as a small needle cannot receive the one that is burdened by the grossness of its body, so also the sacred portal cannot take in the other, who is encumbered by the weight of his offenses. Each has his own burden: the one is weighed down by his physiognomy, the other by his sins. And just as the one cannot pass through the needle's tiny eye, so the other is unfit for the most blessed kingdom of God, except that the camel's body is disordered by nature, while the rich person's will makes him evil. SERMON 32.1.[2]

20:20-30 The Arameans Were Defeated

GOD PUNISHES THE IMPIOUSNESS OF THE ARAMEANS. EPHREM THE SYRIAN:
Here the Scripture relates the two battles of the king of Israel against the Arameans, at which we have already hinted,[3] and the twin slaughters of the

---

[1]1 Kings 20:11 (LXX and VL, used by Maximus; cf. biblical text above).   [2]ACW 50:78.   [3]See 1 Kings 19:18, "The Righteous Will Give Victory to Israel."

Arameans, of which the second caused the death of 127,000 men, as God took his revenge on the impious voice of the Arameans, who said about the true God worshiped by the Israelites, "The Lord is a god of the hills, but he is not a god of the valleys." On the First Book of Kings 20.1.[4]

The Only Author of the Victory. Salvian the Presbyter: Did not the Lord wish Benhadad, king of Syria, whom besides countless thousands of his own people, thirty-two kings and armies of the same number of kings served, to be conquered by a few foot soldiers of the princes in order that he who was the author of such victory would be acknowledged? The Governance of God 7.8.[5]

The Saints Are on the Mountains. Ambrose: Thus the saints go up to the Lord, the wicked go down to sin; the saints are on the mountains, the guilty in the valleys. "For he is the God of the mountains and not the God of the valleys." Those who dwelt in the houses of the plain where God does not dwell could not have the house of God within them, for this is the house that God sought from them so that they might build up themselves and rear within themselves the temple of God from living stones of faith. He did not want buildings made with earthen walls or wooden roofs, for the hand of an enemy would have been able to overthrow them. He wanted that temple that is built in human hearts, to whom it might be said, "You are the temple of God,"[6] in which the Lord Jesus might dwell and from there set out to redeem all humankind. There also could be prepared a sacred chamber in the womb of the Virgin where the King of heaven might live and a human body become the temple of God, which, though it was destroyed, might yet be restored to life on the third day. Letter 80.[7]

20:34 Ahab Made a Treaty

Ahab Believed That His Mercy Was Bet-

ter Than God's Command. John Cassian: No one doubts that when the judgment of the heart goes astray and is seized by the night of ignorance, our thoughts and our deeds, which proceed from the deliberation of discretion, are involved in the greater darkness of sin. Finally, because he never had this eye of discretion, he who by God's judgment first deserved to rule over the people of Israel was cast out of his kingdom like something dark out of a healthy body. Having been deceived by the darkness and error of this light, he decided that his own sacrifices were more acceptable to God than obedience to Samuel's command, and in the very act by which he had hoped that he would propitiate the divine majesty he committed sin instead. Ignorance of this discretion, I say, constrained Ahab, the king of Israel, after the triumph of the glorious victory that had been conceded to him by God's favor, to believe that his own mercy was better than the very severe execution of the divine command, which seemed to him to be a cruel decree. Enfeebled by this thought, he wished to temper a bloody victory with clemency and, having been made dark throughout his body because of his impudent mercy, he was condemned to a death from which there was no recourse. Conference 2.2.6-3.2.[8]

20:35-38 You Have Not Obeyed the Lord

God's Commands Must Be Obeyed. John Chrysostom: Ahab once captured a king of Syria and, contrary to God's decree, saved his life. He had the Syrian king enjoy a seat by his side and sent him off with great honor. About that time a prophet came to his companion and said to him, "In the word of the Lord, strike me." But his companion was not willing to strike him. And the prophet said to him, "Because you would not listen to the word of the Lord, behold, you will depart from me, and a lion will strike you." And

---

[4]ESOO 1:505-6. [5]FC 3:195. [6]1 Cor 3:16. [7]FC 26:449*. [8]ACW 57:86.

he departed from him, and the lion found him and struck him. Then the prophet found another man and said, "Strike me." And the man did strike him and wounded him, and the prophet bandaged up his own face.

What greater paradox than this could there be? The man who struck the prophet was saved; the one who spared the prophet was punished. Why? That you may learn that when God commands, you must not question too much the nature of the action; you have only to obey. So that the first man might not spare him out of reverence, the prophet did not simply say "strike me" but said "strike me, in the word of God." That is, God commands it; seek no further. It is the King who ordains it; reverence the rank of him who commands and with all eagerness heed his word. But the man lacked the courage to strike him and, on this account, he paid the ultimate penalty. But by the punishment he subsequently suffered, he encourages us to yield and obey God's every command. DISCOURSE AGAINST JUDAIZING CHRISTIANS 4.2.1-2.[9]

20:41-43 Your Life Shall Be for His Life

LOOK INTO THE DECREES OF GOD. JOHN CHRYSOSTOM: After the second man had struck and wounded him, the prophet bound his own head with a bandage, covered his eyes and disguised himself. Why did he do this? He was going to accuse the king and condemn him for saving the life of the king of the Syrians. Now Ahab was an impious man and always a foe to the prophets. The prophet did not wish Ahab to recognize him and then drive him from his sight; if the king drove him away, he would not hear the prophet's words of correction. So the prophet concealed his face and any statement of his business in the hope that this would give him the advantage when he did speak and that he might get the king to agree to the terms he wanted.

When the king was passing by, the prophet called aloud to him and said, "Your servant went forth to the campaign of war. Behold, a man brought another man to me and said to me: 'Guard this man for me. If he shall leap away and bound off, it will be your life for his life, or you will pay a talent of silver.' And it happened that as your servant turned his eyes this way and that, the man was not there." And the king of Israel said to him: "This is your judgment before me: You killed the man." And the prophet hurried to take the bandage from his eyes, and the king of Israel recognized that he was one of the sons of the prophets. And he said to the king: "So says the Lord: 'Because you let go from your hand a man worthy of death, it will be your life for his life, and our people for his people.'"

Do you see how not only God but also people make this kind of judgment because both God and people heed the end and the causes rather than the nature of what is done? Certainly even the king said to him, "This is your judgment before me: you killed the man." You are a murderer, he said, because you let an enemy go. The prophet put on the bandage and presented the case as if it were not the king but somebody else on trial, so that the king might pass the proper sentence. And, in fact, this did happen. So after the king condemned him, the prophet tore off the bandage and said, "Because you let go from your hand a man worthy of death, it will be your life for his life and your people for his people." Did you see what a penalty the king paid for his act of kindness? And what punishment he endured in return for his untimely sparing of his foe? The one who spared a life is punished; another, who killed a man, was held in esteem. Phinehas certainly killed two people in a single moment of time—a man and his wife; and after he killed them, he was given the honor of the priesthood.[10] His act of bloodshed did not defile his hand; it even made them cleaner. So you see that he who struck him perishes; you see that he who spared a man's life is punished, while he who refused to spare a life is held in esteem. Therefore, always look into the decrees of God

---

[9]FC 68:74-75. [10]See Num 25:6-13.

before you consider the nature of your own actions. Whenever you find something that accords with his decree, approve that—and only that. DISCOURSE AGAINST JUDAIZING CHRISTIANS 4.2.3-7.[11]

AHAB'S INDULGENCE IS CONDEMNED BY THE PROPHET. EPHREM THE SYRIAN: In the course of these events Ahab's indulgence toward a man who was notoriously impious and an open and arrogant despiser of divine majesty fully deserved to be condemned, just as Saul's clemency toward the king of the Amalekites was reproached with good reason by Samuel;[12] this is especially true if,

as some commentators assert, the same prophet who had promised the victory in the name of God prescribed that a punishment was to be inflicted on Ben-hadad. On the other hand, a mild punishment should have been inflicted on Ahab and his subjects, if they were completely unaware of the will of God. But they could not ignore God's will at all, because the prophet had told them ahead of time that the Arameans would be handed over to them, after the Arameans had violated the majesty of God with their impious insults. ON THE FIRST BOOK OF KINGS 20.1.[13]

---

[11]FC 68:75-77. [12]See 1 Sam 15:8-33. [13]ESOO 1:506.

21:1-29 NABOTH'S VINEYARD*

[1]Now Naboth the Jezreelite had a vineyard in Jezreel, beside the palace of Ahab king of Samaria. [2]And after this Ahab said to Naboth, "Give me your vineyard, that I may have it for a vegetable garden, because it is near my house; and I will give you a better vineyard for it; or, if it seems good to you, I will give you its value in money." [3]But Naboth said to Ahab, "The LORD forbid that I should give you the inheritance of my fathers." [4]And Ahab went into his house vexed and sullen because of what Naboth the Jezreelite had said to him; for he had said, "I will not give you the inheritance of my fathers." And he lay down on his bed, and turned away his face, and would eat no food.

[5]But Jezebel his wife came to him, and said to him, "Why is your spirit so vexed that you eat no food?" [6]And he said to her, "Because I spoke to Naboth the Jezreelite, and said to him, 'Give me your vineyard for money; or else, if it please you, I will give you another vineyard for it'; and he answered, 'I will not give you my vineyard.'" [7]And Jezebel his wife said to him, "Do you now govern Israel? Arise, and eat bread, and let your heart be cheerful; I will give you the vineyard of Naboth the Jezreelite."

[8]So she wrote letters in Ahab's name and sealed them with his seal, and she sent the letters to the elders and the nobles who dwelt with Naboth in his city. [9]And she wrote in the letters, "Proclaim a fast, and set Naboth on high among the people; [10]and set two base fellows opposite him, and let them bring a charge against him, saying, 'You have cursed God and the king.' Then take him out, and stone him to death." [11]And the men of his city, the elders and the nobles who dwelt in

his city, did as Jezebel had sent word to them. As it was written in the letters which she had sent to them, ¹²they proclaimed a fast, and set Naboth on high among the people. ¹³And the two base fellows came in and sat opposite him; and the base fellows brought a charge against Naboth, in the presence of the people, saying, "Naboth cursed God and the king." So they took him outside the city, and stoned him to death with stones. ¹⁴Then they sent to Jezebel, saying, "Naboth has been stoned; he is dead."

¹⁵As soon as Jezebel heard that Naboth had been stoned and was dead, Jezebel said to Ahab, "Arise, take possession of the vineyard of Naboth the Jezreelite, which he refused to give you for money; for Naboth is not alive, but dead." ¹⁶And as soon as Ahab heard that Naboth was dead, Ahab arose to go down to the vineyard of Naboth the Jezreelite, to take possession of it.

¹⁷Then the word of the LORD came to Elijah the Tishbite, saying, ¹⁸"Arise, go down to meet Ahab king of Israel, who is in Samaria; behold, he is in the vineyard of Naboth, where he has gone to take possession. ¹⁹And you shall say to him, 'Thus says the LORD, "Have you killed, and also taken possession?"' And you shall say to him, 'Thus says the LORD: "In the place where dogs licked up the blood of Naboth shall dogs lick your own blood."'"

²⁰Ahab said to Elijah, "Have you found me, O my enemy?" He answered, "I have found you, because you have sold yourself to do what is evil in the sight of the LORD. ²¹Behold, I will bring evil upon you; I will utterly sweep you away, and will cut off from Ahab every male, bond or free, in Israel; ²²and I will make your house like the house of Jeroboam the son of Nebat, and like the house of Baasha the son of Ahijah, for the anger to which you have provoked me, and because you have made Israel to sin. ²³And of Jezebel the LORD also said, 'The dogs shall eat Jezebel within the bounds of Jezreel.' ²⁴Any one belonging to Ahab who dies in the city the dogs shall eat; and any one of his who dies in the open country the birds of the air shall eat."

²⁵(There was none who sold himself to do what was evil in the sight of the LORD like Ahab, whom Jezebel his wife incited. ²⁶He did very abominably in going after idols, as the Amorites had done, whom the LORD cast out before the people of Israel.)

²⁷And when Ahab heard those words, he rent his clothes, and put sackcloth upon his flesh, and fasted and lay in sackcloth, and went about dejectedly. ²⁸And the word of the LORD came to Elijah the Tishbite, saying, ²⁹"Have you seen how Ahab has humbled himself before me? Because he has humbled himself before me, I will not bring the evil in his days; but in his son's days I will bring the evil upon his house."

* This is chapter 20 in the LXX

OVERVIEW: Even though the story of Naboth happened a long time ago, we see that it is constantly repeated nowadays. The real rich man is Naboth, who is able to despise the gold of the king and to condemn his earthly covetousness (AMBROSE). Naboth refused to give Ahab his vineyard, because he knew that the inheritance of the promised land, which all Jews had received through Joshua, was for them as precious as the kingdom of heaven is for us, and so he did not want to be deprived of that divine gift (ISHO'DAD). When Ahab pronounces the words "give to me," he does not express need but only his covetousness for earthly possessions. Ahab is led by insatiable greed, so that he merely desires to exclude others from any property. Ahab and Jezebel perfectly represent the behavior of the rich, who are made sad if they are not seizing the property of others (Ambrose). Elijah pronounces his sentence against the king and the queen and condemns them to be given to the dogs and the house of Ahab to destruction (Ephrem). The punishment decreed by God for Ahab and Jezebel through the words of Elijah is the punishment for all rich and covetous people (Ambrose). God immediately receives the prayer of Ahab and reconciles with him through the mediation of the prophet, because he sees that the king's repentance is sincere (Ephrem). Like all rich people, Ahab is not sorry in heart but only in countenance (Ambrose). Through contrition, fasting and the humility of wearing a sackcloth, Ahab is able to obtain God's forgiveness (Jerome). In his infinite mercifulness the Lord conceded the grace of forgiveness to the unworthy Ahab, but Ahab did not cling to the divine favors conferred on him (Ambrose).

21:1 Naboth Had a Vineyard

The Constant Moral Value of Naboth's Story. Ambrose: The story of Naboth is old in time but daily in practice. For who of the rich does not daily covet the goods of others? Who of the wealthy does not strive to drive off the poor person from his little acre and turn out the needy from the boundaries of his ancestral field? Who is content with his own? What rich person's heart is not set on fire by a neighbor's possession? Not, therefore, was one Ahab born, but, what is worse, daily is Ahab born and never dies in this world. If one perishes, many others spring up; there are more to steal than there are to suffer loss. Not one poor man, Naboth, was killed: daily is Naboth struck down, daily is a poor person put to death. Alarmed by this fear, the human race is now departing from its lands; the poor man, car-

rying his latest born, wanders forth with his little ones; his wife follows in tears, as if accompanying her husband to his tomb. Less, however, does she grieve who weeps over the bodies of her dead: for, although she has not her sons yet she does not mourn for exiles, she does not groan at the hunger of her tender brood, which is worse than death. On Naboth 1.1.[1]

Naboth Owns the True Wealth. Ambrose: An ancient story tells of the two neighbors, King Ahab and a poor man, Naboth. Which of these do we consider the poorer, which the richer: the one who had been endowed with a king's measure of wealth, insatiable and unsatisfied with his wealth, who longed for the little vineyard of the poor man; or the other, heartily despising a "king's fortune of much gold" and imperial wealth, who was satisfied with his vineyard? Does he not seem richer and more a king, since he had enough for himself and regulated his desires so that he wanted nothing that belonged to others? But was he not very poor whose gold was of no account, while he considered the other's vines of priceless value? Understand why he was so very poor: because riches amassed unjustly are disgorged, but the root of the righteous remains and flourishes like a palm tree. Letter 55(38).8.[2]

21:2 Give Me Your Vineyard

Why Did Naboth Refuse to Give Ahab His Vineyard? Isho'dad of Merv: What Ahab said to Naboth, that is, that he would have given him the price of his vineyard or [another vineyard], was a lie. But Naboth did not sell his inheritance, first of all because he knew that [Ahab] would not have given him another vineyard in exchange and would not have kept his promise; second, because the Law forbade that an inheritance could be sold from one person to another;[3] third, because the inheritance of the promised land, which they had received through

---

[1]PSt 15:47. [2]FC 26:306. [3]See Lev 25:23.

the mediation of Joshua, was for them as precious as the kingdom of heaven is for us, and Naboth did not want to be deprived of that divine gift. BOOKS OF SESSIONS 1 KINGS 21.2.[4]

AHAB'S WORDS EXPRESS MERE COVETOUSNESS. AMBROSE:

Let us hear, then, what [Ahab] says: "Give to me," he cries. What other is the cry of one in want? What other is the cry of one asking public alms, if not "Give to me"? That is, "Give to me," because I am in need, "give to me," because I cannot find any other means of sustenance; "give to me," because there is not to me bread for food, money for drink, price for nourishment, substance for raiment; "give to me," because the Lord has given to you from which you should bestow; he has not given to me. "Give to me," because, unless you give, I cannot have; "give to me," because it is written, "Give alms."[5] How abject these words, how mean! For they have not the disposition of humility but the fire of covetousness. But in this very degradation, what effrontery! "Give me," he says, "your vineyard." He confesses it is another's, so that he asks what is not due him. ON NABOTH 2.7.[6]

THE WISH TO EXCLUDE OTHERS. AMBROSE:

"Give me your vineyard," he says, "so that I may have it for a vegetable garden." This, then, was his whole madness; this was his whole passion: that a space should be obtained for paltry herbs. Not so much therefore do you yourself desire to possess, as it were, something useful, but you wish to exclude others. You have a greater concern about the possessions of the poor than about your own gains. You think it a wrong to you if a poor person has anything that is considered worthy of a rich person's ownership. You believe it your loss, whatever is another's. Why do the injuries done to nature delight you? For all has the world been created, which you few rich people are trying to keep for yourselves. For not merely the possession of the earth but the very sky, the air and the sea are claimed for the use of the rich few. ON NABOTH 3.11.[7]

21:9-13 Naboth Is Killed

BEHAVIOR TYPICAL OF THE RICH. AMBROSE: How clearly the custom of the rich is portrayed! They are made sad if they are not seizing the property of others; they renounce food, they fast, not that they may lessen their sin but that they may commit crime. You may see them at such times coming to church, dutiful, humble and assiduous, in order that they may deserve to obtain the accomplishment of their wickedness. But to them God says, "Not this fast have I chosen, not if you should wind your head about like a circle and spread also sackcloth and ashes, and not thus will you call an acceptable fast. Not such a fast have I chosen, says the Lord. Loose every bond of injustice, loose the bonds of violent contracts, let them that are broken go free, and tear asunder every unjust writing. Deal your bread to the hungry, and bring the needy and harborless into your house. If you shall see one naked, cover him, and you shall not despise the domestics of your seed. Then shall your morning light arise, and your health shall speedily arise, and your justice shall go before you, and the majesty of the Lord shall surround you. Then shall you call, and God shall hear you; even while you speak, he shall say, Here I am."[8] Do you hear, O rich person, what the Lord God says? You too come to church, not to bestow anything on a poor person but to take away. You fast, not that the cost of your banquet may profit the needy, but that you may obtain spoil from those in want. ON NABOTH 10.44-45.[9]

21:18-23 I Will Bring Disaster on You

ELIJAH REPROVES THE ASSASSINATION OF NABOTH. EPHREM THE SYRIAN: And the Lord said to Elijah, "Get up,[10] go down to meet King

---

[4]CSCO 229:125. [5]Lk 11:41. [6]PSt 15:51. [7]PSt 15:53. [8]Is 58:5-9 (LXX); Ambrose uses a VL, which is a close translation of the LXX. [9]PSt 15:75-76. [10]These words are added in the Peshitta version used by Ephrem.

Ahab of Israel," and so on. Now, when Jezebel invited Ahab to come and take hold of the vineyard whose owners had been stoned, Elijah went out to meet him, precisely when he did not expect him, and approached him in order to reveal the shameful action which they thought no one else knew about. He reproached the king openly for stealing the vineyard and killing the righteous Naboth. But one may say: Is not Jezebel the one who prepared the death of Naboth? Ahab simply did not accept that his request was rejected by Naboth; he did not want to treat him badly or take his vineyard by force. However, if he claims the vineyard, since the inheritance is due to the king after the heirs are dead, as the law prescribes, we maintain that if Ahab had not sinned at all, it would have been impossible that the justice that absolves those who are oppressed might have wronged him. Nor would the prophet, who reproved him according to the command of the just Judge and had already condemned him twice, [have wronged him].

And Elijah said to him, "Thus says the Lord: In the place where dogs licked up the blood of Naboth, dogs will also lick up your blood, and I will make your house like the house of Jeroboam." To Jezebel too, the Lord said, "The dogs shall eat Jezebel within the boundaries of Jezreel." Such are the judgments that Elijah pronounced against the king and the queen: he gives them to the dogs, and the house of Ahab to destruction. ON THE FIRST BOOK OF KINGS 21.17.[11]

THE SEVERE AND JUST SENTENCE OF GOD.

AMBROSE: By this his divine justice moved, and it condemns the miser with befitting severity, saying, "You have killed, and you have taken possession of his inheritance. Therefore in this place, where the dogs have licked the blood of Naboth, in this place the dogs shall lick your blood and harlots shall wash in your blood."[12] How just, how severe a sentence: that he should be prevented from separating from the horror of his own death the same bitterness of death that he had inflicted on the other! God beholds the poor

man unburied and therefore decrees that the rich man also be without burial; hence, even dead, Ahab may atone for the tribulation of his iniquity, who thought that not even the dead should be spared. Thus his corpse, sprinkled with the gore of his wound, after the manner of a violent death, disclosed the cruelty of his life. When the poor man suffered these things, the rich man was blamed; when the rich man experienced them, the poor man was vindicated. But what does it signify that harlots washed in his blood, unless perhaps that a kind of meretricious perfidy or bloody luxury should be proclaimed to have been in the cruelty of the king, who was so fond of luxury that he desired herbs, and so bloodthirsty that, for the sake of his herbs, he killed a man? A fitting penalty destroyed the miser, a fitting penalty for his avarice. Finally, also, the dogs and the birds of heaven devoured Jezebel, so that it should be made manifest that the spoil of spiritual wickedness becomes the grave of the rich. Flee, therefore, a death of this kind, O rich person. But you will flee a death of this kind only if you flee this kind of crime. Do not be an Ahab and covet a neighbor's possession. Let not Jezebel dwell with you, that deadly avarice that persuades you to bloody deeds; that restrains not your desires but urges you on; that makes you sadder even when you gain possession of what you desire and that makes you destitute when you are rich. ON NABOTH 11.48-49.[13]

21:27 Ahab Tore His Clothes

AHAB'S SINCERE REPENTANCE.

EPHREM THE SYRIAN: And the Lord said to Elijah, "Have you seen how Ahab has humbled himself before me?" and so on. If the repentance of Ahab had not been sincere, it would not have been praised by the Lord nor would the sentence pronounced against him have been diminished. It is true that

---

[11]ESOO 1:508-9. [12]The text of the LXX adds "and harlots shall wash in your blood." This sentence is also in VL, whereas it is omitted in Vg. [13]PSt 15:75-76.

Ahab did not receive his punishment in its entirety: the dogs, in fact, did not rip up his corpse or the birds devour it. Therefore what was said by Elijah as the word of the Lord must be interpreted in the sense of the word addressed to Moses: "I will blot out that nation,"[14] but he did not blot it out. But consider three [different] meanings here.

The first is that Ahab repents and prays, and God immediately receives his prayer and reconciles with him, and he reveals to Ahab the pardon of his fault through the mediation of the prophet. The benevolence of the Lord toward this impious man is truly admirable, and the friend of humankind also shows his mercifulness toward sinners on many occasions. God forgives the faults of David in the same way, and after he has confessed his sin, he hears from the prophet, "Now the Lord has put away your sin; you shall not die."[15] And [the same happens] to Manasseh, whom he enables to leave his captivity after only a short time and to come back to his kingdom from Babylon.[16]

Second, consider that even though the repentance of Ahab was short, the pardon that he asked for was nonetheless granted immediately. His Lord did not act in this manner with Abraham, to whom he conceded an heir only after a prayer lasting one hundred years. See also how a great fault was forgiven Ahab, while Miriam became a leper for a small error. Recognize, then, that the grace of God, which is incomprehensible, does not allow sinners to waste away in their iniquity, and [God] makes the righteous man thrive by not giving him what he wants immediately and by correcting him without delay. See again how Abraham prayed without receiving anything. He does not make his servants rich, so that they might not grow too proud. In the third place, even though God has freed Ahab, who had been condemned by Elijah, from his sentence, he nonetheless says, "But in his sons' days I will bring the disaster on his house." This means that the merciful judge tried to influence the king to live under his good will, for Ahab was an impul-

sive man who changed his mind quickly and turned from goodness to evil. In addition, [he said these words] so that [Ahab] might invoke mercy for his children and turn from them the sentence pronounced against them. On the First Book of Kings 21.28.[17]

THE RICH ONLY PRETEND TO BE SORRY. AMBROSE: Rich people grow angry and calumniate so that they may do injury if they do not obtain what they desire. But when by their calumny they do cause injury, they pretend they are sorry; yet sad and grief-stricken, as it were, not in heart but in countenance, they set out for the place of the stolen estate and take possession by their unjust and violent procedure. On NABOTH 11.47.[18]

THE PROPER WAY TO WEAR SACKCLOTH AND TO FAST. JEROME: A teacher, if he dismisses a child and does not exact obedience from him, hates him; if, on the other hand, he disciplines him and the remedy cures him, his apparent severity turns out to be clemency. Ahab, too, was censured by the Lord when he killed Naboth and took his vineyard and spilled just blood. Elijah, the prophet, was sent to him to say, "You have killed. Moreover, also you have taken possession." Immediately his conscience struck and tormented him; he bowed his head and walked with eyes downcast; and this is an impious king robed in purple. Afterwards, Scripture says, Ahab went about wearing haircloth under his royal attire, and God, seeing him, said, "Because Ahab has humbled himself for my sake, I will not bring evil against him." Just realize the power of haircloth and of fasting, and how much blood is washed away by humble tears! This, then, is the proper way to wear haircloth and the proper way to fast, that no one may observe it. HOMILIES ON THE PSALMS 51 (Ps 140[141]).[19]

---

[14]Deut 9:14 (Peshitta). [15]2 Sam 12:13. [16]See 2 Chron 33:11-13. [17]ESOO 1:511-12. [18]PSt 15:75-76. [19]FC 48:369.

21:29 *Ahab Has Humbled Himself*

GOD'S UNFAILING JUSTICE. AMBROSE: In this place the question comes up: how do we interpret what the Lord said to Elijah: "Have you seen how Ahab has been moved at my presence? I will not bring evils in his days, but in his sons' days will I bring evils"—or how do we say that repentance avails before God? "Behold, the king was moved before the face of the Lord and went away weeping, and he tore his garments, and covered himself with haircloth and put on sackcloth from that day on which he killed Naboth the Jezrehite,"[20] so that mercy moved God, and he changed his decree. Therefore either repentance did not avail and did not turn God to mercy or the prophecy is false, for Ahab was vanquished and killed. But consider that he had a wife, Jezebel, by whose will he was inflamed and who turned his heart and made him execrable by reason of his excessive sacrileges. Accordingly, she checked even this desire of repentance on his part. But the Lord cannot be considered changeable if he did not think that he ought to keep for the one unmindful of his confession what, at his confessing, he had promised him.

But hear another and truer explanation. Even for him in his unworthiness did the Lord keep the tenor of his decree, but Ahab himself did not hold fast to the divine favors conferred on him. The king of Syria[21] made war.[22] He was defeated and kept for pardon. Although a captive, he was even given his liberty and sent back to his kingdom. It was in keeping with the divine decree that Ahab not only escaped harm but even triumphed; it was due to his own stupid want of firmness that he armed against himself the enemy by whom he was to be conquered. And surely he was warned by the prophet, who said, "Know, and see what you do."[23] He was warned, I say, because the help of divine favor was due against the servants of the king of Syria, since he had said, "The God of the mountains is the God of Israel and not the god Baal. Therefore," he says, "they have conquered us. And therefore," he says, "if we shall not completely overcome them, put satraps in the stead of the king of Syria,"[24] so that he might take from them their valor and the power of the king. Hence in the first battle Ahab was victorious, so that he put his enemy to flight; in the second he was also victorious, in which instance he restored the captured king to his power. For this reason there leaped forth a clear prophecy of Ahab's defeat, one of the sons of the prophets saying to his neighbor, "Strike me. But he would not strike him. And he said, Because you would not obey the word of the Lord, behold, you depart from me, and a lion shall kill you. And he departed from him, and a lion found him and killed him."[25] And after this another prophet stood before the king of Israel and said to him, "Thus said the Lord: Because you have let go out of your hand a man of destruction, behold, your life shall be for his life and your people for his people."[26] It is clear, therefore, from these prophecies that the Lord keeps his promises even to the unworthy but the impious are either destroyed by their own folly or are condemned for a second transgression, though they have escaped the snares of the first. But we should so conduct ourselves that, being worthy through good works, we may deserve to receive the promises of the omnipotent God. ON NABOTH 17.70-73.[27]

---

[20]See 1 Kings 21:27 (VL). [21]Aram; LXX, VL and Vg call Aram "Syria" and the Arameans "Syrians." [22]See 1 Kings 20:1, 20-29. [23]1 Kings 20:22. [24]1 Kings 20:23-24. [25]1 Kings 20:35-36. [26]1 Kings 20:42. [27]PSt 15:99-103*.

22:1-53 THE DEATH OF AHAB

¹For three years Syria and Israel continued without war. ²But in the third year Jehoshaphat the king of Judah came down to the king of Israel. ³And the king of Israel said to his servants, "Do you know that Ramoth-gilead belongs to us, and we keep quiet and do not take it out of the hand of the king of Syria?" ⁴And he said to Jehoshaphat, "Will you go with me to battle at Ramoth-gilead?" And Jehoshaphat said to the king of Israel, "I am as you are, my people as your people, my horses as your horses."

⁵And Jehoshaphat said to the king of Israel, "Inquire first for the word of the LORD." ⁶Then the king of Israel gathered the prophets together, about four hundred men, and said to them, "Shall I go to battle against Ramoth-gilead, or shall I forbear?" And they said, "Go up; for the Lord will give it into the hand of the king." ⁷But Jehoshaphat said, "Is there not here another prophet of the LORD of whom we may inquire?" ⁸And the king of Israel said to Jehoshaphat, "There is yet one man by whom we may inquire of the LORD, Micaiah the son of Imlah; but I hate him, for he never prophesies good concerning me, but evil." And Jehoshaphat said, "Let not the king say so." ⁹Then the king of Israel summoned an officer and said, "Bring quickly Micaiah the son of Imlah." ¹⁰Now the king of Israel and Jehoshaphat the king of Judah were sitting on their thrones, arrayed in their robes, at the threshing floor at the entrance of the gate of Samaria; and all the prophets were prophesying before them. ¹¹And Zedekiah the son of Chenaanah made for himself horns of iron, and said, "Thus says the LORD, 'With these you shall push the Syrians until they are destroyed.'" ¹²And all the prophets prophesied so, and said, "Go up to Ramoth-gilead and triumph; the LORD will give it into the hand of the king."

¹³And the messenger who went to summon Micaiah said to him, "Behold, the words of the prophets with one accord are favorable to the king; let your word be like the word of one of them, and speak favorably." ¹⁴But Micaiah said, "As the LORD lives, what the LORD says to me, that I will speak." ¹⁵And when he had come to the king, the king said to him, "Micaiah, shall we go to Ramoth-gilead to battle, or shall we forbear?" And he answered him, "Go up and triumph; the LORD will give it into the hand of the king." ¹⁶But the king said to him, "How many times shall I adjure you that you speak to me nothing but the truth in the name of the LORD?" ¹⁷And he said, "I saw all Israel scattered upon the mountains, as sheep that have no shepherd; and the LORD said, 'These have no master; let each return to his home in peace.'" ¹⁸And the king of Israel said to Jehoshaphat, "Did I not tell you that he would not prophesy good concerning me, but evil?" ¹⁹And Micaiah said, "Therefore hear the word of the LORD: I saw the LORD sitting on his throne, and all the host of heaven standing beside him on his right hand and on his left; ²⁰and the LORD said, 'Who will entice Ahab, that he may go up and fall at Ramoth-gilead?' And one said one thing, and another said another. ²¹Then a spirit came forward and stood before the LORD, saying, 'I will entice him.' ²²And the LORD said to him, 'By what means?' And he said, 'I will go forth, and will

be a lying spirit in the mouth of all his prophets.' And he said, 'You are to entice him, and you shall succeed; go forth and do so.' ²³Now therefore behold, the LORD has put a lying spirit in the mouth of all these your prophets; the LORD has spoken evil concerning you."

²⁴Then Zedekiah the son of Chenaanah came near and struck Micaiah on the cheek, and said, "How did the Spirit of the LORD go from me to speak to you?" ²⁵And Micaiah said, "Behold, you shall see on that day when you go into an inner chamber to hide yourself." ²⁶And the king of Israel said, "Seize Micaiah, and take him back to Amon the governor of the city and to Joash the king's son; ²⁷and say, 'Thus says the king, "Put this fellow in prison, and feed him with scant fare of bread and water, until I come in peace."'" ²⁸And Micaiah said, "If you return in peace, the LORD has not spoken by me." And he said, "Hear, all you peoples!"

²⁹So the king of Israel and Jehoshaphat the king of Judah went up to Ramoth-gilead. ³⁰And the king of Israel said to Jehoshaphat, "I will disguise myself and go into battle, but you wear your robes." And the king of Israel disguised himself and went into battle. ³¹Now the king of Syria had commanded the thirty-two captains of his chariots, "Fight with neither small nor great, but only with the king of Israel." ³²And when the captains of the chariots saw Jehoshaphat, they said, "It is surely the king of Israel." So they turned to fight against him; and Jehoshaphat cried out. ³³And when the captains of the chariots saw that it was not the king of Israel, they turned back from pursuing him. ³⁴But a certain man drew his bow at a venture, and struck the king of Israel between the scale armor and the breastplate; therefore he said to the driver of his chariot, "Turn about, and carry me out of the battle, for I am wounded." ³⁵And the battle grew hot that day, and the king was propped up in his chariot facing the Syrians, until at evening he died; and the blood of the wound flowed into the bottom of the chariot. ³⁶And about sunset a cry went through the army, "Every man to his city, and every man to his country!"

³⁷So the king died, and was brought to Samaria; and they buried the king in Samaria. ³⁸And they washed the chariot by the pool of Samaria, and the dogs licked up his blood, and the harlots washed themselves in it, according to the word of the LORD which he had spoken. ³⁹Now the rest of the acts of Ahab, and all that he did, and the ivory house which he built, and all the cities that he built, are they not written in the Book of the Chronicles of the Kings of Israel? ⁴⁰So Ahab slept with his fathers; and Ahaziah his son reigned in his stead.

⁴¹Jehoshaphat the son of Asa began to reign over Judah in the fourth year of Ahab king of Israel. ⁴²Jehoshaphat was thirty-five years old when he began to reign, and he reigned twenty-five years in Jerusalem. His mother's name was Azubah the daughter of Shilhi. ⁴³He walked in all the way of Asa his father; he did not turn aside from it, doing what was right in the sight of the LORD; yet the high places were not taken away, and the people still sacrificed and burned incense on the high places. ⁴⁴Jehoshaphat also made peace with the king of Israel.

⁴⁵Now the rest of the acts of Jehoshaphat, and his might that he showed, and how he warred, are they not written in the Book of the Chronicles of the Kings of Judah? ⁴⁶And the remnant of the male cult prostitutes who remained in the days of his father Asa, he exterminated from the land.

⁴⁷There was no king in Edom; a deputy was king. ⁴⁸Jehoshaphat made ships of Tarshish to go to

Ophir for gold; but they did not go, for the ships were wrecked at Ezion-geber. ⁴⁹Then Ahaziah the son of Ahab said to Jehoshaphat, "Let my servants go with your servants in the ships," but Jehoshaphat was not willing. ⁵⁰And Jehoshaphat slept with his fathers, and was buried with his fathers in the city of David his father; and Jehoram his son reigned in his stead.

⁵¹Ahaziah the son of Ahab began to reign over Israel in Samaria in the seventeenth year of Jehoshaphat king of Judah, and he reigned two years over Israel. ⁵²He did what was evil in the sight of the Lord, and walked in the way of his father, and in the way of his mother, and in the way of Jeroboam the son of Nebat, who made Israel to sin. ⁵³He served Baal and worshiped him, and provoked the Lord, the God of Israel, to anger in every way that his father had done.

OVERVIEW: The words of the prophet are an invitation to refrain from fighting, but the king is not able to understand them (WALAFRIDIUS STRABO). The host of heaven indicates the angelic powers, both good and evil, who are all subject to the rule of the Lord (RABANUS MAURUS). No prophet ever saw God's essence in its pure state, because each one saw him in a different way (CHRYSOSTOM). The spirit who came forward and stood before the Lord is Michael, the leader of the people (ISHO'DAD). If any spirit is a lying spirit, all similar spirits would be lying spirits in accordance with their falsehood (ORIGEN). The Spirit who stood before God was an evil spirit, because no liar is without an evil spirit (CAESARIUS). The predictions of Elijah about Ahab's death were not entirely fulfilled, as he died in battle but his corpse was not devoured by wild beasts (EPHREM).

22:17 Israel Scattered Like Sheep Without a Shepherd

AN INVITATION TO REFRAIN FROM FIGHTING. WALAFRIDIUS STRABO: "I saw all Israel scattered on the mountains, like sheep that have no shepherd; and the Lord said, 'These have no master; let each one go home in peace.'" Through these words [the prophet] shows that [Ahab's] iniquity is the cause of the slaughter. In fact, if he had been a good and pious shepherd, he would have defeated his enemies with his own forces. Therefore, he shows the way to obtain salvation. "If the Lord is our God," he says to them, "each one

must go home in peace. If you believe in God and want to know from him what you need to do, dismiss the army." GLOSSA ORDINARIA, THIRD BOOK OF KINGS 22.17.[1]

22:19 The Lord with the Host of Heaven

THE ELECT AND THE EVIL ANGELS. RABANUS MAURUS: How should we interpret the "throne of God" but as the angelic powers over whose minds the Lord presides from on high while he arranges everything below? And what does the "host of heaven" signify but the multitude of the attending angels? And what does the text mean when it asserts that the host of heaven is to the right and to the left of him? Indeed God, who is within everything as he is also outside everything, is not enclosed to the right or the left, and therefore the right of God indicates the elect portion of the angels, whereas the left designates the evil portion of the angels. In fact, not only the good ones who help God serve him, but so do those who are distressed because they do not want to return [to be helpful]. . . . Therefore the host of the angels is to the right and to the left, because the will of the elect spirit agrees with the divine sense of justice. Therefore the mind of the evil ones, who serve their own malice is forced to fulfill the orders [of the Lord]. COMMENTARY ON THE THIRD BOOK OF KINGS 22.[2]

---

[1]PL 113:610. [2]PL 109:219.

No One Has Ever Seen God's Essence.
JOHN CHRYSOSTOM: Tell me, John, what do you mean when you say, "No one has ever seen God"?[3] What shall we think about the prophets who say that they saw God? Isaiah said, "I saw the Lord sitting on a high and exalted throne."[4] And, again, Daniel said, "I saw until the thrones were set, and the ancient of days sat."[5] And Micah said, "I saw the God of Israel sitting on his throne." And, again, another prophet said, "I saw the Lord standing on the altar, and he said to me, 'strike the mercy seat.'"[6] And I can gather together many similar passages to show you as witnesses of what I say. How is it, then, that John says, "No one has ever seen God"?[7] He says this so that you may know that he is speaking of a clear knowledge and perfect comprehension of God. All the cases cited were instances of God's condescension and accommodation. That no one of those prophets saw God's essence in its pure state is clear from the fact that each one saw him in a different way. God is a simple being; he is not composed of parts; he is without form or figure. But all these prophets saw different forms and figures. AGAINST THE ANOMOEANS 4.18-19.[8]

22:21-22 I Will Entice Him

Intervention of the Angel Michael.
ISHO'DAD OF MERV: The "spirit" who "came forward and stood [before the Lord]" is an angel and not an evil spirit, namely, Satan, as certain [authors] suggest.[9] In fact, why would an evil spirit stand before the Lord? On the contrary, this spirit is Michael, the leader of the people. It is he who says in his zeal, "I will entice him," that is, "Allow me to leave and abandon the prophets of lies, instead of hindering them, as I have done many times, in order to stop and prevent their false prophecies. As a consequence, the destiny of Ahab will be according to what justice requires, because he will obey [his false prophets] with all his heart, if I do not prevent this." BOOKS OF SESSIONS 1 KINGS 22.20.[10]

All the Words of Evil Spirits Are Lies.
ORIGEN: I think every evil and deceitful spirit is a lie, and whenever anyone of these speaks, it speaks from its own resources and by no means from the resources of God. And the father of these [spirits] is the liar, the devil. We will now present what moved us to say that every inferior spirit is false. It is written in the third book of Kings that at the time Micaiah was called by Ahab to prophesy concerning whether he should go to Ramoth-gilead for war or stay, he said, "I saw the God of Israel sitting on his throne, and all the host of heaven stood around him on his right and on his left. And he said, 'Who will deceive Ahab, king of Israel, and he will go up and fall in Ramoth-gilead?'" And he spoke in this manner. And a spirit came forth and stood before the Lord and said, "I will deceive him." And the Lord said to him, "By what means?" And he said, "I will go forth and will be a false spirit in the mouth of all these prophets of yours.'"

And in the second book of Paralipomenon, the same Micaiah says to Ahab and Jehoshaphat, "Hear the word of the Lord. I saw the Lord sitting on his throne, and every power of heaven stood at his right and at his left. And the Lord said, 'Who will deceive Ahab, king of Israel, and he will go up and fall in Ramoth-gilead?'" And he spoke in this manner. And a spirit came forth and stood before the Lord and said, "I will deceive him." And the Lord said, "By what means?" And he said, "I will go forth and be a false spirit in the mouth of all his prophets."[11]

These words show clearly, then, that if any spirit is the lying spirit, all similar spirits would be lying spirits, indebted to their lying father for being lying spirits in accordance with their falsehood and evil, not because this belongs to their essence. COMMENTARY ON THE GOSPEL OF JOHN 20.257-62.[12]

---

[3]Jn 1:18. [4]Is 6:1. [5]Dan 7:9. [6]Amos 9:1 (LXX). [7]Jn 1:18. [8]FC 72:122. [9]Isho'dad is referring to unknown exegetical sources. [10]CSCO 229:128. [11]2 Chron 18:18-21. [12]FC 89:259-60.

NO SIN IS COMMITTED WITHOUT THE DEVIL'S PROMPTING. CAESARIUS OF ARLES: Perhaps someone says, "How can it happen that one who sins in his flesh by dissipation possesses the devil in his soul?" What we have said, dearly beloved, we will prove with evidence from sacred Scripture. Listen to the Scriptures saying that the proud person is filled with the devil: "Everyone who exalts his own heart is unclean in the sight of God,"[13] and "All pride is the beginning of falling off from God."[14] What does it mean to fall from God, except to depart from him? Moreover, if a person is separated from God, he is necessarily united to the devil. Furthermore, Scripture says that the envious person cannot be without a devil: "By the envy of the devil, death came into the world, and they follow him that are of his side."[15] The canonical writings attest no less that the fornicator is also enslaved by the devil, for the prophet says, "You have been deceived by the spirit of fornication."[16] The fact that no liar can be without an evil spirit is evidenced by Scripture, too: "You will destroy all that speak a lie,"[17] and again: "The mouth that belies kills the soul."[18] In the book of Kings we read that the evil spirit said to the Lord, "I will deceive Ahab." And the Lord said to him, "By what means?" And he answered, "I will go forth and be a lying spirit in the mouth of his prophets." And the Lord said, "You shall deceive him and shall prevail." We should believe that the case is similar with all the other serious sins and offenses, because no one commits them without the devil's prompting. SERMON 79.2.[19]

22:37 Ahab Died and Was Buried in Samaria

ELIJAH'S PREDICTION WAS NOT ENTIRELY FULFILLED. EPHREM THE SYRIAN: You see, not all the humiliations with which Elijah had threatened Ahab were accomplished, thanks to [the king's] profound repentance, nor was Ahab's corpse devoured by birds or wild beasts.[20] Instead he was brought to the royal palace in Samaria, and there, after being celebrated with regal magnificence, was solemnly buried. Ahab died in that battle, which Micaiah had predicted to be fatal and deadly to him, even though he did not die on the battlefield but was taken away from there and survived for several hours, before he finally died in the evening. Therefore it seems clear that the dogs were not prevented from licking the blood that flowed on that day and night from his wound. ON THE FIRST BOOK OF KINGS 22.37.[21]

---

[13]Prov 16:5. [14]See Prov 16:18. [15]Wis 2:24. [16]Hos 4:12. [17]Ps 5:6 (5:7 LXX, Vg). [18]Wis 1:11. [19]FC 31:364-65*. [20]See 1 Kings 21:24. [21]ESOO 1:514.

2 KINGS

1:1-18 ELIJAH PREDICTS
THE DEATH OF AHAZIAH

¹*After the death of Ahab, Moab rebelled against Israel.*

²*Now Ahaziah fell through the lattice in his upper chamber in Samaria, and lay sick; so he sent messengers, telling them, "Go, inquire of Baal-zebub, the god of Ekron, whether I shall recover from this sickness."* ³*But the angel of the LORD said to Elijah the Tishbite, "Arise, go up to meet the messengers of the king of Samaria, and say to them, 'Is it because there is no God in Israel that you are going to inquire of Baal-zebub, the god of Ekron?'* ⁴*Now therefore thus says the LORD, 'You shall not come down from the bed to which you have gone, but you shall surely die.'" So Elijah went.*

⁵*The messengers returned to the king, and he said to them, "Why have you returned?"* ⁶*And they said to him, "There came a man to meet us, and said to us, 'Go back to the king who sent you, and say to him, Thus says the LORD, Is it because there is no God in Israel that you are sending to inquire of Baal-zebub, the god of Ekron? Therefore you shall not come down from the bed to which you have gone, but shall surely die.'"* ⁷*He said to them, "What kind of man was he who came to meet you and told you these things?"* ⁸*They answered him, "He wore a garment of haircloth, with a girdle of leather about his loins." And he said, "It is Elijah the Tishbite."*

⁹*Then the king sent to him a captain of fifty men with his fifty. He went up to Elijah, who was sitting on the top of a hill, and said to him, "O man of God, the king says, 'Come down.'"* ¹⁰*But Elijah answered the captain of fifty, "If I am a man of God, let fire come down from heaven and consume you and your fifty." Then fire came down from heaven, and consumed him and his fifty.*

¹¹*Again the king sent to him another captain of fifty men with his fifty. And he went up*ᵃ *and said to him, "O man of God, this is the king's order, 'Come down quickly!'"* ¹²*But Elijah answered them, "If I am a man of God, let fire come down from heaven and consume you and your fifty." Then the fire of God came down from heaven and consumed him and his fifty.*

¹³*Again the king sent the captain of a third fifty with his fifty. And the third captain of fifty went up, and came and fell on his knees before Elijah, and entreated him, "O man of God, I pray you, let my life, and the life of these fifty servants of yours, be precious in your sight.* ¹⁴*Lo, fire came down from heaven, and consumed the two former captains of fifty men with their fifties; but now*

let my life be precious in your sight." [15]*Then the angel of the* Lord *said to Elijah, "Go down with him; do not be afraid of him." So he arose and went down with him to the king,* [16]*and said to him, "Thus says the* Lord, *'Because you have sent messengers to inquire of Baal-zebub, the god of Ekron,—is it because there is no God in Israel to inquire of his word?—therefore you shall not come down from the bed to which you have gone, but you shall surely die.'"*

[17]*So he died according to the word of the* Lord *which Elijah had spoken. Jehoram,* * *his brother,* [b] *became king in his stead in the second year of Jehoram the son of Jehoshaphat, king of Judah, because Ahaziah had no son.* [18]*Now the rest of the acts of Ahaziah which he did, are they not written in the Book of the Chronicles of the Kings of Israel?*

a Gk Compare verses 9, 13: Heb *answered*   **b** Gk Syr: Heb lacks *his brother*   *Both Jehoram and Joram are simply variants of the same name. To add to the confusion, kings of the same name in Israel and Judah were contemporaries. Jehoram king of Judah (ca. 848-841 B.C.) was the son of Ahab and brother of Ahaziah, who reigned before him without an heir. Readers must give close attention to context in order to discern which king is actually being discussed, though the form Joram more frequently, though not exclusively, refers to the king of Israel.

Overview: Ahaziah follows his father, Ahab, in the practice of idolatry and complies with the impiety of his mother, Jezebel, so that he is punished by God (Ephrem). In the days of the Old Testament, any crimes or offenses committed among the people were ordered to be physically punished. Since the two captains did not give Elijah honor as an old man or reverence him as a prophet, the Holy Spirit spoke through the mouth of the prophet, and they were struck down by a blow sent from heaven (Caesarius). The third captain humbly kneels down before Elijah and repeats the order of the king but gives him the option either to obey or not obey the word of the king. Ahaziah was childless, so that his brother Jehoram became the new king, even though the law did not prescribe this kind of succession, which the Jews borrowed from the Gentile nations (Ephrem).

1:2-4 Inquire of Baal-zebub

Ahaziah Is Punished with Death for His Idolatry. Ephrem the Syrian: "Ahaziah falls from the gallery of his upper chamber in Samaria." . . . Ahaziah is the son of Ahab, and after Ahab's death he takes his place and reigns over his people. Now, he falls from the upper chambers of his palace, and his body is seriously

injured. Therefore Ahaziah sends some messengers to the god of the Ekronites in order to question him about his injury. It seems that such a piece of advice was given to him by his mother, Jezebel, who for her entire life made her children, namely, Ahaziah and Joram, her slaves, just like Ahab, her husband, had been a slave to her. Ahaziah's present action, as well as what his brother did after him—their shameful end and the hardness of their heart in the adoration of their idols until their death—are perfectly in keeping with the abominable actions and wicked will of their mother, Jezebel. So, Elijah, who had learned from a vigilant [i.e., an angel] what Ahaziah was doing, came out to meet his messengers and ordered them, by the word of the Lord, to return to their master and announce to him the news of his departure from this world, because he had rejected the Lord and had taken refuge in the god of Ekron, hoping that he would heal him. On the Second Book of Kings 1.1.[1]

1:9-14 Fire from Heaven

Physical Punishment for the Salvation of the Soul. Caesarius of Arles: These

[1]*ESOO* 1:517.

wretched men[2] are apt to censure the writings of the Old Testament saying, "How was it just for blessed Elijah to burn two captains with their soldiers by means of fire brought down from heaven?" How justly and mercifully this was done, dearly beloved, we want to indicate briefly to your hearts. In the days of the Old Testament, any crimes or offenses committed among the people were ordered to be physically punished. Thus it is written, "Eye for eye, tooth for tooth."[3] Indeed, some were punished in order that the rest might fear bodily punishment and refrain from sins and offenses. Now, in the time of the prophet, blessed Elijah, all the Jewish people had abandoned God and were sacrificing to idols, not only refusing to honor God's prophets but even very frequently trying to kill them. For this reason blessed Elijah was aroused with zeal for God and caused some to be punished physically, so that those who had neglected the salvation of their souls might be healed in heart by fearing bodily death. We should consider that not so much blessed Elijah as the Holy Spirit did this. We know that the same thing was done through blessed Peter in the case of Ananias and Sapphira, for through him they incurred the destruction of death themselves in order that an example might be given to the rest. Therefore, as it is written, "Great fear seized all who heard of this."[4] Examples are given to everyone whenever punishments are inflicted on sinners. Because the Jews thought only of their body and refused to be solicitous for the salvation of their soul, with God as judge they suffered punishment in the very body to which they had devoted so much care. SERMON 125.1.[5]

THE SIN OF PRIDE. CAESARIUS OF ARLES: Now if you consider well, dearly beloved, you will realize that not only the Jewish people fell through pride, but also those two captains perished from the same weakness. With great pride and arrogance but lacking any humility, the latter came to blessed Elijah and said, "Man of God, the king summons you." Because they did

not give him honor as an old man or reverence as a prophet, the Holy Spirit spoke through the mouth of the prophet, and they were struck down by a blow sent from heaven. The third captain, however, coming with great humility and contrition, as was proper, pleaded in a tearful voice and not only merited to escape punishment but even induced blessed Elijah to condescend to go to the king. All this, dearly beloved, happened for the salvation of all the people, since the good and merciful Lord struck a few people in order that he might heal them all. SERMON 125.2.[6]

HUMBLENESS AFTER THE FIRE. EPHREM THE SYRIAN: But the stubborn king did not fear the word of the prophet and said in his heart, "He lies." And so he did not pay attention to his warning, which exhorted him to get rid of the reason of his evils and to repent. He persevered in his stubbornness and, instead of repenting of his pride and being converted, grew more stubborn and sent a captain of fifty with some guards to arrest the prophet of God and lead him to the tribunal. Now, after hearing that the fire had come down and had consumed the captain with his fifty men on the occasion of their effrontery, he sent some others, and again the fire consumed them and made them perish. And [divine] justice decrees this sentence quite rightly, because those who had seen the fire, which had come down at the prayer of Elijah, and had not believed or were converted, were necessarily scorched by the second descent of the fire. And the same punishment was prepared for the third one, who was sent after them, if the terrifying spectacle of the fire had not made him wise. He avoids appearing like his comrades: he arrives after the prophet, humbly kneels down before him and, on the one hand, repeats the order of the king, but on the

---

[2]Caesarius is referring to the Manichaeans, who maintained, like Marcion, that the God of the Old Testament was an inferior divine being (a demiurge), or even a cruel deity, who had formed the world with the darkness of evil. [3]Exod 21:24. [4]Acts 5:11. [5]FC 47:214-15*. [6]FC 47:215.

other, gives him the option whether to obey the word of the king or not. ON THE SECOND BOOK OF KINGS 1.1.[7]

1:17-18 Jehoram Succeeded Ahaziah as King

THE SUCCESSORS OF AHAZIAH. EPHREM THE SYRIAN: After the death of Ahaziah, since he had no children who could inherit the kingdom, his brother Jehoram became king. This did not occur because the Law prescribed anything of the sort, but because this was the custom of their neighbors, which the children of Israel had observed by now for many years. But God gives another rule

for the kingdom of the children of Judah: he binds them to the family of David, and it is in this manner that the kingship was constantly transmitted from the father to the son or the next of kin—but they refused this succession only once, at the time of Jechonias,[8] who became king after Zedekiah,[9] brother of his father, because Jechonias was deported to Babel and Zedekiah was forced to take his place and stop the fall of the monarchy. ON THE SECOND BOOK OF KINGS 1.15.[10]

---

[7]ESOO 1:517-18. [8]Or Jehoiachin; see 2 Kings 24:8. [9]See 2 Kings 24:18; 2 Chron 36:11. [10]ESOO 1:518.

2:1-14 THE LORD TAKES ELIJAH TO HEAVEN

[1]Now when the LORD was about to take Elijah up to heaven by a whirlwind, Elijah and Elisha were on their way from Gilgal. [2]And Elijah said to Elisha, "Tarry here, I pray you; for the LORD has sent me as far as Bethel." But Elisha said, "As the LORD lives, and as you yourself live, I will not leave you." So they went down to Bethel. [3]And the sons of the prophets who were in Bethel came out to Elisha, and said to him, "Do you know that today the LORD will take away your master from over you?" And he said, "Yes, I know it; hold your peace."

[4]Elijah said to him, "Elisha, tarry here, I pray you; for the LORD has sent me to Jericho." But he said, "As the LORD lives, and as you yourself live, I will not leave you." So they came to Jericho. [5]The sons of the prophets who were at Jericho drew near to Elisha, and said to him, "Do you know that today the LORD will take away your master from over you?" And he answered, "Yes, I know it; hold your peace."

[6]Then Elijah said to him, "Tarry here, I pray you; for the LORD has sent me to the Jordan." But he said, "As the LORD lives, and as you yourself live, I will not leave you." So the two of them went on. [7]Fifty men of the sons of the prophets also went, and stood at some distance from them, as they both were standing by the Jordan. [8]Then Elijah took his mantle, and rolled it up, and struck the water, and the water was parted to the one side and to the other, till the two of them could go over on dry ground.

[9]When they had crossed, Elijah said to Elisha, "Ask what I shall do for you, before I am taken from you." And Elisha said, "I pray you, let me inherit a double share of your spirit." [10]And he

said, "You have asked a hard thing; yet, if you see me as I am being taken from you, it shall be so for you; but if you do not see me, it shall not be so." [11]*And as they still went on and talked, behold, a chariot of fire and horses of fire separated the two of them. And Elijah went up by a whirlwind into heaven.* [12]*And Elisha saw it and he cried, "My father, my father! the chariots of Israel and its horsemen!" And he saw him no more.*

Then he took hold of his own clothes and rent them in two pieces. [13]*And he took up the mantle of Elijah that had fallen from him, and went back and stood on the bank of the Jordan.* [14]*Then he took the mantle of Elijah that had fallen from him, and struck the water, saying, "Where is the* LORD, *the God of Elijah?" And when he had struck the water, the water was parted to the one side and to the other; and Elisha went over.*

OVERVIEW: In spite of Elijah's invitation to stop and stay in Gilgal, Elisha follows him first to Bethel and then on the way to Jericho (EPHREM). Elijah was better prepared to be taken up to heaven after crossing the Jordan, since in 1 Corinthians 10:2 Paul calls this incredible passage through water a baptism (ORIGEN). God is everywhere wholly present in himself, not in things of which some have a greater capacity for him, others less (AUGUSTINE). Elijah left a double portion of grace and sanctity to Elisha, although he himself had a single spirit of holiness (MAXIMUS). The word of Elijah came as a preparatory discipline to the people prepared by it, that they might be trained for the reception of the perfect Word (ORIGEN). When Elijah was raised up to the heavens, he let the cloak with which he had been clothed fall to Elisha; when our Lord ascended into heaven, he left the mysteries of the humanity he had assumed to his disciples (BEDE). Relieved of bodily weight by continuous fasting, Elijah flew to heaven as victor over death (CHRYSOLOGUS).

2:1-7 Stay Here

ELISHA REFUSES TO OBEY ELIJAH. EPHREM THE SYRIAN: Elijah, who now lived with Elisha, whom he had also consecrated as prophet according to a divine oracle, as has been said already, was with him every day, inseparably sharing with him the same way of life. When he was about to ascend into the chariots of fire, to leave and be raised to the clouds with that physical mass that drags us to the ground, after he had already crossed Gilgal and was going to reach Bethel, he ordered Elisha to stay in Gilgal. But Elisha did not obey him nor would he separate from him because those words carried him instead of completely imprisoning him. That is why, after all, Elijah took him with him. When both had reached Bethel, where they spent a few days, and Elijah was planning again to visit Jericho by himself, he ordered Elisha not to come along with him for the second time. But just as before, he continued to be disobedient and stubborn, as if he felt torn at the thought of being cut off from his master. Since he did not know what to do, Elijah consented to go again with him. Fifty more followed them. These were the sons of the prophets. ON THE SECOND BOOK OF KINGS 2.2-5.[1]

2:8-9 Elijah Struck the Water with His Mantle

ELIJAH AND ELISHA WERE BAPTIZED IN THE JORDAN. ORIGEN: We must note in addition that when Elijah was about to be taken up in a whirlwind as into heaven, he took his sheepskin and rolled it up and struck the water, and it was divided on this side and that, and both crossed, that is to say, himself and Elisha. He was better

---

[1]ESOO 1:518-19.

prepared to be taken up after he was baptized in the Jordan, since Paul, as we explained previously, called the more incredible passage through water a baptism.[2] It is because of this same Jordan that Elisha is capable of receiving the gift that he has desired through Elijah, for he said, "Let a double portion come on me in your spirit." Perhaps he received the gift in the spirit of Elijah in a double measure on himself because he crossed the Jordan twice, once with Elijah, and a second time when he took the sheepskin of Elijah and struck the water and said, "Where is the Lord, the God of Elijah? And he struck the waters, and they divided on this side and that." COMMENTARY ON THE GOSPEL OF JOHN 6.238-39.[3]

GOD IS EVERYWHERE WHOLLY PRESENT IN HIMSELF. AUGUSTINE: Therefore, he who is everywhere does not dwell in all, and he does not even dwell equally in those in whom he does dwell. Otherwise, what is the meaning of the request made by Elisha that there might be in him double the Spirit of God that was in Elijah? And how is it that among the saints some are more holy than others, except that they have a more abundant indwelling in God? How, then, did we speak the truth when we said above that God is everywhere wholly present if he is more amply present in some, less in others? But it should be noticed with care that we said he is everywhere wholly present in himself, not in things of which some have a greater capacity for him, others less. LETTER 187.17.[4]

2:10 Asking a Hard Thing

A DOUBLE PORTION OF GRACE. MAXIMUS OF TURIN: Angels bring Elijah to heaven, then, and angels watch over Elisha on earth. What is there to wonder at if angels, who carried away the master, protected the disciple? And what is noteworthy in the fact that the deference that they showed to the father they also manifested to the son? For he is the spiritual son of Elijah; he is the inheritor of his holiness. Justifiably is Elisha

called the spiritual son of Elijah because when he went up to heaven Elijah left a double spirit of his grace to him. For when Elisha was given the right to ask for whatever he wanted before Elijah would be taken from him, he asked that a double portion of Elijah might be in him. Then Elijah said, "What you have asked is hard, but so it shall be for you." O precious inheritance in which the inheritor is left more than is possessed and the one who receives obtains more than the giver owned! Clearly this is a precious inheritance that is doubled by a kind of meritorious interest when it is transferred from father to son. Elijah, therefore, left a double portion to Elisha, although he himself had a single spirit of holiness. In a marvelous way, then, Elijah left more grace on earth than he carried with him to heaven. SERMON 84.2.[5]

2:11-14 Elijah Ascended into Heaven

ELIJAH PREPARED THE WORLD TO RECEIVE THE DIVINE DOCTRINE OF CHRIST. ORIGEN: But do not marvel in regard to what is said about Elijah, if, just as something strange happened to him different from all the saints who are recorded, in respect of his having been caught up by a whirlwind into heaven, so his spirit had something of choice excellence, so that not only did it rest on Elisha but also descended along with John at his birth; and that John, separately, "was filled with the Holy Spirit even from his mother's womb," and separately "came before Christ in the spirit and power of Elijah."[6] For it is possible for several spirits not only worse, but also better, to be in the same person. David accordingly asks to be established by a free spirit[7] and that a right spirit be renewed in his inward parts.[8] But if, in order that the Savior may impart to us of the "spirit of wisdom and understanding, the spirit of counsel and might, the spirit of knowledge and reverence,"[9] he was filled also with

---

[2]1 Cor 10:2. [3]FC 80:233. [4]FC 30:233-34. [5]ACW 50:201. [6]Lk 1:15, 17. [7]See Ps 51:12 (50:14 LXX). [8]See Ps 51:10 (50:12 LXX). [9]Is 11:2.

the spirit of the fear of the Lord; it is possible also that these several good spirits may be conceived as being in the person. And this also we have brought forward, because of John having come before Christ "in the spirit and power of Elijah,"[10] in order that the saying "Elijah has already come"[11] may be referred to the spirit of Elijah that was in John; as also the three disciples who had gone up with him understood that he spoke to them about John the Baptist.[12] On Elisha, then, only the spirit of Elijah rested, but John came before, not only in the spirit but also in the power of Elijah. Wherefore, also, Elisha could not have been called Elijah, but John was Elijah himself. But if it is necessary to adduce the Scripture from which the scribes said that Elijah must first come, listen to Malachi, who says, "And behold, I will send to you Elijah the Tishbite," down to the words "Lest I come and strike the earth utterly."[13] And it seems to be indicated by these words that Elijah was to prepare for the glorious coming of Christ by certain holy words and dispositions in their souls, those who had been made fittest for this, which those on earth could not have endured, because of the excellence of the glory, unless they had been prepared beforehand by Elijah. And likewise, by Elijah, in this place, I do not understand the soul of that prophet but his spirit and his power; for these it is by which all things shall be restored, so that when they have been restored, and, as a result of that restoration, become capable of receiving the glory of Christ, the Son of God who shall appear in glory may sojourn with them. But if also Elijah is in some sort a word inferior to "the word who was in the beginning with God, God the Word,"[14] this word also might come as a preparatory discipline to the people prepared by it, that they might be trained for the reception of the perfect Word. COMMENTARY ON THE GOSPEL OF MATTHEW 13.2.[15]

A GLORIOUS TYPE OF THE ASCENSION OF THE SAVIOR. BEDE: The prophets proclaimed the mystery of the Lord's ascension not only by their words but also by their actions. Both Enoch, the seventh [in the line of descent] from Adam,[16] who was transported from the world,[17] and Elijah, who was taken up into heaven, gave evidence that the Lord would ascend above all the heavens. . . .

Elijah presented an image of this festivity of the Lord by a miracle with richer significance. When the time in which he was to be taken away from the world was near, he came to the river Jordan with his disciple Elisha. With his rolled-up cloak he struck the waters, they were divided, and both of them crossed over on dry land. And he said to Elisha, "Ask what you want me to do before I am taken away from you," and Elisha said, "I entreat you that your spirit may become double in me." As they went on conversing together, behold, Elijah was suddenly snatched away, and, as the Scripture says, "He ascended as if into heaven." By this action of his soaring aloft it is meant that [Elijah] was not taken up into heaven itself, as was our Lord, but into the height of the air [above the earth], from where he was borne invisibly to the joys of paradise. Elisha took up the cloak of Elijah that had fallen from him; and, coming to the river Jordan, he struck the water with it, and after calling on God, he divided the water and crossed over.

Let your love take note, my brothers, how the symbolic event agrees point by point with its fulfillment. Elijah came to the river Jordan, and having laid aside his cloak, he struck the waters and divided them. The Lord came to the stream of death, in which the human race ordinarily was immersed, and laying aside from himself for a time the clothing of flesh that he had assumed, struck down death by dying and opened up for us the way to life by rising. The change and decline of our mortal life is properly represented by the river Jordan, since the meaning of Jordan in Latin is "their descent," and since as the river flows into the Dead Sea, it loses its praiseworthy waters. After [the water of the river] Jordan was divided,

---

[10]Lk 1:17. [11]Mt 17:12. [12]Mt 17:13. [13]Mal 4:5-6. [14]Jn 1:1. [15]ANF 9:476. [16]See Gen 5:6-18. [17]See Gen 5:24.

Elijah and Elisha crossed over on dry land; by his rising from the dead the Savior bestowed on his faithful ones the hope of rising too. After they had crossed over the river Jordan, Elijah gave Elisha the option of asking for what he wanted. The Lord too, after the glory of his resurrection had been fulfilled, implanted in his disciples a fuller comprehension of what he had promised previously, that "whatever you ask in my name, I will do [for you]."[18] Elisha asked that the spirit of Elijah might become double in him. The disciples, thoroughly instructed by the Lord, desired to receive the promised gift of the Spirit, which would make them capable of preaching not only to the single nation of Judah, which he himself taught when he was present in the flesh, but to all countries throughout the globe as well. Did he not pledge the double grace of his Spirit when he said, "A person who believes in me will himself also do the works that I do, and he will do even greater ones than these"? As Elijah and Elisha were conversing together, a chariot with fiery horses suddenly snatched Elijah as if into heaven. By the chariot and fiery horses we are to understand the angelic powers, of whom it is written, "He makes the angels his spirits and his ministers a burning fire"[19] (Elijah, being an ordinary human being, had need of them to be raised up from the earth). The Lord too was suddenly taken up as he was speaking with his apostles and as they were looking on; although he was not assisted by the help of angels, he was served by an angelic band of companions. He was truly assumed into heaven with the angels also bearing witness to it, for they said [to the apostles], "This Jesus who has been taken up from you into heaven."[20] When Elijah was raised up to the heavens, he let the cloak with which he had been clothed fall to Elisha. When our Lord ascended into heaven, he left the mysteries of the humanity he had assumed to his disciples, to the entire church in fact, so that it could be sanctified by them and warmed by the power of his love. Elisha took up Elijah's cloak and struck the waters of the river Jordan with it; and when he called on the God of Elijah, [the waters] were divided, and he crossed over. The apostles and the entire church took up the sacraments of their Redeemer that had been instituted through the apostles, so that, spiritually guided by them and cleansed and consecrated by them, they too learned to overcome death's assaults by calling on the name of God the Father and to cross over to undying life, spurning the obstacles of death. HOMILIES ON THE GOSPELS 2.15.[21]

ELIJAH WAS RELIEVED OF BODILY WEIGHT BY FASTING. PETER CHRYSOLOGUS: A burdened stomach drags down the heart toward vices and depresses the mind to keep it unable to experience heavenly piety. Scripture tells us, "The corruptible body is a load on the soul, and the earthly habitation presses down the mind that muses on many things."[22] Hence, the Lord said, too, "Take heed lest your hearts be overburdened with self-indulgence and drunkenness."[23] Therefore, the stomach should be relieved by the tempering influence of a fast, so that the mind can be unburdened and attend to higher things, rise to virtues and like a winged bird fly in its entirety to the very Author of piety. The case of Elijah proves this. Relieved of bodily weight by continuing that fast that the Lord arranged, he flew to heaven as victor over death. SERMON 2.[24]

---

[18]Jn 15:16. [19]Ps 104:4 (103:4 LXX, Vg). [20]Acts 1:11. [21]CS 111:144-47. [22]Wis 9:15. [23]Lk 21:34. [24]FC 17:30-31.

2:15-25 ELISHA IS ACKNOWLEDGED
TO BE ELIJAH'S SUCCESSOR

¹⁵Now when the sons of the prophets who were at Jericho saw him over against them, they said, "The spirit of Elijah rests on Elisha." And they came to meet him, and bowed to the ground before him. ¹⁶And they said to him, "Behold now, there are with your servants fifty strong men; pray, let them go, and seek your master; it may be that the Spirit of the LORD has caught him up and cast him upon some mountain or into some valley." And he said, "You shall not send." ¹⁷But when they urged him till he was ashamed, he said, "Send." They sent therefore fifty men; and for three days they sought him but did not find him. ¹⁸And they came back to him, while he tarried at Jericho, and he said to them, "Did I not say to you, Do not go?"

¹⁹Now the men of the city said to Elisha, "Behold, the situation of this city is pleasant, as my lord sees; but the water is bad, and the land is unfruitful." ²⁰He said, "Bring me a new bowl, and put salt in it." So they brought it to him. ²¹Then he went to the spring of water and threw salt in it, and said, "Thus says the LORD, I have made this water wholesome; henceforth neither death nor miscarriage shall come from it." ²²So the water has been wholesome to this day, according to the word which Elisha spoke.

²³He went up from there to Bethel; and while he was going up on the way, some small boys came out of the city and jeered at him, saying, "Go up, you baldhead! Go up, you baldhead!" ²⁴And he turned around, and when he saw them, he cursed them in the name of the LORD. And two she-bears came out of the woods and tore forty-two of the boys. ²⁵From there he went on to Mount Carmel, and thence he returned to Samaria.

OVERVIEW: Not the soul but the spirit of Elijah rested on Elisha, and Elijah and John the Baptist did not have the same soul but the same spirit (ORIGEN). The city, whose water is purified by Elisha, represents the church that, because of the bad condition of the waters before the coming of Christ, was unable to conceive children for God in its sterility (MAXIMUS). The bitter spring signifies Adam, while the new vessel with salt, which was thrown into the bitter waters by Elisha, is the incarnate Word (CAESARIUS). Elisha, even though he was upset by the rudeness of the children, was much more enraged by the craftiness and the iniquities of their parents, and he corrected both by a harsh and terrible sentence (EPHREM). As under Elisha forty-two boys were killed by two bears, so

forty-two years after the passion of our Lord two bears came, Vespasian and Titus, and besieged and destroyed Jerusalem (CAESARIUS).

2:15-18 The Spirit of Elijah

THE SPIRIT, NOT THE SOUL, OF ELIJAH RESTS ON ELISHA. ORIGEN: I have thought it necessary to dwell some time on the examination of the doctrine of transmigration, because of the suspicion of some who suppose that the soul under consideration was the same in Elijah and in John, being called in the former case Elijah and in the second case John; and that, not apart from God, had he been called John, as is plain from the saying of the angel who appeared to Zacharias, "Fear not, Zacharias, for your supplication is heard, and your wife Elizabeth shall bear you a son, and you shall call his name John";[1] and from the fact that Zacharias regained his speech after he had written in the tablet, that he who had been born should be called John."[2] But if it were the soul of Elijah, then, when he was begotten a second time, he should have been called Elijah; or for the change of name some reason should have been assigned, as in the case of Abram and Abraham, Sarah and Sarai, Jacob and Israel, Simon and Peter. And yet not even thus would their argument in the case be tenable; for ... the changes of name took place in one and the same life. But someone might ask, if the soul of Elijah was not first in the Tishbite and second in John, what might that be in both which the Savior called Elijah? And I say that Gabriel in his words to Zacharias suggested what the substance was in Elijah and John that was the same; for he says, "Many of the children of Israel shall he turn to the Lord their God; and he shall go before his face in the spirit and power of Elijah."[3] For, observe, he did not say in the soul of Elijah, in which case the doctrine might have some ground, but "in the spirit and power of Elijah." For the Scripture well knows the distinction spirit and soul, as, "May God sanctify you wholly, and may your spirit and soul and body be preserved entire, without blame at the coming of our Lord Jesus Christ";[4] and the passage, "Bless the Lord, you spirits and souls of the righteous"[5] as it stands in the book of Daniel, according to the Septuagint, represents the difference between spirit and soul. Elijah, therefore, was not called John because of the soul but because of the spirit and the power, which in no way conflicts with the teaching of the church, though they were formerly in Elijah and afterwards in John; and "the spirits of the prophets are subject to the prophets,"[6] but the souls of the prophets are not subject to the prophets, and "the spirit of Elijah rested on Elisha." COMMENTARY ON THE GOSPEL OF MATTHEW 13.2.[7]

2:19-22 Water Made Wholesome

A FIGURE OF THE CHURCH TO BE CLEANSED BY CHRIST. MAXIMUS OF TURIN: What should we say of the merits of Elisha? This, first of all, is praiseworthy—that he wished to outdo his father in grace, asking that more be given him than he knew that the one who possessed it had. He is, to be sure, covetous in his request but deserving in his merits. For while he demands from his father more than he had, he made him stand out by his own merits more than he was able. For this same Elisha came to Jericho after the ascension of his master and was asked by the townspeople to remain in that city. And when they said to him, "The town is in a good location, but the waters are bad and sterile," he ordered a clay vessel to be given him and, going to the source of the waters, he threw the salt that was kept in it into the waters, saying, "Thus says the Lord: I have cleansed the waters; neither death nor sterility shall come from them. And the waters have been cleansed up until this day." See how great, then, are the merits of Elisha! His first stay in his children's city results in much fruitfulness, because in doing away with the sterility of the waters he makes many people the object of his benefaction. For in accomplishing this Elisha did not cleanse a single person or offer healing to a single household, but he restored the people of the whole city. For if he had done this later the city would have remained without an inhabitant; everyone would have grown old, afflicted with sterility. Therefore Elisha cleansed the people as well when he cleansed the waters, and in blessing the spring of waters he showed favor to the spring, as it were, of souls. For as, by his blessing, water came forth from the earth's hidden channels, so also healthy offspring came forth from the hidden organs of the womb. For Elisha blessed not only those streams alone that were contained in the bowels of the springs but also those that were eventually going to flow later and were still concentrated in the earth's damp soil.

---

[1]Lk 1:13. [2]Lk 1:63. [3]Lk 1:16-17. [4]1 Thess 5:23. [5]Dan 3:86 (Song of the Three Children 5:64 LXX). [6]1 Cor 14:32. [7]ANF 9:475.

Hence Scripture says that Elisha gave a blessing at the source of the waters so that the prophet's sanctifying act might seize the water as it distilled, before the bosom of the spring concealed it.

Therefore, since the holy apostle Paul says that "these things happened to them as a figure,"[8] let us see what the true meaning is of this figure—that is to say, what that city is that suffers sterility and what the vessel means and also why sprinkled salt should confer health. In the same apostle we read that this is said of the church: "Rejoice, you sterile ones who do not bear; break forth and shout, you who do not beget."[9] The church, then, is that sterile city that, because of the bad condition of the waters before the coming of Christ (that is to say, because of the sacrilege of the Gentile peoples), was unable to conceive children for God in its sterility. But when Christ came, taking on a human body like a clay vessel, he cleansed the bad condition of the waters; that is to say, "He cut off the sacrileges of the peoples," and immediately the church, which used to be sterile, began to be fruitful. SERMON 84.3-4.[10]

THE SYMBOLISM OF THE BITTER SPRING, THE BOWL AND THE SALT. CAESARIUS OF ARLES: Let us see what these facts mean, dearly beloved. Elisha, as I have frequently suggested, is the type of our Lord and Savior. That bitter spring seems to signify Adam, from whom the human race has sprung. Before the coming of the true Elisha, that is, our Lord and Savior, the human race remained in barrenness and bitterness through the sin of the first man. Although that new vessel in which salt was thrown represents a type of the apostles, still we can fittingly accept in it the mystery of the Lord's incarnation. Now salt is put there as wisdom, for we read, "Let all your speech be seasoned with salt."[11] Moreover, since Christ is not only "the power of God" but also "the wisdom of God,"[12] the body of Christ like a new vessel was filled with the salt of divine wisdom when the Word was made flesh. Furthermore, the new vessel with salt was thrown into the bitter waters by Elisha, and they were changed into sweetness and

fruitfulness. Similarly, the new vessel, that is, the incarnate Word, was sent by God the Father to recall the human race like bitter flowing waters to sweetness, to lead it to pure charity from evil habits and sterility of good works and to restore it to the fruitfulness of justice. Truly, brothers, does it not seem to you as though the new vessel full of the salt of divine wisdom was put into the water when Christ the Lord went down into the river to be baptized? Then all the waters were changed into sweetness and were sanctified by that new vessel, that is, the body of Christ. As a result, not only were the waters not sterile, but throughout the world by the grace of baptism they have produced a countless number of Christians like abundant fruit and an exceedingly rich harvest.

Although we believe that this truth is fulfilled in things which are seen, still we know that it also takes place spiritually in all people. That the waters signify the people is mentioned in the Apocalypse: "The waters that you saw are peoples and nations."[13] Moreover, that the vessel with salt that was put in the water represents the apostles is very clearly indicated by our Lord in the Gospel when he says, "You are the salt of the earth."[14] Therefore, by his grace he made new apostles out of old people and filled them with the salt of his teachings and divine wisdom, sending them to the whole world as to the spring of the entire human race, to remove its barrenness and bitterness. Finally, from the time that the salt of divine wisdom is afforded to human hearts, all bitterness of relations or sterility in good works is known to be removed.

Therefore, dearly beloved, as we mentioned above, understand Christ our Lord in blessed Elisha and the human race in that spring. Recognize clearly the malice of the devil, which served the first man in what was bitter and sterile. In that new vessel that was put in the spring full of salt, devoutly think of Christ's teaching seasoned with the salt of divine wisdom and through the

---

[8]1 Cor 10:6. [9]Gal 4:27; Is 54:1. [10]ACW 50:202-3. [11]Col 4:6. [12]1 Cor 1:24. [13]Rev 17:15. [14]Mt 5:13.

apostles directed to the human race. We, too, dearly beloved, without any preceding good merits have received such great goods from the Lord through his generous graces and have merited to be changed from bitterness to sweetness, summoned from barrenness to the fruitfulness of good works. SERMON 126.2-5.[15]

2:22-24 Go Away, Baldhead!

REASONS FOR THE PUNISHMENT INFLICTED BY ELISHA. EPHREM THE SYRIAN: "He went up from there to Bethel; and while he was going up on the way, some small boys came out of the city and jeered at him, saying, "Go away, baldhead! Go away, baldhead!" After Elisha had settled the matters concerning his disciples in Jericho, he moved to his dwelling place in Bethel, and during his journey the facts, which the Scripture places here, happened to him. It seems that the impudence of the children resulted from the teaching of their parents, because they were iniquitous and hostile to Elijah and all his disciples. And we may also think that they had been sent by their masters to repeat what they had learned. The word proclaimed according to Elisha by the disciples of Elijah, their fellow citizens, with regard to the ascension of their master grieved the people of Bethel a great deal. That is why, I suppose, those children did not only mention his baldness but also found further insults, which they said before him to outrage his fame, so that nobody might believe his word, if he repeated in Bethel what he had told and about which he had convinced many people in Jericho. In fact, they had meditated on this evil thought and said, "This is the reason for his coming." Now, Elisha, even though he was upset by the effrontery of the children, was much more enraged by the craftiness and the iniquities of their parents, and he corrected both by a harsh and terrible sentence: he punished the former, so that they might not add to their iniquity by growing up to adulthood; the latter, so that they might be corrected and cease from their wickedness. He, who had blessed the children of Jericho and

benefited them to the highest degree for their faith, because, after seeing that he had divided the Jordan through his word, they had said that the spirit of Elijah rested on Elisha, decreed this bitter sentence against the people of Bethel. Indeed, the people of Bethel did not believe, when they heard from children of prophets who were in their city, the news of the ascension of Elijah.

"Then two she-bears came out of the woods and mauled forty-two of the boys." On the day the Lord sent Elijah to anoint Elisha, he said that he would have taken revenge through him on the children of Israel, who had revolted against him, that is, those who escaped from the sword of Hazael[16] and Jehu,[17] Elisha would have caused to perish. This is, therefore, the beginning of the punishment: the word pronounced against the iniquitous began to be fulfilled. ON THE SECOND BOOK OF KINGS 2.20.[18]

A FIGURE OF THE AMENDMENT OF THE JEWS AFTER CHRIST'S PASSION. CAESARIUS OF ARLES: Now according to the letter, dearly beloved, we are to believe, as we mentioned above, that blessed Elisha was aroused with God's zeal to correct the people, rather than moved by unwholesome anger, when he permitted the Jewish children to be torn to pieces. His purpose was not revenge but their amendment, and in this fact, too, the passion of our Lord and Savior was plainly prefigured. Just as those undisciplined children shouted to blessed Elisha, "Go up, you baldhead; go up, you baldhead," so at the time of the passion the insane Jews with impious words shouted to Christ the true Elisha, "Crucify him! Crucify him!"[19] What does "Go up, you baldhead" mean except: Ascend the cross on the site of Calvary? Notice further, brothers, that just as under Elisha forty-two boys were killed, so forty-two years after the passion of our Lord two bears came, Vespasian and Titus, and besieged

---

[15]FC 47:217-18*. [16]See 2 Kings 10:32-33; 13:1-22. [17]See 2 Kings 9:1–10:34. [18]ESOO 1:521-22. [19]Lk 23:21.

Jerusalem. Also consider, brothers, that the siege of Jerusalem took place on the Paschal solemnity. Thus, by the just judgment of God the Jews who had assembled from all the provinces suffered the punishment they deserved, on the very days on which they had hung the true Elisha, our Lord and Savior, on the cross. Indeed, at that time, that is, in the forty-second year after the passion of our Lord, the Jews as if driven by the hand of God assembled in Jerusalem according to their custom to celebrate the Passover. We read in history that three million Jews were then gathered in Jerusalem; eleven hundred thousand of them are read to have been destroyed by the sword of hunger, and one hundred thousand young men were led to Rome in triumph. For two years that city was besieged, and so great was the number of the dead who were cast out of the city that their bodies equaled the height of the walls. This destruction was prefigured by those two bears that are said to have torn to pieces forty-two boys for deriding blessed Elisha. Then was fulfilled what the prophet had said, "The boar from the forest lays it waste, and the beasts of the field feed on it,"[20] for as was indicated, after forty-two years that wicked nation received what it deserved from the two bears, Vespasian and Titus. SERMON 127.2.[21]

---

[20]Ps 80:13 (79:14 LXX, Vg).   [21]FC 47:221-22.

3:1-20 ELISHA PROVIDES JEHORAM'S ARMY WITH WATER

[1]*In the eighteenth year of Jehoshaphat king of Judah, Jehoram the son of Ahab became king over Israel in Samaria, and he reigned twelve years.* [2]*He did what was evil in the sight of the LORD, though not like his father and mother, for he put away the pillar of Baal which his father had made.* [3]*Nevertheless he clung to the sin of Jeroboam the son of Nebat, which he made Israel to sin; he did not depart from it.*

[4]*Now Mesha king of Moab was a sheep breeder; and he had to deliver annually*[c] *to the king of Israel a hundred thousand lambs, and the wool of a hundred thousand rams.* [5]*But when Ahab died, the king of Moab rebelled against the king of Israel.* [6]*So King Jehoram marched out of Samaria at that time and mustered all Israel.* [7]*And he went and sent word to Jehoshaphat king of Judah, "The king of Moab has rebelled against me; will you go with me to battle against Moab?" And he said, "I will go; I am as you are, my people as your people, my horses as your horses."* [8]*Then he said, "By which way shall we march?" Jehoram answered, "By the way of the wilderness of Edom."*

[9]*So the king of Israel went with the king of Judah and the king of Edom. And when they had made a circuitous march of seven days, there was no water for the army or for the beasts which followed them.* [10]*Then the king of Israel said, "Alas! The LORD has called these three kings to give them into the hand of Moab."* [11]*And Jehoshaphat said, "Is there no prophet of the LORD here,*

---

through whom we may inquire of the LORD?" Then one of the king of Israel's servants answered, "Elisha the son of Shaphat is here, who poured water on the hands of Elijah." [12]*And Jehoshaphat said, "The word of the LORD is with him." So the king of Israel and Jehoshaphat and the king of Edom went down to him.*

[13]*And Elisha said to the king of Israel, "What have I to do with you? Go to the prophets of your father and the prophets of your mother." But the king of Israel said to him, "No; it is the LORD who has called these three kings to give them into the hand of Moab."* [14]*And Elisha said, "As the LORD of hosts lives, whom I serve, were it not that I have regard for Jehoshaphat the king of Judah, I would neither look at you, nor see you.* [15]*But now bring me a minstrel." And when the minstrel played, the power of the LORD came upon him.* [16]*And he said, "Thus says the LORD, 'I will make this dry stream-bed full of pools.'* [17]*For thus says the LORD, 'You shall not see wind or rain, but that stream-bed shall be filled with water, so that you shall drink, you, your cattle, and your beasts.'* [18]*This is a light thing in the sight of the LORD; he will also give the Moabites into your hand,* [19]*and you shall conquer every fortified city, and every choice city, and shall fell every good tree, and stop up all springs of water, and ruin every good piece of land with stones."* [20]*The next morning, about the time of offering the sacrifice, behold, water came from the direction of Edom, till the country was filled with water.*

c Tg: Heb lacks *annually*

OVERVIEW: Jehoram marches against Mesha, king of Moab, because he had refused to pay his tribute to the kings of Israel. The musical instrument and the player required by Elisha are means to assert the power of God against idolatry. As in the miracle of Elisha water flowed to fill the wadi, so after Christ's passion the sources were immediately opened and rivers of living water flowed on the nations of the Gentiles (EPHREM).

3:9-14 No Water for the Army

THE KINGS OF ISRAEL, JUDAH AND EDOM CONSULT ELISHA. EPHREM THE SYRIAN: After the death of Ahab, his son Ahaziah died too, and since he had no children, his brother Jehoram took his place. Therefore the Scripture reports that he moved with his army against the king of Moab. He went to war because Mesha, king of Moab, had refused to pay his tribute to the kings of Israel and had not paid both Hezekiah and Jehoram, that is, [he had not paid] one hundred thousand fat lambs and one hundred thousand unshorn rams. The word *noqdo,*[1] which the Scripture mentions here, derives from Hebrew and can be translated as "king of the shepherds of rams," that is, he reared huge herds of them. So Jehoram, who had resolved to assert the rights that his brother had renounced, summoned the kings of the inhabitants of Judea and Edom and marched with them through the territories of the children of Moab. But they found themselves on a barren and arid land, and they had no water for the army. The three kings went to see Elisha, following the advice of righteous Jehoshaphat, and implored him to rescue the suffering people, who were overwhelmed with thirst. The prophet protested and harshly reproached Jehoram but was pleased with Jehoshaphat and gave him hope of salvation. At the same time, he promised that through his mediation, he and his companions would soon obtain the victory through the agency of the Lord. ON THE SECOND BOOK OF KINGS 3.9.[2]

---

[1]2 Kings 3:4 (Peshitta), literally, "herdsman, sheepmaster." [2]ESOO 1:523-24.

3:15 Get Me a Musician

An Instrument to Assert God's Power.
Ephrem the Syrian: The Scripture mentions a
musical instrument that produces sounds, or a
harp, as the Hebrew says,[3] so that, thanks to the
sound of its music, all the soldiers might be
assembled around it and might understand when
they were summoned to destroy their enemies,
and there might be evident testimonies of
[Elisha's] words. In this way, when the miracle
occurred, they could not attribute it to Baal or
the idols they worshiped. Indeed, there were
numerous idolaters in the army. On the Second Book of Kings 3.15.[4]

3:16 I Will Make This Wadi Full of Pools

A Type of the Conversion of the Gentiles. Ephrem the Syrian: "The harpist
played, and the water flowed to the bed of the
streams." Through this figure the voice of Christ
is conveniently foreshadowed, because he kept
the harp of the spirit on the cross. Indeed, our
Lord cried twice and gave up his spirit with a
loud voice.[5] And immediately the pagan centurion gave glory to the Lord,[6] and in this manner
the conversion of the Gentiles was clearly highlighted. After the Christ had brought to perfection on the wood of the cross the new glory of our
Savior,[7] the sources were immediately opened
and rivers of living water flowed on the nations of
the Gentiles, who are symbolized by the "wadi,"
as Jesus had said before his passion: "Let the one
who believes in me drink. As the Scripture has
said, 'Out of the believer's heart shall flow rivers
of living water.' "[8] In this way the word of the
prophet might be fulfilled: He who has played the
harp will play for the Gentiles in the name of the
Lord.[9] On the Second Book of Kings 3.16.[10]

---

[3]Ephrem is referring to a lost Hebrew version of 2 Kings, which is
closer to the translation of LXX. MT reads, "Get me a musician"; LXX,
"Get me a harper"; Peshitta, *naqusho*, "musician, player of musical
instruments." [4]ESOO 1:524. [5]See Mt 27:46-50; Mk 15:34-37. [6]See
Mt 27:54; Mk 15:39. [7]In this sentence it can be noticed how this text
is partly influenced by Nestorianism in its sharp distinction of the two
persons of the Christ and the person of the Savior. [8]Jn 7:37-38. [9]See
Ps 108:3 (107:4 LXX). [10]ESOO 1:524.

3:21-27 THE SACRIFICE OF THE KING OF MOAB

[21]*When all the Moabites heard that the kings had come up to fight against them, all who were
able to put on armor, from the youngest to the oldest, were called out, and were drawn up at the
frontier.* [22]*And when they rose early in the morning, and the sun shone upon the water, the
Moabites saw the water opposite them as red as blood.* [23]*And they said, "This is blood; the kings
have surely fought together, and slain one another. Now then, Moab, to the spoil!"* [24]*But when they
came to the camp of Israel, the Israelites rose and attacked the Moabites, till they fled before them;
and they went forward, slaughtering the Moabites as they went.*[d] [25]*And they overthrew the cities,
and on every good piece of land every man threw a stone, until it was covered; they stopped every
spring of water, and felled all the good trees; till only its stones were left in Kir-haraseth, and the
slingers surrounded and conquered it.* [26]*When the king of Moab saw that the battle was going
against him, he took with him seven hundred swordsmen to break through, opposite the king of*

Edom; but they could not. [27]*Then he took his eldest son who was to reign in his stead, and offered him for a burnt offering upon the wall. And there came great wrath upon Israel; and they withdrew from him and returned to their own land.*

d Gk: Heb uncertain

OVERVIEW: The Moabites erroneously believed that what they saw flowing in the stream was the blood from the carnage of battle. The Moabites came unarmed to plunder the camp of the Israelites but ran away as soon as they saw the army of the enemies appear. The king of Moab offers his firstborn child in sacrifice and wants the Hebrews to see the sacrifice he is making to the God of Abraham according to the teaching of Abraham. God took pity on the king of Moab, since it was in affliction that he made his sacrifice (EPHREM).

3:22-23 Water Red as Blood

THE MOABITES' MISLEADING IMPRESSIONS. EPHREM THE SYRIAN: "The kings fought together and killed one another." After the water had come and the armies of Jehoshaphat and his allied kings had drunk their fill, the Moabites, who had seen that the water was red, said this. But they were wrong, because the color of the water had become red on account of the coming of the sun that oppressed them. When they saw the stream flow, they did not think that water was actually flowing in it, because rain had not fallen in all those days. Consequently they took for granted that no source of water could exist in that dried and scorched region. Therefore they thought that the gods of their homeland had caused the kings and their armies to attack and destroy one another. Indeed, they were easily inclined to religious dissensions. They believed that what they saw flowing in the stream was the blood from the carnage of battle. ON THE SECOND BOOK OF KINGS 3.25.[1]

3:24 The Israelites Attacked the Moabites

THE MOABITES, COMING UNARMED TO PLUN-DER ISRAEL, ARE DEFEATED. EPHREM THE SYRIAN: When the Moabites came to plunder the camp, they convinced themselves that its ruins had been abandoned by their guards. Instead, Jehoshaphat and the kings with him suddenly rose up with drawn swords when they realized that their enemies were approaching and almost upon them. But the Moabites did not persist in their attack. They turned around and ran away because they had come unarmed. They had not come to fight, but to plunder. Therefore they[2] scattered the army of their enemies by simply turning their weapons against them. Then they destroyed and laid waste the land bordering [the Moabites]. And finally, like an overflowing stream, they rushed in to attack Moab, cutting down their trees according to Elisha's order, stopping up the flowing springs, destroying the villages, and demolishing all their houses until they brought down their walls. They surrounded and demolished their fortresses, that is, knocked down the walls and scattered the rubble of the demolition. ON THE SECOND BOOK OF KINGS 3.23.[3]

3:26-27 His Firstborn Son as a Burnt Offering

AN OFFERING TO THE GOD OF ABRAHAM. EPHREM THE SYRIAN: Therefore Mesha, who had lost all his hope in his armies, made an about-face to ask the gods for help, because he had seen that no human being could help him. Certain wise men of his country said to him that it was necessary to implore the mercy of the God of Israel by means of an extraordinary sacrifice, for exactly the same reason which Abraham, the father of

[1]ESOO 1:524-25. [2] That is, the army of Israel. [3]ESOO 1:525.

the Israelites, had made his offering, which had been quite pleasing to God, according to the tradition that is generally renowned among the Canaanites.[4] But the power and the strength of God had already been recognized by all with great admiration for what he had done before all the Moabites. Indeed, no one but him had made the water flow on his people in the desert of Edom, and they had never heard of or known another God who granted his worshipers greater benefits. Therefore the king, who could not deny the miracle that he had seen with his own eyes, did not want to be deprived of sufficient aid in the difficulties that encircled him. He was confirmed [in his hope] and abandoned the worship of idols by taking refuge in the powerful God who had created a new sea in the desert. Therefore he was invited by the word of the wise men and nobles of Moab to make a great sacrifice and to offer his firstborn child, the pillar of his house and the hope of his kingdom, on the city walls, before the armies that besieged him. He wanted the Hebrew to see the sacrifice he was about to make to the God of Abraham according to the teaching of Abraham.

And then the wrath against the Israelites increased, because the calamities, which the Scripture accurately relates after these events, happened to them again. They had seen how God protected them, and the abundance of water that he had made miraculously flow for them and the retreat of their enemies before them. Nevertheless, they persisted in their dishonor, and their hearts were still attached to their calf. ON THE

SECOND BOOK OF KINGS 3.25-27.[5]

WHY DID GOD ACCEPT THE OFFERING?

EPHREM THE SYRIAN: People imitate those who do good deeds, therefore, not out of love for these good deeds but because of their usefulness. For Balaam also flattered [God], in that he had seven altars built because he had heard concerning these ancient ones that, with regard to the sacrifices they had offered to him, their prayers were accepted.[6] The king of Moab took note of Jephthah. But, because it was his firstborn and a human being rather than an animal that he killed, God took pity on him, since it was in affliction that he did it and not through love. In the case of Jephthah, if it had been one of his servants who had been first to encounter him, he would have killed him. But, in order that people would not engage in the sacrifice of their fellow human beings, he caused his own daughter to meet him, so that others would be afraid, lest they offer human beings by vow to God.[7] COMMENTARY ON TATIAN'S DIATESSARON 10.3.[8]

---

[4]See Gen 22:1-18. [5]ESOO 1:525-26. [6]See Num 22:2–24:25. [7]See Judg 11:29-40. [8]ECTD 166. Ephrem discusses how the king of Moab decided to sacrifice his firstborn son. He implies that the king had learned both from Abraham's willingness to sacrifice Isaac and from the vow made by Jephthah when Jephthah had promised to kill the first thing which appeared to him when he returned home if he was victorious in battle. Jephthah's daughter ran to meet her father and one assumes he put her to death to fulfill the rash vow he made. Ephrem's interpretation demonstrates the difficulties in struggling to interpret the final verse of 2 Kings 3 where God allows the king of Moab to prevail over Israel because of the supreme sacrifice he made in sacrificing his oldest son.

4:1-7 ELISHA'S MIRACLE OF THE OIL

[1]*Now the wife of one of the sons of the prophets cried to Elisha, "Your servant my husband is dead; and you know that your servant feared the LORD, but the creditor has come to take my two*

children to be his slaves." ²And Elisha said to her, "What shall I do for you? Tell me; what have you in the house?" And she said, "Your maidservant has nothing in the house, except a jar of oil." ³Then he said, "Go outside, borrow vessels of all your neighbors, empty vessels and not too few. ⁴Then go in, and shut the door upon yourself and your sons, and pour into all these vessels; and when one is full, set it aside." ⁵So she went from him and shut the door upon herself and her sons; and as she poured they brought the vessels to her. ⁶When the vessels were full, she said to her son, "Bring me another vessel." And he said to her, "There is not another." Then the oil stopped flowing. ⁷She came and told the man of God, and he said, "Go, sell the oil and pay your debts, and you and your sons can live on the rest."

OVERVIEW: The woman who asked for the help of Elisha was the widow of Obadiah, treasurer of Ahab and Elijah's secret disciple, who had protected and fed one hundred prophets persecuted by Jezebel (EPHREM). The widow signifies the church, which was a captive because the Redeemer had not yet come; but after Christ our Lord, the true Redeemer, visited the widow, he freed her from all debts (CAESARIUS). The empty vessels symbolize the saints, who have rejected any worldly passion and are filled with the fat of the holy ointment and the oil of happiness (EPHREM). The neighbors are a figure of the Gentiles, who offered empty vessels in order that they might deserve to receive the oil of mercy. The nature of holy love and true charity is such that it increases by being spent, and the more it is paid out to others, the more abundantly it is accumulated in oneself (CAESARIUS).

4:1 The Wife of a Member of the Company of Prophets

OBADIAH'S WIFE CALLS FOR THE HELP OF ELISHA.
EPHREM THE SYRIAN: It is said that this woman was the wife of Obadiah, the treasurer of Ahab and a secret disciple of Elijah, who had taken one hundred prophets away from the rage of Jezebel and had fed them when they were hungry. It seems that in this affair he was entrusted with the gold of the royal house, but after his death his wife was left with a huge debt to be paid to his masters. But since she could not pay, and

the taxmen of the king pressed her and wanted to sell her children, the mother implored Elisha, because she knew he was the father of orphans and the defender of widows,[1] and she thought he would have not drawn back his hands [when asked to help] the sons of a righteous man who had served his companions the prophets. Among other things, the taxmen of the king, who had lent money to Obadiah, in justice, according to the law of the Hebrews, had moved against his children; and this is what our Lord suggested to us in the parable of the creditor king who ordered the children to be sold for the debt of their father, even though he was still alive and only needed some time to pay his debt.[2] ON THE SECOND BOOK OF KINGS 4.1.[3]

THE WIDOW TYPIFIED THE CHURCH.
CAESARIUS OF ARLES: Just as we said concerning blessed Elijah that he typified our Lord and Savior, dearly beloved, so we assert with confidence and assurance that holy Elisha was an image of our Savior. As you heard in the sacred lesson, a certain widow cried to blessed Elisha, beseeching him with tearful voice, "My husband is dead, and behold, the creditors are come and want to take away my sons." Then he asked her what she had in the house. The woman replied, "As the Lord lives, I have nothing but a little oil to anoint me." Then Elisha said, "Borrow vessels of your neighbors, and pour out of that oil into all the vessels,

---

[1]See Ps 68:5 (67:6 LXX). [2]See Mt 18:25. [3]ESOO 1:526.

and when the vessels are full, sell, and pay your creditors." This widow typified the church, beloved brothers, just like the one who merited to receive blessed Elijah. This widow, that is, the church, had contracted a heavy debt of sins, not of material substance. She had a debt, and she endured a most cruel creditor, because she had made herself subject to the devil by many sins. Thus, indeed, the prophet foretold, "It was for your sins that you were sold, for your crimes that your mother was dismissed."[4] For this reason the widow was held captive for such a heavy debt. She was a captive because the Redeemer had not yet come, but after Christ our Lord the true Redeemer visited the widow, he freed her from all debts. Now let us see how that widow was freed—how, except by an increase of oil? In the oil we understand mercy. Notice, brothers: the oil failed, and the debt increased; the oil was increased, and the debt disappeared. Avarice had grown, and charity was lost; charity returned, and iniquity perished. Thus, at the coming of the true Elisha, Christ our Lord, the widow or the church was freed from the debt of sin by an increase of oil, that is, by the gift of grace and mercy or the richness of charity. SERMON 128.1.[5]

4:2-7 Sell the Oil and Pay Your Debts

SYMBOLIC MEANING OF THE MIRACLE OF THE OIL. EPHREM THE SYRIAN: Here the Scripture relates the other miracle that Elisha performed in order to help the widow. He made flow into the vessels an amount of oil sufficient to pay the debt of her husband and abundantly multiplied it for the nourishment of her children.

From the symbolic point of view three aspects must be observed here: first of all it is said that the widow filled the vessels of her neighbors with an oil that gushed out in her house thanks to a gift of God, because the holy church resembles the widow. In fact, she was not abandoned when her husband ascended to heaven, but she filled the hearts of the Gentiles with the oil of the knowledge of salvation which has multiplied and

become abundant in her house thanks to the presence of the Holy Spirit. Moreover, the Gentiles, who were separated before, after being filled with that fat oil, glorified with their lips of cheerfulness that God whom they had ignored before.

In the second place, the widow asked for empty vessels and filled with oil those that her children brought to her, both small and large vessels. This signifies the saints who have rejected any worldly passion and are filled with the fat of the holy ointment and the oil of happiness. So their mother, that is, the grace of God gives oil to each of them, both to the great and the little. For God gives his gifts as he likes, so that everything may be ours,[6] as the apostle says: "We must grow up in Christ according to his gift."[7] But those who are weighed down by their intemperance, drunkenness and worldly interests, those who, as the apostle says, walk in the vanity of their spirit and are obscured in their intelligence, those who have lost their hope and have given themselves to the practice of every sort of paganism and covetousness[8] are deprived of this grace. In fact, they do not desire this oil, and if they desire it, they prepare no vessel to be filled with it. In the third place, the rest of the oil, which the dead husband had left to his widow, signifies the mercy that [Christ] had shown to the saints while he lived on earth. Solomon says that he who associates himself with the Lord has mercy for the poor, and [the Lord] will reward him according to his works.[9] ON THE SECOND BOOK OF KINGS 4.3.[10]

THE NEIGHBORS REPRESENT THE GENTILES.

CAESARIUS OF ARLES: Let us now consider what blessed Elisha said to her: "Borrow many vessels of your neighbors and your friends, shut your door, and pour out of that oil into the vessels of your neighbors." Who were those neighbors, except the Gentiles? Although that widow typified the church, she was still a widow, and so

---

[4]Is 50:1. [5]FC 47:223-24*. [6]See 1 Cor 3:21-22. [7]Eph 4:15. [8]See Eph 4:17-19; Rom 1:21-24. [9]See Prov 19:17. [10]ESOO 1:526-27.

those neighbors from whom she borrowed vessels prefigured the Gentiles. They offered empty vessels in order that they might merit to receive the oil of mercy, because before obtaining the gift of grace all the Gentiles are known to have been without faith, charity and all good works. Finally, all who are offered to the church to receive salutary baptism receive the chrism and oil of benediction, so that they may no longer merit to be empty vessels but full of God as his temples. SERMON 128.2.[11]

THE NATURE OF HOLY LOVE AND TRUE CHARITY. CAESARIUS OF ARLES: Notice, dearly beloved: as long as that widow had oil in her own vessel, it was not enough for her, and she could not pay her debt. It is true, brothers. If a person loves only himself, he does not suffice for himself, and he does not pay the debt of his sins; but when he begins to pour out the oil of charity on all his friends and neighbors and in fact on all people, then he is able to suffice for himself and can free himself from all debts. Truly brothers, such is the nature of holy love and true charity that it increases by being spent, and the more it is paid out to others, the more abundantly it is accumulated in oneself. If you want to give bodily food to the needy, at present you cannot keep what you have given him; but if you offer the bread of charity to one hundred people, it still remains whole. Even if you give it to a thousand, it stays undiminished for you. In fact, if you want to lavish it on the whole world, you will still lose nothing of it; or rather, not only does it not increase, but also the gain of all those on whom you bestowed it increases manifold for you. For example, you had a single loaf of charity; if you had given it to no one you would have it alone, but if you gave it to a thousand you would have acquired a thousand loaves. So great is the possession of charity that it remains entire for each individual and still can be undiminished for them all. Therefore, if you have given to others, you have lost nothing at all; or rather, not only did you not lose anything but also, as I already said, whatever you have conferred on others you have acquired a hundredfold. For this reason, beloved brothers, realize that the widow was freed from her creditors by nothing else than oil; know also that the Catholic church has been freed from its offenses by no other means than the oil of God's mercy. SERMON 128.3.[12]

---

[11]FC 47:224. [12]FC 47:224-25.

4:8-37 THE SHUNAMMITE WOMAN AND HER DEAD CHILD

[8]One day Elisha went on to Shunem, where a wealthy woman lived, who urged him to eat some food. So whenever he passed that way, he would turn in there to eat food. [9]And she said to her husband, "Behold now, I perceive that this is a holy man of God, who is continually passing our way. [10]Let us make a small roof chamber with walls, and put there for him a bed, a table, a chair, and a lamp, so that whenever he comes to us, he can go in there."

[11]One day he came there, and he turned into the chamber and rested there. [12]And he said to

Gehazi his servant, "Call this Shunammite." When he had called her, she stood before him. [13]And he said to him, "Say now to her, See, you have taken all this trouble for us; what is to be done for you? Would you have a word spoken on your behalf to the king or to the commander of the army?" She answered, "I dwell among my own people." [14]And he said, "What then is to be done for her?" Gehazi answered, "Well, she has no son, and her husband is old." [15]He said, "Call her." And when he had called her, she stood in the doorway. [16]And he said, "At this season, when the time comes round, you shall embrace a son." And she said, "No, my lord, O man of God; do not lie to your maidservant." [17]But the woman conceived, and she bore a son about that time the following spring, as Elisha had said to her.

[18]When the child had grown, he went out one day to his father among the reapers. [9]And he said to his father, "Oh, my head, my head!" The father said to his servant, "Carry him to his mother." [20]And when he had lifted him, and brought him to his mother, the child sat on her lap till noon, and then he died. [21]And she went up and laid him on the bed of the man of God, and shut the door upon him, and went out. [22]Then she called to her husband, and said, "Send me one of the servants and one of the asses, that I may quickly go to the man of God, and come back again." [23]And he said, "Why will you go to him today? It is neither new moon nor sabbath." She said, "It will be well." [24]Then she saddled the ass, and she said to her servant, "Urge the beast on; do not slacken the pace for me unless I tell you." [25]So she set out, and came to the man of God at Mount Carmel.

When the man of God saw her coming, he said to Gehazi his servant, "Look, yonder is the Shunammite; [26]run at once to meet her, and say to her, Is it well with you? Is it well with your husband? Is it well with the child?" And she answered, "It is well." [27]And when she came to the mountain to the man of God, she caught hold of his feet. And Gehazi came to thrust her away. But the man of God said, "Let her alone, for she is in bitter distress; and the LORD has hidden it from me, and has not told me." [28]Then she said, "Did I ask my lord for a son? Did I not say, Do not deceive me?" [29]He said to Gehazi, "Gird up your loins, and take my staff in your hand, and go. If you meet any one, do not salute him; and if any one salutes you, do not reply; and lay my staff upon the face of the child." [30]Then the mother of the child said, "As the LORD lives, and as you yourself live, I will not leave you." So he arose and followed her. [31]Gehazi went on ahead and laid the staff upon the face of the child, but there was no sound or sign of life. Therefore he returned to meet him, and told him, "The child has not awaked."

[32]When Elisha came into the house, he saw the child lying dead on his bed. [33]So he went in and shut the door upon the two of them, and prayed to the LORD. [34] Then he went up and lay upon the child, putting his mouth upon his mouth, his eyes upon his eyes, and his hands upon his hands; and as he stretched himself upon him, the flesh of the child became warm. [35]Then he got up again, and walked once to and fro in the house, and went up, and stretched himself upon him; the child sneezed seven times, and the child opened his eyes. [36]Then he summoned Gehazi and said, "Call this Shunammite." So he called her. And when she came to him, he said, "Take up your son." [37]She came and fell at his feet, bowing to the ground; then she took up her son and went out.

OVERVIEW: The Shunammite woman, after hearing the words of her fellow citizens about Elisha and seeing him in her house, understands the advantages of his stay at her place and has a room built for him. Elisha promises the Shunammite woman the blessing of an heir, even though she had not asked for it (EPHREM). Just as the Shunammite woman bore a son at the prayer of Elisha, so the church bore the Christian people when Christ came to it (CAESARIUS). Elisha was profoundly touched by the words of the woman, because he did not suffer so much for the death of the child as for the mockeries he would have been obliged to bear on the part of the prophets of Baal (EPHREM). Elisha, who later came in person to revive the child, was a type of our Lord who had sent his servant ahead of him with a staff that represents the Law (AUGUSTINE). The servant typified Moses, whom God sent into Egypt with a staff: without Christ, Moses could scourge the people with the staff, but he could not free or revive them from original or actual sin (CAESARIUS). Elisha did not raise the child by the mere imposition of the staff but raised him one hour later by adding certain ceremonies to the imposition of the staff, and in that manner he accomplished the type of the Providence of the Word of God (EPHREM). Elisha drew himself together, so that he might fit the little child who lay dead, and what Elisha prefigured in the case of the boy, Christ fulfilled in the entire human race (CAESARIUS, GREGORY THE GREAT). If instead of contracting, Elisha had expanded himself, the widow's son would not have been restored to life; and in the same manner, Christ made himself less in order to give life (JEROME). The prophet did not cause the boy to come back to life by giving him a soul; rather, because he loved him, he got God to do this miracle for him (AUGUSTINE).

4:8-10 A Small Chamber for Elisha

THE SHUNAMMITE WOMAN HAS A ROOM BUILT FOR ELISHA. EPHREM THE SYRIAN: It happened, in the next days, that Elisha arrived at Shunem and passed it. After the ascension of Elijah, Elisha took his place and was appointed as the chief and prefect of the children of the prophets. Duty to his calling obligated him to visit their lodgings in Bethel and Jericho, as well as those along the Jordan. In fact, since the straight line of his route compelled him to pass through the village of Shunem, now and then he made a detour to the house of the Shunammite, because she was an admirable woman. And she, after hearing the words of her fellow citizens about him and seeing him in her house, understood the advantages of his stay at her place. Therefore she asked her husband to build a high room, solitary and separated from the rest of the people of the house. Indeed, she said that it was not proper for a holy prophet to live in an impure place. She called him holy because of his virginity. ON THE SECOND BOOK OF KINGS 4.8.[1]

4:16 You Shall Embrace a Son

ELISHA'S GRATITUDE. EPHREM THE SYRIAN: Elisha said to the Shunammite woman, "At this season, in due time, you shall embrace a son." He wanted to pay his debt for her service and pious assistance to him. Since she was blessed with the goods of the Law but was deprived of children, even though the Law also promised children to those who observed it, she ardently desired to have an heir for those goods. So Elisha promised the Shunammite woman this blessing, even though she had not asked for it. ON THE SECOND BOOK OF KINGS 4.16.[2]

PREFIGURING CHRIST AND THE CHURCH. CAESARIUS OF ARLES: We have heard that after this blessed Elisha passed by Shunem, where a certain woman received him and said to her husband, "I perceive that this is a man of God: let us make him a chamber and put a bed in it for him, and a table, and a stool and a candlestick, that when he comes, he may abide there." Now, that

---

[1]ESOO 1:527-28. [2]ESOO 1:528.

woman was sterile, but at the prayer of Elisha she bore a son. So, too, the church was sterile before the coming of Christ; but just as that other bore a son at the prayer of Elisha, so the church bore the Christian people when Christ came to it. However, the son of that woman died during the absence of Elisha; thus also, the church's son, that is, the Gentiles, died through sin before Christ's advent. When Elisha came down from the mountain, the widow's son was revived; and when Christ came down from heaven, the church's son or the Gentiles were restored to life. Sermon 128.6.[3]

4:17-29 The Shunammite's Son Dies

Reproaches of the Shunammite Woman. Ephrem the Syrian: "The woman conceived and bore a son at that season, in due time, as Elisha had declared to her," but after a few years, the child died. His mother placed the corpse on the bed of the prophet in the high room of her house and then rushed to meet him, blessed him and knelt down at his feet, not in order to make a request but to rebuke him. She said, "Did I ask my lord for a son? Did I not say, 'Do not mislead your servant?'" ["Why did you take me and throw me into the pangs of Eve, when I was free of them, and why did you make death, against which I had risen and for which I had no consideration, reign over me? Indeed, thanks to my unlucky sterility I had been away from those two evils.[4] Because of my fear of death I had not asked you for children, and because of the mockeries of the pagans, among whom I live, I did not desire them. So I have said to you: Do not ask that children be given to me."][5]

From her lips she gave reproaches, while with her hands she implored him and, catching hold of his feet, besieged him. She swore she would not leave him until he had given her his grace and had brought back to life her son, which death had grasped. So Elisha was profoundly touched by the words of the woman. [Because he did not suffer so much for the death of the child as for the

mockeries he would have been obliged to bear on the part of the prophets of Baal.][6]

When he saw her suffering and anguish, he immediately sent his disciple, entrusting him with his staff, and told him to lay it on the dead child and to inform him about the results of his ministry. He wanted the resurrection of the dead to happen by means of the staff of the master and the hands of the disciple, if his servant was sufficient for the miracle. If that were not sufficient, he would blame himself, because he had outraged with his laziness the coat of arms of the house of Moses. On the Second Book of Kings 4.17.[7]

The Symbolic Meaning of the Staff and the Servant. Augustine: There is another representation of the same truth: Elisha's action in first dispatching his servant with his staff to raise the dead child. The son of the woman who had given Elisha hospitality had died; the news was brought to Elisha, and he sent his servant with the staff. "Go," he told him, "lay the staff on the dead child." Was the prophet unsure what to do? The servant went on ahead and placed the staff on the corpse; but the dead child did not revive. "If a law capable of giving life had been granted to us, then of course righteousness would have been obtainable through the law."[8] The law sent through a servant did not bring life. But Elisha, who had sent his staff with his servant, was to follow later himself and bring the child to life. After hearing that the child had not revived, Elisha came in person; he was a type of our Lord, who had sent his servant ahead of him with a staff that represents the Law. He came to the dead child lying there and placed his body over him. But the dead person was an infant and Elisha a grown man, so he contracted

---

[3]FC 47:226-27. [4]The pangs of birth and death. [5]The section in brackets has been translated from the Armenian version of Ephrem's commentary on 1-2 Kings. In the Armenian text (published in Venice in 1836 by the Mekitariste Fathers) we often find passages that perfectly integrate the Syriac text with extremely interesting details: Ephraem Syrus, *Srboyn Ep'remi Matenagrowt'iwnk'*, vol. I, Venezia 1836, p. 453. [6]Ephraem Syrus, *Srboyn Ep'remi Matenagrowt'iwnk'*, vol. I, Venezia 1836, p. 453. [7]ESOO 1:528. [8]Gal 3:21.

his adult stature and somehow curtailed it, making himself like a child so that he matched the corpse in size. The dead child arose when the living man had fitted himself to him; the Lord accomplished what the staff had failed to do; grace achieved what the Law could not. EXPOSITION ON PSALM 70 (EXPOSITION 1).19.[9]

A CROSS WITHOUT CHRIST HAS NO POWER.

CAESARIUS OF ARLES: After the death of her son, that woman went out and prostrated herself at the feet of holy Elisha, but the blessed man gave his staff to his servant and said to him, "Go, and lay my staff on the face of the child. If anyone salutes you, do not return the greeting." At this point, brothers, see to it that no wicked thought overtake anyone by saying that blessed Elisha wanted to practice fortune telling and that for this reason he commanded the boy not to return the greeting if anyone should salute him on the way. We read this frequently in Scripture, but it is said for the sake of speed and is not a command of something superfluous or a wicked practice. It means, in effect: Walk so quickly that you may not presume to busy yourself on the way or slow yourself with gossip. Therefore, the servant departed and laid the staff on the face of the child, but the boy did not rise at all. That servant typified blessed Moses, whom God sent into Egypt with a staff; without Christ, Moses could scourge the people with the staff, but he could not free or revive them from original or actual sin. As the apostle says, "For the law brought nothing to perfection."[10] It was necessary that he who had sent the staff should himself come down. The staff without Elisha availed nothing, because the cross without Christ had no power. EXPOSITION I OF PSALM 70.19.[11]

4:30-37 Take Your Son

ELISHA RAISES THE DEAD CHILD. EPHREM THE SYRIAN: "Then the mother of the child said, 'As the Lord lives, and as you yourself live, I will not leave without you.'" Now, since Elisha had

stayed at home and had sent his disciple, the mother of the [dead] child pressed him to aid her personally. Elisha had mercy on her grief, which was great, and set out to accompany her to the village of Shunem. Gehazi, his disciple, had laid the staff on the child at the time fixed by his master but had not raised him; that is, the resurrection of the dead child had not followed the application of the staff, because Gehazi was a covetous man and was not worthy of being mentioned. Elisha did not raise the child by the mere imposition of the staff either but raised him one hour later by adding certain ceremonies to the imposition of the staff. And in that manner he accomplished the type of the Providence of the Word of God, who came to raise Adam after he had been condemned to death. For he knew that the staff of the prophet represented the wood of the cross. In fact, the salvation of the world was not in the Law, which is only the shadow and the figure of the goods to come,[12] and the dead child was not raised by the application of the staff. Therefore, when the prophet set out to accomplish the resurrection, he diminished his size, lowered his height and adjusted himself to the dimension of the child.

Immediately [the child's] dead flesh became warm. In this figure the incarnation of the only One was represented, as well as the beginning of our salvation, because it was necessary that the Son of God "was made a little lower than the angels"[13] in order to be included in a womb of flesh and to be incarnated, so that he might give life to the flesh through the Spirit. With regard to the fact that the prophet walked back and forth in the house of the dead child, it prefigures the times in which Jesus Christ entered and went out of the houses of humankind and lived with them. Finally the prophet came back and adjusted himself again to the size of the child, and his body covered his body; at that time the dead child was resurrected.

---

[9]WSA 3 17:433-34. [10]Heb 7:19. [11]FC 47:227*. Caesarius here makes an allusion to Christ and his cross, symbolized by the staff. [12]See Heb 10:1. [13]Heb 2:9.

Our Lord accomplished this figure and brought it to perfection, when, still alive, he adjusted his holy limbs to the cross. And after his death he again adjusted his dead body in the tomb to the size of the dead Adam. And so God, through his great love for us, after we had died for our sins, brought us back to life with Christ. By his grace he saved us and raised us from the dead with him and made us sit with him in heaven through Jesus Christ, as the divine Paul says.[14] ON THE SECOND BOOK OF KINGS 4.30-35.[15]

CHRIST HUMBLED HIMSELF TO LIFT THE WORLD. CAESARIUS OF ARLES: Thus, blessed Elisha came and went up to the chamber, because Christ was to come and ascend the gibbet of the cross. Elisha bent down to revive the child; Christ humbled himself to lift up the world that lay in sin. Elisha further put his eyes on [the child's] eyes, his mouth on his mouth and his hands on his hands. Consider, brothers, how much that man of full age drew himself together, so that he might fit the little child who lay dead; for what Elisha prefigured in the case of the boy, Christ fulfilled in the entire human race. Listen to the apostle say, "He humbled himself, becoming obedient to death."[16] Because we were little children, he made himself small; since we lay dead, the kind physician bent down, for, truly, brothers, no one can lift up one who is lying down if he refuses to bend. In the fact that the boy gasped seven times is shown the sevenfold grace of the Holy Spirit that was bestowed on the human race at Christ's advent in order to restore it to life. Concerning the Spirit the apostle says, "If anyone does not have the Spirit of Christ, he does not belong to Christ."[17] Our Lord gave the same Spirit to his disciples when he breathed on them and said, "Receive the Holy Spirit."[18] Truly, in a way he put his mouth on their mouths when he breathed on them and gave them the Spirit. SERMON 128.8.[19]

BROUGHT BACK TO LIFE BY THE SPIRIT OF LOVE. GREGORY THE GREAT: Fear had no power to raise us from the death of sin, but the infused grace of meekness erected us to the seat of life. This is well denoted by Elisha when he raised the child of the Shunammite. He, when he sent his servant with a staff, never restored life to the dead child at all. But, on coming in his own person, spreading himself on the dead body and contracting himself to its limbs, and walking to and fro and breathing seven times into the mouth of the dead body, he forthwith quickened it to the light of new life through the ministering of compassion. For God, the Creator of humankind, as it were grieved for his dead Son, when he beheld us with compassion, killed by the sting of iniquity. And having put forth the terror of the Law by Moses, he, as it were, sent the rod by the servant. But the servant could not raise the dead body with the staff, because, as Paul bears witness, "The law made nothing perfect."[20] But when he came in his own person and spread himself in humility on the body, he contracted himself to match the limbs of the dead body to himself. "Who, being in the form of God, thought it not robbery to be equal with God, but made himself of no reputation, and took on him the form of a servant and was made in the likeness of humankind; and found in fashion as a man."[21] . . . He breathes on the dead body seven times, in that by the publishing of the divine gift, he bestows the Spirit of sevenfold grace on those who lie prostrate in the death of sin. And afterwards it is raised up alive, in that the child, whom the rod of terror could not raise up, has been brought back to life by the Spirit of love. MORALS ON THE BOOK OF JOB 9.40.63.[22]

A COMPARISON BETWEEN JESUS AND ELISHA. JEROME: "Sing to the Lord." Why? What has he done? Why is there a new song due him? "For he has done wondrous deeds." He performed miracles among the Jews: he cured paralytics; he cleansed lepers; he raised the dead to life. But other prophets had done that too. He changed a few loaves

---

[14]See Eph 2:1-6. [15]ESOO 1:529-30. [16]Phil 2:8. [17]Rom 8:9. [18]Jn 20:22. [19]FC 47:227-28. [20]Heb 7:19. [21]Phil 2:6-7. [22]LF 18:542-43*.

into many and fed a countless multitude. But Elisha did that.[23] What new thing, then, did he do to merit a new song? Would you know what he did that was new? God died as man that humankind might live; the Son of God was crucified that he might lift us up to heaven. "For he has done wondrous deeds." Would you know what wondrous deeds he has done? The son of a widow[24] was lying dead in an upper chamber; Elisha came and drew himself together over the child, and he put his mouth on the mouth of the boy, and his hands on his hands and his feet on his feet. If, instead of contracting and decreasing himself, Elisha had expanded and increased himself, the widow's son would not have been restored to life; and so it was, in order to give life, that [Christ] made himself less. Although he was in the form of God, he received the form of humanity; thus did he decrease that through him we might increase. HOMILIES ON THE PSALMS 25 (Ps 97[98]).[25]

How Did Elisha Revive the Dead Child?

AUGUSTINE: What is the point of the addition you thought you should make to this comparison drawn from the example of blessed Elisha, namely, that he raised a dead boy by breathing into his face?[26] Do you really think that the breath of Elisha became the soul of the boy? I would not have thought that you had wandered so far from the truth. If the very same soul, then, that had been taken from the living boy so that he died, was restored to him so that he came back to life, what was the point of your saying that nothing was taken away from Elisha? You imply that we believed that something passed from him into the boy as a result of which the boy was once again alive. But if you said this because he exhaled and still remained whole, what need was there to say this with regard to Elisha raising the dead boy, since you could, in any case, say this of anyone who exhales without raising anyone from the dead? Heaven forbid that you should believe that the breath of Elisha became the soul of the boy when he came back to life! And so, you have certainly spoken without sufficient reflection

when you wanted the only difference between what God first did and what Elisha did to be that God breathed once, while Elisha breathed three times. You did, in fact, say that Elisha breathed into the face of the dead son of that Shunammite woman, just as happened at the first beginnings of our race. "And when the divine power," you said, "had by the breath of the prophet warmed the dead members and restored them to life in their former strength, nothing was taken away from Elisha, though by his breath the dead body received its soul and mind restored to life. The only difference is that the Lord breathed into the man's face and he was alive, while Elisha blew into the face of the dead boy three times."[27] Your words make it sound as if it is only the number of breaths that keep you from believing that the prophet did the same thing as God did. This point too must be corrected. There was a great difference between that action of God and this action of Elisha. God breathed the breath of life by which the man became a living soul; Elisha breathed a breath that was neither sentient nor living but symbolic and intended to signify something else. Moreover, the prophet did not cause the boy to come back to life by giving him a soul; rather, because he loved him, he got God to do this. As for your saying that Elisha breathed three times, either your memory—as often happens—or a faulty manuscript has led you astray. What else can I say? You should not look for examples and arguments to bolster your case; you should, rather, correct and change your position. If you want to be a Catholic, do not believe, do not say, do not teach that God made the soul, not from nothing but from his own nature. THE NATURE AND ORIGIN OF THE SOUL 3.5.7.[28]

---

[23]See below 2 Kings 4:42-44. [24]This detail is not confirmed by the biblical account; it seems that Jerome is confusing the character of the Shunammite woman with the widow in 2 Kings 4:1-7. [25]FC 48:197-98. [26]Augustine is addressing a young disciple, Vincent Victor, whom he wants to instruct on the nature of the soul by correcting his erroneous beliefs. [27]Augustine is quoting from a lost work by Vincent Victor. [28]WSA 1 23:519-20.

4:38-44 ELISHA PURIFIES THE FOOD
AND NOURISHES ONE HUNDRED PEOPLE

³⁸*And Elisha came again to Gilgal when there was a famine in the land. And as the sons of the prophets were sitting before him, he said to his servant, "Set on the great pot, and boil pottage for the sons of the prophets."* ³⁹*One of them went out into the field to gather herbs, and found a wild vine and gathered from it his lap full of wild gourds, and came and cut them up into the pot of pottage, not knowing what they were.* ⁴⁰*And they poured out for the men to eat. But while they were eating of the pottage, they cried out, "O man of God, there is death in the pot!" And they could not eat it.* ⁴¹*He said, "Then bring meal." And he threw it into the pot, and said, "Pour out for the men, that they may eat." And there was no harm in the pot.*

⁴²*A man came from Baal-shalishah, bringing the man of God bread of the first fruits, twenty loaves of barley, and fresh ears of grain in his sack. And Elisha said, "Give to the men, that they may eat."* ⁴³*But his servant said, "How am I to set this before a hundred men?" So he repeated, "Give them to the men, that they may eat, for thus says the* LORD, *'They shall eat and have some left.'"* ⁴⁴*So he set it before them. And they ate, and had some left, according to the word of the* LORD.

OVERVIEW: The steward of the prophets gathered either wild colocynths or squirting cucumbers. Adam gathered bitter fruits as a consequence of his sin, and the Lord changed them into salvation according to divine economy. When Elisha nourished one hundred prophets with a little bit of bread, he prefigured Jesus' miracle of the loaves and the fish (EPHREM).

4:38-40 *Gathering Wild Gourds*[1]

POISONOUS HERBS. EPHREM THE SYRIAN: This was the starving steward of the prophets who was forced by the lack of food to go through the fields in order to gather some herbs. And since he could not find the herbs he knew, he gathered those that he did not know and were not edible. And since it is written that he gathered wild colocynths, some[2] say that he gathered colocynths, others those [herbs] that are called the source of bitterness: with their inside parts, physicians make an effective and purifying medicine. Others

say that perhaps their name comes from the term used by farmers: squirting cucumbers, which have a very bitter taste and resemble a vine. In fact, the Scripture calls a *vine* that plant that the steward found and from which he gathered colocynths. ON THE SECOND BOOK OF KINGS 4.39.[3]

4:40-41 *Bring Some Flour*

A TYPE OF CHRIST. EPHREM THE SYRIAN: Elisha corrects the nature of the cooked foods with some flour and gives them a new taste. Our Lord did the same according to the [divine] economy, so that he might be imitated, as he said for our exhortation, with the result that we might walk the path of the righteous and the pious, and might rejoice because of the great reward he promised us and might heal the diseases and the anguish and the tribulations that constantly sur-

---

[1]In the Peshitta used by Ephrem, "colocynths." [2]Ephrem is referring here to unknown exegetical sources. [3]*ESOO* 1:530.

round us from the beginning of our life. The father of our race, Adam, gathered those [bitter] fruits as a consequence of his sin and proposed and offered them to us in the hour in which he heard [these words] from his Creator: "The ground is cursed because of you; it will bring forth thorns and thistles for you. You are dust, and to dust you shall return."[4] ON THE SECOND BOOK OF KINGS 4.41.[5]

4:42-44 Let the People Eat

THE LOAVES AND THE FISH. EPHREM THE SYRIAN: Here two miracles are proposed, which

Elisha performed while he was among his disciples. He accomplished the first when he caused death to leave the pot, where, as they said, it had hidden. He performed the second when he nourished one hundred prophets with a little bit of bread. In both miracles he prefigures him who multiplies twice some barley loaves[6] and nourishes with them "about five thousand men, besides women and children."[7] ON THE SECOND BOOK OF KINGS 4.38.[8]

---

[4]Gen 3:17-19. [5]ESOO 1:530-31. [6]See Mt 14:13-21. [7]Mt 14:21. [8]ESOO 1:530.

5:1-19 ELISHA CURES NAAMAN OF HIS LEPROSY

[1]Naaman, commander of the army of the king of Syria, was a great man with his master and in high favor, because by him the LORD had given victory to Syria. He was a mighty man of valor, but he was a leper. [2]Now the Syrians on one of their raids had carried off a little maid from the land of Israel, and she waited on Naaman's wife. [3]She said to her mistress, "Would that my lord were with the prophet who is in Samaria! He would cure him of his leprosy." [4]So Naaman went in and told his lord, "Thus and so spoke the maiden from the land of Israel." [5]And the king of Syria said, "Go now, and I will send a letter to the king of Israel."

So he went, taking with him ten talents of silver, six thousand shekels of gold, and ten festal garments. [6]And he brought the letter to the king of Israel, which read, "When this letter reaches you, know that I have sent to you Naaman my servant, that you may cure him of his leprosy." [7]And when the king of Israel read the letter, he rent his clothes and said, "Am I God, to kill and to make alive, that this man sends word to me to cure a man of his leprosy? Only consider, and see how he is seeking a quarrel with me."

[8]But when Elisha the man of God heard that the king of Israel had rent his clothes, he sent to the king, saying, "Why have you rent your clothes? Let him come now to me, that he may know that there is a prophet in Israel." [9]So Naaman came with his horses and chariots, and halted at the door of Elisha's house. [10]And Elisha sent a messenger to him, saying, "Go and wash in the Jordan seven times, and your flesh shall be restored, and you shall be clean." [11]But Naaman was angry, and went away, saying, "Behold, I thought that he would surely come out to me, and stand, and

call on the name of the Lord *his God, and wave his hand over the place, and cure the leper.* ¹²*Are not Abana^e and Pharpar, the rivers of Damascus, better than all the waters of Israel? Could I not wash in them, and be clean?" So he turned and went away in a rage.* ¹³*But his servants came near and said to him, "My father, if the prophet had commanded you to do some great thing, would you not have done it? How much rather, then, when he says to you, 'Wash, and be clean'?"* ¹⁴*So he went down and dipped himself seven times in the Jordan, according to the word of the man of God; and his flesh was restored like the flesh of a little child, and he was clean.*

¹⁵*Then he returned to the man of God, he and all his company, and he came and stood before him; and he said, "Behold, I know that there is no God in all the earth but in Israel; so accept now a present from your servant."* ¹⁶*But he said, "As the* Lord *lives, whom I serve, I will receive none."* *And he urged him to take it, but he refused.* ¹⁷*Then Naaman said, "If not, I pray you, let there be given to your servant two mules' burden of earth; for henceforth your servant will not offer burnt offering or sacrifice to any god but the* Lord. ¹⁸ *In this matter may the* Lord *pardon your servant: when my master goes into the house of Rimmon to worship there, leaning on my arm, and I bow myself in the house of Rimmon, when I bow myself in the house of Rimmon, the* Lord *pardon your servant in this matter."* ¹⁹*He said to him, "Go in peace."*

e Another reading is *Amana*

Overview: Naaman was in favor with the king of Aram and with God, because he had been able to defeat and kill Ahab and to restrain Jezebel's cruelty against the prophets. Naaman was sent to the Jordan, that is, to the remedy capable of healing the whole of humankind, as sin is the leprosy of the soul, which is healed by the power of Christ through baptism (Ephrem). Naaman becomes angry because he does not perceive that it is our Jordan, namely, baptism, and not the prophet, that removes the uncleanness of those who are unclean because of leprosy and heals them (Origen). Naaman's healing clearly prefigures the mystery of the healing, which is freely granted to all nations of the earth by our Lord through the intercession of the apostles (Ephrem). Just as Naaman, although he was an old man, became like a boy by washing seven times in the Jordan, so the Gentiles, although old by reason of their former sins, are renewed by the grace of baptism (Caesarius). Naaman asked for some dust of the promised land in order that the Hebrews might be ashamed that a stranger believed that even the dust of their land was filled

with God, while they did not even believe that God dwelled in the prophets (Ephrem).

5:1 Naaman Powerful and in High Favor

In High Favor with His Master and with the Lord. Ephrem the Syrian: "Naaman, commander of the army of the king of Aram, was a great man and in high favor with his master because by him the Lord had given victory to Aram." Some rely on these words to say that he was the one who had killed Ahab by striking him with an arrow shot by his own hand, when there was war between [Israel] and Aram. This favor was granted him by the Lord as a reward for killing the persecutor of the prophets and for enfeebling the power of Jezebel, [Ahab's] wife, and for restraining her cruelty. And thanks to him the disciples of Elijah had relief too, those whom the fear of Ahab and Jezebel had forced to flee into the desert and take refuge in some caves. And they had returned to their abodes, as the Scripture mentions below. But all these theories are groundless, except for what they say about the persecution of the prophets, which is undoubtedly correct. It is true, nevertheless, what Obadiah says to Elijah: "Has it not been told my lord what I did when Jezebel killed the prophets of the Lord, how I hid a hundred of the Lord's prophets fifty to a cave and provided them with bread and water?"[1] On the Second Book of Kings 5.1.[2]

5:8-12 *Washing in the Jordan*

Elisha's Order to Wash in the Jordan Prefigures Baptism. Ephrem the Syrian:
Naaman was suffering from leprosy, and when he heard that a prophet who lived under the command of Jehoram, king of Israel, could cure him, he left and proceeded to the country of the healer and went to the house of Elisha, because he had learned that he was the prophet who could aid him in his distress and that he had to ask him to be healed. But Elisha did not go out to meet him or speak to him. He informed him through a messenger: If he wanted to be healed, he had to wash his body in the Jordan seven times. Now a question rises: Why did Elisha prevent Naaman from seeing him and did not allow him to come into his house? In the first place, because he had served Ben-hadad[3] in his wars. In fact, the prophet knew that the king of Aram had killed many children of Israel, and how Naaman had destroyed their lands and how his hands were stained with innocent blood, for he was the commander of the army and had received full authority over the Arameans. In the second place, because he was stopped by the corruption of leprosy. Elisha knew that the Law prescribed that no leper could be approached or touched.

Naaman, as a consequence, was enraged. Blaming and accusing Elisha, he left [saying] that he would have never thought to come to a prophet just in order to see him act mysteriously and that he certainly did not expect such words. He believed that his healing would be accomplished through a simple imposition of the hands. So he blamed Elisha and said, "Why did he not come out to meet a man of power who had come

to his house? And why did he prevent me from seeing him, and why did he not judge me worthy of speaking to him? And why did he not heal me with the remedy he uses and which is easy and effortless for me? On the contrary, he sends me to the Jordan, as though that river may really purify me; but are not the rivers of my land, the Amana[4] and the Pharpar, sufficient for such purification?"

It is not surprising that he had such thoughts and rebelled, the man who had heard with his own ears and compared the words of the prophet. A man who had made his career in the army could not have access to the mystery hidden in that unusual healing.

Therefore Naaman was sent to the Jordan as to the remedy capable to heal a human being. Indeed, sin is the leprosy of the soul, which is not perceived by the senses, but intelligence has the proof of it, and human nature must be delivered from this disease by Christ's power which is hidden in baptism. It was necessary that Naaman, in order to be purified from two diseases, that of the soul and that of the body, might represent in his own person the purification of all the nations through the bath of regeneration, whose beginning was in the river Jordan, the mother and originator of baptism. On the Second Book of Kings 5.10-11.[5]

Naaman Does Not Understand the Great Mystery of the Jordan. Origen:
But in addition, that we may accept the interpretation of the Jordan, that river that is so fresh and grants so much grace, it is useful to present both Naaman the Syrian,[6] who was cleansed from leprosy, and the comments made about the rivers by the enemies of religion. It is written of Naaman, therefore: "He came with his horse and chariot and stood at the doors of the house of Elisha. And Elisha sent a messenger to him, saying, 'Go

---

[1]1 Kings 18:13. [2]ESOO 1:531. [3]See 1 Kings 20:1-43. [4]Or Abana. [5]ESOO 1:531-32. [6]In the Greek and Latin biblical tradition the Arameans are usually called Syrians, according to the more recent name of this nation.

and wash seven times in the Jordan, and your flesh will return to you, and you will be cleansed.'" Then Naaman becomes angry because he does not perceive that it is our Jordan, and not the prophet, that removes the uncleanness of those who are unclean because of leprosy and heals them. For the work of a prophet is to send one to that which heals.

Since, therefore, Naaman does not understand the great mystery of the Jordan, he says, "Behold, I said that he will assuredly come out to me and will stand and call on the name of the Lord his God and will place his hand on the place and the leprosy will recover," for placing the hand on leprosy and cleansing it was the work of my Lord Jesus alone. To the man who asked with faith, "If you will, you can make me clean, he not only said "I will, be made clean," but in addition to the word that he spoke, he also touched him, and he was cleansed from leprosy.[7]

Naaman, who is still in error and does not see how inferior the other rivers are to the Jordan for healing the suffering, praises the rivers of Damascus, Abana and Pharphar, saying, "Are not the Abana and the Pharphar, rivers of Damascus, better than all the waters of Israel? Shall I not go and wash in them and be cleansed?" COMMENTARY ON THE GOSPEL OF JOHN 6.242-45.[8]

5:14-16 Naaman's Flesh Restored

A TYPE OF THE HEALING GRANTED BY THE LORD TO ALL NATIONS. EPHREM THE SYRIAN: After Naaman had been persuaded by the prophet and had washed seven times in the Jordan, he eventually acknowledged his error. He was astonished, and a deep bewilderment took him when he realized that he had been delivered from his filthiness. And he thanked God for his healing and testified that the Lord of the universe, in his profound care for him, had conceded him that extraordinary power by simply using water. He also proclaimed that his healing could not have derived from the water of the river but had been caused by Elisha's command. That is

why he offered royal presents, but the prophet did not accept them and was not persuaded by the donor, even though he had pressed him many times. For that magnificently and very clearly prefigured the mystery of the healing, which is freely granted to all nations of the earth by our Lord through the intercession of the apostles. And this had been promised in advance to those masters by the prophet Isaiah, when he said, "You were sold for nothing, and you shall be redeemed without money."[9]

Since all diseases are a sort of bondage, the prophet necessarily fixed the healing at the seventh bath, in parallel with the fact that the Law, too, orders and promises freedom for the slave at the seventh year.[10] ON THE SECOND BOOK OF KINGS 5.15.[11]

THE REGENERATION OF THE GENTILES THROUGH THE BAPTISM OF CHRIST. CAESARIUS OF ARLES: Let us further see what blessed Elisha commanded Naaman the Syrian. "Go," he says, "and wash seven times in the Jordan." When Naaman heard that he was to wash seven times in the Jordan, he was indignant and did not want to comply, but accepting the advice of his friends, he consented to be washed and was cleansed. This signified that before Christ was crucified, the Gentiles did not believe in Christ when he spoke in his own person, but afterwards they devoutly came to the sacrament of baptism after the preaching of the apostles. For this reason Elisha told Naaman to wash seven times in the Jordan. See, brothers: Elisha sent Naaman to the river Jordan because Christ was to send the Gentiles to baptism. Moreover, the fact that Elisha did not touch Naaman himself or baptize him showed that Christ did not come to the Gentiles himself but through his apostles to whom he said, "Go, and baptize all nations in the name of the Father, and of the Son and of the Holy Spirit."[12] Notice further that Naaman, who prefigured the Gen-

---

[7]See Mt 8:2-3. [8]FC 80:234-35. [9]Is 52:3. [10]See Exod 21:1-2; Deut 15:12. [11]ESOO 1:532-33. [12]Mt 28:19.

tiles, recovered his health in the same river that later Christ consecrated by his baptism. However, when Naaman heard that he was to wash seven times in the Jordan, he became angry and said, "Are not the waters of my region better, the rivers of Damascus, the Abana and the Pharphar, that I may wash in them and be made clean?" When he had said this, his servants advised him to agree to the counsel of the prophet. Carefully notice what this means, brothers.

Holy Elisha, as we said, typified our Lord and Savior, while Naaman prefigured the Gentiles. The fact that Naaman believed he would recover his health as the result of his own rivers indicates that the human race presumed on its free will and its own merits; but without the grace of Christ their own merits cannot possess health, although they can have leprosy. For this reason if the human race had not followed the example of Naaman and listened to the advice of Elisha, with humility receiving the gift of baptism through the grace of Christ, they could not be freed from the leprosy of the original and actual sins. "Wash seven times," he said, because of the sevenfold grace of the Holy Spirit, which reposed in Christ our Lord. Moreover, when our Lord was baptized in this river, the Holy Spirit came on him in the form of a dove. When Naaman descended into the river as a figure of baptism, "his flesh became like the flesh of a little child." Notice, beloved brothers, that this likeness was perfected in the Christian people, for you know that all who are baptized are still called infants, whether they are old or young. Those who are born old through Adam and Eve are reborn as young people to death, the second one to life. The former produces children of wrath; the latter generates them again as vessels of mercy. The apostle says, "In Adam all die; in Christ all will be made to live."[13] Therefore, just as Naaman, although he was an old man, became like a boy by washing seven times, so the Gentiles, although old by reason of their former sins and covered with the many spots of iniquity as with leprosy, are renewed by the grace of baptism in such a way that no leprosy of either original or actual sin remains in them. Thus, following the example of Naaman, they are renewed like little children by salutary baptism, although they have always been bent down under the weight of sins. SERMON 129.4-5.[14]

5:17 Naaman Asks for Dust from Israel

FOR THE SHAME OF ISRAEL. EPHREM THE SYRIAN: Naaman the Aramean asked for some dust from the promised land in order to cause the shame of Israel, as I think, so that they might be ashamed that a stranger believed that even the dust of their land was filled with God, while the Hebrews did not even believe that God dwells in the prophets. ON THE SECOND BOOK OF KINGS 5.17.[15]

---

[13]1 Cor 15:22. [14]FC 47:230-31*. [15]ESOO 1:533.

5:20-27 PUNISHMENT OF GEHAZI'S COVETOUSNESS

[20]*Gehazi, the servant of Elisha the man of God, said, "See, my master has spared this Naaman the Syrian, in not accepting from his hand what he brought. As the LORD lives, I will run after him, and get something from him."* [21]*So Gehazi followed Naaman. And when Naaman saw some one*

running after him, he alighted from the chariot to meet him, and said, "Is all well?" [22]*And he said, "All is well. My master has sent me to say, 'There have just now come to me from the hill country of Ephraim two young men of the sons of the prophets; pray, give them a talent of silver and two festal garments.'"* [23]*And Naaman said, "Be pleased to accept two talents." And he urged him, and tied up two talents of silver in two bags, with two festal garments, and laid them upon two of his servants; and they carried them before Gehazi.* [24]*And when he came to the hill, he took them from their hand, and put them in the house; and he sent the men away, and they departed.* [25]*He went in, and stood before his master, and Elisha said to him, "Where have you been, Gehazi?" And he said, "Your servant went nowhere."* [26]*But he said to him, "Did I not go with you in spirit when the man turned from his chariot to meet you? Was it a time to accept money and garments, olive orchards and vineyards, sheep and oxen, menservants and maidservants?* [27]*Therefore the leprosy of Naaman shall cleave to you, and to your descendants for ever." So he went out from his presence a leper, as white as snow.*

OVERVIEW: Gehazi was a covetous man who tried to hide his earthly passions. Elisha gives Gehazi a chance to repent, but he does not take it and denies his fault (EPHREM).

5:21-22 Silver and Fine Clothing

THE COVETOUSNESS OF GEHAZI. EPHREM THE SYRIAN: Gehazi was a covetous man to the bottom of his heart. He had pretended to reject his hidden greed but saw, through the betrayal of his mouth, what his soul was trying to hide. ON THE SECOND BOOK OF KINGS 5.21.[1]

5:25-27 Leprosy Shall Cling to You

ELISHA GIVES GEHAZI A CHANCE TO REPENT. EPHREM THE SYRIAN: After Gehazi had come back from his meeting with Naaman, he entered Elisha's house, and [the prophet] asked him, according to custom, why he had moved away from him. "Where do you come from?" he said to Gehazi. He said this on purpose, so that the justice of the judgment passed on his sin might be evident. If Gehazi repented and swore, he would have been forgiven; but if he denied that he had secretly received money, the leprosy of Naaman would cover him conspicuously. ON THE SECOND BOOK OF KINGS 5.27.[2]

---

[1]ESOO 1:533. [2]ESOO 1:533.

6:1-7 THE MIRACULOUS RECOVERY OF THE AX HEAD

[1]*Now the sons of the prophets said to Elisha, "See, the place where we dwell under your charge is too small for us.* [2]*Let us go to the Jordan and each of us get there a log, and let us make a place for us to dwell there." And he answered, "Go."* [3]*Then one of them said, "Be pleased to go with your servants." And he answered, "I will go."* [4]*So he went with them. And when they came to the Jordan, they cut down trees.* [5]*But as one was felling a log, his axe head fell into the water; and he*

*cried out, "Alas, my master! It was borrowed." ⁶Then the man of God said, "Where did it fall?"
When he showed him the place, he cut off a stick, and threw it in there, and made the iron float.
⁷And he said, "Take it up." So he reached out his hand and took it.*

OVERVIEW: The house of the sacrifices of the
Law is too small for the greatness of the gospel of
Christ (EPHREM). The ax lay in the water, because
the human race had fallen into the abyss of all
vices in miserable ruin, but the piece of wood
thrown into the water by Elisha signifies that
Christ will ascend the gibbet of the cross to lift
up the human race from the depth of hell (CAE-
SARIUS, TERTULLIAN, JUSTIN MARTYR, EPHREM).

6:1-3 A Place Too Small

A TYPE OF THE CHURCH BUILT BY THE APOS-
TLES. EPHREM THE SYRIAN: These words were
fulfilled by the apostles: the house of the sacrifices of the Law was too small for them, and
when they realized that the meeting place of the
Jews was not sufficient for the greatness of the
gospel, they set out to build a holy church where
they gathered the children of God, who are righteous. This is what Isaiah had pointed out to them
in advance by the word of the Lord when he said,
"It is too light a thing that you should be my servant to raise up the tribes of Jacob and to restore
the survivors of Israel; I will give you as a light to
the nations, that my salvation may reach to the
end of the earth."[1] ON THE SECOND BOOK OF
KINGS 6.1.[2]

6:4-7 The Ax Head Fell into the Water

TRUTHS FULFILLED THROUGH THE SACRA-
MENT OF BAPTISM. CAESARIUS OF ARLES:
When the divine lesson was read now, dearly beloved, we heard that as blessed Elisha was going
to the river Jordan with the sons of the prophets
to cut some wood, an ax fell into the water, and
the man from whose hand it slipped cried out to
blessed Elisha, "Alas, my lord, for this was borrowed." After this blessed Elisha threw a piece of

wood into the place where the ax had fallen, and
the iron swam. Elisha typified our Lord and Savior, dearly beloved, as we have frequently mentioned to your charity. Moreover, in the boy who
was from the sons of the prophets and from
whose hand the ax slipped, we not unfittingly understand Christ our Lord. That ax that fell seems
to signify Adam or the whole human race. Therefore, the son of the prophets held the ax in his
hand, because our Lord and Savior had in the
hand of his power the human race, which he had
created. Just as the ax fell out of the prophet's
hand into the water, so the human race through
pride shook off itself free from the hand of almighty God, fell and plunged itself into the river
of dissipation and the waters of every sin. So the
ax lay in the water, because the human race had
fallen into the abyss of all vices in miserable ruin.
As it is written: "I am sunk in the abysmal
swamp," and again: "I have reached the watery
depths; the flood overwhelms me."[3] That river
where the ax fell signifies the pleasure or dissipation of this world, which is passing, fleeting and
descending into the abyss. A river derives its
name from the idea of flowing; since all sinners
are said to flow along clinging to transitory pleasures, for this reason that ax lay sunk in the river
and mud.

At his coming Elisha threw in a piece of wood,
and the iron swam. What does it mean to cast the
piece of wood and bring the iron to light, except
to ascend the gibbet of the cross, to lift up the
human race from the depth of hell and to free it
from the mud of all sins by the mystery of the
cross? After the iron floated, the prophet put in
his hand to recover it, and it returned to the useful service of its master. Thus it also happened to
us, dearly beloved brothers. We who had fallen

---

[1]Is 49:6. [2]*ESOO* 1:533-34. [3]Ps 69:2 (68:3 LXX, Vg).

from the Lord's hand through pride merited to return again to his hand and power through the wood of the cross. Therefore, with his help, let us strive as much as we can not to fall again from his hand through pride. Without any preceding good merits of ours we have been brought from darkness to light, recalled from death to life and brought back to the right path from many errors. For this reason let us run while we still possess the light of life and not neglect the passing times of salvation. Let not the unwholesomely sweet and exceedingly dangerous joy of this world delight us, lest we again fall away from good works and the path of justice as from the hand of the Lord and hasten to the wicked river of this world. Let us not be submerged again in the mud of all sins in unhappy destruction, but let us listen to the apostle say, "If you have risen with Christ, mind the things that are above, where Christ is seated at the right hand of God. Seek the things that are above."[4] Why does he say "if you have risen," unless because we had fallen? Elsewhere the same apostle says, "Awake, sleeper, and arise from among the dead, and Christ will enlighten you."[5] Does it not seem to you as though he is shouting to the ax, which is lying in the mud? Awake, he says, you who sleep in the deep waters, and Christ will enlighten you through the mystery of the cross. All these truths have already been fulfilled in us, beloved brothers, through the sacrament of baptism. SERMON 130.1-3.[6]

FREEDOM THROUGH BAPTISM. TERTULLIAN: And accordingly Elisha, having taken "wood" and cast it into that place where the iron had been submerged, forthwith it rose and swam on the surface, and the "wood" sank, which the sons of the prophets recovered. Thus they understood that the spirit of Elijah was presently conferred on him. What is more manifest than the mystery

of this wood: that the obduracy of this world had been sunk in the profundity of error and is freed in baptism by the wood of Christ, that is, of his passion, in order that what had formerly perished through the tree in Adam should be restored through the tree in Christ? AN ANSWER TO THE JEWS 13.[7]

RAISED BY CHRIST FROM THE MIRE OF SIN. JUSTIN MARTYR: Elisha, by throwing a piece of wood into the river Jordan, brought up to the surface the iron head of the ax with which the sons of the prophets had begun to cut wood for the construction of a building in which they proposed to read and study the precepts of God; just as our Christ, by being crucified on the wood of the cross and by sanctifying us by water raised up us who had been immersed in the mire of our mortal sins and made us a house of prayer and worship. DIALOGUE WITH TRYPHO 86.[8]

A SYMBOL OF THE SALVATION IN CHRIST. EPHREM THE SYRIAN: This is a symbol signifying the fall of Adam. For water represents the type of sin. Indeed, through water, sin was redeemed by the deluge at the time of Noah[9] and at the fulfillment of times. It was washed in the water of holy baptism by our Lord when he was baptized in the Jordan by John, when he was received and ate with sinners and in his passion was counted among the reprobates. The wood descended, the iron has emerged, because Emmanuel died, was buried and went down to the infernal regions of earth, and from there he has come back, and in his ascension he has lifted up Adam from the deep towards the heights. ON THE SECOND BOOK OF KINGS 6.5.[10]

---

[4]Col 3:1-2. [5]Eph 5:14. [6]FC 47:233-34*. [7]ANF 3:170*. [8]FC 6:286*. [9]See Gen 6:17. [10]ESOO 1:534.

6:8-23 A NEW WAR AGAINST THE ARAMEANS
[See commentary on 1 Kings 20:1-43; 22:1-40]

⁸Once when the king of Syria was warring against Israel, he took counsel with his servants, saying, "At such and such a place shall be my camp." ⁹But the man of God sent word to the king of Israel, "Beware that you do not pass this place, for the Syrians are going down there." ¹⁰And the king of Israel sent to the place of which the man of God told him. Thus he used to warn him, so that he saved himself there more than once or twice.

¹¹And the mind of the king of Syria was greatly troubled because of this thing; and he called his servants and said to them, "Will you not show me who of us is for the king of Israel?" ¹²And one of his servants said, "None, my lord, O king; but Elisha, the prophet who is in Israel, tells the king of Israel the words that you speak in your bedchamber." ¹³And he said, "Go and see where he is, that I may send and seize him." It was told him, "Behold, he is in Dothan." ¹⁴So he sent there horses and chariots and a great army; and they came by night, and surrounded the city.

¹⁵When the servant of the man of God rose early in the morning and went out, behold, an army with horses and chariots was round about the city. And the servant said, "Alas, my master! What shall we do?" ¹⁶He said, "Fear not, for those who are with us are more than those who are with them." ¹⁷Then Elisha prayed, and said, "O LORD, I pray thee, open his eyes that he may see." So the LORD opened the eyes of the young man, and he saw; and behold, the mountain was full of horses and chariots of fire round about Elisha. ¹⁸And when the Syrians came down against him, Elisha prayed to the LORD, and said, "Strike this people, I pray thee, with blindness." So he struck them with blindness in accordance with the prayer of Elisha. ¹⁹And Elisha said to them, "This is not the way, and this is not the city; follow me, and I will bring you to the man whom you seek." And he led them to Samaria.

²⁰As soon as they entered Samaria, Elisha said, "O LORD, open the eyes of these men, that they may see." So the LORD opened their eyes, and they saw; and lo, they were in the midst of Samaria. ²¹When the king of Israel saw them he said to Elisha, "My father, shall I slay them? Shall I slay them?" ²²He answered, "You shall not slay them. Would you slay those whom you have taken captive with your sword and with your bow? Set bread and water before them, that they may eat and drink and go to their master." ²³So he prepared for them a great feast; and when they had eaten and drunk, he sent them away, and they went to their master. And the Syrians came no more on raids into the land of Israel.

OVERVIEW: Elisha did the most glorious thing: he brought the battle to an end without using the force of the soldiers but with the help of God thanks to his merits before him. Faith and justice should be observed even in war, and it could not but be a disgraceful thing if faith were violated (AMBROSE). Adversaries are conquered more by merits than by strength and are overcome not so much by power as by holiness, just as holy Elisha overcame his foes not by arms but by prayer

(Maximus). Where there is perfidy there is blindness, so rightly the army of the unbelievers was blind; but where there is faith there is an army of angels (AMBROSE).

6:16-23 *Strike This People with Blindness*

ELISHA BROUGHT A BATTLE TO AN END.
AMBROSE: But, as many delight in warfare, which is the most glorious, to bring a battle to an end by the strength of a great army or by merits before God alone? Elisha rested in one place while the king of Syria waged a great war against the people of our ancestors, and was adding to its terrors by various treacherous plans and was endeavoring to catch them in an ambush. But the prophet found out all their preparations, and being by the grace of God present everywhere in mental vigor, he told the thoughts of their enemies to his countrymen and warned them of what places to beware. And when this was known to the king of Syria, he sent an army and shut in the prophet. Elisha prayed and caused all of them to be struck with blindness and made those who had come to besiege him enter Samaria as captives. DUTIES OF THE CLERGY 3.1.5.[1]

FAITH AND JUSTICE. AMBROSE: If, then, justice is binding, even in war, how much more ought we to observe it in time of peace. Such favor the prophet showed to those who came to seize him. We read that the king of Syria had sent his army to lie in wait for him, for he had learned that it was Elisha who had made known to all his plans and consultations. And Gehazi, the prophet's servant, seeing the army, began to fear that his life was in danger. But the prophet said to him, "Do not fear, for they who are with us are more than they who are with them." And when the prophet asked that the eyes of his servant might be opened, they were opened. Then Gehazi saw the whole mountain full of horse and chariots round about Elisha. As they came down to him the prophet says, "Strike, O God, the army of Syria with blindness." And this prayer being granted, he says to the Syrians, "Follow me, and I will bring you to the man whom you seek." Then they saw Elisha, whom they were endeavoring to lay hold of, and seeing him they could not hold him fast. It is clear from this that faith and justice should be observed even in war; and that it could not but be a disgraceful thing if faith were violated. DUTIES OF THE CLERGY 1.29.140.[2]

THE DIVINE PROTECTION MERITED BY HOLINESS. MAXIMUS OF TURIN: Thus, when the king of Syria wanted to capture holy Elisha the prophet and subject him to his power and had surrounded him with many warriors and troops, he was not terrified or disturbed but said to the servant who brought him the information: *Do not fear, for there are more on our side than on theirs.* O the faith of the holy prophet! He does not fear the adversaries whom he sees because he knows that angels are with Him in whom he believes; he is not afraid of earthly plots because he knows that heavenly auxiliaries are present to him. *There are more on our side,* he says, *than on theirs.* What a remarkable thing! There are more defenders from heaven merited by holiness than there are attackers on earth produced by wickedness. See the merit of blessedness! The prophet already speaks of a multitude while his servant is still uncertain of salvation. How much more do spiritual eyes discern than fleshly ones! The one perceives a throng of warriors, and the other catches sight of a sign of protection. How great is the divine mercy! A benefit is conferred upon human beings, and it is not seen; those in danger obtain help, and they do not know it. For this is the kindness of the Savior, that He should intervene for the sake of salvation and not let Himself be seen, that He should be sensed through His benefits and not be discerned through sight.

Hence he errs who thinks that when he has waged a war successfully, he has overcome by his own power. For he ought to know that adversaries are conquered more by merits than by

---

[1]NPNF 2 10:68. [2]NPNF 2 10:24*.

strength and are overcome not so much by power as by holiness, just as holy Elisha overcame his foes not by arms but by prayer. For when he said to his servant, in order to drive out his fear, that there were more defenders present, but his fear could not be removed, then he prayed to the Lord and said: *Lord, open his eyes that he may see! And his eyes were opened and he saw, and behold, there was a whole mountain full of horsemen,* and so forth. The prayer of the prophet, then, opened his servant's eyes. It is not to be wondered at if prayer, which opened heaven for an army to come, opened his eyes so that he could see the army. It is not to be wondered at, I say, if he who promises new auxiliaries inserts new eyes. Or why would not he who furnished an army of angels produce an army of seers? Why, I say, would not he who penetrated the darkness of the clouds by his merits cleanse dullness of vision by his prayer? Necessarily, then, with this deed holy Elisha offered safety to his frightened servant, to whom he had already given clearness of vision. SERMON 83.2-3.[3]

WHERE THERE IS FAITH. AMBROSE: Elsewhere, also, that is, in the books of Kings we read that Elisha was in Samaria, and suddenly an army of Syrians surrounded and set on him. Gehazi saw them and said to his master, "O master, what shall we do?" And Elisha the prophet said, "Do not fear, for there are more with us than with them." And he prayed that the Lord would open the eyes of Gehazi. And his eyes were opened, and he saw the mountain full of horses and chariots around Elisha. And Elisha prayed that God would strike them with blindness. And they were struck, and they entered into the city whither they were going, seeing not at all. Surely, you soldiers who have been surrounded have heard that where there is perfidy, there is blindness. Rightly, therefore, was the army of the unbeliever blind. But where there is faith, there is an army of angels. Good, then, is faith, which often exercises its power among the dead.[4] Hence our adversary [the devil] and his

legions are daily hurled back by the virtue of the martyrs. ON THE DEATH OF THEODOSIUS 10.[5]

THE JEWS CONVERTED BY CHRIST WILL LOSE THEIR BLINDNESS. EPHREM THE SYRIAN: Elisha prayed before the Lord and said, "strike this people with blindness." And he struck them with blindness according to the words of Elisha. Ben-hadad, king of the Arameans, sent a large army to surround the city of Dothan and ordered them to arrest Elisha, who lived there at that time. Now his servant saw the army of the Arameans and was horrified. But Elisha opened the eyes of the young man and showed him the ranks of fire that the Lord had erected around him against the Arameans, and his fear disappeared. At the same time [the enemies] were struck in their eyes and did not know the route of their march. They asked Elisha to be their guide; he led them to Samaria, and they were imprisoned inside walls. Then their eyes opened and they realized the danger into which they had voluntarily thrown themselves. But Elisha ordered that nobody should hurt them, and by his command, king Jehoram warmly received them. After offering them a banquet, he sent them back to their land in peace.

This is the symbolic meaning [of this passage]: God had predicted through the prophet Isaiah, "The heart of these people was hardened; they have stopped their ears and have shut their eyes, so that they cannot see with their eyes."[6] The people of Abraham had been blinded by a just sentence of God, because of their perverse will. They asked that the Savior of the world be killed and tried to delete any memory of him completely, but Christ has converted them from their perversity to good behavior. He has delivered his persecutors from their blindness and has given them the bread of heaven. Then he has scattered them through the earth to announce his wonders. Such were those who came back from the mount

---

[3]ACW 50:198-99. [4]See Col 2:12; Acts 17:31. [5]FC 22:311. [6]Is 6:10 (Peshitta).

of Golgotha, beating their own chest.[7] They said to Simon and the other apostles with contrite hearts, "Brothers, what should we do?"[8] And such was Saul, the persecutor of the church whose eyes were open without seeing[9] and whose eyes God wondrously closed but opened again very soon,[10] and to whom he ordered to bring his name before the nations, the kings and the children of Israel.[11] On the Second Book of Kings 6.18.[12]

---

[7]See Lk 23:48. [8]Acts 2:37. [9]See Acts 9:8. [10]See Acts 9:18. [11]See Acts 9:15. [12]ESOO 1:534-35.

6:24–7:1 ATROCIOUS ACTS COMMITTED DURING THE SIEGE OF SAMARIA

[24]*Afterward Ben-hadad king of Syria mustered his entire army, and went up, and besieged Samaria.* [25]*And there was a great famine in Samaria, as they besieged it, until an ass's head was sold for eighty shekels of silver, and the fourth part of a kab of dove's dung for five shekels of silver.* [26]*Now as the king of Israel was passing by upon the wall, a woman cried out to him, saying, "Help, my lord, O king!"* [27]*And he said, "If the Lord will not help you, whence shall I help you? From the threshing floor, or from the wine press?"* [28]*And the king asked her, "What is your trouble?" She answered, "This woman said to me, 'Give your son, that we may eat him today, and we will eat my son tomorrow.'* [29]*So we boiled my son, and ate him. And on the next day I said to her, 'Give your son, that we may eat him'; but she has hidden her son."* [30]*When the king heard the words of the woman he rent his clothes—now he was passing by upon the wall—and the people looked, and behold, he had sackcloth beneath upon his body—*[31]*and he said, "May God do so to me and more also, if the head of Elisha the son of Shaphat remains on his shoulders today."*

[32]*Elisha was sitting in his house, and the elders were sitting with him. Now the king had dispatched a man from his presence; but before the messenger arrived Elisha said to the elders, "Do you see how this murderer has sent to take off my head? Look, when the messenger comes, shut the door, and hold the door fast against him. Is not the sound of his master's feet behind him?"* [33]*And while he was still speaking with them, the king[f] came down to him and said, "This trouble is from the Lord! Why should I wait for the Lord any longer?"* **7** *But Elisha said, "Hear the word of the Lord: thus says the Lord, Tomorrow about this time a measure of fine meal shall be sold for a shekel, and two measures of barley for a shekel, at the gate of Samaria."*

f See 7.2: Heb *messenger*

Overview: The famine, which forced the Samaritans to practice cannibalism, symbolizes the lack of heavenly nourishment, which affected in those days all the nations of the earth. The donkey's head signifies the teaching coming from the philosophers and scientists of the world, and it was an abominable and rotting food but was very precious until the famine reigned over the earth (EPHREM). When famine prevails over a land, not only does it not prevail over the just, but rather through them, a remedy is brought to the threatened destruction (ORIGEN).

6:24-32 Gruesome Effects of the Famine

A FAMINE OF HEAVENLY FOOD. EPHREM THE SYRIAN: "Some time later King Ben-hadad of Aram mustered his entire army; he marched against Samaria and laid siege to it." This is that Ben-hadad who had been condemned to death by God; and Ahab had received the order to execute him.[1] But he spared his life and sent him back in peace. Therefore the Arameans besieged the city and prolonged the siege for many days, because their army occupied the whole surrounding area, so that bread began to be more and more scarce, and famine ruled. And when [the citizens] did not find the usual sustenance and food, they fell on the corpses of the dead. For the Scripture relates that there were certain mothers who decided to kill their children to assuage their hunger. And after one of them had put her son to death, when her companion in crime hid her own son (in order to save him) and broke the contract, an argument rose between them, and they both went before the judge. And they began to expound their reasons before the king, that is, Jehoram, the son of Ahab. The king, seeing that that was a harsh trial for him, was taken over by a violent rage against Elisha. For he thought [the prophet] was the cause of his disaster. Therefore he said, "Yesterday he gave abundant goods to Aramean robbers, and today has given sufficient bread to his disciples, and they are not lacking food, but he has no care for the people of his city and abandons them in their need." And he swore that on that day itself he would take revenge on Elisha for the blood of his people. But Jehoram had no right to accuse the prophet, but rather Ahab, his father, who had

scorned the prophets. In fact, if he had been persuaded by their words and had killed Ben-hadad, that [king] would have never besieged Samaria and would have never thrown him into such calamities.

From the symbolic point of view the atrocious famine which tortured the Samaritans for so many days and forced them to eat in such an abominable manner shows the lack of heavenly nourishment, which affected in those days all the nations of the earth. So the city of Samaria signifies the whole of humankind, and its famine represents the famine of all. But Elisha made it disappear through his prayer, as well as through the grace of Christ. The sick were fortified by his strength, and "those who were full hired themselves out for bread."[2] This means that the apostles, announcers [of the gospel], have transmitted to the Gentiles the knowledge of salvation, and it has flowed, as Isaiah predicted, like "the waters covering the sea."[3] In the same manner it had been decreed before God that the hungry should eat the crop of the foolish and that the thirsty should absorb his goods, as the friend of the righteous Job said.[4] Indeed, as the Samaritans plundered the food that they had collected for the Arameans and the needs of their army and brought it into their army, so the church of the Gentiles took the holy books which were preserved in the Hebrew synagogues, and gave them for the benefit of their descendants. ON THE SECOND BOOK OF KINGS 6.24.[5]

PAGAN PHILOSOPHERS AND THE LAW OF MOSES. EPHREM THE SYRIAN: "Famine in Samaria became so great that a donkey's head was sold for eighty shekels of silver." The donkey's head, which the Scripture reports here to be so expensive, signifies the teaching coming from the ravings of the philosophers and the scientists of the world. And it was an abominable and rotting food but was very precious when the famine reigned over the earth, and there was no one to break and give the bread to those children who

---

[1]See 1 Kings 20 (21):28-34. [2]1 Sam 2:5. [3]Is 11:9. [4]See Job 5:5. [5]ESOO 1:535-36.

asked for it, that is, until the advent of Christ.

"And one-fourth of a kab of dove's dung [was sold] for five shekels of silver." Even though the symbol is contrary—in fact, it does not fit in with the Word—but because the righteous are likened to a dove, we say that the kab of dove's dung represents the teaching of the law of Moses, if we compare it with the gospel of Christ. So it can be said that it was mud, a mud precious to the Jews at that time, with which they covered their eyes, which were to be opened soon by the spiritual bath and the gospel of Christ. On the Second Book of Kings 6.25.[6]

7:1 Choice Meal Shall Be Sold for a Shekel

Famine Does Not Prevail over the Just.
Origen: You will also find similar things in the times of Elisha, when the son of Jader, king of Syria, came up against Samaria and besieged it.

"And there was a great famine in Samaria for so long," Scripture says, "that a donkey's head became worth fifty shekels of silver and a quarter of pigeon dung five pieces of silver." But suddenly an amazing change occurs through the word of the prophet, who says, "Hear the word of the Lord. Thus says the Lord: 'Tomorrow, at this hour a measure of the finest wheat flour shall be one shekel and two measure of barley shall be one shekel, in the gates of Samaria.'"

Notice, therefore, what is inferred from all these texts: when famine prevails over a land, not only does it not prevail over the just, but rather through them, a remedy is brought to the threatened destruction. Homilies on Genesis 16.3.[7]

---

[6]ESOO 1:536. [7]FC 71:219.

7:2-20 END OF THE FAMINE IN SAMARIA

[2]*Then the captain on whose hand the king leaned said to the man of God, "If the Lord himself should make windows in heaven, could this thing be?" But he said, "You shall see it with your own eyes, but you shall not eat of it."*

[3]*Now there were four men who were lepers at the entrance to the gate; and they said to one another, "Why do we sit here till we die? [4]If we say, 'Let us enter the city,' the famine is in the city, and we shall die there; and if we sit here, we die also. So now come, let us go over to the camp of the Syrians; if they spare our lives we shall live, and if they kill us we shall but die." [5]So they arose at twilight to go to the camp of the Syrians; but when they came to the edge of the camp of the Syrians, behold, there was no one there. [6]For the Lord had made the army of the Syrians hear the sound of chariots, and of horses, the sound of a great army, so that they said to one another, "Behold, the king of Israel has hired against us the kings of the Hittites and the kings of Egypt to come upon us." [7]So they fled away in the twilight and forsook their tents, their horses, and their asses, leaving the camp as it was, and fled for their lives. [8]And when these lepers came to the edge of the camp, they went into a tent, and ate and drank, and they carried off silver and gold and*

---

clothing, and went and hid them; then they came back, and entered another tent, and carried off things from it, and went and hid them.

⁹*Then they said to one another, "We are not doing right. This day is a day of good news; if we are silent and wait until the morning light, punishment will overtake us; now therefore come, let us go and tell the king's household." *¹⁰*So they came and called to the gatekeepers of the city, and told them, "We came to the camp of the Syrians, and behold, there was no one to be seen or heard there, nothing but the horses tied, and the asses tied, and the tents as they were." *¹¹*Then the gatekeepers called out, and it was told within the king's household. *¹²*And the king rose in the night, and said to his servants, "I will tell you what the Syrians have prepared against us. They know that we are hungry; therefore they have gone out of the camp to hide themselves in the open country, thinking, 'When they come out of the city, we shall take them alive and get into the city.' " *¹³*And one of his servants said, "Let some men take five of the remaining horses, seeing that those who are left here will fare like the whole multitude of Israel that have already perished; let us send and see." *¹⁴*So they took two mounted men, and the king sent them after the army of the Syrians, saying, "Go and see." *¹⁵*So they went after them as far as the Jordan; and lo, all the way was littered with garments and equipment which the Syrians had thrown away in their haste. And the messengers returned, and told the king.*

¹⁶*Then the people went out, and plundered the camp of the Syrians. So a measure of fine meal was sold for a shekel, and two measures of barley for a shekel, according to the word of the LORD. *¹⁷*Now the king had appointed the captain on whose hand he leaned to have charge of the gate; and the people trod upon him in the gate, so that he died, as the man of God had said when the king came down to him. *¹⁸*For when the man of God had said to the king, "Two measures of barley shall be sold for a shekel, and a measure of fine meal for a shekel, about this time tomorrow in the gate of Samaria," *¹⁹*the captain had answered the man of God, "If the LORD himself should make windows in heaven, could such a thing be?" And he had said, "You shall see it with your own eyes, but you shall not eat of it." *²⁰*And so it happened to him, for the people trod upon him in the gate and he died.*

OVERVIEW: The officer prefigures the fall of the people of Abraham, those who could see "the bread" of life "descended from heaven," but without profit. By announcing goods for the inhabitants of their city, the four leprous men fittingly represent the four holy Evangelists (EPHREM). The Lord knows how to bring to naught the counsels of the nations, as he did when he made the Arameans flee, so that they left a great abundance of food in Samaria (BASIL).

7:2 You Shall See but Not Eat

THE FALL OF THE PEOPLE OF ABRAHAM.

EPHREM THE SYRIAN: Elisha said, "Tomorrow there will be relief from the siege and the famine in the city of Samaria." But an officer of the house of king Jehoram mocked these words and derided the word [of the prophet]. Elisha answered him what the Scripture relates here. Some say that this man was the one whose story is reported by the biblical text above.[1] He had sent to Elisha a messenger or a captain of the guard [of the king]

---

[1]See 2 Kings 6:32-33. The story of this officer resumes at 2 Kings 7:17-20.

to arrest him or to kill him but later had repented of his evil scheme and had run after him, preventing him from executing his command. This poor man, therefore, had seen the delivery of the town and the consequent abundance of which he had not profited, because on that same day the inhabitants of the city, who were coming out to plunder, had trampled him, and he had died. In his miserable fate he prefigures the fall of the people of Abraham, those who could see "the bread" of life "descended from heaven"[2] to them but in large number were not worthy of enjoying that vivifying abundance, even though, at the same time, it was abundantly given to all those who asked for it through the grace of our Savior Jesus Christ. ON THE SECOND BOOK OF KINGS 7.1.[3]

7:3-15 Four Leprous Men

THE FOUR EVANGELISTS PREFIGURED.
EPHREM THE SYRIAN: Even though the four lepers are loathsome, if we symbolically recognize in them the fact that they announced goods for the inhabitants of their city, they do no wrong to the symbol but correctly represent the four holy Evangelists. Indeed, we must bear in mind that through their books the grace of our Savior and source of life Jesus Christ was known, and freedom was given to all people according to his divine plan. And so those whose flesh was leprous shone in their interior look with the splendor of their righteousness. In addition, they symbolically represent the first attitude of the apostles in the fact that leprosy had corrupted their skin. But they also represent them in the fact that their interior was adorned with righteous behavior because the old man has been

transformed by the coming of the Holy Spirit and renewed. Therefore they have clothed themselves with the garment shining with the colors of heaven and have been sent to show the work of the hands of God. ON THE SECOND BOOK OF KINGS 7.3.[4]

7:16 Measures and Prices

THE LORD OVERTURNS THE COUNSELS OF THE NATIONS.
BASIL THE GREAT: "The Lord brings to nothing the counsels of nations, and he rejects the devices of people."[5] . . . If you will read the things in each history that God did to the faithless nations, you will find that the statement has much force even according to our corporal intelligence. When Joram, son of Ahab, was king in Israel, then his son Ader, king of Syria, carrying on a war with a great force and a heavy hand, besieged Samaria, so that even the necessaries of life were wanting to them, and the head of a donkey was sold for fifty shekels of silver and the fourth part of a cabe[6] of pigeon dung for five shekels of silver.[7] At that time, therefore, in order that the promise of Elisha might be fulfilled, the counsels of Syria were brought to nothing, and abandoning their tents and all their supplies, they fled, leaving such a great abundance in Samaria that a measure of fine flour and two measures of barley were sold for one shekel. Thus, then, the Lord knew how to bring to nothing the counsels of the nations. HOMILIES ON THE PSALMS 15.6 (Ps 32).[8]

---

[2]Jn 6:58. [3]ESOO 1:537-38. [4]ESOO 1:538. [5]Ps 33:10 (32:10 LXX). [6]A cabe was about four pints. [7]See 2 Kings 6:25. [8]FC 46:239-40*.

8:1-29 THE NEW PROPHECIES OF ELISHA

¹Now Elisha had said to the woman whose son he had restored to life, "Arise, and depart with your household, and sojourn wherever you can; for the LORD has called for a famine, and it will come upon the land for seven years." ²So the woman arose, and did according to the word of the man of God; she went with her household and sojourned in the land of the Philistines seven years. ³And at the end of the seven years, when the woman returned from the land of the Philistines, she went forth to appeal to the king for her house and her land. ⁴Now the king was talking with Gehazi the servant of the man of God, saying, "Tell me all the great things that Elisha has done." ⁵And while he was telling the king how Elisha had restored the dead to life, behold, the woman whose son he had restored to life appealed to the king for her house and her land. And Gehazi said, "My lord, O king, here is the woman, and here is her son whom Elisha restored to life." ⁶And when the king asked the woman, she told him. So the king appointed an official for her, saying, "Restore all that was hers, together with all the produce of the fields from the day that she left the land until now."

⁷Now Elisha came to Damascus. Ben-hadad the king of Syria was sick; and when it was told him, "The man of God has come here," ⁸the king said to Hazael, "Take a present with you and go to meet the man of God, and inquire of the LORD through him, saying, 'Shall I recover from this sickness?'" ⁹So Hazael went to meet him, and took a present with him, all kinds of goods of Damascus, forty camel loads. When he came and stood before him, he said, "Your son Ben-hadad king of Syria has sent me to you, saying, 'Shall I recover from this sickness?'" ¹⁰And Elisha said to him, "Go, say to him, 'You shall certainly recover'; but the LORD has shown me that he shall certainly die." ¹¹And he fixed his gaze and stared at him, until he was ashamed. And the man of God wept. ¹²And Hazael said, "Why does my lord weep?" He answered, "Because I know the evil that you will do to the people of Israel; you will set on fire their fortresses, and you will slay their young men with the sword, and dash in pieces their little ones, and rip up their women with child." ¹³And Hazael said, "What is your servant, who is but a dog, that he should do this great thing?" Elisha answered, "The LORD has shown me that you are to be king over Syria." ¹⁴Then he departed from Elisha, and came to his master, who said to him, "What did Elisha say to you?" And he answered, "He told me that you would certainly recover." ¹⁵But on the morrow he took the coverlet and dipped it in water and spread it over his face, till he died. And Hazael became king in his stead.

¹⁶In the fifth year of Joram the son of Ahab, king of Israel,ᵍ Jehoram the son of Jehoshaphat, king of Judah, began to reign. ¹⁷He was thirty-two years old when he became king, and he reigned eight years in Jerusalem. ¹⁸And he walked in the way of the kings of Israel, as the house of Ahab had done, for the daughter of Ahab was his wife. And he did what was evil in the sight of the LORD. ¹⁹Yet the LORD would not destroy Judah, for the sake of David his servant, since he promised to give a lamp to him and to his sons for ever.

^{20}*In his days Edom revolted from the rule of Judah, and set up a king of their own.* ^{21}*Then Joram passed over to Zair with all his chariots, and rose by night, and he and his chariot commanders smote the Edomites who had surrounded him; but his army fled home.* ^{22}*So Edom revolted from the rule of Judah to this day. Then Libnah revolted at the same time.* ^{23}*Now the rest of the acts of Joram, and all that he did, are they not written in the Book of the Chronicles of the Kings of Judah?* ^{24}*So Joram slept with his fathers, and was buried with his fathers in the city of David; and Ahaziah his son reigned in his stead.*

^{25}*In the twelfth year of Joram the son of Ahab, king of Israel, Ahaziah the son of Jehoram, king of Judah, began to reign.* ^{26}*Ahaziah was twenty-two years old when he began to reign, and he reigned one year in Jerusalem. His mother's name was Athaliah; she was a granddaughter of Omri king of Israel.* ^{27}*He also walked in the way of the house of Ahab, and did what was evil in the sight of the LORD, as the house of Ahab had done, for he was son-in-law to the house of Ahab.*

^{28}*He went with Joram the son of Ahab to make war against Hazael king of Syria at Ramoth-gilead, where the Syrians wounded Joram.* ^{29}*And King Joram returned to be healed in Jezreel of the wounds which the Syrians had given him at Ramah, when he fought against Hazael king of Syria. And Ahaziah the son of Jehoram king of Judah went down to see Joram the son of Ahab in Jezreel, because he was sick.*

g Gk Syr: Heb Israel, Jehoshaphat being king of Judah

OVERVIEW: Palestine, where the Shunammite woman moves, symbolizes the world that hates the saints and constantly persecutes them. Ben-hadad's illness derived from his unhappiness, because he had been deeply afflicted by the fact that his armies had been defeated and his people had been driven out of the city. Ben-hadad was misled by Hazael, his ambassador, who spread the bed cover on his master, killed him and reigned in his place, as Elisha had predicted (EPHREM).

8:1-6 The Shunammite Woman Settled in the Land of the Philistines

THE WORLD HATES THE SAINTS AND CONSTANTLY PERSECUTES THEM. EPHREM THE SYRIAN: "Now Elisha had said to the woman whose son he had restored to life, 'Get up and go with your household.' " This is the Shunammite woman who had received Elisha in her home. And [the prophet] had taken care of her son too, who had died, by reviving him. Elisha predicted to her that a seven-year famine would occur and

invited her to find a new home by emigrating. He chose for her Palestine, a close and fertile region, whose inhabitants were rich thanks to their maritime commerce. For the land of the Philistines is entirely situated along the coast, and it had, at that time, some renowned harbors which were full of countless vessels, as is testified by the Scripture in many passages. That is why the patriarchs Abraham and Isaac had looked there for their refuge.[1]

From the allegorical point of view, Palestine, which received the righteous who were in exile and symbolically far from the Lord,[2] was a figure of the world. And the people of Palestine detested the people of God and ill-treated the children of Israel who feared God. Later they were defeated by David and gave up their weapons of war, but they took them up again now and then. The world hates the saints and constantly persecutes them. And even after our Lord has defeated it and its prince [the devil] has been thrown out,

---

[1]See Gen 12:1. [2]See 2 Cor 5:6.

these two never cease from fighting against his servants, grabbing and destroying the idle and the ignorant. On the Second Book of Kings 8.1.[3]

8:7-15 Ben-hadad Will Certainly Die

Ben-hadad Was Upset by His Failure in the War. Ephrem the Syrian: "Elisha went to Damascus while King Ben-hadad was ill." His illness had derived from his unhappiness. For he had been deeply afflicted by the fact that, in the war of Samaria, his armies had been defeated and that, at the same time, his people had been chased from the city when he had hoped that his victory would occur immediately. His entire army had fled and sunk into shame and dishonor, and he was troubled in his mind because of this. In addition, the anguish of his thoughts was due to something that was not responsible for his fall: he had been deceived in believing that a countless and powerful army would march against him, whereas it was later shown that there was no army at all to oppress him.

Therefore the king, when he heard of the coming of Elisha, sent Hazael, one of his noble men, to meet him. He ordered him to persuade the prophet to take care of his healing, and since he thought that this request must be accompanied with gifts and offerings, according to secular customs, he sent him, through his ambassador, all sorts of goods from Damascus and forty camels. But certainly the prophets refused, just as Elisha had refused and had not accepted the offerings of Naaman, the Aramean. On the Second Book of Kings 8.7.[4]

The Words of Elisha. Ephrem the Syrian: "Go, say to him, 'You shall certainly recover;' but the Lord has shown me that he shall certainly die." These were the words of Elisha to the king, who asked him, "Will I live after this illness?" But it seems that they do not agree with the truth of the events, and not even with each other. However, after the words reported above in the story of the prophet Micah,[5] it is evident that they do not cancel each other out or contradict each other. In fact, both prophets answer in the same manner, and the words of their reply pursue the same aim in the fact that they announce to their interlocutor good and death at the same time. But in the reply of Micah a particular aspect must be considered, that is, the fact that Ahab could not escape from death, because he so ardently and savagely wanted to go to the war, which was the real cause of his fall.

But the case of Ben-hadad is quite different: it would have been easy for him to get rid of his illness, because it was not serious or fatal. He would have recovered from his illness, as Elisha had said to him and as Ben-Hadad had asked him by saying, "Will I live after my illness?" However, he died in a natural course but by a hostile means: he was misled by Hazael, his ambassador, the one who spread the bed cover[6] on his master, killed him and reigned in his place, as Elisha had predicted. On the Second Book of Kings 8.10.[7]

---

[3]ESOO 1:538. [4]ESOO 1:538-39. [5]See 1 Kings 22:15. [6]The Syriac text reads "hand," but it seems that Ephrem refers to the entire action of spreading the wet bed cover. [7]ESOO 1:539.

9:1-37 JEHU TAKES REVENGE AGAINST JEZEBEL

¹Then Elisha the prophet called one of the sons of the prophets and said to him, "Gird up your loins, and take this flask of oil in your hand, and go to Ramoth-gilead. ²And when you arrive, look there for Jehu the son of Jehoshaphat, son of Nimshi; and go in and bid him rise from among his fellows, and lead him to an inner chamber. ³Then take the flask of oil, and pour it on his head, and say, 'Thus says the LORD, I anoint you king over Israel.' Then open the door and flee; do not tarry."

⁴So the young man, the prophet,ᵇ went to Ramoth-gilead. ⁵And when he came, behold, the commanders of the army were in council; and he said, "I have an errand to you, O commander." And Jehu said, "To which of us all?" And he said, "To you, O commander." ⁶So he arose, and went into the house; and the young man poured the oil on his head, saying to him, "Thus says the LORD the God of Israel, I anoint you king over the people of the LORD, over Israel. ⁷And you shall strike down the house of Ahab your master, that I may avenge on Jezebel the blood of my servants the prophets, and the blood of all the servants of the LORD. ⁸For the whole house of Ahab shall perish; and I will cut off from Ahab every male, bond or free, in Israel. ⁹And I will make the house of Ahab like the house of Jeroboam the son of Nebat, and like the house of Baasha the son of Ahijah. ¹⁰And the dogs shall eat Jezebel in the territory of Jezreel, and none shall bury her." Then he opened the door, and fled.

¹¹When Jehu came out to the servants of his master, they said to him, "Is all well? Why did this mad fellow come to you?" And he said to them, "You know the fellow and his talk." ¹²And they said, "That is not true; tell us now." And he said, "Thus and so he spoke to me, saying, 'Thus says the LORD, I anoint you king over Israel.'" ¹³Then in haste every man of them took his garment, and put it under him on the bareⁱ steps, and they blew the trumpet, and proclaimed, "Jehu is king."

¹⁴Thus Jehu the son of Jehoshaphat the son of Nimshi conspired against Joram. (Now Joram with all Israel had been on guard at Ramoth-gilead against Hazael king of Syria; ¹⁵but King Joram had returned to be healed in Jezreel of the wounds which the Syrians had given him, when he fought with Hazael king of Syria.) So Jehu said, "If this is your mind, then let no one slip out of the city to go and tell the news in Jezreel." ¹⁶Then Jehu mounted his chariot, and went to Jezreel, for Joram lay there. And Ahaziah king of Judah had come down to visit Joram.

¹⁷Now the watchman was standing on the tower in Jezreel, and he spied the company of Jehu as he came, and said, "I see a company." And Joram said, "Take a horseman, and send to meet them, and let him say, 'Is it peace?'" ¹⁸So a man on horseback went to meet him, and said, "Thus says the king, 'Is it peace?'" And Jehu said, "What have you to do with peace? Turn round and ride behind me." And the watchman reported, saying, "The messenger reached them, but he is not coming back." ¹⁹Then he sent out a second horseman, who came to them, and said, "Thus the king has said, 'Is it peace?'" And Jehu answered, "What have you to do with peace? Turn round and ride

behind me." ²⁰Again the watchman reported, "He reached them, but he is not coming back. And the driving is like the driving of Jehu the son of Nimshi; for he drives furiously."

²¹Joram said, "Make ready." And they made ready his chariot. Then Joram king of Israel and Ahaziah king of Judah set out, each in his chariot, and went to meet Jehu, and met him at the property of Naboth the Jezreelite. ²²And when Joram saw Jehu, he said, "Is it peace, Jehu?" He answered, "What peace can there be, so long as the harlotries and the sorceries of your mother Jezebel are so many?" ²³Then Joram reined about and fled, saying to Ahaziah, "Treachery, O Ahaziah!" ²⁴And Jehu drew his bow with his full strength, and shot Joram between the shoulders, so that the arrow pierced his heart, and he sank in his chariot. ²⁵Jehu said to Bidkar his aide, "Take him up, and cast him on the plot of ground belonging to Naboth the Jezreelite; for remember, when you and I rode side by side behind Ahab his father, how the LORD uttered this oracle against him: ²⁶'As surely as I saw yesterday the blood of Naboth and the blood of his sons—says the LORD—I will requite you on this plot of ground.' Now therefore take him up and cast him on the plot of ground, in accordance with the word of the LORD."

²⁷When Ahaziah the king of Judah saw this, he fled in the direction of Beth-haggan. And Jehu pursued him, and said, "Shoot him also"; and they shot him^j in the chariot at the ascent of Gur, which is by Ibleam. And he fled to Megiddo, and died there. ²⁸His servants carried him in a chariot to Jerusalem, and buried him in his tomb with his fathers in the city of David.

²⁹In the eleventh year of Joram the son of Ahab, Ahaziah began to reign over Judah.

³⁰When Jehu came to Jezreel, Jezebel heard of it; and she painted her eyes, and adorned her head, and looked out of the window. ³¹And as Jehu entered the gate, she said, "Is it peace, you Zimri, murderer of your master?" ³²And he lifted up his face to the window, and said, "Who is on my side? Who?" Two or three eunuchs looked out at him. ³³He said, "Throw her down." So they threw her down; and some of her blood spattered on the wall and on the horses, and they trampled on her. ³⁴Then he went in and ate and drank; and he said, "See now to this cursed woman, and bury her; for she is a king's daughter." ³⁵But when they went to bury her, they found no more of her than the skull and the feet and the palms of her hands. ³⁶When they came back and told him, he said, "This is the word of the LORD, which he spoke by his servant Elijah the Tishbite, 'In the territory of Jezreel the dogs shall eat the flesh of Jezebel; ³⁷and the corpse of Jezebel shall be as dung upon the face of the field in the territory of Jezreel, so that no one can say, This is Jezebel.'"

h Gk Syr: Heb *the young man, the young man, the prophet*   **i** The meaning of the Hebrew word is uncertain   **j** Syr Vg Compare Gk: Heb lacks *and they shot him*

OVERVIEW: Elisha's servant is sent to the city of Ramoth-gilead, where he anoints Jehu and orders him to take revenge against the house of Ahab. When Jezebel heard that Jehu had come to her city, she painted her eyes and adorned her head with a miter, thinking that she might still seduce him with her look. Jezebel, who had terrified prophets and enslaved kings, was thrown by slaves into shame and dishonor, and her body was lacerated by the teeth of dogs (EPHREM).

9:1-26 Jehu Anointed King of Israel

JEHU IS ANOINTED TO TAKE REVENGE AGAINST THE HOUSE OF AHAB. EPHREM THE SYRIAN: "Then the prophet Elisha called a member of the company of prophets and said to him, 'Gird up your loins; take this flask of oil in your hand, and go to Ramoth-gilead.'" Here the Scripture reports the just sentence that befalls the house of Ahab. Immediately it speaks about the choice of the judge and executor of the judgment. And this was Jehu, the son of Nimshi, who, on the word of the Lord, anointed one of the prophets for the royalty. And this was the disciple of Elisha who was sent by his master to the city of Ramoth-gilead, which was under the siege of the Israelites. He entered their camp and went to the tent where the commanders of the army gathered and standing before them, he naively said, "I have a message for you, commander." Jehu said in reply, "For which one of us?" The servant realized that he was the one indicated by Elisha. In fact, he did not know his name, but even though the son of the prophet did not know him nor had ever seen him, he saw the importance of this situation, and his mind was troubled, so that he said, "For you, commander." He showed that through the revelation of God he had realized that he was the one chosen by God. And immediately he took him into an inner chamber, according to the order of his master. And two things were also hidden: Jehu understood that that affair had to remain secret and that the news [of the anointing] should not be divulged at that time among the people. Therefore he anointed him and ordered him to take revenge against the house of Ahab. Then the prophet fled at once from the camp, and shortly later the entire assembly was in an admirable unanimity before king Jehu against Israel.

So he went out with a group of select men. But he met Joram, king of Israel, in the course of his journey, and little later Ahaziah, king of Judah. He was able to defeat them after the first attack and killed them both. Jehu said to Bidkar, "'Lift him out, and throw him on the plot of ground belonging to Naboth the Jezreelite,' because last night I saw the blood of Naboth and the blood of his children." He is thinking here about what had been said to him at night, or maybe he believes that this vengeance and the fact that he would kill

Joram had been predicted to him at night through a vision. Jehu had also indicated to Bidkar another reason for killing Joram in his place and for ordering him to throw him on the plot of Naboth, saying, "When you and I rode side by side behind his father Ahab how the Lord uttered this oracle against him: 'For the blood of Naboth and for the blood of his children that I saw yesterday, says the Lord, I swear I will repay you on this very plot of ground,'" that is, outside the walls of Jezreel where the goods of Naboth were. After this action accomplished outside the gates of Jezreel, he entered the city to complete what he had successfully begun. ON THE SECOND BOOK OF KINGS 9.1-24.[1]

9:30-31 Jezebel Adorns Herself

JEZEBEL TRIES TO SEDUCE JEHU. EPHREM THE SYRIAN: They thought that she would have wept over her dead son, but in the very hour in which she heard that the king had come, she painted her eyes, a raving old woman, adorned her head with a miter and looked from her window so that she might be looked at. She thought that maybe [Jehu] would be seduced by her look and would take her among his wives. Maybe she had heard of the story of Adonijah,[2] who at the time of Solomon was aided by Abishag the Shunammite and demanded that she became his wife, so that, through the queen, he might be elevated to the throne of the kingdom. So she believed that Jehu too, in order to confirm and pacify his troubled and agitated new reign, would walk the path of Adonijah. These were the thoughts of Jezebel until she was still able to control herself.

But after seeing Jehu, who was entering the gate, she remembered the horrible murder of her son and could not stand the sight of his murderer any longer nor could she restrain her fury but insulted him angrily and abused him before the crowd by saying, "Is it peace, Zimri, murderer of your master?" Indeed, nothing could break the

---

[1]ESOO 1:539-40. [2]See 1 Kings 2:17.

violence of that insolent woman, neither the hope of marriage, nor the fear of an imminent death, nor the fear of her adversary who brandished his sword while threatening her. She, who tortured the others, was not able to save herself, but she provoked the king like a madwoman, addressing him with insulting words, so that she kindled his rage even more and greater resentment rose against her. ON THE SECOND BOOK OF KINGS 9.30.[3]

9:32-37 The Dogs Shall Eat the Flesh of Jezebel

THE HARSH PUNISHMENT OF UNREPENTANT WICKEDNESS. EPHREM THE SYRIAN: Jehu, who had seen the woman who had spoken to him and had recognized her to be Jezebel, ordered the eunuchs who were beside her to throw her out of the window, and they immediately threw her with force and spattered the wall with her blood. Horses passed there and trampled her corpse, and, a little later, dogs lacerated her flesh, so that nobody could say, This was Jezebel.

[Let us see] the symbolic meaning [of this passage]. Ahab was struck in battle and fell, and after his fall, his servants came to mourn and weep over him, and they placed him into the tomb of the kings with honor.[4] But the same thing did not happen to Jezebel. After the eunuchs had thrown her to the ground and her bones were broken in the fall, horses trampled her and dogs lacerated her. The reason for this difference is that Ahab, even though he committed many crimes, showed repentance now and then.[5] Jezebel, by contrast, did not only violate justice and cause rage with her abominable behavior but also drove her husband to crime and exhorted him to commit iniquities. And later, she never repented in the times of her prosperity or in those of calamity, nor [did she turn] away from her path of perversity. Even in the very time of her condemnation to death, she became furious like a madwoman. Therefore there were many reasons why justice should be particularly harsh against her.

In addition, observe and understand how Jezebel, who had terrified prophets and enslaved kings, was thrown by slaves into shame and dishonor and was lacerated by the teeth of dogs. That happened so that the mouth of liars might be stopped, and they might not say, "Why does the way of the guilty prosper? Why do all who are treacherous thrive?"[6] ON THE SECOND BOOK OF KINGS 9.32.[7]

---

[3]ESOO 1:540-41. [4]See 1 Kings 22:34-37. [5]See 1 Kings 20 (21):27. [6]Jer 12:1. [7]ESOO 1:540-41.

10:1-36 DESTRUCTION OF THE HOUSE OF AHAB AND THE PRIESTS OF BAAL

[1]Now Ahab had seventy sons in Samaria. So Jehu wrote letters, and sent them to Samaria, to the rulers of the city,[k] to the elders, and to the guardians of the sons of Ahab, saying, [2]"Now then, as soon as this letter comes to you, seeing your master's sons are with you, and there are with you chariots and horses, fortified cities also, and weapons, [3]select the best and fittest of your master's

sons and set him on his father's throne, and fight for your master's house." ⁴But they were exceedingly afraid, and said, "Behold, the two kings could not stand before him; how then can we stand?" ⁵So he who was over the palace, and he who was over the city, together with the elders and the guardians, sent to Jehu, saying, "We are your servants, and we will do all that you bid us. We will not make any one king; do whatever is good in your eyes." ⁶Then he wrote to them a second letter, saying, "If you are on my side, and if you are ready to obey me, take the heads of your master's sons, and come to me at Jezreel tomorrow at this time." Now the king's sons, seventy persons, were with the great men of the city, who were bringing them up. ⁷And when the letter came to them, they took the king's sons, and slew them, seventy persons, and put their heads in baskets, and sent them to him at Jezreel. ⁸When the messenger came and told him, "They have brought the heads of the king's sons," he said, "Lay them in two heaps at the entrance of the gate until the morning." ⁹Then in the morning, when he went out, he stood, and said to all the people, "You are innocent. It was I who conspired against my master, and slew him; but who struck down all these? ¹⁰Know then that there shall fall to the earth nothing of the word of the LORD, which the LORD spoke concerning the house of Ahab; for the LORD has done what he said by his servant Elijah." ¹¹So Jehu slew all that remained of the house of Ahab in Jezreel, all his great men, and his familiar friends, and his priests, until he left him none remaining.

¹²Then he set out and went to Samaria. On the way, when he was at Beth-eked of the Shepherds, ¹³Jehu met the kinsmen of Ahaziah king of Judah, and he said, "Who are you?" And they answered, "We are the kinsmen of Ahaziah, and we came down to visit the royal princes and the sons of the queen mother." ¹⁴He said, "Take them alive." And they took them alive, and slew them at the pit of Beth-eked, forty-two persons, and he spared none of them.

¹⁵And when he departed from there, he met Jehonadab the son of Rechab coming to meet him; and he greeted him, and said to him, "Is your heart true to my heart as mine is to yours?"^l And Jehonadab answered, "It is." Jehu said,^m "If it is, give me your hand." So he gave him his hand. And Jehu took him up with him into the chariot. ¹⁶And he said, "Come with me, and see my zeal for the LORD." So heⁿ had him ride in his chariot. ¹⁷And when he came to Samaria, he slew all that remained to Ahab in Samaria, till he had wiped them out, according to the word of the LORD which he spoke to Elijah.

¹⁸Then Jehu assembled all the people, and said to them, "Ahab served Baal a little; but Jehu will serve him much. ¹⁹Now therefore call to me all the prophets of Baal, all his worshipers and all his priests; let none be missing, for I have a great sacrifice to offer to Baal; whoever is missing shall not live." But Jehu did it with cunning in order to destroy the worshipers of Baal. ²⁰And Jehu ordered, "Sanctify a solemn assembly for Baal." So they proclaimed it. ²¹And Jehu sent throughout all Israel; and all the worshipers of Baal came, so that there was not a man left who did not come. And they entered the house of Baal, and the house of Baal was filled from one end to the other. ²²He said to him who was in charge of the wardrobe, "Bring out the vestments for all the worshipers of Baal." So he brought out the vestments for them. ²³Then Jehu went into the house of Baal with Jehonadab the son of Rechab; and he said to the worshipers of Baal, "Search, and see that there is no servant

of the Lord *here among you, but only the worshipers of Baal.”* [24]*Then he*[o] *went in to offer sacrifices and burnt offerings.*

Now Jehu had stationed eighty men outside, and said, “The man who allows any of those whom I give into your hands to escape shall forfeit his life.” [25]*So as soon as he had made an end of offering the burnt offering, Jehu said to the guard and to the officers, “Go in and slay them; let not a man escape.” So when they put them to the sword, the guard and the officers cast them out and went into the inner room*[p] *of the house of Baal* [26]*and they brought out the pillar that was in the house of Baal, and burned it.* [27]*And they demolished the pillar of Baal, and demolished the house of Baal, and made it a latrine to this day.*

[28]*Thus Jehu wiped out Baal from Israel.* [29]*But Jehu did not turn aside from the sins of Jeroboam the son of Nebat, which he made Israel to sin, the golden calves that were in Bethel, and in Dan.* [30]*And the* Lord *said to Jehu, “Because you have done well in carrying out what is right in my eyes, and have done to the house of Ahab according to all that was in my heart, your sons of the fourth generation shall sit on the throne of Israel.”* [31]*But Jehu was not careful to walk in the law of the* Lord *the God of Israel with all his heart; he did not turn from the sins of Jeroboam, which he made Israel to sin.*

[32]*In those days the* Lord *began to cut off parts of Israel. Hazael defeated them throughout the territory of Israel:* [33]*from the Jordan eastward, all the land of Gilead, the Gadites, and the Reubenites, and the Manassites, from Aroer, which is by the valley of the Arnon, that is, Gilead and Bashan.* [34]*Now the rest of the acts of Jehu, and all that he did, and all his might, are they not written in the Book of the Chronicles of the Kings of Israel?* [35]*So Jehu slept with his fathers, and they buried him in Samaria. And Jehoahaz his son reigned in his stead.* [36]*The time that Jehu reigned over Israel in Samaria was twenty-eight years.*

k Gk Vg: Heb *Jezreel*   l Gk: Heb *Is it right with your heart, as my heart is with your heart?*   m Gk: Heb lacks *Jehu said*   n Gk Syr Tg: Heb *they*   o Gk Compare verse 25: Heb *they*   p Cn: Heb *city*

Overview: From the case of Jehonadab it clearly appears that also among the ten tribes there were people endowed with piety, and thanks to them God tolerated all the others (Theodoret). Jehu, who by an impious lie and a sacrilegious sacrifice sought to kill the impious and the sacrilegious, is not a model that Christians should imitate (Augustine). Since Jehu did not want anybody to escape his revenge, he lied, so that all the priests of Baal might come confidently to the temple and be killed there (Theodoret).

10:15-17 Jehu Took Jehonadab into His Chariot

Jehonadab Was a Pious Man. Theodoret of Cyr: This was also a pious man, and a relative of his. Indeed, his family constantly lived in tents and kept away from drunkenness. The prophet Jeremiah mentions them with praise, and history shows their piety. Therefore king Jehu, as soon as he saw him, blessed him, that is, greeted him. Then he asked, “Is your heart as true to mine as mine is to yours?” When he had answered, “It is,” Jehu said to him, “If it is, give me your hand.” Then, while he was taking him into his chariot, he said, “‘Come with me and see my zeal for the Lord.’ So he had him ride in his chariot.” From this it clearly appears that also among the ten tribes there were people endowed with piety, and thanks to them, God, who rules everything with wisdom, tolerated all the others. QUESTION 33, ON 2 KINGS.[1]

10:18-24 Worshipers of Baal Summoned

JEHU CANNOT BE A MODEL OF BEHAVIOR FOR CHRISTIANS. AUGUSTINE: This opinion dishonors the holy martyrs; no, altogether removes the possibility of holy martyrdom. For, according to the Priscillianists,[2] the martyrs would act more justly and wisely if they did not confess to their persecutors that they were Christians and by their confession make homicides of their persecutors, but rather, if by lying and by denying what they were, they preserved the advantage of the flesh and the intention of the heart and did not allow their persecutors to perform the wicked deed they had in mind. For these persecutors were enemies of the truth itself, not neighbors of theirs in the Christian faith to whom they were obliged to speak the truth with their tongue that they spoke in their heart. For if Jehu (whom as an example of lying they look on with greater show of prudence than on the others) falsely declared that he was a servant of Baal in order to kill the servants of Baal, how much more justly, according to the perversity of the Priscillianists, would the servants of Christ in time of persecution declare falsely that they are servants of demons in order that the servants of demons not kill the servant of Christ! And if Jehu sacrificed to Baal in order to kill people, how much more justly would they sacrifice to idols in order that people not be killed! Why, according to the remarkable doctrine of these liars, should it be prejudicial to them to profess falsely the worship of the devil in the open, provided they preserved the worship of God in their heart? But not in this manner have the true martyrs, the holy martyrs, understood the apostle. They have seen and kept what has been said, "With the heart a person believes unto justice, and with the mouth profession of faith is made unto salvation,"[3] and, "In their mouth was

found no lie."[4] So, they have departed irreprehensibly where they will no longer have to be on guard against being tempted by liars, because they will have no more liars, whether strangers or neighbors, in their celestial gatherings. As for Jehu, who by an impious lie and a sacrilegious sacrifice sought to kill the impious and the sacrilegious—him they would not imitate, not even if the same Scripture had said nothing about what kind of man he was. But, since it has been written that he did not have a righteous heart in the sight of God, what did it profit him to receive some transitory reward of temporal rule for some obedience that he displayed in utterly destroying the house of Ahab in accordance with his lust for Ahab's dominion? I exhort you, brother, rather to defend the true opinion of the martyrs, that you may be against liars; not a teacher of falsehood, but an advocate of truth. Pay close attention, I beseech you, to what I say, in order that you may find out, despite your laudable zeal to apprehend and correct or else to shun the impious, how much you must be on guard against a doctrine that you are rather injudicious in thinking should be taught. AGAINST LYING 2.3.[5]

JEHU'S LIES WERE JUSTIFIED. THEODORET OF CYR: "Then Jehu assembled all the people and said to them, 'Ahab offered Baal small service; but Jehu will offer much more.'" We need to examine

---

[1]PG 80:769. [2]This is a heretical sect founded by the Spanish priest Priscillian at the end of fourth century. Augustine also wrote a short work against them (*Ad Orosium Contra Priscillianistas et Origenistas*), after his disciple Orosius had written a pamphlet on this heretical sect (*Commonitorium de Errore Priscillianistarum et Origenistarum*). According to the extant historical sources, the Priscillianists were in general accused of being loose in their behavior and too indulgent in their doctrine. However, the documents written by Priscillian or by members of his sect, discovered only at the end of nineteenth century and published by Schepss (CSEL 18 [1889]), reveal a sort of ascetic Christian sect with a certain inclination for esotericism but give no evidence of any loose or indulgent or particularly heretical behavior. This is even more surprising if we consider that Priscillian was the first heretic to be formally condemned to death by a tribunal and to be executed. However, a certain number of scholars believe that Priscillian or his disciples tried not to reveal their real doctrines in their writings, especially in order not to give ground to the accusations made against them. [3]Rom 10:10. [4]Rev 14:5. [5]FC 16:128-29.

the purpose of words and actions. And this must be done here too. In fact, since he did not want anyone to escape his revenge, Jehu used these words, so that all the priests of Baal might come confidently. In addition, in order that no priest of God might share with them the same punishment, he ordered that they be driven away as though they were not worthy of that celebration, and so he killed only [the idolatrous priests]. He also burned the statue of Baal, cut down its sacred groves and freed the whole land of Israel from other idols. However, he continued to worship the two golden calves[6] and gave the name of Baalim to the sanctuary of Baal. QUESTION 34, ON 2 KINGS.[7]

---

[6]See 1 Kings 12:28-33. [7]PG 80:769-72.

11:1-21 THE REIGN OF ATHALIAH

[1]Now when Athaliah the mother of Ahaziah saw that her son was dead, she arose and destroyed all the royal family. [2]But Jehosheba, the daughter of King Joram, sister of Ahaziah, took Joash* the son of Ahaziah, and stole him away from among the king's sons who were about to be slain, and she put[q] him and his nurse in a bedchamber. Thus she[r] hid him from Athaliah, so that he was not slain; [3]and he remained with her six years, hid in the house of the LORD, while Athaliah reigned over the land.

[4]But in the seventh year Jehoiada sent and brought the captains of the Carites and of the guards, and had them come to him in the house of the LORD; and he made a covenant with them and put them under oath in the house of the LORD, and he showed them the king's son. [5]And he commanded them, "This is the thing that you shall do: one third of you, those who come off duty on the sabbath and guard the king's house [6](another third being at the gate Sur and a third at the gate behind the guards), shall guard the palace; [7]and the two divisions of you, which come on duty in force on the sabbath and guard the house of the LORD,[s] [8]shall surround the king, each with his weapons in his hand; and whoever approaches the ranks is to be slain. Be with the king when he goes out and when he comes in."

[9]The captains did according to all that Jehoiada the priest commanded, and each brought his men who were to go off duty on the sabbath, with those who were to come on duty on the sabbath, and came to Jehoiada the priest. [10]And the priest delivered to the captains the spears and shields that had been King David's, which were in the house of the LORD; [11]and the guards stood, every man with his weapons in his hand, from the south side of the house to the north side of the house, around the altar and the house.[t] [12]Then he brought out the king's son, and put the crown upon him, and gave him the testimony; and they proclaimed him king, and anointed him; and they clapped their hands, and said, "Long live the king!"

¹³*When Athaliah heard the noise of the guard and of the people, she went into the house of the Lord to the people;* ¹⁴*and when she looked, there was the king standing by the pillar, according to the custom, and the captains and the trumpeters beside the king, and all the people of the land rejoicing and blowing trumpets. And Athaliah rent her clothes, and cried, "Treason! Treason!"* ¹⁵*Then Jehoiada the priest commanded the captains who were set over the army, "Bring her out between the ranks; and slay with the sword any one who follows her." For the priest said, "Let her not be slain in the house of the Lord."* ¹⁶*So they laid hands on her; and she went through the horses' entrance to the king's house, and there she was slain.*

¹⁷*And Jehoiada made a covenant between the Lord and the king and people, that they should be the Lord's people; and also between the king and the people.* ¹⁸*Then all the people of the land went to the house of Baal, and tore it down; his altars and his images they broke in pieces, and they slew Mattan the priest of Baal before the altars. And the priest posted watchmen over the house of the Lord.* ¹⁹*And he took the captains, the Carites, the guards, and all the people of the land; and they brought the king down from the house of the Lord, marching through the gate of the guards to the king's house. And he took his seat on the throne of the kings.* ²⁰*So all the people of the land rejoiced; and the city was quiet after Athaliah had been slain with the sword at the king's house.*

^{21u}*Jehoash was seven years old when he began to reign.*

q With 2 Chron 22.11: Heb lacks *and she put* r Gk Syr Vg Compare 2 Chron 22.11: Heb *they* s Heb *the Lord to the king* t Heb *the house to the king* u Ch 12.1 in Heb *"Joash": this name has the alternative spelling "Jehoash." As in the case of "Joram/Jehoram," contemporaries of the same name who ruled in Israel (ca. 798-782 B.C.) and in Judah (ca. 835-796 B.C.).

Overview: Athaliah's scheme against the house of David resembles that of the devil against humankind (Isho'dad). After Athaliah had been executed and the kingdom had been pacified, Jehoiada devoted himself to restoring the religion of God, which had been destroyed by Joram and his successors (Ephrem).

beginning against the chief of our race. However, her scheme was not accomplished, but after seven years the kingdom returned to the family of David, thanks to a righteous man, Jehoiada, the husband of Jehosheba, Joram's daughter, who had brought up Joash, son of Ahaziah. Books of Sessions 2 Kings 11.1.[1]

11:1-3 Athaliah Destroys the Royal Family

The Devilish Wickedness of Athaliah. Isho'dad of Merv: Athaliah exterminated all the royal children. In fact, after her son had been killed by Jehu, she had conceived an extremely perfidious and vicious scheme, saying to herself with anger, "I will reign just the same against the will of God by fighting God's promises, and I will make the posterity of David's house perish, as the descendants of my father's house have perished and have been exterminated." That scheme resembled the treachery that Satan plotted at the

11:13-18 Jehoiada Makes a Covenant

Jehoiada Restores the True Religion of God. Ephrem the Syrian: While these things were happening in the temple, Athaliah, being alarmed by the shouts of the gathering people and by the noise of the crowds, ran to the temple. But while she was trying to restrain the riot with her presence and voice, she was arrested by the guards of the king and was brought outside the walls of the temple, where she was killed by order

[1]CSCO 229:139-40.

of the high priest, lest her blood might pollute the house of God. So the prophetic predictions about the annihilation of the family of Ahab were gradually accomplished through different deaths.

After the kingdom had been pacified and its problems settled down, Jehoiada devoted himself to restore the religion of God, which had been destroyed by Joram and his successors. Therefore, in the first place, he persuaded the king and the entire people to renew the covenant made with God by their ancestors according to the words used in the traditional rite and to take an oath of reciprocal trust with one another. After that he turned to erase all the new cults and found that the people consented with him in an admirable manner. And so, after gathering a corps of soldiers, he immediately entered the sanctuary of Baal and destroyed its altars, smashed its statues and killed Mattan, the priest of that impious cult. Therefore, thanks to the authority of Jehoiada and his pious observation of the Law, the order of the sacred ministry, the sacrifices and the ceremonies were nearly brought back to the same honor that they had during the reign of David. On the Second Book of Kings 11.13.[2]

[2]ESOO 1:545.

12:1-21 JEHOASH REIGNED FOR FORTY YEARS

[1]In the seventh year of Jehu Jehoash began to reign, and he reigned forty years in Jerusalem. His mother's name was Zibiah of Beer-sheba. [2]And Jehoash did what was right in the eyes of the Lord all his days, because Jehoiada the priest instructed him. [3]Nevertheless the high places were not taken away; the people continued to sacrifice and burn incense on the high places.

[4]Jehoash said to the priests, "All the money of the holy things which is brought into the house of the Lord, the money for which each man is assessed—the money from the assessment of persons—and the money which a man's heart prompts him to bring into the house of the Lord, [5]let the priests take, each from his acquaintance; and let them repair the house wherever any need of repairs is discovered." [6]But by the twenty-third year of King Jehoash the priests had made no repairs on the house. [7]Therefore King Jehoash summoned Jehoiada the priest and the other priests and said to them, "Why are you not repairing the house? Now therefore take no more money from your acquaintances, but hand it over for the repair of the house." [8]So the priests agreed that they should take no more money from the people, and that they should not repair the house.

[9]Then Jehoiada the priest took a chest, and bored a hole in the lid of it, and set it beside the altar on the right side as one entered the house of the Lord; and the priests who guarded the threshold put in it all the money that was brought into the house of the Lord. [10]And whenever they saw that there was much money in the chest, the king's secretary and the high priest came up and they counted and tied up in bags the money that was found in the house of the Lord. [11]Then they would give the money that was weighed out into the hands of the workmen who had the oversight of the house of the Lord; and they paid it out to the carpenters and the builders who

worked upon the house of the Lord, ¹²and to the masons and the stonecutters, as well as to buy timber and quarried stone for making repairs on the house of the Lord, and for any outlay upon the repairs of the house. ¹³But there were not made for the house of the Lord basins of silver, snuffers, bowls, trumpets, or any vessels of gold, or of silver, from the money that was brought into the house of the Lord, ¹⁴for that was given to the workmen who were repairing the house of the Lord with it. ¹⁵And they did not ask an accounting from the men into whose hand they delivered the money to pay out to the workmen, for they dealt honestly. ¹⁶The money from the guilt offerings and the money from the sin offerings was not brought into the house of the Lord; it belonged to the priests.

¹⁷At that time Hazael king of Syria went up and fought against Gath, and took it. But when Hazael set his face to go up against Jerusalem, ¹⁸Jehoash king of Judah took all the votive gifts that Jehoshaphat and Jehoram and Ahaziah his fathers, the kings of Judah, had dedicated, and his own votive gifts, and all the gold that was found in the treasuries of the house of the Lord and of the king's house, and sent these to Hazael king of Syria. Then Hazael went away from Jerusalem.

¹⁹Now the rest of the acts of Joash, and all that he did, are they not written in the Book of the Chronicles of the Kings of Judah? ²⁰His servants arose and made a conspiracy, and slew Joash in the house of Millo, on the way that goes down to Silla. ²¹It was Jozacar the son of Shimeath and Jehozabad the son of Shomer, his servants, who struck him down, so that he died. And they buried him with his fathers in the city of David, and Amaziah his son reigned in his stead.

OVERVIEW: The money for the assessment, which derives from a form of contribution introduced by Moses, is given to the priests to repair the house of the Lord (ISHO'DAD). Joash wanted to restore the temple after the damages caused by Athaliah and her predecessors, who had forced the priests to abandon the house of the Lord and to worship Baal and other idols. Joash, being persuaded by the advice of some of his princes, abandons the true religion, which he had piously served when Jehoiada was alive. However, his apostasy is punished later, when he is killed in a plot (EPHREM).

12:4 Money from Assessments

A TRADITION DATING FROM THE TIME OF MOSES. ISHO'DAD OF MERV: "The money for the assessment." [The Scripture] uses [this term] for the money which is voluntarily given by the people for the "assessment" of their own person and whose payment has survived from the time of

Moses who, after the [Israelites] were counted in the census, prescribed that four *zouzē*[1] should be deducted from each of them.[2] This form of contribution was perpetuated up to the days of our Lord as a memory of the kindness of God toward them. But at the time of our Lord they only gave two *zouzē*, because they had become poor.[3] BOOKS OF SESSIONS 2 KINGS 12.4.[4]

12:6-8 Repairing the Lord's House

JOASH WANTS TO REPAIR THE DAMAGES CAUSED BY ATHALIAH. EPHREM THE SYRIAN: "Therefore King Joash summoned the priest Jehoiada with the other priests and said to them, 'Why are you not repairing the house?'" The reason why king Joash and the high priest Jehoiada called a meeting to discuss the repairing of the house of God is revealed in the second book of

---

[1]Equivalent to the drachma or denarius. [2]See Exod 30:13. [3]See Mt 17:23. [4]CSCO 229:140.

the Annals[5] with these words: "Athaliah instructed the children of iniquity, and undermined the house of the Lord and drove all the priests who were in the house of the Lord to the worship of the idols."[6] And it is not surprising that Athaliah, a woman endowed with audacity and shrewdness, made that attempt in order to aspire to power and take hold of the kingdom. Therefore, when everything was under her control and the king Ahaziah himself obeyed her blindly, nothing was neglected by her in order to draw the Jews away from the divine worship and to drive them to the ancient religion of the Sidonians. For this reason, while the temple of the true God remained abandoned after the introduction of the foreign cult, it had begun to be in ruin in many spots and was in danger of collapsing because of that. So the king, in order to remedy this serious situation, together with the authority of the high priest, gathered a large sum of money freely offered by the people and entrusted with it some priests elected to accomplish that task. But later on, when he realized that they were not making the progress he had hoped for in the task they had received, he transferred the care of the temple to other men of certain integrity who could work on that assignment with the highest perseverance and dedication. From the allegorical point of view you can recognize here a type of the saints who, after receiving from God the gift of knowledge, set out to repair that same house shaken by vain cults and various crimes. ON THE SECOND BOOK OF KINGS 12.7.[7]

12:19-21 Joash Killed by His Servants

JOASH LOSES HIS FAITH AND IS PUNISHED.

EPHREM THE SYRIAN: "His servants arose, devised a conspiracy and killed Joash in the house of Millo, on the way that goes down to Silla." When he reached the age of 130 years, the priest Jehoiada died. Joash, being persuaded by the advice of some of his princes, abandoned the true religion which he had piously served when Jehoiada was alive, and restored the idolatry introduced by the women of Sidon, which he had gloriously banished with the help of the high priest himself. And while Zechariah, son of Jehoiada, attempted to prevent [that impiety] with all his might, and being inflamed with the divine spirit and standing between the temple and the altar, reproached the king and his princes, he was stoned to death in the hall itself of the house of God. And that was an act of extreme cruelty on the part of Joash, and every person's mind was disturbed because he, being oblivious of the benefits received from Jehoiada, allowed that the son of that very holy man was treated with such brutality before him and even incited [the crowd to stone him]. And [Zechariah], calling God as the witness of his innocence and his avenger, said, "May the Lord see and avenge."[8] The holy man foresaw the calamities that would shortly befall the king and his kingdom. One year later the Syrians[9] invaded Judah and plundered the land so that Joash, in order to save his life, was forced to deprive himself of the goods of the royal house and of the temple but was, nevertheless, shamefully ill treated by his enemies; and eventually he fell ill and lay in bed. While Joash was ill in his own bed, he was the victim of a plot of his servants, who stabbed him to death.[10] ON THE SECOND BOOK OF KINGS 12.20.[11]

---

[5]This is the Syriac name of the books of Chronicles, which is directly taken from the Hebrew (see 1 Kings 14:19; 14:29; etc.). However, the passage quoted by Ephrem is not attested in the Peshitta and probably derives from a lost Syriac version of 2 Chronicles. [6]See 2 Chron 22. This passage quoted by Ephrem is not found in the Hebrew text or in the Syriac Peshitta and probably belongs to a lost Syriac version of Chronicles. [7]ESOO 1:545-46. [8]2 Chron 24:22. [9]Or Arameans. [10]See 2 Chron 24:17-25. [11]ESOO 1:546-47.

13:1-25 THE DEATH OF ELISHA

¹In the twenty-third year of Joash the son of Ahaziah, king of Judah, Jehoahaz the son of Jehu began to reign over Israel in Samaria, and he reigned seventeen years. ²He did what was evil in the sight of the LORD, and followed the sins of Jeroboam the son of Nebat, which he made Israel to sin; he did not depart from them. ³And the anger of the LORD was kindled against Israel, and he gave them continually into the hand of Hazael king of Syria and into the hand of Ben-hadad the son of Hazael. ⁴Then Jehoahaz besought the LORD, and the LORD hearkened to him; for he saw the oppression of Israel, how the king of Syria oppressed them. ⁵ (Therefore the LORD gave Israel a savior, so that they escaped from the hand of the Syrians; and the people of Israel dwelt in their homes as formerly. ⁶Nevertheless they did not depart from the sins of the house of Jeroboam, which he made Israel to sin, but walked*ᵛ* in them; and the Asherah also remained in Samaria.) ⁷For there was not left to Jehoahaz an army of more than fifty horsemen and ten chariots and ten thousand footmen; for the king of Syria had destroyed them and made them like the dust at threshing. ⁸Now the rest of the acts of Jehoahaz and all that he did, and his might, are they not written in the Book of the Chronicles of the Kings of Israel? ⁹So Jehoahaz slept with his fathers, and they buried him in Samaria; and Joash his son reigned in his stead.

¹⁰In the thirty-seventh year of Joash king of Judah Jehoash the son of Jehoahaz began to reign over Israel in Samaria, and he reigned sixteen years. ¹¹He also did what was evil in the sight of the LORD; he did not depart from all the sins of Jeroboam the son of Nebat, which he made Israel to sin, but he walked in them. ¹²Now the rest of the acts of Joash, and all that he did, and the might with which he fought against Amaziah king of Judah, are they not written in the Book of the Chronicles of the Kings of Israel? ¹³So Joash slept with his fathers, and Jeroboam sat upon his throne; and Joash was buried in Samaria with the kings of Israel.

¹⁴Now when Elisha had fallen sick with the illness of which he was to die, Joash king of Israel went down to him, and wept before him, crying, "My father, my father! The chariots of Israel and its horsemen!" ¹⁵And Elisha said to him, "Take a bow and arrows"; so he took a bow and arrows. ¹⁶Then he said to the king of Israel, "Draw the bow"; and he drew it. And Elisha laid his hands upon the king's hands. ¹⁷And he said, "Open the window eastward"; and he opened it. Then Elisha said, "Shoot"; and he shot. And he said, "The LORD's arrow of victory, the arrow of victory over Syria! For you shall fight the Syrians in Aphek until you have made an end of them." ¹⁸And he said, "Take the arrows"; and he took them. And he said to the king of Israel, "Strike the ground with them"; and he struck three times, and stopped. ¹⁹Then the man of God was angry with him, and said, "You should have struck five or six times; then you would have struck down Syria until you had made an end of it, but now you will strike down Syria only three times."

²⁰So Elisha died, and they buried him. Now bands of Moabites used to invade the land in the spring of the year. ²¹And as a man was being buried, lo, a marauding band was seen and the man

was cast into the grave of Elisha; and as soon as the man touched the bones of Elisha, he revived, and stood on his feet.

²²Now Hazael king of Syria oppressed Israel all the days of Jehoahaz. ²³But the LORD was gracious to them and had compassion on them, and he turned toward them, because of his covenant with Abraham, Isaac, and Jacob, and would not destroy them; nor has he cast them from his presence until now.

²⁴When Hazael king of Syria died, Ben-hadad his son became king in his stead. ²⁵Then Jehoash the son of Jehoahaz took again from Ben-hadad the son of Hazael the cities which he had taken from Jehoahaz his father in war. Three times Joash defeated him and recovered the cities of Israel.

v Gk Syr Tg Vg: Heb *he walked*

OVERVIEW: The apostasy of Joash and the people and their rebellious will in the worship of idols is the cause that hindered the gift of grace signified in the sign of Elisha. From the spiritual point of view, "the Lord's arrow of victory" in Elisha's sign signifies our Savior hanging from the wood and giving up his spirit, while the fact that the arrow is shot from the window placed eastwards means that the accomplishment of our salvation has been obtained through the ascension of our Lord, as he rides higher than the heavens of the eastern heavens. It seems that the prophet Hosea took Elisha's place and ruled the sons of the prophets after him, because Hosea says at the beginning of his oracles that he prophesied at the time of Jeroboam, son of Joash. The power that the Lord gives to the bones of Elisha is symbolic of the seed of resurrection. Temporal death is a mercy for the righteous, since it is subjugated to them like a slave. This is demonstrated by Elisha, who resurrected a man after he was already dead (EPHREM). The bodies of the saints are holy and filled with grace, so that they can still perform miracles from the sepulcher (APOSTOLIC CONSTITUTIONS, CHRYSOSTOM). The case of Elisha demonstrates once more that the prescriptions of the law concerning dead bodies and the pollution deriving from them are meaningless (ORIGEN).

13:10-19 Striking Aram Three Times

THE SYMBOLISM OF ELISHA'S LAST PROPH-

ECY. EPHREM THE SYRIAN: "Now when Elisha had fallen sick with the illness from which he was to die, King Joash of Israel went down to him and wept before him, crying, "My father, my father! The chariots of Israel and its horsemen!" And Jehu, king of Israel, died, and Jehoahaz, his son, took his place for seventeen years[1] and died. And his son Joash reigned; he reestablished the kingship which had been troubled by his father, and fought impiety. Elisha helped him with words and actions. And when the prophet was struck with a fatal disease, the king came to him and, seeing that his death was imminent, began to weep like a son deprived of his father and said, "My father, my father," and so on. This is also the word that Elisha said at the moment of Elijah's ascension to heaven. And the meaning of both words is one, and we have explained it above.[2]

Then he calls the prophet "chariots and horsemen of Israel," because the peace of the kingdom and the victories of Israel depended on his prayer and rule. The prophet, on his part, rewarded the love of his tears and "said to him, 'Take a bow and arrows.' Elisha laid his hands on the king's hands" and ordered him to open the window turned eastwards and to shoot the arrow. And he shot the arrow. And Elisha said, "The Lord's arrow of vic-

---

[1] 2 Kings 10:35. [2] See ESOO 1:520. Ephrem asserts that this word pronounced by Joash at the departure of Elisha from the world and pronounced by Elisha at the departure of Elijah (2 Kings 2:12) clearly shows that with the disappearance of the two prophets, a great protection for the children of Israel vanishes.

tory, the arrow of victory over Aram!" Indeed, the window was turned towards Aram. "You shall fight the Arameans in Aphek until you have made an end of them."

This passage suggests two spiritual meanings. The first is that God has bound the victory of the children of Israel to that sign, which is not a new thing: it existed for many centuries, [as was demonstrated] a few centuries before when the Lord made the plagues of Egypt and the liberation of the people depend on the lifting of the rod of Moses,[3] and the destruction of Amalek on the lifting of his hands during the prayer[4] and the destruction of the city of Ai on the lifting of the javelin of Joshua.[5] It was appropriate that that situation was carried out in that manner, so that the people might clearly recognize with certainty the aid that God had given them and, at the moment of receiving such grace, the memory of grace might penetrate into their hearts. But only Elisha clearly knew the mystery, whereas it was hidden to the king; otherwise, he would have not struck the ground three times but ten. And since he was hesitant and drew back, Elisha blamed him—not because he had committed any fault but because his mistake deprived the children of his people of the victory and the great profit that would have derived from the extermination of the Arameans and the overthrowing of their kingdom that Elisha strongly desired. He is sad for being frustrated in his hope by the king who had stopped and had not multiplied the prescribed strokes. But the real motive which prevented the grace was the apostasy of the king and the people and their rebellious will in the worship of idols. That was again the cause that hindered the gift of the grace that was signified in that sign.

The fact that Elisha laid his hands on the hands of the king shows that the weak hands of the king would be strengthened by the power that dwelled in the hands of the prophet, who stood here in the place of his master, so that those hands might be capable of destroying Aram and to exterminate it after it had destroyed and exterminated Israel. It is clear that the children of

Israel, at the time of Joram, had diminished a great deal because in the royal city only 5 horses, and at the time of his son, only 10 chariots were available in their entire land and 50 horsemen, and only 10,000 foot soldiers, as the Scripture says, because the king of Aram had made them perish and had made them like the dust at threshing. Now the Hebrews, at the time of Solomon, had 52,000 horses in the stables of the king, and Jeroboam sent to war 800,000 men, and Abijah lined up against them 400,000 brave men whom he had gathered from the two tribes of Judah and Benjamin.

The second spiritual meaning is the following: this sign is divided into two figures, and each of them possesses its own meaning: "The Lord's arrow of victory" clearly signifies our Lord and Savior hanging from the wood and giving up his spirit. In his spirit he descends into the fortresses and the castle of Sheol and delivers the righteous, who were imprisoned there, and after his resurrection, he subdues the entire universe through the holy apostles and gives new life to those who believe in his name.

On the other hand, the fact that the arrow was shot from the window placed eastwards means that the accomplishment of our salvation has been obtained through the ascension of our Lord, as he rides higher than the heavens of the eastern heavens,[6] and through his ascension he raises the eternal gates and makes us ascend as a host of the captives of heaven.[7] Again the arrow stuck into the ground and then pulled out or departing from the ground signifies the burial of our Lord and his resurrection after he had descended and remained in the heart of the Sheol and in the land of the dead. Observe also, with discernment, that the land of Israel has been struck with three arrows, but the kingdom of Aram has been defeated in three battles, in the likeness of the adorable body of our Lord, which was tried with the thorns, the nails and the sword but was not

---

[3]See Exod 4:17. [4]See Exod 17:9-13. [5]See Josh 8:18-19. [6]See Ps 68:34 (67:35 LXX). [7]See Eph 4:8.

corrupted. The power of death, of Satan, has been crushed three times. Indeed, [the Lord] annihilated Satan and banished sin and death. Again the arrow is shot three times and stays on the ground, but the Lord raises up the people of the Lord who had been thrown onto the ground, as also Christ was placed in the tomb and gave the hope of resurrection to the saints. On the Second Book of Kings 13.14-19.[8]

13:20 Elisha Died and Was Buried

Hosea Takes the Place of Elisha. Ephrem the Syrian: His disciples, the sons of the prophets, buried him. It seems that Joash accompanied him to his grave, because he had stayed beside him at the time of his illness and had showed a deep love for him, weeping before him and composing lamentations for his death. It also seems that the prophet Hosea took his place and ruled the sons of the prophets, because Hosea says at the beginning of his oracles that he prophesied at the time of Jeroboam, son of Joash.[9] On the Second Book of Kings 13.20.[10]

13:21 A Dead Man Comes to Life

The Symbol and Seed of Resurrection. Ephrem the Syrian: Now also Elijah raised somebody from the dead, and Elisha, too, performed that miracle during his lifetime. But none of the prophets, after dying, ever resurrected anyone. Therefore see how the spirit of Elijah doubly rests on Elisha. In fact, the power that the Lord gives to the bones of Elisha is the symbol and seed of resurrection. And the honor devoted to them shows the glory with which the bodies of the saints will be clothed on the day of the resurrection of all the dead. On the Second Book of Kings 13.21.[11]

Death Is Subjugated to the Power of Saints. Ephrem the Syrian: And because temporal death is a mercy for the righteous, they therefore despise death, since it is subjugated to

them like a slave. In what manner did death harm Elisha who descended into hades? For, while he was in the pit of death, he snatched a dead man from its mouth. Because they entrust both body and spirit to God, they do not become downcast in the face of bodily afflictions. Homily on the Solitaries 253-64.[12]

Those Who Live with God. Apostolic Constitutions: Wherefore, of those that live with God, even their very relics are not without honor. For even Elisha the prophet, after he was fallen asleep, raised up a dead man who was slain by the pirates of Syria. For his body touched the bones of Elisha, and he arose and revived. Now this would not have happened unless the body of Elisha were holy. Constitutions of the Holy Apostles 6.30.[13]

Spiritual Grace Fills the Sepulchers of Saints. John Chrysostom: For not the bodies only but also the very sepulchers of the saints have been filled with spiritual grace. For if in the case of Elisha this happened, and a corpse, when it touched the sepulcher, burst the bands of death and returned to life again, much rather now, when grace is more abundant, when the energy of the spirit is greater, is it possible that one touching a sepulcher, with faith, should win great power. On this account God allowed us the remains of the saints, wishing to lead us by them to the same emulation and to afford us a kind of haven and a secure consolation for the evils that are ever overtaking us. Therefore I beseech you all, if any is in despondency, if in disease, if under insult, if in any other circumstance of this life, if in the depth of sins, let him come here with faith, and he will lay aside all those things and will return with much joy, having procured a lighter conscience from the sight alone. But more, it is not only necessary that those who are in affliction should come here, but if any one be in cheerful-

---

[8]ESOO 1:547-49. [9]See Hos 1:1. [10]ESOO 1:549-50. [11]ESOO 1:549. [12]AHSIS 475*. [13]ANF 7:464.

ness, in glory, in power, in much assurance toward God, let not this person despise the benefit. For coming here and beholding this saint, he will keep these noble possessions unmoved, persuading his own soul to be moderate by the recollection of this person's mighty deeds and not suffering his conscience by the mighty deeds to be lifted up to any self-conceit. HOMILIES ON ST. IGNATIUS AND ST. BABYLAS 5.[14]

USELESSNESS OF THE LAW'S PRESCRIPTIONS.
ORIGEN: After this, another law is published. It says, "Whatever soul touches anything unclean, or the carcass of unclean beasts, and conceals it and is defiled, or if he touches the uncleanness of [a person] or anything unclean by which he is defiled,"[15] and so forth. These, to be sure, are

observed by the Jews indecently and uselessly enough. And why should one who, for example, touches a dead animal or the body of a dead person be held to be impure? What if it is the body of a prophet? What if it is the body of a patriarch or even the body of Abraham himself? What if he touches the bones, will he be unclean? What if he should touch the bones of Elisha, which raise a dead person? Will that one be unclean who touches the bones of the prophets and likewise do they make that one himself unclean whom they raise from the dead? See how unsuitable the Jewish interpretation is. HOMILIES ON LEVITICUS 3.3.1.[16]

---

[14]NPNF 1 9:140. [15]Lev 5:2-3. [16]FC 83:55-56.

14:1-29 THE REIGNS OF AMAZIAH IN JUDAH AND JEROBOAM IN ISRAEL

[1]*In the second year of Joash the son of Joahaz, king of Israel, Amaziah the son of Joash, king of Judah, began to reign.* [2]*He was twenty-five years old when he began to reign, and he reigned twenty-nine years in Jerusalem. His mother's name was Jeho-addin of Jerusalem.* [3]*And he did what was right in the eyes of the LORD, yet not like David his father; he did in all things as Joash his father had done.* [4]*But the high places were not removed; the people still sacrificed and burned incense on the high places.* [5]*And as soon as the royal power was firmly in his hand he killed his servants who had slain the king his father.* [6]*But he did not put to death the children of the murderers; according to what is written in the book of the law of Moses, where the LORD commanded, "The fathers shall not be put to death for the children, or the children be put to death for the fathers; but every man shall die for his own sin."*

[7]*He killed ten thousand Edomites in the Valley of Salt and took Sela by storm, and called it Jok-the-el, which is its name to this day.*

[8]*Then Amaziah sent messengers to Jehoash the son of Jehoahaz, son of Jehu, king of Israel, saying, "Come, let us look one another in the face."* [9]*And Jehoash king of Israel sent word to Amaziah king of Judah, "A thistle on Lebanon sent to a cedar on Lebanon, saying, 'Give your daughter to my*

son for a wife'; and a wild beast of Lebanon passed by and trampled down the thistle. ¹⁰*You have indeed smitten Edom, and your heart has lifted you up. Be content with your glory, and stay at home; for why should you provoke trouble so that you fall, you and Judah with you?"*

¹¹*But Amaziah would not listen. So Jehoash king of Israel went up, and he and Amaziah king of Judah faced one another in battle at Beth-shemesh, which belongs to Judah. ¹²And Judah was defeated by Israel, and every man fled to his home. ¹³And Jehoash king of Israel captured Amaziah king of Judah, the son of Jehoash, son of Ahaziah, at Beth-shemesh, and came to Jerusalem, and broke down the wall of Jerusalem for four hundred cubits, from the Ephraim Gate to the Corner Gate. ¹⁴And he seized all the gold and silver, and all the vessels that were found in the house of the LORD and in the treasuries of the king's house, also hostages, and he returned to Samaria.*

¹⁵*Now the rest of the acts of Jehoash which he did, and his might, and how he fought with Amaziah king of Judah, are they not written in the Book of the Chronicles of the Kings of Israel? ¹⁶And Jehoash slept with his fathers, and was buried in Samaria with the kings of Israel; and Jeroboam his son reigned in his stead.*

¹⁷*Amaziah the son of Joash, king of Judah, lived fifteen years after the death of Jehoash son of Jehoahaz, king of Israel. ¹⁸Now the rest of the deeds of Amaziah, are they not written in the Book of the Chronicles of the Kings of Judah? ¹⁹And they made a conspiracy against him in Jerusalem, and he fled to Lachish. But they sent after him to Lachish, and slew him there. ²⁰And they brought him upon horses; and he was buried in Jerusalem with his fathers in the city of David. ²¹And all the people of Judah took Azariah, who was sixteen years old, and made him king instead of his father Amaziah. ²²He built Elath and restored it to Judah, after the king slept with his fathers.*

²³*In the fifteenth year of Amaziah the son of Joash, king of Judah, Jeroboam the son of Joash, king of Israel, began to reign in Samaria, and he reigned forty-one years. ²⁴And he did what was evil in the sight of the LORD; he did not depart from all the sins of Jeroboam the son of Nebat, which he made Israel to sin. ²⁵He restored the border of Israel from the entrance of Hamath as far as the Sea of the Arabah, according to the word of the LORD, the God of Israel, which he spoke by his servant Jonah the son of Amittai, the prophet, who was from Gath-hepher. ²⁶For the LORD saw that the affliction of Israel was very bitter, for there was none left, bond or free, and there was none to help Israel. ²⁷But the LORD had not said that he would blot out the name of Israel from under heaven, so he saved them by the hand of Jeroboam the son of Joash.*

²⁸*Now the rest of the acts of Jeroboam, and all that he did, and his might, how he fought, and how he recovered for Israel Damascus and Hamath, which had belonged to Judah, are they not written in the Book of the Chronicles of the Kings of Israel? ²⁹And Jeroboam slept with his fathers, the kings of Israel, and Zechariah his son reigned in his stead.*

OVERVIEW: When his reign began to be very prosperous, Amaziah rejected his fear of God, which he had conceived after witnessing his father's punishment, and embraced foreign cults (EPHREM). Jehoash compares Amaziah with a thorn bush, which is a puny plant, because he wants to suggest that his power is weak and ineffective (ISHO'DAD). God, wishing to punish Amaziah's sin of idolatry, influenced his heart so that he would not heed salutary advice but would engage in battle, there to perish together with his army (Augustine). Jeroboam honors the prophet Jonah in the course of his reign and restores the power of Israel in Samaria (Ephrem).

14:1-7 Amaziah Reigned Twenty-nine Years

Amaziah Turned to Idolatry. Ephrem the Syrian: "In the second year of King Joash son of Ahaziah of Israel, King Amaziah son of Joash of Judah began to reign," who avenged the death of his father, but with moderation, so that he spared the life of the relatives of the conspirators according to the prescriptions of the Law and was careful that the punishment might not be too excessive for the authors of the crime. Therefore Amaziah was pious, as long as he had before his eyes his father's unhappy end, whose cause he could not ignore: offense against the true religion [of God]. However, when his reign began to be very prosperous, [Amaziah] rejected his fear of God which he had conceived after witnessing his father's punishment, and embraced foreign cults. In the second book of the Annals, the Scripture relating his victory against the Edomites confirms that this was the reason of his apostasy: "But Amaziah took courage, and led out his people, and went to the Valley of Salt and smote ten thousand men of Seir. The men of Judah captured another ten thousand alive and took them to the top of a rock, and all were enchained."[1] And the text adds, "After Amaziah came from the slaughter of the Edomites, he brought the gods of the men of Seir, and set them up as his gods and worshiped them, making offerings to them."[2] On the Second Book of Kings 16.1.[3]

14:8-9 A Thorn Bush Sent to a Cedar

Meaning of Jehoash's Words to Amaziah. Isho'dad of Merv: The thorn bush [mentioned here] is a tiny plant and herb and is not the blackberry bush, [whose fruits] we eat.

"Since, if ever," he says, "the thorn bush were sent to a cedar, saying, 'Give your daughter to my son for a wife,' it would be an insult and an act of derision, since the thorn bush is much smaller than the cedar, so you, Amaziah, do not differ at all from the thorn bush, if compared with my power." By the cedar and the wild beast Jehoash signifies himself. Books of Sessions 2 Kings 12.4.[4]

14:10-14 Judah Defeated by Israel

God Works in Human Hearts. Augustine: The Almighty, who cannot possibly will anything unjust, is able to set in motion even the inclinations of their will in people's hearts in order to accomplish through these people whatever he wishes to achieve through their agency. What meaning can these words have that the man of God addressed to King Amaziah: "Do not allow the army of Israel to go out with you, for the Lord is not with Israel and all the children of Ephraim. And if you think to prevail over them, God will put you to flight before your enemies; for it belongs to God both to help and to put to flight"?[5]

How does the power of God help some in war by giving them confidence and turns others to flight by instilling them with fear, except for this reason, that he who has made all things as he willed in heaven and on earth, also works in the human hearts? We also read of what Joash, king of Israel, said when he dispatched a messenger to King Amaziah, who had a mind to go to war with him. Having mentioned certain things, he went on to say, "Sit at home. Why do you provoke evil that you should fall and Judah with you?" The Scripture then went on to add, "And Amaziah would not listen to him because it was the Lord's will that he should be delivered into the hands of enemies because he sought after the gods of Edom."[6]

---

[1] 2 Chron 25:11 (Peshitta). [2] 2 Chron 25:14. [3] ESOO 1:550. [4] CSCO 229:140. [5] 2 Chron 25:7-8. [6] 2 Chron 25:20.

There you see how God, wishing to punish the sin of idolatry, influenced the heart of this man with whom he was justly angry, that he would not heed salutary advice but, in his contempt for it, would engage in battle, there to perish together with his army. ON GRACE AND FREE WILL 21.42.[7]

14:23-26 Jeroboam Restored the Border of Israel

JEROBOAM HONORED THE PROPHET JONAH.
EPHREM THE SYRIAN: "In the fifteenth year of King Amaziah son of Joash of Judah, King Jeroboam son of Joash of Israel began to reign in Samaria; he reigned forty-one years. He restored the border of Israel from Lebo-hamath as far as the Sea of the Arabah, according to the word of the Lord, the God of Israel, which he spoke by his servant Jonah son of Amittai, the prophet." This is the same Jonah who preached the repentance of Nineveh. And the Sea of Arabah[8] is the same that the Scripture calls elsewhere the "salt sea,"[9] situated on the border with Canaan, of which the city of Hamath, beside the Mount Lebanon, is the other northern border. Jeroboam honored the prophet Jonah as his father had honored Elisha and recurred to his useful work, so that, being encouraged by his predictions and advice, was able to conquer back the cities occupied by the Syrians.[10] ON THE SECOND BOOK OF KINGS 14.23.[11]

---

[7]FC 59:301-2. [8]In Syriac, "sea of loneliness." [9]I.e., the Dead Sea. [10]Or Arameans. See 2 Kings 13. [11]ESOO 1:550-51.

15:1-38 DIFFERENT KINGS ON THE THRONES OF JUDAH AND ISRAEL

[1]*In the twenty-seventh year of Jeroboam king of Israel Azariah* the son of Amaziah, king of Judah, began to reign.* [2]*He was sixteen years old when he began to reign, and he reigned fifty-two years in Jerusalem. His mother's name was Jecoliah of Jerusalem.* [3]*And he did what was right in the eyes of the LORD, according to all that his father Amaziah had done.* [4]*Nevertheless the high places were not taken away; the people still sacrificed and burned incense on the high places.* [5]*And the LORD smote the king, so that he was a leper to the day of his death, and he dwelt in a separate house. And Jotham the king's son was over the household, governing the people of the land.* [6]*Now the rest of the acts of Azariah, and all that he did, are they not written in the Book of the Chronicles of the Kings of Judah?* [7]*And Azariah slept with his fathers, and they buried him with his fathers in the city of David, and Jotham his son reigned in his stead.*

[8]*In the thirty-eighth year of Azariah king of Judah Zechariah the son of Jeroboam reigned over Israel in Samaria six months.* [9]*And he did what was evil in the sight of the LORD, as his fathers had done. He did not depart from the sins of Jeroboam the son of Nebat, which he made Israel to sin.* [10]*Shallum the son of Jabesh conspired against him, and struck him down at Ibleam,ʷ and killed*

him, and reigned in his stead. [11]*Now the rest of the deeds of Zechariah, behold, they are written in the Book of the Chronicles of the Kings of Israel.* [12](*This was the promise of the* LORD *which he gave to Jehu, "Your sons shall sit upon the throne of Israel to the fourth generation." And so it came to pass.*)

[13]*Shallum the son of Jabesh began to reign in the thirty-ninth year of Uzziah king of Judah, and he reigned one month in Samaria.* [14]*Then Menahem the son of Gadi came up from Tirzah and came to Samaria, and he struck down Shallum the son of Jabesh in Samaria and slew him, and reigned in his stead.* [15]*Now the rest of the deeds of Shallum, and the conspiracy which he made, behold, they are written in the Book of the Chronicles of the Kings of Israel.* [16]*At that time Menahem sacked Tappuah*[x] *and all who were in it and its territory from Tirzah on; because they did not open it to him, therefore he sacked it, and he ripped up all the women in it who were with child.*

[17]*In the thirty-ninth year of Azariah king of Judah Menahem the son of Gadi began to reign over Israel, and he reigned ten years in Samaria.* [18]*And he did what was evil in the sight of the* LORD; *he did not depart all his days from all the sins of Jeroboam the son of Nebat, which he made Israel to sin.* [19]*Pul the king of Assyria came against the land; and Menahem gave Pul a thousand talents of silver, that he might help him to confirm his hold of the royal power.* [20]*Menahem exacted the money from Israel, that is, from all the wealthy men, fifty shekels of silver from every man, to give to the king of Assyria. So the king of Assyria turned back, and did not stay there in the land.* [21]*Now the rest of the deeds of Menahem, and all that he did, are they not written in the Book of the Chronicles of the Kings of Israel?* [22]*And Menahem slept with his fathers, and Pekahiah his son reigned in his stead.*

[23]*In the fiftieth year of Azariah king of Judah Pekahiah the son of Menahem began to reign over Israel in Samaria, and he reigned two years.* [24]*And he did what was evil in the sight of the* LORD; *he did not turn away from the sins of Jeroboam the son of Nebat, which he made Israel to sin.* [25]*And Pekah the son of Remaliah, his captain, conspired against him with fifty men of the Gileadites, and slew him in Samaria, in the citadel of the king's house;*[y] *he slew him, and reigned in his stead.* [26]*Now the rest of the deeds of Pekahiah, and all that he did, behold, they are written in the Book of the Chronicles of the Kings of Israel.*

[27]*In the fifty-second year of Azariah king of Judah Pekah the son of Remaliah began to reign over Israel in Samaria, and he reigned twenty years.* [28]*And he did what was evil in the sight of the* LORD; *he did not depart from the sins of Jeroboam the son of Nebat, which he made Israel to sin.*

[29]*In the days of Pekah king of Israel Tiglath-pileser king of Assyria came and captured Ijon, Abel-beth-maacah, Jan-oah, Kedesh, Hazor, Gilead, and Galilee, all the land of Naphtali; and he carried the people captive to Assyria.* [30]*Then Hoshea the son of Elah made a conspiracy against Pekah the son of Remaliah, and struck him down, and slew him, and reigned in his stead, in the twentieth year of Jotham the son of Uzziah.* [31]*Now the rest of the acts of Pekah, and all that he did, behold, they are written in the Book of the Chronicles of the Kings of Israel.*

[32]*In the second year of Pekah the son of Remaliah, king of Israel, Jotham the son of Uzziah, king of Judah, began to reign.* [33]*He was twenty-five years old when he began to reign, and he*

reigned sixteen years in Jerusalem. His mother's name was Jerusha the daughter of Zadok. [34]*And he did what was right in the eyes of the LORD, according to all that his father Uzziah had done.* [35]*Nevertheless the high places were not removed; the people still sacrificed and burned incense on the high places. He built the upper gate of the house of the LORD.* [36]*Now the rest of the acts of Jotham, and all that he did, are they not written in the Book of the Chronicles of the Kings of Judah?* [37]*In those days the LORD began to send Rezin the king of Syria and Pekah the son of Remaliah against Judah.* [38]*Jotham slept with his fathers, and was buried with his fathers in the city of David his father; and Ahaz his son reigned in his stead.*

w Gk Compare 9.27: Heb *before the people*   x Compare Gk: Heb *Tiphsah*   y Heb adds *Argob and Arieh,* which probably belong to the list of places in verse 29   * In the Syriac version of the Bible (Peshitta), King Azariah is called "Uzziah" and is identified with the "Uzziah" described in 2 Chronicles 26:1-23, as is evident from the comments of Isho'dad of Merv (cf. below: 2 Kings 15:1-7).

OVERVIEW: King Azariah (Uzziah) was struck with leprosy because, besides kingship, he dared arrogate priesthood, without remembering what had happened to the people of Dathan and Korah and what had happened to Jeroboam (ISHO'DAD). Jotham restores the power in Judah and builds new fortifications in the city of Jerusalem (EPHREM).

15:1-7 Azariah Was Sixteen

THE REIGN OF AZARIAH (UZZIAH)[1] IN JUDAH.
ISHO'DAD OF MERV: In the book of Chronicles [it is written]: Uzziah "did what was right in the sight of the Lord, just as his father David,[2] and God made him prosper."[3] "He built" fortresses "and palaces and high towers which were reinforced with iron bolts."[4] "But when he had become strong, he grew proud; he became an infidel to the Lord his God and entered the temple of the Lord to make the censer-bearers of perfumes smoke. But the priest Azariah went in after him and said to him, 'It is not for you, king, [to make offerings].' And the king was angered with the priests and ordered them to be driven out of the sanctuary. But at the same time a leprous disease broke out of the holy place on his forehead."[5] And when he died, "they did not bury him in the burial field that belonged to the kings, for they said, 'He is leprous.'"[6]

He was struck with leprosy because, besides kingship, he dared arrogate priesthood, without remembering what had happened to the people of Dathan and Korah[7] and what had happened to Jeroboam.[8] That is why he received a punishment on a part of his body that was conspicuous.[9] And since no prophet had reproached him, except for the priest Azariah, the gift of prophecy was withheld from [all prophets] until the death of Uzziah. And the bronze bull which they worshiped bellowed and produced a tremendous noise, while blood, ravaging and plagues reigned among the people. And the prophet Zechariah referred to these events when he said, "And you shall flee as you fled from the earthquake in the days of King Uzziah of Judah."[10] BOOKS OF SESSIONS 2 KINGS 15.3.[11]

15:32-36 Jotham Worshiped the Lord

RENAISSANCE OF JUDAH. EPHREM THE SYRIAN:
"In the second year of King Pekah son of Remaliah of Israel, King Jotham son of Uzziah of Judah began to reign." After rising to power in that year, Jotham administered the government [of Judah] for sixteen years, earning great praise. While the second book of the Annals has shown all the feats

[1]See textual note to 2 Kings 15:1-38. [2]This is the reading of the Peshitta. Hebrew reads "Amaziah." [3]2 Chron 26:4-5. [4]2 Chron 26:9 (Peshitta). [5]2 Chron 26:16-19 (Peshitta). [6]2 Chron 26:23 (Peshitta). [7]See Num 16:1-50. [8]See 1 Kings 12:22–13:6; 14:1-18. [9]On his forehead. [10]Zech 14:5. [11]CSCO 229:141-42.

illustriously accomplished by him, the Scripture never reproaches him in this passage[12] for any error, except for his toleration of the high places,[13] which was a fault common to all the most praised kings of Judah. In the first place, he strengthened Jerusalem with new fortifications and built towers and castles in desert places. He conquered the Ammonites, who were perpetual enemies of the Jews, and ordered them for the future to pay the kings of Judah an annual tribute. ON THE SECOND BOOK OF KINGS 15.32.[14]

---

[12]See 2 Chron 27:1-9.   [13]See 1 Kings 12:31-32; 2 Kings 12:3; etc.
[14]ESOO 1:553.

16:1-20 THE IMPIETY AND CRUELTY OF AHAZ

[1]*In the seventeenth year of Pekah the son of Remaliah, Ahaz the son of Jotham, king of Judah, began to reign. [2]Ahaz was twenty years old when he began to reign, and he reigned sixteen years in Jerusalem. And he did not do what was right in the eyes of the LORD his God, as his father David had done, [3]but he walked in the way of the kings of Israel. He even burned his son as an offering,[z] according to the abominable practices of the nations whom the LORD drove out before the people of Israel. [4]And he sacrificed and burned incense on the high places, and on the hills, and under every green tree.*

[5]*Then Rezin king of Syria and Pekah the son of Remaliah, king of Israel, came up to wage war on Jerusalem, and they besieged Ahaz but could not conquer him. [6]At that time[a] the king of Edom[b] recovered Elath for Edom,[b] and drove the men of Judah from Elath; and the Edomites came to Elath, where they dwell to this day. [7]So Ahaz sent messengers to Tiglath-pileser king of Assyria, saying, "I am your servant and your son. Come up, and rescue me from the hand of the king of Syria and from the hand of the king of Israel, who are attacking me." [8]Ahaz also took the silver and gold that was found in the house of the LORD and in the treasures of the king's house, and sent a present to the king of Assyria. [9]And the king of Assyria hearkened to him; the king of Assyria marched up against Damascus, and took it, carrying its people captive to Kir, and he killed Rezin.*

[10]*When King Ahaz went to Damascus to meet Tiglath-pileser king of Assyria, he saw the altar that was at Damascus. And King Ahaz sent to Uriah the priest a model of the altar, and its pattern, exact in all its details. [11]And Uriah the priest built the altar; in accordance with all that King Ahaz had sent from Damascus, so Uriah the priest made it, before King Ahaz arrived from Damascus. [12]And when the king came from Damascus, the king viewed the altar. Then the king drew near to the altar, and went up on it, [13]and burned his burnt offering and his cereal offering, and poured his drink offering, and threw the blood of his peace offerings upon the altar. [14]And the bronze altar which was before the LORD he removed from the front of the house, from the place between his altar and the house of the LORD, and put it on the north side of his altar. [15]And King*

Ahaz commanded Uriah the priest, saying, "Upon the great altar burn the morning burnt offering, and the evening cereal offering, and the king's burnt offering, and his cereal offering, with the burnt offering of all the people of the land, and their cereal offering, and their drink offering; and throw upon it all the blood of the burnt offering, and all the blood of the sacrifice; but the bronze altar shall be for me to inquire by." [16]*Uriah the priest did all this, as King Ahaz commanded.*

[17]*And King Ahaz cut off the frames of the stands, and removed the laver from them, and he took down the sea from off the bronze oxen that were under it, and put it upon a pediment of stone.* [18]*And the covered way for the sabbath which had been built inside the palace, and the outer entrance for the king he removed from^c the house of the LORD, because of the king of Assyria.* [19]*Now the rest of the acts of Ahaz which he did, are they not written in the Book of the Chronicles of the Kings of Judah?* [20]*And Ahaz slept with his fathers, and was buried with his fathers in the city of David; and Hezekiah his son reigned in his stead.*

z *Or made his son to pass through the fire* a *Heb At that time Rezin* b *Heb Aram (Syria)* c *Cn: Heb turned to*

OVERVIEW: King Ahaz embraces all the worst practices of idolatry and does not hesitate to offer his own son as a human sacrifice (CHRYSOSTOM). The people of Israel, instead of serving the true God, worshiped foreign idols from different nations (ORIGEN). The words "the bronze altar shall be for me to inquire by," that is, to consult God, were pronounced by Ahaz in a purely formal manner, and not seriously (ISHO'DAD). Ahaz's impiety was such that he removed the genuine altar of bronze, which Solomon had built, and put in its place another one made according to the model of the Assyrian altar he had seen in Damascus (THEODORET).

16:1-4 Ahaz Made His Son Pass Through Fire

THE ABOMINATION OF MAKING SACRIFICES TO DEMONS. JOHN CHRYSOSTOM: Do you see that demons dwell in their souls and that these demons are more dangerous than the ones of old? And this is very reasonable. In the old days the Jews acted impiously toward the prophets; now they outrage the Master of the prophets.[1] Tell me this. Do you not shudder to come into the same place with people possessed, who have so many unclean spirits, who have been reared amid slaughter and bloodshed? Must you share a greeting with them and exchange a bare word? Must you not turn away from them since they are the common disgrace and infection of the whole world? Have they not come to every form of wickedness? Have not all the prophets spent themselves making many and long speeches of accusation against them?[2] What tragedy, what manner of lawlessness have they not eclipsed by their blood guilt? They sacrificed their own sons and daughters to demons. They refused to recognize nature, they forgot the pangs of birth, they trod underfoot the rearing of their children, they overturned from their foundations the laws of kinship, they became more savage than any wild beast. DISCOURSES AGAINST JUDAIZING CHRISTIANS 1.6.7.[3]

16:10-14 Ahaz Offered His Burnt Offering

---

[1]Chrysostom uses this historical testimony in the second book of Kings to explain the cruelty of the Jews in condemning Christ. His position revealing an extreme form of anti-Semitism must be interpreted in the context of rhetorical amplification and exaggerated emotionality, which alter the actual historical testimony. In its unpleasantness and incorrectness, this is an existing component of ancient biblical exegesis. [2]See Is 1:1-31; 2:6-4:6; 9:8-10:4; 28:1-29:16; Jer 2:1-6:30; Ezek 4:1-24:27. [3]FC 68:24-25.

They Served Idols. Origen: "And when you say, 'Why did the Lord God do all of these bad things to us?' And you will say to them, 'As you have forsaken me and served other gods in your land, so you shall serve in a land not your own.' "[4] Let one consider the literal sense, and it will suffice at the present to refresh the memory from the literal sense for those who can understand. Surely then, the people of Israel possessed the holy land, the temple, the house of prayer. They ought to have served God, but when they transgressed the divine commandments they served idols, both the idols acquired from Damascus, as it is written in Kings, and the other idols brought from other pagan nations into the holy land. Due to the fact that they received these pagan idols, they made themselves worthy to be rejected to the land of the idols, to dwell there where they worship the idols. Homilies on Jeremiah 7.3.1.[5]

16:15-16 The Bronze Altar

A Purely Formal Assertion. Isho'dad of Merv: The words "the bronze altar shall be for me to inquire by," that is, in order to consult [God]: [the king] says these words in a purely formal manner, and not seriously. Books of Sessions 2 Kings 16.15.[6]

16:17-20 Ahaz Changes the Temple

Ahaz's Profanations of the Temple. Theodoret of Cyr: I certainly do not think that he built [the altar] for the God of all things but just for certain of those who are falsely called gods. This is what the book of Chronicles points out. It reads, "In the time of his distress this king Ahaz became yet more faithless to the Lord. For he sacrificed to the gods of Damascus, which had defeated him, and said, "Because the gods of the kings of Aram helped them, I will sacrifice to them so that they may help me." But they were the ruin of him and of all Israel."[7] And this is also signified by the next verse: "Ahaz gathered together the utensils of the house of God and cut in pieces the utensils of the house of God. He shut up the doors of the house of the Lord and made himself altars in every corner of Jerusalem."[8] He did these and other similar things, as is also confirmed in the book of Chronicles:[9] "When King Ahaz went to Damascus to meet King Tiglath-pileser of Assyria, he saw the altar that was at Damascus. King Ahaz sent to the priest Uriah a model of the altar, and its pattern, exact in all its details." He removed the genuine altar of bronze, which Solomon had built, and put in its place another one recently made. And what happened to the stands is revealed by what follows: "King Ahaz cut off the frames of the stands," the text says, "and removed the laver from them." And he even dared to commit another act of impiety: he moved the entrance of the royal house into the divine temple, transforming the sacred enclosure into a thoroughfare. Question 48, On 2 Kings.[10]

---

[4]Jer 5:19. [5]FC 97:71*. [6]CSCO 229:142. [7]2 Chron 28:22-23. [8]2 Chron 28:24. [9]See 2 Chron 28:22-25. [10]PG 80:780-81.

17:1-41 THE FALL OF SAMARIA

---

[1]*In the twelfth year of Ahaz king of Judah Hoshea the son of Elah began to reign in Samaria over Israel, and he reigned nine years.* [2]*And he did what was evil in the sight of the Lord, yet not*

---

as the kings of Israel who were before him. ³Against him came up Shalmaneser king of Assyria; and Hoshea became his vassal, and paid him tribute. ⁴But the king of Assyria found treachery in Hoshea; for he had sent messengers to So, king of Egypt, and offered no tribute to the king of Assyria, as he had done year by year; therefore the king of Assyria shut him up, and bound him in prison. ⁵Then the king of Assyria invaded all the land and came to Samaria, and for three years he besieged it. ⁶In the ninth year of Hoshea the king of Assyria captured Samaria, and he carried the Israelites away to Assyria, and placed them in Halah, and on the Habor, the river of Gozan, and in the cities of the Medes.

⁷And this was so, because the people of Israel had sinned against the Lord their God, who had brought them up out of the land of Egypt from under the hand of Pharaoh king of Egypt, and had feared other gods ⁸and walked in the customs of the nations whom the Lord drove out before the people of Israel, and in the customs which the kings of Israel had introduced.ᵈ ⁹And the people of Israel did secretly against the Lord their God things that were not right. They built for themselves high places at all their towns, from watchtower to fortified city; ¹⁰they set up for themselves pillars and Asherim on every high hill and under every green tree; ¹¹and there they burned incense on all the high places, as the nations did whom the Lord carried away before them. And they did wicked things, provoking the Lord to anger, ¹²and they served idols, of which the Lord had said to them, "You shall not do this." ¹³Yet the Lord warned Israel and Judah by every prophet and every seer, saying, "Turn from your evil ways and keep my commandments and my statutes, in accordance with all the law which I commanded your fathers, and which I sent to you by my servants the prophets." ¹⁴But they would not listen, but were stubborn, as their fathers had been, who did not believe in the Lord their God. ¹⁵They despised his statutes, and his covenant that he made with their fathers, and the warnings which he gave them. They went after false idols, and became false, and they followed the nations that were round about them, concerning whom the Lord had commanded them that they should not do like them. ¹⁶And they forsook all the commandments of the Lord their God, and made for themselves molten images of two calves; and they made an Asherah, and worshiped all the host of heaven, and served Baal. ¹⁷And they burned their sons and their daughters as offerings,ᵉ and used divination and sorcery, and sold themselves to do evil in the sight of the Lord, provoking him to anger. ¹⁸Therefore the Lord was very angry with Israel, and removed them out of his sight; none was left but the tribe of Judah only.

¹⁹Judah also did not keep the commandments of the Lord their God, but walked in the customs which Israel had introduced. ²⁰And the Lord rejected all the descendants of Israel, and afflicted them, and gave them into the hand of spoilers, until he had cast them out of his sight.

²¹When he had torn Israel from the house of David they made Jeroboam the son of Nebat king. And Jeroboam drove Israel from following the Lord and made them commit great sin. ²²The people of Israel walked in all the sins which Jeroboam did; they did not depart from them, ²³until the Lord removed Israel out of his sight, as he had spoken by all his servants the prophets. So Israel was exiled from their own land to Assyria until this day.

²⁴And the king of Assyria brought people from Babylon, Cuthah, Avva, Hamath, and Sephar-

vaim, and placed them in the cities of Samaria instead of the people of Israel; and they took possession of Samaria, and dwelt in its cities. ^{25}And at the beginning of their dwelling there, they did not fear the Lord; therefore the Lord sent lions among them, which killed some of them. ^{26}So the king of Assyria was told, "The nations which you have carried away and placed in the cities of Samaria do not know the law of the god of the land; therefore he has sent lions among them, and behold, they are killing them, because they do not know the law of the god of the land." ^{27}Then the king of Assyria commanded, "Send there one of the priests whom you carried away thence; and let him^f go and dwell there, and teach them the law of the god of the land." ^{28}So one of the priests whom they had carried away from Samaria came and dwelt in Bethel, and taught them how they should fear the Lord.

^{29}But every nation still made gods of its own, and put them in the shrines of the high places which the Samaritans had made, every nation in the cities in which they dwelt; ^{30}the men of Babylon made Succoth-benoth, the men of Cuth made Nergal, the men of Hamath made Ashima, ^{31}and the Avvites made Nibhaz and Tartak; and the Sepharvites burned their children in the fire to Adrammelech and Anammelech, the gods of Sepharvaim. ^{32}They also feared the Lord, and appointed from among themselves all sorts of people as priests of the high places, who sacrificed for them in the shrines of the high places. ^{33}So they feared the Lord but also served their own gods, after the manner of the nations from among whom they had been carried away. ^{34}To this day they do according to the former manner.

They do not fear the Lord, and they do not follow the statutes or the ordinances or the law or the commandment which the Lord commanded the children of Jacob, whom he named Israel. ^{35}The Lord made a covenant with them, and commanded them, "You shall not fear other gods or bow yourselves to them or serve them or sacrifice to them; ^{36}but you shall fear the Lord, who brought you out of the land of Egypt with great power and with an outstretched arm; you shall bow yourselves to him, and to him you shall sacrifice. ^{37}And the statutes and the ordinances and the law and the commandment which he wrote for you, you shall always be careful to do. You shall not fear other gods, ^{38}and you shall not forget the covenant that I have made with you. You shall not fear other gods, ^{39}but you shall fear the Lord your God, and he will deliver you out of the hand of all your enemies." ^{40}However they would not listen, but they did according to their former manner.

^{41}So these nations feared the Lord, and also served their graven images; their children likewise, and their children's children—as their fathers did, so they do to this day.

d Heb obscure   e Or made their sons and their daughters pass through the fire   f Syr Vg: Heb them

OVERVIEW: Samaria takes its name from the mountain Semer; its inhabitants, however, were not originally from that region but were Babylonians who had been transferred there by their king Shalmaneser (CHRYSOSTOM). The Samaritans take their name from the Hebrew word somer, which means "guard," because they were the guards sent by Shalmaneser to control the territory of Israel (ORIGEN). Idolatry and every form of impiety were amply widespread in all Israel (ISHO'DAD). The Lord was offended with the Israelites and gave them over to perdition because they had been dispersed from unity (CYPRIAN). Both Israel and Judah sinned so much that they were sentenced by providence to become captives to the Assyrians and Babylonians. The first lion is the antagonistic devil; the second lion, at the completion of the age, is "the man of sin, the son of perdition" (ORIGEN). The Samaritans thought that God was confined to a place and divisible and worshiped him in that way (CHRYSOSTOM).

17:1-6 The King of Assyria Captured Samaria

WHERE DID THE SAMARITANS ORIGINATE?
JOHN CHRYSOSTOM: At this point it is also appropriate to tell where the Samaritans originated. I say this because the entire region is called Samaria. From what source, then, did they derive this name? The mountain is called Semer from the man who had taken possession of it,[1] as Isaiah also said: "And the head of Samaria, Ephraim."[2] The inhabitants, however, were called not Samaritans but Israelites. But as time went on, they transgressed against God, and during the reign of Pekah, Tiglath-pileser went up and seized many cities.[3] After attacking and killing Elah, he gave the kingdom over to Hoshea. Later, Shalmaneser came and captured other cities and made them subject and tributary. However, though Hoshea at first yielded, he revolted afterwards from subjection and took refuge in the aid of the Ethiopians.[4] The Assyrian learned this and, having made an expedition and taken them captive, forbade the nation to remain there any longer, because he suspected the possibility of another such revolt. These inhabitants, moreover, he transported to Babylon and Medea and, having brought from various regions the people dwelling in that vicinity, he caused them to dwell in Samaria so that his power might be safeguarded for the future, with loyal inhabitants in possession of the place.

When these things had taken place, God, wishing to show his power and that he had given over the Jews not because of any lack of power on his part but because of the sins of those whom he had surrendered to their enemies, sent lions on the barbarians, and these preyed on the entire nation. This was reported to the king, and he sent a certain priest to give to them the laws of God. Nevertheless, not even then were they freed entirely from their impiety, but only partly. However, as time went on they turned away from idols and worshiped God. When things had reached this point, the Jews, finally returning, showed a contentious spirit toward them as foreigners and enemies and named them "Samaritans" after the mountain. HOMILIES ON THE GOSPEL OF JOHN 31.2.[5]

A DIFFERENT ETYMOLOGY.
ORIGEN: The Hebrews, however, call a guard *somer*, and thus they also hand on in their tradition that the Samaritans first received this name because the king of the Assyrians sent them to be guards of the land of Israel after the captivity, that is, that other Israel besides Judah, which was taken captive into Assyria because of their many sins. COMMENTARY ON THE GOSPEL OF JOHN 20.321.[6]

17:7-12 They Built High Places

A WIDESPREAD PRACTICE OF IDOLATRY.
ISHO'DAD OF MERV: With the words "from watchtower to fortified city" [the Scripture] denounces the large number of their idols, that is, [there were] idols from border to border. The text refers to the "fortified city" as Jerusalem, but other [interpreters] say Antioch. BOOKS OF SESSIONS 2 KINGS 16.15.[7]

17:20-28 The Lord Punished Israel

THE ESSENTIAL SACRAMENT OF UNITY.
CYPRIAN: Finally, how inseparable is the sacrament of unity and how hopeless are they and what greatest perdition they seek for themselves from the indignation of God—they who make a schism and, after having abandoned their bishop, ap-

---

[1]See 1 Kings 16:24. [2]Is 7:9. [3]See 2 Kings 15:29. [4]The Egyptians (2 Kings 17:4). [5]FC 33:301-2. [6]FC 89:272. [7]CSCO 229:142.

point for themselves another false bishop from without—the divine Scripture declares in the book of Kings, when from the tribe of Judah and Benjamin ten tribes were separated and, abandoning their king, appointed themselves another from without. "And the Lord was offended," it says, "at all the seed of Israel, and afflicted them and delivered them up to plunder till he cast them away from his face because Israel was torn from the house of David, and they made Jeroboam son of Nabath their king."[8] It said that the Lord was offended and gave them over to perdition because they had been dispersed from unity and had appointed another king for themselves.

And so great indignation of the Lord remained against those who had made the schism that even when the man of God had been sent to Jeroboam to upbraid him for his sins and to foretell future vengeance, he was forbidden also to eat bread and to drink water among them. Since he had not heeded this and had dined contrary to the precept of God, he was immediately stricken by the majesty of divine censure; on his return, he was killed on the journey by the attack and bite of a lion. And does anyone of you dare to say that the life-giving water of baptism and heavenly grace can be common with schismatics with whom neither earthly food nor worldly drink ought to be common?

Moreover, the Lord satisfies us in his gospel and reveals a greater light of understanding that the same people who then had separated themselves from the tribe of Judah and Benjamin and, after having abandoned Jerusalem, had withdrawn to Samaria should be reputed among the profane and the Gentiles. For when he first sent his disciples upon the ministry of salvation, he commanded and said, "Do not go in the direction of the Gentiles or enter the town of the Samaritans."[10] Sending first to the Jews, he orders the Gentiles to be passed over as yet; but, adding that the city of the Samaritans, where there were schismatics, ought to be omitted, he shows that the schismatics were in the same category as the Gentiles. LETTER 69.6.[10]

THE WICKEDNESS OF JUDAH AND ISRAEL.
ORIGEN: "Faithless Israel has shown itself less guilty than false Judah."[11] The letter of the text just read has something unclear that we need to understand first. Then, after this, if God wills, we shall know his mystical plan. He wants us then to know in these words, just as it is written in Kings, that the people were divided in those times into the kingdom of ten tribes under Jeroboam and the kingdom of two tribes under Roboam.[12] And those under Jeroboam were called Israel, and those under Roboam Judah. And the division of the people persisted, according to the history, until today. For we know of nothing in the history that united Israel and Judah "into the same nation."[13] Then Israel first, under Jeroboam and under his successors, sinned excessively, and Israel sinned so much beyond Judah that they were sentenced by providence to become captives "to the Assyrians until the sign,"[14] as the Scripture says. After this, the people of Judah also sinned, and as captives they were sentenced to Babylon, not until a sign, as Israel, but for "seventy years,"[15] as Jeremiah prophesied and Daniel also mentioned.[16] HOMILIES ON JEREMIAH 4.1.1-2.[17]

THE SYMBOLIC MEANING OF THE LIONS. ORIGEN: [The Lord] takes hold of two principal lions, the Assyrians and the Babylonians. According to the history in the fourth book of Kings, there are two. For Assyria removed the sons of Israel to Assyria "until today," but Babylon removed the sons of Judah "to Babylon."[18] Except he did not say here first and second, but first and last. For the first lion is the antagonistic devil; he is a murderer.[19] The very last lion at the completion of the age is "the man of sin, the son of perdition, who exalts himself above every so-called god or object of worship."[20] FRAGMENTS FROM THE CATENA ON JEREMIAH 28.2.[21]

---

[8]2 Kings 17:20-21 (VL). [9]Mt 10:5. [10]FC 51:248-49*. [11]Jer 3:11. [12]I.e., Rehoboam. [13]Jer 3:18. [14]2 Kings 17:23 (LXX). [15]Jer 25:11. [16]See Dan 9:2. [17]FC 97:30. [18]2 Kings 25:7, 11. [19]See Jn 8:44. [20]2 Thess 2:3-4. [21]FC 97:296.

17:29-34 They Worshiped the Lord and Their Own Gods

ERRORS OF THE SAMARITANS IN WORSHIP-ING GOD. JOHN CHRYSOSTOM: How, then, did the Samaritans not know what they worshiped? Because they thought that God was confined to a place and divisible; at least it was in that way that they worshiped him. And it was in this spirit that they sent to the Persians and announced that the God of this place was displeased with them.[22]

According to this, their idea of him was no greater than their conception of their idols. Therefore, they continued to worship both evil spirit and him, combining things that were altogether incompatible. But the Jews for the most part were free of this taint and knew that he is God of the universe, even though not all of them [were faithful]. HOMILIES ON THE GOSPEL OF JOHN 33.1.[23]

---

[22]2 Kings 17:26 (LXX). [23]FC 33:323.

18:1-37 THE RIGHTEOUSNESS OF HEZEKIAH

[1]*In the third year of Hoshea son of Elah, king of Israel, Hezekiah the son of Ahaz, king of Judah, began to reign.* [2]*He was twenty-five years old when he began to reign, and he reigned twenty-nine years in Jerusalem. His mother's name was Abi the daughter of Zechariah.* [3]*And he did what was right in the eyes of the LORD, according to all that David his father had done.* [4]*He removed the high places, and broke the pillars, and cut down the Asherah. And he broke in pieces the bronze serpent that Moses had made, for until those days the people of Israel had burned incense to it; it was called Nehushtan.* [5]*He trusted in the LORD the God of Israel; so that there was none like him among all the kings of Judah after him, nor among those who were before him.* [6]*For he held fast to the LORD; he did not depart from following him, but kept the commandments which the LORD commanded Moses.* [7]*And the LORD was with him; wherever he went forth, he prospered. He rebelled against the king of Assyria, and would not serve him.* [8]*He smote the Philistines as far as Gaza and its territory, from watchtower to fortified city.*

[9]*In the fourth year of King Hezekiah, which was the seventh year of Hoshea son of Elah, king of Israel, Shalmaneser king of Assyria came up against Samaria and besieged it* [10]*and at the end of three years he took it. In the sixth year of Hezekiah, which was the ninth year of Hoshea king of Israel, Samaria was taken.* [11]*The king of Assyria carried the Israelites away to Assyria, and put them in Halah, and on the Habor, the river of Gozan, and in the cities of the Medes,* [12]*because they did not obey the voice of the LORD their God but transgressed his covenant, even all that Moses the servant of the LORD commanded; they neither listened nor obeyed.*

[13]*In the fourteenth year of King Hezekiah Sennacherib king of Assyria came up against all the fortified cities of Judah and took them.* [14]*And Hezekiah king of Judah sent to the king of Assyria at Lachish, saying, "I have done wrong; withdraw from me; whatever you impose on me I will bear."*

And the king of Assyria required of Hezekiah king of Judah three hundred talents of silver and thirty talents of gold. ¹⁵And Hezekiah gave him all the silver that was found in the house of the Lord, and in the treasuries of the king's house. ¹⁶At that time Hezekiah stripped the gold from the doors of the temple of the Lord, and from the doorposts which Hezekiah king of Judah had overlaid and gave it to the king of Assyria. ¹⁷And the king of Assyria sent the Tartan, the Rabsaris, and the Rabshakeh with a great army from Lachish to King Hezekiah at Jerusalem. And they went up and came to Jerusalem. When they arrived, they came and stood by the conduit of the upper pool, which is on the highway to the Fuller's Field. ¹⁸And when they called for the king, there came out to them Eliakim the son of Hilkiah, who was over the household, and Shebnah the secretary, and Joah the son of Asaph, the recorder.

¹⁹And the Rabshakeh said to them, "Say to Hezekiah, 'Thus says the great king, the king of Assyria: On what do you rest this confidence of yours? ²⁰Do you think that mere words are strategy and power for war? On whom do you now rely, that you have rebelled against me? ²¹Behold, you are relying now on Egypt, that broken reed of a staff, which will pierce the hand of any man who leans on it. Such is Pharaoh king of Egypt to all who rely on him. ²²But if you say to me, "We rely on the Lord our God," is it not he whose high places and altars Hezekiah has removed, saying to Judah and to Jerusalem, "You shall worship before this altar in Jerusalem"? ²³Come now, make a wager with my master the king of Assyria: I will give you two thousand horses, if you are able on your part to set riders upon them. ²⁴How then can you repulse a single captain among the least of my master's servants, when you rely on Egypt for chariots and for horsemen? ²⁵Moreover, is it without the Lord that I have come up against this place to destroy it? The Lord said to me, Go up against this land, and destroy it.'"

²⁶Then Eliakim the son of Hilkiah, and Shebnah, and Joah, said to the Rabshakeh, "Pray, speak to your servants in the Aramaic language, for we understand it; do not speak to us in the language of Judah within the hearing of the people who are on the wall." ²⁷But the Rabshakeh said to them, "Has my master sent me to speak these words to your master and to you, and not to the men sitting on the wall, who are doomed with you to eat their own dung and to drink their own urine?"

²⁸Then the Rabshakeh stood and called out in a loud voice in the language of Judah: "Hear the word of the great king, the king of Assyria! ²⁹Thus says the king: 'Do not let Hezekiah deceive you, for he will not be able to deliver you out of my hand. ³⁰Do not let Hezekiah make you to rely on the Lord by saying, The Lord will surely deliver us, and this city will not be given into the hand of the king of Assyria.' ³¹Do not listen to Hezekiah; for thus says the king of Assyria: 'Make your peace with me and come out to me; then every one of you will eat of his own vine, and every one of his own fig tree, and every one of you will drink the water of his own cistern; ³²until I come and take you away to a land like your own land, a land of grain and wine, a land of bread and vineyards, a land of olive trees and honey, that you may live, and not die. And do not listen to Hezekiah when he misleads you by saying, The Lord will deliver us. ³³Has any of the gods of the nations ever delivered his land out of the hand of the king of Assyria? ³⁴Where are the gods of

Hamath and Arpad? Where are the gods of Sepharvaim, Hena, and Ivvah? Have they delivered Samaria out of my hand? [35]*Who among all the gods of the countries have delivered their countries out of my hand, that the LORD should deliver Jerusalem out of my hand?'"*

[36]*But the people were silent and answered him not a word, for the king's command was, "Do not answer him."* [37]*Then Eliakim the son of Hilkiah, who was over the household, and Shebna the secretary, and Joah the son of Asaph, the recorder, came to Hezekiah with their clothes rent, and told him the words of the Rabshakeh.*

OVERVIEW: Hezekiah served God by destroying the groves and temples of idols. He was the first king who completely destroyed the high places. The bronze serpent was preserved intact in memory of Moses' miracle but afterwards was worshiped as an idol by the unfaithful people until Hezekiah destroyed it (AUGUSTINE). Hezekiah did not hesitate, in the face of stern necessity, to give the Assyrian king all that he had consecrated to the Lord (JEROME). Sennacherib is a type of the devil, and this is confirmed by the words that the Rabshakeh boastfully speaks against God (EPHREM).

18:1-7 Hezekiah Removed the High Places

HEZEKIAH SERVED GOD. AUGUSTINE: A sovereign serves God one way as man, another way as king; he serves him as man by living according to faith, he serves him as king by exerting the necessary strength to sanction laws that command goodness and prohibit its opposite. It was thus that Hezekiah served him by destroying the groves and temples of idols and the high places that had been set up contrary to the commandments of God. LETTER 185.19.[1]

THE FIRST KING TO DESTROY THE HIGH PLACES. AUGUSTINE: But because he goes on to add "of this man's seed God, according to his promise, has raised up to Israel a Savior, Jesus,"[2] he indicates that that testimony must have a deeper meaning in the Lord Jesus, who truly does all the will of God the Father, rather than in the great King David, who, even though according to

the previous discussion his sins had been remitted and not imputed and also because of the holy penitence mentioned, could not unjustly be said to have been found according to the heart of God. Yet, how did he do all the will of God? Even if he was exceptionally praised when Scripture relates his times and his deeds, he is marked because he did not destroy the high places where the people of God used to sacrifice contrary to the command of God, who had ordered that sacrifices be offered to him only in the tabernacle of the testament, although in these same high places sacrifice is offered to the same God. The king Hezekiah, himself sprung from the seed of David, afterwards destroyed these places, accompanied by the testimony of his great praise. EIGHT QUESTIONS OF DULCITIUS 5.[3]

THE BRONZE SERPENT. AUGUSTINE: Then there were the miracles . . . of the deadly bites of serpents, inflicted as just punishment for sin, and healed when a brazen serpent was raised on a wooden pole in sight of all,[4] so that not only did relief come to an afflicted people but also the destruction of death by death was symbolized by this image of the crucifixion. This serpent was preserved intact in memory of the miracle but afterwards was worshiped as an idol by the unfaithful people until King Hezekiah, religiously using his power in the service of God, destroyed it and thus gained great renown for his piety. CITY OF GOD 10.8.[5]

---

[1]FC 30:160. [2]Acts 13:23. [3]FC 16:465-66. [4]See Num 21:8-9. [5]FC 14:131*.

18:13-16 *Hezekiah Gave Sennacherib All the Silver from the Temple*

HEZEKIAH'S NOBLE DEEDS. JEROME: Of Hezekiah it is written, "And he did that which was right in the eyes of the Lord, according to all that David his father had done. He destroyed the high places, and broke the statues in pieces, and burned the groves and broke the brazen serpent that Moses had made." And again, "He trusted in the Lord the God of Israel, and after him there was none like him among all the kings of Judah who were before him. He stuck to the Lord, and departed not from him and kept his commandments, which the Lord commanded Moses, and the Lord was with him, and in all things to which he went forth, he behaved himself wisely." And, when Sennacherib, the king of the Assyrians, had taken all the cities of Judah, "Hezekiah sent messengers to him, to Lachish, saying, 'I have sinned, depart from me, and all that you shall command of me, I will give.' And the king of the Assyrians put a tax on Hezekiah, king of Judah, of three hundred talents of silver and thirty talents of gold. And Hezekiah gave him all the money that was found in the house of the Lord and in the treasure houses of the king. At that time, he broke the doors of the temple of the Lord and the plates of gold and gave them all to the king of the Assyrians." Although such great demands were placed on him, Hezekiah did not hesitate, in the face of stern necessity, to give the Assyrian king all that he had consecrated to the Lord, and it is said to him, "I will protect this city for my own sake and for David my servant's sake."[6] Not for your sake, for you had already performed a noble deed when 185,000 soldiers of the Assyrian army were laid low and slaughtered by an angel.[7] AGAINST THE PELAGIANS 2.21.[8]

18:19-37 *Make Your Peace with Me*

SENNACHERIB AS A TYPE OF THE DEVIL. EPHREM THE SYRIAN: As I have already said, Sennacherib is a type of the devil, and this hypothesis is perfectly confirmed by the words that in this passage the Rabshakeh boastfully speaks against God when he makes false promises to the people, trying to take away from [God] the praise of his supreme power and giving assurance of a land of fertile soil and abundant crops in order to persuade them to abandon the region given to them by God and to move to the new dwelling places promised by the Assyrian. With a very similar artifice the accomplices and envoys of the devil endeavor to seduce a simple soul. And for this reason, in the first place, they try to uproot all the opinions that are inspired by divine providence. ON THE SECOND BOOK OF KINGS 18.19.[9]

---

[6]2 Kings 20:6. [7]See 2 Kings 18:17–19:37. [8]FC 53:330. [9]ESOO 1:557.

19:1-37 THE DEFEAT OF SENNACHERIB

---

[1]*When King Hezekiah heard it, he rent his clothes, and covered himself with sackcloth, and went into the house of the LORD. [2]And he sent Eliakim, who was over the household, and Shebna the secretary, and the senior priests, covered with sackcloth, to the prophet Isaiah the son of Amoz. [3]They said to him, "Thus says Hezekiah, This day is a day of distress, of rebuke, and of disgrace;*

---

children have come to the birth, and there is no strength to bring them forth. ⁴It may be that the LORD your God heard all the words of the Rabshakeh, whom his master the king of Assyria has sent to mock the living God, and will rebuke the words which the LORD your God has heard; therefore lift up your prayer for the remnant that is left." ⁵When the servants of King Hezekiah came to Isaiah, ⁶Isaiah said to them, "Say to your master, 'Thus says the LORD: Do not be afraid because of the words that you have heard, with which the servants of the king of Assyria have reviled me. ⁷Behold, I will put a spirit in him, so that he shall hear a rumor and return to his own land; and I will cause him to fall by the sword in his own land.'"

⁸The Rabshakeh returned, and found the king of Assyria fighting against Libnah; for he heard that the king had left Lachish. ⁹And when the king heard concerning Tirhakah king of Ethiopia, "Behold, he has set out to fight against you," he sent messengers again to Hezekiah, saying, ¹⁰"Thus shall you speak to Hezekiah king of Judah: 'Do not let your God on whom you rely deceive you by promising that Jerusalem will not be given into the hand of the king of Assyria. ¹¹Behold, you have heard what the kings of Assyria have done to all lands, destroying them utterly. And shall you be delivered? ¹²Have the gods of the nations delivered them, the nations which my fathers destroyed, Gozan, Haran, Rezeph, and the people of Eden who were in Telassar? ¹³Where is the king of Hamath, the king of Arpad, the king of the city of Sepharvaim, the king of Hena, or the king of Ivvah?'"

¹⁴Hezekiah received the letter from the hand of the messengers, and read it; and Hezekiah went up to the house of the LORD, and spread it before the LORD. ¹⁵And Hezekiah prayed before the LORD, and said: "O LORD the God of Israel, who art enthroned above the cherubim, thou art the God, thou alone, of all the kingdoms of the earth; thou hast made heaven and earth. ¹⁶Incline thy ear, O LORD, and hear; open thy eyes, O LORD, and see; and hear the words of Sennacherib, which he has sent to mock the living God. ¹⁷Of a truth, O LORD, the kings of Assyria have laid waste the nations and their lands, ¹⁸and have cast their gods into the fire; for they were no gods, but the work of men's hands, wood and stone; therefore they were destroyed. ¹⁹So now, O LORD our God, save us, I beseech thee, from his hand, that all the kingdoms of the earth may know that thou, O LORD, art God alone."

²⁰Then Isaiah the son of Amoz sent to Hezekiah saying, "Thus says the LORD, the God of Israel: Your prayer to me about Sennacherib king of Assyria I have heard. ²¹This is the word that the LORD has spoken concerning him:

"She despises you, she scorns you—
    the virgin daughter of Zion;
she wags her head behind you—
    the daughter of Jerusalem.

²²"Whom have you mocked and reviled?
    Against whom have you raised your voice
and haughtily lifted your eyes?
    Against the Holy One of Israel!

²³By your messengers you have mocked the Lord,
>   and you have said, 'With my many chariots
I have gone up the heights of the mountains,
>   to the far recesses of Lebanon;
I felled its tallest cedars,
>   its choicest cypresses;
I entered its farthest retreat,
>   its densest forest.
²⁴I dug wells
>   and drank foreign waters,
and I dried up with the sole of my foot
>   all the streams of Egypt.'

²⁵"Have you not heard
>   that I determined it long ago?
I planned from days of old
>   what now I bring to pass,
that you should turn fortified cities
>   into heaps of ruins,
²⁶while their inhabitants, shorn of strength,
>   are dismayed and confounded,
and have become like plants of the field,
>   and like tender grass,
like grass on the housetops;
>   blighted before it is grown?

²⁷"But I know your sitting down
>   and your going out and coming in,
>   and your raging against me.
²⁸Because you have raged against me
>   and your arrogance has come into my ears,
I will put my hook in your nose
>   and my bit in your mouth,
and I will turn you back on the way
>   by which you came.

²⁹"And this shall be the sign for you: this year you shall eat what grows of itself, and in the second year what springs of the same; then in the third year sow, and reap, and plant vineyards, and eat their fruit. ³⁰And the surviving remnant of the house of Judah shall again take root downward, and bear fruit upward; ³¹for out of Jerusalem shall go forth a remnant, and out of Mount Zion a

band of survivors. The zeal of the LORD will do this.

[32]*"Therefore thus says the LORD concerning the king of Assyria, He shall not come into this city or shoot an arrow there, or come before it with a shield or cast up a siege mound against it.* [33]*By the way that he came, by the same he shall return, and he shall not come into this city, says the LORD.* [34]*For I will defend this city to save it, for my own sake and for the sake of my servant David."*

[35]*And that night the angel of the LORD went forth, and slew a hundred and eighty-five thousand in the camp of the Assyrians; and when men arose early in the morning, behold, these were all dead bodies.* [36]*Then Sennacherib king of Assyria departed, and went home, and dwelt at Nineveh.* [37]*And as he was worshiping in the house of Nisroch his god, Adrammelech and Sharezer, his sons, slew him with the sword, and escaped into the land of Ararat. And Esarhaddon his son reigned in his stead.*

OVERVIEW: Sennacherib fled from Hezekiah through the agency of the prophet Isaiah, even though he was far removed in another district, because at that time Isaiah was the mediator for Hezekiah before God (PAULINUS). Through prayer Hezekiah added to the days of his life as king and routed the mighty army of the Assyrians (SAHDONA). When an ear is ascribed to God, it is implied that he hears all things (NOVATIAN). The Lord's goodness is so great that he often finds his way to grant the salvation of the majority on account of a few just people. When Hezekiah was about to run the greatest possible risk, although he was a righteous man, God said that he would aid him for the sake of David (CHRYSOSTOM). The true angel sent by the Lord against the Assyrians had no need of crowds or apparitions or loud noises, like demons have, but he used his power quietly and destroyed 185,000 at one time (ATHANASIUS). Because God was gracious to the Jews, without battle or war the barbarian king left 185,000 of his slain soldiers among them and fled (CHRYSOSTOM).

19:1-7 God Will Cause Him to Fall

ISAIAH WAS THE MEDIATOR BETWEEN GOD AND HEZEKIAH. PAULINUS OF NOLA: Faith unguarded is armed by God. Hezekiah, through the power of faith, proved stronger with his puny force than Sennacherib, king of Babylon and rich Nineveh, with his thousands. Sennacherib had enlisted the forces of Assyria and the realm of the Medes. Laying waste with his huge legions all the neighbouring kingdoms, he proceeded towards the city sacred to the Lord and against it alone concentrated his whole massive war machine. But as he made preparations for this, God hindered him, for warfare delayed his unholy designs. He sent to Jerusalem a letter brusque in its arrogant threats. Hezekiah received it with grief and bore it to the Lord before the altar. There in prostrate prayer accompanied by his people in mourning black, he read out those harsh words and bedewed the letter with abundant tears, and so he prevailed on God. By prayer alone, though absent from the scene, he won a shattering victory over the Assyrians, who suffered a grievous death when God warred on them. This favour he won was so considerable that he did not even clap eyes on the enemy he conquered. Once his tears of complaint had passed above the constellations, once his lament from a humble heart had risen beyond the stars and his devoted words had assailed the ears of highest Father, the lofty doors of heaven swung open and a winged angel glided down, breathing the fragrant air on his smooth descent. Armed with the sword of the Word, he smote that wicked army, and glorying in the silent slaughter of the sleeping foe, he brought simultaneous death to one hundred and eighty thousand men. A single night was the accomplice engagement on that scale. Next morning the king arose still threatening but then took flight with his depleted column, wretched because his army was

thus stripped of its slaughtered soldiers. He fled from Hezekiah, though the prophet was far removed in another district, and though he had only recently in his presence threatened to clap his fetters on him. At that time Isaias was mediator for Hezekiah. POEMS 26.166-95.[1]

19:15-18 Hezekiah Prayed to the Lord

THE POWER OF PRAYER. SAHDONA: Prayer sometimes brings the dead back to life, but sometimes it may slay the living, as happened with the godly Peter: he brought Tabitha back to life[2] by prayer, but he effected the death of Ananias and Sapphira.[3] Elisha, that spiritual man, brought to life the young son of the Shunammite woman,[4] but he brought to their end the wicked children, through the bears that he brought out against them with the course.[5] The case of Hezekiah was also astonishing: through prayer he added to the days of his life as king[6] and routed the mighty army of the Assyrians with the help of a spiritual being. BOOK OF PERFECTION 41.[7]

19:20-31 God Punishes the Arrogance of Sennacherib

GOD HEARS ALL THINGS. NOVATIAN: When eyes are ascribed to God, it is implied that he sees all things;[8] an ear, to show that he hears all things; a finger,[9] to reveal a certain signification of the will; nostrils, to show that he is aware of our prayers as one is of odors;[10] hands, to prove that he is the author of every created thing; an arm,[11] to make it known that no nature can resist his power; and finally feet,[12] to make it clear that he fills all things and that there is no thing in which God is not. ON THE TRINITY 6.6.[13]

19:32-34 God Will Defend Jerusalem

SALVATION ON ACCOUNT OF THE VIRTUE OF THE DEPARTED. JOHN CHRYSOSTOM: The Lord's goodness is immense, and frequently he finds his way to grant the salvation of the majority on account of a few just people. Why do I say on account of a few just people? Frequently, when a just person cannot be found in the present life, he takes pity on the living on account of the virtue of the departed and cries aloud in the words, "I will protect this city for my own sake and the sake of my servant David." Even if they do not deserve to be saved, he is saying, and have no claim on salvation, yet since showing love is habitual with me and I am prompt to have pity and rescue them from disaster, for my own sake and the sake of my servant David I will act as a shield; he who passed on from this life many years before will prove the salvation of those who have fallen victim to their own indifference. HOMILIES ON GENESIS 42.24.[14]

THE FORCE OF REPENTANCE TRANSCENDS GENERATIONS. JOHN CHRYSOSTOM: For the blessed David also had a fall like that which has now happened to you; and not this only but another also that followed it. I mean that of murder. What then? Did he remain prostrate? Did he not immediately rise up again with energy and place himself in position to fight the enemy? In fact, he wrestled with him so bravely that even after his death he was the protector of his offspring. For when Solomon had perpetrated great iniquity and had deserved countless deaths, God said that he would leave him the kingdom intact, thus speaking: "I will surely rend the kingdom out of your hand and will give it to your servant. Nevertheless I will not do this in your days." Wherefore? "For David your father's sake, I will take it out of the hand of your son."[15] And again when Hezekiah was about to run the greatest possible risk, although he was a righteous man, God said that he would aid him for the sake of this saint. "For I will cast my shield," he says, "over this city to save it for my own sake and for my servant David's sake." LETTER TO THE FALLEN THEODORE 1.14.[16]

---

[1]ACW 40:260-61. [2]See Acts 9:40. [3]See Acts 5:3-10. [4]See 2 Kings 4:32-36. [5]See 2 Kings 2:23-24. [6]See Is 38:1-5. [7]CS 101:219. [8]Ps 33:15 (32:15 LXX); 34:15 (33:16 LXX, Vg). [9]See Exod 31:18. [10]See Gen 8:21. [11]See Ps 136:12 (135:12 LXX, Vg); Deut 5:15. [12]See Is 66:1. [13]FC 67:36. [14]FC 82:431. [15]1 Kings 11:11. [16]NPNF 1 9:105*.

19:35-37 *The Angel of the Lord*

THE TRUE STRENGTH OF THE ANGEL. ATHANASIUS: Since the evil spirits have no power, they play as on a stage, changing their shapes and frightening children by the apparition of crowds and by their changed forms. This is why they are to be despised the more for their powerlessness. The true angel sent by the Lord against the Assyrians had no need of crowds or apparitions from without, or loud noises or clappings, but he used his power quietly and destroyed 185,000 at one time. Powerless demons such as these, however, try to frighten, if only by empty phantoms. LIFE OF ST. ANTHONY 28.9-10.[17]

THE POWER OF GOD SAVED THE JEWS AT THE TIME OF HEZEKIAH. JOHN CHRYSOSTOM: But the Jews will say, "Where is the evidence that God has turned away from us?" Does this still need proof in words? Tell me this. Do not the facts themselves shout it out? Do they not send forth a sound clearer than the trumpet's call? Do you still ask for proof in words when you see the destruction of your city, the desolation of your temple and all the other misfortunes that have come on you? "But people brought these things on us, not God." Rather it was God above all others who did these things. If you attribute them to people, then you must consider that even if people were to have the boldness, they would not have had the power to bring these things to accomplishment, unless it were by God's decree. The barbarian came down on you and brought all Persia[18] with him. He expected that he would catch you all by the suddenness of his attack, and he kept you all locked in the city as if you were caught in the net of a hunter or fisherman. Because God was gracious to you at the time—I repeat, at that time—without a battle, without a war, without a hostile encounter, the barbarian king left 185,000 of his slain soldiers among you and fled, contented that he alone was saved. And God often decided countless other battles in this way. So also now, if God had not deserted you once and for all, your enemies would not have had the power to destroy your city and leave your temple desolate. If God had not abandoned you, the ruin of desolation would not have lasted so long a time, nor would your frequent efforts to rebuild the temple have been in vain. DISCOURSES AGAINST JUDAIZING CHRISTIANS 6.3.6-7.[19]

---

[17]FC 15:162*. [18]Sennacherib was king of Assyria, not Persia. This is probably a slip on the part of Chrysostom. [19]FC 68:157-58.

20:1-21 THE END OF THE REIGN OF HEZEKIAH

[1]*In those days Hezekiah became sick and was at the point of death. And Isaiah the prophet the son of Amoz came to him, and said to him, "Thus says the LORD, 'Set your house in order; for you shall die, you shall not recover.'"* [2]*Then Hezekiah turned his face to the wall, and prayed to the LORD, saying,* [3]*"Remember now, O LORD, I beseech thee, how I have walked before thee in faithfulness and with a whole heart, and have done what is good in thy sight." And Hezekiah wept bitterly.* [4]*And before Isaiah had gone out of the middle court, the word of the LORD came to him:* [5]*"Turn back, and say to Hezekiah the prince of my people, Thus says the LORD, the God of David*

your father: I have heard your prayer, I have seen your tears; behold, I will heal you; on the third day you shall go up to the house of the LORD. ⁶*And I will add fifteen years to your life. I will deliver you and this city out of the hand of the king of Assyria, and I will defend this city for my own sake and for my servant David's sake."* ⁷*And Isaiah said, "Bring a cake of figs. And let them take and lay it on the boil, that he may recover."*

⁸*And Hezekiah said to Isaiah, "What shall be the sign that the LORD will heal me, and that I shall go up to the house of the LORD on the third day?"* ⁹*And Isaiah said, "This is the sign to you from the LORD, that the LORD will do the thing that he has promised: shall the shadow go forward ten steps, or go back ten steps?"* ¹⁰*And Hezekiah answered, "It is an easy thing for the shadow to lengthen ten steps; rather let the shadow go back ten steps."* ¹¹*And Isaiah the prophet cried to the LORD; and he brought the shadow back ten steps, by which the sun*^g *had declined on the dial of Ahaz.*

¹²*At that time Merodach-baladan the son of Baladan, king of Babylon, sent envoys with letters and a present to Hezekiah; for he heard that Hezekiah had been sick.* ¹³*And Hezekiah welcomed them, and he showed them all his treasure house, the silver, the gold, the spices, the precious oil, his armory, all that was found in his storehouses; there was nothing in his house or in all his realm that Hezekiah did not show them.* ¹⁴*Then Isaiah the prophet came to King Hezekiah, and said to him, "What did these men say? And whence did they come to you?" And Hezekiah said, "They have come from a far country, from Babylon."* ¹⁵*He said, "What have they seen in your house?" And Hezekiah answered, "They have seen all that is in my house; there is nothing in my storehouses that I did not show them."*

¹⁶*Then Isaiah said to Hezekiah, "Hear the word of the LORD:* ¹⁷*Behold, the days are coming, when all that is in your house, and that which your fathers have stored up till this day, shall be carried to Babylon; nothing shall be left, says the LORD.* ¹⁸*And some of your own sons, who are born to you, shall be taken away; and they shall be eunuchs in the palace of the king of Babylon."* ¹⁹*Then said Hezekiah to Isaiah, "The word of the LORD which you have spoken is good." For he thought, "Why not, if there will be peace and security in my days?"*

²⁰*The rest of the deeds of Hezekiah, and all his might, and how he made the pool and the conduit and brought water into the city, are they not written in the Book of the Chronicles of the Kings of Judah?* ²¹*And Hezekiah slept with his fathers; and Manasseh his son reigned in his stead.*

g Syr See Is 38.8 and Tg: Heb lacks *the sun*

OVERVIEW: The Lord, with a view to mercy and kindness, chooses to break his word and to extend the life of Hezekiah (CASSIAN). Hezekiah does not cease from penitence, for he remembers the words of Isaiah: "In the hour that you turn and lament, you shall be saved" (CYRIL OF JERUSALEM). When Hezekiah was sick, he did not call to mind sumptuous feasting or glory or royalty but righteousness (CHRYSOSTOM). Hezekiah is commanded to make a plaster with a lump of figs, because the fig tree symbolizes the Holy Spirit (METHODIUS). Hezekiah showed God's treasure to the Assyrians, who ought never to have seen what they were sure to covet (JEROME). Hezekiah did not rejoice for the disaster of the captivity, but he could not oppose the will of the Lord and received the Lord's commands with patience like a humble servant (AMBROSE).

20:1-6 I Will Heal You

IN HIS INFINITE MERCY, GOD REMAINS FREE TO REVISE HIS JUDGMENTS. JOHN CASSIAN: Now let us rise to still more sublime examples. Speaking in the person of God, the prophet Isaiah addressed King Hezekiah as he was lying in bed and laboring under a grave illness: "The Lord says this: Set your house in order, because you shall die, and you shall not live. And Hezekiah," it says, "turned his face to the wall and prayed to the Lord and said, I beseech you, Lord, remember, I pray, how I walked before you in truth and with a perfect heart and did what was good in your sight. And Hezekiah wept with much weeping." After this it was said to him again: "Turn back and speak to Hezekiah, king of Judah, and say, The Lord, the God of David your father, says this: I have heard your prayer, I have seen your tears, and behold, I will add fifteen years to your days, and I will free you from the hand of the king of the Assyrians, and I will defend this city for my own sake and for the sake of my servant David." What is clearer than this text, according to which the Lord, with a view to mercy and kindness, chose to break his own word and to extend the life of the one praying by fifteen years beyond the appointed time of his death rather than show himself inexorable because of an inflexible decree? CONFERENCE 17.25.10-11.[1]

HEZEKIAH IS SAVED BY THE POWER OF HIS REPENTANCE. CYRIL OF JERUSALEM: Would you know the power of repentance? Would you understand this strong weapon of salvation and the might of confession? By confession Hezekiah routed 185,000 of the enemy.[2] That was important, but it was little compared with what shall be told. The same king's repentance won the repeal of the sentence God had passed on him. For when he was sick, Isaiah said to him, "Give charge concerning your house, for you shall die and not live." What

expectation was left? What hope of recovery was there, when the prophet said, "For you shall die"? But Hezekiah did not cease from penitence, for he remembered what was written: "In the hour that you turn and lament, you shall be saved."[3] He turned his face to the wall, and from his bed of pain his mind soared up to heaven—for no wall is so thick as to stifle reverent prayer—"Lord," he said, "remember me. You are not subject to circumstance, but are yourself the legislator of life. For not on birth and conjunction of stars, as some vainly say, does our life depend. No, you are the arbiter, according to your will, of life and the duration of life." He whom the prophet's sentence had forbidden to hope was granted fifteen further years of life, the sun turning back its course in witness thereof. Now while the sun retraced its course for Hezekiah, for Christ it was eclipsed, the distinction marking the difference between the two, I mean Hezekiah and Jesus. Now if even Hezekiah could revoke God's decree, shall not Jesus grant the remission of sins? Turn and lament, shut your door, and beg for pardon, that God may remove from the scorching flames. For confession has the power to quench even fire; it can tame even lions. CATECHETICAL LECTURES 2.15.[4]

A PIOUS PERSON WILL EXULT IN RIGHTEOUSNESS. JOHN CHRYSOSTOM: For which of the things in our present life seems to you pleasant? A sumptuous table, and health of body, and glory and wealth? No, these delights, if you set them by that pleasure, will prove the bitterest of all things, compared with what is to come. For nothing is more pleasurable than a sound conscience and a good hope. And if you would learn this, let us inquire of him who is on the point of departing hence or of him that is grown old; and when we have reminded him of sumptuous banqueting that he had enjoyed, and of glory and honor and of good works that he had some time practiced and wrought, let us ask in which he exults the more; and we shall see him for the

---

[1]ACW 57:607. [2]See 2 Kings 19:35. [3]Is 30:15. [4]FC 61:104-5.

other ashamed and covering his face but for these soaring and leaping with joy. So Hezekiah, too, when he was sick, called not to mind sumptuous feasting or glory or royalty but righteousness. For "remember," he said, "how I walked before you in an upright way." HOMILIES ON THE GOSPEL OF MATTHEW 53.6-7.[5]

20:7-11 A Lump of Figs

THE FIG TREE IS A SYMBOL OF THE HOLY SPIRIT. METHODIUS: The vine, and that not in a few places, refers to the Lord himself,[6] and the fig tree to the Holy Spirit, as the Lord makes glad the hearts of people and heals them. And therefore Hezekiah is commanded first to make a plaster with a lump of figs—that is, the fruit of the Spirit—that he may be healed—that is, according to the apostle—by love; for he says, "The fruit of the Spirit is love, joy, peace, longsuffering, gentleness, goodness, faith, meekness, temperance;"[7] which, on account of their great pleasantness the prophet calls figs. Micah also says, "They shall sit everyone under his vine and under his fig tree; and none shall make them afraid."[8] Now it is certain that those who have taken refuge and rested under the Spirit and under the shadow of the Word shall not be alarmed or frightened by him who troubles the hearts of humankind. SYMPOSIUM OR BANQUET OF THE TEN VIRGINS 10.5.[9]

20:12-15 Hezekiah's Treasure House

THE EYES OF COVETOUSNESS. JEROME: And assuredly no gold or silver vessel was ever so dear to God as is the temple of a virgin's body. The shadow went before, but now the reality has come. You indeed may speak in all simplicity, and from motives of amiability you may treat with courtesy the truest strangers, but unchaste eyes see nothing aright. They fail to appreciate the beauty of the soul and value only that of the body. Hezekiah showed God's treasure to the Assyrians, who ought never to have seen what they were sure to covet. The consequence was that Judea was torn by continual wars and that the very first things carried away to Babylon were these vessels of the Lord. We find Belshazzar at his feast and among his concubines (vice always glories in defiling what is noble) drinking out of these sacred cups.[10] LETTER 22.23.[11]

20:17-21 Some of Hezekiah's Sons Will Be Exiled

HEZEKIAH RECEIVES THE LORD'S COMMANDS. AMBROSE: Surely the just Hezekiah did not rejoice that the disaster of the captivity had fallen on his children, but he could not oppose the will of the Lord, and so he received the Lord's commands with patience like a humble servant. Thus it happens that one could judge that merit and virtue could be evident even in captivity. For Jeremiah was not less happy in captivity,[12] nor was Daniel,[13] nor Ezra,[14] nor were Ananias and Azariah and Misael less happy than if they had not fallen into captivity.[15] They entered into captivity in such a way that they brought to their people both present consolations in captivity and the hope of escaping from it. JACOB AND THE HAPPY LIFE 8.36.[16]

---

[5]NPNF 1 10:331. [6]See Jn 15:1. [7]Gal 5:22-23. [8]Mic 4:4. [9]ANF 6:350. [10]Dan 5:1-3. [11]NPNF 2 6:31. [12]See Jer 37-38. [13]See Dan 1:6. [14]See Ezra 7:6. [15]See Dan 3:19-96 (Vg). [16]FC 65:141-42.

21:1-26 THE RETURN TO IDOLATRY
UNDER MANASSEH AND AMON

[1]*Manasseh was twelve years old when he began to reign, and he reigned fifty-five years in Jerusalem. His mother's name was Hephzibah.* [2]*And he did what was evil in the sight of the LORD, according to the abominable practices of the nations whom the LORD drove out before the people of Israel.* [3]*For he rebuilt the high places which Hezekiah his father had destroyed; and he erected altars for Baal, and made an Asherah, as Ahab king of Israel had done, and worshiped all the host of heaven, and served them.* [4]*And he built altars in the house of the LORD, of which the LORD had said, "In Jerusalem will I put my name."* [5]*And he built altars for all the host of heaven in the two courts of the house of the LORD.* [6]*And he burned his son as an offering, and practiced soothsaying and augury, and dealt with mediums and with wizards. He did much evil in the sight of the LORD, provoking him to anger.* [7]*And the graven image of Asherah that he had made he set in the house of which the LORD said to David and to Solomon his son, "In this house, and in Jerusalem, which I have chosen out of all the tribes of Israel, I will put my name for ever;* [8]*and I will not cause the feet of Israel to wander any more out of the land which I gave to their fathers, if only they will be careful to do according to all that I have commanded them, and according to all the law that my servant Moses commanded them."* [9]*But they did not listen, and Manasseh seduced them to do more evil than the nations had done whom the LORD destroyed before the people of Israel.*

[10]*And the LORD said by his servants the prophets,* [11]*"Because Manasseh king of Judah has committed these abominations, and has done things more wicked than all that the Amorites did, who were before him, and has made Judah also to sin with his idols;* [12]*therefore thus says the LORD, the God of Israel, Behold, I am bringing upon Jerusalem and Judah such evil that the ears of every one who hears of it will tingle.* [13]*And I will stretch over Jerusalem the measuring line of Samaria, and the plummet of the house of Ahab; and I will wipe Jerusalem as one wipes a dish, wiping it and turning it upside down.* [14]*And I will cast off the remnant of my heritage, and give them into the hand of their enemies, and they shall become a prey and a spoil to all their enemies,* [15]*because they have done what is evil in my sight and have provoked me to anger, since the day their fathers came out of Egypt, even to this day."*

[16]*Moreover Manasseh shed very much innocent blood, till he had filled Jerusalem from one end to another, besides the sin which he made Judah to sin so that they did what was evil in the sight of the LORD.*

[17]*Now the rest of the acts of Manasseh, and all that he did, and the sin that he committed, are they not written in the Book of the Chronicles of the Kings of Judah?* [18]*And Manasseh slept with his fathers, and was buried in the garden of his house, in the garden of Uzza; and Amon his son reigned in his stead.*

[19]*Amon was twenty-two years old when he began to reign, and he reigned two years in Jerusa-*

lem. His mother's name was Meshullemeth the daughter of Haruz of Jotbah. ²⁰*And he did what was evil in the sight of the LORD, as Manasseh his father had done.* ²¹*He walked in all the way in which his father walked, and served the idols that his father served, and worshiped them;* ²²*he forsook the LORD, the God of his fathers, and did not walk in the way of the LORD.* ²³*And the servants of Amon conspired against him, and killed the king in his house.* ²⁴*But the people of the land slew all those who had conspired against King Amon, and the people of the land made Josiah his son king in his stead.* ²⁵*Now the rest of the acts of Amon which he did, are they not written in the Book of the Chronicles of the Kings of Judah?* ²⁶*And he was buried in his tomb in the garden of Uzza; and Josiah his son reigned in his stead.*

OVERVIEW: For a period of time, the Lord God punished Manasseh, who was addicted to idols and had slain many innocent persons, but received him when he repented and forgave him his offenses (APOSTOLIC CONSTITUTIONS, CHRYSOSTOM). Amon did evil in the sight of the Lord above all who were before him, and the Lord soon destroyed him utterly from his good land (APOSTOLIC CONSTITUTIONS).

21:1-17 Manasseh More Wicked Than the Amorites

WICKEDNESS AND FINAL REPENTANCE OF MANASSEH. APOSTOLIC CONSTITUTIONS: For it is written thus in the fourth book of Kings and the second book of Chronicles, or of Days: "Manasseh was twelve years old when he began to reign; he reigned fifty-five years in Jerusalem. His mother's name was Hephzibah. He did what was evil in the sight of the Lord, following the abominable practices of the nations that the Lord drove out before the people of Israel. For he rebuilt the high places that his father Hezekiah had destroyed; he erected altars for Baal, made a sacred pole, as King Ahab of Israel had done, worshiped all the host of heaven and served them. He built altars in the house of the Lord, of which the Lord had said, 'In Jerusalem I will put my name.' He built altars for all the host of heaven in the two courts of the house of the Lord."[1] And Manasseh raised altars and served Baal there and said, "My name will last forever." "He built altars for all the host of heaven in the two courts of the house of the Lord. He made his son pass through fire; he practiced soothsaying and augury and dealt with mediums and with wizards. He did much evil in the sight of the Lord, provoking him to anger. The carved image of Asherah that he had made he set in the house of which the Lord said to David and to his son Solomon, 'In this house and in Jerusalem, which I have chosen out of all the tribes of Israel, I will put my name forever; I will not cause the feet of Israel to wander any more out of the land that I gave to their ancestors, if only they will be careful to do according to all that I have commanded them and according to all the law that my servant Moses commanded them.'" But they did not listen; Manasseh misled them to do more evil than the nations had done that the Lord destroyed before the people of Israel.

The Lord said by his servants the prophets, "Because King Manasseh of Judah has committed these abominations, has done things more wicked than all that the Amorites did, who were before him, and has caused Judah also to sin with his idols; therefore thus says the Lord, the God of Israel, I am bringing on Jerusalem and Judah such evil that the ears of everyone who hears of it will tingle. I will stretch over Jerusalem the measuring line for Samaria and the plumb line for the house of Ahab; I will wipe Jerusalem as one wipes a dish, wiping it and turning it upside down. I will

---

[1]2 Chron 33:1-4.

cast off the remnant of my heritage and give them into the hand of their enemies; they shall become a prey and a spoil to all their enemies, because they have done what is evil in my sight and have provoked me to anger, since the day their ancestors came out of Egypt, even to this day." Moreover Manasseh shed very much innocent blood, until he had filled Jerusalem from one end to another, besides the sin that he caused Judah to sin so that they did what was evil in the sight of the Lord."[2] "Therefore the Lord brought against them the commanders of the army of the king of Assyria, who took Manasseh captive in manacles, bound him with fetters and brought him to Babylon."[3] And he was bound and shackled all over with iron in the house of the prison. And bread made of bran was given to him scantly and by weight, and water mixed with vinegar but a little and by measure, so much as would keep him alive; and he was in straits and sore afflictions. "While he was in distress he entreated the favor of the Lord his God and humbled himself greatly before the God of his ancestors. He prayed to him,"[4] saying, "O Lord, almighty God of our fathers Abraham, Isaac and Jacob and of their righteous seed, who have made heaven and earth, with all the ornaments thereof, who have bound the sea by the word of your commandment, who have shut up the deep and sealed it by your terrible and glorious name, whom all people fear and tremble before your power; for the majesty of your glory cannot be borne, and your angry threatening toward the sinner is insupportable. But your merciful promise is unmeasurable and unsearchable; for you are the most high Lord, of great compassion, long suffering, very merciful and who repents of the evils of humankind. You, O Lord, according to your great goodness, have promised repentance and forgiveness to them who have sinned against you, and of your infinite mercy you have appointed repentance to sinners, that they may be saved. You therefore, O Lord, that are the God of the just, have not appointed repentance to the just as to Abraham and Isaac and Jacob, who have not sinned against you; but

you have appointed repentance to me that am a sinner: for I have sinned above the number of the sands of the sea. My transgressions, O Lord, are multiplied; my transgressions are multiplied, and I am not worthy to behold and see the height of heaven for the multitude of my iniquity. I am bowed down with many iron bands; for I have provoked your wrath and done evil before you, setting up abominations and multiplying offenses. Now, therefore, I bow the knee of my heart, beseeching you of grace. I have sinned, O Lord, I have sinned, and I acknowledge my iniquities; wherefore I humbly beseech you, forgive me, O Lord, forgive me, and do not destroy me with my iniquities. Be not angry with me forever, by reserving evil for me; neither condemn me into the lower part of the earth. For you are the God, even the God of them that repent, and in me you will show your goodness; for you will save me that am unworthy, according to your great mercy. Therefore I will praise you forever all the days of my life; for all the powers of the heavens do praise you, and yours is the glory forever and ever. Amen."

"And God heard his plea"[5] and had compassion on him. And there appeared a flame of fire about him, and all the iron shackles and chains that were about him fell off; and the Lord healed Manasseh from his affliction and "restored him again to Jerusalem and to his kingdom. Then Manasseh knew that the Lord indeed was God."[6] And he worshiped the Lord God alone with all his heart and with all his soul, and all the days of his life; and he was esteemed righteous. "He took away the foreign gods and the idol from the house of the Lord and all the altars that he had built on the mountain of the house of the Lord and in Jerusalem, and he threw them out of the city. He also restored the altar of the Lord and offered on it sacrifices of well-being and of thanksgiving; and he commanded Judah to serve the Lord the God of Israel."[7] . . . You have heard, our beloved chil-

---

[2]2 Chron 33:5-10. [3]2 Chron 33:11. [4]2 Chron 33:12. [5]2 Chron 33:13. [6]2 Chron 33:13. [7]2 Chron 33:15-16.

dren, how the Lord God for a while punished him who was addicted to idols and had slain many innocent persons; and yet that he received him when he repented, and forgave him his offenses and restored him to his kingdom. For he not only forgives the penitent, but also reinstates them in their former dignity. CONSTITUTIONS OF THE HOLY APOSTLES 2.22.[8]

REPENTANCE GIVES WAY TO THE GRACE OF CHRIST. JOHN CHRYSOSTOM: For so Manasseh had perpetrated innumerable pollutions, having both stretched out his hands against the saints, and brought abominations into the temple, and filled the city with murders and wrought many other things beyond excuse; yet nevertheless after so long and so great wickedness, he washed away from himself all these things. How and in what matter? By repentance and self-examination. For there is no sin that does not yield and give way to the power of repentance, or rather to the grace of Christ. Since if we would but only change, we have him to assist us. And if you are desirous to become good, there is none to hinder us; or rather there is one to hinder us, the devil, yet he has no power, so long as you choose what is best and so attract God to your aid. HOMILIES ON THE GOSPEL OF MATTHEW 22.6.[9]

21:19-24 *Amon Served Idols*

PUNISHMENT FOR THE UNREPENTANT. APOSTOLIC CONSTITUTIONS: There is no sin more grievous than idolatry, for it is an impiety against God, and yet even this sin has been forgiven, on sincere repentance. But if anyone sins in direct opposition and on purpose to try whether God will punish the wicked or not, such a one shall have no remission, although he says to himself, "All is well, and I will walk according to the customs of my evil heart."[10] Such a one was Amon the son of Manasseh. For the Scripture says, "And Amon reasoned an evil reasoning of transgression and said, My father from his childhood was a great transgressor and repented in his old age; and now I will walk as my soul lusts, and afterwards I will return to the Lord." And he did evil in the sight of the Lord above all who were before him. And the Lord God soon destroyed him utterly from his good land. And his servants conspired against him and killed him in his own house, and he reigned two years only. CONSTITUTIONS OF THE HOLY APOSTLES 2.23.[11]

---

[8]ANF 7:406-7**. [9]NPNF 1 10:154-55*. [10]Deut 29:19. [11]ANF 7:408.

22:1-20 THE PIOUS RULE OF JOSIAH

[1]*Josiah was eight years old when he began to reign, and he reigned thirty-one years in Jerusalem. His mother's name was Jedidah the daughter of Adaiah of Bozkath.* [2]*And he did what was right in the eyes of the LORD, and walked in all the way of David his father, and he did not turn aside to the right hand or to the left.*

[3]*In the eighteenth year of King Josiah, the king sent Shaphan the son of Azaliah, son of Meshullam, the secretary, to the house of the LORD, saying,* [4]*"Go up to Hilkiah the high priest, that he may reckon the amount of the money which has been brought into the house of the LORD, which the keepers of the threshold have collected from the people;* [5]*and let it be given into the hand of the*

workmen who have the oversight of the house of the LORD; and let them give it to the workmen who are at the house of the LORD, repairing the house, ⁶that is, to the carpenters, and to the builders, and to the masons, as well as for buying timber and quarried stone to repair the house. ⁷But no accounting shall be asked from them for the money which is delivered into their hand, for they deal honestly."

⁸And Hilkiah the high priest said to Shaphan the secretary, "I have found the book of the law in the house of the LORD." And Hilkiah gave the book to Shaphan, and he read it. ⁹And Shaphan the secretary came to the king, and reported to the king, "Your servants have emptied out the money that was found in the house, and have delivered it into the hand of the workmen who have the oversight of the house of the LORD." ¹⁰Then Shaphan the secretary told the king, "Hilkiah the priest has given me a book." And Shaphan read it before the king.

¹¹And when the king heard the words of the book of the law, he rent his clothes. ¹²And the king commanded Hilkiah the priest, and Ahikam the son of Shaphan, and Achbor the son of Micaiah, and Shaphan the secretary, and Asaiah the king's servant, saying, ¹³"Go, inquire of the LORD for me, and for the people, and for all Judah, concerning the words of this book that has been found; for great is the wrath of the LORD that is kindled against us, because our fathers have not obeyed the words of this book, to do according to all that is written concerning us."

¹⁴So Hilkiah the priest, and Ahikam, and Achbor, and Shaphan, and Asaiah went to Huldah the prophetess, the wife of Shallum the son of Tikvah, son of Harhas, keeper of the wardrobe (now she dwelt in Jerusalem in the Second Quarter); and they talked with her. ¹⁵And she said to them, "Thus says the LORD, the God of Israel: 'Tell the man who sent you to me, ¹⁶Thus says the LORD, Behold, I will bring evil upon this place and upon its inhabitants, all the words of the book which the king of Judah has read. ¹⁷Because they have forsaken me and have burned incense to other gods, that they might provoke me to anger with all the work of their hands, therefore my wrath will be kindled against this place, and it will not be quenched. ¹⁸But as to the king of Judah, who sent you to inquire of the LORD, thus shall you say to him, Thus says the LORD, the God of Israel: Regarding the words which you have heard, ¹⁹because your heart was penitent, and you humbled yourself before the LORD, when you heard how I spoke against this place, and against its inhabitants, that they should become a desolation and a curse, and you have rent your clothes and wept before me, I also have heard you, says the LORD. ²⁰Therefore, behold, I will gather you to your fathers, and you shall be gathered to your grave in peace, and your eyes shall not see all the evil which I will bring upon this place.'" And they brought back word to the king.

OVERVIEW: Josiah destroys the pagan temples rebuilt by Manasseh and refurbishes the house of the Lord, which had been neglected during the impious reign of his predecessor (EPHREM). It is not without a reason that the book of Deuteronomy was discovered in the house of the Lord at the time of Josiah, because he, more than all the other kings, showed a real fervor against the priests of Baal (ISHOʻDAD). In the Scripture, women are praised when holy men fail, so that this may be a reproach for all men (JEROME). It is possible that Huldah's power of prophecy was superior to that of Jeremiah (ISHOʻDAD). The dead undergo no evils either by enduring them themselves or by compassionate suffering for others but are liberated from all evils that when they lived here they endured for themselves and out of compassion for others (AUGUSTINE).

22:1-7 Josiah Did What Was Right

THE RIGHTEOUSNESS AND PIETY OF JOSIAH. EPHREM THE SYRIAN: "Josiah was eight years old when he began to reign; and he did what was right in the sight of the Lord" for the thirty-one years in which he reigned. In the eighteenth year from the beginning of his rule, he began to purify Judah and the inhabitants of Jerusalem. In fact, he removed the foreign religions introduced by Manasseh and overturned the sanctuaries and altars. In the same eighteenth year he ordered an expiation of the temple and commanded the priests to make repairs. He brought in workers, gathered stones, materials and other things useful to building and supplied the money for the expected expenses, and in this case he religiously emulated the pious zeal of his great-grandfather Jehoash.[1] And at that time the refurbishment of the temple was not less necessary than it had been before, because for the fifty years in which Manasseh had reigned,[2] it had been neglected or given to profane uses. ON THE SECOND BOOK OF KINGS 22.1.[3]

22:8-10 The Book of the Law

DEUTERONOMY WAS THE BOOK FOUND. ISHO'DAD OF MERV: The book that was discovered was the Deuteronomy that Moses had placed in the ark as a precaution.[4] It was brought out through a divine action, in order to show the people that it cried and argued against them because of their great iniquity and therefore did not want to stay in its place. Hilkiah, who found the book, was the father of the prophet Jeremiah.[5] It is not without a reason that the book was discovered at the time of Josiah because he, more than all the other kings, showed a real fervor against the priests of Baal, especially against

those of the ten tribes, that is, those that had survived among them. Indeed, if [the book] had been found at the time of the other kings, they would not have accepted it. They might have even torn it up, as Zedekiah tore the prophecy of Jeremiah and threw it into the fire.[6] [Another reason] is that the time of their captivity had come. For the seventy years of the Babylonian captivity are usually counted from the eighteenth year of Josiah, the year in which the book was discovered: as if the captivity was about to come in those days but was hindered because of Josiah's virtue. BOOKS OF SESSIONS 2 KINGS 22.8.[7]

22:11-14 The Prophet Huldah

WHEN HOLY MEN FAIL, WOMEN ARE PRAISED. JEROME: We need not wonder that Huldah, the prophet and wife of Shallum, was consulted by Josiah, king of Judah, when the captivity was approaching and the wrath of the Lord was falling on Jerusalem: since it is the rule of Scripture, when holy men fail, to praise women to the reproach of men. AGAINST JOVINIANUS 1.25.[8]

HULDAH'S GIFT OF PROPHECY. ISHO'DAD OF MERV: "They went to the prophet Huldah," and not to Jeremiah, even though he was already well known as a prophet, probably because Jeremiah was not there at the moment, or maybe because this woman surpassed him with the power of her gift of prophecy. BOOKS OF SESSIONS 2 KINGS 22.14.[9]

22:18-20 Gathered to His Grave in Peace

THE DEAD ARE NOT AFFECTED BY EVILS AMONG THE LIVING. AUGUSTINE: How do we say that they have been advised who have died

---

[1]See 2 Kings 12:4-16. [2]See 2 Kings 21:1-18. [3]ESOO 1:564-65. [4]See Deut 31:26. [5]This assertion of Isho'dad appears to be historically groundless. [6]Jer 36:23. [7]CSCO 229:146-47. [8]NPNF 2 6:364*. [9]CSCO 229:147.

before the coming of the evils that followed their death, if after death they perceive whatever misfortunes befall the human life? Or is it that we are mistaken when we imagine that they are at rest when the restless life of the living concerns them? What is this, then, that God promised to the most devout king, Josiah, for a great reward, telling him that he would soon die in order that he might not see the evils that he was threatening to send on that place and that people? The words of God are these: "Thus says the Lord the God of Israel: My words, which you have heard and which you feared from my mouth when you heard what I said about this place and those who dwell in it, that it be forsaken and become a curse, and you rent your garments and wept in my sight, shall not come to pass, says the Lord of hosts. Behold I shall bring you to your fathers, and you shall be brought with peace, and your eyes shall not see all the evils that I bring upon this place and those who dwell in it." And Josiah, alarmed at the dire threats of God, wept and tore his garments and then was made secure by an early death from all future ills, because he would so rest in peace that he would not see those evils. The souls of the dead, then, are in a place where they do not see the things that go on and transpire in this mortal life. How, then, do they see their own graves or their own bodies, whether they are buried or lie exposed? How do they take part in the misery of the living, when either they are suffering their own evil deserts, if such they have merited, or they rest in peace, such as was promised to this Josiah? For there they undergo no evils either by enduring them themselves or by compassionate suffering for others, but they are liberated from all evils that when they lived here they endured for themselves and out of compassion for others. THE CARE TO BE TAKEN FOR THE DEAD 13.16.[10]

[10]FC 27:374-75.

23:1-30 JOSIAH IS KILLED BY THE EGYPTIANS

[1]Then the king sent, and all the elders of Judah and Jerusalem were gathered to him. [2]And the king went up to the house of the LORD, and with him all the men of Judah and all the inhabitants of Jerusalem, and the priests and the prophets, all the people, both small and great; and he read in their hearing all the words of the book of the covenant which had been found in the house of the LORD. [3]And the king stood by the pillar and made a covenant before the LORD, to walk after the LORD and to keep his commandments and his testimonies and his statutes, with all his heart and all his soul, to perform the words of this covenant that were written in this book; and all the people joined in the covenant.

[4]And the king commanded Hilkiah, the high priest, and the priests of the second order, and the keepers of the threshold, to bring out of the temple of the LORD all the vessels made for Baal, for Asherah, and for all the host of heaven; he burned them outside Jerusalem in the fields of the Kidron, and carried their ashes to Bethel. [5]And he deposed the idolatrous priests whom the kings of Judah had ordained to burn incense in the high places at the cities of Judah and round about

Jerusalem; those also who burned incense to Baal, to the sun, and the moon, and the constellations, and all the host of the heavens. ⁶And he brought out the Asherah from the house of the LORD, outside Jerusalem, to the brook Kidron, and burned it at the brook Kidron, and beat it to dust and cast the dust of it upon the graves of the common people. ⁷And he broke down the houses of the male cult prostitutes which were in the house of the LORD, where the women wove hangings for the Asherah. ⁸And he brought all the priests out of the cities of Judah, and defiled the high places where the priests had burned incense, from Geba to Beer-sheba; and he broke down the high places of the gates that were at the entrance of the gate of Joshua the governor of the city, which were on one's left at the gate of the city. ⁹However, the priests of the high places did not come up to the altar of the LORD in Jerusalem, but they ate unleavened bread among their brethren. ¹⁰And he defiled Topheth, which is in the valley of the sons of Hinnom, that no one might burn his son or his daughter as an offering to Molech. ¹¹And he removed the horses that the kings of Judah had dedicated to the sun, at the entrance to the house of the LORD, by the chamber of Nathan-melech the chamberlain, which was in the precincts;ʰ and he burned the chariots of the sun with fire. ¹²And the altars on the roof of the upper chamber of Ahaz, which the kings of Judah had made, and the altars which Manasseh had made in the two courts of the house of the LORD, he pulled down and broke in pieces,ⁱ and cast the dust of them into the brook Kidron. ¹³And the king defiled the high places that were east of Jerusalem, to the south of the mount of corruption, which Solomon the king of Israel had built for Ashtoreth the abomination of the Sidonians, and for Chemosh the abomination of Moab, and for Milcom the abomination of the Ammonites. ¹⁴And he broke in pieces the pillars, and cut down the Asherim, and filled their places with the bones of men.

¹⁵Moreover the altar at Bethel, the high place erected by Jeroboam the son of Nebat, who made Israel to sin, that altar with the high place he pulled down and he broke in pieces its stones,ʲ crushing them to dust; also he burned the Asherah. ¹⁶And as Josiah turned, he saw the tombs there on the mount; and he sent and took the bones out of the tombs, and burned them upon the altar, and defiled it, according to the word of the LORD which the man of God proclaimed, who had predicted these things. ¹⁷Then he said, "What is yonder monument that I see?" And the men of the city told him, "It is the tomb of the man of God who came from Judah and predicted these things which you have done against the altar at Bethel." ¹⁸And he said, "Let him be; let no man move his bones." So they let his bones alone, with the bones of the prophet who came out of Samaria. ¹⁹And all the shrines also of the high places that were in the cities of Samaria, which kings of Israel had made, provoking the LORD to anger, Josiah removed; he did to them according to all that he had done at Bethel. ²⁰And he slew all the priests of the high places who were there, upon the altars, and burned the bones of men upon them. Then he returned to Jerusalem.

²¹And the king commanded all the people, "Keep the passover to the LORD your God, as it is written in this book of the covenant." ²²For no such passover had been kept since the days of the judges who judged Israel, or during all the days of the kings of Israel or of the kings of Judah; ²³but in the eighteenth year of King Josiah this passover was kept to the LORD in Jerusalem.

²⁴Moreover Josiah put away the mediums and the wizards and the teraphim and the idols and

all the abominations that were seen in the land of Judah and in Jerusalem, that he might establish the words of the law which were written in the book that Hilkiah the priest found in the house of the LORD. ²⁵Before him there was no king like him, who turned to the LORD with all his heart and with all his soul and with all his might, according to all the law of Moses; nor did any like him arise after him.

²⁶Still the LORD did not turn from the fierceness of his great wrath, by which his anger was kindled against Judah, because of all the provocations with which Manasseh had provoked him. ²⁷And the LORD said, "I will remove Judah also out of my sight, as I have removed Israel, and I will cast off this city which I have chosen, Jerusalem, and the house of which I said, My name shall be there."

²⁸Now the rest of the acts of Josiah, and all that he did, are they not written in the Book of the Chronicles of the Kings of Judah? ²⁹In his days Pharaoh Neco king of Egypt went up to the king of Assyria to the river Euphrates. King Josiah went to meet him; and Pharaoh Neco slew him at Megiddo, when he saw him. ³⁰And his servants carried him dead in a chariot from Megiddo, and brought him to Jerusalem, and buried him in his own tomb. And the people of the land took Jehoahaz the son of Josiah, and anointed him, and made him king in his father's stead.

h The meaning of the Hebrew word is uncertain   **i** Heb *pieces from there*   **j** Gk: Heb *he burned the high place*

OVERVIEW: In zeal Josiah was superior to those who went before him (AMBROSE). Josiah served the Lord as a king when he performed acts in his service that none but kings can perform (AUGUSTINE). By abolishing all human sacrifices, Josiah abolished every form of the cult of the devil and the demons (ISHO'DAD). The old prophet, who had led the true prophet to transgression, knew that the time would have come according to the prophecy of that man of God when Josiah, king of the Jews, would dig up in the land the bones of many dead and with them defile the sacrilegious altars that had been set up for graven images but would have spared that tomb where the prophet lay[1] (AUGUSTINE). Because grievous destruction threatened the Jewish people, the just king Josiah was taken away beforehand (AMBROSE).

23:1-3 Josiah Made a Covenant

JOSIAH'S RELIGIOUS ZEAL. AMBROSE: Love faith. For by his devotion and faith Josiah won great love for himself from his enemies. For he celebrated the Lord's Passover when he was eighteen years old, as no one had done it before him. As then in zeal he was superior to those who went before him, so do you, my children, show zeal for God. Let zeal for God search you through and devour you, so that each one of you may say, "The zeal of your house has eaten me up."[2] An apostle of Christ was called the zealot.[3] But why do I speak of an apostle? The Lord himself said, "The zeal of your house has eaten me up."[4] Let it then be real zeal for God, not mean earthly zeal, for that causes jealousy. DUTIES OF THE CLERGY 2.30.154.[5]

23:4-9 Destroying the Vessels Made for Baal

JOSIAH USES HIS ROYAL POWER. AUGUSTINE: How, then, do kings serve the Lord with fear except by forbidding and restraining with religious severity all acts committed against the commandments of the Lord? A sovereign serves God

---

[1]See 1 Kings 13:29-32. [2]Ps 69:9 (68:10 LXX, Vg). [3]Lk 6:15. [4]Jn 2:17; the text of John says, "The disciples remembered that it was written." [5]NPNF 2 10:67.

one way as man, another way as king; he serves him as man by living according to faith, he serves him as king by exerting the necessary strength to sanction laws that command goodness and prohibit its opposite. It was thus that Hezekiah served him by destroying the groves and temples of idols and the high places that had been set up contrary to the commandments of God;[6] thus Josiah served him by performing similar acts. . . . It is thus that kings serve the Lord as kings when they perform acts in his service that none but kings can perform. LETTER 185.19.[7]

23:10-15 Topheth Defiled

ABOLISHMENT OF THE WORSHIP OF DEMONS.
ISHO'DAD OF MERV: "No one would make a son or a daughter pass through fire." The passage through fire is the symbol of combustion. In fact, the demons demanded that [their worshipers] burn their own children, and sometimes they were immolated, sometimes they only underwent the symbolic rite mentioned above,[8] as if they had been actually placed into the fire and consumed, and so the expectations of the demons were satisfied. Sometimes fire was also passed above somebody to signify that he was by now enveloped in fire. Then salt was thrown, too, according to the customs of those who worship the devil. BOOKS OF SESSIONS 2 KINGS 23.10.[9]

23:16-18 The Tomb of the Man of God

A FULFILLED PROPHECY. AUGUSTINE: Yet from that love of the human heart, because of which "no one ever hated his own flesh,"[10] if people believe that anything would be lacking to their bodies after death that in their own people or country the solemnity of burial demands, they become sad, and before death they fear for their bodies that which has no effect on them after death. Thus we read in the book of Kings that God through a prophet threatens another prophet who transgressed his word, that his body should not be returned to the sepulcher of his

ancestors. Scripture records it in these words: "Thus says the Lord: Because you have not been obedient to the Lord and have not kept the commandment that the Lord your God commanded you, and have returned and eaten bread and drunk water in the place wherein he commanded you that you should not eat bread or drink water, your dead shall not be brought in the sepulcher of your ancestors."[11] If we consider the extent of this punishment according to the Evangelist where we learn that after the body has been slain there is no occasion to fear that the lifeless members will suffer, it should not be called punishment. But, if we consider it in relation to the love of a person for his own flesh, then he might have been frightened and saddened while living at what he was not to feel when dead. This, then, was the nature of the punishment: The soul grieved that something would happen to its body, although, when it did happen, the soul did not grieve. Only to this extent did the Lord wish to punish his servant, for it was not from his own obstinacy that he refused to carry out the command, but, because of the deceit of another person who was deceiving him, he thought he obeyed when he did not obey. THE CARE TO BE TAKEN FOR THE DEAD 7.9.[12]

23:25-30 Pharaoh Neco Killed Josiah

JOSIAH IS TAKEN AWAY BEFOREHAND.
AMBROSE: Nobody must think that anything was detracted to the celerity of death because of one's merits. Enoch was kidnapped,[13] lest malice might spoil his heart,[14] and Josiah, who celebrated the Passover of the Lord in the eighteenth year of his reign in such a manner that he overcame in piousness all the previous kings, did not survive longer through the merits of his faith. No, rather, because grievous destruction threatened the Jewish people, the just king was taken away before-

---

[6]See 2 Kings 18:4. [7]FC 30:160. [8]That is, the passage through fire. [9]CSCO 229:147. [10]Lk 12:4. [11]1 Kings 13:21-22. [12]FC 27:362-63. [13]See Gen 5:24. [14]Wis 4:11.

hand. I fear that you, too, were snatched away from us because of some offense on our part, so that, as a just person, you might escape in the eighteenth year of your reign the bitterness of impending evil.[15] CONSOLATION ON THE DEATH

of EMPEROR VALENTINIAN 57.[16]

[15]In this funeral oration Ambrose is addressing the emperor Valentinian (reigned 364-375), who supported his religious activity. [16]FC 22:289-90**.

23:31–24:20 UNDER THE DOMINATION OF THE EGYPTIANS AND THE BABYLONIANS

[31]*Jehoahaz was twenty-three years old when he began to reign, and he reigned three months in Jerusalem. His mother's name was Hamutal the daughter of Jeremiah of Libnah.* [32]*And he did what was evil in the sight of the* LORD, *according to all that his fathers had done.* [33]*And Pharaoh Neco put him in bonds at Riblah in the land of Hamath, that he might not reign in Jerusalem, and laid upon the land a tribute of a hundred talents of silver and a talent of gold.* [34]*And Pharaoh Neco made Eliakim the son of Josiah king in the place of Josiah his father, and changed his name to Jehoiakim. But he took Jehoahaz away; and he came to Egypt, and died there.* [35]*And Jehoiakim gave the silver and the gold to Pharaoh, but he taxed the land to give the money according to the command of Pharaoh. He exacted the silver and the gold of the people of the land, from every one according to his assessment, to give it to Pharaoh Neco.*

[36]*Jehoiakim was twenty-five years old when he began to reign, and he reigned eleven years in Jerusalem. His mother's name was Zebidah the daughter of Pedaiah of Rumah.* [37]*And he did what was evil in the sight of the* LORD, *according to all that his fathers had done.*

24 *In his days Nebuchadnezzar king of Babylon came up, and Jehoiakim became his servant three years; then he turned and rebelled against him.* [2]*And the* LORD *sent against him bands of the Chaldeans, and bands of the Syrians, and bands of the Moabites, and bands of the Ammonites, and sent them against Judah to destroy it, according to the word of the* LORD *which he spoke by his servants the prophets.* [3]*Surely this came upon Judah at the command of the* LORD, *to remove them out of his sight, for the sins of Manasseh, according to all that he had done,* [4]*and also for the innocent blood that he had shed; for he filled Jerusalem with innocent blood, and the* LORD *would not pardon.* [5]*Now the rest of the deeds of Jehoiakim, and all that he did, are they not written in the Book of the Chronicles of the Kings of Judah?* [6]*So Jehoiakim slept with his fathers, and Jehoiachin his son reigned in his stead.* [7]*And the king of Egypt did not come again out of his land, for the king of Babylon had taken all that belonged to the king of Egypt from the Brook of Egypt to the river Euphrates.*

[8]*Jehoiachin was eighteen years old when he became king, and he reigned three months in Jerusa-*

lem. His mother's name was Nehushta the daughter of Elnathan of Jerusalem. ⁹And he did what was evil in the sight of the LORD, according to all that his father had done.

¹⁰At that time the servants of Nebuchadnezzar king of Babylon came up to Jerusalem, and the city was besieged. ¹¹And Nebuchadnezzar king of Babylon came to the city, while his servants were besieging it; ¹²and Jehoiachin the king of Judah gave himself up to the king of Babylon, himself, and his mother, and his servants, and his princes, and his palace officials. The king of Babylon took him prisoner in the eighth year of his reign, ¹³and carried off all the treasures of the house of the LORD, and the treasures of the king's house, and cut in pieces all the vessels of gold in the temple of the LORD, which Solomon king of Israel had made, as the LORD had foretold. ¹⁴He carried away all Jerusalem, and all the princes, and all the mighty men of valor, ten thousand captives, and all the craftsmen and the smiths; none remained, except the poorest people of the land. ¹⁵And he carried away Jehoiachin to Babylon; the king's mother, the king's wives, his officials, and the chief men of the land, he took into captivity from Jerusalem to Babylon. ¹⁶And the king of Babylon brought captive to Babylon all the men of valor, seven thousand, and the craftsmen and the smiths, one thousand, all of them strong and fit for war. ¹⁷And the king of Babylon made Mattaniah, Jehoiachin's uncle, king in his stead, and changed his name to Zedekiah.

¹⁸Zedekiah was twenty-one years old when he became king, and he reigned eleven years in Jerusalem. His mother's name was Hamutal the daughter of Jeremiah of Libnah. ¹⁹And he did what was evil in the sight of the LORD, according to all that Jehoiakim had done. ²⁰For because of the anger of the LORD it came to the point in Jerusalem and Judah that he cast them out from his presence.

And Zedekiah rebelled against the king of Babylon.

OVERVIEW: Jehoahaz leaves his country and never comes back, according to the prophecy that Jeremiah had spoken against him[1] (ISHO'DAD). Nebuchadnezzar, king of Babylon, came against Jerusalem and assaulted it, and the Lord gave it into his hand: power is given to evil against us according to our sins (CYPRIAN). It is more difficult to escape from the domination of vainglory than from that of lust, as is demonstrated by the case of Nebuchadnezzar (CASSIAN). It is much better that the priests melt the holy vessels of gold for the sustenance of the poor, if a sacrilegious enemy threatens to carry them off and defile them (AMBROSE).

23:31-36 Jehoahaz Reigned Three Months

JEHOAHAZ IS DEPORTED TO EGYPT. ISHO'DAD

OF MERV: Jehoahaz, also called Shalom,[2] reigned three months until the Egyptians came back from Mabboug.[3] At that stage [Pharaoh] enchained him and brought him to Egypt. So [Jehoahaz] left his country and never came back, according to the prophecy that Jeremiah had spoken against him.[4] Pharaoh appointed his brother Heliakim as the new king and gave him the name of Jehoiakim. BOOKS OF SESSIONS 2 KINGS 23.31.[5]

24:1-3 For the Sins of Manasseh

NOTHING EVIL IS PERMITTED OUTSIDE THE WILL OF GOD. CYPRIAN: Necessarily, too, the

---

[1]See Jer 22:10-12. [2]See Jer 22:11. [3]Probably Larchemish or Cerablus, the ancient capital of the Hurrians; the city was situated in the north of Mesopotamia. [4]See Jer 22:10-12. [5]CSCO 229:148-49.

Lord gives us this admonition, to say in our prayer, "And lead us not into temptation." In this part it is shown that the adversary has no power against us, unless God has previously permitted it, in order that all our fear and devotion and obedience may be turned to God, since in temptations nothing evil is permitted, unless the power is granted by him. Scripture proves this when it says, "Nebuchadnezzar, king of Babylon, came against Jerusalem and assaulted it, and the Lord gave it into his hand." Moreover, power is given to evil against us according to our sins; as it is written, "Who has given Jacob for a spoil and Israel to those who despoiled him? Has not God, against whom they have sinned and were unwilling to walk in his ways and to hear his law, even poured out on them the indignation of his fury?"[6] THE LORD'S PRAYER 25.[7]

24:8-16 The King of Babylon Assaulted Jerusalem

A SYMBOLIC REPRESENTATION OF VAINGLORY. JOHN CASSIAN: There is an illustration of this—namely, of the fact that when vainglory makes its appearance the vice of fornication is expelled, as we have said—that is put in beautiful and clear language in the book of Kings. It occurs when Nebuchadnezzar, king of the Assyrians,[8] has come up from Egypt and taken the captive people of Israel away from Neco,[9] king of Egypt, to his own country, not in order to restore to them their former freedom and their birthplace but to lead those who would be transported to his own land, which was still further away than where they had been held captive in the land of Egypt. This illustration can be well understood in the following way. Although it is more tolerable to be subject to the vice of vainglory than to that of fornication, yet it is more difficult to escape from the domination of vainglory. For, so to say, one who has been held captive for a relatively long time will return less easily to his native soil and to his old-established freedom, and rightly is that prophetic rebuke directed to him: "Why have you grown in a foreign land?" Whoever is not removed from earthly vices is appropriately said to have grown old in a foreign land. CONFERENCE 5.12.4-5.[10]

TREASURES MUST BE SPENT FOR THE SUSTENANCE OF THE POOR. AMBROSE: The church has gold, not stored up but to lay out and to spend on those who need. What necessity is there to guard what is of no good? Do we not know how much gold and silver the Assyrians took out of the temple of the Lord? Is it not much better that the priests should melt it down for the sustenance of the poor, if other supplies fail, than that of a sacrilegious enemy should carry it off and defile it? Would not the Lord say, Why did you allow so many needy to die of hunger? Surely you had gold? You should have given them sustenance. Why are so many captives brought to the slave market, and why are so many unredeemed left to be slain by the enemy? It had been better to preserve living vessels than gold ones. DUTIES OF THE CLERGY 2.28.137.[11]

---

[6]Is 42:24-25. [7]FC 36:149. [8]Babylonians. [9]See 2 Kings 24:7. [10]ACW 57:193. [11]NPNF 2 10:64*.

25:1-30 THE SIEGE AND DESTRUCTION
OF JERUSALEM

[1]And in the ninth year of his reign, in the tenth month, on the tenth day of the month, Nebuchadnezzar king of Babylon came with all his army against Jerusalem, and laid siege to it; and they built siegeworks against it round about. [2]So the city was besieged till the eleventh year of King Zedekiah. [3]On the ninth day of the fourth month the famine was so severe in the city that there was no food for the people of the land. [4]Then a breach was made in the city; the king with all the men of war fled[k] by night by the way of the gate between the two walls, by the king's garden, though the Chaldeans were around the city. And they went in the direction of the Arabah. [5]But the army of the Chaldeans pursued the king, and overtook him in the plains of Jericho; and all his army was scattered from him. [6]Then they captured the king, and brought him up to the king of Babylon at Riblah, who passed sentence upon him. [7]They slew the sons of Zedekiah before his eyes, and put out the eyes of Zedekiah, and bound him in fetters, and took him to Babylon.

[8]In the fifth month, on the seventh day of the month—which was the nineteenth year of King Nebuchadnezzar, king of Babylon—Nebuzaradan, the captain of the bodyguard, a servant of the king of Babylon, came to Jerusalem. [9]And he burned the house of the LORD, and the king's house and all the houses of Jerusalem; every great house he burned down. [10]And all the army of the Chaldeans, who were with the captain of the guard, broke down the walls around Jerusalem. [11]And the rest of the people who were left in the city and the deserters who had deserted to the king of Babylon, together with the rest of the multitude, Nebuzaradan the captain of the guard carried into exile. [12]But the captain of the guard left some of the poorest of the land to be vinedressers and plowmen.

[13]And the pillars of bronze that were in the house of the LORD, and the stands and the bronze sea that were in the house of the LORD, the Chaldeans broke in pieces, and carried the bronze to Babylon. [14]And they took away the pots, and the shovels, and the snuffers, and the dishes for incense and all the vessels of bronze used in the temple service, [15]the firepans also, and the bowls. What was of gold the captain of the guard took away as gold, and what was of silver, as silver. [16]As for the two pillars, the one sea, and the stands, which Solomon had made for the house of the LORD, the bronze of all these vessels was beyond weight. [17]The height of the one pillar was eighteen cubits, and upon it was a capital of bronze; the height of the capital was three cubits; a network and pomegranates, all of bronze, were upon the capital round about. And the second pillar had the like, with the network.

[18]And the captain of the guard took Seraiah the chief priest, and Zephaniah the second priest, and the three keepers of the threshold; [19]and from the city he took an officer who had been in command of the men of war, and five men of the king's council who were found in the city; and the secretary of the commander of the army who mustered the people of the land; and sixty men of the

people of the land who were found in the city. [20]*And Nebuzaradan the captain of the guard took them, and brought them to the king of Babylon at Riblah.* [21]*And the king of Babylon smote them, and put them to death at Riblah in the land of Hamath. So Judah was taken into exile out of its land.*

[22]*And over the people who remained in the land of Judah, whom Nebuchadnezzar king of Babylon had left, he appointed Gedaliah the son of Ahikam, son of Shaphan, governor.* [23]*Now when all the captains of the forces in the open country[l] and their men heard that the king of Babylon had appointed Gedaliah governor, they came with their men to Gedaliah at Mizpah, namely, Ishmael the son of Nethaniah, and Johanan the son of Kareah, and Seraiah the son of Tanhumeth the Netophathite, and Ja-azaniah the son of the Ma-acathite.* [24]*And Gedaliah swore to them and their men, saying, "Do not be afraid because of the Chaldean officials; dwell in the land, and serve the king of Babylon, and it shall be well with you."* [25]*But in the seventh month, Ishmael the son of Nethaniah, son of Elishama, of the royal family, came with ten men, and attacked and killed Gedaliah and the Jews and the Chaldeans who were with him at Mizpah.* [26]*Then all the people, both small and great, and the captains of the forces arose, and went to Egypt; for they were afraid of the Chaldeans.*

[27]*And in the thirty-seventh year of the exile of Jehoiachin king of Judah, in the twelfth month, on the twenty-seventh day of the month, Evil-merodach king of Babylon, in the year that he began to reign, graciously freed Jehoiachin king of Judah from prison;* [28]*and he spoke kindly to him, and gave him a seat above the seats of the kings who were with him in Babylon.* [29]*So Jehoiachin put off his prison garments. And every day of his life he dined regularly at the king's table;* [30]*and for his allowance, a regular allowance was given him by the king, every day a portion, as long as he lived.*

k Gk Compare Jer 39.4; 52.7: Heb lacks *the king and fled*   l With Jer 40.7: Heb lacks *in the open country*

OVERVIEW: When Nebuchadnezzar acknowledged the most high God, uttered words of thanksgiving to God, repented of his past wickedness and recognized his own weakness, in that hour God restored to him his royal dignity (CYRIL OF JERUSALEM). Jehoiachin and Evil-merodach made friends while they were in prison. When Evil-merodach was appointed as the new king, he granted Jehoiachin favors and gifts (ISHO'DAD). After Jehoiachin brought with him his mother and the mighty men of the kingdom, he left Jerusalem, deserting to the Babylonians. However, he displayed, at the same time, a mature repentance, so that he became "a seal of righteousness in circumcision"[1] (ORIGEN). Some of the prophets continued to prophesy in Israel, while others prophesied in Babylon and later in the kingdom of the Persians (CLEMENT OF ALEXANDRIA).

25:1-11 Nebuchadnezzar Laid Siege to Jerusalem

GOD WAS MERCIFUL EVEN WITH NEBUCHADNEZZAR. CYRIL OF JERUSALEM: What think you of Nebuchadnezzar? Have you not heard from Scripture that he was bloodthirsty, fierce, with the disposition of a lion? Have you not heard that he disinterred the kings?[2] Have you not heard that he brought the people away into captivity? Have you not heard that he put the king's sons to the sword before Zedekiah's eyes and then

[1]Rom 4:11. [2]See Jer 8:1; Bar 2:24-25.

blinded him? Have you not heard that he shattered the cherubim?[3] I do not mean the invisible cherubim—it is blasphemy to think it—but the sculptured images and the mercy seat in the Holy of Holies, from the midst of which God was apt to speak with his voice. He trampled on the veil of sanctification, he took the censer and carried it away to a temple of idols; he seized all the offerings; he burned the temple to its foundations. What punishment did he not deserve for slaying kings, for burning the holy object, for reducing the people to captivity, for putting the sacred vessels in the temples of the idols? Did he not deserve ten thousand deaths?

You have seen the enormity of his crimes. Turn now to the loving-kindness of God. Nebuchadnezzar was turned into a wild beast; he dwelled in the wilderness; God scourged him to save him. He had claws like a lion's, for he had preyed on the saints. He had a lion's mane, for he had been a ravening, roaring lion. He ate grass like an ox, for he had behaved like a brute beast, not knowing him who had given him his kingdom. His body was drenched with dew, because, after seeing the fire quenched by the dew, he had not believed. And what happened? Afterwards he says, "I, Nebuchadnezzar, raised my eyes to heaven . . . and I blessed the Most High, and I praised and glorified him who lives forever."[4] When therefore he acknowledged the Most High, and uttered words of thanksgiving to God, and repented of his past wickedness and recognized his own weakness, in that hour God restored to him his royal dignity.

What then? If God granted pardon and a kingdom to Nebuchadnezzar after such terrible crimes, when he had made confession, will he not grant you the remission of your sins if you repent and the kingdom of heaven if you live worthily? God is merciful and quick to forgiveness but slow to vengeance. Therefore let no one despair of salvation. Peter, the chief and foremost of the apostles, denied the Lord thrice before a little serving maid; but, moved to repentance, he wept bitterly. His weeping revealed his heartfelt repentance,

and for that reason not only did he receive pardon for his denial but also retained his apostolic prerogative. CATECHETICAL LECTURES 2.17-19.[5]

25:22-30 Jehoiachin Dined in the King's Presence

THE FRIENDSHIP BETWEEN JEHOIACHIN AND EVIL-MERODACH. ISHO'DAD OF MERV: Evil-merodach was the son of Nebuchadnezzar. Since he had ruled the kingdom badly and had, in addition, troubled the land with a severe conflict, when his father came back [from his military campaign], his father imprisoned him, fearing that he might rebel against him. Now he was imprisoned in the same place where also Jehoiachin was imprisoned. There they kept each other company for a long time and became friends. Therefore, after Nebuchadnezzar was dead and Evil-merodach was appointed as the new king, he granted [Jehoiachin] favors and gifts. And this was a reward given to Jehoiachin, because he had obeyed the prophecy and had surrendered, so that God did not refuse him the wage that he had earned.[6] BOOKS OF SESSIONS 2 KINGS 25.27.[7]

THE ROLE OF JEHOIACHIN. ORIGEN: Jeremiah calls this son of Jehoiakim Jeconiah,[8] and the Pharaoh Neco called the father of this man, though named Eliakim, Jehoiakim, whom Babylon, having carried off, cast forth before the gate, as the present prophet and Josephus in the tenth book of his Antiquities says.[9] And the other editions have given the signet ring as a seal. And every person who through repentance makes shine again what is according to the image becomes a

---

[3]This is not attested by the biblical narrative and must be considered an assumption on the part of Cyril. [4]Dan 4:34. [5]FC 61:106-7*. [6]Jehoiachin had given himself up to Nebuchadnezzar before the end of the siege (see 2 Kings 24:10-12). According to Isho'dad, he did that in obedience to the order of Jeremiah. There is no explicit reference to an order in the biblical text, but the Syriac author is probably referring to Jeremiah 21:9: "Those who go out and surrender to the Chaldeans who are besieging you shall live." [7]CSCO 229:150. [8]This is the Greek spelling (LXX) of the name Jehoiachin. See also 2 Kings 24:8-12. [9]Josephus Antiquities of the Jews 10.5.2; 6.3; Jer 22:24.

seal, a ring on the "right hand of God."[10] For good works are understood as the part on the right of God, who places "the sheep at the right."[11] The father gave this kind of seal to the profligate son who returned.[12] If Jeconiah had become this way, he would have been a model for those who are subjects of devotion. But that did not happen. Yet he seemed to be persuaded by what the prophet said: "He who goes out to surrender to the Chaldeans who besieged you shall live."[13] For after he brought with him his mother and the mighty men, he left, deserting to the Babylonians. But if he also displays mature repentance, so that he becomes "a seal of righteousness in circumcision."[14] So that, according to this, he seems to be on the right hand of God, he would be delivered, since he did pay a penalty for his recent sins, though one more moderate. For in Babylon, after he chastised in prison and in chains, due to Evil-merodach, he was then set free, becoming one who ate with the king, and thus in a foreign land he finished life. FRAGMENTS FROM THE CATENA ON JEREMIAH 14.[15]

THE PROPHETS AT THE TIME OF THE CAPTIVITY IN BABYLON.

CLEMENT OF ALEXANDRIA: In the twelfth year of king Zedekiah, seventy years before the dominance of the Persians, Nebuchadnezzar campaigned against the Phoenicians and Jews, as Berossus says in his "Researches on the Chaldeans."[16] Juba,[17] writing "On the Assyrians," admits that he took his account from Berossus, testifying to its accuracy. Nebuchadnezzar blinded Zedekiah and removed him to Babylon, deporting the whole people except a few who escaped to Egypt. The captivity lasted for seventy years. Jeremiah and Habakkuk continued to prophesy under Zedekiah, and in the fifth year of his reign Ezekiel was prophesying in Babylon. After him came the prophet Nahum, then Daniel, and again after him, Haggai and Zechariah prophesied for two years under Darius I, and after him, one of the twelve, the Herald.[18] STROMATEIS 1.122.1-4.[19]

---

[10]Jer 22:24. [11]Mt 25:33. [12]See Lk 15:22. [13]Jer 21:9 (LXX). [14]Rom 4:11. [15]FC 97:286-87. [16]Berossus was a Babylonian priest of Bel, who wrote a history of his country in Greek in the early Alexandrian age (around 290 B.C.). [17]King of Mauretania and learned historian (c. 50 B.C.-A.D. 23). [18]Malachi. [19]FC 85:114.

1 CHRONICLES

1:1–10:14 THE GENEALOGIES OF THE PEOPLE OF GOD FROM ADAM TO SAUL

¹Adam, Seth, Enosh; ²Kenan, Mahalalel, Jared; ³Enoch, Methuselah, Lamech; ⁴Noah, Shem, Ham, and Japheth.

⁵The sons of Japheth: Gomer, Magog, Madai, Javan, Tubal, Meshech, and Tiras. ⁶The sons of Gomer: Ashkenaz, Diphath, and Togarmah. ⁷The sons of Javan: Elishah, Tarshish, Kittim, and Rodanim.

⁸The sons of Ham: Cush, Egypt, Put, and Canaan. ⁹The sons of Cush: Seba, Havilah, Sabta, Raama, and Sabteca. The sons of Raamah: Sheba and Dedan. ¹⁰Cush was the father of Nimrod; he began to be a mighty one in the earth. . . .

²⁴Shem, Arpachshad, Shelah; ²⁵Eber, Peleg, Reu; ²⁶Serug, Nahor, Terah; ²⁷Abram, that is, Abraham.

²⁸The sons of Abraham: Isaac and Ishmael. ²⁹These are their genealogies: the first-born of Ishmael, Nebaioth; and Kedar, Adbeel, Mibsam, ³⁰Mishma, Dumah, Massa, Hadad, Tema, ³¹Jetur, Naphish, and Kedemah. These are the sons of Ishmael. ³²The sons of Keturah, Abraham's concubine: she bore Zimran, Jokshan, Medan, Midian, Ishbak, and Shuah. The sons of Jokshan: Sheba and Dedan. ³³The sons of Midian: Ephah, Epher, Hanoch, Abida, and Eldaah. All these were the descendants of Keturah.

³⁴Abraham was the father of Isaac. The sons of Isaac: Esau and Israel. ³⁵The sons of Esau: Eliphaz, Reuel, Jeush, Jalam, and Korah. ³⁶The sons of Eliphaz: Teman, Omar, Zephi, Gatam, Kenaz, Timna, and Amalek. ³⁷The sons of Reuel: Nahath, Zerah, Shammah, and Mizzah. . . .

⁴³These are the kings who reigned in the land of Edom before any king reigned over the Israelites: Bela the son of Beor, the name of whose city was Dinhabah. ⁴⁴When Bela died, Jobab the son of Zerah of Bozrah reigned in his stead. ⁴⁵When Jobab died, Husham of the land of the Temanites reigned in his stead. ⁴⁶When Husham died, Hadad the son of Bedad, who defeated Midian in the country of Moab, reigned in his stead; and the name of his city was Avith. ⁴⁷When Hadad died, Samlah of Masrekah reigned in his stead. ⁴⁸When Samlah died, Shaul of Rehoboth on the Euphrates reigned in his stead. ⁴⁹When Shaul died, Baal-hanan, the son of Achbor, reigned in his stead. ⁵⁰When Baal-hanan died, Hadad reigned in his stead; and the name of his city was Pai, and

his wife's name Mehetabel the daughter of Matred, the daughter of Mezahab. [51]And Hadad died.

The chiefs of Edom were: chiefs Timna, Aliah, Jetheth, [52]Oholibamah, Elah, Pinon, [53]Kenaz, Teman, Mibzar, [54]Magdiel, and Iram; these are the chiefs of Edom.

2 These are the sons of Israel: Reuben, Simeon, Levi, Judah, Issachar, Zebulun, [2]Dan, Joseph, Benjamin, Naphtali, Gad, and Asher. [3]The sons of Judah: Er, Onan, and Shelah; these three Bath-shua the Canaanitess bore to him. Now Er, Judah's first-born, was wicked in the sight of the LORD, and he slew him. [4]His daughter-in-law Tamar also bore him Perez and Zerah. Judah had five sons in all. . . .

3 These are the sons of David . . . . [5]These were born to him in Jerusalem: Shime-a, Shobab, Nathan, and Solomon, four by Bath-shua, the daughter of Ammiel; then Ibhar, Elishama, Eliphelet, [7]Nogah, Nepheg, Japhia, [8]Elishama, Eliada, and Eliphelet, nine. [9]All these were David's sons, besides the sons of the concubines; and Tamar was their sister. . . .

5 The sons of Reuben the first-born of Israel (for he was the first-born; but because he poluted his father's couch, his birthright was given to the sons of Joseph the son of Israel, so that he is not enrolled in the genealogy according to the birthright; [2]though Judah became strong among his brothers and a prince was from him, yet the birthright belonged to Joseph). . . .

[18]The Reubenites, the Gadites, and the half-tribe of Manasseh had valiant men, who carried shield and sword, and drew the bow, expert in war, forty-four thousand seven hundred and sixty, ready for service. [19]They made war upon the Hagrites, Jetur, Naphish, and Nodab; [20]and when they received help against them, the Hagrites and all who were with them were given into their hands, for they cried to God in the battle, and he granted their entreaty because they trusted in him. [21]They carried off their livestock: fifty thousand of their camels, two hundred and fifty thousand sheep, two thousand asses, and a hundred thousand men alive. [22]For many fell slain, because the war was of God. And they dwelt in their place until the exile. . . .

6 The sons of Levi: Gershom, Kohath, and Merari. [2]The sons of Kohath: Amram, Izhar. . . . [3]The children of Amram: Aaron, Moses, and Miriam. . . . [10]Azariah (it was he who served as priest in the house that Solomon built in Jerusalem). . . . [15]And Jehozadak went into exile when the LORD sent Judah and Jerusalem into exile by the hand of Nebuchadnezzar.

. . . [18]The sons of Kohath: Amram, Izhar, Hebron, and Uzziel. . . . [21]The sons of Kohath: Amminadab his son, Korah his son. . . .

[33]Heman the singer the son of Joel, son of Samuel. . . . [39]Asaph. . . . [44]Ethan. . . .

[49]But Aaron and his sons made offerings upon the altar of burnt offering and upon the altar of incense for all the work of the most holy place, and to make atonement for Israel, according to all that Moses the servant of God had commanded. [50]These are the sons of Aaron: Eleazar his son, Phinehas his son, Abishua his son, [51]Bukki his son, Uzzi his son, Zerahiah his son, [52]Meraioth his son, Amariah his son, Ahitub his son, [53]Zadok his son, Ahima-az his son. . . .

7 [14]The sons of Manasseh: Asri-el, whom his Aramean concubine bore; she bore Machir the father of Gilead. [15]And Machir took a wife for Huppim and for Shuppim. The name of his sister was Maacah. And the name of the second was Zelophehad; and Zelophehad had daughters. ¹⁶And Maacah the wife of Machir bore a son, and she called his name Peresh; and the name of his brother was Sheresh; and his sons were Ulam and Rakem. ¹⁷The sons of Ulam: Bedan. These were the sons of Gilead the son of Machir, son of Manasseh. ¹⁸And his sister Hammolecheth bore Ishhod, Abi-ezer, and Mahlah. ¹⁹The sons of Shemida were Ahian, Shechem, Likhi, and Aniam. . . .

8 Benjamin was the father of Bela his first-born, Ashbel the second, Aharah the third, ²Nohah the fourth, and Rapha the fifth. ³And Bela had sons: Addar, Gera, Abihud, ⁴Abishua, Naaman, Ahoah, ⁵Gera, Shephuphan, and Huram. ⁶These are the sons of Ehud (they were heads of fathers' houses of the inhabitants of Geba, and they were carried into exile to Manahath): ⁷Naaman,' Ahijah, and Gera, that is, Heglam,' who was the father of Uzza and Ahihud. ⁸And Shaharaim had sons in the country of Moab after he had sent away Hushim and Baara his wives. . . .

9 So all Israel was enrolled by genealogies; and these are written in the Book of the Kings of Israel. And Judah was taken into exile in Babylon because of their unfaithfulness. ²Now the first to dwell again in their possessions in their cities were Israel, the priests, the Levites, and the temple servants. . . .

¹⁰Of the priests: Jedaiah, Jehoiarib, Jachin. . . .

¹⁴Of the Levites: Shemaiah the son of Hasshub, son of Azrikam. . . .

¹⁹Shallum the son of Kore, son of Ebiasaph, son of Korah, and his kinsmen of his fathers' house, the Korahites, were in charge of the work of the service, keepers of the thresholds of the tent, as their fathers had been in charge of the camp of the Lord, keepers of the entrance. . . . ²²All these, who were chosen as gatekeepers at the thresholds, were two hundred and twelve. They were enrolled by genealogies in their villages. David and Samuel the seer established them in their office of trust. ²³So they and their sons were in charge of the gates of the house of the Lord, that is, the house of the tent, as guards. ²⁴The gatekeepers were on the four sides, east, west, north, and south. . . .

²⁸Some of them had charge of the utensils of service, for they were required to count them when they were brought in and taken out. ²⁹Others of them were appointed over the furniture, and over all the holy utensils, also over the fine flour, the wine, the oil, the incense, and the spices. ³⁰Others, of the sons of the priests, prepared the mixing of the spices. . . .

10 Now the Philistines fought against Israel; and the men of Israel fled before the Philistines, and fell slain on Mount Gilboa. ²And the Philistines overtook Saul and his sons; and the Philistines slew Jonathan and Abinadab and Malchishua, the sons of Saul. ³The battle pressed hard upon Saul, and the archers found him; and he was wounded by the archers. ⁴Then Saul said to his armor-bearer, "Draw your sword, and thrust me through with it, lest these uncircumcised come and make sport of me." But his armor-bearer would not; for he feared greatly. Therefore Saul took his own sword, and fell upon it. ⁵And when his armor-bearer saw that Saul was dead, he also fell upon his sword, and died. ⁶Thus Saul died; he and his three sons and all his house died together. ⁷And when all the men of Israel who were in the valley saw that the army^w had fled and that Saul and his

sons were dead, they forsook their cities and fled; and the Philistines came and dwelt in them.

⁸On the morrow, when the Philistines came to strip the slain, they found Saul and his sons fallen on Mount Gilboa. ⁹And they stripped him and took his head and his armor, and sent messengers throughout the land of the Philistines, to carry the good news to their idols and to the people. ¹⁰And they put his armor in the temple of their gods, and fastened his head in the temple of Dagon. ¹¹But when all Jabesh-gilead heard all that the Philistines had done to Saul, ¹²all the valiant men arose, and took away the body of Saul and the bodies of his sons, and brought them to Jabesh. And they buried their bones under the oak in Jabesh, and fasted seven days.

¹³So Saul died for his unfaithfulness; he was unfaithful to the LORD in that he did not keep the command of the LORD, and also consulted a medium, seeking guidance, ¹⁴and did not seek guidance from the LORD. Therefore the LORD slew him, and turned the kingdom over to David the son of Jesse.

n Ch 5.27 in Heb y   s Heb and Naaman   t Or he carried them into exile   w Heb the

---

OVERVIEW: The book of Chronicles reports a detailed genealogy of the kingdom of Judah, demonstrating how all human beings are derived from a single man and how our Savior the Son of God descended from it. In addition, it describes the cities and the tribes that followed one another in the land of God after the captivity in Egypt (THEODORET).

THE GENEALOGY OF JUDAH. THEODORET OF CYR: There is abundant information in the books of Chronicles which were written to continue the books of the Kings and to preserve the memory of such important events. The first book begins with a genealogy that sets out to demonstrate how the human race came from a single man. Since it focuses only on the single kingdom of Judah,[1] it can tell us about its cities and the villages, and from where they took their names. Here we come to know Nathan,[2] from whom the blessed Luke[3] constructed the beginning of his genealogy of our Lord and Savior, Son of David and Solomon's brother[4] on his mother's side: "The following children were born to him in Jerusalem: Shimeah, Shobab, Nathan and Solomon, that is, the four children he fathered with Bersabea,[5] daughter of Ammiel." And Rechab[6] herself, who is mentioned in many books of Scripture, is said to have come from the tribe of Judah.

It also clearly explains why Reuben lost his birthright and Joseph gained it and also, finally, the reason why the tribe of Judah obtained the highest honor: "The sons of Reuben the firstborn of Israel. He was the firstborn, but because he defiled his father's bed his birthright was given to the sons of Joseph son of Israel, so that he is not enrolled in the genealogy according to the birthright; though Judah became prominent among his brothers and a ruler came from him, yet the birthright belonged to Joseph." It also explains the reason why such a great honor was conceded to Joseph. By the will of God Judah had the dignity of receiving the Lord who was born from him according to the flesh. This is the sense tacitly expressed with the words "a leader from him." Indeed the passage seems to assert that not only the kings of the earth derived from Judah, but also the eternal king himself who had no beginning and will never end.

---

[1]Num 10:14; Judg 15:10; 2 Sam 2:4, 7; Ezra 5:8; Neh 1:3; 3:1-32; 2 Kings 18ff. [2]Sir 47:1; 2 Sam 7:3, 8-17; 12:1-14; 1 Kings 1:11, 14, 22, 27, 32-38. [3]Lk 3:23-38. [4]Jesus thus becomes Solomon's brother as the Son of David. [5]More commonly known as Bathsheba. [6]Theodore equates the Rechab of 1 Chronicles 2:55 with Rahab the harlot, although her name is spelled differently in Greek.

It also describes the situation of the tribes beyond the Jordan, those of Reuben and Gad, and even the tribes of Manasseh which later were received into those of the Hagarites and the Itureans, and talks about the tribes of the Naphiseans, and all those peoples who entered into conflict with them. In addition the text relates how they fought and won, and made the Hagarites flee. And it also reports the reason for the victory: "When they received help against them, the Hagarites and all who were with them were given into their hands, for they cried to God in the battle, and he granted their entreaty because they trusted in him." It also describes the amount of the spoils of war: "They captured their livestock: 50,000 of their camels, 250,000 sheep, 2,000 donkeys and 100,000 captives. Many were slain because the war was from God. And they lived in their territory until the exile." Questions on 1 Chronicles, Prologue.[7]

The Genealogy of the Priests and the Levites. Theodoret of Cyr: The genealogy of the priests and the Levites comes after this. It relates that Zadok,[8] who was high priest at the time of David, had been the eleventh from Aaron; that Azariah, nephew of Zadok, had been the first to receive the priestly anointing in the temple built by Solomon. Among them there was also Jehozadak, who was brought to Babylon as a war prisoner. Jesus[9] was his son, a high priest as well, who delivered the people from bondage together with Zerubbabel,[10] and built a temple for the Lord. Here we also learn that Korah, who revolted against the great Moses, was a nephew of Isaar,[11] son of Caath and brother of Amram, Aaron's and Moses' father. According to this lineage he was related to the first legislator.[12] But he himself paid in the desert for his errors, although his children did not share the punishment of their father. From here Samuel[13] came and then Aeman, who intoned Psalms and was a nephew of the prophet Samuel. In fact he was the son of Joel, son of Samuel. On the other hand, Asaph,[14] one

of the singers, came from the lineage of Gerson, son of Levi and brother of Caath. Aetham, who also belonged to the group of the singers, had Merari, the third son of Levi, as great-grandfather.

The text also explains the difference between the priests and the Levites. It relates that the Levites were initiated into all the ministries of the holy altar of God: "But Aaron and his sons made offerings on the altar of burnt offering and on the altar of incense, doing all the work of the most holy place, to make atonement for Israel, according to all that Moses the servant of God had commanded." It seems to me, in fact, that this book was written after the return from Babylon. For this reason it also talks about the bondage and explains its cause: "So all Israel was enrolled by genealogies; and these are written in the book of the Kings of Israel. And Judah was taken into exile in Babylon because of their unfaithfulness. Now the first to live again in their possessions in their towns were Israelites, priests, Levites, and temple servants." These accounts show that the book was begun after the captivity. Indeed no historian ever relates facts that happened afterwards, but what happened before or during his times. And actually only the prophets have the power to foretell the future. In addition it says that also those who had inhabited that land before them had been enslaved. And actually many of them still live with them: the Canaanites, Chettites,[15] Jebusites, who had been their companions in such a misfortune. Also the priests and the Levites were brought into captivity with the Israelites. I believe that those who were called "the saints' servants" were then called Nathinim. Many of them, in fact, consecrated themselves to the ministries of the priests and the Levites. There were among them also those who were

---

[7]PG 80:801-3. [8]2 Sam 8:17; 15:35-36; 17:15; 1 Kings 1:7-45. [9]Joshua. [10]Ezra 3:2, 8; 5:2; 2:2; 6:7; 3:1-9; 6:7; Hag 2:18; Hag 2:21-23; Zech 6:12-13. [11]Izhar. [12]I.e., Moses. [13]1 Sam 1:9, 20, 25-28; 8:5, 11-22; 9:26–10:8; 15:35; 16:1-13; 25:1. [14]1 Chron 15:17; 16:5, 7, 37. [15]Hittites.

entrusted with the carrying of the water, the gathering of wood and other necessary duties. Indeed, if it was imposed to the Gabaonites,[16] who were foreigners, to follow Joshua in the praises and to perform some works as porters or carpenters, this task was even more the duty of the Israelites. As a proof of this I have found in the interpretation of Hebrew names that this name means "house of *Iaō*," that is, "of the God who is." The text, in fact, mentions the children of Israel and among them Judah and Benjamin,[17] and Ephraim[18] and Manasseh. It also mentions the priests and the Levites, who inhabited those cities. About the *Korēnites*[19] it says that they derived from Korah. It also says that among them there had been the guardians of the temple of God as well, and it seems that this custom had been introduced by Samuel and David. "All these, who were chosen as gatekeepers at the thresholds, were two hundred twelve. They were enrolled by genealogies in their villages. David and the prophet Samuel established them in their office of trust. So they and their descendants were in charge of the gates of the house of the Lord, that is, the house of the tent, as guards. The gatekeepers were on the four sides, east, west, north, and south." QUESTIONS ON 1 CHRONICLES, PROLOGUE.[20]

THE TABERNACLE AND FURNISHINGS FOR WORSHIP. THEODORET OF CYR: The Chronicles also speak about the tabernacle because a temple of the Lord had not yet been built by either Samuel or David. The text also adds that that the holy services were held in the tabernacle. Worship was observed at that time according to the number of the days of the week. For it also says, "and their kindred who were in their villages were obliged to come in every seven days, in turn, to be with them." With regard to the holy utensils it says, "Some of them had charge of the utensils of service, for they were required to count them when they were brought in and taken out. Others of them were appointed over the furniture, and over all the holy utensils, also over the choice flour, the wine, the oil, the incense and the spices." And about the priests it says, "Others, of the sons of the priests, prepared the mixing of the spices." With regard to the tomb of Saul the Chronicles gives us much information, and in the Book of Kings itself we read that his bones were gathered and buried in the land of Jabesh.[21] QUESTIONS ON FIRST CHRONICLES, PROLOGUE.[22]

---

[16]Gibeonites. [17]Gen 25:26; 32:23-32. [18]Gen 41:52; 48:5; 2 Sam 20:1; 1 Kings 12:15-17, 20; Is 7:1-17; Ps 78:67 (77:67 LXX). [19]Korahites. [20]PG 80:803-5. [21]1 Sam 31:13. [22]PG 80:805-8.

11:1-9 DAVID KING OF HEBRON

¹*Then all Israel gathered together to David at Hebron, and said, "Behold, we are your bone and flesh.* ²*In times past, even when Saul was king, it was you that led out and brought in Israel; and the LORD your God said to you, 'You shall be shepherd of my people Israel, and you shall be prince over my people Israel.'"* ³*So all the elders of Israel came to the king at Hebron; and David made a covenant with them at Hebron before the LORD, and they anointed David king over Israel, according to the word of the LORD by Samuel.*

⁴*And David and all Israel went to Jerusalem, that is Jebus, where the Jebusites were, the inhabitants of the land.* ⁵*The inhabitants of Jebus said to David, "You will not come in here." Neverthe-*

less David took the stronghold of Zion, that is, the city of David. ⁶David said, "Whoever shall smite the Jebusites first shall be chief and commander." And Joab the son of Zeruiah went up first, so he became chief. ⁷And David dwelt in the stronghold; therefore it was called the city of David. ⁸And he built the city round about from the Millo in complete circuit; and Joab repaired the rest of the city. ⁹And David became greater and greater, for the LORD of hosts was with him.

OVERVIEW: Jerusalem is our inheritance (GREGORY OF NAZIANZUS). We have to add to this wisdom and eloquence a careful study and knowledge of Scripture (JEROME). There is no doubt that human wills cannot resist the will of God. God, who was with David, brought people to make him king over all Israel. Human hearts are inclined to God's will with the result that they will be welcomed in the heavenly kingdom (AUGUSTINE).

11:4 David and Israel Marched to Jerusalem

OUR NEW INHERITANCE. GREGORY OF NAZIANZUS: Farewell likewise, grand and renowned temple, our new inheritance, whose greatness is now due to the Word, which once was a Jebus and has now been made by us a Jerusalem. THE LAST FAREWELL, ORATION 42.26.[1]

11:5 The Stronghold of Zion

YOU HAVE DAVID'S WISDOM AND STRENGTH. JEROME: You have a great intellect and an inexhaustible store of language, your diction is fluent and pure, your fluency and purity are mingled with wisdom. Your head is clear and all your senses keen. Were you to add to this wisdom and eloquence a careful study and knowledge of Scripture, I should soon see you holding our citadel against all comers; you would go up with Joab on the roof of Zion and sing on the housetops what you had learned in the secret chambers.[2] LETTER 58:11.[3]

11:9 David Increased in Greatness

HUMAN WILLS CANNOT RESIST THE WILL OF GOD. AUGUSTINE: There is no doubt that human

wills cannot resist the will of God, "who has done whatsoever he pleased in heaven and on earth"[4] and who has even "done the things that are to come."[5] Nor can the human will prevent him from doing what he wills, seeing that even with human wills he does what he wills, when he wills to do it. . . . There is the case of David, whom God with happier outcome set up over the kingdom. We read of him: "And David went on growing and increasing, and the Lord of hosts was with him." Then, shortly thereafter, it is said, "But the spirit came on Amasai, the chief among thirty, and he said, We are yours, O David, and for you, O son of Isay; peace, peace be to you, and peace to your helpers; for your God helped you." Could Amasai have opposed the will of God, instead of doing his will, since God, through his spirit, with which Amasai was clothed, wrought in his heart that he should so will and speak and act? In like fashion, a little later on, Scripture says, "And all these men of war, well appointed to fight, came with a perfect heart to Hebron, to make David king over all Israel." Obviously, it was of their own will that these men made David king; the fact is clear and undeniable. Nevertheless, it was God, who effects in human hearts whatsoever he wills, who wrought this will in them. This is why Scripture first says, "And David went on growing and increasing, and the Lord of hosts was with him." The Lord God, therefore, who was with David, brought these men to make him king. And how did he bring them to this? Surely it was not by binding them with any material chains. Rather, he worked within them; he seized their hearts; he drew

---

[1]NPNF 2 7:394. [2]See Lk 12:3. [3]NPNF 2 6:123. [4]Ps 135:6 (134:6 LXX). [5]Is 45:11.

them on by means of their own wills, which he had himself created within them. When, therefore, God wills to set up kings on earth, he holds the wills of people more in his own power than they are in the power of people themselves. And if this is so, it is surely he, and no other, who makes admonitions salutary and effects amendment in the heart of one who is admonished, with the result that he is established in the heavenly kingdom. ADMONITION AND GRACE 14.45.[6]

HUMAN HEARTS ARE INCLINED TO GOD'S WILL. AUGUSTINE: In vain also do they object that what we have established from Scripture in the books of Kings and Chronicles—that when God wills the accomplishment of something which ought not to be done except by people who will it, their hearts will be inclined to will this, with God producing this inclination, who in a marvelous and ineffable way works also in us that we will—is not pertinent to the subject with which we are dealing. PREDESTINATION OF THE SAINTS 20.42.[7]

---

[6]FC 2:299-300*. [7]FC 86:268.

11:10-47 THE HEROES OF DAVID

[10]*Now these are the chiefs of David's mighty men, who gave him strong support in his kingdom, together with all Israel, to make him king, according to the word of the LORD concerning Israel.* [11]*This is an account of David's mighty men: Jashobe-am, a Hachmonite, was chief of the three;[x] he wielded his spear against three hundred whom he slew at one time.*

[12]*And next to him among the three mighty men was Eleazar the son of Dodo, the Ahohite.* [13]*He was with David at Pas-dammim when the Philistines were gathered there for battle. There was a plot of ground full of barley, and the men fled from the Philistines.* [14]*But he[y] took his[y] stand in the midst of the plot, and defended it, and slew the Philistines; and the LORD saved them by a great victory.*

[15]*Three of the thirty chief men went down to the rock to David at the cave of Adullam, when the army of Philistines was encamped in the valley of Rephaim.* [16]*David was then in the stronghold; and the garrison of the Philistines was then at Bethlehem.* [17]*And David said longingly, "O that some one would give me water to drink from the well of Bethlehem which is by the gate!"* [18]*Then the three mighty men broke through the camp of the Philistines, and drew water out of the well of Bethlehem which was by the gate, and took and brought it to David. But David would not drink of it; he poured it out to the LORD,* [19]*and said, "Far be it from me before my God that I should do this. Shall I drink the lifeblood of these men? For at the risk of their lives they brought it." Therefore he would not drink it. These things did the three mighty men.*

[20]*Now Abishai, the brother of Joab, was chief of the thirty.[z] And he wielded his spear against three hundred men and slew them, and won a name beside the three.* [21]*He was the most renowned[a]*

of the thirty,^z and became their commander; but he did not attain to the three.

²²*And Benaiah the son of Jehoiada was a valiant man^b of Kabzeel, a doer of great deeds; he smote two ariels^c of Moab. He also went down and slew a lion in a pit on a day when snow had fallen.* ²³*And he slew an Egyptian, a man of great stature, five cubits tall. The Egyptian had in his hand a spear like a weaver's beam; but Benaiah went down to him with a staff, and snatched the spear out of the Egyptian's hand, and slew him with his own spear.* ²⁴*These things did Benaiah the son of Jehoiada, and won a name beside the three mighty men.* ²⁵*He was renowned among the thirty, but he did not attain to the three. And David set him over his bodyguard.*

²⁶*The mighty men of the armies were Asahel the brother of Joab, Elhanan the son of Dodo of Bethlehem,* ²⁷*Shammoth of Harod,^d Helez the Pelonite,* ²⁸*Ira the son of Ikkesh of Tekoa, Abi-ezer of Anathoth,* ²⁹*Sibbecai the Hushathite, Ilai the Ahohite,* ³⁰*Maharai of Netophah, Heled the son of Baanah of Netophah,* ³¹*Ithai the son of Ribai of Gibeah of the Benjaminites, Benaiah of Pirathon,* ³²*Hurai of the brooks of Gaash, Abiel the Arbathite,* ³³*Azmaveth of Baharum, Eliahba of Sha-albon,* ³⁴*Hashem^e the Gizonite, Jonathan the son of Shagee the Hararite,* ³⁵*Ahiam the son of Sachar the Hararite, Eliphal the son of Ur,* ³⁶*Hepher the Mecherathite, Ahijah the Pelonite,* ³⁷*Hezro of Carmel, Naarai the son of Ezbai,* ³⁸*Joel the brother of Nathan, Mibhar the son of Hagri,* ³⁹*Zelek the Ammonite, Naharai of Be-eroth, the armor-bearer of Joab the son of Zeruiah,* ⁴⁰*Ira the Ithrite, Gareb the Ithrite,* ⁴¹*Uriah the Hittite, Zabad the son of Ahlai,* ⁴²*Adina the son of Shiza the Reubenite, a leader of the Reubenites, and thirty with him,* ⁴³*Hanan the son of Maacah, and Joshaphat the Mithnite,* ⁴⁴*Uzzia the Ashterathite, Shama and Je-iel the sons of Hotham the Aroerite,* ⁴⁵*Jedia-el the son of Shimri, and Joha his brother, the Tizite,* ⁴⁶*Eliel the Mahavite, and Jeribai, and Joshaviah, the sons of Elna-am, and Ithmah the Moabite,* ⁴⁷*Eliel, and Obed, and Ja-asiel the Mezoba-ite.*

x Compare 2 Sam 23.8: Heb *thirty* or *captains*   y Compare 2 Sam 23.12: Heb *they . . . their*   z Syr: Heb *three*   a Compare 2 Sam 23.19: Heb *more renowned among the two*   b Syr: Heb *the son of a valiant man*   c The meaning of the word *ariel* is unknown   d Compare 2 Sam 23.25: Heb *the Harorite*   e Compare Gk and 2 Sam 23.32: Heb *the sons of Hashem*

OVERVIEW: The observance of fasting becomes not the curbing of old passions but an opportunity for new pleasures (AUGUSTINE). The judgment of almighty God prefers innocence to gold; we, as David, have to scorn to receive gold in accordance with the will of our Lord. But also as David we have to respect the law (GREGORY THE GREAT).

11:17-19 David Poured Out Water as an Offering

OBSERVANCE OF FASTING. AUGUSTINE: The observance of Lent becomes not the curbing

of old passions but an opportunity for new pleasures. Take measures in advance with as much diligence as possible to prevent these attitudes from creeping on you. Let frugality be joined to fasting. As satisfying the stomach is to be censured, so stimulants of the appetite must be eliminated. It is not that certain kinds of food are to be detested but that bodily pleasure is to be checked. . . . And holy King David repented of having excessively desired water. SERMON 207.2.[1]

---

[1]FC 38:91*.

YOU HAVE TO SATISFY THE JUDGMENT OF ALMIGHTY GOD. GREGORY THE GREAT: I must tell you that I have been led to praise God the more for your work by what I have learned from the report of my most believed son Probinus the presbyter; namely that, your excellency, having issued a certain ordinance against the perfidy of the Jews, those to whom it related attempted to bend the rectitude of your mind by offering a sum of money, which your excellency scorned, and, seeking to satisfy the judgment of almighty God, preferred innocence to gold. With regard to this, what was done by King David recurs to my mind, who, when he longed for water from the cistern of Bethlehem, which was wedged in by the enemy, had been brought him by obedient soldiers, said, "God forbid that I should drink the blood of righteous men." And, because he poured it out and would not drink it, it is written, "He offered it a libation to the Lord." If, then, water was scorned by the armed king and turned into a sacrifice to God, we may estimate what manner of sacrifice to almighty God has been offered by the king who for his love has scorned to receive not water but gold. LETTER 122.[2]

WATER POURED AS A LIBATION TO GOD. GREGORY THE GREAT: David desired long afterwards to drink water from the cistern of Bethlehem, which, when his bravest soldiers had brought to him, he refused to drink and poured it out as a libation to the Lord. For it was lawful for him to drink it, had he been so minded; but, because he remembered having done what was unlawful, he laudably abstained even from what was lawful. And he, who to his guilt previously feared not that the blood of dying soldiers should be shed, afterwards considered that, were he to drink the water, he would have shed the blood of living soldiers, saying, "Shall I drink the blood of these men who have put their lives in jeopardy?" LETTER 45.[3]

---

[2]NPNF 2 13:35-36* (CCL 140A references this as *Letter* 229).
[3]NPNF 2 13:66 (CCL 140A references this as *Letter* 27).

12:1-22 THE FOLLOWERS OF DAVID

[1]*Now these are the men who came to David at Ziklag, while he could not move about freely because of Saul the son of Kish; and they were among the mighty men who helped him in war.* [2]*They were bowmen, and could shoot arrows and sling stones with either the right or the left hand; they were Benjaminites, Saul's kinsmen.* [3]*The chief was Ahi-ezer, then Joash, both sons of Shemaah of Gibe-ah; also Jezi-el and Pelet the sons of Azmaveth; Beracah, Jehu of Anathoth,* [4]*Ishmaiah of Gibeon, a mighty man among the thirty and a leader over the thirty; Jeremiah,ʲ Jahaziel, Johanan, Jozabad of Gederah,* [5]*Eluzai,ᵍ Jerimoth, Bealiah, Shemariah, Shephatiah the Haruphite;* [6]*Elkanah, Isshiah, Azarel, Jo-ezer, and Jashobe-am, the Korahites;* [7]*And Joelah and Zebadiah, the sons of Jeroham of Gedor.*

[8]*From the Gadites there went over to David at the stronghold in the wilderness mighty and experienced warriors, expert with shield and spear, whose faces were like the faces of lions, and who were swift as gazelles upon the mountains:* [9]*Ezer the chief, Obadiah second, Eliab third,*

251

[10]*Mishmannah fourth, Jeremiah fifth,* [11]*Attai sixth, Eliel seventh,* [12]*Johanan eighth, Elzabad ninth,* [13]*Jeremiah tenth, Machbannai eleventh.* [14]*These Gadites were officers of the army, the lesser over a hundred and the greater over a thousand.* [15]*These are the men who crossed the Jordan in the first month, when it was overflowing all its banks, and put to flight all those in the valleys, to the east and to the west.*

[16]*And some of the men of Benjamin and Judah came to the stronghold to David.* [17]*David went out to meet them and said to them, "If you have come to me in friendship to help me, my heart will be knit to you; but if to betray me to my adversaries, although there is no wrong in my hands, then may the God of our fathers see and rebuke you."* [18]*Then the Spirit came upon Amasai, chief of the thirty, and he said,*

> *"We are yours, O David;*
> *and with you, O son of Jesse!*
> *Peace, peace to you,*
> *and peace to your helpers!*
> *For your God helps you."*

Then David received them, and made them officers of his troops.

[19]*Some of the men of Manasseh deserted to David when he came with the Philistines for the battle against Saul. (Yet he did not help them, for the rulers of the Philistines took counsel and sent him away, saying, "At peril to our heads he will desert to his master Saul.")* [20]*As he went to Ziklag these men of Manasseh deserted to him: Adnah, Jozabad, Jedia-el, Michael, Jozabad, Elihu, and Zillethai, chiefs of thousands in Manasseh.* [21]*They helped David against the band of raiders;[h] for they were all mighty men of valor, and were commanders in the army.* [22]*For from day to day men kept coming to David to help him, until there was a great army, like an army of God.*

f *Heb verse 5* g *Heb verse 6* h *Or as officers of his troops*

Overview: We are not seeking our own glory but the Lord's, and when God prevails we also triumph (Augustine).

12:17-18 *Peace to the One Who Helps You!*

When God Wins, You Prevail. Augustine: "The Lord shall give the Word to them that preach good tidings, with great power."[1] Of you, also, I venture to make this prayer, that, in this struggle of ours, truth may prevail. For you are not seeking your own glory but Christ's,[2] and when you win the victory, I also shall win it if I recognize my own error, and, contrarily, you prevail when I win, "for neither ought the children to lay up for the parents, but the parents for the children."[3] And in the book of Paralipomenon we read that the sons of Israel went out to fight with peaceful heart, in the very midst of swords and blood shedding and the bodies of the slain, because they were thinking of the victory of peace, not their own. Letter 75.[4]

---

[1]Ps 68:11 (67:12 LXX, Vg). [2]Jn 7:18. [3]2 Cor 12:14. [4]FC 12:343-44*.

12:23-40 DAVID KING OF ALL ISRAEL

38All these, men of war, arrayed in battle order, came to Hebron with full intent to make David king over all Israel; likewise all the rest of Israel were of a single mind to make David king. 39And they were there with David for three days, eating and drinking, for their brethren had made preparation for them. 40And also their neighbors, from as far as Issachar and Zebulun and Naphtali, came bringing food on asses and on camels and on mules and on oxen, abundant provisions of meal, cakes of figs, clusters of raisins, and wine and oil, oxen and sheep, for there was joy in Israel.

OVERVIEW: The tongue is a sword. It slays human souls (JEROME).

12:38 *Warriors Arrayed for Battle Order*

MY OWN IS MY ENEMY. JEROME: "O Lord, deliver me from lying lip, from treacherous tongue": not from another's tongue but from my own. Another's tongue does not injure me; my own is my enemy. Deliver me; deliver me from my own tongue. My tongue is a sword, and it is slaying my soul. I think that I am harming my enemy; I do not realize that I am killing myself. My adversaries may contradict me when I speak to them, but I shall speak peace. Their spirit may be hostile, but let our spirit be that of peacemakers. It is written in Paralipomenon: "The sons of Israel came to fight with peaceful heart." HOMILIES ON THE PSALMS 41 (Ps 119[120]).[1]

---

[1]FC 48:315.

[13:1-14 THE ARK IS BROUGHT TO THE HOUSE OF OBED-EDOM]
[See commentary on 2 Samuel 6]

[14:1-17 THE REIGN OF DAVID]
[See commentary on 2 Samuel 5:11-25]

[15:1-29 PREPARATIONS FOR CARRYING THE ARK]
[See commentary on 2 Samuel 6]

16:1-36 OFFERINGS FOR THE TRANSFER OF THE ARK

¹And they brought in the ark of God, and set it inside the tent which David had pitched for it; and they offered burnt offerings and peace offerings before God. ²And when David had finished offering the burnt offerings and the peace offerings, he blessed the people in the name of the LORD, ³and distributed to all Israel, both men and women, to each a loaf of bread, a portion of meat,° and a cake of raisins.

⁴Moreover he appointed certain of the Levites as ministers before the ark of the LORD, to invoke, to thank, and to praise the LORD, the God of Israel. ⁵Asaph was the chief, and second to him were Zechariah, Je-iel, Shemiramoth, Jehiel, Mattithiah, Eliab, Benaiah, Obed-edom, and Je-iel, who were to play harps and lyres; Asaph was to sound the cymbals, ⁶and Benaiah and Jahaziel the priests were to blow trumpets continually, before the ark of the covenant of God.

⁷Then on that day David first appointed that thanksgiving be sung to the LORD by Asaph and his brethren.

⁸O give thanks to the LORD, call on his name,
    make known his deeds among the peoples!
⁹Sing to him, sing praises to him,
    tell of all his wonderful works!
¹⁰Glory in his holy name;
    let the hearts of those who seek the LORD rejoice!
¹¹Seek the LORD and his strength,
    seek his presence continually!
¹²Remember the wonderful works that he has done,
    the wonders he wrought, the judgments he uttered,
¹³O offspring of Abraham his servant,
    sons of Jacob, his chosen ones!

¹⁴He is the LORD our God;
    his judgments are in all the earth.
¹⁵He is mindful of his covenant for ever,
    of the word that he commanded, for a thousand generations,
¹⁶the covenant which he made with Abraham,
    his sworn promise to Isaac,
¹⁷which he confirmed as a statute to Jacob,

as an everlasting covenant to Israel,
¹⁸saying, "To you I will give the land of Canaan,
as your portion for an inheritance."

¹⁹When they were few in number,
and of little account, and sojourners in it,
²⁰wandering from nation to nation,
from one kingdom to another people,
²¹he allowed no one to oppress them;
he rebuked kings on their account,
²²saying, "Touch not my anointed ones,
do my prophets no harm!"

²³Sing to the LORD, all the earth!
Tell of his salvation from day to day.
²⁴Declare his glory among the nations,
his marvelous works among all the peoples!
²⁵For great is the LORD, and greatly to be praised,
and he is to be held in awe above all gods.
²⁶For all the gods of the peoples are idols;
but the LORD made the heavens.
²⁷Honor and majesty are before him;
strength and joy are in his place.

²⁸Ascribe to the LORD, O families of the peoples,
ascribe to the LORD glory and strength!
²⁹Ascribe to the LORD the glory due his name;
bring an offering, and come before him!
Worship the LORD in holy array;
³⁰tremble before him, all the earth;
yea, the world stands firm, never to be moved.
³¹Let the heavens be glad, and let the earth rejoice,
and let them say among the nations, "The LORD reigns!"
³²Let the sea roar, and all that fills it,
let the field exult, and everything in it!
³³Then shall the trees of the wood sing for joy
before the LORD, for he comes to judge the earth.
³⁴O give thanks to the LORD, for he is good;
for his steadfast love endures for ever!

^{35}Say also:

"Deliver us, O God of our salvation,
 and gather and save us from among the nations,
that we may give thanks to thy holy name,
 and glory in thy praise.
^{36}Blessed be the Lord, the God of Israel,
 from everlasting to everlasting!"
Then all the people said, "Amen!" and praised the Lord.

o Compare Gk Syr Vg: Heb uncertain

Overview: The prophets sing a unique prayer to the Lord (Origen). The divine Spirit inspires people when they sing hymns to God (Eusebius). The action of the Lord makes one church out of the two peoples (Cassiodorus). As there are many antichrists in the world, in the same way, knowing that Christ has come, we see that there are many christs in the world, who, like him, love righteousness and hate iniquity (Origen). Glory and praise are before Christ, and strength and pride are in the place of his sanctification. So there will be joy for those who will look forward to the incorruption that he has promised (Justin).

16:8 Give Thanks to the Lord

The Praises of Asaph and His Brothers. Origen: The sixth song is in 1 Chronicles, where David first established Asaph and his brothers for praising the Lord. The beginning of the song is as follows, "Praise the Lord, give thanks to him, and call on his name; make known his purposes among the peoples. Sing to him, sing praises to him, tell of all his wonderful works, which the Lord has done," and so forth. It should, however, be known that the song in 2 Samuel is very much like Psalm 18. Furthermore, the first part of the text in 1 Chronicles, up to the place where it says "and do my prophets no harm," is like Psalm 105, and the latter part of it, following the verse just mentioned, bears a likeness to the first part of Psalm 96, where it says, "Sing to the Lord, all the earth," up to the place where it says "for he comes to judge the earth."[1] Commentary on the Song of Songs, Prologue 4.[2]

Chronicles and Psalms. Origen: In the first book of Chronicles the psalm praising the Lord attributed to Asaph and his brothers, which begins "O give thanks to the Lord, call on his name,"[3] is, for the most part, the same as Psalm 104, down to the words "Do my prophets no harm!"[4] After that it is almost identical to Psalm 95 from the beginning, "Sing to the Lord, all the earth!"[5] Letter to Julius Africanus 21.[6]

16:15 Remembering God's Covenant

Many Prophecies of the Future. Eusebius of Caesarea: As it has been supposed by some that the book of Psalms merely consists of hymns to God and sacred songs and that we shall look in vain in it for predictions and prophecies of the future, let us realize distinctly that it contains many prophecies, far too many to be quoted now, and it must suffice for proof of what Isaiah to make use of two psalms ascribed to Asaph, written in the time of David. For Asaph was one of the temple musicians then, as is stated in the book of Chronicles, and was inspired by the divine Spirit to speak the psalms inscribed with his name. Proof of the Gospel 10.1.[7]

---

[1]Ps 96:1, 13 (95:1, 13 LXX). [2]OSW 238-39. [3]Ps 105:1 (104:1 LXX). [4]Ps 105:15 (104:15 LXX). [5]Ps 96:1 (95:1 LXX). [6]MFC 9:134. [7]POG 2:191-92.

16:22 Do Not Harm the Prophets of God

ONE CHURCH OUT OF THE TWO PEOPLES.
CASSIODORUS: How splendidly joined to each
other are the sections proceeding from the same
source to achieve the salvation of the human race.
Who would not be amazed that what is said earlier
in different psalms is clearly assembled so harmo-
niously here? Similarly David himself in the
Chronicles is filled with the holy Spirit and made
the Lord's praises resound with great expressions
of joy by assembling sections of Psalms 95, 104 and
105, so that incense compounded of different aro-
mas could happily rise to the Lord's presence; for
sentiments that are clear, in no sense at odds with
each other are united without difficulty. . . . My
judgment is that there is another apt feature in the
present instance: the action of the Lord made one
church out of the two peoples. EXPLANATION OF
THE PSALMS, CONCLUSION.[8]

**CHRIST LOVES RIGHTEOUSNESS AND HATES
INIQUITY.** ORIGEN: There was no need that
there should everywhere exist many bodies and
many spirits like Jesus, in order that the entire
humankind might be enlightened by the Word of
God. For the one Word was enough, having
arisen as the "Sun of righteousness," to send forth
from Judea his coming rays into the souls of all
who were willing to receive him. But if anyone
desires to see many bodies filled with a divine
Spirit, similar to the one Christ, ministering to
the salvation of people everywhere, let him take
note of those who teach the Gospel of Jesus in all
lands in soundness of doctrine and uprightness of
life and who are themselves termed "christs" by
the holy Scriptures in the passage "Do not touch
my anointed, and do not harm my prophets."[9] For
as we have heard that Antichrist comes and yet
have learned that there are many antichrists in
the world, in the same way, knowing that Christ
has come, we see that, owing to him, there are
many christs in the world, who, like him, have
loved righteousness and hated iniquity, and therefore God, the God of Christ, anointed them also

with the "oil of gladness." AGAINST CELSUS
6.79.[10]

16:23-31 Tell of God's Salvation

**THE SPIRIT SPEAKS OF THINGS TO COME AS
ALREADY HAVING HAPPENED.** JUSTIN MAR-
TYR: In another prophecy the prophetic Spirit, testifying through the same David that after being
crucified, Christ would reign, said, "O sing to the
Lord, all the earth, and proclaim his salvation from
day to day; for great is the Lord and highly to be
praised, terrible beyond all the gods. For all the
gods of the nations are images of demons, but God
made the heavens. Glory and praise are before him,
and strength and pride in the place of his sanctification. Give glory to the Lord, the Father of the
ages. Receive favor, and go in before his face, and
worship in his holy courts. Let all the earth fear
before him and be set upright and not shaken. Let
them exult among the nations; the Lord has
reigned from the tree."[11] Now when the prophetic
Spirit speaks of things to come as already having
happened, as is illustrated in the passages quoted, I
will explain this too so that those who come on it
will have no excuse for not understanding. Things
he fully knows are to happen he speaks of in
advance as if they had already occurred. Give careful attention to the passages quoted, and you will
see that this is the way they must be taken. David
uttered the words quoted above fifteen hundred
years before Christ, made man, was crucified, and
none of those who were crucified before him gave
joy to the nations, nor of those crucified after him
either. But in our time Jesus Christ, who was crucified and died, rose again and, ascending into
heaven, began to reign; and on account of what
was proclaimed by the apostles in all nations as
coming from him, there is joy for those who look
forward to the incorruption that he has promised.
FIRST APOLOGY 41-42.[12]

---

[8]ACW 53:102. [9]See Ps 105:15 (104:15 LXX). [10]ANF 4:609*. [11]See also Ps 96:1-2, 4-10 (95:1-2, 4-10 LXX). [12]LCC 1:268-69.

A New Song. Augustine: "O sing unto the Lord a new song; sing unto the Lord, all the earth." If all the earth sings a new song, it is thus building while it sings; the very act of singing is building, but only if it sings not the old song. The lust of the flesh sings the old song; the love of God sings the new. Hear why it is a new song: the Lord says, "A new commandment I give to you, that you love one another."[13] The whole earth then sings a new song: there the house of God is built. All the earth is the house of God. If all the earth is the house of God, he who clings not to all the earth is a ruin, not a house; that old ruin whose shadow that ancient temple represented. For there what was old was destroyed, that what was new might be built up. Expositions of the Psalms 96.2.[14]

---

[13]Jn 15:12. [14]NPNF 1 8:470.

16:37-43 ORDERS OF LEVITES

[37]*So David left Asaph and his brethren there before the ark of the covenant of the Lord to minister continually before the ark as each day required,* [38]*and also Obed-edom and his*[p] *sixty-eight brethren; while Obed-edom, the son of Jeduthun, and Hosah were to be gatekeepers.* [39]*And he left Zadok the priest and his brethren the priests before the tabernacle of the Lord in the high place that was at Gibeon,* [40]*to offer burnt offerings to the Lord upon the altar of burnt offering continually morning and evening, according to all that is written in the law of the Lord which he commanded Israel.* [41]*With them were Heman and Jeduthun, and the rest of those chosen and expressly named to give thanks to the Lord, for his steadfast love endures for ever.* [42]*Heman and Jeduthun had trumpets and cymbals for the music and instruments for sacred song. The sons of Jeduthun were appointed to the gate.*

[43]*Then all the people departed each to his house, and David went home to bless his household.*

p Heb *their*

Overview: We think that the composition of the work is owed to David; that was given to Idithun for his use that he might correct the passions of his soul (Basil).

16:41 *Rendering Thanks to the Lord*

Idithun Was a Singer in the Temple. Basil the Great: We know two psalms with the title "For Idithun," the sixty-first and the thirty-eighth. We think that the composition of the work is owed to David; that was given to Idithun for his use that he might correct the passions of his soul and also as a choral song to be sung in the presence of the people. Through it, also, God was glorified, and those who heard it amended their habits. Now, Idithun was a singer in the temple, as the history of the Paralipomenon testifies to us, saying, "And after them Heman and Idithun sounded the trumpets and played on the cymbals and all kinds of musical instruments to sing praises to God." And a little later it says, "Moreover David the king and the chief officers of the army separated for the ministry the sons of Asaph, and of Heman and of Idithun: to prophesy with harps, and with psalteries and with tym-

pana."[1] Homilies on the Psalms 21.1 (Ps 61).[2]

---

[1] 1 Chron 25:1. [2] FC 46:341.

17:1-27 THE PROPHECY OF NATHAN
[See commentary on 2 Samuel 7]

[1]Now when David dwelt in his house, David said to Nathan the prophet, "Behold, I dwell in a house of cedar, but the ark of the covenant of the Lord is under a tent." [2]And Nathan said to David, "Do all that is in your heart, for God is with you."
[3]But that same night the word of the Lord came to Nathan, [4]"Go and tell my servant David, 'Thus says the Lord: You shall not build me a house to dwell in. [5]For I have not dwelt in a house since the day I led up Israel to this day, but I have gone from tent to tent and from dwelling to dwelling. [6]In all places where I have moved with all Israel, did I speak a word with any of the judges of Israel, whom I commanded to shepherd my people, saying, "Why have you not built me a house of cedar?" ' [7]Now therefore thus shall you say to my servant David, 'Thus says the Lord of hosts, I took you from the pasture, from following the sheep, that you should be prince over my people Israel; [8]and I have been with you wherever you went, and have cut off all your enemies from before you; and I will make for you a name, like the name of the great ones of the earth. [9]And I will appoint a place for my people Israel, and will plant them, that they may dwell in their own place, and be disturbed no more; and violent men shall waste them no more, as formerly, [10]from the time that I appointed judges over my people Israel; and I will subdue all your enemies. Moreover I declare to you that the Lord will build you a house. [11]When your days are fulfilled to go to be with your fathers, I will raise up your offspring after you, one of your own sons, and I will establish his kingdom. [12]He shall build a house for me, and I will establish his throne for ever. [13]I will be his father, and he shall be my son; I will not take my steadfast love from him, as I took it from him who was before you, [14]but I will confirm him in my house and in my kingdom for ever and his throne shall be established for ever.' " [15]In accordance with all these words, and in accordance with all this vision, Nathan spoke to David.

Overview: Nathan prophesies of one after David who would build the house of David. Although Solomon built the temple, Nathan must have been referring not to Solomon but to Christ, who was the only one worthy to build the house

of God (Eusebius).

17:11-13 Nathan's Prophecy of the House of David

NOT SOLOMON BUT CHRIST WILL BUILD THE

HOUSE. EUSEBIUS OF CAESAREA: There is no doubt that Solomon was the son of David and his successor in the kingdom. And he first built the temple of God at Jerusalem, and perhaps the Jews understand him to be the subject of the prophecy. But we may fairly ask them whether the oracle applies to Solomon, which says, "And I will set up his throne for ever," and also where God swore with the affirmation of an oath by his holy one, "The throne of him that is foretold shall be as the sun and the days of heaven." For if the years of the reign of Solomon are reckoned, they will be found to be forty and no more. Even if the reigns of all his successors are added up, they do not altogether come to 500 years. And even if we suppose that their line continued down to the final attack on the Jewish nation by the Romans, how can they fulfill a prophecy which says, "Your throne shall remain for ever, and be as the sun and the days of heaven"? And the words, "I will be to him a father, and he shall be to me a son," how can they refer to Solomon? For his history tells us much about him that is foreign and opposed to the adoption of God. No. Hear the indictment against him: "And Solomon loved women, and took many strange wives, even the daughter of Pharaoh, Moabites, Ammonites, and Idumaeans, Syrians and Chatteans, and Amorites, from the nations of whom the Lord said to the children of Israel, that they should not go in to them."[1]

And in addition to this: "And his heart was not right with the Lord his God, as was the heart of David his father; and Solomon went after Astarte, the abomination of the Sidonians and after their king, the idol of the sons of Ammon. And Solomon did evil before the Lord."[2] And again further on he adds, "And the Lord raised Satan against Solomon, Ader the Idumaean." Now who would venture to call God his father, who lay under such grievous charges, and to call himself the firstborn son of the God of the Universe? Or how could these sayings apply first to David, if you reflect. Therefore we require someone else, here revealed to arise from the seed of David. But there was no other born of him, as is recorded, save only our Lord and Savior Jesus the Christ of God, who alone of the kings of David's line is called through the whole world the Son of David according to his earthly birth, and whose kingdom continues and will continue, lasting for endless time. It is attacked by many, but always by its divine superhuman power proves itself inspired and invincible as the prophecy foretold. PROOF OF THE GOSPEL 7.3.[3]

---

[1]1 Kings 11:1. [2]1 Kings 11:4. [3]POG 2:86-87.

[18:1-17 THE VICTORIES OF DAVID]
[See commentary on 2 Samuel 8]

[19:1-19 WARS AGAINST THE AMMONITES AND THE ARAMEANS]
[See commentary on 2 Samuel 10; 12:26-31]

[20:1-8 OVERTHROW OF RABBAH
AND VICTORIES OVER THE PHILISTINES]
[See commentary on 2 Samuel 12:26-31]

[21:1-17 GUILT OF DAVID AND PUNISHMENT
OF THE LORD]
[See commentary on 2 Samuel 24:1-25]

21:18-30 DAVID BUYS THE THRESHING FLOOR
OF ORNAN

[18]Then the angel of the Lord commanded Gad to say to David that David should go up and rear an altar to the Lord on the threshing floor of Ornan the Jebusite. [19]So David went up at Gad's word, which he had spoken in the name of the Lord. [20]Now Ornan was threshing wheat; he turned and saw the angel, and his four sons who were with him hid themselves. [21]As David came to Ornan, Ornan looked and saw David and went forth from the threshing floor, and did obeisance to David with his face to the ground. [22]And David said to Ornan, "Give me the site of the threshing floor that I may build on it an altar to the Lord—give it to me at its full price—that the plague may be averted from the people." [23]Then Ornan said to David, "Take it; and let my lord the king do what seems good to him; see, I give the oxen for burnt offerings, and the threshing sledges for the wood, and the wheat for a cereal offering. I give it all." [24]But King David said to Ornan, "No, but I will buy it for the full price; I will not take for the Lord what is yours, nor offer burnt offerings which cost me nothing." [25]So David paid Ornan six hundred shekels of gold by weight for the site. [26]And David built there an altar to the Lord and presented burnt offerings and peace offerings, and called upon the Lord, and he answered him with fire from heaven upon the altar of burnt offering. [27]Then the Lord commanded the angel; and he put his sword back into its sheath.

[28]At that time, when David saw that the Lord had answered him at the threshing floor of Ornan the Jebusite, he made his sacrifices there. [29]For the tabernacle of the Lord, which Moses had made in the wilderness, and the altar of burnt offering were at that time in the high place at

Gibeon; [30]*but David could not go before it to inquire of God, for he was afraid of the sword of the angel of the LORD.*

OVERVIEW: Christ's church would grow up not in Israel but among the Gentiles (JEROME). It is appropriate that the place for building the temple should be on the threshing floor of Ornan the Jebusite because the church is customarily designated by the term "threshing floor." Jebus is the same city as Jerusalem, but Jebus means "trampled on" and Jerusalem "the vision of peace." Therefore, while Ornan still held sway in this city it was called Jebus, but when he sold the site of his threshing floor together with his oxen and threshing sledges to David, it took the name Jerusalem because the Gentiles who still persisted in their obstinacy were trampled on as worthless and contemptible by the wicked spirits (BEDE).

21:18 *An Altar on a Threshing Floor*

THE CHURCH OF GOD GROWS UP AMONG THE GENTILES. JEROME: When of old the Philistines had been overcome, when their devilish audacity had been destroyed, when their champion had fallen on his face to the earth,[1] it was from this city that there went forth a procession of jubilant souls, a harmonious choir to sing our David's victory over tens of thousands.[2] Here, too, it was that the angel grasped his sword, and while he laid waste the whole of the ungodly city, he marked out the temple of the Lord in the threshing floor of Ornan, king of the Jebusites. Thus early was it made plain that Christ's church would grow up not in Israel but among the Gentiles. LETTER 46.2.[3]

21:25-26 *David Built an Altar to the Lord*

WHY DID THE LORD CHOOSE THE CITY OF JEBUS FOR THE CONSTRUCTION OF HIS TEMPLE? BEDE: David had prepared by singing psalms, and the other prophets too by prophesying prepared for the Lord who was indeed the true Solomon a place that he might build a house, because they taught the hearts of their hearers by true faith, earnestly urging them to receive with faith and devotion the Son of God who was coming in the flesh. . . . It is appropriate that this place should be on the threshing floor of Ornan the Jebusite because the church is customarily designated by the term "threshing floor," as John says of the Lord: "His winnowing fork is in his hand, and he will clear his threshing floor."[4] Ornan, whose name means "enlightened" and who was a Jebusite by origin, signifies the Gentiles by his origin, and by his name he indicates these same [Gentiles] who were to be enlightened by the Lord and transformed into children of the church to whom the apostle rightly says, "Once you were darkness, but now you are light in the Lord."[5] Jebus is the same city as Jerusalem. Now Jebus means "trampled on" but Jerusalem "the vision of peace." As long as the Gentile Ornan reigned there it was called Jebus; but when David bought a place of burnt offering there, when Solomon built a temple to the Lord there, it was no longer called Jebus but Jerusalem, because, that is, as long as the Gentiles continued in ignorance of divine worship they were trampled on and made a mockery of by the unclean spirits, following mute idols according as they were led to do;[6] but when they called to mind the grace of their Creator, they immediately found in themselves both the place and the name of peace, as the Lord says of them, "Blessed are the peacemakers, for they shall be called the children of God."[7] Therefore, while Ornan still held sway in this city it was called Jebus, but when he sold the site of his threshing floor together with his oxen and threshing

---

[1]See 1 Sam 17:49. [2]See 1 Sam 18:7. [3]NPNF 2 6:61. [4]Mt 3:12. [5]Eph 5:8. [6]See 1 Cor 12:2. [7]Mt 5:9.

sledges to king David, it took the name Jerusalem because the Gentiles who still persisted in their obstinacy were trampled on as worthless and contemptible by the wicked spirits; but when they learned to sell all they had and offer it to the true king, they could no longer be tram-

pled on by the demons and vices but were given a greater share of inner peace, which they possessed with their Creator. ON THE TEMPLE I. 5.4-5.[8]

---

[8]TTH 21:20-22*.

22:1-19 PREPARATIONS FOR BUILDING THE TEMPLE

[1]Then David said, "Here shall be the house of the LORD God and here the altar of burnt offering for Israel."

[2]David commanded to gather together the aliens who were in the land of Israel, and he set stonecutters to prepare dressed stones for building the house of God. [3]David also provided great stores of iron for nails for the doors of the gates and for clamps, as well as bronze in quantities beyond weighing, [4]and cedar timbers without number; for the Sidonians and Tyrians brought great quantities of cedar to David. [5]For David said, "Solomon my son is young and inexperienced, and the house that is to be built for the LORD must be exceedingly magnificent, of fame and glory throughout all lands; I will therefore make preparation for it." So David provided materials in great quantity before his death.

[6]Then he called for Solomon his son, and charged him to build a house for the LORD, the God of Israel. [7]David said to Solomon, "My son, I had it in my heart to build a house to the name of the LORD my God. [8]But the word of the LORD came to me, saying, 'You have shed much blood and have waged great wars; you shall not build a house to my name, because you have shed so much blood before me upon the earth. [9]Behold, a son shall be born to you; he shall be a man of peace. I will give him peace from all his enemies round about; for his name shall be Solomon, and I will give peace and quiet to Israel in his days. [10]He shall build a house for my name. He shall be my son, and I will be his father, and I will establish his royal throne in Israel for ever.' [11]Now, my son, the LORD be with you, so that you may succeed in building the house of the LORD your God, as he has spoken concerning you. [12]Only, may the LORD grant you discretion and understanding, that when he gives you charge over Israel you may keep the law of the LORD your God. [13]Then you will prosper if you are careful to observe the statutes and the ordinances which the LORD commanded Moses for Israel. Be strong, and of good courage. Fear not; be not dismayed. [14]With great pains I have provided for the house of the LORD a hundred thousand talents of gold, a million talents of silver, and bronze and iron beyond weighing, for there is so much of it; timber and stone too I have

provided. To these you must add. ¹⁵*You have an abundance of workmen: stonecutters, masons, carpenters, and all kinds of craftsmen without number, skilled in working* ¹⁶*gold, silver, bronze, and iron. Arise and be doing! The Lord be with you!"*

¹⁷*David also commanded all the leaders of Israel to help Solomon his son, saying,* ¹⁸ *"Is not the Lord your God with you? And has he not given you peace on every side? For he has delivered the inhabitants of the land into my hand; and the land is subdued before the Lord and his people.* ¹⁹*Now set your mind and heart to seek the Lord your God. Arise and build the sanctuary of the Lord God, so that the ark of the covenant of the Lord and the holy vessels of God may be brought into a house built for the name of the Lord."*

Overview: Because of his guilt, David could not build a temple of God (Jerome), although he occupied himself with gathering of the material of the temple (Origen). Solomon was a man of peace, and so he was able to construct the famous temple for God, although his kingdom would not last as long as his descendant Christ's would (Theodoret of Cyr) who would be the ultimate man of peace (Eusebius).

22:8 David Not Allowed to Build the Temple

The Guilt of David. Jerome: Because he was a man of blood—the reference is not, as some think, to his wars, but to the murder [of Uriah]—he was not permitted to build a temple of the Lord. Against Jovinianus 1.24.[1]

The Construction of the Temple. Origen: As a man of blood, David was prevented from constructing it; he seems, at least, to have been occupied concerning the gathering of the material of the temple. Commentary on the Gospel of John 10.257.[2]

22:9 A Man of Peace

Christ's Peace More Lasting than Solomon's. Theodoret of Cyr: Solomon means "peaceable"; as you can find in the Chronicles: God said to David when he wanted to build the new temple, "Lo, a son is born to you; he will be a man of repose, and I shall give him peace

from all his enemies round about because his name is Solomon, and I shall give peace and tranquility to Israel in his days. He will build a house for my name, and he will be a son to me, and I shall be a father to him, and I shall assure the throne of his kingdom in Israel forever." It is well known, however, that Solomon died without living long, and that his throne came to an end. He gives the name Solomon, therefore, to our peaceable Lord, of whom blessed Paul says, "For he is our peace, who has made the two one and has broken down the dividing wall."[3] . . . Now it was not Solomon who had dominion to the ends of the world [either] but he who sprang from Solomon in his humanity, Jesus Christ, and was called Solomon on account of his peaceable and gentle nature and his being the cause of peace. Commentary on the Song of Songs 3.[4]

The Ultimate Man of Peace is Christ. Eusebius of Caesarea: This [passage quoted, 1 Kings 8:26-27] is also found in the same words in Chronicles. God then promised David he would raise up a king from his body and would be his father, so that the offspring of the seed of David should be called the Son of God and should have his throne in an eternal kingdom. This was prophesied to David by Nathan in the Second Book of Kings.[5] . . . The same is also said

---

[1]NPNF 2 6:363. [2]FC 80:312. [3]Eph 2:14. [4]ECS 2:73. [5]2 Sam 7:12. [6]Eusebius also quotes Ps 89:4-5, 27-29, 36-37 (88:4-5, 27-29, 36-37 LXX) along with Ps 132:1-2, 11, 17 (131:1-2, 11, 17 LXX) as further references to Christ fulfilling this promise.

in Chronicles, and in the 88th [89th] Psalm.[6] . . . And so Solomon, being unique in wisdom, understanding this oracle given to his father, and perceiving it to be no slight thing, but something beyond human nature, and more suitable to God than to himself, son of David though he was, and knowing who was meant by God by the Firstborn, and who was clearly foretold as the Son of God, was overjoyed at the message and prayed that the words of the prophecy might be confirmed and that he who was foretold might come, calling him Firstborn and Son of God. PROOF OF THE GOSPEL 6.12.[7]

---

[7]POG 2:11-12.

23:1-32 DAVID ESTABLISHES THE RULES OF PRIESTHOOD

[1]*When David was old and full of days, he made Solomon his son king over Israel.*

[2]*David assembled all the leaders of Israel and the priests and the Levites.* [3]*The Levites, thirty years old and upward, were numbered, and the total was thirty-eight thousand men. . . .* [6]*And David organized them in divisions corresponding to the sons of Levi: Gershom, Kohath, and Merari.*

. . . [12]*The sons of Kohath: Amram, Izhar, Hebron, and Uzziel, four.* [13]*The sons of Amram: Aaron and Moses. Aaron was set apart to consecrate the most holy things, that he and his sons for ever should burn incense before the LORD, and minister to him and pronounce blessings in his name for ever.* [14]*But the sons of Moses the man of God were named among the tribe of Levi.* [15]*The sons of Moses: Gershom and Eliezer.*

OVERVIEW: From the lineage of Moses the high priest was chosen to consecrate at the altar of the Lord (PROCOPIUS).

23:3 The Levites Were Counted

THE LINEAGE OF MOSES. PROCOPIUS OF GAZA: The text of Chronicles makes a list of the Levites according to the importance and dignity given them by the great Moses. It demonstrates how the successors of Moses were chosen for this purpose and how Zadok was appointed as the high priest, along with his nephew Eleazari, and also Abimelech, nephew of Itamari. It includes two lineages, one of which is connected with Itamari which it attributes to those who descend from them. Also Luke mentions this genealogy in his Gospel, considering Zechariah as belonging to the lineage of Abijah. The aforementioned book [of Chronicles] shows that Abija was the seventh to obtain by lot this inheritance.[1] COMMENTARY ON 1 CHRONICLES 23.[2]

---

[1]See 1 Chron 24:10. The LXX has Abijah listed as eighth. Procopius, as well as Theodoret (PG 80:813), may reflect an alternate textual tradition. [2]PG 87:1205.

24:1-31 THE DIVISIONS OF THE PRIESTS

¹The divisions of the sons of Aaron were these. The sons of Aaron: Nadab, Abihu, Eleazar, and Ithamar. ²But Nadab and Abihu died before their father, and had no children, so Eleazar and Ithamar became the priests. ³With the help of Zadok of the sons of Eleazar, and Ahimelech of the sons of Ithamar, David organized them according to the appointed duties in their service. ⁴Since more chief men were found among the sons of Eleazar than among the sons of Ithamar, they organized them under sixteen heads of fathers' houses of the sons of Eleazar, and eight of the sons of Ithamar. ⁵They organized them by lot, all alike, for there were officers of the sanctuary and officers of God among both the sons of Eleazar and the sons of Ithamar. ⁶And the scribe Shemaiah the son of Nethanel, a Levite, recorded them in the presence of the king, and the princes, and Zadok the priest, and Ahimelech the son of Abiathar, and the heads of the fathers' houses of the priests and of the Levites; one father's house being chosen for Eleazar and one chosen for Ithamar.

⁷The first lot fell to Jehoiarib, the second to Jedaiah, ⁸the third to Harim, the fourth to Se-orim, ⁹the fifth to Malchijah, the sixth to Mijamin, ¹⁰the seventh to Hakkoz, the eighth to Abijah, ¹¹the ninth to Jeshua, the tenth to Shecaniah, ¹²the eleventh to Eliashib, the twelfth to Jakim, ¹³the thirteenth to Huppah, the fourteenth to Jeshebe-ab, ¹⁴the fifteenth to Bilgah, the sixteenth to Immer, ¹⁵the seventeenth to Hezir, the eighteenth to Happizzez, ¹⁶the nineteenth to Pethahiah, the twentieth to Jehezkel, ¹⁷the twenty-first to Jachin, the twenty-second to Gamul, ¹⁸the twenty-third to Delaiah, the twenty-fourth to Ma-aziah. ¹⁹These had as their appointed duty in their service to come into the house of the LORD according to the procedure established for them by Aaron their father, as the LORD God of Israel had commanded him.

²⁰And of the rest of the sons of Levi: of the sons of Amram, Shuba-el; of the sons of Shuba-el, Jehdeiah. ²¹Of Rehabiah: of the sons of Rehabiah, Isshiah the chief. ²²Of the Izharites, Shelomoth; of the sons of Shelomoth, Jahath. ²³The sons of Hebron:ʸ Jeriah the chief,ᶻ Amariah the second, Jahaziel the third, Jekameam the fourth. ²⁴The sons of Uzziel, Micah; of the sons of Micah, Shamir. ²⁵The brother of Micah, Isshiah; of the sons of Isshiah, Zechariah. ²⁶The sons of Merari: Mahli and Mushi. The sons of Ja-aziah: Beno. ²⁷The sons of Merari: of Ja-aziah, Beno, Shoham, Zaccur, and Ibri. ²⁸Of Mahli: Eleazar, who had no sons. ²⁹Of Kish, the sons of Kish: Jerahmeel. ³⁰The sons of Mushi: Mahli, Eder, and Jerimoth. These were the sons of the Levites according to their fathers' houses. ³¹These also, the head of each father's house and his younger brother alike, cast lots, just as their brethren the sons of Aaron, in the presence of King David, Zadok, Ahimelech, and the heads of fathers' houses of the priests and of the Levites.

y See 23.19: Heb lacks *Hebron* z See 23.19: Heb lacks *the chief*

OVERVIEW: As the worship and magnificence of the temple increased, the graceful exercise of the ministry and the assembly of those ministering might also increase, and David would organize his reign establishing the rules of priesthood and dividing his priests in sections (BEDE).

24:1 The Divisions of the Priests

PREPARATION FOR SOLOMON'S REIGN. BEDE:
If you of the brotherhood would take delight in
hearing who that Abijah was from whose priestly
division it is said that Zechariah derived his rank,
he was the high priest during the time of King
David. By the Lord's order, Aaron was the first
single high priest appointed by Moses under the
law; after his death his son, Eleazar, received the
gift of the high priesthood.[1] When he too had
died, his son, Phinehas, became his successor as
high priest.[2] Thus up to the time of King David,
over a period of about 470 years, one after the
other became heir of the high priesthood. When
David, burning with great zeal for religion,
wanted to fashion a temple for the Lord, the Lord
willed this to be carried out by his son Solomon
instead. David himself nevertheless was concerned carefully to make ready everything that
pertained to the future construction and reverent
ceremonies of this temple.[3] He also arranged for
singers to chant the psalms daily at the time of
sacrifice, to the tune of musical instruments. This
was to arouse the minds of the people in attendance to remembrance and love of heavenly matters, not only by the sublimity of the words that
were sung, but also by the sweetness of the
sounds by which they were sung. Desiring that,
as the worship and magnificence of the temple increased, the graceful exercise of the ministry and
the assembly of those ministering might also increase, David called together all the descendants
of the sons of Aaron, those descending from the
stock of Eleazar and those from the stock of Ithamar, and he divided them into twenty-four sections, choosing individuals from each section as

high priests; the rest, who were in the sections of
the lower priesthood (which is now called that of
priest), he ordered to exercise their offices with
this provision, namely, that when any one of the
high priests departed this life, whoever was considered the best in his section should succeed him
in the high priesthood.

David set up these sections in such a way that
the individual high priests, along with the priests
who were under them, should minister for eight
successive days, that is, from sabbath to sabbath.[4]
And although all in the priestly class were equal,
yet one of them who seemed to be more worthy of
special reverence and more outstanding and in
power was to have the name of "high priest." As
to the order that was to be observed among these
sections, it was determined by the casting of lots
in the presence of King David and the leading
persons of the priestly and Levitical families. In
this distribution of lots, it is found that Abijah,
from whose priestly division and generation
Zechariah sprang, occupied the eighth place. It
was fitting that the herald of the new covenant, in
which the glory of the resurrection was declared
to the world, was born in the place of the eighth
lot, both because our Lord rose from the dead on
the day after the sabbath, which is the eighth day
following the seven days of creation, and because
we are promised at the end of time an eighth age
of everlasting resurrection, following the six ages
of this world and a seventh of tranquility for
souls, which comes in the next life. HOMILIES ON
THE GOSPELS 2.19.[5]

---

[1]See Exod 28:1; Num 3:2-4; 20:25-28; Deut 10:6. [2]Josh 24:33; Judg
20:28. [3]See 2 Sam 7:4-13; 1 Chron 22:1-10. [4]2 Chron 23:8. [5]CS
111:190-91.

25:1-31 THE DIVISIONS OF THE MUSICIANS

¹David and the chiefs of the service also set apart for the service certain of the sons of Asaph, and of Heman, and of Jeduthun, who should prophesy with lyres, with harps, and with cymbals.

Overview: The division of singers point to a rational part consisting of the human voice, an irrational part comprising musical instruments and a common part resulting from the fusion of the two (Cassiodorus).

25:1 Set Apart for Service

A Threefold Division. Cassiodorus: We read in the first book of Paralipomena that when the prophet David grew old in years devoted to the Lord, he chose four thousand young men from the people of Israel to render the psalms, which he had composed through the Lord's inspiration, so as to attain the great sweetness of heavenly grace by means of pipes, lyres, harps, timbrels, cymbals, trumpets, and their own voices. This sweet harmony clearly comprised a threefold division: a rational part consisting of the human voice, an irrational part comprising musical instruments and a common part resulting from the fusion of the two, such that the human voice issued forth in fixed melody and the tune of the instruments joined in harmonious accompaniment. With this performance the sweet and pleasant music presaged the Catholic church, which by the Lord's gift was to believe with varied tongues and diverse blending in the single harmony of faith. Explanation of the Psalms, Preface 2.[1]

---

[1] ACW 51:29.

[26:1-31 THE DIVISIONS OF THE GATEKEEPERS]

[27:1-34 MILITARY AND CIVIL ORGANIZATION]

28:1-21 DAVID'S INSTRUCTIONS FOR
BUILDING THE TEMPLE

¹David assembled at Jerusalem all the officials of Israel, the officials of the tribes, the officers of the divisions that served the king, the commanders of thousands, the commanders of hundreds, the stewards of all the property and cattle of the king and his sons, together with the palace officials, the mighty men, and all the seasoned warriors. ²Then King David rose to his feet and said: "Hear me, my brethren and my people. I had it in my heart to build a house of rest for the ark of the covenant of the Lord, and for the footstool of our God; and I made preparations for building. ³But God said to me, 'You may not build a house for my name, for you are a warrior and have shed blood.' ⁴Yet the Lord God of Israel chose me from all my father's house to be king over Israel for ever; for he chose Judah as leader, and in the house of Judah my father's house, and among my father's sons he took pleasure in me to make me king over all Israel. ⁵And of all my sons (for the Lord has given me many sons) he has chosen Solomon my son to sit upon the throne of the kingdom of the Lord over Israel. ⁶He said to me, 'It is Solomon your son who shall build my house and my courts, for I have chosen him to be my son, and I will be his father. ⁷I will establish his kingdom for ever if he continues resolute in keeping my commandments and my ordinances, as he is today.' ⁸Now therefore in the sight of all Israel, the assembly of the Lord, and in the hearing of our God, observe and seek out all the commandments of the Lord your God; that you may possess this good land, and leave it for an inheritance to your children after you for ever.

⁹"And you, Solomon my son, know the God of your father, and serve him with a whole heart and with a willing mind; for the Lord searches all hearts, and understands every plan and thought. If you seek him, he will be found by you; but if you forsake him, he will cast you off for ever. ¹⁰Take heed now, for the Lord has chosen you to build a house for the sanctuary; be strong, and do it."

¹¹Then David gave Solomon his son the plan of the vestibule of the temple, and of its houses, its treasuries, its upper rooms, and its inner chambers, and of the room for the mercy seat; ¹²and the plan of all that he had in mind for the courts of the house of the Lord, all the surrounding chambers, the treasuries of the house of God, and the treasuries for dedicated gifts; ¹³for the divisions of the priests and of the Levites, and all the work of the service in the house of the Lord; for all the vessels for the service in the house of the Lord, ¹⁴the weight of gold for all golden vessels for each service, the weight of silver vessels for each service, ¹⁵the weight of the golden lampstands and their lamps, the weight of gold for each lampstand and its lamps, the weight of silver for a lampstand and its lamps, according to the use of each lampstand in the service, ¹⁶the weight of gold for each table for the showbread, the silver for the silver tables, ¹⁷and pure gold for the forks, the basins, and the cups; for the golden bowls and the weight of each; for the silver bowls and the weight of each; ¹⁸for the altar of incense made of refined gold, and its weight; also his plan for the golden

chariot of the cherubim that spread their wings and covered the ark of the covenant of the Lord. [19]*All this he made clear by the writing from the hand of the Lord concerning it,[h] all the work to be done according to the plan.*

[20]*Then David said to Solomon his son, "Be strong and of good courage, and do it. Fear not, be not dismayed; for the Lord God, even my God, is with you. He will not fail you or forsake you, until all the work for the service of the house of the Lord is finished.* [21]*And behold the divisions of the priests and the Levites for all the service of the house of God; and with you in all the work will be every willing man who has skill for any kind of service; also the officers and all the people will be wholly at your command."*

h Cn: Heb *upon me*

OVERVIEW: As political prosperity is the business of emperors, so the condition of the church is the concern of shepherds and teachers (JOHN OF DAMASCUS). The temple of the Lord was built during the reigns in which the peace dominated (ORIGEN). We receive God's grace as grace alone, not according to our merit (AUGUSTINE). The Spirit of God dwells in our soul (JEROME). The fact that the entire height of the temple was 120 cubits refers to the same mystery as when the primitive church in Jerusalem, after the passion and resurrection and ascension of the Lord into heaven, received the grace of the Holy Spirit in the same number of men (BEDE).

28:3 You Are a Warrior and Have Shed Blood

GOD GAVE THE KINGDOM TO DAVID. JOHN OF DAMASCUS: "Remember your leaders, those who spoke to you the Word of God; consider the outcome of their life and imitate their faith."[1] Emperors have not preached the word to you, but apostles and prophets, shepherds and teachers. When God gave commands to David concerning the house David intended to build for him, he said to him, "You may not build a house for my name, for you are a warrior and have shed blood." "Pay all of them their dues," the apostle Paul says, "taxes to whom taxes are due, revenue to whom revenue is due, respect to whom respect is due, honor to whom honor is due."[2] Political prosper-

ity is the business of emperors; the condition of the church is the concern of shepherds and teachers. Any other method is piracy, brothers. Saul tore Samuel's cloak, and what was the consequence? God tore the kingdom away from him and gave it to David the meek.[3] ON DIVINE IMAGES, SECOND APOLOGY 12.[4]

THE TEMPLE OF PEACE. ORIGEN: Consider whether the story about David and Solomon concerning the temple hints at something like this. For when David, who wages the wars of the Lord and stands firm against many personal enemies and enemies of Israel, wishes to build a temple for God, he is prevented by God through Nathan, who says to him, "You shall not build me a house, because you are a man of blood."

Solomon, however, who saw God in a dream and received wisdom in a dream (for the reality [of God] was reserved for him who said, "Behold, a greater than Solomon is here"),[5] who enjoyed the profoundest peace so that each person at that time rested under his own vine and under his own fig tree and who was named after the peace in his time (for Solomon means "peaceful"),[6] because of this peace has time to construct the famous temple for God. The temple for God is also rebuilt in the times of Esdras, when the truth overcomes wine along with the hostile king

[1]Heb 13:7. [2]Rom 13:7. [3]1 Sam 15:27-28. [4]JDDI 59-60. [5]Mt 12:42. [6]See 1 Chron 22:9.

and the women.[7] Commentary on the Gospel of John 6.4-5.[8]

28:9 If You Seek God

Being with God. Augustine: There is a passage in the first book of the same Chronicles that declares the choice of the will: "And you, Solomon, my son, know you the God of your father and serve him with a perfect heart and with a willing mind, for the Lord searches all hearts and understands all the imaginations of the thoughts; if you seek him, he will be found of you; but if you forsake him, he will cast you off forever." But these people find some room for human merit in the clause "if you seek him," and then the grace is thought to be given according to this merit in what is said in the ensuing words, "he will be found of you." And so they labor with all their might to show that God's grace is given according to our merits, in other words, that grace is not grace. For, as the apostle most expressly says, to them who receive reward according to merit "the recompense is not reckoned of grace but of debt."[9] On Grace and Free Will 11.[10]

The Spirit of God Dwells in You. Jerome: "Do you know that you are the temple of God and that the Spirit of God dwells in you? If anyone destroys the temple of God, him will God destroy."[11] And in another place: "The Lord is with you as long as you are with him. If you abandon him, he also will abandon you." Against the Pelagians 3.1.[12]

28:11-12 David Gave to Solomon the Plan of the Temple

The Plan for Building the Temple. Bede: It is to be noted, of course, that the thirty cubits of height spoken of above reached to the middle story; from there on to the third story another thirty cubits were added until the portico that was around the temple on the south and north and east reached the roof, as we learn from Jose-

phus's account;[13] from there to the top of the temple roof was another sixty cubits, and so the total height of the house according to the book of Paralipomenon amounted to 120 cubits.[14] Also the portico that was in front of the temple to the east, according to the account of the aforesaid volume, was the same number of cubits in height. That is, the porticoes around the temple of which we have just spoken, this book calls treasuries and inner chambers. David, it says, "gave his son Solomon a plan of the portico, and of the temple, and of the treasuries, and of the upper room, and of the inner chambers and of the room for the mercy seat"; here too he refers to the outer houses that were outside the courtyard of the priests surrounding the temple, when he adds, "As also of all the courts that he had in mind, and of the surrounding chambers for the treasuries of the house of the Lord and for the treasuries for dedicated objects." The fact that the entire height of the temple was 120 cubits refers to the same mystery as when the primitive church in Jerusalem after the passion and resurrection and ascension of the Lord into heaven received the grace of the Holy Spirit in the same number of men.[15] For fifteen, which is the sum of seven and eight, is sometimes taken to signify the life that is now lived in the sabbath rest of the souls of the faithful[16] but will be brought to perfection at the end of the world by the resurrection of their immortal bodies. Now this fifteen arranged in a triangle, that is, numbered with all its parts, makes 120. Hence by the number 120 the great happiness of the elect in the life to come is aptly represented, and by it the third story of the Lord's house is aptly completed because after the present hardships of the faithful and after their souls receive their rest in the life to come, the complete happiness of the whole church will be achieved in the glory of the resurrection. To this mystery likewise refers, as we have said, the fact that the Lord on rising from

---

[7]See 1 Ezra 4:36-38 (LXX). [8]FC 80:168-69. [9]Rom 4:4. [10]NPNF 1 5:448*. [11]1 Cor 3:16-17. [12]FC 53:348. [13]Josephus *Antiquities of the Jews* 8.3.2. [14]See 2 Chron 3:4. [15]See Acts 1:16. [16]See Heb 4:9.

the dead and ascending into heaven sent to this number of men in tongues of fire the Holy Spirit, who enabled them, though differing from each other on account of the diversity of their languages, suddenly to speak in his praise in a common tongue by giving them a knowledge of all languages.[17] For the church too in its own turn rising from the dead and ascending to heaven in incorruptible flesh will be fully and perfectly enlightened by the gift of the Holy Spirit when,

according to the promise of the apostle, "God" will be "all in all."[18] Then there will be complete unity of languages universally for the preaching of the wonderful works of God because all join with one mind and voice in praising the glory of the divine majesty that they see before them. On the Temple 1.8.2.[19]

---

[17]See Acts 2:3-4. [18]1 Cor 15:28. [19]TTH 21:30-32.

29:1-30 FROM DAVID TO SOLOMON

[1]And David the king said to all the assembly, "Solomon my son, whom alone God has chosen, is young and inexperienced, and the work is great; for the palace will not be for man but for the Lord God. [2]So I have provided for the house of my God, so far as I was able, the gold for the things of gold, the silver for the things of silver, and the bronze for the things of bronze, the iron for the things of iron, and wood for the things of wood, besides great quantities of onyx and stones for setting, antimony, colored stones, all sorts of precious stones, and marble."

Overview: The stones of which the temple was made were white and precious because they were produced on the island of Paros (Bede).

29:2 Precious Stones

The Stones for Building the Temple.
Bede: What color the stones were with which the temple was made is openly stated in the book of Paralipomenon when David said to Solomon on showing him the materials of the temple that he

had procured, "I have prepared all manner of precious stones and marble of Paros in great abundance." White marble is called Parian marble because it was produced on the island of that name. Hence the poet writes of it: "[past the] Isle of Olives, and then past snow-white Paros and the Cyclades sprinkled about the sea we sped o'er the waters tossed by many a wind."[1] On the Temple 1.4.5.[2]

---

[1]Virgil Aeneid 3:126-27. [2]TTH 21:17.

2 CHRONICLES

1:1-17 THE SOLEMN OFFERING OF SOLOMON

[1]Solomon the son of David established himself in his kingdom, and the LORD his God was with him and made him exceedingly great.

[2]Solomon spoke to all Israel, to the commanders of thousands and of hundreds, to the judges, and to all the leaders in all Israel, the heads of fathers' houses. [3]And Solomon, and all the assembly with him, went to the high place that was at Gibeon; for the tent of meeting of God, which Moses the servant of the LORD had made in the wilderness, was there. [4](But David had brought up the ark of God from Kiriath-jearim to the place that David had prepared for it, for he had pitched a tent for it in Jerusalem.) [5]Moreover the bronze altar that Bezalel the son of Uri, son of Hur, had made, was there before the tabernacle of the LORD. And Solomon and the assembly sought the LORD. [6]And Solomon went up there to the bronze altar before the LORD, which was at the tent of meeting, and offered a thousand burnt offerings upon it.

[7]In that night God appeared to Solomon, and said to him, "Ask what I shall give you." [8]And Solomon said to God, "Thou hast shown great and steadfast love to David my father, and hast made me king in his stead. [9]O LORD God, let thy promise to David my father be now fulfilled, for thou hast made me king over a people as many as the dust of the earth. [10]Give me now wisdom and knowledge to go out and come in before this people, for who can rule this thy people, that is so great?" [11]God answered Solomon, "Because this was in your heart, and you have not asked possessions, wealth, honor, or the life of those who hate you, and have not even asked long life, but have asked wisdom and knowledge for yourself that you may rule my people over whom I have made you king, [12]wisdom and knowledge are granted to you. I will also give you riches, possessions, and honor, such as none of the kings had who were before you, and none after you shall have the like." [13]So Solomon came from[a] the high place at Gibeon, from before the tent of meeting, to Jerusalem. And he reigned over Israel.

[14]Solomon gathered together chariots and horsemen; he had fourteen hundred chariots and twelve thousand horsemen, whom he stationed in the chariot cities and with the king in Jerusalem. [15]And the king made silver and gold as common in Jerusalem as stone, and he made cedar as plentiful as the sycamore of the Shephelah. [16]And Solomon's import of horses was from Egypt and Kue, and the king's traders received them from Kue for a price. [17]They imported a chariot from Egypt

for six hundred shekels of silver, and a horse for a hundred and fifty; likewise through them these were exported to all the kings of the Hittites and the kings of Syria.

a Gk Vg: Heb *to*

OVERVIEW: Ask and you will receive (CHRYSOSTOM). The truth is full of difficulty and obscurity. Solomon entered into the depth and declared the furthest point of wisdom to be the discovery of how very far off wisdom was from him (GREGORY OF NAZIANZUS). Solomon might judge his people "in wisdom" because the Lord had given him an abundance of prudence (ORIGEN).

1:7 God Appeared to Solomon

SPIRITUAL GIFTS. JOHN CHRYSOSTOM: You also therefore should ask nothing worldly, but all things spiritual, and you will surely receive. For so Solomon, because he asked what he ought, behold, how quickly he received. Two things now, you see, should be in one who prays: asking earnestly and asking what he ought, "since you too," said he, "though you are parents, wait for your children to ask; and if they should ask of you anything inexpedient, you refuse the gifts; just as, if it be expedient, you consent and bestow it." Do you too, considering these things, not withdraw until you receive; until you have found, do not retire; do not relax your diligence until the door is opened. For if you approach with this mind and say, "Except I receive, I will not depart," you will surely receive, provided you ask such things as are both suitable for him of whom you asked to give and expedient for you the petitioner. But what are these? To seek the things spiritual, all of them; to forgive them who have trespassed, and so to draw near asking forgiveness; "to lift up holy hands without wrath and doubting."[1] If we thus ask, we shall receive. As it is, surely our asking is a mockery and the act of drunken rather than of sober people.

"What then," said one, "if I ask even spiritual things, and do not receive?" You did not surely knock with earnestness; or you made yourself unworthy to receive; or did quickly stop asking.

"And wherefore," it may be inquired, "did he not say, what things we ought to ask"? No, truly, he has mentioned them all in what precedes and has signified for what things we ought to draw near. Do not say, then, "I drew near and did not receive." For in no case is it owing to God that we receive not, God who loves us so much as to surpass even parents, to surpass them as far as goodness does this evil nature. HOMILIES ON THE GOSPEL OF MATTHEW 23.5.[2]

1:10 Give Wisdom and Knowledge

THE SUBJECT OF GOD IS HARDER TO APPROACH. GREGORY OF NAZIANZUS: The truth, and the whole Word, is full of difficulty and obscurity; and as it were with a small instrument we are undertaking a great work, when with merely human wisdom we pursue the knowledge of the self-existent, and in company with, or not apart from, the senses, by which we are borne hither and thither and led into error, we apply ourselves to the search after things that are only to be grasped by the mind, and we are unable by meeting bare realities with bare intellect to approximate somewhat more closely to the truth and to mold the mind by its concepts. Now the subject of God is harder to come at, in proportion as it is more perfect than any other and is open to more objections, and the solutions of them are more laborious. For every objection, however small, stops and hinders the course of our argument and cuts off its further advance, just like people who suddenly check with the rein the horses in full career and turn them right round by the unexpected shock. Thus Solomon, who was the wisest of all people, whether before him or in

---

[1] Tim 2:8. [2] NPNF 1 10:161*.

his own time, to whom God gave breadth of heart and a flood of contemplation, more abundant than the sand, even he, the more he entered into the depth, the more dizzy he became, and he declared the furthest point of wisdom to be the discovery of how very far off it was from him.[3] On Theology, Theological Oration 2(28).21.[4]

A Man of Prudence. Origen: "There was no

wise man like you before you, and there will not be after you." Therefore, because the Lord had given [Solomon] an abundance of prudence, "like the sand of the sea,"[5] that he might judge his people "in wisdom," thus he could exercise many virtues at the same time. Homilies on Genesis 11.2.[6]

---

[3]Eccles 7:23. [4]NPNF 2 7:296. [5]See Gen 22:17. [6]FC 71:171*.

2:1-18 LAST PREPARATIONS FOR BUILDING THE TEMPLE

[1b]Now Solomon purposed to build a temple for the name of the Lord, and a royal palace for himself. [2c]And Solomon assigned seventy thousand men to bear burdens and eighty thousand to quarry in the hill country, and three thousand six hundred to oversee them. [3]And Solomon sent word to Huram the king of Tyre: "As you dealt with David my father and sent him cedar to build himself a house to dwell in, so deal with me. [4]Behold, I am about to build a house for the name of the Lord my God and dedicate it to him for the burning of incense of sweet spices before him, and for the continual offering of the showbread, and for burnt offerings morning and evening, on the sabbaths and the new moons and the appointed feasts of the Lord our God, as ordained for ever for Israel. [5]The house which I am to build will be great, for our God is greater than all gods. [6]But who is able to build him a house, since heaven, even highest heaven, cannot contain him? Who am I to build a house for him, except as a place to burn incense before him? [7]So now send me a man skilled to work in gold, silver, bronze, and iron, and in purple, crimson, and blue fabrics, trained also in engraving, to be with the skilled workers who are with me in Judah and Jerusalem, whom David my father provided. [8]Send me also cedar, cypress, and algum timber from Lebanon, for I know that your servants know how to cut timber in Lebanon. And my servants will be with your servants, [9]to prepare timber for me in abundance, for the house I am to build will be great and wonderful. [10]I will give for your servants, the hewers who cut timber, twenty thousand cors of crushed wheat, twenty thousand cors of barley, twenty thousand baths of wine, and twenty thousand baths of oil."

[11]Then Huram the king of Tyre answered in a letter which he sent to Solomon, "Because the Lord loves his people he has made you king over them." [12]Huram also said, "Blessed be the Lord God of Israel, who made heaven and earth, who has given King David a wise son, endued with

discretion and understanding, who will build a temple for the Lord, and a royal palace for himself.

[13]*"Now I have sent a skilled man, endued with understanding, Huramabi,* [14]*the son of a woman of the daughters of Dan, and his father was a man of Tyre. He is trained to work in gold, silver, bronze, iron, stone, and wood, and in purple, blue, and crimson fabrics and fine linen, and to do all sorts of engraving and execute any design that may be assigned him, with your craftsmen, the craftsmen of my lord, David your father.* [15]*Now therefore the wheat and barley, oil and wine, of which my lord has spoken, let him send to his servants;* [16]*and we will cut whatever timber you need from Lebanon, and bring it to you in rafts by sea to Joppa, so that you may take it up to Jerusalem."*

[17]*Then Solomon took a census of all the aliens who were in the land of Israel, after the census of them which David his father had taken; and there were found a hundred and fifty-three thousand six hundred.* [18]*Seventy thousand of them he assigned to bear burdens, eighty thousand to quarry in the hill country, and three thousand six hundred as overseers to make the people work.*

b Ch 1.18 in Heb   c Ch 2.1 in Heb

Overview: By overseers' teaching authority we are instructed in all things how best to teach the ignorant and correct the contemptuous. The aforesaid overseers are rightly recorded as numbering seven thousand and eight thousand, but the perfect works of good people are appropriately symbolized by the number six. Nor should we pass over the fact that these seventy and eighty thousand hod carriers and stonemasons with their overseers were not from Israel but from among the proselytes (Bede).

2:17-18 Solomon Took a Census

The Perfect Works of Good People.

Bede: Now the overseers who were in charge of each operation are the writers of sacred Scripture by whose teaching authority we are instructed in all things as to how best to teach the ignorant and correct the contemptuous, to bear each other's burdens so that we may fulfill the law of Christ. But the more each one labors in giving his neighbors support in their needs or in correcting their mistakes, the more surely may he expect in the life to come the rewards whether of peace of soul after death or of blessed immortality of body. Consequently, the aforesaid overseers are rightly

recorded as numbering 70,000 and 80,000: 70,000 because of the sabbath rest of souls for the seventh day is consecrated to the sabbath, that is, rest; 80,000 because of the hope of resurrection on the eighth day, that is, after the sabbath, has already taken place in the Lord, and, it is hoped, will take place in us also on the eighth day and in the eighth age to come. The overseers, on the other hand, were 3,300, doubtless because of faith in the holy Trinity that the holy Scriptures proclaim to us. But the fact that in the book of Paralipomenon the number 3,000 is written instead of 3,300 has to do with the very same perfection of people of sublime virtue. For because the Lord completed the adornment of the world in the number six, the perfect works of good people are rightly apt to be symbolized by the same number, and because holy Scripture teaches that we must have the works of piety as well as true faith, the overseers of the temple works are rightly said to be 3,600. Nor should we pass over the fact that these 70,000 and 80,000 hod carriers[1] and stonemasons with their overseers were not from Israel but from among the prose-

---

[1] A hod was a kind of wooden tray with a handle, used for carrying mortar or bricks on one's shoulders.

lytes, that is, strangers who sojourned among them. For it is written in the book of Paralipomenon, "And Solomon took a census of all the proselytes resident in the land of Israel, on the model of the census that David his father had taken; and it was found that they numbered 153,600. And he put 70,000 of them carrying burdens on their shoulders," and so forth. ON THE TEMPLE 1.3.4.[2]

---

[2]TTH 21:12-13*.

[3:1-17 THE BUILDING OF THE TEMPLE]
[See commentary on 1 Kings 6-7]

[4: 1-22 THE SACRED FURNISHINGS OF THE TEMPLE]
[See commentary on 1 Kings 7:13-51]

[5:1-14 TRANSPORT OF THE ARK]
[See commentary on 2 Samuel 6:1-11]

[6:1-12 SOLOMON CONSECRATES THE TEMPLE]
[See commentary on 1 Kings 8:12-53]

[7:1-22 CELEBRATION IN ISRAEL AND APPEARANCE OF GOD]
[See commentary on 1 Kings 8-9]

[8:1-17 WORKS OF SOLOMON]
[See commentary on 1 Kings 9]

[9:1-28 VISIT OF THE QUEEN OF SHEBA
AND MAGNIFICENCE OF SOLOMON]
[See commentary on 1 Kings 10]

[9:29-31 DEATH OF SOLOMON]
[1 Kings 11:41-43]

[10:1-19 POLITICIANS' SCHISM]
[See commentary on 1 Kings 12]

[11:1-23 THE REIGN AND THE FAMILY]
OF REHOBOAM
[See commentary on 1 Kings 12; 14:21-31]

[12:1-16 INFIDELITY OF REHOBOAM]

[13:1-22 ABIJAH, KING OF JUDAH]

14:1-15 THE REIGN OF ASA

⁹*Zerah the Ethiopian came out against them with an army of a million men and three hundred chariots, and came as far as Mareshah. ¹⁰And Asa went out to meet him, and they drew up their lines of battle in the valley of Zephathah at Mareshah. ¹¹And Asa cried to the LORD his God, "O LORD, there is none like thee to help, between the mighty and the weak. Help us, O LORD our God, for we rely on thee, and in thy name we have come against this multitude. O LORD, thou art our God; let not man prevail against thee." ¹²So the LORD defeated the Ethiopians before Asa and before Judah, and the Ethiopians fled.*

OVERVIEW: The vast army was defeated by the power of Asa's prayer (APHRAHAT).

14:10-15 In God's Name

THE POWER OF PRAYER. APHRAHAT: Asa prayed, and his prayer manifested great power: when Zerah the Indian [Ethiopian] went out against him with an army of one million with him, Asa then prayed, saying, "By this shall your power be known, O our God, when you finish off a vast people by means of a small people." God heard his prayer and sent his angel to rout them. Thus the vast army was defeated by the power of Asa's prayer. DEMONSTRATION 4.8.[1]

[1]CS 101:12.

15:1-19 THE REFORMS OF ASA

¹*The Spirit of God came upon Azariah the son of Oded, ²and he went out to meet Asa, and said to him, "Hear me, Asa, and all Judah and Benjamin: The LORD is with you, while you are with him. If you seek him, he will be found by you, but if you forsake him, he will forsake you. ³For a long time Israel was without the true God, and without a teaching priest, and without law; ⁴but when in their distress they turned to the LORD, the God of Israel, and sought him, he was found by them. ⁵In those times there was no peace to him who went out or to him who came in, for great disturbances afflicted all the inhabitants of the lands. ⁶They were broken in pieces, nation against*

nation and city against city, for God troubled them with every sort of distress. ⁷But you, take courage! Do not let you hands be weak, for your work shall be rewarded."

⁸When Asa heard these words, the prophecy of Azariah the son of Oded,ᶜ he took courage, and put away the abominable idols from all the land of Judah and Benjamin and from the cities which he had taken in the hill country of Ephraim, and he repaired the altar of the LORD that was in front of the vestibule of the house of the LORD.ᵈ ⁹And he gathered all Judah and Benjamin, and those from Ephraim, Manasseh, and Simeon who were sojourning with them, for great numbers had deserted to him from Israel when they saw that the LORD his God was with him. ¹⁰They were gathered at Jerusalem in the third month of the fifteenth year of the reign of Asa. ¹¹They sacrificed to the LORD on that day, from the spoil which they had brought, seven hundred oxen and seven thousand sheep. ¹²And they entered into a covenant to seek the LORD, the God of their fathers, with all their heart and with all their soul; ¹³and that whoever would not seek the LORD, the God of Israel, should be put to death, whether young or old, man or woman. ¹⁴They took oath to the LORD with a loud voice, and with shouting, and with trumpets, and with horns. ¹⁵And all Judah rejoiced over the oath; for they had sworn with all their heart, and had sought him with their whole desire, and he was found by them, and the LORD gave them rest round about.

¹⁶Even Maacah, his mother, King Asa removed from being queen mother because she had made an abominable image for Asherah. Asa cut down her image, crushed it, and burned it at the brook Kidron. ¹⁷But the high places were not taken out of Israel. Nevertheless the heart of Asa was blameless all his days. ¹⁸And he brought into the house of God the votive gifts of his father and his own votive gifts, silver, and gold, and vessels. ¹⁹And there was no more war until the thirty-fifth year of the reign of Asa.

c Compare Syr Vg: Heb *the prophecy, Oded the prophet*   d Heb *the vestibule of the* LORD

OVERVIEW: Persevering in faith and virtue, we may attain to the palm and the crown (CYPRIAN). As humans have many facial expressions, so also do the feelings of their hearts vary. If it were possible for us to be always immersed in the waters of baptism, sins would fly over our heads and leave us untouched (JEROME). Impiety always leads us to worship false idols and to drive us away from the ineffable goodness of God (THEODORET).

15:2 The Lord Is with You

WE MUST PERSEVERE IN FAITH. CYPRIAN: We must press on and persevere in faith and virtue and in completion of heavenly and spiritual grace, that we may attain to the palm and the crown. In

the book of Chronicles [we read], "The Lord is with you so long as you also are with him; but if you forsake him, he will forsake you." EXHORTATION TO MARTYRDOM 8.[1]

IF WE WERE CONTINUALLY IMMERSED IN WATERS OF BAPTISM. JEROME: When we have been baptized we are told, "Behold, you are made whole; sin no more lest a worse thing happen to you."[2] And again, "Don't you know that you are a temple of God and that the Spirit of God dwells in you? If anyone profanes the temple of God, God shall destroy him."[3] And in another place, "The Lord is with you so long as you are with him: if you forsake him, he will also forsake you." Where is the

---

[1]FC 36:326*. [2]Jn 5:14. [3]1 Cor 3:16-17.

person, do you suppose, in whom as in a shrine and sanctuary the purity of Christ is permanent and in whose case the serenity of the temple is saddened by no cloud of sin? We cannot always have the same countenance, though the philosophers falsely boast that this was the experience of Socrates; how much less can our minds be always the same! As people have many facial expressions, so also do the feelings of their hearts vary. If it were possible for us to be always immersed in the waters of baptism, sins would fly over our heads and leave us untouched. The Holy Spirit would protect us. But the enemy assails us, and when conquered he does not depart but is ever lying in ambush, that he may secretly shoot the upright in heart. AGAINST THE PELAGIANS 3.1.[4]

15:3 Israel Was Without the True God

THE DAMAGES OF IMPIETY. THEODORET OF CYR: The passage shows the impiety of the ten tribes: "For a long time Israel was without the true God, and without a teaching priest and without law; but when in their distress they turned to the Lord, the God of Israel, and sought him, he was found by them." Do not imitate, the Scripture says, the impiety of your brothers. They do not preach the true God but pursue false idols. For this reason they have been deprived of the priests and the teachers, who could teach them the law of God. Experience, therefore, becomes our guide in showing the damages of impiety. For after being afflicted by any kind of calamity they implore now the help of God, giving themselves entirely to the ineffable goodness of the Lord. QUESTION I, ON 2 CHRONICLES.[5]

---

[4]NPNF 2 6:472*. [5]PG 80:828.

[16:1-14 LAST ACTS OF ASA]

17:1-19 JEHOSHAPHAT, THE NEW KING OF JUDAH

³The LORD was with Jehoshaphat, because he walked in the earlier ways of his father;[e] he did not seek the Baals, ⁴but sought the God of his father and walked in his commandments, and not according to the ways of Israel. ⁵Therefore the LORD established the kingdom in his hand; and all Judah brought tribute to Jehoshaphat; and he had great riches and honor. ⁶His heart was courageous in the ways of the LORD; and furthermore he took the high places and the Asherim out of Judah.

e Another reading is *his father David*

OVERVIEW: Jehoshaphat possessed the justice that David later committed, and the Lord established the kingdom in his hand (JEROME).

17:3-6 Jehoshaphat Followed the Way of the Lord

JEHOSHAPHAT, SUCCESSOR OF DAVID IN JUSTICE AND GLORY. JEROME: Of Jehoshaphat, the king of Judah, it is written, "And the Lord was with Jehoshaphat, who walked in the first ways of David, his father." From this it is clear that Jehoshaphat possessed the justice that David first possessed and that he did not commit the sins that David later committed. "He trusted not in Baalim," he says, "but in the God of his father and walked in his commandments, and not according to the sins of Israel. And the Lord established the kingdom in his hand and all Judah brought presents to Jehoshaphat. And he acquired immense wealth and riches and much glory." "And when his heart had taken courage for the ways of the Lord, he took away also the high places and the groves out of Judah." AGAINST THE PELAGIANS 2.21.[1]

---

[1]FC 53:329.

18:1-34 JEHOSHAPHAT MAKES A COVENANT WITH AHAB

[18]And Micaiah said, "Therefore hear the word of the LORD: I saw the LORD sitting on his throne, and all the host of heaven standing on his right hand and on his left; [19]and the LORD said, 'Who will entice Ahab the king of Israel, that he may go up and fall at Ramoth-gilead?' And one said one thing, and another said another. [20]Then a spirit came forward and stood before the LORD, saying, 'I will entice him.' And the LORD said to him, 'By what means?' [21]And he said, 'I will go forth, and will be a lying spirit in the mouth of all his prophets.' And he said, 'You are to entice him, and you shall succeed; go forth and do so.'"

OVERVIEW: God is so merciful that for the sake of our salvation he foregoes being spoken of in terms befitting his dignity (CHRYSOSTOM).

18:18-21 A Lying Spirit in the Mouth of the Prophets

IN ACCORDANCE WITH HIS DIGNITY. JOHN CHRYSOSTOM: In the case of Ahab, God said, "Who shall deceive Ahab for me?" In addition, there is also the fact that he always made himself available for comparison with the pagan gods, and all this is below the dignity of God. However, viewed in another way, it becomes worthy of him. I say this for he is so merciful that for the sake of our salvation he foregoes being spoken of in terms befitting his dignity. HOMILIES ON THE GOSPEL OF JOHN 64.2.[1]

---

[1]FC 41:195*.

19:1-11 PEACE IN THE REIGN OF JEHOSHAPHAT

¹*Jehoshaphat the king of Judah returned in safety to his house in Jerusalem.* ²*But Jehu the son of Hanani the seer went out to meet him, and said to King Jehoshaphat, "Should you help the wicked and love those who hate the* LORD? *Because of this, wrath has gone out against you from the* LORD. ³*Nevertheless some good is found in you, for you destroyed the Asherahs out of the land, and have set your heart to seek God."*

⁴*Jehoshaphat dwelt at Jerusalem; and he went out again among the people, from Beer-sheba to the hill country of Ephraim, and brought them back to the* LORD, *the God of their fathers.* ⁵*He appointed judges in the land in all the fortified cities of Judah, city by city,* ⁶*and said to the judges, "Consider what you do, for you judge not for man but for the* LORD; *he is with you in giving judgment.* ⁷*Now then, let the fear of the* LORD *be upon you; take heed what you do, for there is no perversion of justice with the* LORD *our God, or partiality, or taking bribes."*

⁸*Moreover in Jerusalem Jehoshaphat appointed certain Levites and priests and heads of families of Israel, to give judgment for the* LORD *and to decide disputed cases. They had their seat at Jerusalem.* ⁹*And he charged them: "Thus you shall do in the fear of the* LORD, *in faithfulness, and with your whole heart:* ¹⁰*whenever a case comes to you from your brethren who live in their cities, concerning bloodshed, law or commandment, statutes or ordinances, then you shall instruct them, that they may not incur guilt before the* LORD *and wrath may not come upon you and your brethren. Thus you shall do, and you will not incur guilt.* ¹¹*And behold, Amariah the chief priest is over you in all matters of the* LORD; *and Zebadiah the son of Ishmael, the governor of the house of Judah, in all the king's matters; and the Levites will serve you as officers. Deal courageously, and may the* LORD *be with the upright!"*

OVERVIEW: God does not examine us according to the part, because by examining the whole and not taking the part only into account, you will find that your neighbor is better than you (BASIL). Moreover, the Lord alone cannot err in his judgment because he cannot be deceived in his knowledge (AUGUSTINE).

19:3 Some Good Is Found

GOD DOES NOT EXAMINE US ACCORDING TO THE PART. BASIL THE GREAT: If you see your neighbor committing sin, take care not to dwell exclusively on his sin, but think of the many things he has done and continues to do rightly. Many times, by examining the whole and not taking the part only into account, you will find that he is better than you. God does not examine humans according to the part, for he says, "I come to gather together their works and thoughts."[1] Furthermore, when he rebuked Josaphat for a sin committed in an unguarded moment, he mentioned also the good he had done, saying, "But good works are found in you." ON HUMILITY.[2]

---

[1]Is 66:18. [2]FC 9:483*.

19:7 No Perversion of Justice

GOD CANNOT ERR IN HIS JUDGMENT. AUGUSTINE: Do not doubt that this duty of ours is a part of religion because God, "with whom there is no iniquity," whose power is supreme, who not only sees what each one is but also foresees what he will be, who alone cannot err in his judgment because he cannot be deceived in his knowledge, nevertheless acts as the Gospel expresses it, "He makes his sun to rise on the good and bad, and rains on the just and unjust."³ LETTER 153.⁴

---

³Mt 5:45. ⁴FC 20:282-83*.

[20:1-37 WARS AND VICTORIES OF JEHOSHAPHAT UNTIL HIS DEATH]

21:1-20 THE IMPIOUS JEHORAM SUCCEEDS JEHOSHAPHAT

> ¹⁶*And the LORD stirred up against Jehoram the anger of the Philistines and of the Arabs who are near the Ethiopians;* ¹⁷*and they came up against Judah, and invaded it, and carried away all the possessions they found that belonged to the king's house, and also his sons and his wives, so that no son was left to him except Jehoahaz, his youngest son.*

OVERVIEW: When Philistines and Arabs came to the land of Judah and wasted it, we had a clear indication of how God stirs up enemies to lay waste those countries that he judges to be deserving of such punishment (AUGUSTINE).

21:16-17 Philistines and Arabs Invade Judah

THE JUDGMENT OF THE LORD. AUGUSTINE: Just read the books of Paralipomenon and this is what you will find written in the second book: "And the Lord stirred up against Jehoram the spirit of the Philistines and of the Arabians who border on the Ethiopians. And they came up to the land of Judah and wasted it, and they carried away all substance that was found in the king's house." Here we have a clear indication of how God stirs up enemies to lay waste those countries that he judges to be deserving of such punishment. And yet, was it not of their own will that the Philistines and Arabs came to lay waste the country of Judah? Or did they so come of their own will that the Scripture lies where it tells us that the Lord stirred up their spirit to do so? On the contrary. Both statements are true because they did come of their own will and God did stir up their spirit. The same thing could also be expressed by saying that God both stirred up their spirit and that they came nevertheless of their own will. For the Almighty, who cannot possibly will anything unjust, is able to set in motion even the inclinations of their will in human hearts in order to accomplish through these people whatever he wishes to achieve through their agency. ON GRACE AND FREE WILL 21.42.[1]

---

[1]FC 59:301.

22:1-12 THE REIGN OF AHAZIAH AND THE USURPATION OF ATHALIAH

[2]Ahaziah was forty-two years old when he began to reign, and he reigned one year in Jerusalem. [8]And when Jehu was executing judgment upon the house of Ahab, he met the princes of Judah and the sons of Ahaziah's brothers, who attended Ahaziah, and he killed them. [9]He searched for Ahaziah, and he was captured while hiding in Samaria, and he was brought to Jehu and put to death. They buried him, for they said, "He is the grandson of Jehoshaphat, who sought the LORD with all his heart." And the house of Ahaziah had no one able to rule the kingdom.

OVERVIEW: The justice one possesses in the past is destroyed by the fact that he has committed sin and has refused the God's law (JEROME).

22:8-9 Jehu Executed Judgment on the House of Ahab

SON OF JEHOSHAPHAT. JEROME: The Lord established the kingdom in Jehoshaphat's hand, and all Judah brought presents to him. And he acquired immense wealth and riches and much glory.... And, lest we suppose that the justice he possessed in the past was destroyed by the fact that he committed this sin and was reproved by the prophet, it is written subsequently of Uzziah, his descendant, that Jehu found him lying in Samaria, and, when he was brought in, he killed him: "And they buried him," he says, "because he was the son of Jehoshaphat, who has sought the Lord with all his heart." AGAINST THE PELAGIANS 2.21.[1]

---

[1]FC 53:329-30*.

[23:1-21 JEHOIADA PROCLAIMS JOASH KING]

24:1-27 JOASH IS THE NEW KING OF JUDAH

[1]*Joash was seven years old when he began to reign, and he reigned forty years in Jerusalem; his mother's name was Zibiah of Beer-sheba.* [2]*And Joash did what was right in the eyes of the* LORD *all the days of Jehoiada the priest.* [3]*Jehoiada got for him two wives, and he had sons and daughters.*

[4]*After this Joash decided to restore the house of the* LORD. [5]*And he gathered the priests and the Levites, and said to them, "Go out to the cities of Judah, and gather from all Israel money to repair the house of your God from year to year; and see that you hasten the matter." But the Levites did not hasten it.* [6]*So the king summoned Jehoiada the chief, and said to him, "Why have you not required the Levites to bring in from Judah and Jerusalem the tax levied by Moses, the servant of the* LORD, *on*[m] *the congregation of Israel for the tent of testimony?"* [7]*For the sons of Athaliah, that wicked woman, had broken into the house of God; and had also used all the dedicated things of the house of the* LORD *for the Baals.*

[8]*So the king commanded, and they made a chest, and set it outside the gate of the house of the* LORD. [9]*And proclamation was made throughout Judah and Jerusalem, to bring in for the* LORD *the tax that Moses the servant of God laid upon Israel in the wilderness.* [10]*And all the princes and all the people rejoiced and brought their tax and dropped it into the chest until they had finished.* [11]*And whenever the chest was brought to the king's officers by the Levites, when they saw that there was much money in it, the king's secretary and the officer of the chief priest would come and empty the chest and take it and return it to its place. Thus they did day after day, and collected money in abundance.* [12]*And the king and Jehoiada gave it to those who had charge of the work of the house of the* LORD, *and they hired masons and carpenters to restore the house of the* LORD, *and also workers in iron and bronze to repair the house of the* LORD. [13]*So those who were engaged in the work labored, and the repairing went forward in their hands, and they restored the house of God to its proper condition and strengthened it.* [14]*And when they had finished, they brought the rest of the money before the king and Jehoiada, and with it were made utensils for the house of the* LORD, *both for the service and for the burnt offerings, and dishes for incense, and vessels of gold and silver. And they offered burnt offerings in the house of the* LORD *continually all the days of Jehoiada.*

[15]*But Jehoiada grew old and full of days, and died; he was a hundred and thirty years old at his death.* [16]*And they buried him in the city of David among the kings, because he had done good in Israel, and toward God and his house.*

[17]*Now after the death of Jehoiada the princes of Judah came and did obeisance to the king; then the king harkened to them.* [18]*And they forsook the house of the* LORD, *the God of their fathers, and served the Asherim and the idols. And wrath came upon Judah and Jerusalem for this their guilt.* [19]*Yet he sent prophets among them to bring them back to the* LORD; *these testified against them, but they would not give heed.*

²⁰Then the Spirit of God took possession ofⁿ Zechariah the son of Jehoiada the priest; and he stood above the people, and said to them, "Thus says God, 'Why do you transgress the commandments of the LORD, so that you cannot prosper? Because you have forsaken the LORD, he has forsaken you.'" ²¹But they conspired against him, and by command of the king they stoned him with stones in the court of the house of the LORD. ²²Thus Joash the king did not remember the kindness which Jehoiada, Zechariah's father, had shown him, but killed his son. And when he was dying, he said, "May the LORD see and avenge!"

²³ At the end of the year the army of the Syrians came up against Joash. They came to Judah and Jerusalem, and destroyed all the princes of the people from among the people, and sent all their spoil to the king of Damascus. ²⁴Though the army of the Syrians had come with few men, the LORD delivered into their hand a very great army, because they had forsaken the LORD, the God of their fathers. Thus they executed judgment on Joash.

²⁵When they had departed from him, leaving him severely wounded, his servants conspired against him because of the blood of the son^o of Jehoiada the priest, and slew him on his bed. So he died; and they buried him in the city of David, but they did not bury him in the tombs of the kings. ²⁶Those who conspired against him were Zabad the son of Shime-ath the Ammonitess, and Jehozabad the son of Shimrith the Moabitess. ²⁷Accounts of his sons, and of the many oracles against him, and of the rebuilding^p of the house of God are written in the Commentary on the Book of the Kings. And Amaziah his son reigned in his stead.

m Compare Vg: Heb *and*   n Heb *clothed itself with*   o Gk Vg: Heb *sons*   p Heb *founding*

OVERVIEW: Although the king is young, he could be meek, gentle and quiet (APOSTOLIC CONSTITUTIONS). Joash forsook the temple of the Lord and served groves and idols, and the consequence of his sin was that he was given over to shocking and filthy passions (CASSIAN). The church of the Lord remains closed against terrors. The camp of Christ, invincible and brave and fortified by the protecting Lord, does not yield to threats (CYPRIAN). Zechariah was a man of God (BEDE).

24:1 Joash Was Seven Years Old

AN EXAMPLE OF A YOUNG KING. APOSTOLIC CONSTITUTIONS: If in a small parish one advanced in years is not to be found, let some younger person who has a good report among his neighbors and is esteemed by them worthy of the office of a bishop—who has carried himself from his youth with meekness and regularity, like a much elder person—after examination and a general good report, be ordained in peace. . . . Joash governed the people at seven years of age. Wherefore, although the person is young, let him be meek, gentle and quiet. CONSTITUTIONS OF THE HOLY APOSTLES 2.1.[1]

24:17-25 Perversion of Joash

THE CONSEQUENCE OF JOASH'S PRIDE. JOHN CASSIAN: Some such thing we read of in the book of Chronicles. For Joash the king of Judah at the age of seven was summoned by Jehoiada the priest to the kingdom and by the witness of Scripture is commended for all his actions as long as the aforesaid priest lived. But hear what Scripture relates of him after Jehoiada's death and how he was puffed up with pride and given over to a

---

[1]ANF 7:396.

most disgraceful state. "But after the death of Jehoiada the princes went in and worshiped the king: and he was soothed by their services and hearkened to them. And they forsook the temple of the Lord, the God of their fathers, and served groves and idols, and great wrath came on Judah and Jerusalem because of this sin." And after a little: "When a year was come about, the army of Syria came up against him: and they came to Judah and Jerusalem and killed all the princes of the people, and they sent all the spoils to the king to Damascus. And whereas there came a very small number of the Syrians, the Lord delivered into their hands an infinite multitude, because they had forsaken the Lord the God of their fathers; and on Joash they executed shameful judgments. And departing they left him in great diseases." You see how the consequence of pride was that he was given over to shocking and filthy passions. For he who is puffed up with pride and has permitted himself to be worshiped as God, is (as the apostle says) "given over to shameful passions and a reprobate mind to do those things that are not convenient."[2] And because, as Scripture says, "everyone who exalts his heart is unclean before God,"[3] he who is puffed up with swelling pride of heart is given over to most shameful confusion to be deluded by it, that when thus humbled he may know that he is unclean through impurity of the flesh and knowledge of impure desires, a thing that he had refused to recognize in the pride of his heart; and also that the shameful infection of the flesh may disclose the hidden impurity of the heart, which he contracted through the sin of pride, and that through the patent pollution of his body he may be proved to be impure, who did not formerly see that he had become unclean through the pride of his spirit. INSTITUTES 12.21.[4]

OBSERVING THE WILL OF GOD. CYPRIAN: If there are any who think that they can return to the church without prayers but with threats, or think that they can make an entrance for themselves, not by lamentations and reparations but by terrors, let them certainly consider that the church of the Lord remains closed against such and that the camp of Christ, invincible and brave and fortified by the protecting Lord, does not yield to threats. The bishop of God, holding the gospel, can be killed as observing the precepts of Christ; he cannot be conquered. Zachariah, the high priest of God, suggests and gives to us examples of virtue and of faith. When he could not be terrified by threats and stoning, he was killed in the temple of God, crying out and saying the same thing that we shout also against heretics and say, "Thus says the Lord: You have forsaken the ways of the Lord, and the Lord will forsake you." LETTER 59.17.[5]

ZECHARIAH, A HOLY MAN. BEDE: Zechariah was son of high priest Jehoiada, a man who was likewise very holy. They stoned Zechariah between the temple and the altar, as the Lord himself bore witness when he made mention of the blessed martyrs in the Gospel.[6] HOMILIES ON THE GOSPELS 1.3.[7]

---

[2]Rom 1:28. [3]Prov 16:5 (LXX). [4]NPNF 2 11:286-87. [5]FC 51:189. [6]See Lk 11:47. [7]CS 110:26*.

25:1-28 WARS UNDER AMAZIAH

[5]*Then Amaziah assembled the men of Judah, and set them by fathers' houses under commanders of thousands and of hundreds for all Judah and Benjamin. He mustered those twenty years old and upward, and found that they were three hundred thousand picked men, fit for war, able to handle spear and shield. [6]He hired also a hundred thousand mighty men of valor from Israel for a hundred talents of silver. [7]But a man of God came to him and said, "O king, do not let the army of Israel go with you, for the* Lord *is not with Israel, with all these Ephraimites. [8]But if you suppose that in this way you will be strong for war,[q] God will cast you down before the enemy; for God has power to help or to cast down." [9]And Amaziah said to the man of God, "But what shall we do about the hundred talents which I have given to the army of Israel?" The man of God answered, "The* Lord *is able to give you much more than this." [10]Then Amaziah discharged the army that had come to him from Ephraim, to go home again. And they became very angry with Judah, and returned home in fierce anger. [11]But Amaziah took courage, and led out his people, and went to the Valley of Salt and smote ten thousand men of Seir. [12]The men of Judah captured another ten thousand alive, and took them to the top of a rock and threw them down from the top of the rock; and they were all dashed to pieces. [13]But the men of the army whom Amaziah sent back, not letting them go with him to battle, fell upon the cities of Judah, from Samaria to Beth-horon, and killed three thousand people in them, and took much spoil.*

[14]*After Amaziah came from the slaughter of the Edomites, he brought the gods of the men of Seir, and set them up as his gods, and worshiped them, making offerings to them. [15]Therefore the* Lord *was angry with Amaziah and sent to him a prophet, who said to him, "Why have you resorted to the gods of a people, which did not deliver their own people from your hand?" [16]But as he was speaking the king said to him, "Have we made you a royal counselor? Stop! Why should you be put to death?" So the prophet stopped, but said, "I know that God has determined to destroy you, because you have done this and have not listened to my counsel."*

[17]*Then Amaziah king of Judah took counsel and sent to Joash the son of Jehoahaz, son of Jehu, king of Israel, saying, "Come, let us look one another in the face." [18]And Joash the king of Israel sent word to Amaziah king of Judah, "A thistle on Lebanon sent to a cedar on Lebanon, saying, 'Give your daughter to my son for a wife'; and a wild beast of Lebanon passed by and trampled down the thistle. [19]You say, 'See, I have smitten Edom,' and your heart has lifted you up in boastfulness. But now stay at home; why should you provoke trouble so that you fall, you and Judah with you?"*

[20]*But Amaziah would not listen; for it was of God, in order that he might give them into the hand of their enemies, because they had sought the gods of Edom.*

q Gk: Heb *But if you go, act, be strong for the battle*

OVERVIEW: The Lord, wishing to punish the sin of idolatry, wrought this in this man's heart, with whom he was indeed justly angry, not to listen to sound advice but to despise it, and go to the battle, in which he with his army was routed. Besides, the refusal to hear the truth leads to commission of sin, and this sin is also punishment for preceding sin (AUGUSTINE).

25:7-20 The Unfaithfulness of Amaziah

AMAZIAH WOULD NOT HEAR THE PRESCRIPTIONS OF GOD. AUGUSTINE: For the Almighty sets in motion even in the innermost hearts of people the movement of their will, so that he does through their agency whatsoever he wishes to perform through them—even he who knows not how to will anything in unrighteousness. What, again, is the purport of that which the man of God said to King Amaziah: "Let not the army of Israel go with you; for the Lord is not with Israel, even with all the children of Ephraim: for if you shall think to obtain with these, the Lord shall put you to flight before your enemies: for God has power either to strengthen or to put to flight"? Now, how does the power of God help some in war by giving them confidence and put others to flight by injecting fear into them, except it be that he who has made all things according to his own will, in heaven and on earth,[1] also works in human hearts? We read also what Joash, king of Israel, said when he sent a message to Amaziah, king of Judah, who wanted to fight with him. After certain other words, he added, "Now

stay at home; why do you challenge me to your hurt, that you should fall, you and Judah with you?"[2] Then the Scripture has added this sequel: "But Amaziah would not hear; for it came of God, that he might be delivered into their hands, because they sought after the gods of Edom." Behold, now, how God, wishing to punish the sin of idolatry, wrought this in this man's heart, with whom he was indeed justly angry, not to listen to sound advice but to despise it and go to the battle in which he with his army was routed. ON GRACE AND FREE WILL 42 [21].[3]

FROM A HIDDEN JUDGMENT OF GOD COMES PERVERSITY OF HEART. AUGUSTINE: Is not sin also punishment for sin where Amaziah, king of Judah, did not wish to hear the good advice of Jehoahaz, king of Israel, not to go to war? We read, "Amaziah would not listen to him because it was the Lord's will that he should be delivered into their hands, because they sought the god of Edom." We can recount many other events clearly showing that from a hidden judgment of God comes perversity of heart, with the result that refusal to hear the truth leads to commission of sin, and this sin is also punishment for preceding sin. For to believe a lie and not believe the truth is indeed sin, but it comes from the blindness of heart that by a hidden but just judgment of God is also punishment for sin. AGAINST JULIAN 5.3.12.[4]

---

[1]Ps 135:6 (134:6 LXX, Vg). [2]2 Kings 14:10. [3]NPNF 1 5:462*. [4]FC 35:254.

26:1-23 THE REIGN OF UZZIAH

[1]*And all the people of Judah took Uzziah, who was sixteen years old, and made him king instead of his father Amaziah. [2]He built Eloth and restored it to Judah, after the king slept with*

his fathers. ³Uzziah was sixteen years old when he began to reign, and he reigned fifty-two years in Jerusalem. His mother's name was Jecoliah of Jerusalem. ⁴And he did what was right in the eyes of the LORD, according to all that his father Amaziah had done. ⁵He set himself to seek God in the days of Zechariah, who instructed him in the fear of God; and as long as he sought the LORD, God made him prosper.

⁶He went out and made war against the Philistines, and broke down the wall of Gath and the wall of Jabneh and the wall of Ashdod; and he built cities in the territory of Ashdod and elsewhere among the Philistines. ⁷God helped him against the Philistines, and against the Arabs that dwelt in Gurbaal, and against the Me-unites. ⁸The Ammonites paid tribute to Uzziah, and his fame spread even to the border of Egypt, for he became very strong. ⁹Moreover Uzziah built towers in Jerusalem at the Corner Gate and at the Valley Gate and at the Angle, and fortified them. ¹⁰And he built towers in the wilderness, and hewed out many cisterns, for he had large herds, both in the Shephelah and in the plain, and he had farmers and vinedressers in the hills and in the fertile lands, for he loved the soil. ¹¹Moreover Uzziah had an army of soldiers, fit for war, in divisions according to the numbers in the muster made by Je-iel the secretary and Ma-aseiah the officer, under the direction of Hananiah, one of the king's commanders. ¹²The whole number of the heads of fathers' houses of mighty men of valor was two thousand six hundred. ¹³Under their command was an army of three hundred and seven thousand five hundred, who could make war with mighty power, to help the king against the enemy. ¹⁴And Uzziah prepared for all the army shields, spears, helmets, coats of mail, bows, and stones for slinging. ¹⁵In Jerusalem he made engines, invented by skilful men, to be on the towers and the corners, to shoot arrows and great stones. And his fame spread far, for he was marvelously helped, till he was strong.

¹⁶But when he was strong he grew proud, to his destruction. For he was false to the LORD his God, and entered the temple of the LORD to burn incense on the altar of incense. ¹⁷But Azariah the priest went in after him, with eighty priests of the LORD who were men of valor; ¹⁸and they withstood King Uzziah, and said to him, "It is not for you, Uzziah, to burn incense to the LORD, but for the priests the sons of Aaron, who are consecrated to burn incense. Go out of the sanctuary; for you have done wrong, and it will bring you no honor from the LORD God." ¹⁹Then Uzziah was angry. Now he had a censer in his hand to burn incense, and when he became angry with the priests leprosy broke out on his forehead, in the presence of the priests in the house of the LORD, by the altar of incense. ²⁰And Azariah the chief priest, and all the priests, looked at him, and behold, he was leprous in his forehead! And they thrust him out quickly, and he himself hastened to go out, because the LORD had smitten him. ²¹And King Uzziah was a leper to the day of his death, and being a leper dwelt in a separate house, for he was excluded from the house of the LORD. And Jotham his son was over the king's household, governing the people of the land.

²²Now the rest of the acts of Uzziah, from first to last, Isaiah the prophet the son of Amoz wrote. ²³And Uzziah slept with his fathers, and they buried him with his fathers in the burial field which belonged to the kings, for they said, "He is a leper." And Jotham his son reigned in his stead.

Overview: Uzziah was branded by the Lord's anger on that part of the body on which those who win the Lord's favor are sealed (Cyprian). Those who in the conflict of battle have escaped the danger of death fall before their own trophies and triumphs (Cassian). It is lawful only for the priests to do offerings and to approach the altar (Apostolic Constitutions). Only the chief priest has the right to enter the Holy of Holies (Pseudo-Dionysius). Sacred offices are conferred only by the laying on of the hands of the bishop (Apostolic Constitutions). Because of their sin, Adam and Uzziah fled and hid in shame of their bodies (Ephrem). Uzziah is described as at first having been righteous, and then it is related that he was lifted up in mind and dared to offer sacrifice to God himself, and his face became leprous in consequence. Also among the Jews who rejected the Christ of God, the true High Priest, a kind of leprosy infected their souls, as in the days of Uzziah (Eusebius).

26:16-23 A Leprous Disease

Uzziah Knew God's Indignation. Cyprian: When King Uzziah carried a censer and violently took on himself to sacrifice, against the law of God, and refused to submit or give place, despite the opposition of Azariah the priest, he was confounded by God's indignation and defiled with the markings of leprosy on his forehead, branded by the Lord's anger on that part of the body on which those who win the Lord's favor are sealed. The Unity of the Church 18.[1]

Uzziah Was Cast Down by Pride. John Cassian: Of Uzziah, the ancestor of this king of whom we have been speaking, himself also praised in all things by the witness of the Scripture, after great commendation for his virtue, after countless triumphs that he achieved by the merit of his devotion and faith, learn how he was cast down by the pride of vainglory. "And," we are told, "the name of Uzziah went forth, for the Lord helped him and had strengthened him. But

when he was made strong, his heart was lifted up to his destruction, and he neglected the Lord his God." . . . You see how dangerous the successes of prosperity generally are, so that those who could not be injured by adversity are ruined, unless they are careful, by prosperity; and those who in the conflict of battle have escaped the danger of death fall before their own trophies and triumphs. Institutes 11.11.[2]

Nobody Can Offer Anything Without the Priest. Apostolic Constitutions: As, therefore, it was not lawful for one of another tribe that was not a Levite to offer anything or to approach the altar without the priest, so also do you do nothing without the bishop; for if anyone does anything without the bishop, he does it to no purpose. For it will not be esteemed as of any avail to him. . . . For as Uzziah the king, who was not a priest and yet would exercise the functions of the priests, was smitten with leprosy for his transgression; so every lay person shall not be unpunished who despises God, and is so mad as to affront his priests and unjustly to snatch that honor to himself: not imitating Christ, "who glorified not himself to be made an high priest"[3] but waited till he heard from his Father, "The Lord swore and will not repent, You are a priest forever, after the order of Melchizedek."[4] If, therefore, Christ did not glorify himself without the Father, how dare anyone thrust himself into the priesthood who has not received that dignity from his superior and do such things that it is lawful only for the priests to do? Constitutions of the Holy Apostles 2.27.[5]

Everyone Must Remain Within the Order of His Ministry. Pseudo-Dionysius: This, then, is what must be said whenever someone acts out of place, even when he seems to be doing something right, for no one may get out of line in this way. Surely, there was nothing

---

[1]LCC 5:136-37. [2]NPNF 2 11:277-78. [3]Heb 5:5. [4]Ps 110:4 (109:4 LXX). [5]ANF 7:410*.

unseemly in the fact that Uzziah burned incense in honor of God. . . . And yet the Word of God bars anyone who has taken over a task that is not for him. It teaches that everyone must remain within the order of his ministry,[6] that only the chief priest has the right to enter the Holy of Holies, and this only once a year and in the state of hierarchical purity which Law demands.[7] The priests cover the holy things, and the Levites "do not touch the holy things, lest they die."[8] That is why the Lord was angered by the boldness of Uzziah. . . . To sum up, The perfect justice of God rejects those who break the law. LETTER 8.[9]

HOW SACRED OFFICES ARE CONFERRED.

APOSTOLIC CONSTITUTIONS: Neither do we permit the laity to perform any of the offices belonging to the priesthood, as, for instance, neither the sacrifice, nor baptism, nor the laying on of hands nor the blessing, whether the smaller or the greater, for "no one takes this honor to himself, but he that is called of God."[10] For such sacred offices are conferred by the laying on of the hands of the bishop. But a person to whom such an office is not committed but seizes on it for himself, he shall undergo the punishment of Uzziah. CONSTITUTIONS OF THE HOLY APOSTLES 3.10.[11]

ADAM LIKE UZZIAH.

EPHREM THE SYRIAN: In the midst of paradise God had planted the Tree of Knowledge to separate off, above and below, sanctuary from Holy of Holies. Adam made bold to touch and was smitten like Uzziah: the king became leprous, Adam was tripped. Being struck like Uzziah, he hastened to leave: both kings fled and hid, in shame of their bodies. HYMNS ON PARADISE 3.14.[12]

A DOUBLE LOSS.

EPHREM THE SYRIAN: Remember Uzziah, how he entered the sanctuary; by seeking to seize the priesthood he lost his kingdom. Adam, by wishing to enrich himself, incurred a double loss. Recognize in the sanctuary the Tree, in the censer the fruit and in the lep-rosy the nakedness. From these two treasures there proceeded harm in both cases. HYMNS ON PARADISE 12.4.[13]

IN THE DAYS OF UZZIAH.

EUSEBIUS OF CAESAREA: Uzziah is described as at first having been righteous, and then it is related that he was lifted up in mind and dared to offer sacrifice to God himself, and his face became leprous in consequence. But Josephus carefully studied the additional comments of the expounders as well, and a Hebrew of the Hebrews as he was, hear his description of the events of those times. He tells: "Though the priests urged Uzziah to go out of the temple and not to break the law of God, he angrily threatened them with death unless they held their peace. And meanwhile an earthquake shook the earth, and a bright light shone through a breach in the temple and struck the king's face, so that at once it became leprous. And before the city at the place called Eroga, the western half of the Mount was split asunder and rolling four *stadia* stopped at the eastern mountain, so as to block up the royal approach and gardens."[14] This I take from the work of Josephus on Jewish antiquities. And I found in the beginning of the prophet Amos the statement that he began to prophecy "in the days of Uzziah, king of Judah, two years before the earthquake."[15] What earthquake he does not clearly say. But I think the same prophet further on suggests this earthquake when he says, "I saw the Lord standing on the altar. And he said, Strike the altar, and the doors shall be shaken, and strike the heads of all, and the remnant I will slay with the sword."[16]

Here I understand a prediction of the earthquake, and of the destruction of the ancient solemnities of the Jewish race and of the worship practiced by them in Jerusalem, the ruin that should overtake them after the coming of our Savior, when, since they rejected the Christ of

---

[6]Num 7:5. [7]Lev 16:34; Exod 30:10; Heb 9:7. [8]Num 4:15. [9]*PDCW* 273-74. [10]Heb 5:4. [11]ANF 7:429. [12]*HOP* 95. [13]*HOP* 161-62. [14]Josephus *Antiquities of the Jews* 9.10.4. [15]Amos 1:1. [16]Amos 9:1.

God, the true High Priest, leprosy infected their souls, as in the days of Uzziah, when the Lord himself standing on the altar gave leave to him that struck, saying, "Strike the altar." Proof of

the Gospel 6.18.[17]

---

[17]*POG 2:32-33*.*

[27:1-9 REIGN OF JOHAM]
[See commentary on 2 Kings 15:32-38]

[28:1-27 AHAZ BEGINS TO REIGN]
[See commentary on 2 Kings 16]

29:1–32:33 THE RETURN OF PASSOVER AND HEZEKIAH'S REIGN
[See commentary on 2 Kings 18-20]

[1]*Hezekiah began to reign when he was twenty-five years old, and he reigned twenty-nine years in Jerusalem. His mother's name was Abijah the daughter of Zechariah.* [2]*And he did what was right in the eyes of the* Lord, *according to all that David his father had done.*

[3]*In the first year of his reign, in the first month, he opened the doors of the house of the* Lord, *and repaired them.* [4]*He brought in the priests and the Levites, and assembled them in the square on the east,* [5]*and said to them, "Hear me, Levites! Now sanctify yourselves, and sanctify the house of the* Lord, *the God of your fathers, and carry out the filth from the holy place.* [6]*For our fathers have been unfaithful and have done what was evil in the sight of the* Lord *our God. . . ."*

[12]*Then the Levites arose. . . .* [15]*They gathered their brethren, and sanctified themselves, and went in as the king had commanded, by the words of the* Lord, *to cleanse the house of the* Lord. [16]*The priests went into the inner part of the house of the* Lord *to cleanse it. . . .*

[20]*Then Hezekiah the king rose early and gathered the officials of the city, and went up to the house of the* Lord. [21]*And they brought seven bulls, seven rams, seven lambs, and seven he-goats*

for a sin offering for the kingdom and for the sanctuary and for Judah. And he commanded the priests the sons of Aaron to offer them on the altar of the Lord. . . .

[25] And he stationed the Levites in the house of the Lord *with cymbals, harps, and lyres. . . . [30] And they sang praises with gladness, and they bowed down and worshiped.*

[35] . . . Thus the service of the house of the Lord *was restored. [36] And Hezekiah and all the people rejoiced because of what God had done for the people; for the thing came about suddenly.*

30

Hezekiah sent to all Israel and Judah, and wrote letters also to Ephraim and Manasseh, that they should come to the house of the Lord at Jerusalem, to keep the passover to the Lord the God of Israel. . . .

[12] The hand of God was also upon Judah to give them one heart to do what the king and the princes commanded by the word of the Lord.

[13] And many people came together in Jerusalem to keep the feast of unleavened bread in the second month, a very great assembly. [14] They set to work and removed the altars that were in Jerusalem, and all the altars for burning incense they took away and threw into the Kidron valley. [15] And they killed the passover lamb on the fourteenth day of the second month. And the priests and the Levites were put to shame, so that they sanctified themselves, and brought burnt offerings into the house of the Lord. . . .

[23] Then the whole assembly agreed together to keep the feast for another seven days; so they kept it for another seven days with gladness. . . . [26] So there was great joy in Jerusalem, for since the time of Solomon the son of David king of Israel there had been nothing like this in Jerusalem. [27] Then the priests and the Levites arose and blessed the people, and their voice was heard, and their prayer came to his holy habitation in heaven.

31

Now when all this was finished, all Israel who were present went out to the cities of Judah and broke in pieces the pillars and hewed down the Asherim and broke down the high places and the altars throughout all Judah and Benjamin, and in Ephraim and Manasseh, until they had destroyed them all. . . .

[20] Thus Hezekiah did throughout all Judah; and he did what was good and right and faithful before the Lord *his God. [21] And every work that he undertook in the service of the house of God and in accordance with the law and the commandments, seeking his God, he did with all his heart, and prospered.*

32

After these things and these acts of faithfulness Sennacherib king of Assyria came and invaded Judah and encamped against the fortified cities, thinking to win them for himself. . . .

[9] After this Sennacherib king of Assyria, who was besieging Lachish with all his forces, sent his servants to Jerusalem to Hezekiah king of Judah and to all the people of Judah that were in Jerusalem, saying, [10] "Thus says Sennacherib king of Assyria, 'On what are you relying, that you stand siege in Jerusalem? [11] Is not Hezekiah misleading you, that he may give you over to die by famine and by thirst, when he tells you, "The Lord *our God will deliver us from the hand of the king of Assyria"? [12] Has not this same Hezekiah taken away his high places and his altars and commanded*

Judah and Jerusalem, "Before one altar you shall worship, and upon it you shall burn your sacrifices"? [13]Do you not know what I and my fathers have done to all the peoples of other lands? Were the gods of the nations of those lands at all able to deliver their lands out of my hand? [14]Who among all the gods of those nations which my fathers utterly destroyed was able to deliver his people from my hand, that your God should be able to deliver you from my hand? [15]Now therefore do not let Hezekiah deceive you or mislead you in this fashion, and do not believe him, for no god of any nation or kingdom has been able to deliver his people from my hand or from the hand of my fathers. How much less will your God deliver you out of my hand!" . . .

[20]Then Hezekiah the king and Isaiah the prophet, the son of Amoz, prayed because of this and cried to heaven. [21]And the LORD sent an angel, who cut off all the mighty warriors and commanders and officers in the camp of the king of Assyria. . . .

[24]In those days Hezekiah became sick and was at the point of death, and he prayed to the LORD; and he answered him and gave him a sign. [25]But Hezekiah did not make return according to the benefit done to him, for his heart was proud. Therefore wrath came upon him and Judah and Jerusalem. [26]But Hezekiah humbled himself for the pride of his heart, both he and the inhabitants of Jerusalem, so that the wrath of the LORD did not come upon them in the days of Hezekiah.

. . . [33]And Hezekiah slept with his fathers, and they buried him in the ascent of the tombs of the sons of David; and all Judah and the inhabitants of Jerusalem did him honor at his death. And Manasseh his son reigned in his stead.

Overview: Hezekiah reinstituted the celebration of Passover. As a man of prayer, he demonstrated where true strength was to be found and this is why he was able to defeat Sennacherib (Pseudo-Tertullian). Judah itself would have been resistant to such change had God not changed their hearts (Augustine). Hezekiah grew proud of his accomplishments, however, therefore God humbled him and Hezekiah repented. Had he not done so, he would have lost everything (Cassian).

30:1 Hezekiah's Invitation to Celebrate the Passover

The Man of Prayer Defeats Sennacherib. Pseudo-Tertullian:

As corrector of an inert People
That emulator [of David] Hezekiah arose;
He restored the Law to a sinful, forgetful
  people
All God's mandates of old, he first

Commanded the people to observe,
Who ended war by his prayers,[1]
Not by steel's point: he, dying, had a grant
Of years and times of life made to his tears:
Deservedly such honor his career obtained.
Five Books in Reply to Marcion 3.176-183.[2]

30:12 God Changes Judah's Mind

God Brings Judah Back. Augustine: For who is "drawn," if he was already willing? And yet no one comes unless he is willing. Therefore he is drawn in wondrous ways to will by the one who knows how to work within the very hearts of individuals. Not that people who are unwilling should believe—which cannot be—but that they should be made willing from being unwilling.

That this is true we do not surmise by human

---

[1]When one compares the sequence of events in Scripture, it will be seen that Hezekiah's reforms preceded his war with Sennacherib and Sennacherib's subsequent defeat. [2]ANF 4:153**.

conjecture but discern by the most evident authority of the divine Scriptures. It is read in the books of the Chronicles, "Also in Judah, the hand of God was made to give them one heart, to do the commandment of the king and of the princes in the word of the Lord." . . . Did the men of God who wrote these things—in fact, did the Spirit of God himself, under whose guidance such things were written by them—assail human free will? Away with the notion! But God has commended both the most righteous judgment and the most merciful aid of the Omnipotent in all cases. For it is enough for human beings to know that there is no unrighteousness with God. But how he dispenses those benefits, making some deservedly vessels of wrath, others graciously vessels of mercy—who has known the mind of the Lord, or who has been his counselor?[3] If, then, we attain to the honor of grace, let us not be ungrateful by attributing to ourselves what we have received. "For what do we have which we have not received?"?[4] AGAINST TWO LETTERS OF THE PELAGANS 37-38.[5]

32:24-26 Hezekiah's Pride

THE IMPORTANCE OF HUMILITY. JOHN CASSIAN: "In those days," we are told, "Hezekiah was sick unto death, and he prayed to the Lord, and the Lord heard him and gave him a sign," that, namely of which we read in the fourth book of the kingdoms, which was given by Isaiah the prophet through the going back of the sun. "But," it says, "he did not respond to the benefits which he had received, for his heart was proud. And wrath was kindled against him and against Judah and Jerusalem. He humbled himself afterwards because his heart had been proud, both he and the inhabitants of Jerusalem, and therefore the wrath of the Lord did not come upon them in the days of Hezekiah." How dangerous, how terrible is the malady of vanity! So much goodness, so many virtues, faith and devotion, great enough to prevail to change nature itself and the laws of the whole world—all destroyed by a single act of pride! The result would have been that all his good deeds would have been forgotten as if they had never existed, and he would at once have been subject to the wrath of the Lord unless he had appeased him by recovering his humility. Thus, he who, at the suggestion of pride, had fallen from so great a height of excellence, could only mount again to the height he had lost by the same steps of humility. INSTITUTES 11.10.[6]

---

[3]1 Cor 2:15. [4]1 Cor 4:7. [5]NPNF 1 5:389-90**. [6]NPNF 2 11:277**.

33:1-25 MANASSEH AND AMON
[See commentary on 2 Kings 21]

[1]*Manasseh was twelve years old when he began to reign, and he reigned fifty-five years in Jerusalem.* [2]*He did what was evil in the sight of the LORD, according to the abominable practices of the nations whom the LORD drove out before the people of Israel.* [3]*For he rebuilt the high places which his father Hezekiah had broken down, and erected altars to the Baals, and made Asherahs, and worshiped all the host of heaven, and served them.* [4]*And he built altars in the house of the LORD, of which the LORD had said, "In Jerusalem shall my name be for ever."* [5]*And he built altars for all*

the host of heaven in the two courts of the house of the Lord. ⁶And he burned his sons as an offering in the valley of the son of Hinnom, and practiced soothsaying and augury and sorcery, and dealt with mediums and with wizards. He did much evil in the sight of the Lord, provoking him to anger. ⁷And the image of the idol which he had made he set in the house of God, of which God said to David and to Solomon his son, "In this house, and in Jerusalem, which I have chosen out of all the tribes of Israel, I will put my name for ever; ⁸and I will no more remove the foot of Israel from the land which I appointed for your fathers, if only they will be careful to do all that I have commanded them, all the law, the statutes, and the ordinances given through Moses." ⁹Manasseh seduced Judah and the inhabitants of Jerusalem, so that they did more evil than the nations whom the Lord destroyed before the people of Israel.

¹⁰The Lord spoke to Manasseh and to his people, but they gave no heed. ¹¹Therefore the Lord brought upon them the commanders of the army of the king of Assyria, who took Manasseh with hooks and bound him with fetters of bronze and brought him to Babylon. ¹²And when he was in distress he entreated the favor of the Lord his God and humbled himself greatly before the God of his fathers. ¹³He prayed to him, and God received his entreaty and heard his supplication and brought him again to Jerusalem into his kingdom. Then Manasseh knew that the Lord was God.

¹⁴Afterwards he built an outer wall for the city of David west of Gihon, in the valley, and for the entrance into the Fish Gate, and carried it round Ophel, and raised it to a very great height; he also put commanders of the army in all the fortified cities in Judah. ¹⁵And he took away the foreign gods and the idol from the house of the Lord, and all the altars that he had built on the mountain of the house of the Lord and in Jerusalem, and he threw them outside of the city. ¹⁶He also restored the altar of the Lord and offered upon it sacrifices of peace offerings and of thanksgiving; and he commanded Judah to serve the Lord the God of Israel. ¹⁷Nevertheless the people still sacrificed at the high places, but only to the Lord their God.

¹⁸Now the rest of the acts of Manasseh, and his prayer to his God, and the words of the seers who spoke to him in the name of the Lord the God of Israel, behold, they are in the Chronicles of the Kings of Israel. ¹⁹And his prayer, and how God received his entreaty, and all his sin and his faithlessness, and the sites on which he built high places and set up the Asherim and the images, before he humbled himself, behold, they are written in the Chronicles of the Seers.ᵛ ²⁰So Manasseh slept with his fathers, and they buried him in his house; and Amon his son reigned in his stead.

²¹Amon was twenty-two years old when he began to reign, and he reigned two years in Jerusalem. ²²He did what was evil in the sight of the Lord, as Manasseh his father had done. Amon sacrificed to all the images that Manasseh his father had made, and served them. ²³And he did not humble himself before the Lord, as Manasseh his father had humbled himself, but this Amon incurred guilt more and more. ²⁴And his servants conspired against him and killed him in his house. ²⁵But the people of the land slew all those who had conspired against King Amon; and the people of the land made Josiah his son king in his stead.

v One Ms: Gk: Heb of Hozai

OVERVIEW. Hezekiah's son Manasseh shed much innocent blood, but he, like his father and others in the history of the faith, repented of what he had done, was forgiven and had his kingdom restored (JEROME). His baptism of repentant tears was accepted by God, washing away the wickedness he had committed (GREGORY OF NAZIANZUS). If he had despaired, he would have missed all he obtained, but he contended with the devil and finished the race (JOHN CHRYSOSTOM).

33:10-12 *The Punishment of Manasseh*

THE PATTERN OF REPENTANCE AND FORGIVENESS. JEROME: O happy penitence which has drawn down upon itself the eyes of God, and which has by confessing its error changed the sentence of God's anger! The same conduct is in the Chronicles attributed to Manasseh, and in the book of the prophet Jonah[1] to Nineveh, and in the gospel to the publican.[2] The first of these not only was allowed to obtain forgiveness but also recovered his kingdom, the second broke the force of God's impending wrath, while the third, striking his breast with his hands, "would not lift up so much as his eyes to heaven."[3] Yet for all that the publican with his humble confession of his faults went back justified far more than the Pharisee with his arrogant boasting of his virtues. LETTER 77.4.[4]

A BAPTISM OF REPENTANT TEARS. GREGORY OF NAZIANZUS: I know of a fifth baptism[5] also, which is that of tears and takes much more work. It is received by one who washes his bed every night and his couch with tears;[6] whose bruises sting through his wickedness;[7] and who goes about mourning and is of a sad disposition. It is received by one who imitates the repentance of Manasseh[8] and the humiliation of the Ninevites[9] upon whom God had mercy; who utters the words of the Publican in the Temple, and is justified rather than the stiff-necked Pharisee;[10] who like the Canaanite woman bends down and asks for mercy and crumbs, the food of a dog that is very hungry.[11] ON THE HOLY LIGHTS, ORATION 39.17.[12]

33:10-20 *The Punishment of Manasseh*

REPENTANCE AFTER PUNISHMENT. JOHN CHRYSOSTOM: What sort of comfort, to be every day looking for punishment and vengeance? No, if you would have some comfort from this delay, take it by gathering for yourself the fruit of amendment after repentance. Since if the mere delay of vengeance seems to you a sort of refreshment, far more is it gain not to fall into the vengeance. Let us then make full use of this delay, in order to have a full deliverance from the dangers that press on us. For none of the things enjoined is either burdensome or grievous, but all are so light and easy that if we only bring a genuine purpose of heart, we may accomplish all, though we be chargeable with countless offenses. For so Manasseh had perpetrated innumerable pollutions, having both stretched out his hands against the saints, and brought abominations into the temple, and filled the city with murders and wrought many other things beyond excuse; yet nevertheless after so long and so great wickedness, he washed away from himself all these things. How and in what manner? By repentance and consideration. HOMILIES ON THE GOSPEL OF MATTHEW 22.6.[13]

GOD PUNISHED THE ENORMITY OF MANASSEH'S TRANSGRESSIONS. JOHN CHRYSOSTOM: Manasseh, having exceeded all in fury and tyranny, and having subverted the legal form of worship, and shut up the temple and caused the deceit of idolatry to flourish and having become more ungodly than all who were before him, when he afterwards repented was ranked among the friends of God. Now if, looking to the magnitude of his own iniquities, he had despaired of restoration and repentance, he would have missed all that he afterwards obtained; but as it was, looking to the boundlessness of God's ten-

---

[1]Jon 3:5-10. [2]Lk 18:9-14. [3]Lk 18:13. [4]NPNF 2 6:159. [5]Gregory has just spoken of four previous types of baptism: that of (1) Moses, (2) the Jews, (3) Jesus' baptism of the Spirit; (4) Martyr's baptism by blood. [6]Ps 6:6. [7]Ps 37:5. [8]2 Chron 33:12. [9]Jn 3:7-10. [10]Lk 18:13. [11]Mt 15:27. [12]NPNF 2 7:358. [13]NPNF 1 10:154*.

der mercy instead of the enormity of his transgressions, and having broken in two the bonds of
the devil, he rose up and contended with him and
finished the good course. Letter to the Fallen

Theodore 1.6.[14]

_____

[14]NPNF 1 9:95*.

34:1-33 THE PIOUS REIGN OF JOSIAH

[1]Josiah was eight years old when he began to reign, and he reigned thirty-one years in Jerusalem.
[2]He did what was right in the eyes of the Lord, and walked in the ways of David his father; and
he did not turn aside to the right or to the left.

[8]Now in the eighteenth year of his reign, when he had purged the land and the house, he sent
Shaphan the son of Azaliah, and Ma-aseiah the governor of the city, and Joah the son of Joahaz,
the recorder, to repair the house of the Lord his God.

[14]While they were bringing out the money that had been brought into the house of the Lord,
Hilkiah the priest found the book of the law of the Lord given through Moses. [18]. . . And Shaphan
read it before the king.

[19]When the king heard the words of the law he rent his clothes. [20]And the king commanded
Hilkiah, Ahikam the son of Shaphan, Abdon the son of Micah, Shaphan the secretary, and Asaiah the king's servant, saying, [21]"Go, inquire of the Lord for me and for those who are left in Israel
and in Judah, concerning the words of the book that has been found; for great is the wrath of the
Lord that is poured out on us, because our fathers have not kept the word of the Lord, to do
according to all that is written in this book."

[22]So Hilkiah and those whom the king had sent[x] went to Huldah the prophetess, the wife of
Shallum the son of Tokhath, son of Hasrah, keeper of the wardrobe (now she dwelt in Jerusalem in
the Second Quarter) and spoke to her to that effect. [23]And she said to them, "Thus says the Lord,
the God of Israel: 'Tell the man who sent you to me, [24]Thus says the Lord, Behold, I will bring
evil upon this place and upon its inhabitants, all the curses that are written in the book which was
read before the king of Judah.' "

x Syr Vg: Heb lacks had sent

Overview: Josiah demonstrated his zeal for the
Lord in the many reforms he enacted against the
idol worship of Israel (Pseudo-Tertullian).
Through Huldah, God reproved the king, priest
and indeed all men (Jerome).

34:1-8 Josiah's Reforms

The Zeal of Josiah. Pseudo-Tertullian:
> With zeal immense, Josiah,
> Himself a prince, acted in such a way

As no one before or after him had ever
done!— Idols he
Dethroned; destroyed unhallowed temples;
burned
With fire priests on their altars; all the
bones
Of false prophets were dug up; the altars
burned,
The carcasses to be consumed did serve
For fuel!

FIVE BOOKS IN REPLY TO MARCION 3.184-191.[1]

34:22-23 Predictions of Huldah

THE JUST POSSESSES THIS TITLE. JEROME: It is
written in the book of Days: "Hezekiah fell
because his heart was lifted up."[2] Certainly, no
one but the ungodly will deny that Hezekiah was
a just man. You may say, "He sinned in certain
things, and, therefore, he ceased to be just." But
Scripture does not say this. For he did not lose
the title of just because he committed small sins,
but he possessed the title of just because he performed many good deeds. Say all this to prove,
with the testimonies of sacred Scripture, that the
just are not sinners simply because they have
sinned on occasions, but they remain just because
they flourish in many virtues. Of Josiah it is written, "He did that which was right in the sight of
the Lord, and walked in the way of David his
father. He declined neither to the right nor to the
left"; and yet, although he was a just man, in a
time of need and dire necessity, he sent Hilkiah to
Huldah, the prophet, the wife of Shallum, the
son of Tokhath, the son of Hasrah, keeper of the
wardrobe. "And she dwelled," he says, "in Jerusalem in the second part" (a reference, undoubtedly,
to that part of the city that is enclosed by an
inner wall). "And she answered, 'Thus says the
Lord the God of Israel: Go and tell the man that
sent you to me.'" There is contained in these
words a secret reproof of the king and priests and
all men, because never was there any saint found
among people who could predict the future.
AGAINST THE PELAGIANS 2.22.[3]

---

[1]ANF 4:153-54**. [2]2 Chron 32:25. [3]FC 53:332*.

35:1-27 THE DEATH OF JOSIAH

[20]*After all this, when Josiah had prepared the temple, Neco king of Egypt went up to fight at
Carchemish on the Euphrates and Josiah went out against him.* [21]*But he sent envoys to him, saying,
"What have we to do with each other, king of Judah? I am not coming against you this day, but
against the house with which I am at war; and God has commanded me to make haste. Cease
opposing God, who is with me, lest he destroy you."* [22]*Nevertheless Josiah would not turn away
from him, but disguised himself in order to fight with him. He did not listen to the words of Neco
from the mouth of God, but joined battle in the plain of Megiddo.* [23]*And the archers shot King
Josiah; and the king said to his servants, "Take me away, for I am badly wounded."* [24]*So his servants took him out of the chariot and carried him in his second chariot and brought him to Jerusalem. And he died, and was buried in the tombs of his fathers. All Judah and Jerusalem mourned for*

Josiah. [25]*Jeremiah also uttered a lament for Josiah; and all the singing men and singing women have spoken of Josiah in their laments to this day. They made these an ordinance in Israel; behold, they are written in the Laments.* [26]*Now the rest of the acts of Josiah, and his good deeds according to what is written in the law of the Lord,* [27]*and his acts, first and last, behold, they are written in the Book of the Kings of Israel and Judah.*

Overview: Josiah did not listen to the words of the Lord. If God gives you grace, give a full explanation in the work that you have promised; so your faults are eclipsed by your virtues (Jerome).

35:22-25 The Death of Josiah

In the Monument of His Ancestors. Jerome: Finally, Josiah is killed by Pharaoh, the king of Egypt, because he would not listen to the words of the Lord from the mouth of the prophet Jeremiah, or, as it is written in the Paralipomenon: "Josiah would not return but prepared to fight against him and did not listen to the words of Neco from the mouth of God." And it is stated, "And he died and was buried in the monument of his ancestors. And all Judah and Jerusalem mourned for him, particularly Jeremiah, whose lamentations for Josiah all the singing men and singing women repeat to this day. And it became like a law in Israel: 'Behold, it is found written in the Lamentations.'" Against the Pelagians 2.22.[1]

For Many Righteous the Virtues Eclipse Their Faults. Jerome: It is true that in the holy Scriptures many are called righteous, as Zachariah and Elizabeth, Job, Jehosaphat, Josiah, and many others who are mentioned in the sacred writings. Of this fact I shall, if God gives me grace, give a full explanation in the work that I have promised; in this letter it must suffice to say that they are called righteous, not because they are faultless but because their faults are eclipsed by their virtues. In fact Zachariah is punished with dumbness,[2] Job is condemned out of his own mouth,[3] and Jehoshaphat and Josiah who are beyond a doubt described as righteous are narrated to have done things displeasing to the Lord. The first aligned himself with the ungodly Ahab and brought on himself the rebuke of Micaiah;[4] and the second, though forbidden by the word of the Lord spoken by Jeremiah, went against Pharaoh Neco, king of Egypt, and was killed by him. Letter 133.13.[5]

---

[1]FC 53:332-33*. [2]Lk 1:20-22. [3]Job 42:6. [4]1 Kings 22:19-25. [5]NPNF 2 6:280.

[36:1-23 THE LAST KINGS AND THE DESTRUCTION OF JERUSALEM]

[See commentary on 2 Kings 23:31-25]

E Z R A

1:1-11 CYRUS GIVES FREEDOM TO THE PEOPLE OF GOD

¹*In the first year of Cyrus king of Persia, that the word of the* LORD *by the mouth of Jeremiah might be accomplished, the* LORD *stirred up the spirit of Cyrus king of Persia so that he made a proclamation throughout all his kingdom and also put it in writing:*

²*"Thus says Cyrus king of Persia: The* LORD*, the God of heaven, has given me all the kingdoms of the earth, and he has charged me to build him a house at Jerusalem, which is in Judah.* ³*Whoever is among you of all his people, may his God be with him, and let him go up to Jerusalem, which is in Judah, and rebuild the house of the* LORD*, the God of Israel—he is the God who is in Jerusalem;* ⁴*and let each survivor, in whatever place he sojourns, be assisted by the men of his place with silver and gold, with goods and with beasts, besides freewill offerings for the house of God which is in Jerusalem."*

⁵*Then rose up the heads of the fathers' houses of Judah and Benjamin, and the priests and the Levites, every one whose spirit God had stirred to go up to rebuild the house of the* LORD *which is in Jerusalem;* ⁶*and all who were about them aided them with vessels of silver, with gold, with goods, with beasts, and with costly wares, besides all that was freely offered.* ⁷*Cyrus the king also brought out the vessels of the house of the* LORD *which Nebuchadnezzar had carried away from Jerusalem and placed in the house of his gods.* ⁸*Cyrus king of Persia brought these out in charge of Mithredath the treasurer, who counted them out to Shesh-bazzar the prince of Judah.* ⁹*And this was the number of them: a thousandᵃ basins of gold, a thousand basins of silver, twenty-nine censers,* ¹⁰*thirty bowls of gold, two thousandᵇ four hundred and ten bowls of silver, and a thousand other vessels;* ¹¹*all the vessels of gold and of silver were five thousand four hundred and sixty-nine.ᶜ All these did Shesh-bazzar bring up, when the exiles were brought up from Babylonia to Jerusalem.*

a 1 Esdras 2.13: Heb *thirty*   b 1 Esdras 2.13: Heb *of a second sort*   c 1 Esdras 2.14: Heb *five thousand four hundred*

OVERVIEW: Cyrus testifies publicly that the God of Israel is truly the maker of all kingdoms. The Lord made Cyrus foreshadow his only-begotten Son, because as he, after destroying the empire of the Chaldeans, freed the people of God, so Christ, after destroying the kingdom of death and sin, freed all humankind. In his words Cyrus shows his faith, because he understands that the people of Israel are the people of God before all nations. Cyrus also demonstrates his piety, by allowing all to go back to their homeland. The basins, the knives and the bowls typologically indicate different kinds of pious Christians (BEDE).

1:1-2 Cyrus Told to Build a House for the Lord

CYRUS PROCLAIMS THE POWER OF GOD.
BEDE: The ancient histories, with which also the Scripture of Daniel agrees, relate that Cyrus, king of the Persians, after allying with Darius, king of the Medians, destroyed the empire of the Babylonians and killed their last king, Balthazar, and razed and ransacked their capital. And therefore Cyrus, knowing that the kingdom of Israel had been entrusted to him by God, as soon as he defeated that kingdom that had captured the people of Israel and kept them in bondage, gave the Israelites permission to return to their homeland and to rebuild the house of their God, which had been set on fire. And not only did he proclaim by words that sentence of release to those present, but also he communicated it to those who were away in all the provinces of his kingdom by means of letters and testified through public voice that he who is the God of Israel was truly the maker of all kingdoms. ON EZRA AND NEHEMIAH 1.1.[1]

CYRUS AS A TYPE OF JESUS CHRIST. BEDE: Therefore the Lord made Cyrus similar to his only-begotten Son, our God and Lord Jesus Christ. Just as Cyrus, after destroying the empire of the Chaldeans, freed the people of God, and sent them back to their homeland and ordered them to rebuild the temple, which had been set on fire in Jerusalem, taking care that his edict was proclaimed everywhere through letters, so that Jeremiah's[2] words might be fulfilled, through which he had predicted what would have happened in the future; so the mediator between God and humanity, after destroying all over the

world the kingdom of the devil, called back from that tyranny his elect, who had been scattered, and now gathers them in his church. ON EZRA AND NEHEMIAH 1.1.[3]

1:3-7 God's People Are Permitted to Go to Jerusalem

THE MEANING OF CYRUS'S WORDS. BEDE: In these words the great faith of the king and his great piety shine. His faith, certainly, because he understood that the people of Israel was the people of God before all nations. And his piety because without exception he allowed all who wanted to to go back to their homeland. And again his faith, because he testified that that same Lord God dwelled in heaven and was in Jerusalem and moved to Jerusalem together with all those who were coming back from Babylon. Is it not clearer than light that he conceived him not as a corporeal being that can be enclosed in a place but as a Spirit that is everywhere? Indeed Cyrus confessed that [God] was in Jerusalem and in the temple, without doubting that he also ruled the kingdom of heaven at the same time. So he believed that he reigned in heaven but was nevertheless on earth with his faithful, in order to direct their minds and hands to make the good works of salvation. In addition, all the words of this Scripture are fragrant with spiritual meanings. To whom is it not obviously clear that only those with whom God is can actually move from the "confusion"[4] of sin to the works of virtue, as from the bondage of Babylon to the freedom of Jerusalem? ON EZRA AND NEHEMIAH 1.1.[5]

1:8-11 Gold and Silver Vessels

SYMBOLISM OF THE VESSELS. BEDE: Therefore the basins, which are large vessels, signify the

---

[1]PL 91:810. [2]See Jer 29:10-14. [3]PL 91:811 [4]"Confusion" is the meaning of the name Babylon: see Jerome Nom. Heb. CCL 72:62.18. Bede often refers to this meaning in the course of his commentary on Ezra and Nehemiah. [5]PL 91:812.

clear hearts of the simple, who do not know how to hide in themselves any covert thought but always declare with a pure tongue the things they have in their mind . . . The knives, which they used to cut and divide in a right measure the members of the victims, so that, after everything had been prepared according to the ritual, a part might be consumed on the altar by the holy fire and a part might be given to the use of those who had made the offering, indicate those in the church, who are renowned for the grace of discretion, who know perfectly how to distinguish the sacrifice of salvation, which is Christ. . . . The bowls, which are vessels for drinking, figuratively express those who are usually inebriated by a greater ardor of interior charity. ON EZRA AND NEHEMIAH 1.1.[6]

---

[6]PL 91:816-17.

2:1-70 A LIST OF THOSE WHO RETURN TO JERUSALEM

[1]*Now these were the people of the province who came up out of the captivity of those exiles whom Nebuchadnezzar the king of Babylon had carried captive to Babylonia; they returned to Jerusalem and Judah, each to his own town.* [2]*They came with Zerubbabel, Jeshua, Nehemiah, Seraiah, Reel-aiah, Mordecai, Bilshan, Mispar, Bigvai, Rehum, and Baanah.*

[64]*The whole assembly together was forty-two thousand three hundred and sixty,* [65]*besides their menservants and maidservants, of whom there were seven thouand three hundred and thirty-seven; and they had two hundred male and female singers.* [66]*Their horses were seven hundred and thirty-six, their mules were two hundred and forty-five,* [67]*their camels were four hundred and thirty-five, and their asses were six thousand seven hundred and twenty.*

[68]*Some of the heads of families, when they came to the house of the LORD which is in Jerusalem, made freewill offerings for the house of God, to erect it on its site;* [69]*according to their ability they gave to the treasury of the work sixty-one thousand darics of gold, five thousand minas of silver, and one hundred priests' garments.*

[70]*The priests, the Levites, and some of the people lived in Jerusalem and its vicinity;[e] and the singers, the gatekeepers, and the temple servants lived in their towns, and all Israel in their towns.*

e 1 Esdras 5.46: Heb lacks *lived in Jerusalem and its vicinity*

OVERVIEW: Not only those who had migrated from Judah to Babylon belonged to Judah, but also those who were born in Babylon from their stock because, even though they were bodily born in Babylon, they longed for Judah and Jerusalem. Jerusalem signifies the universal state of the holy church, which is all over the world, while the towns, which belong to Jerusalem, signify each of the virtues of the faithful (BEDE). The return of the Jews from captivity symbolically represents the restoration of the soul after the captivity of sin (Cassiodorus).

2:1-34 Returning to Jerusalem and Judah

Born in Babylon but Longing for Jerusalem. Bede: "Now these were the people of the province who came from those captive exiles...." The text calls them children of the province of Judah, and not of Babylon. Indeed, not only those who had migrated from Judah to Babylon belonged to it, but also those who were born in Babylon from their stock. Even though they were bodily born in Babylon, they longed with all their heart for Judah and Jerusalem. And the one who represented them was their distinguished leader Zerubbabel, who showed with his name that he was born in Babylon but demonstrated with his intentions and actions that he was a citizen of Jerusalem.

In a different sense, they are the children of the church, the children of the heavenly homeland, not only those who have been already imbued with the sacraments of the church but also those who have erred among the impious for a long time but have been chosen for life before the centuries by divine election and in time are to be consecrated to the mysteries of divine grace. On Ezra and Nehemiah 1.2.[1]

The Allegorical Meaning of Jerusalem and the Towns. Bede: "All to their own towns," because they certainly lived in each of their towns, as they all belonged to Jerusalem and Judah in general. Therefore Jerusalem signifies the universal state of the holy church, which is all over the world. The towns, which belong to Jerusalem, signify each of the virtues of the faithful, in which they are defended from the temptations and attacks of the evil spirits as in a fortress made of different towns.

Finally the towns, in which lived those who had come to Jerusalem and Judah from the exile, may be interpreted as the different churches of Christ, by all of which together the one universal church is formed. On Ezra and Nehemiah 1.2.[2]

2:64-70 Offerings for the Temple

The Restoration of the Soul. Cassiodorus: "A canticle of David, when the house was built after the captivity."[3] So far as the literal sense is concerned, the heading points to the time when the temple at Jerusalem is known to have been refurbished by Zerubbabel, son of Salathiel, after it had been leveled to the ground by a hostile band of Chaldeans. But since he says nothing of this kind in what follows, and since the headings of psalms are never at variance with their content, it remains for us to investigate it in the spiritual sense. A destroyed house is built up when a soul following the captivity of sin begins to return to an understanding of the truth through the generosity of the Lord. This house, which is the universal church in which Christ dwells, is always raised up on living stones, because every day it gains increase in building from its confessors and does not cease to be built up until the number of the predestined is attained at the end of the world. We must store this psalm in our minds as the second of those proclaiming the first and the second coming of the Lord. Explanation of the Psalms 95.1.[4]

---

[1]PL 91:817-18. [2]PL 91:818. [3]Ps 95, title (Cassidorus quotes this title from Jerome's Vg). [4]ACW 52:415.

3:1-7 ZERUBBABEL AND JESHUA SET ABOUT
TO REBUILD THE TEMPLE

¹When the seventh month came, and the sons of Israel were in the towns, the people gathered as one man to Jerusalem. ²Then arose Jeshua the son of Jozadak, with his fellow priests, and Zerubbabel the son of She-alti-el with his kinsmen, and they built the altar of the God of Israel, to offer burnt offerings upon it, as it is written in the law of Moses the man of God. ³They set the altar in its place, for fear was upon them because of the peoples of the lands, and they offered burnt offerings upon it to the LORD, burnt offerings morning and evening. ⁴And they kept the feast of booths, as it is written, and offered the daily burnt offerings by number according to the ordinance, as each day required, ⁵and after that the continual burnt offerings, the offerings at the new moon and at all the appointed feasts of the LORD, and the offerings of every one who made a freewill offering to the LORD. ⁶From the first day of the seventh month they began to offer burnt offerings to the LORD. But the foundation of the temple of the LORD was not yet laid. ⁷So they gave money to the masons and the carpenters, and food, drink, and oil to the Sidonians and the Tyrians to bring cedar trees from Lebanon to the sea, to Joppa, according to the grant which they had from Cyrus king of Persia.

OVERVIEW: The seventh month symbolizes the Holy Spirit's grace, which is described in the prophet Isaiah and in the Revelation of Saint John as sevenfold (BEDE). Even though the rebuilding of the temple was still in progress, prayers, rituals and celebrations were regularly performed in it (ATHANASIUS).

3:1 When the Seventh Month Came

AN ALLEGORICAL REFERENCE TO THE HOLY SPIRIT. BEDE: In a higher sense, the seventh month suggests the Holy Spirit's grace, which is described in the prophet Isaiah and in the Revelation of Saint John as sevenfold. And certainly in that month, after our captivity, we gather in Jerusalem, where we are washed from our filthiness and the errors of vice, and protected by the defense of good works and finally are illumined by the greater grace of that same Spirit, so that we are lit in the love of supreme peace, which is contained in the true unity: Jerusalem, indeed,

means "vision of peace." ON EZRA AND NEHEMIAH 1.3.[1]

3:2-7 Making Offerings to the Lord

RITUALS WERE PERFORMED AS THE TEMPLE WAS BUILT. ATHANASIUS: Or rather let them learn of you, who are so well instructed in such histories, how that Jeshua the son of Josedek the priest, and his brother, and Zerubbabel the wise, the son of Salathiel, and Ezra the priest and scribe of the law, as the temple was being built after the captivity, the feast of tabernacles being at hand (which was a great feast and time of assembly and prayer in Israel), gathered the people together with one accord in the great court within the first gate, which is toward the east, and prepared the altar to God, and there offered their gifts and kept the feast. And so afterwards they brought hither their sacrifices, on the sab-

[1]PL 91:825.

baths and the new moons, and the people offered up their prayers. And yet the Scripture says expressly that when these things were done, the temple of God was not yet built; but rather while they thus prayed, the building of the house was advancing. So neither were their prayers deferred in expectation of the dedication, nor was the dedication prevented by the assemblies held for the sake of prayer. But the people thus continued to pray; and when the house was entirely finished, they celebrated the dedication, and brought their gifts for that purpose and all kept the feast for the completion of the work. DEFENSE BEFORE CONSTANTIUS 18.[2]

TYPOLOGICAL INTERPRETATION OF THE FOUNDING OF THE TEMPLE. BEDE: Typologically, in this passage, the founding of God's temple holds a figure of those who, recently converted to the faith, prepare a place or abode in their heart and body for the Lord, as the apostle says: "Do you not know that your limbs are the temple of the Holy Spirit, which is in you";[3] and again, "That by faith Christ dwells in your hearts."[4] Accordingly, those who when freed from captivity had come up to Jerusalem had indeed arranged to build a temple, which, by their labor, they eventually achieved, but first they built an altar and commended themselves to the Lord with daily burnt offerings, so that in this way being made more pure they might deserve to start the work of building the temple. Likewise with respect to the spiritual edifice too it is necessary in every way that whoever has decided to teach others should first teach himself, and one who aims to instruct his neighbors to fear and love God should first make himself worthy for the office of teacher by serving God more eagerly, lest by chance he should hear from the apostle, "You, then, who teach others, do you not teach yourself? You who preach against stealing, do you steal?"[5] This is why the apostle says in regard to himself, "But I chastise my body and bring it into subjection, in case when preaching to others I myself should be found wanting."[6] Consequently, it is fitting that the descendants of the exile are found to have offered God no victims or sacrifices other than entire burnt offerings . . . , because whoever lives an evil life yet desires to teach others to refrain from illicit acts must give himself over entirely to his Creator by living well and refraining even from things that are permissible, so that he might not only by the merit of good action more copiously obtain heavenly help in preaching but also, by the example of that same good work, encourage his hearers to follow more effectively what he teaches. ON EZRA AND NEHEMIAH 1.3.[7]

[2]NPNF 2 4:245*. [3]1 Cor 6:19. [4]Eph 3:17. [5]Rom 2:21-22. [6]1 Cor 9:27. [7]TTH 47:54-55; PL 91:835.

3:8-13 NEW FOUNDATIONS ARE LAID

[8]*Now in the second year of their coming to the house of God at Jerusalem, in the second month, Zerubbabel the son of She-alti-el and Jeshua the son of Jozadak made a beginning, together with the rest of their brethren, the priests and the Levites and all who had come to Jerusalem from the captivity. They appointed the Levites, from twenty years old and upward, to have the oversight of the work of the house of the LORD.* [9]*And Jeshua with his sons and his kinsmen, and Kadmi-el and*

his sons, the sons of Judah, together took the oversight of the workmen in the house of God, along with the sons of Henadad and the Levites, their sons and kinsmen.

[10]And when the builders laid the foundation of the temple of the LORD, the priests in their vestments came forward with trumpets, and the Levites, the sons of Asaph, with cymbals, to praise the LORD, according to the directions of David king of Israel; [11]and they sang responsively, praising and giving thanks to the LORD,

"For he is good,

for his steadfast love endures for ever toward Israel."

And all the people shouted with a great shout, when they praised the LORD, because the foundation of the house of the LORD was laid. [12]But many of the priests and Levites and heads of fathers' houses, old men who had seen the first house, wept with a loud voice when they saw the foundation of this house being laid, though many shouted aloud for joy; [13]so that the people could not distinguish the sound of the joyful shout from the sound of the people's weeping, for the people shouted with a great shout, and the sound was heard afar.

OVERVIEW: The founding of God's temple figuratively points to those who, recently converted to the faith, prepare a place or abode in their heart and body for the Lord. The phases in the reconstruction of the temple typologically refer to the phases of Christ's passion and resurrection (BEDE). When Salathiel and Zerubbabel returned, they led the people more democratically, transferring the rule to the priesthood because of the intermingling of the priestly and royal tribes (BASIL). The Jews rejoiced because they had been freed from captivity and had received the authority to restore the temple, but they wept because they knew that the first temple had been destroyed on account of their wickedness (BEDE).

3:8-9 Zerubbabel and Jeshua Made a Beginning

THE SPIRITUAL MEANING OF THE PHASES IN THE RECONSTRUCTION. BEDE: [The text] says they came to the temple of God not because they found the temple already built, since, to be sure, it was said earlier that it did not yet have foundations. Rather, "to the temple of God" means to the place of God's temple—to the work by which

they desired to rebuild the temple. And so modern Jews[1] who habitually claim that not the temple walls but only the roof was destroyed by the Chaldeans are mistaken, since Ezra plainly writes that the descendants of the exiles rebuilt the temple from its foundations. However, since it was said above that they came to Jerusalem on the seventh month,[2] and here it is added that "in the second year of their arrival" they began the work of the temple "in the second month," it is clear that for seven months they prepared the stones, cement, timber and other necessary materials, but when the eighth month began they started to press on at last with their longed-for work: for there were six months in the first year and the seventh in the following. Any learned person will very easily find a great mystery in this. For seven pertains to the sabbath, on which day the Lord either rested from all his works after he created the earth[3] or when he redeemed the world through his passion and rested in the tomb. Eight refers to the first day after the sabbath[4] on which he rose from the dead; seven looks to the hope of our sabbath rest after death, eight to the joy of

---

[1]These *moderni Judaei* mentioned by Bede cannot be identified (see TTH 47:60 n. 4). [2]See Ezra 3:1-2. [3]Gen 2:2. [4]See Mt 28:1.

our everlasting happiness after resurrection. ON EZRA AND NEHEMIAH 1.4.[5]

A MORE DEMOCRATIC REGIME. BASIL THE GREAT: When Jerusalem was demolished by Nebuchadnezzar, the kingdom was destroyed, and no longer were there hereditary successions to the sovereignty as formerly; at that time, moreover, being out of power, the posterity of David were living in captivity. But, when the followers of Salathiel and Zerubbabel returned, they led the people more democratically, transferring the rule henceforth to the priesthood because of the intermingling of the priestly and royal tribes. LETTER 236.2.[6]

3:10-13 Old People Wept or Shouted for Joy

CRIES OF WEEPING MIXED WITH CRIES OF JOY. BEDE: Of those who had seen the first temple, some were uttering cries of weeping, others of joy when the foundation of this temple too was laid before their eyes—of joy, indeed, because the temple of the Lord that had been destroyed had now begun to be restored; of weeping because they were distressed when they realized what a difference there was between the poverty of the undertaking of that time and the former most magnificent power of Solomon, whereby the original temple was founded. They rejoiced greatly

because they had been freed from captivity and had received the authority to restore the temple, but they wept loudly because they knew that the first temple, whose size and beauty they could in no way equal, had been destroyed on account of their wickedness. For the prophet's words, "The glory of this new house will be greater than that of the first,"[7] pertain not to the greatness or decoration of the house but to the act of building itself, because the fact that the few surviving captives were able to accomplish such a great undertaking even as their enemies were opposing them was a greater and more obvious miracle of divine power than that a very rich king who had no adversaries at all but rather the very powerful and wealthy king of Tyre as a collaborator,[8] did this with most accomplished craftsmen, just as he desired. So too, the glory of that most recent house will be greater than the first because the worshipers in the first house preached to the peoples the writings of the Old Testament, namely, the Law and the Prophets, whereas in the second house Christ and the apostles spread the good news of the grace of the New Testament and coming of the kingdom of heaven. ON EZRA AND NEHEMIAH 1.4.[9]

---

[5]TTH 47:60-61; PL 91:835. [6]FC 28:168-69. [7]Hag 2:9. [8]See 1 Kings 5:1-18. [9]TTH 47:66; PL 91:838-39.

4:1-24 AN INTERMISSION IN THE WORK OF RECONSTRUCTION

[1]*Now when the adversaries of Judah and Benjamin heard that the returned exiles were building a temple to the LORD, the God of Israel,* [2]*they approached Zerubbabel and the heads of fathers' houses and said to them, "Let us build with you; for we worship your God as you do, and we have*

been sacrificing to him ever since the days of Esar-haddon king of Assyria who brought us here." ³But Zerubbabel, Jeshua, and the rest of the heads of fathers' houses in Israel said to them, "You have nothing to do with us in building a house to our God; but we alone will build to the LORD, the God of Israel, as King Cyrus the king of Persia has commanded us."

⁴Then the people of the land discouraged the people of Judah, and made them afraid to build, ⁵and hired counselors against them to frustrate their purpose, all the days of Cyrus king of Persia, even until the reign of Darius king of Persia.

⁶And in the reign of Ahasu-erus, in the beginning of his reign, they wrote an accusation against the inhabitants of Judah and Jerusalem.

⁷And in the days of Ar-ta-xerxes, Bishlam and Mithredath and Tabeel and the rest of their associates wrote to Ar-ta-xerxes king of Persia; the letter was written in Aramaic and translated. ⁸Rehum the commander and Shimshai the scribe wrote a letter against Jerusalem to Ar-ta-xerxes the king as follows—⁹then wrote Rehum the commander, Shimshai the scribe, and the rest of their associates, the judges, the governors, the officials, the Persians, the men of Erech, the Babylonians, the men of Susa, that is, the Elamites, ¹⁰and the rest of the nations whom the great and noble Osnappar deported and settled in the cities of Samaria and in the rest of the province Beyond the River, and now ¹¹this is a copy of the letter that they sent—"To Ar-ta-xerxes the king: Your servants, the men of the province Beyond the River, send greeting. And now ¹²be it known to the king that the Jews who came up from you to us have gone to Jerusalem. They are rebuilding that rebellious and wicked city; they are finishing the walls and repairing the foundations. ¹³Now be it known to the king that, if this city is rebuilt and the walls finished, they will not pay tribute, custom, or toll, and the royal revenue will be impaired. ¹⁴Now because we eat the salt of the palace and it is not fitting for us to witness the king's dishonor, therefore we send and inform the king, ¹⁵in order that search may be made in the book of the records of your fathers. You will find in the book of the records and learn that this city is a rebellious city, hurtful to kings and provinces, and that sedition was stirred up in it from of old. That was why this city was laid waste. ¹⁶We make known to the king that, if this city is rebuilt and its walls finished, you will then have no possession in the province Beyond the River."

¹⁷The king sent an answer: "To Rehum the commander and Shimshai the scribe and the rest of their associates who live in Samaria and in the rest of the province Beyond the River, greeting. And now ¹⁸the letter which you sent to us has been plainly read before me. ¹⁹And I made a decree, and search has been made, and it has been found that this city from of old has risen against kings, and that rebellion and sedition have been made in it. ²⁰And mighty kings have been over Jerusalem, who ruled over the whole province Beyond the River, to whom tribute, custom, and toll were paid. ²¹Therefore make a decree that these men be made to cease, and that this city be not rebuilt, until a decree is made by me. ²²And take care not to be slack in this matter; why should damage grow to the hurt of the king?"

²³Then, when the copy of King Ar-ta-xerxes' letter was read before Rehum and Shimshai the scribe and their associates, they went in haste to the Jews at Jerusalem and by force and power

made them cease. ²⁴*Then the work on the house of God which is in Jerusalem stopped; and it ceased until the second year of the reign of Darius king of Persia.*

f Heb adds *in Aramaic,* indicating that 4.8–6.18 is in Aramaic. Another interpretation is *The letter was written in the Aramaic script and set forth in the Aramaic language*

OVERVIEW: The Samaritans, who offer their help in the construction of the temple, figuratively represent false brothers, that is, heretics and evil Catholics. According to Josephus, the Artaxerxes to whom letters were sent was Cambyses. He also took the power of Ahasuerus, as this other king died in the first year of his reign. The number of forty-six years for the completion of the temple typologically refers to different phases of the perfecting of our Lord's physical body (BEDE).

4:1-5 Let Us Build with You

THE SAMARITANS AS A TYPE OF CHRISTIAN HERETICS. BEDE: The story is well known, because the text declares that the adversaries of Judah and Benjamin are the Samaritans, whom the king of the Assyrians, during the captivity of the ten tribes, assembled from different nations and moved into their cities and lands.[1] And while they had accepted the law of God and partly served it . . . , they still worshiped their old idols. Therefore those who abhorred the true followers of God promised that they would have helped in the reconstruction of the temple, so that, after being received in their society, they might cause a loss of funds. It is obviously clear to everybody that these people figuratively represent the false brothers, that is, the heretics and the evil Catholics. In fact, they are the adversaries of Judah, that is, of the confession and praise that now the church offers to the Lord through orthodox faith and works that are worthy of faith. They are also enemies of Benjamin, that is, of the son of the right, because they separate the people who listen to them from the fate of the faithful people who will receive the blessing and the eternal kingdom at the right hand of the Judge. ON EZRA AND NEHEMIAH 1.4.[2]

4:7-12 Letters Written to King Artaxerxes of Persia

LETTERS SENT TO AHASUERUS AND ARTAXERXES. BEDE: Josephus[3] believes that this Artaxerxes, who forbade that the temple might be reconstructed in Jerusalem after receiving the letter from the Samaritans, was Cambyses, son of Cyrus, who took power after his father had reigned for thirty years and ruled the kingdom for eight years. Then the magi reigned one year after him, until Darius, son of Hystaspis, succeeded. And in the second year of his reign, in which he allowed the temple to be rebuilt, the angel said through the prophet Zechariah before the people: "O Lord of hosts, how long will you withhold mercy from Jerusalem and the cities of Judah, with which you have been angry these seventy years?"[4] With regard to Ahasuerus, to whom it is said that a letter of accusation was sent as well, it is not mentioned whether he replied or wrote anything back, because he died in the same year in which he had begun to reign, so that he left to Artaxerxes all the power and also the care of this case. ON EZRA AND NEHEMIAH 1.5.[5]

4:17-24 Work on the Temple Stopped

THE WORK WAS FINISHED AFTER FORTY-SIX YEARS. BEDE: The Jews said, "This temple was built in forty-six years, and you will raise it up in three days?"[6] They answered as they understood. But lest we too should perceive our Lord's spiritual word in a carnal way, the Evangelist subsequently explained what temple it was of which he was speaking. As for their stating that the temple was built in forty-six years, they meant not its

[1]See 2 Kings 17:24-41. [2]PL 91:839. [3]See Josephus *Antiquities of the Jews* 11.2.3. [4]Zech 1:12. [5]PL 91:841–42. [6]Jn 2:20.

first but its second building. For Solomon, the first [builder], finished the temple very rapidly within seven years, during a time of great peace in his kingdom.[7] It was destroyed by the Chaldeans,[8] but after seventy years it began to be rebuilt, at the bidding of Cyrus the Persian, when the captivity was lightened.[9] But the descendants of those who were deported were unable to finish the work that they were doing under the rulers Zerubbabel and Jeshua before forty-six years had passed, on account of the resistance of the neighboring nations.

This number [forty-six] of years is also most apt for the perfecting of our Lord's physical body. Writers on natural history tell us that the form of the human body is completed within this number of days. During the first six days after conception it has a likeness to milk; during the following nine days it is changed into blood; next, in twelve days, it becomes solid; during the remaining eighteen days it is formed into the perfect features of all its members; and after this, during the time remaining until birth, it increases in size. Six plus nine plus twelve plus eighteen makes forty-five. If to this we add one, that is, the day on which the body, divided into its separate members, begins to grow, we find the same number of days in the building up of our Lord's body as there were years in the construction of the temple. HOMILIES ON THE GOSPELS 2.1.[10]

---

[7]1 Kings 6:38. [8]See 2 Kings 25:9. [9]Ezra 1:1-3. [10]CS 111:8.

5:1-17 ZERUBBABEL AND JESHUA RESUME THE BUILDING OF THE TEMPLE

[1]Now the prophets, Haggai and Zechariah the son of Iddo, prophesied to the Jews who were in Judah and Jerusalem, in the name of the God of Israel who was over them. [2]Then Zerubbabel the son of She-alti-el and Jeshua the son of Jozadak arose and began to rebuild the house of God which is in Jerusalem; and with them were the prophets of God, helping them.

[3]At the same time Tattenai the governor of the province Beyond the River and Shethar-bozenai and their associates came to them and spoke to them thus, "Who gave you a decree to build this house and to finish this structure?" [4]They[g] also asked them this, "What are the names of the men who are building this building?" [5]But the eye of their God was upon the elders of the Jews, and they did not stop them till a report should reach Darius and then answer be returned by letter concerning it.

[6]The copy of the letter which Tattenai the governor of the province Beyond the River and Shethar-bozenai and his associates the governors who were in the province Beyond the River sent to Darius the king; [7]they sent him a report, in which was written as follows: "To Darius the king, all peace. [8]Be it known to the king that we went to the province of Judah, to the house of the great God. It is being built with huge stones, and timber is laid in the walls; this work goes on diligently and prospers in their hands. [9]Then we asked those elders and spoke to them thus, 'Who gave you a

decree to build this house and to finish this structure?' ¹⁰We also asked them their names, for your information, that we might write down the names of the men at their head. ¹¹And this was their reply to us: 'We are the servants of the God of heaven and earth, and we are rebuilding the house that was built many years ago, which a great king of Israel built and finished. ¹²But because our fathers had angered the God of heaven, he gave them into the hand of Nebuchadnezzar king of Babylon, the Chaldean, who destroyed this house and carried away the people to Babylonia. ¹³However in the first year of Cyrus king of Babylon, Cyrus the king made a decree that this house of God should be rebuilt. ¹⁴And the gold and silver vessels of the house of God, which Nebuchadnezzar had taken out of the temple that was in Jerusalem and brought into the temple of Babylon, these Cyrus the king took out of the temple of Babylon, and they were delivered to one whose name was Shesh-bazzar, whom he had made governor; ¹⁵and he said to him, "Take these vessels, go and put them in the temple which is in Jerusalem, and let the house of God be rebuilt on its site." ¹⁶Then this Shesh-bazzar came and laid the foundations of the house of God which is in Jerusalem; and from that time until now it has been in building, and it is not yet finished.' ¹⁷Therefore, if it seem good to the king, let search be made in the royal archives there in Babylon, to see whether a decree was issued by Cyrus the king for the rebuilding of this house of God in Jerusalem. And let the king send us his pleasure in this matter."

g Gk Syr: Aramaic We

OVERVIEW: Thanks to the exhortations of Haggai and Zechariah, Zerubbabel and Jeshua together with the entire people set out to rebuild the house of the Lord. In the holy church, when those who have been held back by the attacks of wicked people or spirits are suddenly set straight by the words of faithful teachers, they begin to burn so greatly for righteous pursuits that they cannot be overcome by any temptation. The fact that the temple was built from old and new stones can rightly be interpreted as corresponding to the fact that the one church of Christ is assembled from both peoples, namely, Jews and Gentiles (BEDE).

5:1-2 Zerubbabel and Jeshua Set Out to Rebuild the Temple

THE EXHORTATIONS OF HAGGAI AND ZECHARIAH. BEDE: "Now the prophets Haggai and Zechariah, son of Iddo, prophesied to the Jews." . . . These things are reported in full detail in the books of the same prophets. And with their words they reproached the laziness of those who had been negligent in the reconstruction of the temple and exhorted them to work with the help of God. And thanks to their exhortation and devotion, Zerubbabel and Jeshua together with the entire people set out to rebuild the house of the Lord. And certainly the prophet Haggai began with these words: "In the second year of King Darius, in the sixth month, on the first day of the month, the word of the Lord came by the prophet Haggai to Zerubbabel, son of Shealtiel, and to Joshua,¹ son of Jehozadak, the high priest: Thus says the Lord of the hosts: These people say the time has not yet come to rebuild the Lord's house. Then the word of the Lord came by the prophet Haggai, saying: Is it a time for you yourselves to live in your paneled houses while this house lies in ruins?"² And a bit further: "And the Lord stirred up the spirit of Zerubbabel, son of Shealtiel, governor of Judah, and the spirit of

---

¹The NRSV, from which is quoted the text of Haggai, indifferently uses the two alternate spellings of this name: Jeshua-Joshua. ²Hag 1:1-4.

Joshua, son of Jehozadak, the high priest, and the spirit of all the remnant of the people; and they came and worked on the house of the Lord of hosts, their God, on the twenty-fourth day of the month, in the sixth month."[3] And as a sequel to the words that we have quoted above: "The latter splendor of this house shall be greater than the former, says the Lord of hosts."[4] In the same way Zechariah begins: "In the eighth month, in the second year of Darius, the word of the Lord came to the prophet Zechariah son of Berechiah son of Iddo. Thus says the Lord of hosts: Return to me, says the Lord of hosts, and I will return to you."[5] ON EZRA AND NEHEMIAH 2.6.[6]

5:3-5 Who Gave You a Decree to Build This House?

TO BURN FOR RIGHTEOUS PURSUITS. BEDE: The literal meaning is clear, namely, that the leaders of the Jews, strengthened by the prophets' words, could not be hindered by the harrying of the enemies from the holy work, from which they had ceased out of fear of the enemies when the prophets still remained silent. This occurs in the same way in the holy church now when those who have been held back by the attacks of wicked people or spirits and have remained for a while rather lax with respect to good deeds are suddenly set straight by the words either of faithful teachers or of the divine Scriptures and begin to burn so greatly for righteous pursuits that they cannot be overcome by any wiles of temptations or be called back from what they intended to do. ON EZRA AND NEHEMIAH 2.6.[7]

5:6-17 The Temple Built of Hewn Stone

OLD AND NEW STONES. BEDE: This letter that Tattenai writes to Darius is very different from the one Rehum and Shimsahi[8] wrote to Artaxerxes. That letter was filled with accusation of the people of Jerusalem, this one with praise not only of the people but also of almighty God. Indeed, it begins as follows: "To Darius the king, all peace: Let it be known to the king that we went to the province of Judah, to the house of the great God, which is built with unfinished stone, and the timbers are being laid in the walls; and the work is being carried on with diligence and is making rapid progress in their hands. So we questioned those elders and spoke to them as follows, 'Who gave you the authority to build this house?' and so on. In these words we should also note in what sense it is said that God's house was built from 'unfinished stone,'[9] when it is evident that such a great work could only have been built from finished stones. Yet by 'unfinished stone' we should understand new stone, which they themselves discovered unhewn but, by shaping it up, made it suitable for the building of the Lord's house. For even though some of the old stones remained, which, as the lamenting Jeremiah shows, were scattered 'at the end of every street,'"[10] yet no one can doubt that new stones also had to be shaped to complete the work of the temple. The mystery of this matter is undoubtedly plain, since we have seen that God's church is built not only from those who by repenting regain their senses and return to the life of holiness that they have previously squandered by sinning, but also from those who have recently been called to the faith, arranged by the instruction of teachers as though with the measuring rod of builders and so inserted into the edifice of the Lord's house in a place appropriate to themselves. Yet the fact that the temple was built from both old and new stones, that is, both from stones that had been finished long previously and from those that had remained unfinished for longer, can also rightly be interpreted as corresponding to the fact that the one church of Christ is assembled from both peoples, namely, Jews and Gentiles—the

---

[3]Hag 1:14-15. [4]Hag 2:9. [5]Zech 1:1, 3. In the original text of Bede, only the first verse (Zech 1:1) is quoted, but it seems clear that Bede forgot to add the exhortation of Zechariah (Zech 1:3). [6]PL 91:843-44. [7]TTH 47:81; PL 91:845-46. [8]See Ezra 4:6-24. [9]The Hebrew reads "hewn stone," while Vg text reads *lapide impolito*, which Bede seems to interpret as "unfinished stone" but might be also intended as "unpolished stone," that is, "roughly cut stone." [10]Lam 4:1.

Jews who long since had been as though finished through knowledge and mindfulness of God's law, the Gentiles who, being enslaved to idolatry, had not by any industry of spiritual architects or any cultivation of piety divested themselves of the ugliness of a rustic and earthly mind. On Ezra and Nehemiah 2.6.[11]

---

[11]TTH 47:82-83; PL 91:846-47.

6:1-22 THE TEMPLE IS COMPLETED

[1]*Then Darius the king made a decree, and search was made in Babylonia, in the house of the archives where the documents were stored.* [2]*And in Ecbatana, the capital which is in the province of Media, a scroll was found on which this was written: "A record.* [3]*In the first year of Cyrus the king, Cyrus the king issued a decree: Concerning the house of God at Jerusalem, let the house be rebuilt, the place where sacrifices are offered and burnt offerings are brought; its height shall be sixty cubits and its breadth sixty cubits,* [4]*with three courses of great stones and one course of timber; let the cost be paid from the royal treasury.* [5]*And also let the gold and silver vessels of the house of God, which Nebuchadnezzar took out of the temple that is in Jerusalem and brought to Babylon, be restored and brought back to the temple which is in Jerusalem, each to its place; you shall put them in the house of God."*

[6]*"Now therefore, Tattenai, governor of the province Beyond the River, Shethar-bozenai, and your associates the governors who are in the province Beyond the River, keep away;* [7]*let the work on this house of God alone; let the governor of the Jews and the elders of the Jews rebuild this house of God on its site.* [8]*Moreover I make a decree regarding what you shall do for these elders of the Jews for the rebuilding of this house of God; the cost is to be paid to these men in full and without delay from the royal revenue, the tribute of the province from Beyond the River.* [9]*And whatever is needed—young bulls, rams, or sheep for burnt offerings to the God of heaven, wheat, salt, wine, or oil, as the priests at Jerusalem require—let that be given to them day by day without fail,* [10]*that they may offer pleasing sacrifices to the God of heaven, and pray for the life of the king and his sons.* [11]*Also I make a decree that if any one alters this edict, a beam shall be pulled out of his house, and he shall be impaled upon it, and his house shall be made a dunghill.* [12]*May the God who has caused his name to dwell there overthrow any king or people that shall put forth a hand to alter this, or to destroy this house of God which is in Jerusalem. I Darius make a decree; let it be done with all diligence."*

[13]*Then, according to the word sent by Darius the king, Tattenai, the governor of the province Beyond the River, Shethar-bozenai, and their associates did with all diligence what Darius the king had ordered.* [14]*And the elders of the Jews built and prospered, through the prophesying of*

Haggai the prophet and Zechariah the son of Iddo. They finished their building by command of the God of Israel and by decree of Cyrus and Darius and Ar-ta-xerxes king of Persia; [15]*and this house was finished on the third day of the month of Adar, in the sixth year of the reign of Darius the king.*

[16]*And the people of Israel, the priests and the Levites, and the rest of the returned exiles, celebrated the dedication of this house of God with joy.* [17]*They offered at the dedication of this house of God one hundred bulls, two hundred rams, four hundred lambs, and as a sin offering for all Israel twelve he-goats, according to the number of the tribes of Israel.* [18]*And they set the priests in their divisions and the Levites in their courses, for the service of God at Jerusalem, as it is written in the book of Moses.*

[19]*On the fourteenth day of the first month the returned exiles kept the passover.* [20]*For the priests and the Levites had purified themselves together; all of them were clean. So they killed the passover lamb for all the returned exiles, for their fellow priests, and for themselves;* [21]*it was eaten by the people of Israel who had returned from exile, and also by every one who had joined them and separated himself from the pollutions of the peoples of the land to worship the LORD, the God of Israel.* [22]*And they kept the feast of unleavened bread seven days with joy; for the LORD had made them joyful, and had turned the heart of the king of Assyria to them, so that he aided them in the work of the house of God, the God of Israel.*

OVERVIEW: Cyrus proposed a plan for the temple from his own ideas and noted the measurements and arrangements of the work as seemed appropriate to him. Darius designates the dutiful devotion of those kings who, recognizing the will of God, endeavored not only not to resist the Christian faith but also to assist it with their decrees. All the writers of sacred Scripture promise good things for the builders of the holy church (i.e., teachers) if they do not tire from adversities and cease from their holy labor. The priests and the Levites and all the people rejoice in the dedication of the Lord's restored house because all the orders of the holy church must share in the rejoicing when those who have sinned are reconciled by repenting (BEDE).

6:1-4 The Height and Width Were Sixty Cubits

DISCREPANCIES IN CYRUS'S MEASUREMENTS OF THE TEMPLE. BEDE: "And so that they lay foundations that may support a height of 60

cubits and a breadth of 60 cubits, three rows of unfinished stones[1] and in the same way rows of new timber": we need not comment on it because neither in the building of the first temple nor of the subsequent one are any of these measurements or works of this sort found.[2] It can thus be inferred that Cyrus proposed this from his own ideas and that he noted the measurements and arrangement of the work as seemed appropriate to him. Indeed, as Chronicles relates, in the first measurement (that is, inside the inner walls) the temple was 60 cubits long and 20 cubits wide,[3] but the height, as the history of Kings explains, was 30 cubits to the upper room;[4] from there to the high chamber an additional 30 cubits, which was the level reached by the top of the porticos, as Josephus attests;[5] and from there another 60 to the top of the roof, which is to say, 120 cubits all

---

[1]See commentary on Ezra 5:6-17. [2]Even though some modern scholars share Bede's doubts over these figures, the height and width may be correct; see TTH 47:86 n. 1. [3]2 Chron 3:3. [4]See 1 Kings 6:2. [5]Josephus *Antiquities of the Jews* 8.3.2.

together, as Chronicles explains.[6] Yet how does it say that three rows of unfinished stones and in the same way rows of new timbers are to be laid, when all inside the temple was lined with cedar, unless perhaps it was a custom of the Persians to make temples with varied work in such a way that there were three rows of stones throughout the walls and a fourth made skillfully from timbers, and Cyrus thought that this should be done too in the same manner in the Jerusalem temple; or perhaps we should understand that he spoke of the courtyard of the priests, which, built in a circle around the temple, had three rows of finished stones and a fourth of cedar wood[7] and was as high as a man's chest; or else of the portico of the Lord's house that was in the front of the temple, concerning which Scripture, when King Solomon's palace was being built, relates thus: "And he made the greater courtyard round with three rows of hewn stones and one row of planks of cedar, and also in the inner courtyard of the Lord's house and in the portico of the house."[8] ON EZRA AND NEHEMIAH 2.7.[9]

6:6-8 Let the Jews Rebuild the Temple

DARIUS APPROVES AND SUPPORTS THE REBUILDING OF THE TEMPLE. BEDE: The sequence of events in the text is as if Darius himself had read Cyrus's letter and, having perused it, immediately endorsed it with his authority, in such a way that suppressing all their adversaries, he ordered the temple of God to be rebuilt on its site just as the letter said, and himself, with a most devout mind in all things, assisted God's worshipers to serve his will. Let Artaxerxes, therefore, who above forbade that the house or city of God be built,[10] designate those lords of worldly affairs who by inciting persecutions opposed the construction of the holy church, while in the upheaval of these persecutions that church flourished chiefly by the triumph of martyrs. Let Darius designate the dutiful devotion of those kings who, recognizing the will of God, endeavored not only not to resist the Christian

faith but also to assist it with their decrees; and many of them, forbidding the persecutions of their predecessors, wished that they themselves along with the people under their sway might be consecrated in the sacraments of the same faith. ON EZRA AND NEHEMIAH 2.7.[11]

6:13-15 The Jews Built and Prospered

GIFTS FOR THE BUILDERS OF THE HOLY CHURCH. BEDE: For these prophets had predicted that if they persisted in building the temple, soon, with the Lord's assistance, they not only would complete the work itself but also have a more abundant supply of all good things as a reward for their devotion. Among their proclamations are Zechariah's words: "The hands of Zerubbabel have laid the foundation of this house, and his hands will complete it, and you will know that the Lord of Hosts has sent me to you,"[12] which is to say, "When you see that the temple has been completed by Zerubbabel, by whom it was begun, then you will understand that I was sent by the Lord and that what I have said I have said at his command." And Haggai says, "From this twenty-fourth day of the ninth month, from the day when the foundations of the Lord's temple were laid, store it in your heart. Is the seed as yet to sprout? Or have the vine, the fig tree, the pomegranate and the olive tree not blossomed? From this day on I will bless you."[13] What happened in the event shows that this prediction was correct. But all the prophets, indeed all the writers of sacred Scripture, promise good things for the builders of the holy church (i.e., teachers) if they do not tire from adversities and cease from their holy labor. For divine help will be present, by which the Lord's house that has been begun may be brought to completion in the heart of their listeners by their believing and living well; and to the architects themselves will come the

---

[6]2 Chron 3:4. [7]See 1 Kings 6:36. [8]1 Kings 7:12. [9]TTH 47:85-87; PL 91:848. [10]See Ezra 4:17-24. [11]TTH 47:88; PL 91:848-49. [12]Zech 4:9. [13]Hag 2:18-19.

blessing of crops, the vine, the fig tree, the pomegranate and the olive [i.e., more abundance of spiritual gifts], which without any doubt will be more copiously granted to us by the Lord the more diligently we have endeavored to establish the abode of his glory either in ourselves or in the hearts of our neighbors. ON EZRA AND NEHEMIAH 2.7.[14]

6:17-22 The Dedication of the Temple

THE SPIRITUAL MEANING OF THE DEDICATION. BEDE: But since the rebuilding of the house after the captivity, as has often been said, designates the correction of those who through sin have wandered from the path of truth that they had only just set out on, it is fitting that when the temple has been restored in this way it is dedicated by the priests and Levites and the rest of the descendants of the exiles with joy. For when those who have sinned are set straight,

"there is great joy" in heaven "in the presence of the angels of God";[15] there is joy also for the teachers who have labored for the salvation of those who go astray, and there is joy for all those who have migrated in their thoughts and deeds from Babylon [i.e., from "the confusion of sinners"] to the citadel of the virtues, which is truly the promised land. So both the priests and the Levites and all the people rejoice in the dedication of the Lord's restored house because all the orders of the holy church must share in the rejoicing when those who have sinned are reconciled by repenting. They offer victims for this dedication when they bring vows of thanks to God for the efforts of sinners to lead a holy life and when many, observing their life devoted to God, are themselves spurred on to works of greater virtue. ON EZRA AND NEHEMIAH 2.8.[16]

---

[14]TTH 47:92-93; PL 91:851. [15]Lk 15:10. [16]TTH 47:100; PL 91:859.

7:1-26 EZRA LEAVES BABYLONIA

[1]Now after this, in the reign of Ar-ta-xerxes king of Persia, Ezra the son of Seraiah, son of Azariah, son of Hilkiah, [2]son of Shallum, son of Zadok, son of Ahitub, [3]son of Amariah, son of Azariah, son of Meraioth, [4]son of Zerahiah, son of Uzzi, son of Bukki, [5]son of Abishua, son of Phinehas, son of Eleazar, son of Aaron the chief priest—[6]this Ezra went up from Babylonia. He was a scribe skilled in the law of Moses which the LORD the God of Israel had given; and the king granted him all that he asked, for the hand of the LORD his God was upon him.

[7]And there went up also to Jerusalem, in the seventh year of Ar-ta-xerxes the king, some of the people of Israel, and some of the priests and Levites, the singers and gatekeepers, and the temple servants. [8]And he came to Jerusalem in the fifth month, which was in the seventh year of the king; [9]for on the first day of the first month he began[b] to go up from Babylonia, and on the first day of the fifth month he came to Jerusalem, for the good hand of his God was upon him. [10]For Ezra had set his heart to study the law of the LORD, and to do it, and to teach his statutes and ordinances in Israel.

¹¹This is a copy of the letter which King Ar-ta-xerxes gave to Ezra the priest, the scribe, learned in matters of the commandments of the LORD and his statutes for Israel: ¹² "Ar-ta-xerxes, king of kings, to Ezra the priest, the scribe of the law of the God of heaven.ˣ And now ¹³I make a decree that any one of the people of Israel or their priests or Levites in my kingdom, who freely offers to go to Jerusalem, may go with you. ¹⁴For you are sent by the king and his seven counselors to make inquiries about Judah and Jerusalem according to the law of your God, which is in your hand, ¹⁵and also to convey the silver and gold which the king and his counselors have freely offered to the God of Israel, whose dwelling is in Jerusalem, ¹⁶with all the silver and gold which you shall find in the whole province of Babylonia, and with the freewill offerings of the people and the priests, vowed willingly for the house of their God which is in Jerusalem. ¹⁷With this money, then, you shall with all diligence buy bulls, rams, and lambs, with their cereal offerings and their drink offerings, and you shall offer them upon the altar of the house of your God which is in Jerusalem. ¹⁸Whatever seems good to you and your brethren to do with the rest of the silver and gold, you may do, according to the will of your God. ¹⁹The vessels that have been given you for the service of the house of your God, you shall deliver before the God of Jerusalem. ²⁰And whatever else is required for the house of your God, which you have occasion to provide, you may provide it out of the king's treasury.

²¹"And I, Ar-ta-xerxes the king, make a decree to all the treasurers in the province Beyond the River: Whatever Ezra the priest, the scribe of the law of the God of heaven, requires of you, be it done with all diligence, ²²up to a hundred talents of silver, a hundred cors of wheat, a hundred baths of wine, a hundred baths of oil, and salt without prescribing how much. ²³Whatever is commanded by the God of heaven, let it be done in full for the house of the God of heaven, lest his wrath be against the realm of the king and his sons. ²⁴We also notify you that it shall not be lawful to impose tribute, custom, or toll upon any one of the priests, the Levites, the singers, the doorkeepers, the temple servants, or other servants of this house of God.

²⁵"And you, Ezra, according to the wisdom of your God which is in your hand, appoint magistrates and judges who may judge all the people in the province Beyond the River, all such as know the laws of your God; and those who do not know them, you shall teach. ²⁶Whoever will not obey the law of your God and the law of the king, let judgment be strictly executed upon him, whether for death or for banishment or for confiscation of his goods or for imprisonment."

h Vg See Syr: Heb *that was the foundation of the going up*   x Aramaic adds a word of uncertain meaning

OVERVIEW: According to Josephus, Artaxerxes was called Xerxes, and he reigned for twenty years after his father, Darius. Ezra rewrote not only the Law but also, as the common tradition of our forebears holds, the whole sequence of sacred Scripture. Ezra typologically represents Christ because, as the Jews are brought from captivity in Babylon to freedom in Jerusalem by him, so the faithful are brought from the "confusion" of the vices to the "peace" and serenity of the virtues by Christ. Artaxerxes, who in his own way pays homage to God's temple and priests with a most devout mind and offers willing service to him, like his predecessor Darius, signifies Christian rulers (BEDE).

7:1-5 Ezra Left Babylon

THE CHRONOLOGICAL POSITION OF ARTA-XERXES' REIGN. BEDE: This Artaxerxes,[1] under whom Ezra came up from Babylon to Jerusalem, Josephus believes to be Xerxes son of Darius, who reigned after him.[2] Moreover, the books of the *Chronicon*[3] hold that the successor of this same Xerxes, who also among them was called Artaxerxes, is designated here. Now Darius, under whom the temple was built, ruled thirty-six years; after him Xerxes ruled for twenty years; after him Artabanus ruled for seven months (which the chroniclers set down as a year); and after him Artaxerxes ruled for forty years.[4] ON EZRA AND NEHEMIAH 2.9.[5]

7:6 A Scribe Skilled in the Law

EZRA THE RESTORER OF THE LAW. BEDE: Now Ezra, who is called "a swift scribe in the law of Moses" for having restored the Law that had been destroyed, rewrote not only the Law but also, as the common tradition of our forebears holds, the whole sequence of sacred Scripture that had likewise been destroyed by fire, in accordance with the way that seemed to him to meet the needs of readers.[6] ON EZRA AND NEHEMIAH 2.9.[7]

7:7-10 Some People of Israel Also Went to Jerusalem

EZRA AS A TYPE OF CHRIST. BEDE: By his name too, which means "helper," Ezra openly stands for the Lord. For it is he by whom alone the people of the faithful are constantly liberated from tribulations and, as though from captivity in Babylon to freedom in Jerusalem, are brought from the "confusion" of the vices to the "peace" and serenity of the virtues as they advance by the steps of meritorious deeds. In the second psalm of the same *anabathmoi*[8] [i.e., of the Ascents], the psalmist proclaims to all those who strive for the highest under whose leadership they ought to strive to attain it when he suggests, "My help is

from the Lord who made heaven and earth."[9] In his actions, too, Ezra was a figure of the Lord, since Ezra led back no small portion of the people from the captivity to Jerusalem and at the same time conveyed money and vessels consecrated to God for the glory of his temple; and through his pontifical authority[10] he purged these people of their foreign wives.[11] What all this suggests with regard to what is done or is going to be done in the church by the Lord is clear to the learned reader, but we will take pains to make them accessible to the less learned as well. For the fact that Ezra goes up from Babylon, and some of the children of Israel and descendants of the priests and the Levites go up with him. This signifies the merciful provision of our Redeemer by which, appearing in the flesh, he entered into the "confusion" of this world though he himself was free from the confusion of sins so that, when he returned, he might free us from all "confusion" and lead us with him into the restfulness of celestial "peace." ON EZRA AND NEHEMIAH 2.9.[12]

7:11-26 A Copy of the Letter That Artaxerxes Gave to Ezra

A FIGURE OF CHRISTIAN RULERS. BEDE: This Artaxerxes, who in his own way pays homage to God's temple and priests with a most devout mind and offers willing service to him, like his predecessor Darius signifies Christian rulers. Nor should one marvel if we have said that the successors of Cyrus, who caused the Lord's temple and city to be built, who loved and assisted his servants and law, contain a figure of Christian

---

[1]This Artaxerxes is a successor to the Artaxerxes who stopped the rebuilding of the temple; see Ezra 4:17-24. [2]Josephus *Antiquities of the Jews* 11.5.1. [3]Jerome *Chronicon* 110.18-21. [4]See Jerome *Chronicon* 104a.25–110.21. [5]TTH 47:109; PL 91:859. [6]The idea that Ezra rewrote the entire sequence of holy Scripture is based on apocryphal sources, especially 4 Ezra 14:9-48; see TTH 47:109 n. 6. [7]TTH 47:109*; PL 91:859. [8]Ps 120–134 (119–133 Vg). [9]Ps 121 (120:2 LXX, Vg). [10]By using the term "pontifical," Bede compares Ezra's authority with that of the pope and bishops in their role as representatives of Christ's power on earth. [11]See Ezra 10:6-44. [12]TTH 47:113-14; PL 91:861.

kings, since the Lord himself said through the prophet that Cyrus came as a figure of his own Son and deigned that Cyrus should be honored through his name: "Thus the Lord says to my anointed Cyrus,"[13] and the other things about him that we have spoken about more extensively above.[14] ON EZRA AND NEHEMIAH 2.9.[15]

---

[13]Is 45:1. [14]See Bede *In Ezr.* 1.108-215; see commentary on Ezra 6:6-8; TTH 47:88 n. 4. [15]TTH 47:117; PL 91:863.

7:27–8:36 JERUSALEM IS FINALLY REACHED

[27]*Blessed be the* LORD, *the God of our fathers, who put such a thing as this into the heart of the king, to beautify the house of the* LORD *which is in Jerusalem,* [28]*and who extended to me his steadfast love before the king and his counselors, and before all the king's mighty officers. I took courage, for the hand of the* LORD *my God was upon me, and I gathered leading men from Israel to go up with me.*

8 *These are the heads of their fathers' houses, and this is the genealogy of those who went up with me from Babylonia, in the reign of Ar-ta-xerxes the king:* [2]*Of the sons of Phinehas, Gershom. Of the sons of Ithamar, Daniel. Of the sons of David, Hattush,* [3]*of the sons of Shecaniah. Of the sons of Parosh, Zechariah, with whom were registered one hundred and fifty men.* [4]*Of the sons of Pahath-moab, Eli-e-ho-enai the son of Zerahiah, and with him two hundred men.* [5]*Of the sons of Zattu,[i] Shecaniah the son of Jahaziel, and with him three hundred men.* [6]*Of the sons of Adin, Ebed the son of Jonathan, and with him fifty men.* [7]*Of the sons of Elam, Jeshaiah the son of Athaliah, and with him seventy men.* [8]*Of the sons of Shephatiah, Zebadiah the son of Michael, and with him eighty men.* [9]*Of the sons of Joab, Obadiah the son of Jehiel, and with him two hundred and eighteen men.* [10]*Of the sons of Bani,[j] Shelomith the son of Josiphiah, and with him a hundred and sixty men.* [11]*Of the sons of Bebai, Zechariah, the son of Bebai, and with him twenty-eight men.* [12]*Of the sons of Azgad, Johanan the son of Hakkatan, and with him a hundred and ten men.* [13]*Of the sons of Adonikam, those who came later, their names being Eliphelet, Jeuel, and Shemaiah, and with them sixty men.* [14]*Of the sons of Bigvai, Uthai and Zaccur, and with them seventy men.*

[15]*I gathered them to the river that runs to Ahava, and there we encamped three days. As I reviewed the people and the priests, I found there none of the sons of Levi.* [16]*Then I sent for Eliezer, Ariel, Shemaiah, Elnathan, Jarib, Elnathan, Nathan, Zechariah, and Meshullam, leading men, and for Joiarib and Elnathan, who were men of insight,* [17]*and sent them to Iddo, the leading man at the place Casiphia, telling them what to say to Iddo and his brethren the temple servants[k] at the place Casiphia, namely, to send us ministers for the house of our God.* [18]*And by the good hand of our God upon us, they brought us a man of discretion, of the sons of Mahli the son*

of Levi, son of Israel, namely Sherebiah with his sons and kinsmen, eighteen; [19]also Hashabiah and with him Jeshaiah of the sons of Merari, with his kinsmen and their sons, twenty; [20]besides two hundred and twenty of the temple servants, whom David and his officials had set apart to attend the Levites. These were all mentioned by name.

[21]Then I proclaimed a fast there, at the river Ahava, that we might humble ourselves before our God, to seek from him a straight way for ourselves, our children, and all our goods. [22]For I was ashamed to ask the king for a band of soldiers and horsemen to protect us against the enemy on our way; since we had told the king, "The hand of our God is for good upon all that seek him, and the power of his wrath is against all that forsake him." [23]So we fasted and besought our God for this, and he listened to our entreaty.

[24]Then I set apart twelve of the leading priests: Sherebiah, Hashabiah, and ten of their kinsmen with them. [25]And I weighed out to them the silver and the gold and the vessels, the offering for the house of our God which the king and his counselors and his lords and all Israel there present had offered; [26]I weighed out into their hand six hundred and fifty talents of silver, and silver vessels worth a hundred talents, and a hundred talents of gold, [27]twenty bowls of gold worth a thousand darics, and two vessels of fine bright bronze as precious as gold. [28]And I said to them, "You are holy to the LORD, and the vessels are holy; and the silver and the gold are a freewill offering to the LORD, the God of your fathers. [29]Guard them and keep them until you weigh them before the chief priests and the Levites and the heads of fathers' houses in Israel at Jerusalem, within the chambers of the house of the LORD." [30]So the priests and the Levites took over the weight of the silver and the gold and the vessels, to bring them to Jerusalem, to the house of our God.

[31]Then we departed from the river Ahava on the twelfth day of the first month, to go to Jerusalem; the hand of our God was upon us, and he delivered us from the hand of the enemy and from ambushes by the way. [32]We came to Jerusalem, and there we remained three days. [33]On the fourth day, within the house of our God, the silver and the gold and the vessels were weighed into the hands of Meremoth the priest, son of Uriah, and with him was Eleazar the son of Phinehas, and with them were the Levites, Jozabad the son of Jeshua and No-adiah the son of Binnui. [34]The whole was counted and weighed, and the weight of everything was recorded.

[35]At that time those who had come from captivity, the returned exiles, offered burnt offerings to the God of Israel, twelve bulls for all Israel, ninety-six rams, seventy-seven lambs, and as a sin offering twelve he-goats; all this was a burnt offering to the LORD. [36]They also delivered the king's commissions to the king's satraps and to the governors of the province Beyond the River; and they aided the people and the house of God.

i Gk: 1 Esdras 8.32: Heb lacks *of Zattu* j Gk: 1 Esdras 8.36: Heb lacks *Bani* k Heb *nethinim*

OVERVIEW: The heads of the families spiritually symbolize all teachers of God's people, who receive increases in their eternal reward commensurate with the number of souls they have acquired for the Lord. Ezra carefully provides for himself a sufficient supply of ministers of God in order to carry out those things that touched on the needs of the temple. As a result of the captivity of the

Assyrians, the descendants of Israel are shown to have reached even as far as the region of Casiphia, since Ezra sent to that place for ministers of the Lord's house to be brought to him. The silver and gold and the vessels that were being sent from Babylon to Jerusalem designate souls that are converted to the Lord from the confusion and sins of this world. The three days of tarrying in Jerusalem are the excellent virtues of faith, hope and love that all the faithful should possess (BEDE).

7:27–8:14 Family Heads and Genealogy

THE SYMBOLISM OF THE HEADS OF THE FAMILIES. BEDE: "These are their family heads, and this is the genealogy of those who went up with me from Babylonia, in the reign of King Artaxerxes: Of the descendants of Phinehas, Gershom," and so on until the end of the genealogy. He carefully enumerates the leaders who came up with him from Babylon and unfolds their genealogy. He takes pains, too, to add their total, which reached 1,440, to suggest that the names of those who come up from the "confusion" of this world are contained in the book of life of the Lamb.[1] But also all teachers [i.e., the heads of the families] of God's people receive increases in their eternal reward commensurate with the number of souls they have acquired for the Lord, according to that parable in the Gospel wherein the good and wise servant said, "Master, your pound has earned ten pounds," and the master replied, "Take charge of ten cities,"[2] which is to say, "appear more glorious in the heavenly kingdom because of the life of those whom you have taught." ON EZRA AND NEHEMIAH 2.10.[3]

8:15-16 No Descendants of Levi

MINISTERS OF GOD WERE NEEDED. BEDE: Ezra fittingly arranged that before he began so great a journey, he might carefully provide for himself a sufficient supply of ministers of God's house in order to carry out those things that were necessary for the needs of the temple when he arrived in Jerusalem. ON EZRA AND NEHEMIAH 2.10.[4]

8:17-20 At the Place Called Casiphia

EZRA RECRUITS MINISTERS IN THE CASPIAN REGION. BEDE: It is worth noting here that although historians write Caspian,[5] Ezra in this passage calls it Casiphia. For the Hebrews, not having the letter *p*, use the letter *ph* in Greek or barbarian names, as in Phetrus or Philatus. Thus, as a result of the captivity of the Assyrians and Chaldeans, the descendants of Israel are shown to have reached even as far as the region of Casiphia, since Ezra sent to that place for ministers of the Lord's house to be brought to him, namely, Levites and Nathinnites, whom Josephus calls "sacred servants."[6] Concerning these people it should be noted that they were living very freely and peacefully even among foreigners, since, at Ezra's command or requests, they were immediately able to appoint so great an army. For the catalogue of them that follows shows that there were 258 men chosen in that expedition; when these were added, Ezra is found to have had a total of nearly 1,700 men in his army. ON EZRA AND NEHEMIAH 2.10.[7]

8:24-25 Weighing Silver and Gold for the Temple

SOULS CONVERTED TO THE LORD. BEDE: It has frequently been said that the silver and gold and the vessels that were being sent from Babylon to Jerusalem designate souls that are converted to the Lord from the confusion and sins of this world. So it is fitting that Ezra entrusts vessels of this kind to the priests to convey them to Jerusalem, because all who desire to join the community of the holy church must be washed in baptism

---

[1]See Rev 21:27. [2]Lk 19:16-17. [3]TTH 47:127; PL 91:868. [4]TTH 47:127-28; PL 91:868. [5]See Orosius *Hist.* 1.2.47-50 (CSEL 5:207-13). [6]Josephus *Antiquities of the Jews* 11.5.1. [7]TTH 47:128-29; PL 91:869.

and consecrated to the Lord through the hands of priests. Equally, those who by sinning have been drawn away from the church's fellowship into the devil's servitude, and who by remaining in their sins have fallen into the captivity of the king of Babylon, must be reconciled to the holy church by doing penance through the office of a priest. And it is well that there are twelve priests to whom this charge was assigned because there are twelve apostles by whose teaching the church was first established throughout the world and by whose successors it does not cease to be built until the end of the world. ON EZRA AND NEHEMIAH 2.11.[8]

8:31-33 Arriving at Jerusalem

THE VIRTUES OF FAITH, HOPE AND LOVE.
BEDE: Appropriately, it is added that when those who came up from Babylon arrived at Jerusalem, they remained there for a period of three days and only then offered and weighed out in the Lord's house the silver and the gold and the vessels that they had brought. For the three days of tarrying in Jerusalem are the excellent virtues of faith, hope and love that all the faithful should possess.[9] Teachers, therefore, must first of all manifest these in themselves and only then offer those whom they have taught and educated in these same virtues to the Fathers who have preceded them in Christ for their approval. For when the holy church finds that those whom we are catechizing are sound in faith and action, it is as if, on weighing the vessels that we offer in the temple through the hands of the priests, [the church] discovers them to be both of pure metal and of perfect weight. This is not only done in this church by the elect every day in examining the life of believers, but, as we said above,[10] is also completed more perfectly in the heavenly Jerusalem in those who have deserved to enter it. For in this life, holy teachers, as though after remaining for three days in the silver and the gold that they brought as an offering when they reveal that they themselves are strong in faith, sublime in hope and fervent in love and show that their hearers shine forth like tested silver through the confession of true faith, gleam in the manner of the best gold through the purity of inviolate understanding and stand out as though they were vessels consecrated to God through the reception of spiritual gifts in themselves. In the heavenly homeland too, these same teachers, when they receive a reward first of all for their own faith, hope and love and then for those whom they have taught, it is as though after the joy of a three-day stay in Jerusalem they are honored more handsomely for the gifts and precious vessels worthy of God they have brought. ON EZRA AND NEHEMIAH 2.11.[11]

---

[8]TTH 47:129-30*; PL 91:869-70. [9]See 1 Cor 13:13. [10]See Bede *In Ezr.* 2.1340-54. [11]TTH 47:133*; PL 91:871.

9:1-15 EZRA CONDEMNS THE PRACTICE OF MIXED MARRIAGES

[1]*After these things had been done, the officials approached me and said, "The people of Israel and the priests and the Levites have not separated themselves from the peoples of the lands with their abominations, from the Canaanites, the Hittites, the Perizzites, the Jebusites, the Ammonites, the Moabites, the Egyptians, and the Amorites. *[2]For they have taken some of their daughters*

to be wives for themselves and for their sons; so that the holy race has mixed itself with the peoples of the lands. And in this faithlessness the hand of the officials and chief men has been foremost." ³*When I heard this, I rent my garments and my mantle, and pulled hair from my head and beard, and sat appalled.* ⁴*Then all who trembled at the words of the God of Israel, because of the faithlessness of the returned exiles, gathered round me while I sat appalled until the evening sacrifice.* ⁵*And at the evening sacrifice I rose from my fasting, with my garments and my mantle rent, and fell upon my knees and spread out my hands to the LORD my God,* ⁶*saying:*

"O my God, I am ashamed and blush to lift my face to thee, my God, for our iniquities have risen higher than our heads, and our guilt has mounted up to the heavens. ⁷*From the days of our fathers to this day we have been in great guilt; and for our iniquities we, our kings, and our priests have been given into the hand of the kings of the lands, to the sword, to captivity, to plundering, and to utter shame, as at this day.* ⁸*But now for a brief moment favor has been shown by the LORD our God, to leave us a remnant, and to give us a secure hold*[l] *within his holy place, that our God may brighten our eyes and grant us a little reviving in our bondage.* ⁹*For we are bondmen; yet our God has not forsaken us in our bondage, but has extended to us his steadfast love before the kings of Persia, to grant us some reviving to set up the house of our God, to repair its ruins, and to give us protection*[m] *in Judea and Jerusalem.*

¹⁰*"And now, O our God, what shall we say after this? For we have forsaken thy commandments,* ¹¹*which thou didst command by thy servants the prophets, saying, 'The land which you are entering, to take possession of it, is a land unclean with the pollutions of the peoples of the lands, with their abominations which have filled it from end to end with their uncleanness.* ¹²*Therefore give not your daughters to their sons, neither take their daughters for your sons, and never seek their peace or prosperity, that you may be strong, and eat the good of the land, and leave it for an inheritance to your children for ever.'* ¹³*And after all that has come upon us for our evil deeds and for our great guilt, seeing that thou, our God, hast punished us less than our iniquities deserved and hast given us such a remnant as this,* ¹⁴*shall we break thy commandments again and intermarry with the peoples who practice these abominations? Wouldst thou not be angry with us till thou wouldst consume us, so that there should be no remnant, nor any to escape?* ¹⁵*O LORD the God of Israel, thou art just, for we are left a remnant that has escaped, as at this day. Behold, we are before thee in our guilt, for none can stand before thee because of this."*

l Heb *nail* or *tent-pin*   m Heb *a wall*

OVERVIEW: Through Ezra's condemnation of mixed marriages the Jews realize that their holiness had been polluted by the detestable actions of the Gentiles and even the leaders by whom they ought to have been corrected were the first to have gone astray. In the fact that Ezra falls on his knees and turns the mind of very many to repentance by pouring out prayers and tears, he represents the Lord Savior, who deigned to pray before and at the time of his passion (BEDE).

9:1-3 Not Separated from the Peoples of the Lands

MIXED MARRIAGES HAVE POLLUTED THE PEOPLE OF GOD. BEDE: The crime of this transgression is also plainly described in the prophet Malachi and is denounced by prophetic authority.[1] For when they had returned from captivity in Babylonia, not only the leaders and priests and Levites but also the remaining people cast aside their wives who were of the Israelite race, who were exhausted and unable to work due to their poverty and the privations of too long a journey and the weakness of their sex, and so their bodies had become weak and unattractive. And they joined in marriage with foreigners either because of the care they took of their bodies, or because they were the daughters of powerful and rich men. These Israelites, it should be understood, were not from among those who had come up with Ezra on that occasion but from those who had long since come up from captivity with Zerubbabel and Jeshua.[2] For those who had come up with Ezra could not have come so rapidly to despise the teaching of such a great guide and leader that, having remained in their homeland for not even five months, they would have abandoned their own wives and accepted foreign ones; rather, those leaders must be understood to have been from the number of those who were anxious to condemn this crime by reporting to Ezra. Nor should one be surprised how it is the people of Israel along with the priests and Levites who are said to have committed this crime, when the earlier return consisted more of people from Judah and Benjamin than from the ten tribes who were called Israel. "For it should be known that when Israel [i.e., the ten tribes] was led into captivity, the two tribes of Judah and Benjamin were without distinction also called by the former name 'Israel.'"[3] In this verse, therefore, "the people of Israel" should not be interpreted as referring to the ten tribes (as opposed to Judah and Benjamin) but in a general way as referring to the people of God (as opposed to the people of the surrounding lands), who polluted the dignity of their heavenly name by associating with people of the lands. For the same prophet Malachi, whom the Hebrews declare to be none other than Ezra,[4] also mentions this transgression in the book of his prophecy as follows:

"Judah has sinned, and a detestable thing has been committed in Israel and in Jerusalem; for Judah has desecrated the holiness of the Lord whom he loved and has married the daughter of a foreign god. May the Lord cut off the man who has done this, both the teacher and the disciple, from the tents of Jacob, even though he brings a gift to the Lord of Hosts."[5] When he says "Judah" here, he clearly means that the people of the first return had been defiled by this crime. But by adding, "May the Lord cut off the man who has done this, both the teacher and the disciple, from the tents of Jacob," he showed by the words *master* and *disciple* that both the rulers and the people were polluted by this sin and that both, if they will not reform, must be rooted out from the fellowship of the holy. And when he added, "even though he brings a gift to the Lord of Hosts," he warns that those who do not shrink from submitting themselves to the devil by sinning offer victims to the Lord in vain.

In this episode we should admire the faith and excellent resolution of the people who were freed from captivity, who refer to themselves as "the holy seed" but the other nations in distinction to their own as "the people of the lands," so that they might openly imply that they themselves, although born from the earth, nevertheless have their dwelling not on earth but in heaven insofar as they, more than other nations, believed in the God of heaven and hoped to obtain heavenly blessings from him. Thus they rightly grieve that their holiness had been polluted by the detestable actions of the Gentiles, and, what is worse, they acknowledge that even the leaders by whom they ought to have been corrected were the first to have gone astray. And it should be carefully noted and used as an example of good works that while some leaders sinned and caused the common people who were entrusted to them to sin, other leaders who were of more wholesome view for their part do their best to correct those sins; but

---

[1]Mal 2:11-12. [2]See Ezra 1:1–2:70. [3]Jerome *In Mal.* 1.1 (CCL 76A:903.18-20). [4]According to the Talmud and Targums. [5]Mal 2:11-12.

because they cannot do this themselves they refer the matter to their *pontifex* [i.e., their archbishop][6] through whose authority so grave, so manifold and so long-lasting a sin can be expiated. No one can doubt, in fact, that the foreign wives figuratively stand for the heresies and superstitious sects of philosophers, which, when they are recklessly admitted into the church, often greatly contaminate the holy seed of catholic truth and pure action with their errors. ON EZRA AND NEHEMIAH 2.12.[7]

9:5-15 Ezra Ashamed and Embarrassed

EZRA IN HIS AFFLICTION SYMBOLIZES THE SAVIOR'S INTERCESSION. BEDE: Ezra had prepared himself through compunction of heart and through bodily affliction so that he might be made worthy to hear heavenly mercy, and only then did he begin to break forth in words of prayer. He bends his knees, spreads out his hands and pours forth prayers to the Lord at the time of the evening sacrifice, not doubting that this sacrifice that is offered with a humble spirit and contrite heart would be more pleasing to God than one offered with the flesh or blood of cattle. Typologically, however, in the fact that with his garment torn he falls on his knees, spreads out his hands to God and turns the mind of very many to repentance by pouring out prayers and tears, as is written in what follows, he represents the Lord Savior, who deigned to pray for our sins both before and at the very time of his passion and who allowed his hands to be stretched out on the cross and the garment of his own flesh to be torn with wounds and mortified at the appointed time on behalf of our restoration, so that, as the apostle says, he who "died on behalf of our sins" might rise "for our justification."[8] This was aptly done at the time of evening sacrifice either because the Lord at the end of the age[9] offered the sacrifice of his own flesh and blood to the Father and ordered that it should be offered by us in bread and wine or because with legal sacrifice coming to an end, he freed us through his own passion and, separating us from the people of the lands, made us become heavenly and allowed those who are chaste in heart and body to adhere to him. ON EZRA AND NEHEMIAH 2.12.[10]

---

[6]Again Bede compares the figure of Ezra with that of a Christian archbishop or the pope. [7]TTH 47:136-39; PL 91:873-74. [8]Rom 4:25; 1 Cor 15:3. [9]That is, at the end of the fifth age of the so-called six world ages; see Bede *In Ezr.* 1.1220-27. [10]TTH 47:141-42; PL 91:875-76.

10:1-44 THE RESTORATION OF MORALITY AND PURITY AMONG THE PEOPLE

[1]*While Ezra prayed and made confession, weeping and casting himself down before the house of God, a very great assembly of men, women, and children, gathered to him out of Israel; for the people wept bitterly.* [2]*And Shecaniah the son of Jehiel, of the sons of Elam, addressed Ezra: "We have broken faith with our God and have married foreign women from the peoples of the land, but even now there is hope for Israel in spite of this.* [3]*Therefore let us make a covenant with our God to put away all these wives and their children, according to the counsel of my lord and of those who tremble at the commandment of our God; and let it be done according to the law.* [4]*Arise, for it is your*

task, and we are with you; be strong and do it." ⁵Then Ezra arose and made the leading priests and Levites and all Israel take oath that they would do as had been said. So they took the oath.

⁶Then Ezra withdrew from before the house of God, and went to the chamber of Jehohanan the son of Eliashib, where he spent the night,ⁿ neither eating bread nor drinking water; for he was mourning over the faithlessness of the exiles. ⁷And a proclamation was made throughout Judah and Jerusalem to all the returned exiles that they should assemble at Jerusalem, ⁸and that if any one did not come within three days, by order of the officials and the elders all his property should be forfeited, and he himself banned from the congregation of the exiles.

⁹Then all the men of Judah and Benjamin assembled at Jerusalem within the three days; it was the ninth month, on the twentieth day of the month. And all the people sat in the open square before the house of God, trembling because of this matter and because of the heavy rain. ¹⁰And Ezra the priest stood up and said to them, "You have trespassed and married foreign women, and so increased the guilt of Israel. ¹¹Now then make confession to the LORD the God of your fathers, and do his will; separate yourselves from the peoples of the land and from the foreign wives." ¹²Then all the assembly answered with a loud voice, "It is so; we must do as you have said. ¹³But the people are many, and it is a time of heavy rain; we cannot stand in the open. Nor is this a work for one day or for two; for we have greatly transgressed in this matter. ¹⁴Let our officials stand for the whole assembly; let all in our cities who have taken foreign wives come at appointed times, and with them the elders and judges of every city, till the fierce wrath of our God over this matter be averted from us." ¹⁵Only Jonathan the son of Asahel and Jahzeiah the son of Tikvah opposed this, and Meshullam and Shabbethai the Levite supported them.

¹⁶Then the returned exiles did so. Ezra the priest selected men,º heads of fathers' houses, according to their fathers' houses, each of them designated by name. On the first day of the tenth month they sat down to examine the matter; ¹⁷and by the first day of the first month they had come to the end of all the men who had married foreign women.

¹⁸Of the sons of the priests who had married foreign women were found Ma-aseiah, Eliezer, Jarib, and Gedaliah, of the sons of Jeshua the son of Jozadak and his brethren. ¹⁹They pledged themselves to put away their wives, and their guilt offering was a ram of the flock for their guilt. ²⁰Of the sons of Immer: Hanani and Zebadiah. ²¹Of the sons of Harim: Ma-aseiah, Elijah, Shemaiah, Jehiel, and Uzziah. ²²Of the sons of Pashhur: Eli-o-enai, Ma-aseiah, Ishmael, Nethanel, Jozabad, and Elasah.

²³Of the Levites: Jozabad, Shime-i, Kelaiah (that is, Kelita), Petha-hiah, Judah, and Eliezer. ²⁴Of the singers: Eliashib. Of the gatekeepers: Shallum, Telem, and Uri.

²⁵And of Israel: of the sons of Parosh: Ramiah, Izziah, Malchijah, Mijamin, Eleazar, Hashabiah,ᴾ and Benaiah. ²⁶Of the sons of Elam: Mattaniah, Zechariah, Jehiel, Abdi, Jeremoth, and Elijah. ²⁷Of the sons of Zattu: Eli-o-enai, Eliashib, Mattaniah, Jeremoth, Zabad, and Aziza. ²⁸Of the sons of Bebai were Jehohanan, Hananiah, Zabbai, and Athlai. ²⁹Of the sons of Bani were Meshullam, Malluch, Adaiah, Jashub, Sheal, and Jeremoth. ³⁰Of the sons of Pahath-moab: Adna, Chelal, Benaiah, Ma-aseiah, Mattaniah, Bezalel, Binnui, and Manasseh. ³¹Of the sons of Harim: Eliezer,

Isshijah, Malchijah, Shemaiah, Shime-on, [32]Benjamin, Malluch, and Shemariah. [33]Of the sons of
Hashum: Mattenai, Mattattah, Zabad, Eliphelet, Jeremai, Manasseh, and Shime-i. [34]Of the sons
of Bani: Ma-adai, Amram, Uel, [35]Benaiah, Bedeiah, Chelubi, [36]Vaniah, Meremoth, Eliashib,
[37]Mattaniah, Mattenai, Jaasu. [38]Of the sons of Binnui:[q] Shime-i, [39]Shelemiah, Nathan, Adaiah,
[40]Machnadebai, Shashai, Sharai, [41]Azarel, Shelemiah, Shemariah, [42]Shallum, Amariah, and
Joseph. [43]Of the sons of Nebo: Je-iel, Mattithiah, Zabad, Zebina, Jaddai, Joel, and Benaiah. [44]All
these had married foreign women, and they put them away with their children.[r]

n 1 Esdras 9.2: Heb *where he went* **o** 1 Esdras 9.16: Syr: Heb *and there were selected Ezra, etc.* **p** 1 Esdras 9.26: Gk: Heb *Malchijah* **q** Gk: Heb *Bani, Binnui* **r** 1 Esdras 9.36: Heb obscure

Overview: After Ezra's prayers and grief for the pollution of Israel, a very great crowd of weeping people of both sexes and of all ages gathered around him. When the people assembled in the middle of winter, they trembled "because of their sin and the rain," and this was done to admonish for them and all other sinners. The sin of the Jews shows us how the minds of the faithful are tempted inwardly with much greater danger when they are seduced and enticed by their own lust. The different deeds accomplished by Ezra demonstrate in all their aspects that he was a type of Christ our Savior (Bede).

10:1-5 *The People Wept*

Effects of Ezra's Prayer. Bede: How much Ezra's prayer, tears and sorrow accomplished is shown when it relates that a very great crowd of weeping people of both sexes and of all ages immediately gathered around him. They were weeping either because those who had sinned were doing penance for their sin or because those who had remained pure were sorrowing over the transgression and downfall of their brothers. But whether it was the former or the latter or both groups who were weeping, all are shown to have been greatly troubled by the prayers and laments of their *pontifex*,[1] since even the women and children are said to have been present here as well. The event can also be understood to have happened in this way, namely, that first those who were innocent and righteous flocked to Ezra when he says, "And all who feared the word of God concerning this transgression of those who had come up from captivity gathered around me,"[2] but now those who had sinned also came to do penance, together with their wives and children. On Ezra and Nehemiah 2.13.[3]

10:7-14 *The People Assembled*

The Ninth Month Signifies One Admonition for All. Bede: The ninth month is the one that is called Casleu [Chislev] by the Hebrews and December by the Romans. Who does not know that this month comes in the middle of winter and is rainy and surprisingly stormy? Hence we should note all the more carefully that when the people assembled in the middle of winter, it is recorded that they trembled "because of their sin and the rain." For when they noticed that the rains were pouring down more than was usual even for this wet season, they were brought back to their conscience and understood that this had happened because of their sins and that heavenly wrath was imminent. Admonished by this disturbance of the sky, they grew frightened, and for this reason they had not dared to carry on their business in their own homes but sat down in the courtyard of the Lord's house and put on penitential and humble garb. This was done as a lesson for those who,

[1]Again Bede compares Ezra with an archbishop or the pope. [2]Ezra 9:4. [3]TTH 47:142-43; PL 91:876.

even when the elements are stirred up and weather deteriorates into violent winds, floods of rain, heavy snowstorms, parching drought or even the death of people and animals, and when the judge himself threatens the force of his anger through open signs, do not at all seek to correct their behavior so as to placate that judge and escape the destruction hanging over them but instead merely busy themselves to find some means to avoid or overcome the adverse conditions raging outside on account of their sins. ON EZRA AND NEHEMIAH 2.13.[4]

10:15-44 They Pledged to Send Away Their Wives

REJECTION OF THE FOREIGN WIVES AND EXPIATION OF THE SIN. BEDE: First they put away the unlawful wives, and only then do they offer a ram on their behalf so that, cleansed from the crime, they might approach the altar in a state of purity. For it is difficult for a person's offering to be acceptable to God if he does not first strive to abandon the misdeed for which he offers it, as Isaiah says: "Cease to act perversely; learn to do well."[5] And because they who were the first to sin were the descendants or brothers of the high priest, it is right that they offer a ram from their flock as a punishment for their crime in order that by such a victim they might indicate that they themselves who were seen to be the teachers and rulers of the people, as it were the leaders of a flock of followers, had arranged to sacrifice themselves with respect to their former way of life and, purged by appropriate penance, to offer themselves to God through a better way of life. Meanwhile, it should be noted with what great art of warfare the devil constantly assails the faithful and how he never leaves them any time secure from battle. For consider how those who could not be overcome by misfortunes were overcome by enticements; they conquered their public enemies when the Lord's temple was built and dedicated but were conquered by a desire for Gentile women, so that they did not keep the temples of

their own hearts and bodies worthy for God to inhabit. Very clearly there is a complete allegorical interpretation of this for our own times. For we see that the minds of the faithful are tempted inwardly with much greater danger now when they are seduced and enticed by their own lust than when they were previously tempted outwardly when their brutal opponent was raging against their constancy by sword and fire. But the mercy of the Lord will be present, so that just as it then endowed those people with the virtue of patience against open battles of those who raged against them, in the same way it may also give us the protection of caution against the snares of enticements that catch us unawares. Accordingly, when the *pontifex*[6] and all those who feared the Lord acted zealously, those who had sinned "were pricked in the heart,"[7] and they cast out their foreign wives. Once they expelled the baseness of self-indulgence, the beauty of chasteness returned; once they cast out the debris of the vices, the flowers and spices of the virtues were strewn in the Lord's city. ON EZRA AND NEHEMIAH 2.14.[8]

EZRA'S DEEDS FORESHADOWED THOSE OF THE SAVIOR. BEDE: Now Ezra himself was clearly a type of the Lord Savior too, inasmuch as he restored sacred Scripture, recalled the people out from captivity to Jerusalem, enriched the Lord's house with greater gifts, appointed leaders and guardians beyond the river Euphrates who were familiar with God's law and purified the descendants of the exiles from their foreign wives. For the Lord restored sacred Scripture, because when the scribes and the Pharisees either had defiled it by their traditions or taught that it should be understood according to the letter alone, he showed it was full of spiritual meaning, according as to whether it was written by Moses or by the prophets; and by sending the Holy

---

[4]TTH 47:145-46; PL 91:878. [5]Is 1:16-17. [6]Ezra, who is compared with a Christian archbishop or the pope. [7]Acts 2:37. [8]TTH 47:150-51*; PL 91:880-81.

Spirit on them he also caused the New Testament to be written down by apostles and apostolic men. He led the people out from captivity in Babylonia and brought them now liberated to Jerusalem and the promised land, not only because by suffering on that one occasion on the cross he redeemed the world through his own blood, and descending into hell he rescued all true Israelites [i.e., the elect] he found there and, leading them to the walls of the heavenly city, granted them the joys of inheritance they had once been promised; but also because daily gathering the faithful from the turmoil of this world, he calls them together to the fellowship of the holy church and the eternal kingdom. He increased the riches of the temple with gold and silver and precious vessels that either the people of Israel or rulers of the Persians had sent there through him, because by bringing those who believe in him from both peoples [i.e., Jews and Gentiles] into the church, he does not cease to adorn and glorify her always through the splendor of their faith and good works. He appointed leaders and guardians for all the people beyond the river who knew and taught God's law because in the holy church, which not only has been cleansed in the river of sacred baptism but also by

the sincerity of its faith has transcended the Babylonian river (that is, the turmoil of this changing world), he placed apostles, evangelists, pastors and teachers.[9] He purified the descendants of the exiles from their foreign wives because he forbade that those who by professing the faith had renounced the world should be enslaved any more to the enticements of the world. He also cast out the children of these mothers from the assembly of the returned exiles in case by chance when they grew up they might follow the faithlessness of their mothers rather than the faith of their fathers, because he taught that even those of our works that seem good to people are spurious if they are mixed with carnal pleasure or originate from the contagion of human favor, and so are not worthy of the fellowship of those who, completely renouncing the world with their whole mind, move on to the things of heaven and who rejoice not to be weakened by temporal enticements but on the contrary to be made stronger through adversities and to be prepared by them for their heavenly rest. ON EZRA AND NEHEMIAH 2.14.[10]

---

[9]See Eph 4:11. [10]TTH 47:151-52*; PL 91:881-82.

NEHEMIAH

1:1-11 NEHEMIAH'S PRAYER FOR GOD'S MERCY

¹*The words of Nehemiah the son of Hacaliah.*

Now it happened in the month of Chislev, in the twentieth year, as I was in Susa the capital, ²*that Hanani, one of my brethren, came with certain men out of Judah; and I asked them concerning the Jews that survived, who had escaped exile, and concerning Jerusalem.* ³*And they said to me, "The survivors there in the province who escaped exile are in great trouble and shame; the wall of Jerusalem is broken down, and its gates are destroyed by fire."*

⁴*When I heard these words I sat down and wept, and mourned for days; and I continued fasting and praying before the God of heaven.* ⁵*And I said, "O LORD God of heaven, the great and terrible God who keeps covenant and steadfast love with those who love him and keep his commandments;* ⁶*let thy ear be attentive, and thy eyes open, to hear the prayer of thy servant which I now pray before thee day and night for the people of Israel thy servants, confessing the sins of the people of Israel, which we have sinned against thee. Yea, I and my father's house have sinned.* ⁷*We have acted very corruptly against thee, and have not kept the commandments, the statutes, and the ordinances which thou didst command thy servant Moses.* ⁸*Remember the word which thou didst command thy servant Moses, saying, 'If you are unfaithful, I will scatter you among the peoples;* ⁹*but if you return to me and keep my commandments and do them, though your dispersed be under the farthest skies, I will gather them thence and bring them to the place which I have chosen, to make my name dwell there.'* ¹⁰*They are thy servants and thy people, whom thou hast redeemed by thy great power and by thy strong hand.* ¹¹*O Lord, let thy ear be attentive to the prayer of thy servant, and to the prayer of thy servants who delight to fear thy name; and give success to thy servant today, and grant him mercy in the sight of this man."*

Now I was cupbearer to the king.

OVERVIEW: By his words and deeds and person Nehemiah plainly designates the mediator of God and people, our Lord Jesus Christ. The city of Susa symbolizes the defenses of the mind of the faithful, especially of those who are charged with the salvation of the souls that are occasionally snatched away from the church by the attacks of the devil. The words of Nehemiah literally describe his concern for Jerusalem, which was still undefended before its enemies, but typologically indicate the concern of those people in the holy church who are rightly afflicted because some of their neighbors still are subject to sins (BEDE). The salvation in Christ is open to Jews and Gentiles (ORIGEN).

1:1-2 Certain Men from Judah

NEHEMIAH FORESHADOWS CHRIST THE MEDIATOR. BEDE: Nehemiah is interpreted in Latin as "My consoler is the Lord" or "the consoler from the Lord." For when Nehemiah restored Jerusalem's walls and, after delivering them from the disdain of their enemies, raised up the people of God to the observance of the divine law, it is surely clear that by his word and deed and person he not unsuitably designates the mediator of God and people, the man Christ Jesus,[1] who indicates that he was sent to console the poor in spirit when he said to his disciples as he was about to ascend to heaven: "I will ask the Father, and he will give you another Paraclete,"[2] that is, a Consoler, by whom the psalmist showed that God's holy city (namely, the church) would be rebuilt and also those who mourn would be consoled when he said, "The Lord builds up Jerusalem; he gathers the exiles of Israel. He heals the brokenhearted,"[3] and so on. ON EZRA AND NEHEMIAH 3.15.[4]

THE DEFENSES OF THE MIND OF THE FAITHFUL. BEDE: Nehemiah writes that he was in the fortress of Susa when the men came who brought the news about Jerusalem. Susa is the capital city of the kingdom of the Persians, as we read in the book of Esther.[5] Not only Nehemiah but also the prophet Daniel calls it a "fortress," "not because the city itself is a fortress, for as we have stated it is a capital city and a very powerful one, but because it is so solidly built that it looks like a fortress."[6] Now Susa means "riding" or "returning." The name aptly befits the defenses of the mind of the faithful, especially of those who are charged with the capture of Jerusalem, that is, for the salvation of those who are occasionally snatched away from the church through the devil's attacks but by repenting are brought back

to the church again by the grace of God. For such people are in a returning fortress—that is, in the strength of a mind called back from the lowest delights to a longing for the heavenly homeland, from which they had fallen in their first parent; such people are in the very strong cavalry of the hearts of the saints who carry God as their rider, according to the prophet's saying: "Mounting your horses, and your riding is salvation."[7] For the Lord indeed mounts his horses when he illuminates the hearts of preachers with the grace of his mercy so that he can rule them; and his riding is salvation because he not only carries to eternal salvation those over whom he presides by ruling them but also, so that he may likewise preside over them too, and through them makes others sharers of this same everlasting salvation as well. ON EZRA AND NEHEMIAH 3.15.[8]

1:3-4 The Wall of Jerusalem

LITERAL AND ALLEGORICAL MEANING OF NEHEMIAH'S WORDS. BEDE: The literal meaning is evident, namely, that those who had remained after the capture, even though they seemed to be living at peace in view of the fact that the king of the Persians had shown himself to be their friend and not long previously had sent to them Ezra the scribe with letters in order that he should have authority over all the region beyond the river,[9] nonetheless were in great distress because their enemies were blaming them and because the holy city still remained in ruins.[10] But even now in the holy church, people are rightly afflicted and pricked by a salutary sense of remorse when, even though they themselves have repented of their past wrongdoings, they consider the fact that their neighbors still are subject to sins, so that, through the negligence of those who, having reformed, could have been profitable

---

[1]See 1 Tim 2:5. [2]Jn 14:16. [3]Ps 147 (146:2-3 LXX, Vg). [4]TTH 47:154*; PL 91:883. [5]See Esther 1:2. [6]Jerome In Danielem 2.8.2 (CCL 75A:851.770-73). [7]Hab 3:8. [8]TTH 47:155-56; PL 91:883-84. [9]See Ezra 7:25. [10]This is the emendation proposed by DeGregorio; see TTH 47:156 n. 2.

to many, the devil has free entry into the church, as through the walls of a ruined city. It is even more lamentable if those very ones who should have been profiting others through their teaching and personal example show to observers an example of destruction in themselves by living corruptly. For this is what is meant by the fact that the gates of Jerusalem were burned down by enemy flames: that those who ought, by living and teaching well, to have been introducing worthy people into the assembly of the elect and keeping unworthy people out, perish instead in the fire of avarice, self-indulgence, pride, strife, envy, and the rest of the vices that the evil enemy is apt to bring in. ON EZRA AND NEHEMIAH 3.15.[11]

1:5-11 God Will Gather His People

SALVATION IN GOD IS OPEN TO ALL. ORIGEN: But I say, Has the Lord used iniquity to snatch the nations from the power of his enemies and recall them to faith in him and to his dominion? By no means. For "Israel" was once "the Lord's portion,"[12] but they made Israel turn from their God in sin, and because of their sins God said to them, "Behold, you have been separated by your sins and because of your sins you have been scattered under the whole heaven." But again he says to them, "If your dispersion should be from one end of heaven to the other, from there I will gather you, says the Lord." Because, therefore, "the princes of this world"[13] had first invaded "the Lord's portion," "the good shepherd"[14] had, necessarily, the ninety and nine having been left on the heights,[15] to descend to the lands and seek the one sheep that was lost, and when it was found and carried back on his shoulders, to recall it to the sheepfold of perfection on high. HOMILIES ON GENESIS 9.7.[16]

---

[11]TTH 47:156-57*; PL 91:884. [12]Sir 17:17 (LXX). [13]Jn 16:11. [14]Jn 10:11. [15]See Mt 18:12. [16]FC 71:155.

2:1-20 NEHEMIAH IS SENT TO JERUSALEM TO REBUILD THE WALLS

[1]*In the month of Nisan, in the twentieth year of King Ar-ta-xerxes, when wine was before him, I took up the wine and gave it to the king. Now I had not been sad in his presence.* [2]*And the king said to me, "Why is your face sad, seeing you are not sick? This is nothing else but sadness of the heart." Then I was very much afraid.* [3]*I said to the king, "Let the king live for ever! Why should not my face be sad, when the city, the place of my fathers' sepulchres, lies waste, and its gates have been destroyed by fire?"* [4]*Then the king said to me, "For what do you make request?" So I prayed to the God of heaven.* [5]*And I said to the king, "If it pleases the king, and if your servant has found favor in your sight, that you send me to Judah, to the city of my fathers' sepulchres, that I may rebuild it."* [6]*And the king said to me (the queen sitting beside him), "How long will you be gone, and when will you return?" So it pleased the king to send me; and I set him a time.* [7]*And I said to the king, "If it pleases the king, let letters be given me to the governors of the province Beyond the*

River, that they may let me pass through until I come to Judah; ⁸and a letter to Asaph, the keeper of the king's forest, that he may give me timber to make beams for the gates of the fortress of the temple, and for the wall of the city, and for the house which I shall occupy." And the king granted me what I asked, for the good hand of my God was upon me.

⁹Then I came to the governors of the province Beyond the River, and gave them the king's letters. Now the king had sent with me officers of the army and horsemen. ¹⁰But when Sanballat the Horonite and Tobiah the servant, the Ammonite, heard this, it displeased them greatly that some one had come to seek the welfare of the children of Israel.

¹¹So I came to Jerusalem and was there three days. ¹²Then I arose in the night, I and a few men with me; and I told no one what my God had put into my heart to do for Jerusalem. There was no beast with me but the beast on which I rode. ¹³I went out by night by the Valley Gate to the Jackal's Well and to the Dung Gate, and I inspected the walls of Jerusalem which were broken down and its gates which had been destroyed by fire. ¹⁴Then I went on to the Fountain Gate and to the King's Pool; but there was no place for the beast that was under me to pass. ¹⁵Then I went up in the night by the valley and inspected the wall; and I turned back and entered by the Valley Gate, and so returned. ¹⁶And the officials did not know where I had gone or what I was doing; and I had not yet told the Jews, the priests, the nobles, the officials, and the rest that were to do the work.

¹⁷Then I said to them, "You see the trouble we are in, how Jerusalem lies in ruins with its gates burned. Come, let us build the wall of Jerusalem, that we may no longer suffer disgrace." ¹⁸And I told them of the hand of my God which had been upon me for good, and also of the words which the king had spoken to me. And they said, "Let us rise up and build." So they strengthened their hands for the good work. ¹⁹But when Sanballat the Horonite and Tobiah the servant, the Ammonite, and Geshem the Arab heard of it, they derided us and despised us and said, "What is this thing that you are doing? Are you rebelling against the king?" ²⁰Then I replied to them, "The God of heaven will make us prosper, and we his servants will arise and build; but you have no portion or right or memorial in Jerusalem."

OVERVIEW: We can properly take Artaxerxes, who with the same devotion of his predecessor Cyrus ordered that the city of Jerusalem be rebuilt, as a type of the Lord, who builds a city for himself from living stones. Sanballat and Tobias, who became greatly distressed because they realized that the buildings of Jerusalem were about to be restored, rightly signify the heretics and enemies of the church. As Nehemiah wanders around inspecting the various parts of the devastated city, so it is fitting for spiritual teachers to get up regularly at night and inspect with careful scrutiny the state of the holy church. Also holy teachers, just like Nehemiah, are in the greatest distress as long as they discern that Jerusalem, that is the "vision of peace" that the Lord has commended to us, lies deserted due to wars of disagreements (BEDE).

2:1-8 The King Granted Nehemiah's Request

ARTAXERXES IS A TYPE OF CHRIST. BEDE: We have plainly learned from the teaching of Isaiah how Cyrus, the first king of the Persians, represents a figure of the Lord Savior because he ended the captivity of the people of God and decreed that the temple be restored.[1] So too, we can properly take the successor of this same empire, Artaxerxes, who with the same devotion ordered that the city of Jerusalem be rebuilt, as a type of the Lord, who builds a city for himself from living stones (that is, the one church made from all the elect) through the service of preachers. Thus it is appropriate that the name Artaxerxes means "a light that tests silently."[2] For the Lord is indeed the light of life who tests the hearts of his faithful silently, at times illuminating them with the sweetness of celestial grace, at others clouding them with the burdens of this life, so that, instructed by temporal adversities, they might desire eternal goods more ardently. On EZRA AND NEHEMIAH 3.16.[3]

2:10 Sanballat's and Tobiah's Displeasure

FIGURES OF HERETICS AND ENEMIES OF THE CHURCH. BEDE: Heretics and all enemies of the church are also saddened whenever they notice the elect laboring for the catholic faith or the correction of morality so that the walls of the church may be rebuilt. Note how different their mood and situation was now from what it had been earlier, because above it was said that those who had remained from the captivity of Judea were "in great distress and disgrace"[4] and that Nehemiah also conducted a prolonged fast with weeping and prayers because the walls of Jerusalem had been destroyed and its gates burned down by fire. But now, by contrast, the enemies of this same holy city were saddened and became greatly distressed because they realized that its buildings were about to be restored and at the same time that the citizens would be delivered from the insults of their enemies. Hence we should recollect that, even in this life, that saying of the Lord can be fulfilled in which he said, "Amen, Amen, I say to you, that you will weep and mourn but the world will rejoice. You will grieve," he adds at once, "but your grief will be turned into joy."[5] For surely, as the world that used to rejoice weeps, the sadness of the

just will be turned into joy when it is learned that the affairs of the holy church are prospering and those who by sinning have gone astray are returning to it by doing penance. On EZRA AND NEHEMIAH 3.16.[6]

2:11-13 The Inspection of the Walls

NEHEMIAH AS A MODEL FOR SPIRITUAL TEACHERS. BEDE: He wanders around inspecting the various parts of the devastated city and examines carefully in his mind how each of these should be repaired. Similarly, it is fitting for spiritual teachers also to get up regularly at night and inspect with careful scrutiny the state of the holy church while others are resting, so that they might vigilantly investigate how they might repair and rebuild through chastening those things that have been defiled or destroyed in it by the warfare of sins. Jerusalem's wall lies in ruins, and the way of life of the faithful is soiled by earthly and base desires. The gates are consumed by fire when, as a result of their abandoning instruction in the truth, even those who ought to have been opening up the entrance of life to others also by teaching them now grow idle with the same laziness as everyone else and become slaves to temporal concerns. On EZRA AND NEHEMIAH 3.17.[7]

2:17-18 Jerusalem in Ruins

AN EXHORTATION TO RESTORE THE BUILDINGS OF FAITH. BEDE: These words are plain and exceedingly adaptable to a spiritual meaning because holy teachers—indeed, all who burn with zeal for God—are in the greatest distress as long as they discern that Jerusalem (that is, the "vision of peace"[8] that the Lord has bequeathed and commended to us) lies deserted due to wars

---

[1]See Is 44:28; Ezra 1:1-4. [2]See Jerome *Nom. Hebr.* (CCL 72:129.3). [3]TTH 47:158-59; PL 91:885. [4]Neh 1:3. [5]Jn 16:20. [6]TTH 47:160-61*; PL 91:886. [7]TTH 47:161; PL 91:886. [8]This is the meaning in Hebrew of the name Jerusalem.

of disagreements, and they behold that the gates of the virtues (which, according to Isaiah, "praise" should occupy)[9] have been destroyed and subjected to insults while the gates of hell prevail. Hence they work hard to unite the ministers of the word in a single purpose so that those build-ings of faith and good action that seemed to have been destroyed can rise again. ON EZRA AND NEHEMIAH 3.17.[10]

---

[9]Is 60:18. [10]TTH 47:161-62; PL 91:886.

3:1-32 THE RESTORATION OF JERUSALEM'S WALLS

[1]*Then Eliashib the high priest rose up with his brethren the priests and they built the Sheep Gate. They consecrated it and set its doors; they consecrated it as far as the Tower of the Hundred, as far as the Tower of Hananel.* [2]*And next to him the men of Jericho built. And next to them[a] Zaccur the son of Imri built.*

[3]*And the sons of Hassenaah built the Fish Gate; they laid its beams and set its doors, its bolts, and its bars.* [4]*And next to them Meremoth the son of Uriah, son of Hakkoz repaired. And next to them Meshullam the son of Berechiah, son of Meshezabel repaired. And next to them Zadok the son of Baana repaired.* [5]*And next to them the Tekoites repaired; but their nobles did not put their necks to the work of their LORD.[b]*

[6]*And Joiada the son of Paseah and Meshullam the son of Besodeiah repaired the Old Gate; they laid its beams and set its doors, its bolts, and its bars.* [7]*And next to them repaired Melatiah the Gibeonite and Jadon the Meronothite, the men of Gibeon and of Mizpah, who were under the jurisdiction of the governor of the province Beyond the River.* [8]*Next to them Uzziel the son of Harhaiah, goldsmiths, repaired. Next to him Hananiah, one of the perfumers, repaired; and they restored[c] Jerusalem as far as the Broad Wall.* [9]*Next to them Rephaiah the son of Hur, ruler of half the district of[d] Jerusalem, repaired.* [10]*Next to them Jedaiah the son of Harumaph repaired opposite his house; and next to him Hattush the son of Hashabneiah repaired.* [11]*Malchijah the son of Harim and Hasshub the son of Pahath-moab repaired another section and the Tower of the Ovens.* [12]*Next to him Shallum the son of Hallohesh, ruler of half the district of[d] Jerusalem, repaired, he and his daughters.*

[13]*Hanun and the inhabitants of Zanoah repaired the Valley Gate; they rebuilt it and set its doors, its bolts, and its bars, and repaired a thousand cubits of the wall, as far as the Dung Gate.*

[14]*Malchijah the son of Rechab, ruler of the district of[d] Beth-haccherem, repaired the Dung Gate; he rebuilt it and set its doors, its bolts, and its bars.*

¹⁵*And Shallum the son of Colhozeh, ruler of the district of*^d *Mizpah, repaired the Fountain Gate; he rebuilt it and covered it and set its doors, its bolts, and its bars; and he built the wall of the Pool of Shelah of the king's garden, as far as the stairs that go down from the City of David.* ¹⁶*After him Nehemiah the son of Azbuk, ruler of half the district of*^d *Beth-zur, repaired to a point opposite the sepulchres of David, to the artificial pool, and to the house of the mighty men.* ¹⁷*After him the Levites repaired: Rehum the son of Bani; next to him Hashabiah, ruler of half the district of*^d *Keilah, repaired for his district.* ¹⁸*After him their brethren repaired: Bavvai the son of Henadad, ruler of half the district of*^d *Keilah;* ¹⁹*next to him Ezer the son of Jeshua, ruler of Mizpah, repaired another section opposite the ascent to the armory at the Angle.* ²⁰*After him Baruch the son of Zabbai repaired another section from the Angle to the door of the house of Eliashib the high priest.* ²¹*After him Meremoth the son of Uriah, son of Hakkoz repaired another section from the door of the house of Eliashib to the end of the house of Eliashib.* ²²*After him the priests, the men of the Plain, repaired.* ²³*After them Benjamin and Hasshub repaired opposite their house. After them Azariah the son of Ma-aseiah, son of Ananiah repaired beside his own house.* ²⁴*After him Binnui the son of Henadad repaired another section, from the house of Azariah to the Angle* ²⁵*and to the corner. Palal the son of Uzai repaired opposite the Angle and the tower projecting from the upper house of the king at the court of the guard. After him Pedaiah the son of Parosh* ²⁶*and the temple servants living*^e *on Ophel repaired to a point opposite the Water Gate on the east and the projecting tower.* ²⁷*After him the Tekoites repaired another section opposite the great projecting tower as far as the wall of Ophel.*

²⁸*Above the Horse Gate the priests repaired, each one opposite his own house.* ²⁹*After them Zadok the son of Immer repaired opposite his own house. After him Shemaiah the son of Shecaniah, the keeper of the East Gate, repaired.* ³⁰*After him Hananiah the son of Shelemiah and Hanun the sixth son of Zalaph repaired another section. After him Meshullam the son of Berechiah repaired opposite his chamber.* ³¹*After him Malchijah, one of the goldsmiths, repaired as far as the house of the temple servants and of the merchants, opposite the Muster Gate,*^f *and to the upper chamber of the corner.* ³²*And between the upper chamber of the corner and the Sheep Gate the goldsmiths and the merchants repaired.*

a Heb *him*   b Or *lords*   c Or *abandoned*   d Or *foreman of half the portion assigned to*   e Cn: Heb *were living*   f Or *Hammiphkad Gate*

OVERVIEW: It was right that the restoration of the city was begun by a high priest and his brothers, in order that those who were highest in rank might themselves in their good works become an example for all. The Fish Gate typologically refers to the community of Christians, because just as a flock stands for the Lord's faithful, so in the same way they are frequently called fish. They who build the Dung Gate in Jerusalem prefigure the ones who ordain to the ministry of the holy church those through whom the filth of the vices is removed from the minds of the elect. The Pool of Shelah (which means "sent"), where the man born blind was given light, stands for the Lord Savior who was sent by God the Father for our illumination. The builders of the Gate of the Horses foreshadow the holy teachers, who show satisfactory examples of living to those who enter the doors of the holy church (BEDE).

3:1-2 Priests Rebuild the Sheep Gate

High Priests Must Be an Example for All. Bede: This Elijahhib was the high priest at the time. He was the son of Joiakim, who, after his own father, Jeshua the high priest son of Jozadak, himself bore the insignia of the priesthood for a long time. And it was right that the restoration of the city was begun by a high priest and his brothers, in order that those who were highest in rank might themselves in their good works become an example for all. And it is well that, as the priests are building, it adds, "And as far as the Tower of One Hundred Cubits they sanctified it, as far as the Tower of Hanenel." For priests build to the number of one hundred cubits when they enflame all those whom they are instructing with love and desire for eternal things. For the number one hundred, which in counting on the fingers moves from the left hand to right, represents celestial rewards, which, in comparison with temporal and base rewards, are as the right hand is to the left. They are also said to have sanctified the gate that they built. For it is the duty of priests to make their own actions more worthy than others through a special sanctification and to do this earnestly so that those who are joined with them might sanctify the Lord's name in themselves by living well. On Ezra and Nehemiah 3.18.[1]

3:3-5 Building the Fish Gate

Typological Meaning of the Fish Gate. Bede: He gives the name Fish Gate to the gate that faced Joppa and Diospolis (i.e., Lydda).[2] It was nearest to the sea of all of Jerusalem's roads;[3] today it is said to be called the Gate of David and is the first of the gates to the west of Mount Zion. This view appears to be borne out in Chronicles, in which it is written about Manasseh king of Judah: "After this he built a wall outside the City of David,[4] to the west of Gihon in the valley, from the entrance of the Gate of the Fish in a circuit as far as Ophel, and he erected it much higher."[5] Typologically, however,

just as a flock stands for the Lord's faithful, so in the same way they are frequently called fish. Thus, just as he says to Peter, "Feed my sheep,"[6] so too he promises Peter together with Andrew and the rest of the apostles, "Come, follow me, and I will make you become fishers of people."[7] In a parable he likewise says about these same fishermen, "They collected the good fish in baskets but threw the bad away."[8] Therefore, the Fish Gate is built in Jerusalem when those orders are established in the church through which the elect, separated from the reprobate like good fish from the bad, may be brought into the fellowship of perpetual peace; and the Fish Gate is built when they rescue their neighbors, who observe them, from the waves of worldly agitation and desire and introduce them to the tranquility and peace of the spiritual life. On Ezra and Nehemiah 3.18.[9]

3:13-14 Malchijah Repaired the Dung Gate

Those Through Whom the Filth of Vice Is Removed. Bede: They say the site of the city of Jerusalem, being laid out on a gentle slope, inclines toward the north and east in such a way that rainfall does not accumulate there at all but rather flows out like rivers through the eastern gates and swells the torrent of Kidron in the valley of Jehoshaphat, taking with it all the waste of the streets. And so it appears likely that the Dung Gate is the one through which refuse and filth were generally to be driven out. It is not in any way of less virtue and usefulness for all impure things to be removed from the city of the Lord than for those things that are pure to be collected into it. They who build the Dung Gate in Jerusalem, therefore, are the ones who ordain to the ministry of the holy church those

---

[1]TTH 47:162-63; PL 91:887. [2]Lydda, now Lod, is a city in Palestine about ten miles from the sea. [3]Jerome In Sophoniam 1.10 (CCL 76A:666.388-89). [4]The City of David was the part of Jerusalem on the ridge to the south of the Temple Mount; see TTH 47:165 n. 1. [5]2 Chron 33:14. [6]Jn 21:17. [7]Mt 4:19. [8]Mt 13:48. [9]TTH 47:164-65; PL 91:888.

through whom the filth of the vices is removed from the minds of the elect, but also through whom people of corrupt mind are kept away from the boundaries of the church while a shower of heavenly grace helps them and weakens every impurity, so that, according to the psalmist, "all who do evil" are eliminated "from the city of the Lord."[10] On Ezra and Nehemiah 3.18.[11]

3:15 The Wall of the Pool of Shelah

DIVINE MYSTERIES FORESHADOWED IN THE POOL OF SHELAH. BEDE: The Pool of Siloa[12] (which means "sent"), where the man born blind was given light,[13] stands for the Lord Savior who was sent by God the Father for our illumination. The spring of this pool can be very aptly understood as the same Father from whom he was born, about which the psalmist well says, "For with you is the spring of life; in your light we shall see light."[14] And the Spring Gate is built in Jerusalem when teachers are ordained in the church to preach belief in divine eternity to the nations. The walls of the Pool of Siloa are built too when the very firm and invincible testimonies of the Scriptures, in which the mystery of the Lord's incarnation is described, are rooted in the mind of the faithful. Moreover these walls of divine utterances reach as far as the King's Garden when, having recognized the mysteries of the Lord's dispensation, we begin to bring forth shoots of the virtues with the help of that same king, our Lord God. On Ezra and Nehemiah 3.18.[15]

3:28 The Priests Repair the Horse Gate

THE SPIRITUAL CONSTRUCTION OF THE CHURCH. BEDE: Jeremiah mentions this gate and indicates that it is in the eastern part of the city when he writes typologically about the church, "And the city shall be rebuilt for the Lord from the Tower of Hananel";[16] and a little afterwards: "up to the torrent of Kidron and as far as the corner of the Gate of the Horse on the east."[17] Now horses, when they are put to good use, just as donkeys, camels and mules also do, sometimes represent peoples of the Gentiles who have been converted to the Lord, and at other times concerns for temporal matters that have been duly subjugated to the rule of the soul. And the priests built the wall of God's city up to the gate of the horses when, after the calling of the Jewish people, holy teachers by spreading the word went on to lead the peoples of the Gentiles into the holy church. Similarly, they build up to the gate of the horses when they show satisfactory examples of living to those who enter the doors of the holy church in order to bridle the wanton motions of their flesh or soul, or perhaps when they control their own thoughts with which they consider it necessary to worry about their own and their family's food and clothing[18] in such a way that these thoughts in no way impede the freedom of that mind with which they have resolved always to seek heavenly things. On Ezra and Nehemiah 3.18.[19]

---

[10]Ps 101:8 (100:8 LXX, Vg). [11]TTH 47:169; PL 91:890-91. [12]This is the Latin spelling (derived from the Greek in the LXX) of the name "shelah." [13]Jn 9:7. [14]Ps 36:9 (35:10 LXX, Vg). [15]TTH 47:170-71*; PL 91:891. [16]Jer 31:38. [17]Jer 31:40. [18]See Mt 6:31. [19]TTH 47:177; PL 91:895.

4:1-23 PLOTS AGAINST JERUSALEM

[1g]Now when Sanballat heard that we were building the wall, he was angry and greatly enraged, and he ridiculed the Jews. [2]And he said in the presence of his brethren and of the army of Samaria, "What are these feeble Jews doing? Will they restore things? Will they sacrifice? Will they finish up in a day? Will they revive the stones out of the heaps of rubbish, and burned ones at that?" [3]Tobiah the Ammonite was by him, and he said, "Yes, what they are building—if a fox goes up on it he will break down their stone wall!" [4]Hear, O our God, for we are despised; turn back their taunt upon their own heads, and give them up to be plundered in a land where they are captives. [5]Do not cover their guilt, and let not their sin be blotted out from thy sight; for they have provoked thee to anger before the builders.

[6]So we built the wall; and all the wall was joined together to half its height. For the people had a mind to work.

[7b]But when Sanballat and Tobiah and the Arabs and the Ammonites and the Ashdodites heard that the repairing of the walls of Jerusalem was going forward and that the breaches were beginning to be closed, they were very angry; [8]and they all plotted together to come and fight against Jerusalem and to cause confusion in it. [9]And we prayed to our God, and set a guard as a protection against them day and night.

[10]But Judah said, "The strength of the burden-bearers is failing, and there is much rubbish; we are not able to work on the wall." [11]And our enemies said, "They will not know or see till we come into the midst of them and kill them and stop the work." [12]When the Jews who lived by them came they said to us ten times, "From all the places where they live[i] they will come up against us."[j] [13]So in the lowest parts of the space behind the wall, in open places, I stationed the people according to their families, with their swords, their spears, and their bows. [14]And I looked, and arose, and said to the nobles and to the officials and to the rest of the people, "Do not be afraid of them. Remember the Lord, who is great and terrible, and fight for your brethren, your sons, your daughters, your wives, and your homes."

[15]When our enemies heard that it was known to us and that God had frustrated their plan, we all returned to the wall, each to his work. [16]From that day on, half of my servants worked on construction, and half held the spears, shields, bows, and coats of mail; and the leaders stood behind all the house of Judah, [17]who were building on the wall. Those who carried burdens were laden in such a way that each with one hand labored on the work and with the other held his weapon. [18]And each of the builders had his sword girded at his side while he built. The man who sounded the trumpet was beside me. [19]And I said to the nobles and to the officials and to the rest of the people, "The work is great and widely spread, and we are separated on the wall, far from one another. [20]In the place where you hear the sound of the trumpet, rally to us there. Our God will fight for us."

[21]So we labored at the work, and half of them held the spears from the break of dawn till the

stars came out. [22] *I also said to the people at that time, "Let every man and his servant pass the night within Jerusalem, that they may be a guard for us by night and may labor by day."* [23] *So neither I nor my brethren nor my servants nor the men of the guard who followed me, none of us took off our clothes; each kept his weapon in his hand.*[k]

g Ch 3.33 in Heb h Ch 4.1 in Heb i Cn: Heb *you return* j Compare Gk Syr: Heb uncertain k Cn: Heb *each his weapon the water*

OVERVIEW: The Samaritans exhorted by Sanballat to oppose the construction of the wall openly represent the heretics, who are separated from the unity of Christ and the church by schisms or wicked works. The sole refuge against all enemies of the church is prayer to God and the zeal of teachers. Against all the enemies of the church we must, according to the apostle, take up the armor of God, "so that" we may be able to "resist on the evil day and stand perfect in all things."[1] We must keep a constant watch lest we may fall back into sins through the devil's seduction (BEDE).

4:1-5 What Are These Jews Doing?

OBVIOUS FIGURES OF HERETICS. BEDE: Obviously this is the anger of heretics, these the words of those who in vain call themselves "samaritans" (that is, the "guardians of God's law")[2] despite the fact that they are greatly opposed to God and his laws inasmuch as, having been long separated from the House of David (that is, from the unity of Christ and the church) by heresies or schisms or wicked works, they are afraid to see the walls of the faith being built lest their own irreverence might be attacked and excluded; this is the ridicule of all who claim that "they know God, but in their deeds they deny him,"[3] for indeed the Samaritans used to serve the Lord but without repudiating their own ancient gods. Typologically, they are imitated today by Christians but in such a way that they also consider their stomach a god[4] and pursue greed (which the apostle clearly calls "slavery to idols")[5] and, being slaves to the remaining allurements of the world, serve "created things" more "than the Creator, who is praised forever."[6] And so, just like heretics, such people do not want the walls of the church to be restored in case they are forced by the growing state of piety to retreat from their own impiety; such ones are apt to call the Jews (that is, confessors of the faith)[7] "feeble" and say that they will be easily overthrown by the Gentiles, since in the daily battle of souls they love sins more than obtaining the victory palm of virtue. ON EZRA AND NEHEMIAH 3.19.[8]

4:6-9 The Jews Pray to God

THE PROTECTION OF PRAYER. BEDE: This is the sole refuge against all enemies of the church—namely, prayer to God and the zeal of teachers, who, meditating day and night on his law, fortify the hearts of the faithful against the attacks of the devil and his soldiers by preaching, consoling and exhorting. ON EZRA AND NEHEMIAH 3.19.[9]

4:10-15 The People Stationed According to Their Families

WE MUST TAKE UP THE ARMOR OF GOD. BEDE: These things are also always done in the spiritual edifice. For the unwearied enemy lies in waiting with his unclean companions (namely, malicious spirits and people) who constantly endeavor to impede and, insofar as they can, to assault the works of the faith and virtues whenever we are incautious, and they attempt to kill the mind of the faithful with the sword of depraved suggestion. But against these we must, according to the apostle, take up the armor of

---

[1]Eph 6:13. [2]Jerome *Nom. Hebr.* (CCL 72:142.3). [3]Tit 1:16. [4]Phil 3:19. [5]Eph 5:5. [6]Rom 1:25. [7]Isidore *Etymol.* 8.4.2. [8]TTH 47:179*; PL 91:896. [9]TTH 47:180-81; PL 91:897.

God, "so that" we may be able to "resist on the evil day and stand perfect in all things."[10] Now it is well said that he stationed the people "behind the wall in a circuit" with weapons so that, surrounded by a troop of armed men, the builders might press on in building the wall with a freer and securer hand. For the grades of the faithful are divided up: some build up the church by adorning it with good works on the inside, while others, armed with the weapons of sacred reading, keep vigilant for heretics who attack the same church. The former in religious devotion strengthen their neighbors in the truth of the faith, while the latter wage a necessary battle against the weapons of the devil or of the vices with which they struggle to assault this same faith and with pastoral solicitude repel the wolves lying in ambush from the Lord's sheepfold. ON EZRA AND NEHEMIAH 3.19.[11]

4:15 The Enemies' Plot Was Known

A VICTORY OBTAINED. BEDE: In the spiritual edifice too, if we are always clothed with the apostolic armor,[12] the stratagem of the devil and his angels who desire to subdue us will be foiled. ON EZRA AND NEHEMIAH 3.19.[13]

4:16-23 Working and Watching

A CONSTANT WATCH AGAINST THE DEVIL'S MACHINATIONS. BEDE: For it should be noted not only that half of the young men did the work and half were prepared to fight, but also that these same young men who were doing the work were all equipped with a sword. For so great is the ancient enemy's craftiness, so great the fury of his malice when he fights against the church, that

not only preachers of the truth but even the very people of God themselves must always keep watch against his machinations, as though standing firm in battle. For the builders gird their loins with a sword when those who take pains to persevere in good works and who take pains to govern those in their charge by means of an ordered regimen (that is, to place the living stones in the edifice of the holy city in suitable arrangement) endeavor to restrain in themselves the laxness of wanton behavior with the sharpness of God's Word. And we should not pass over the fact that when David and Solomon were building this same city, nothing is said about armed builders or attacking adversaries; rather, the city destroyed by their wrongdoings is restored with greater labor and effort, first because the spiritual edifice, which is concerned with the salvation of souls, is such that, as soon as we are reborn in baptism through the faith and confession of the Holy Trinity, we are made, through God's grace, his city and house without any effort of our own; but if after our ablution in the sacred font we fall back into sins through the devil's seduction and the victorious enemy demolishes the defenses of our virtue with the fire of the vices, it is necessary for us to repair those buildings of good works that we have lost through more serious efforts of prayer, mortification, vigils, alms and a stricter life. For it is harder for us to be free of known enticements of the vices than unknown, and it takes less effort to avoid an unknown pleasure of the flesh than to reject a familiar one. ON EZRA AND NEHEMIAH 3.20.[14]

---

[10]Eph 6:13. [11]TTH 47:181-82; PL 91:897-98. [12]See Eph 6:13. [13]TTH 47:182; PL 91:898. [14]TTH 47:182-83; PL 91:898.

5:1-19 NEHEMIAH FIGHTS AGAINST USURY AND SOCIAL OPPRESSION

[1]Now there arose a great outcry of the people and of their wives against their Jewish brethren. [2]For there were those who said, "With our sons and our daughters, we are many; let us get grain, that we may eat and keep alive." [3]There were also those who said, "We are mortgaging our fields, our vineyards, and our houses to get grain because of the famine." [4]And there were those who said, "We have borrowed money for the king's tax upon our fields and our vineyards. [5]Now our flesh is as the flesh of our brethren, our children are as their children; yet we are forcing our sons and our daughters to be slaves, and some of our daughters have already been enslaved; but it is not in our power to help it, for other men have our fields and our vineyards."

[6]I was very angry when I heard their outcry and these words. [7]I took counsel with myself, and I brought charges against the nobles and the officials. I said to them, "You are exacting interest, each from his brother." And I held a great assembly against them, [8]and said to them, "We, as far as we are able, have bought back our Jewish brethren who have been sold to the nations; but you even sell your brethren that they may be sold to us!" They were silent, and could not find a word to say. [9]So I said, "The thing that you are doing is not good. Ought you not to walk in the fear of our God to prevent the taunts of the nations our enemies? [10]Moreover I and my brethren and my servants are lending them money and grain. Let us leave off this interest. [11]Return to them this very day their fields, their vineyards, their olive orchards, and their houses, and the hundredth of money, grain, wine, and oil which you have been exacting of them." [12]Then they said, "We will restore these and require nothing from them. We will do as you say." And I called the priests, and took an oath of them to do as they had promised. [13]I also shook out my lap and said, "So may God shake out every man from his house and from his labor who does not perform this promise. So may he be shaken out and emptied." And all the assembly said "Amen" and praised the LORD. And the people did as they had promised.

[14]Moreover from the time that I was appointed to be their governor in the land of Judah, from the twentieth year to the thirty-second year of Ar-ta-xerxes the king, twelve years, neither I nor my brethren ate the food allowance of the governor. [15]The former governors who were before me laid heavy burdens upon the people, and took from them food and wine, besides forty shekels of silver. Even their servants lorded it over the people. But I did not do so, because of the fear of God. [16]I also held to the work on this wall, and acquired no land; and all my servants were gathered there for the work. [17]Moreover there were at my table a hundred and fifty men, Jews and officials, besides those who came to us from the nations which were about us. [18]Now that which was prepared for one day was one ox and six choice sheep; fowls likewise were prepared for me, and every ten days skins of wine in abundance; yet with all this I did not demand the food allowance of the governor, because the servitude was heavy upon this people. [19]Remember for my good, O my God, all that I have done for this people.

Overview: The famine is caused not only by a scarcity of crops but also by the greed of the rulers, since they were demanding greater taxes from these people than they were able to pay. Nehemiah's words warn us that we should take care, whenever a general time of famine and destitution has afflicted the people, not only to give poor people what we can but also to forgive that tribute that we have been accustomed to exact from our subjects. Labors performed without piety cannot become fruitful before the Lord. Nehemiah's honest and moderate behavior mystically suggests that a work is an apostolic one when someone who has been promoted to be a ruler of God's people nobly undertakes the work of the ruler by building the church but does not seek a reward for his work (Bede).

5:1-5 Having to Pledge Land and Houses

The Scarcity of Crops and the Greed of the Rulers. Bede: The people desired to construct the city wall but were being hindered from the holy work by the severity of the famine. This famine had been caused not only by a scarcity of crops but also by the greed of the rulers, since they were demanding greater taxes from these people than they were able to pay. We see that this occurs among us in the same manner every day. For how many are there among God's people who willingly desire to obey the divine commands but are hindered from being able to fulfill what they desire not only by lack of temporal means and by poverty but also by the examples of those who seem to be endowed with the garb of religion but who exact an immense tax and weight of worldly goods from those whom they claim to be in charge of while giving nothing for their eternal salvation, either by teaching them or by providing them with examples of good living or by devoting effort to works of piety for them? Would that some Nehemiah (i.e., a "consoler from the Lord") might come in our own days and restrain our errors, kindle our breasts to love of the divine and strengthen our hands by turning

them away from our own pleasures to establishing Christ's city!

But we should observe according to the literal meaning that the unhappy outcry of the afflicted people was attended by a threefold distinction. For some, compelled by the famine, were proposing to sell their own children to the more wealthy for food; others, sparing their children, wished rather to give up their fields and own homes for food; and some, by contrast, prohibiting the sale of both children and fields, were urging that they should merely borrow money for the king's taxes, giving their fields and vineyards as a pledge until a fruitful supply of crops returned and they could restore the moneylenders what they had borrowed. On Ezra and Nehemiah 3.21.[1]

5:6-11 Stop This Taking of Interest

An Exhortation to Charity and Social Solidarity. Bede: As the most excellent leader of the heavenly militia and "wise architect"[2] of God's city, he first of all declared that he himself had done what he wished the nobles and magistrates of the people to do, namely, to give alms to the poor and seek nothing from them except faithfulness to God's law and the building of his city. In this passage, we do not need to scrutinize the allegorical meaning but to observe the literal meaning of the text itself by performing it as diligently as we can, namely, so that quite apart from the daily fruits of almsgiving, we should take care whenever a general time of famine and destitution has afflicted the people, not only to give poor people what we can but also to forgive that tribute that we have been accustomed to exact from our subjects as though by right, in order that the Father might forgive us our debts too.[3] On Ezra and Nehemiah 3.21.[4]

5:12-13 Holding the Wealthy to Their Promise

---

[1]TTH 47:183-85; PL 91:899. [2]1 Cor 3:10. [3]See Mt 6:12. [4]TTH 47:185*; PL 91:899.

THE PUNISHMENT OF THE UNMERCIFUL.
BEDE: For [if one] either refuses to show mercy on poor people or is not ashamed to demand from them, as if lawfully, what they do not have to give, this person is shaken from his house (namely, is cast and shaken out from the fellowship of the holy church in which he believed he would remain forever) and deprived of his labors, doubtless, that is, of the fruit of good works in which he believed that he had toiled admirably. For labors performed without piety cannot become fruitful before the Lord. ON EZRA AND NEHEMIAH 3.21.[5]

5:13 All the People Praise the Lord

A PROFOUND EFFECT. BEDE: When on hearing his declaration they all responded "Amen" and, praising God, did what Nehemiah had commanded, it is surely evident that they had not been forced by fear but had received his words in the inmost affection of their heart. ON EZRA AND NEHEMIAH 3.21.[6]

5:14-19 Not Eating the Food Allowance

THE MYSTICAL MEANING OF NEHEMIAH'S GENEROUS BEHAVIOR. BEDE: Explaining this by means of a type, the apostle says that "the Lord has commanded that those who preach the gospel should receive their living from the gospel. But I have not used any of these things."[7] For twelve years, Nehemiah and his brothers so lived under his leadership that they would not eat "the yearly provisions that were due to the governors," so that by this he might mystically suggest that that work is an apostolic one when someone who has been promoted to be a ruler of God's people nobly undertakes the work of the ruler by building the church but does not seek a reward for his work by asking for earthly goods from those whom he rules by preaching and living well. ON EZRA AND NEHEMIAH 3.22.[8]

---

[5]TTH 47:185-86; PL 91:899-900. [6]TTH 47:186; PL 91:900. [7]1 Cor 9:14-15. [8]TTH 47:186*; PL 91:900.

6:1-14 NEW PLOTS OF THE ENEMIES

¹Now when it was reported to Sanballat and Tobiah and to Geshem the Arab and to the rest of our enemies that I had built the wall and that there was no breach left in it (although up to that time I had not set up the doors in the gates), ²Sanballat and Geshem sent to me, saying, "Come and let us meet together in one of the villages in the plain of Ono." But they intended to do me harm. ³And I sent messengers to them, saying, "I am doing a great work and I cannot come down. Why should the work stop while I leave it and come down to you?" ⁴And they sent to me four times in this way and I answered them in the same manner. ⁵In the same way Sanballat for the fifth time sent his servant to me with an open letter in his hand. ⁶In it was written, "It is reported among the nations, and Geshem¹ also says it, that you and the Jews intend to rebel; that is why you are building the wall; and you wish to become their king, according to this report. ⁷And you have also set up prophets to proclaim concerning you in Jerusalem, 'There is a king in Judah.' And now it will be

reported to the king according to these words. So now come, and let us take counsel together." ⁸Then I sent to him, saying, "No such things as you say have been done, for you are inventing them out of your own mind." ⁹For they all wanted to frighten us, thinking, "Their hands will drop from the work, and it will not be done." But now, O God, strengthen thou my hands.

¹⁰Now when I went into the house of Shemaiah the son of Delaiah, son of Mehetabel, who was shut up, he said, "Let us meet together in the house of God, within the temple, and let us close the doors of the temple; for they are coming to kill you, at night they are coming to kill you." ¹¹But I said, "Should such a man as I flee? And what man such as I could go into the temple and live?ᵐ I will not go in." ¹²And I understood, and saw that God had not sent him, but he had pronounced the prophecy against me because Tobiah and Sanballat had hired him. ¹³For this purpose he was hired, that I should be afraid and act in this way and sin, and so they could give me an evil name, in order to taunt me. ¹⁴Remember Tobiah and Sanballat, O my God, according to these things that they did, and also the prophetess No-adiah and the rest of the prophets who wanted to make me afraid.

l Heb *Gashmu*   m Or *would go into the temple to save his life*

OVERVIEW: Sanballat, Tobiah and Geshem are like the heretics and false Christians who want to have a fellowship of peace with true believers but do not agree to follow ecclesiastical faith and, on the contrary, compel those who are on the peak of virtues to go down to the lowest depths of wicked works. Shemaiah, who invites Nehemiah to his house, is a traitor and an enemy who has been corrupted by the gifts of friendship with foreigners (BEDE).

6:1-9 A Request for a Meeting

NEHEMIAH'S ENEMIES FORESHADOW HERETICS AND FALSE CHRISTIANS. BEDE: The enemies of the holy city are urging Nehemiah to go down to the plains and to enter into a peace pact with them by together slaughtering calves as testimony to the arranged treaty, but he perseveres in the mountains so that the devout work is not neglected. So too, heretics and false catholics want to have a fellowship of peace with true catholics but with this stipulation, that they do not agree to ascend to the citadel of ecclesiastical faith or duty themselves but rather they compel those whom they see dwelling on the peak of the virtues to go down to the lowest depths of wicked works or dogmas. And it is well that they want to enter into a pact with Nehemiah on one plain, doubtless because they desire that all those whom they are able to seduce be relaxed in the same freedom of the broader life that they themselves follow; and it is well that they wish to enter into a pact with him by together slaughtering calves, because false brothers are eager to offer the sacrifices of their prayer and action to God together with true catholics, so that, when they are believed to be genuinely faithful, they might be able to corrupt these same true catholics through the proximity of their association. But Nehemiah, representing the person of faithful teachers, by no means agrees to go down to the impious or to be defiled with their sacrifices but remains devout in the virtuous works he has undertaken; and the more severely his enemies tried to frighten him, the more he himself strove to become terrifying to these same enemies by doing a good work. ON EZRA AND NEHEMIAH 3.23.[1]

---

[1]TTH 47:187*; PL 91:900-901.

6:10-14 *Intimidation*

AN ATTEMPT AGAINST NEHEMIAH'S VIRTUE.
BEDE: Pressured by the attacks of his enemies, Nehemiah enters the house of Shemaiah as though Shemaiah were his friend and brother but discovers that Shemaiah himself is a traitor and enemy, inasmuch as he had been corrupted by the gifts of friendship with foreigners. For the elect always have "conflicts without and fears within,"[2] and not just the apostles but the prophets too lived a life fraught "with dangers from the nation, with dangers from Gentiles, with dangers from false brothers."[3] ON EZRA AND NEHEMIAH 3.23.[4]

---

[2]2 Cor 7:5. [3]2 Cor 11:26. [4]TTH 47:188*; PL 91:901.

6:15-19 COMPLETION OF THE WALL

[15]*So the wall was finished on the twenty-fifth day of the month Elul, in fifty-two days.* [16]*And when all our enemies heard of it, all the nations round about us were afraid[n] and fell greatly in their own esteem; for they perceived that this work had been accomplished with the help of our God.* [17]*Moreover in those days the nobles of Judah sent many letters to Tobiah, and Tobiah's letters came to them.* [18]*For many in Judah were bound by oath to him, because he was the son-in-law of Shecaniah the son of Arah: and his son Jehohanan had taken the daughter of Meshullam the son of Berechiah as his wife.* [19]*Also they spoke of his good deeds in my presence, and reported my words to him. And Tobiah sent letters to make me afraid.*

n Another reading is *saw*

OVERVIEW: The wall is completed on the twenty-fifth day of the month Elul, after fifty-two days of work: both numbers have different mystical meanings. As in Jerusalem, where the sturdy structure of the wall was built, the enemies were hindered and stopped, so too in the holy church, when the sturdy structure of charity, self-restraint and peace is erected, unclean spirits grow afraid and their temptation is repelled (BEDE).

6:15 *Twenty-five Days and Fifty-two Days*

THE MYSTICAL MEANING OF THE NUMBERS.
BEDE: According to the Hebrews, the month of Elul is the sixth month of the year, which is called September by the Romans. And it is right that the wall of the holy city is completed in the sixth month of the year, so that by this number the perfected action of the faithful, whether penitents or the innocent, might also be designated. For the perfection of a good work is usually designated by the number six, either because the Lord completed the creation of the world on the sixth day and rested on the seventh or because he wished us to sweat with good actions within the six ages[1] of this world but to hope for a sabbath rest for our souls in the seventh, which comes in the next life. It is rightly completed on the twenty-fifth day of that same month, namely, on account of

---

[1]For the theory of the six ages of the world, see Bede *In Ezr.* (CCL 119A:1.1201-28); *De Templ.* 66-71 (CCL 123B:445.1-544.98).

---

the five bodily senses, by the aid of which we ought to do good works outwardly: for just as the simple number five is often a figure of these senses, so when this is multiplied by itself to make twenty-five it designates these same senses with greater perfection. Therefore, we complete the wall of Jerusalem on the twenty-fifth day of the sixth month when, diligently surrendering all of our bodily senses to divine servitude, we bring the pursuits of the virtues that we have begun to a sure end and, with the Lord's help, effectively complete whatever things have begun to do faithfully in defense of catholic peace.

It is also fitting that the wall is said to have been completed in fifty-two days. For the fiftieth psalm—in which the prophet also prays specifically for the construction of this city, saying, "Deal favorably, O Lord, in your good will with Zion, that the walls of Jerusalem may be built up"[2]—is one of repentance and forgiveness. On the fiftieth day of the Lord's resurrection, the Holy Spirit, through whom not only the desire to repent is poured into us but also the gift of pardon is conferred on those who repent, came to the primitive church. Now there are two precepts concerning charity, namely, love of God and of neighbors, in which, once pardon for sins has been granted to us by the Holy Spirit, we are commanded to endeavor to attain eternal life. It is therefore most appropriate that when rebuilding the wall of the holy city that had been destroyed by the enemies, its citizens restore it in fifty-two days, because this, undoubtedly, is the perfection of the righteous in this life, namely, that they should not only, by repenting through the grace of divine inspiration, set right whatever sins they have committed but afterwards adorn themselves with good works in love of God and neighbors. On Ezra and Nehemiah 3.23.[3]

6:16-19 All the Nations Were Afraid

The Sturdy Structure of Virtue Repels Temptation. Bede: Those who previously were seeking to frighten the builders of the holy city in order to hinder them from working now are themselves frightened when the construction of this same city is completed, and they are disheartened when they realize that its construction was begun and completed through God's authority. So too in the holy church, when the sturdy structure of charity, self-restraint, peace and the rest of virtues is erected, unclean spirits grow afraid and their temptation, put to flight by our strength, is repelled and makes our victory all the greater. This can be understood to apply equally to heretics and to false catholics, who, through the steadfast faith of good people that works through love, are either set straight and reformed or, having been exposed so that people can be on their guard against them, are expelled from the boundaries of the church. On Ezra and Nehemiah 3.24.[4]

---

[2]Ps 51:18 (50:20 LXX, Vg). [3]TTH 47:188-89; PL 91:901-2. [4]TTH 47:189-90; PL 91:902.

7:1-3 GATEKEEPERS AND GUARDS
ARE APPOINTED TO WATCH THE WALL

¹Now when the wall had been built and I had set up the doors, and the gatekeepers, the singers, and the Levites had been appointed, ²I gave my brother Hanani and Hananiah the governor of the castle charge over Jerusalem, for he was a more faithful and God-fearing man than many. ³And I said to them, "Let not the gates of Jerusalem be opened until the sun is hot; and while they are still standing guard° let them shut and bar the doors. Appoint guards from among the inhabitants of Jerusalem, each to his station* and each opposite his own house."

o Heb obscure   * Heb *some at their watch posts* Vg *each in his own turn*

OVERVIEW: The gatekeepers are those who have received "the keys to the kingdom of heaven" so that they might receive those who are worthy and humble but prevent the proud and the impure from entry into the heavenly city. The guardianship of the holy church is duly achieved only if everyone shows concern for all the faithful but makes a particularly diligent effort to take care of those over whom he has been put in charge by God's authority (BEDE).

7:1-2 Gatekeepers Chosen

THE DOORS OF REGULAR DISCIPLINE. BEDE: In the spiritual sense too, whenever the walls of the church have been built by gathering new nations to the faith or by setting straight those who have erred, immediately the doors of regular discipline must be set in place so that the ancient enemy, who "prowls around like a roaring lion,"[1] might not in any place be able to invade the fold of the faithful. Gatekeepers, singers and Levites must be appointed to guard these same doors; it is clear that the character of all these accords with holy teachers. For the gatekeepers are those who have received "the keys to the kingdom of heaven"[2] so that they might receive those who are worthy and humble but prevent the proud and the impure from entry into the heavenly city by

saying, "You have no part or lot in this business, for your heart is not right before God."[3] The singers are those who with a devout voice preach the sweetness of this same heavenly homeland to their hearers; the Levites are those who always remain vigilant in regard to the observance of divine worship. Now Nehemiah ordered that "the gates of Jerusalem are not to be opened until the sun is hot"[4] (that is, throughout the whole night), doubtless either in case the enemy invaded under the cover of darkness or else in case any of the citizens were to go out incautiously and be captured by the enemy and killed. Likewise, throughout the night of this age also, guardians of souls must act diligently to ensure that the observance of devout living is not neglected, allowing the devil to sneak in to disturb the company of the faithful or to seize and destroy one of their number. But when the "Sun of righteousness"[5] appears and the light of future blessedness shines forth, no longer will there be a need for barriers of self-restraint, because adversaries will no longer be given the ability to attack or tempt the faithful, since they will be condemned to eternal punishment along with their leader. Thus in his Apocalypse John says about the future glory of the holy city, "And its gates

---

[1] 1 Pet 5:8. [2] Mt 16:19. [3] Acts 8:21. [4] Neh 7:3. [5] Mal 4:2.

will not be shut ever, for there will be no night in that place."[6] ON EZRA AND NEHEMIAH 3.24.[7]

7:3 Guards Appointed

GUARDIAN OF SOULS MUST BE WELL TRAINED. BEDE: Guardians of souls must not be appointed from recent converts or from the common crowd but from those who, freed by the grace of God from the battle of vices, have already trained themselves to keep their mind in Jerusalem (that is, in the "vision of serene peace") and who can say with the apostle, "But our dwelling is in heaven."[8] About this people is well said that they appointed "each in his own turn," namely, so that when their course has been completed and they have been removed from this light, others may immediately be chosen in their place to rule over the faithful; and that there may at no time be a shortage of those who make an effort to keep watch on behalf of the peace of the holy church "because of night-time fears,"[9] since the truth of prophetic words, in which it is said to the same church, "In the place of your fathers, sons are born to you,"[10] runs continuously to the end of the age. It is also well added, "and each opposite his own house." For the guardianship of the holy church is duly achieved only if everyone shows concern for all the faithful but makes a particularly diligent effort to take care of those over whom he has been put in charge by God's authority. ON EZRA AND NEHEMIAH 3.24.[11]

---

[6]Rev 21:25. [7]TTH 47:190-91; PL 91:902. [8]Phil 3:20. [9]Song 3:8. [10]Ps 45:16 (44:17 Vg). [11]TTH 47:191; PL 91:902-3.

7:4-73 A CENSUS OF THE CITIZENS

[4]*The city was wide and large, but the people within it were few and no houses had been built.* [5]*Then God put it into my mind to assemble the nobles and the officials and the people to be enrolled by genealogy. . . .*

OVERVIEW: The fact that Jerusalem was still devoid of houses foreshadows the time when God's word was spread far and wide by the apostles but churches had not yet been built. Nehemiah makes a review of the total of all the people, so that he might be able to determine which ones should dwell in the city of Jerusalem and which in the other cities (BEDE).

7:4 Few People and No Houses

A FOURESHADOWING OF THE FIRST CONVERSIONS TO CHRIST. BEDE: Typologically, these details correspond to that time when, as a result of God's word being spread far and wide by the apostles, the whole world received the new seed of the faith and when churches had not yet been built but the peoples, as yet uninstructed, had merely begun to hear and receive the sacraments of the word. ON EZRA AND NEHEMIAH 3.25.[1]

7:5 Assembling the Nobles and the People

---

[1]TTH 47:191-92; PL 91:903.

NEHEMIAH'S CENSUS. BEDE: When, therefore, not only the nobles and officials but also all the common people had assembled before him, he diligently endeavored to make a census of their number so that, having made a review of the total of all the people, he might be able to determine which ones should dwell in the city of Jerusalem and which in the other cities. ON EZRA AND NEHEMIAH 3.25.[2]

[2]TTH 47:192; PL 91:903.

8:1-18 EZRA PROCLAIMS THE WORDS OF THE LAW BEFORE THE PEOPLE

[1]*And all the people gathered as one man into the square before the Water Gate; and they told Ezra the scribe to bring the book of the law of Moses which the LORD had given to Israel.* [2]*And Ezra the priest brought the law before the assembly, both men and women and all who could hear with understanding, on the first day of the seventh month.* [3]*And he read from it facing the square before the Water Gate from early morning until midday, in the presence of the men and the women and those who could understand; and the ears of all the people were attentive to the book of the law.* [4]*And Ezra the scribe stood on a wooden pulpit which they had made for the purpose; and beside him stood Mattithiah, Shema, Anaiah, Uriah, Hilkiah, and Ma-aseiah on his right hand; and Pedaiah, Misha-el, Malchijah, Hashum, Hash-baddanah, Zechariah, and Meshullam on his left hand.* [5]*And Ezra opened the book in the sight of all the people, for he was above all the people; and when he opened it all the people stood.* [6]*And Ezra blessed the LORD, the great God; and all the people answered, "Amen, Amen," lifting up their hands; and they bowed their heads and worshiped the LORD with their faces to the ground.* [7]*Also Jeshua, Bani, Sherebiah, Jamin, Akkub, Shabbethai, Hodiah, Ma-aseiah, Kelita, Azariah, Jozabad, Hanan, Pelaiah, the Levites,[r] helped the people to understand the law, while the people remained in their places.* [8]*And they read from the book, from the law of God, clearly;[s] and they gave the sense, so that the people understood the reading.*

[9]*And Nehemiah, who was the governor, and Ezra the priest and scribe, and the Levites who taught the people said to all the people, "This day is holy to the LORD your God; do not mourn or weep." For all the people wept when they heard the words of the law.* [10]*Then he said to them, "Go your way, eat the fat and drink sweet wine and send portions to him for whom nothing is prepared; for this day is holy to our Lord; and do not be grieved, for the joy of the LORD is your strength."* [11]*So the Levites stilled all the people, saying, "Be quiet, for this day is holy; do not be grieved."* [12]*And all the people went their way to eat and drink and to send portions and to make great rejoicing, because they had understood the words that were declared to them.*

¹³*On the second day the heads of fathers' houses of all the people, with the priests and the Levites, came together to Ezra the scribe in order to study the words of the law.* ¹⁴*And they found it written in the law that the LORD had commanded by Moses that the people of Israel should dwell in booths during the feast of the seventh month,* ¹⁵*and that they should publish and proclaim in all their towns and in Jerusalem, "Go out to the hills and bring branches of olive, wild olive, myrtle, palm, and other leafy trees to make booths, as it is written."* ¹⁶*So the people went out and brought them and made booths for themselves, each on his roof, and in their courts and in the courts of the house of God, and in the square at the Water Gate and in the square at the Gate of Ephraim.* ¹⁷*And all the assembly of those who had returned from the captivity made booths and dwelt in the booths; for from the days of Jeshua the son of Nun to that day the people of Israel had not done so. And there was very great rejoicing.* ¹⁸*And day by day, from the first day to the last day, he read from the book of the law of God. They kept the feast seven days; and on the eighth day there was a solemn assembly, according to the ordinance.*

r 1 Esdras 9.48 Vg: Heb *and the Levites*   s Or *with interpretation*

OVERVIEW: The people gather before the Water Gate, because they are to be given spiritual drink by Ezra their high priest from the streams of Scripture. By the command to eat fat food and drink sweet drink, Ezra invites us to rejoice over the abundance of good action bestowed on us by God and over the very sweetness of hearing God's Word. In the Festival of Booths there is a foreshadowing of Christ's passion and the deliverance of humankind from the death of sin. The feast and assembly, which were held on the eighth day, symbolize the moment when all the obscurities of our mind are dispersed by the most luminous light of Christ and our resurrection (BEDE).

8:1-4 Ezra Reads the Law to the People

INSTRUCTION THROUGH DIVINE DISCOURSES. BEDE: As Nehemiah was seeking to make plans and decide who should reside in the city that they had built, the seventh month arrived, for it was not far off. For since the wall had been completed on the twenty-fifth day of the sixth month, not more than five days remained until the beginning of the seventh month. The whole of this seventh month, from its first day until the twenty-second, was conse-

crated with ceremonies prescribed by the Law; when these had been duly celebrated, only then did he return with the leaders and common people to decide who should be residents of the rebuilt city. The point to note here is the devotion and also the like-mindedness of the people who as one person (that is, with one and the same faith and love) came together at the Lord's temple; and they themselves asked their *pontifex*[1] to bring the book and recount for them the commandments of the Law that they must observe, so that along with the rebuilt city, a structure of good works pleasing to God might spring up in case, just as before, neglect of religion should lead to the ruination of the city as well. And it is appropriate that the city was completed in the sixth month and that the people gathered in it to hear the Law in the seventh; for in the Law there are six days for working and a seventh for resting.[2] And this, after we have done good work, is the form of our rest that is most beloved and most acceptable to the Lord: to abstain from servile work (that is, from sin) and devote ourselves to hearing and fulfilling his commandments with due diligence. This is

---

[1]Bede is comparing Ezra with an archbishop or the pope; see also Ezra 9:1-3; 10:1-5; 10:15-44.   [2]See Exod 20:9-11.

why the Feast of Trumpets, by whose blast the people, amid their prayers and offerings, were more fervently moved to remembrance of the divine law, was placed in the beginning of this seventh month also.

Even today too, according to the spiritual meaning, the construction of the holy city should be followed by divine reading and the frequent sounding of trumpets, no doubt because it is necessary that when a people has been initiated into the heavenly sacraments they should also, as occasion requires, be carefully instructed by divine discourses how they should live. Now he says that the people assembled "in the square that is before the Water Gate." I think that by the Water Gate is meant the gate in the courtyard of the priests that surrounded the temple on all its sides in a square, especially on the temple's eastern side, where there was the bronze sea for washing the hands and feet of those going into the temple, the ten bronze washbasins for washing the victims and the altar of burnt offering between which and the temple Zechariah son of Berechiah was stoned to death.[3] The people did not have permission to enter inside the gate of this court but only the priests and ministers of the Lord; the people were accustomed to stand outside of this gate and especially in the square that was at its eastern side, in order to listen to the word or to pray. Therefore, it is appropriate that the people gathered before the Water Gate, because they were to be given spiritual drink by their high priest from the streams of Scripture. ON EZRA AND NEHEMIAH 3.26.[4]

8:9-12 Eat the Fat and Drink Sweet Wine

TO REJOICE IN HOPE. BEDE: For it is a holy day of the Lord for us when we take pains to hear and carry out his words. On this day it is proper that, however much outwardly we have endured the obstacles of tribulations, we should be "rejoicing in hope,"[5] in keeping with the apostle's saying: "As if sorrowful, yet always rejoicing."[6]

On this day we are also commanded to eat fat food and drink sweet drink, that is, to rejoice over the abundance of good action bestowed on us by God and over the very sweetness of hearing God's Word. ON EZRA AND NEHEMIAH 3.26.[7]

8:13-17 Written in the Law

MYSTERIES FORESHADOWED IN THE FESTIVAL OF BOOTHS. BEDE: These matters are written about more fully in Leviticus,[8] and it is also written that they were ordered to be done in memory of that very long journey, on which the Lord, leading his people out of Egypt, made them dwell in tabernacles in the desert for forty years, daily revealing to them the precepts of his law through Moses. Moreover it was ordered that the setting up of tabernacles (which in Greek is called *skēnopēgia*) was to be done every year for seven days, that is, from the fifteenth day of the seventh month to the twenty-second. It is well worth our while to make a thorough examination of the mystery of this observance through spiritual investigation, especially since in the Gospel the Lord deigned to attend this same feast and, as he addressed the people who gathered there, dedicated it with his most holy words.[9] Our ancestors too, therefore, were set free from slavery in Egypt through the blood of a lamb and were led through the desert for forty years that they come to the promised land when through the Lord's passion the world was set free from slavery to the devil and through the apostles the primitive church was gathered and was led as it were through the desert for forty years until it came to the homeland promised in heaven, because in imitation of the forty-day fast that Moses and Elijah and the Lord himself fulfilled,[10] the primitive church used to lead a

---

[3]See Mt 23:35; cf. Lk 11:51; 2 Chron 24:20-21. [4]TTH 47:192-93*; PL 91:903-4. [5]Rom 12:12. [6]2 Cor 6:10. [7]TTH 47:195; PL 91:905. [8]See Lev 23:34-43. [9]See Jn 7:2-14. [10]See Exod 24:18; 34:28; Deut 9:9; 1 Kings 19:8; Mt 4:2.

life of great continence, thirsting always for its eternal homeland, and having set itself completely apart from all the distractions of this world, conducted its life as though in secret in daily meditation on the divine law. In remembrance of this time, we, too, ought to dwell in tabernacles, leaving our homes, that is, having forsaken the cares and pleasures of the world, we ought to confess that we are pilgrims in this life and have our homeland in heaven and desire that we may arrive there all the more quickly; this, too, in a holy feast in the seventh month (i.e., in the light of celestial joy) when the grace of the Holy Spirit, which was commended by the prophet as sevenfold,[11] fills our heart. We are ordered to remain in these tabernacles for seven days because during the entire time of this life, which we accomplish in as many days, we must bear in mind that, like our ancestors, we are dwellers and pilgrims on earth in the eyes of the Lord. ON EZRA AND NEHEMIAH 3.27.[12]

8:18 On the Eighth Day, a Solemn Assembly

A FIGURE OF THE ASSEMBLY OF THE SAINTS.
BEDE: The literal sense is clear to this extent: the Feast of Tabernacles[13] itself was customarily celebrated for seven days (i.e., from the fifteenth moon of the seventh month to the twenty-first); then, on the eighth day (i.e., the twenty-second day of the month), a second assembly of the people was held, an assembly notable for its greater festivity. For it is written in Leviticus, "From the fifteenth day of the seventh month, when you have gathered in all the crops of your land, you shall celebrate a festival of the Lord for seven days; on the first day and on the eighth there will be a sabbath, that is, a day of rest. And on the first day you shall take for yourselves the fruits of the most beautiful tree,"[14] and so on. Therefore, for the seven days of the Feast of Tabernacles, Ezra read to the people from the Book of the Law of God, doubtless because this is our true feast of the mind in this life—that each day (i.e., through all the good works by which we are illuminated by the Lord), we should make time for reading, hearing and performing his words with a resolute heart. But this feast begins "on the fifteenth day of the month when the moon is at its fullest in the evening,"[15] when all the obscurities of our mind are dispersed by the most luminous light of Christ. And the eighth day of the sabbath (i.e., of rest) follows it, namely, at the moment of our resurrection in the life to come by whose joys in our present life we are uplifted in hope but that we will then enjoy in reality when the most longed-for gathering, the whole assembly of the saints (both of angels and of human beings), having been gathered in their Creator's sight and never to be separated, will rejoice. ON EZRA AND NEHEMIAH 3.27.[16]

---

[11]Is 11:2-3. [12]TTH 47:196-97; PL 91:905-6. [13]Or booths. [14]Lev 23:39-40. [15]Jerome *In Zachariam* 3.14.16 (CCL 76A:895.690-91). [16]TTH 47:199; PL 91:907-8.

9:1-38 THE PEOPLE OF ISRAEL MAKE A PUBLIC CONFESSION

[1]*Now on the twenty-fourth day of this month the people of Israel were assembled with fasting and in sackcloth, and with earth upon their heads.* [2]*And the Israelites separated themselves from*

all foreigners, and stood and confessed their sins and the iniquities of their fathers. ³And they stood up in their place and read from the book of the law of the LORD their God for a fourth of the day*; for another fourth of it† they made confession and worshiped the LORD their God. ⁴Upon the stairs of the Levites stood Jeshua, Bani, Kadmi-el, Shebaniah, Bunni, Sherebiah, Bani, and Chenani; and they cried with a loud voice to the LORD their God. ⁵Then the Levites, Jeshua, Kadmiel, Bani, Hashabneiah, Sherebiah, Hodiah, Shebaniah, and Pethahiah, said, "Stand up and bless the LORD your God from everlasting to everlasting. Blessed be thy glorious name which is exalted above all blessing and praise."

⁶And Ezra said:ᵗ "Thou art the LORD, thou alone; thou hast made heaven, the heaven of heavens, with all their host, the earth and all that is on it, the seas and all that is in them; and thou preservest all of them; and the host of heaven worships thee. ⁷Thou art the LORD, the God who didst choose Abram and bring him forth out of Ur of the Chaldeans and give him the name Abraham; ⁸and thou didst find his heart faithful before thee, and didst make with him the covenant to give to his descendants the land of the Canaanite, the Hittite, the Amorite, the Perizzite, the Jebusite, and the Girgashite; and thou hast fulfilled thy promise, for thou art righteous.

⁹"And thou didst see the affliction of our fathers in Egypt and hear their cry at the Red Sea, ¹⁰and didst perform signs and wonders against Pharaoh and all his servants and all the people of his land, for thou knewest that they acted insolently against our fathers; and thou didst get thee a name, as it is to this day. ¹¹And thou didst divide the sea before them, so that they went through the midst of the sea on dry land; and thou didst cast their pursuers into the depths, as a stone into mighty waters. ¹²By a pillar of cloud thou didst lead them in the day, and by a pillar of fire in the night to light for them the way in which they should go. ¹³Thou didst come down upon Mount Sinai, and speak with them from heaven and give them right ordinances and true laws, good statutes and commandments, ¹⁴and thou didst make known to them thy holy sabbath and command them commandments and statutes and a law by Moses thy servant. ¹⁵Thou didst give them bread from heaven for their hunger and bring forth water for them from the rock for their thirst, and thou didst tell them to go in to possess the land which thou hadst sworn to give them.

¹⁶"But they and our fathers acted presumptuously and stiffened their neck and did not obey thy commandments; ¹⁷they refused to obey, and were not mindful of the wonders which thou didst perform among them; but they stiffened their neck and appointed a leader to return to their bondage in Egypt. But thou art a God ready to forgive, gracious and merciful, slow to anger and abounding in steadfast love, and didst not forsake them. ¹⁸Even when they had made for themselves a molten calf and said, 'This is your God who brought you up out of Egypt,' and had committed great blasphemies, ¹⁹thou in thy great mercies didst not forsake them in the wilderness; the pillar of cloud which led them in the way did not depart from them by day, nor the pillar of fire by night which lighted for them the way by which they should go. ²⁰Thou gavest thy good Spirit to instruct them, and didst not withhold thy manna from their mouth, and gavest them water for their thirst. ²¹Forty years didst thou sustain them in the wilderness, and they lacked nothing; their clothes did not wear out and their feet did not swell. ²²And thou didst give them kingdoms and peoples, and didst allot to them every corner; so they

took possession of the land of Sihon king of Heshbon and the land of Og king of Bashan. ²³Thou didst multiply their descendants as the stars of heaven, and thou didst bring them into the land which thou hadst told their fathers to enter and possess. ²⁴So the descendants went in and possessed the land, and thou didst subdue before them the inhabitants of the land, the Canaanites, and didst give them into their hands, with their kings and the peoples of the land, that they might do with them as they would. ²⁵And they captured fortified cities and a rich land, and took possession of houses full of all good things, cisterns hewn out, vineyards, olive orchards and fruit trees in abundance; so they ate, and were filled and became fat, and delighted themselves in thy great goodness.

²⁶"Nevertheless they were disobedient and rebelled against thee and cast thy law behind their back and killed thy prophets, who had warned them in order to turn them back to thee, and they committed great blasphemies. ²⁷Therefore thou didst give them into the hand of their enemies, who made them suffer; and in the time of their suffering they cried to thee and thou didst hear them from heaven; and according to thy great mercies thou didst give them saviors who saved them from the hand of their enemies. ²⁸But after they had rest they did evil again before thee, and thou didst abandon them to the hand of their enemies, so that they had dominion over them; yet when they turned and cried to thee thou didst hear from heaven, and many times thou didst deliver them according to thy mercies. ²⁹And thou didst warn them in order to turn them back to thy law. Yet they acted presumptuously and did not obey thy commandments, but sinned against thy ordinances, by the observance of which a man shall live, and turned a stubborn shoulder and stiffened their neck and would not obey. ³⁰Many years thou didst bear with them, and didst warn them by thy Spirit through thy prophets; yet they would not give ear. Therefore thou didst give them into the hand of the peoples of the lands. ³¹Nevertheless in thy great mercies thou didst not make an end of them or forsake them; for thou art a gracious and merciful God.

³²"Now therefore, our God, the great and mighty and terrible God, who keepest covenant and steadfast love, let not all the hardship seem little to thee that has come upon us, upon our kings, our princes, our priests, our prophets, our fathers, and all thy people, since the time of the kings of Assyria until this day. ³³Yet thou hast been just in all that has come upon us, for thou hast dealt faithfully and we have acted wickedly; ³⁴our kings, our princes, our priests, and our fathers have not kept thy law or heeded thy commandments and thy warnings which thou didst give them. ³⁵They did not serve thee in their kingdom, and in thy great goodness which thou gavest them, and in the large and rich land which thou didst set before them; and they did not turn from their wicked works. ³⁶Behold, we are slaves this day; in the land that thou gavest to our fathers to enjoy its fruit and its good gifts, behold, we are slaves. ³⁷And its rich yield goes to the kings whom thou hast set over us because of our sins; they have power also over our bodies and over our cattle at their pleasure, and we are in great distress."

³⁸ᵘ"Because of all this we make a firm covenant and write it, and our princes, our Levites, and our priests set their seal to it.

s Gk: Heb lacks *and Ezra said*   t Gk: Heb lacks *and Ezra said*   u Ch 10.1 in Heb   * Heb *for a fourth part of the day* Vg *four times a day*   † Heb *and for another fourth* Vg *four times a nigh*

OVERVIEW: Following the examples of the people of Israel, we should search out with careful scrutiny the ways we can fulfill each duty with the reproof of our heart and body. From the public reading of the Book of the Law at the time of Ezra and Nehemiah a most beautiful custom has developed in the church, namely, that through each hour of daily psalmody a passage from Old or New Testament is recited by heart for all to hear. After the Feast of the Tabernacles (Booths) and after purging themselves with resolved purpose from the contagions of their wrongdoings, the people of Israel unite themselves to the divine covenant and confirm its terms by word and in writing (BEDE).

9:1-2 The People Assembled in Sackcloth

COMMITMENT TO RIGHTEOUSNESS. BEDE: One should note the devotion of the people reformed after the captivity: when the feast that had been commanded by the Lord's law had been duly completed, after just one day's intermission, they immediately came together of their own accord with fasting and with repentance, and they diligently carried out what on the days of sacred readings and rejoicing they had heard must be done by separating themselves in mind and body from the fellowship of those who were proven to be alienated from the Lord and his worship, lest through the association and examples of the wicked they should again fall into the evils of captivity and hardship that, they discerned, they had just at that time barely escaped after long revolutions of times and ages. And what are we to reflect on mystically about these matters except that, following the examples of such people, whatever we have learned in a public meeting or reading should be done, we should reflect on again with mutual discussion among ourselves, and we should search out with careful scrutiny the ways we can fulfill each duty with the reproof of our heart and body. ON EZRA AND NEHEMIAH 3.28.[1]

9:3 Reading from the Book of the Law

A BEAUTIFUL EXAMPLE FOR THE CHURCH. BEDE: "And they rose up to stand, and they read from the Book of the Law of the Lord their God four times a day, and four times a night they confessed and prayed to the Lord their God." For who would not be amazed that such a great people had such extraordinary concern for devotion that four times a day—that is, at the first hour of the morning, the third, the sixth and the ninth, when time was to be made for prayer and psalmody—they gave themselves over to listening to the divine law in order to renew their mind in God and come back purer and more devout for imploring his mercy; but also four times a night they would shake off their sleepiness and get up in order to confess their sins and to beg pardon. From this example, I think, a most beautiful custom has developed in the church, namely, that through each hour of daily psalmody a passage from Old or New Testament is recited by heart for all to hear, and thus strengthened by the words of the apostles or the prophets, they bend their knees to perseverance in prayer, but also at night, when people cease from the labors of doing good works, they turn willing ears to listen to divine readings. ON EZRA AND NEHEMIAH 3.28.[2]

9:6-38 An Agreement in Writing

NEW UNITY IN THE DIVINE COVENANT. BEDE: "And Ezra said, 'You yourself, O Lord, you alone made the heaven, the heaven of heavens, and all their host, the earth and all that is on it,'" and so on up until the end of his prayer or confession. It was said above that they were confessing their sins and the sins of their ancestors; here, when Ezra prays, it is shown more fully how this was done. But where he says at the end, "Because of all this, therefore, we ourselves are making a covenant and writing it down, and our leaders, our Levites and our priests are signing it," and so on,

---

[1]TTH 47:200; PL 91:908.   [2]TTH 47:200-201; PL 91:908.

it is shown more clearly with what gracious devotion all the various persons made a new assembly after the Feast of the Tabernacles, namely, so that after purging themselves with resolved purpose from the contagions of their wrongdoings, they might unite themselves to the divine covenant and confirm its terms by word and in writing. Thus separated from association with the ungodly, they would more confidently complete the work they began long ago, that is, to choose citizens from among the devout who were suitable to rebuild the city. ON EZRA AND NEHEMIAH 3.29.[3]

---

[3]TTH 47:201*; PL 91:908-9.

10:1-39 A NEW COVENANT IS SIGNED

[28]*The rest of the people, the priests, the Levites, the gatekeepers, the singers, the temple servants, and all who have separated themselves from the peoples of the lands to the law of God, their wives, their sons, their daughters, all who have knowledge and understanding, [29]join with their brethren, their nobles, and enter into a curse and an oath to walk in God's law which was given by Moses the servant of God, and to observe and do all the commandments of the LORD our Lord and his ordinances and his statutes. [30]We will not give our daughters to the peoples of the land or take their daughters for our sons; [31]and if the peoples of the land bring in wares or any grain on the sabbath day to sell, we will not buy from them on the sabbath or on a holy day; and we will forego the crops of the seventh year and the exaction of every debt.*

[32]We also lay upon ourselves the obligation to charge ourselves yearly with the third part of a shekel for the service of the house of our God: [33]for the showbread, the continual cereal offering, the continual burnt offering, the sabbaths, the new moons, the appointed feasts, the holy things, and the sin offerings to make atonement for Israel, and for all the work of the house of our God. [34]We have likewise cast lots, the priests, the Levites, and the people, for the wood offering, to bring it into the house of our God, according to our fathers' houses, at times appointed, year by year, to burn upon the altar of the LORD our God, as it is written in the law. [35]We obligate ourselves to bring the first fruits of our ground and the first fruits of all fruit of every tree, year by year, to the house of the LORD; [36]also to bring to the house of our God, to the priests who minister in the house of our God, the first-born of our sons and of our cattle, as it is written in the law, and the firstlings of our herds and of our flocks; [37]and to bring the first of our coarse meal, and our contributions, the fruit of every tree, the wine and the oil, to the priests, to the chambers of the house of our God; and to bring to the Levites the tithes from our ground, for it is the Levites who collect the tithes in all our rural towns. [38]And the priest, the son of Aaron, shall be with the Levites when the Levites receive the tithes; and the Levites shall bring up the tithe of the tithes to the house of our God, to

the chambers, to the storehouse. [39]*For the people of Israel and the sons of Levi shall bring the contribution of grain, wine, and oil to the chambers, where are the vessels of the sanctuary, and the priests that minister, and the gatekeepers and the singers. We will not neglect the house of our God.*

OVERVIEW: We also, as Ezra commands, should always keep a spiritual sabbath, should always take a rest from servile work (i.e., sin), should always make time for and consider that the Lord is God. The excellent order of religious life established at the time of Ezra and Nehemiah ought to be imitated by us, too, in a spiritual manner (BEDE).

10:30-31 Not Buying Merchandise on the Sabbath

A WARNING AGAINST THE ENTICEMENTS OF SIN. BEDE: We, too, should always keep a spiritual sabbath, should always take a rest from servile work (i.e., sin), should always make time for and consider that the Lord is God, so that after such a sabbath, when we have been freed from the sins of conscience, we may come to the sabbath of future glory in heaven. But the peoples of the land seek a way to profane our sabbath by bringing in all sorts of things to sell us on the holy day because unclean spirits try hard to pollute the cleanness of our heart; and once they have received the payment of our consent, they heap on us the enticements of the vices in order to defile the day of greatest holiness (i.e., to darken the light of our devout thought or action with the sins they have sent in). But we should entirely shun merchandise of this sort with the walls of our closed-off city, that is, with the pro-

tection of a more perfected life. ON EZRA AND NEHEMIAH 3.30.[1]

10:32-39 Committed to the Service of God

A MODEL TO BE IMITATED IN A SPIRITUAL MANNER. BEDE: All these matters that are contained in this chapter are relevant to the care of the Lord's house and his ministers and services. This excellent order of religious life ought to be imitated by us, too, in a spiritual manner today, namely, that first the descendants of the exiles purified themselves from the pollution caused by the Gentiles, then they were sanctified by keeping the sabbath (which stood prominently among the first commandments of the Law)[2] and only then did they turn all their attention to carrying out the observance of divine worship in other respects, for we must first be cleansed from evils and only then equip ourselves for good works. However, it would take quite a long time to discuss allegorically in what order we must carry out each of these in a spiritual manner with respect to the worship of the Lord, and this should be done rather in the Book of the Law itself.[3] ON EZRA AND NEHEMIAH 3.30.[4]

---

[1]TTH 47:202; PL 91:909. [2]See Exod 20:8. [3]The Pentateuch: Genesis, Exodus, Leviticus, Numbers and Deuteronomy. [4]TTH 47:203*; PL 91:909.

11:1-36 A NEW ARRANGEMENT IN
THE DISTRIBUTION OF THE PEOPLE

[1]*Now the leaders of the people lived in Jerusalem; and the rest of the people cast lots to bring one out of ten to live in Jerusalem the holy city, while nine tenths remained in the other towns.* [2]*And the people blessed all the men who willingly offered to live in Jerusalem.*

[3]*These are the chiefs of the province who lived in Jerusalem; but in the towns of Judah every one lived on his property in their towns: Israel, the priests, the Levites, the temple servants, and the descendants of Solomon's servants.* [4]*And in Jerusalem lived certain of the sons of Judah and of the sons of Benjamin. Of the sons of Judah: Athaiah the son of Uzziah, son of Zechariah, son of Amariah, son of Shephatiah, son of Mahalalel, of the sons of Perez;* [5]*and Ma-aseiah the son of Baruch, son of Col-hozeh, son of Hazaiah, son of Adaiah, son of Joiarib, son of Zechariah, son of the Shilonite.* [6]*All the sons of Perez who lived in Jerusalem were four hundred and sixty-eight valiant men.*

[7]*And these are the sons of Benjamin: Sallu the son of Meshullam, son of Joed, son of Pedaiah, son of Kolaiah, son of Ma-aseiah, son of Ithi-el, son of Jeshaiah.* [8]*And after him Gabbai, Sallai, nine hundred and twenty-eight.* [9]*Joel the son of Zichri was their overseer; and Judah the son of Hassenuah was second over the city.*

[10]*Of the priests: Jedaiah the son of Joiarib, Jachin,* [11]*Seraiah the son of Hilkiah, son of Meshullam, son of Zadok, son of Meraioth, son of Ahitub, ruler of the house of God,* [12]*and their brethren who did the work of the house, eight hundred and twenty-two; and Adaiah the son of Jeroham, son of Pelaliah, son of Amzi, son of Zechariah, son of Pashhur, son of Malchijah,* [13]*and his brethren, heads of fathers' houses, two hundred and forty-two; and Amashsai, the son of Azarel, son of Ahzai, son of Meshillemoth, son of Immer,* [14]*and their brethren, mighty men of valor, a hundred and twenty-eight; their overseer was Zabdiel the son of Haggedolim.*

[15]*And of the Levites: Shemaiah the son of Hasshub, son of Azrikam, son of Hashabiah, son of Bunni;* [16]*and Shabbethai and Jozabad, of the chiefs of the Levites, who were over the outside work of the house of God;* [17]*and Mattaniah the son of Mica, son of Zabdi, son of Asaph, who was the leader to begin the thanksgiving in prayer, and Bakbukiah, the second among his brethren; and Abda the son of Shammua, son of Galal, son of Jeduthun.* [18]*All the Levites in the holy city were two hundred and eighty-four.*

[19]*The gatekeepers, Akkub, Talmon and their brethren, who kept watch at the gates, were a hundred and seventy-two.* [20]*And the rest of Israel, and of the priests and the Levites, were in all the towns of Judah, every one in his inheritance.* [21]*But the temple servants lived on Ophel; and Ziha and Gishpa were over the temple servants.*

[22]*The overseer of the Levites in Jerusalem was Uzzi the son of Bani, son of Hashabiah, son of Mattaniah, son of Mica, of the sons of Asaph, the singers, over the work of the house of God.* [23]*For there was a command from the king concerning them, and a settled provision for the singers, as*

every day required. ²⁴*And Pethahiah the son of Meshezabel, of the sons of Zerah the son of Judah, was at the king's hand in all matters concerning the people.*

²⁵*And as for the villages, with their fields, some of the people of Judah lived in Kiriath-arba and its villages, and in Dibon and its villages, and in Jekabzeel and its villages,* ²⁶*and in Jeshua and in Moladah and Beth-pelet,* ²⁷*in Hazar-shual, in Beer-sheba and its villages,* ²⁸*in Ziklag, in Meconah and its villages,* ²⁹*in En-rimmon, in Zorah, in Jarmuth,* ³⁰*Zanoah, Adullam, and their villages, Lachish and its fields, and Azekah and its villages. So they encamped from Beer-sheba to the valley of Hinnom.* ³¹*The people of Benjamin also lived from Geba onward, at Michmash, Aija, Bethel and its villages,* ³²*Anathoth, Nob, Ananiah,* ³³*Hazor, Ramah, Gittaim,* ³⁴*Hadid, Zeboim, Neballat,* ³⁵*Lod, and Ono, the valley of craftsmen.* ³⁶*And certain divisions of the Levites in Judah were joined to Benjamin.*

OVERVIEW: Those living in the remaining cities of Israel represent the devout lifestyle of the common people of God, whereas those settling in Jerusalem specifically signify the conduct of those who, having already overcome the struggle of the vices, draw near to the vision of heavenly peace. The fact that some of the people dwelled partly in Jerusalem and partly in cities given to them by God foreshadows the fact that the stages of progress of the Christian faithful will be many and diverse (BEDE).

11:1-19 *The Rest of the People Cast Lots*

THE SYMBOLISM OF THE NEW DISTRIBUTION OF THE PEOPLE. BEDE: The arrangement was now completed. It was begun as soon as the city was made, but until the total number of the people had been counted and the feast of the seventh month had been completed, it was impossible to determine who should reside in the holy city itself and who in the other cities. Now it is consistent with the figures of the sacraments that the rulers of the people are reported to have settled in Jerusalem. For it is proper that those in charge of the holy church should surpass the common people in the merits of their life by as much as they surpass them in the greatness of their power. For the remaining cities of Israel represent the devout lifestyle of the common people of God, whereas the act of settling in Jerusalem specifically repre-

sents the conduct of those who, having already overcome the struggle of the vices, draw near to the vision of heavenly peace with an unimpeded mind according to the psalmist's saying: "The Lord loves the gates of Zion above all the tabernacles of Jacob."[1] Thus it follows that the reason that a tenth part of the people chosen by lot take their dwelling in Jerusalem but the remaining nine parts reside in their cities is doubtless that it is a mark of the perfect (namely, of those who wholly keep the precepts of the Decalogue in the love of God and neighbor) to draw near in mind to the heavenly secrets and, so to speak, to imitate the peace of the highest blessedness amid the whirlwinds of this transient life; and yet the door to eternal life also remains open to those who keep God's general commandments, according to what the Lord declares in the Gospel to the rich man who questioned him.[2] For such people dwell as it were in cities given to them by the Lord because by keeping the sacred law they remain constantly vigilant to defend themselves from the attacks of the ancient enemy. But those who wish to be perfect and follow the Lord by selling all their belongings and giving them as alms for the poor are those who dwell as it were "in the citadel of Jerusalem"[3] and next to the temple of God and the ark of the covenant because they approach the grace of their Creator in a more sublime way. It is

[1]Ps 87:2 (86:2 LXX, Vg). [2]See Mt 19:17. [3]1 Macc 13:49.

well said that their dwelling in the holy city was granted to them not by the foresight of human choice but by the outcome of a lot, just as during Joshua's time the ownership of the rest of the cities was given to the children of Israel by lot,[4] no doubt because both the small things of the small man and the great things of the great man come about not through the freedom or industriousness of his own will but by the gift of the hidden judge and provider. On Ezra and Nehemiah 3.31.[5]

11:20-36 Living in Kiriath-arba

The Stages of Progress of the Faithful Are Many. Bede: "Some of the children of Judah settled in Kiriath and its daughters," and so on until it says, "And they made their home in Beer-sheba as far as the Valley of Hinnom." For Beer-sheba was the boundary of Judah on the southern side, whereas the valley of the descendants of Hinnom was to the north next to Jerusalem on the east side. Finally, the cities of the descendants of Benjamin are recounted in a similar order, and the sentence that is added after they have been counted, "And of the Levites portions of Judah and Benjamin," means that the Levites according to the decree of the Law received a lot on the property of the descendants of Judah and Benjamin. Let this much be said briefly concerning the historical sense. Concerning all these matters, if it delights you to hear also some allegorical meaning that is appropriate for our actions, Judah is interpreted as "he who confesses," Benjamin "the son of the right hand" and Levi "accepted."[6] The reason that the tribes of all of these dwell partly in Jerusalem and partly in cities given to them by God is that the stages of progress of the faithful are many and diverse, and for them there are also many mansions in our Father's house in heaven, as we have taught above.[7] Some are content to observe God's general commandments: not to commit murder, not to commit adultery, not to steal, not to speak false testimony against a neighbor, to honor father and mother, and to love neighbors as themselves.[8] Others try to lay hold of the narrower stronghold of the perfect life, yet they all, each person according to his own calling, praise and confess the grace of their Creator, and they are children of the everlasting kingdom that is in his right hand and are taken up by him to life when the moment of that separation will come in which "two men will be in the field; one will be taken and the other left behind. Two women will be grinding at the mill; one will be taken and the other left behind."[9] On Ezra and Nehemiah 3.31.[10]

---

[4]See Josh 1:6. [5]TTH 47:203-4*; PL 91:909-10. [6]Bede, as usual, takes these etymologies from Jerome *Nom. Hebr.* (CCL 72:152.15; 62.24; 68.7-8). [7]See Bede *In Ezr.* (CCL 119A:3.755-66). [8]See Mt 19:17-19. [9]Mt 24:40-41. [10]TTH 47:205-6; PL 91:911.

12:1-26 A COMPLETE LIST OF PRIESTS AND LEVITES

[1]*These are the priests and the Levites who came up with Zerubbabel the son of She-alti-el, and Jeshua: Seraiah, Jeremiah, Ezra,* [2]*Amariah, Malluch, Hattush,* [3]*Shecaniah, Rehum, Meremoth,* [4]*Iddo, Ginnethoi, Abijah,* [5]*Mijamin, Ma-adiah, Bilgah,* [6]*Shemaiah, Joiarib, Jedaiah,* [7]*Sallu, Amok, Hilkiah, Jedaiah. These were the chiefs of the priests and of their brethren in the days of Jeshua.*

⁸*And the Levites: Jeshua, Binnui, Kadmi-el, Sherebiah, Judah, and Mattaniah, who with his brethren was in charge of the songs of thanksgiving. ⁹And Bakbukiah and Unno their brethren stood opposite them in the service. ¹⁰And Jeshua was the father of Joiakim, Joiakim the father of Eliashib, Eliashib the father of Joiada, ¹¹Joiada the father of Jonathan, and Jonathan the father of Jaddu-a.*

¹²*And in the days of Joiakim were priests, heads of fathers' houses: of Seraiah, Meraiah; of Jeremiah, Hananiah; ¹³of Ezra, Meshullam; of Amariah, Jehohanan; ¹⁴of Malluchi, Jonathan; of Shebaniah, Joseph; ¹⁵of Harim, Adna; of Meraioth, Helkai; ¹⁶of Iddo, Zechariah; of Ginnethon, Meshullam; ¹⁷of Abijah, Zichri; of Miniamin, of Moadiah, Piltai; ¹⁸of Bilgah, Shammu-a; of Shemaiah, Jehonathan; ¹⁹of Joiarib, Mattenai; of Jedaiah, Uzzi; ²⁰of Sallai, Kallai; of Amok, Eber; ²¹of Hilkiah, Hashabiah; of Jedaiah, Nethanel.*

²²*As for the Levites, in the days of Eliashib, Joiada, Johanan, and Jaddu-a, there were recorded the heads of fathers' houses; also the priests until the reign of Darius the Persian. ²³The sons of Levi, heads of fathers' houses, were written in the Book of the Chronicles until the days of Johanan the son of Eliashib. ²⁴And the chiefs of the Levites: Hashabiah, Sherebiah, and Jeshua the son of Kadmi-el, with their brethren over against them, to praise and to give thanks, according to the commandment of David the man of God, watch corresponding to watch. ²⁵Mattaniah, Bakbukiah, Obadiah, Meshullam, Talmon, and Akkub were gatekeepers standing guard at the storehouses of the gates. ²⁶These were in the days of Joiakim the son of Jeshua son of Jozadak, and in the days of Nehemiah the governor and of Ezra the priest the scribe.*

OVERVIEW: Jaddua, who was the last of the high priests, and lived at the time of Alexander the Great, could have been born when Nehemiah was still alive. It was not done without the understanding of a more sacred mystery that the rebuilt city of Jerusalem deserved a greater multitude of citizens, as in this aspect it foreshadowed the holy church (BEDE).

12:1-11 The Priests Who Returned with Zerubbabel and Jeshua

FROM THE TIME OF EZRA TO THE BEGINNING OF THE KINGDOM OF THE MACEDONIANS.

BEDE: "Now these are the priests and Levites who went up with Zerubbabel son of Shealtiel and Jeshua: Seraiah, Jeremiah," and so on. Here leaders of the priests are described together with their brothers (i.e., the lesser priests and Levites), those who came up from the Babylonian captivity with Zerubbabel and Jeshua son of Jehozadak. Once these have been set forth, there are also added those who, from this time until the beginning of the kingdom of the Macedonians, succeeded each other in turn in the leadership of the priesthood. For there follows "Jeshua begot Joiakim, Joiakim begot Elijahhib, Elijahhib begot Joiada, Joiada begot Jonathan, and Jonathan begot Jaddua." In fact, Josephus writes that Jaddua, who was the last of these, was the high priest in the time of Alexander the Great, and when Jaddua with his brothers met him, Alexander received him humbly and with honor. Josephus, who spells his name Jaddus, says that he was the father of the high priest Onias,[1] who is mentioned in the book of Maccabees.[2] This not to say that Nehemiah, the author of this book, could have

---

[1]Josephus *Antiquities of the Jews* 11.8.1-7. [2]1 Macc 12:6-7.

lived right up to that time in the flesh but that he knew Jaddua when he was an infant, and Jaddua could have reached the rank of priesthood long after Nehemiah's death. For at the end of this book[3] mention also is made of the sons of Joiada son of Elijahhib, to the effect that one of these was the son-in-law of Sanballat the Horonite, though the name of his son-in-law is not recorded. But because this Joiada is the grandfather of Jaddua, it is clear that the son-in-law who is mentioned was either Jaddua's father or parental uncle, and so he could have been born when Nehemiah was still alive. On Ezra and Nehemiah 3.31-32.[4]

12:12-26 In the Days of Joiakim

A Typological Comparison with the Holy Church. Bede: After the succession of the high priests has been described, a catalogue of the lesser priests and Levites who existed in their time is also added so that we may know that after a large number of citizens were gathered in Jerusalem, there was also an excellent and most noble assembly of priests and Levites sufficient to provide for the services of the temple and altar, to confess and praise God, for the guardianship of the temple and city and to educate the people. And it was not done without the understanding of a more sacred mystery that the rebuilt city of Jerusalem deserved a greater multitude of citizens in every rank and order that it is ever said to have lost when the enemy was attacking and destroying it. For in the same way the holy church often receives greater gains from its losses when, by one person's lapse through carelessness into sin, many are frightened by his example and become more careful to continue steadfastly in the purity of faith; often these same people who have sinned begin, after they have done penance, to bear greater fruits of good works than they used to bear before the invasion of sin; often, when the church has been ravaged by heretics and after it recovers the light of truth through the perseverance of catholic teachers, it has given birth to more children in order that they might come to know and uphold the reason of this same truth that has been restored. On Ezra and Nehemiah 3.32.[5]

---

[3]See Neh 13:28. [4]TTH 47:206-7*; PL 91:911-12. [5]TTH 47:207-8; PL 91:912.

12:27-43 THE DEDICATION OF THE WALL OF JERUSALEM

[27]And at the dedication of the wall of Jerusalem they sought the Levites in all their places, to bring them to Jerusalem to celebrate the dedication with gladness, with thanksgivings and with singing, with cymbals, harps, and lyres. [28]And the sons of the singers gathered together from the circuit round Jerusalem and from the villages of the Netophathites; [29]also from Beth-gilgal and from the region of Geba and Azmaveth; for the singers had built for themselves villages around Jerusalem. [30]And the priests and the Levites purified themselves; and they purified the people and the gates and the wall.

[31]Then I brought up the princes of Judah upon the wall, and appointed two great companies

which gave thanks and went in procession. One went to the right upon the wall to the Dung Gate; [32]*and after them went Hoshaiah and half of the princes of Judah,* [33]*and Azariah, Ezra, Meshullam,* [34]*Judah, Benjamin, Shemaiah, and Jeremiah,* [35]*and certain of the priests' sons with trumpets: Zechariah the son of Jonathan, son of Shemaiah, son of Mattaniah, son of Micaiah, son of Zaccur, son of Asaph;* [36]*and his kinsmen, Shemaiah, Azarel, Milalai, Gilalai, Maai, Nethanel, Judah, and Hanani, with the musical instruments of David the man of God; and Ezra the scribe went before them.* [37]*At the Fountain Gate they went up straight before them by the stairs of the city of David, at the ascent of the wall, above the house of David, to the Water Gate on the east.*

[38]*The other company* of those who gave thanks went to the left, and I followed them with half of the people, upon the wall, above the Tower of the Ovens, to the Broad Wall,* [39]*and above the Gate of Ephraim, and by the Old Gate, and by the Fish Gate and the Tower of Hananel and the Tower of the Hundred, to the Sheep Gate; and they came to a halt at the Gate of the Guard.* [40]*So both companies of those who gave thanks stood in the house of God, and I and half of the officials with me;* [41]*and the priests Eliakim, Ma-aseiah, Miniamin, Micaiah, Eli-o-enai, Zechariah, and Hananiah, with trumpets;* [42]*and Ma-aseiah, Shemaiah, Eleazar, Uzzi, Jehohanan, Malchijah, Elam, and Ezer. And the singers sang with Jezrahiah as their leader.* [43]*And they offered great sacrifices that day and rejoiced, for God had made them rejoice with great joy; the women and children also rejoiced. And the joy of Jerusalem was heard afar off.*

* Heb *company* Vg *choir*

OVERVIEW: The holy city, after being built, is dedicated when, after the number of the elect is completed at the end of the world, the church in its entirety is introduced into heaven. The leaders of Judah foreshadow all those more perfect teachers who will be proven through their holy deeds to have risen above the ordinary life of the holy church. When Nehemiah walks with his choir of praisers over the Tower of the Ovens, in whose structure they once used to sweat, he symbolizes the teachers of the truth who rejoice over the sublime rewards of those whom they have taught. We pay our vows to the Lord in the midst of Jerusalem in the sight of all his people when, in the heavenly homeland, after the whole multitude of the saints has congregated, we offer those praises of thanksgiving to him (BEDE).

12:27-28 The Levites in Their Places

A TYPE OF THE CHURCH AT THE END OF THE

WORLD. BEDE: The city had been built long before, but it was not proper that it be dedicated before the inhabitants had been gathered and ministers suitable for the temple and guardians for the gates and vestibules had been appointed. The holy city, after being built, is dedicated when, after the number of the elect is completed at the end of the world, the church in its entirety is introduced in heaven to the sight of its Creator, and whenever in this life we are uplifted with desire for that future life, it is as if we are rejoicing over the future dedication of our city. Thus this same dedication also can be interpreted in a twofold way, namely, at the present time the hope of those who desire and purify the eyes of their heart so that they can see God, but then in the reality of blessed persons in spiritual bodies who enjoy a vision of God amid hosts of angelic spirits. ON EZRA AND NEHEMIAH 3.33.[1]

[1]TTH 47:209*; PL 91:913.

12:31 *The Leaders of Judah*

THE PERFECT TEACHERS OF THE CHURCH.
BEDE: The leaders of Judah (i.e., "confession" or
"praise")[2] are all those more perfect teachers of
the holy church who at the dedication of the city
go up on top of the wall because when the time of
retribution appears, they will be proven to have
risen above the ordinary life of the holy church by
their more exalted manner of living. For they are
the ones concerning whom the Lord promises
this holy church through the prophet, saying, "I
have posted guardians on your walls."[3] Thus it is
just that those today who have been placed in the
office of watchman over the holy church's walls
will at that time also be distinguished by the
glory of this same reward. ON EZRA AND
NEHEMIAH 3.33.[4]

12:37 *The Company of Those Who Gave Thanks*

**THE SPIRITUAL MEANING OF THE CHOIR AND
THE TOWER OF THE OVENS.** BEDE: It would
take a long time to discuss all the gates and towers individually. Let it suffice to have said that
those who completed the gates, towers and city
wall amid great toil, hardship, famine, cold and
vigils by day and night while the tireless enemy
fights against and assails them, afterwards, once
the enemy has been beaten back and thrown into
disarray, go walking together through the gates,
towers and buildings of this city and rejoice with
songs, hymns, harps, cymbals, lyres, and trumpets and thanksgivings together with those very
teachers who were the authors of the project and
the teachers of God's law. No one can doubt that
in the same sequence, this takes place in the spiritual building too when, as the hour of final retribution approaches as though it were the long-
desired dedication of God's city, the faithful
obtain eternal rewards for their works when,
much like Nehemiah and Ezra and the other
priests and Levites as they each bring forth their
workers, all the teachers of faithful peoples con-

duct their listeners whom they have acquired for
the Lord into the fortifications of the heavenly
homeland. Then, as well as the other fortifications of the holy city, Nehemiah also walks with
his choir of praisers over the Tower of the Ovens
in whose structure they once used to sweat, when
teachers of the truth rejoice over the sublime
rewards of those whom they have taught. For if
the loaves of the furnace that are baked in secret
signify the inward devotion of the mind of the
faithful that is strengthened by the fire of love,
which is why such loaves were also commanded
by the Law to be offered as a sacrifice to the
Lord,[5] what could be more aptly figured by the
ovens in which these loaves are baked than their
very hearts that are accustomed always to burn
with the flame of inner love and to beget deeds or
words of the virtues? ON EZRA AND NEHEMIAH
3.33.[6]

12:43 *Sacrifices and Rejoicing*

**THE ELECT SHALL OFFER SACRIFICE OF
PRAISE TO THE LORD.** BEDE: For on that day of
perpetual light about which Zechariah said,
"And there shall be one day that is known to the
Lord, not day or night"[7] (that is, a day that is
remote from the usual experience of passing
time), the elect sacrifice great victims to the
Lord, namely, those about which the psalmist,
tasting them in the hope of things to come, said,
"You have broken my bonds; I will offer to you
the sacrifice of praise."[8] He properly also reveals
where he was hoping that he would offer this
sacrifice when he immediately adds, "I will pay
my vows to the Lord in the courtyards of the
Lord's house, in the sight of all his people, in the
midst of you, O Jerusalem."[9] For we pay our
vows to the Lord in the midst of Jerusalem in
the sight of all his people when, in the heavenly
homeland, after the whole multitude of the

---

[2]See Jerome *Nom. Hebr.* (CCL 72:67.19). [3]Is 62:6. [4]TTH 47:211; PL
91:914. [5]See Lev 2:4. [6]TTH 47:213-14*; PL 91:916. [7]Zech 14:7.
[8]Ps 116:16-17 (115:7-8 LXX, Vg). [9]Ps 116:18-19 (115:9-10 LXX, Vg).

saints has congregated, we offer those praises of thanksgiving to him whom in this present life we sigh for and thirst for with daily desire. ON

EZRA AND NEHEMIAH 3.33.[10]

[10]TTH 47:216-17; PL 91:917-18.

12:44-47 JUDAH REJOICES OVER THE PRIESTS AND LEVITES WHO MINISTER

[44]On that day men were appointed over the chambers for the stores, the contributions, the first fruits, and the tithes, to gather into them the portions required by the law for the priests and for the Levites according to the fields of the towns; for Judah rejoiced over the priests and the Levites who ministered. [45]And they performed the service of their God and the service of purification, as did the singers and the gatekeepers, according to the command of David and his son Solomon. [46]For in the days of David and Asaph of old there was a chief of the singers, and there were songs of praise and thanksgiving to God. [47]And all Israel in the days of Zerubbabel and in the days of Nehemiah gave the daily portions for the singers and the gatekeepers; and they set apart that which was for the Levites; and the Levites set apart that which was for the sons of Aaron.

OVERVIEW: Woe to those priests and ministers who are happy to take from the people the payments due to their rank but are not eager to labor for the salvation of this same people or to offer them any holy guidance by living uprightly (BEDE).

12:44-47 People Appointed over the Chambers

A WARNING TO THE MINISTERS OF THE CHURCH. BEDE: The reason that the people liked the priests, Levites and other ministers of holy things to dwell in Jerusalem is that they rejoiced in the good works of those by whose God-devoted perseverance not only had the people been corrected from their sins but also the city rebuilt and dedicated with great praise and joy. The allegorical exposition of this chapter is clear to us because the Lord stated that those "who preach the gospel should live by the gospel."[1] But woe to those priests and ministers of holy things who are happy to take from the people the payments due to their rank but are not at all eager to labor for the salvation of this same people, not to offer them any holy guidance by living uprightly or to sing of the pleasantness of the heavenly kingdom by preaching something delightful to them; instead, so far from opening the doors of the heavenly city for them by having citizenship in heaven, they are proven rather to shut these doors by acting perversely, and so far from rejoicing in the works of these ministers when confessing or praising the Lord, the people are compelled to be all the more afflicted. ON EZRA AND NEHEMIAH 3.33.[2]

[1]1 Cor 9:14. [2]TTH 47:218; PL 91:919.

13:1-31 NEHEMIAH COMPLETES
HIS RELIGIOUS REFORMS

[1]On that day they read from the book of Moses in the hearing of the people; and in it was found written that no Ammonite or Moabite should ever enter the assembly of God; [2]for they did not meet the children of Israel with bread and water, but hired Balaam against them to curse them— yet our God turned the curse into a blessing. [3]When the people heard the law, they separated from Israel all those of foreign descent.

[4]Now before this, Eliashib the priest, who was appointed over the chambers of the house of our God, and who was connected with Tobiah, [5]prepared for Tobiah a large chamber where they had previously put the cereal offering, the frankincense, the vessels, and the tithes of grain, wine, and oil, which were given by commandment to the Levites, singers, and gatekeepers, and the contributions for the priests. [6]While this was taking place I was not in Jerusalem, for in the thirty-second year of Ar-ta-xerxes king of Babylon I went to the king. And after some time I asked leave of the king [7]and came to Jerusalem, and I then discovered the evil that Eliashib had done for Tobiah, preparing for him a chamber in the courts of the house of God. [8]And I was very angry, and I threw all the household furniture of Tobiah out of the chamber. [9]Then I gave orders and they cleansed the chambers; and I brought back thither the vessels of the house of God, with the cereal offering and the frankincense.

[10]I also found out that the portions of the Levites had not been given to them; so that the Levites and the singers, who did the work, had fled each to his field. [11]So I remonstrated with the officials and said, "Why is the house of God forsaken?" And I gathered them together and set them in their stations. [12]Then all Judah brought the tithe of the grain, wine, and oil into the storehouses. [13]And I appointed as treasurers over the storehouses Shelemiah the priest, Zadok the scribe, and Pedaiah of the Levites, and as their assistant Hanan the son of Zaccur, son of Mattaniah, for they were counted faithful; and their duty was to distribute to their brethren. [14]Remember me, O my God, concerning this, and wipe not out my good deeds that I have done for the house of my God and for his service.

[15]In those days I saw in Judah men treading wine presses on the sabbath, and bringing in heaps of grain and loading them on asses; and also wine, grapes, figs, and all kinds of burdens, which they brought into Jerusalem on the sabbath day; and I warned them on the day when they sold food. [16]Men of Tyre also, who lived in the city, brought in fish and all kinds of wares and sold them on the sabbath to the people of Judah, and in Jerusalem. [17]Then I remonstrated with the nobles of Judah and said to them, "What is this evil thing which you are doing, profaning the sabbath day? [18]Did not your fathers act in this way, and did not our God bring all this evil on us and on this city? Yet you bring more wrath upon Israel by profaning the sabbath."

[19]When it began to be dark at the gates of Jerusalem before the sabbath, I commanded that the

doors should be shut and gave orders that they should not be opened until after the sabbath. And I set some of my servants over the gates, that no burden might be brought in on the sabbath day. ²⁰Then the merchants and sellers of all kinds of wares lodged outside Jerusalem once or twice. ²¹But I warned them and said to them, "Why do you lodge before the wall? If you do so again I will lay hands on you." From that time on they did not come on the sabbath. ²²And I commanded the Levites that they should purify themselves and come and guard the gates, to keep the sabbath day holy. Remember this also in my favor, O my God, and spare me according to the greatness of thy steadfast love.

²³In those days also I saw the Jews who had married women of Ashdod, Ammon, and Moab; ²⁴and half of their children spoke the language of Ashdod, and they could not speak the language of Judah, but the language of each people. ²⁵And I contended with them and cursed them and beat some of them and pulled out their hair; and I made them take oath in the name of God, saying, "You shall not give your daughters to their sons, or take their daughters for your sons or for yourselves. ²⁶Did not Solomon king of Israel sin on account of such women? Among the many nations there was no king like him, and he was beloved by his God, and God made him king over all Israel; nevertheless foreign women made even him to sin. ²⁷Shall we then listen to you and do all this great evil and act treacherously against our God by marrying foreign women?"

²⁸And one of the sons of Jehoiada, the son of Eliashib the high priest, was the son-in-law of Sanballat the Horonite; therefore I chased him from me. ²⁹Remember them, O my God, because they have defiled the priesthood and the covenant of the priesthood and the Levites.

³⁰Thus I cleansed them from everything foreign, and I established the duties of the priests and Levites, each in his work; ³¹and I provided for the wood offering, at appointed times, and for the first fruits. Remember me, O my God, for good.

OVERVIEW: The Moabites and the Ammonites, because they were born from incest, figuratively represent heretics, whose authors corrupt the teaching of the Fathers through their faulty understanding. The zeal of Nehemiah in cleansing and purifying the temple can be compared with that of the Lord Savior, who made a whip from cords and drove all vendors and buyers outside the house of God. The spiritual meaning of the sabbath is that all the elect should labor for eternal rest but on a day that is to come should hope for that rest from the Lord. The citizens of the Holy City must be purified from all the filth of foreign pollution, which is alien to God (BEDE).

13:1-3 Ammonites and Moabites Excluded from the Assembly of God

LIBERATION FROM HERESY AND NEW LIFE IN THE CHRISTIAN PEACE. BEDE: It is known that the Moabites and the Ammonites, because they were born from incest,[1] figuratively represent heretics, whose authors through their faulty understanding corrupt the teaching of the Fathers from which they themselves were instructed, just as the daughters of Lot secretly and in darkness and illegitimately use the seed of their father; and for this reason the offspring of such ones (i.e., adherents of heresies) can never have any part in the Lord's church. For those who are set straight from these heresies will no longer be the offspring of such mothers. Now they would meet the children of Israel with food and water as they are

[1]See Gen 19:31-38.

coming from Egypt if they themselves, living well and dwelling in catholic peace, were to bestow the solace of God's Word on those who, recently rescued from the servitude of sins through the water of baptism as if through the waves of the sea, are panting for the freedom of the celestial homeland. ON EZRA AND NEHEMIAH 3.33.[2]

13:4-9 The Chambers Cleansed

A TYPE OF THE TRUE CONSOLER AND CLEANSER. BEDE: You also, whatever infidelity and uncleanness you discover among the faithful, immediately cast it out so that after the hearts of believers (which are the Lord's storerooms, since they are full of the riches of the virtues), have been purified, the vessels of the Lord may be brought in—that is to say, those same hearts that just before were vessels of error through sin may again become vessels of the Lord through correction, and there let the sacrifice of good works and the incense of pure prayer be found where before there was a den of thieves.[3] But the vessels of Tobiah the Ammonite are also cast out from the temple storeroom, and God's vessels as well as the sacrifice and the incense are returned to that place by those who, after they have excommunicated or anathematized heretics and false catholics and expelled them from the church, substitute in their place catholic servants of Christ such as may serve him faithful deeds and prayers. Clearly, we ought to compare this zeal of Nehemiah with that of the Lord Savior, when finding vendors and buyers in the temple, he made a whip from cords and drove them all outside.[4] Nehemiah, in this as in his other undertakings, aptly conveyed a type of true consoler and cleanser. ON EZRA AND NEHEMIAH 3.35.[5]

13:15-22 Treading Wine Presses on the Sabbath

THE SPIRITUAL MEANING OF THE SABBATH. BEDE: We are commanded by the Law to do for six days the things that are necessary and to rest on the seventh.[6] The general mystery of this command is clear: namely, that in this world, which lasts for six ages,[7] all the elect should labor for eternal rest, but on a day that is to come, as it were on the seventh, should hope for that rest itself from the Lord. But according to tropology (i.e., the moral sense), the elect even in this life keep the sabbath holy for the Lord when, having separated themselves at the appropriate time from worldly concerns, they make time for prayer and raise their minds, which have been purified, to the contemplation of heavenly things. For when we lawfully carry out those things that care for the body's demands with a sincere heart and not with desires contrary to the precept of the apostle,[8] we are, so to speak, performing our necessary work in the six days, since we are occupied with those things that we have need of in this world. ON EZRA AND NEHEMIAH 3.36.[9]

13:23-30 Cleansed from Everything Foreign

PURIFICATION FROM ALL THAT IS ALIEN TO GOD. BEDE: It is in all respects an apt and appropriate end to the work of building the holy city and the temple of the Lord that when the citizens have been purified by God from all the filth of foreign pollution, which is alien to God, the orders of the priests and the Levites should be duly preserved in their own ministry in order that the teachers of the church who have been instructed according to rule may continually exhort the people now cleansed from all sin to remain henceforth in goodness and to grow. Among other things, the people offer wood to the Lord to feed the fire of the altar when they perform works of virtues that are assuredly worthy of divine consecration. For if wood did not

---

[2]TTH 47:219-20; PL 91:919-20. [3]See Jer 7:11. [4]See Mt 21:12; Jn 2:14-15. [5]TTH 47:222; PL 91:921. [6]See Exod 20:9-10. [7]For the theory of the six ages of the world, see Bede *In Ezr.* (CCL 119A:1.1201-28); *De Templ.* 66-71 (CCL 123B:445.1-544.98). [8]See Rom 13:14. [9]TTH 47:222-23*; PL 91:921.

sometimes symbolize something good, the prophet would not say, "Then shall all the wood of the forests rejoice in the presence of the Lord."[10] Now the wood burns and is consumed in the altar of the burnt offering when in the hearts of the elect works of righteousness are perfected in the flame of love. ON EZRA AND NEHEMIAH 3.37.[11]

---

[10]Ps 96:12-13 (95:12-13 LXX, Vg). [11]TTH 47:225-26*; PL 91:924.

ESTHER

1:1-8 THE MAGNIFICENCE OF AHASUERUS'S REIGN

¹In the days of Ahasu-erus, the Ahasu-erus who reigned from India to Ethiopia over one hundred and twenty-seven provinces, ²in those days when King Ahasu-erus sat on his royal throne in Susa the capital, ³in the third year of his reign he gave a banquet for all his princes and servants, the army chiefs^a of Persia and Media and the nobles and governors of the provinces being before him, ⁴while he showed the riches of his royal glory and the splendor and pomp of his majesty for many days, a hundred and eighty days. ⁵And when these days were completed, the king gave for all the people present in Susa the capital, both great and small, a banquet lasting for seven days, in the court of the garden of the king's palace. ⁶There were white cotton curtains and blue hangings caught up with cords of fine linen and purple to silver rings^b and marble pillars, and also couches of gold and silver on a mosaic pavement of porphyry, marble, mother-of-pearl and precious stones. ⁷Drinks were served in golden goblets, goblets of different kinds, and the royal wine was lavished according to the bounty of the king. ⁸And drinking was according to the law, no one was compelled; for the king had given orders to all the officials of his palace to do as every man desired.

a Heb *the army*   **b** Or *rods*

OVERVIEW: Ahasuerus was called Artaxerxes and reigned after Darius for forty years. The city of Susa takes its name from the river Susis, along whose banks lies the royal palace of Cyrus. From the spiritual point of view, Ahasuerus's magnificent banquet signifies the greatness of the spiritual riches and the excellence of the living treasures given by Christ to humanity (RABANUS MAURUS).

1:1 *In the Days of Ahasuerus*

THE TIME OF AHASUERUS'S REIGN. RABANUS MAURUS: Not only the Holy Scriptures, but the Jewish Antiquities of Josephus as well contain the

story of Esther, although they differ in some of the historical details. Therefore, there is some question as to the actual identity of that Ahasuerus who ruled from India to Ethiopia over one hundred twenty-seven provinces. In fact, when Josephus mentions him, he relates that he was Cyrus son of King Xerxes who reigned over Persia after his father Darius. He also adds that this Cyrus was called Artaxerxes by the Greeks, having the nickname "Long-handed,"[1] and was in power for forty years. But I do not think that Esther lived at that time. Ezra writes that he had

---

[1] "Longimanus" in the Latin text.

returned at that time from Babylonia, but he would never have omitted mentioning Esther if she had actually accomplished the things which are attributed to her. Therefore Eusebius, in his Chronicles, thinks that this Ahasuerus was called Artaxerxes and reigned after Darius for forty years, having the nickname Nothus as his father had. Explanation on the Book of Esther 1.[2]

1:2 In the Citadel of Susa

The City of Susa. Rabanus Maurus: Susa is the metropolis of Persia which the historians say was founded by the brother of Memnon. It is called Susa because it lies along the river Susis where the royal palace of Cyrus was constructed with glittering white stone as well as other varieties. It is conspicuous for its golden columns and roofs and for its precious stones. It also contains the sculpture of a sky full of shining stars and other incredible things to the human mind. This is the place where it is said that the king gave a lavish banquet and displayed his great wealth to his subjects. Explanation on the Book of Esther 1.[3]

1:3-8 Ahasuerus Displayed the Wealth of His Kingdom

The Spiritual Meaning of the Banquet. Rabanus Maurus: Even though from the historical point of view it simply appears to show the abundance of riches and the luxury of delights of a powerful king, . . . according to the holier mystery of our most powerful king, namely, Our Lord Christ, this preparation of a most magnificent banquet signifies the greatness of the spiritual riches and the excellence of the living treasures that he distributes according to the measure of his dispensation to each of his faithful. Explanation on the Book of Esther 1.[4]

---

[2]PL 109:636D-637A. [3]PL 109:637A. [4]PL 109:637.

1:9-22 QUEEN VASHTI'S OUTRAGE

[9]*Queen Vashti also gave a banquet for the women in the palace which belonged to King Ahasuerus.*

[10]*On the seventh day, when the heart of the king was merry with wine, he commanded Mehuman, Biztha, Harbona, Bigtha and Abagtha, Zethar and Carkas, the seven eunuchs who served King Ahasu-erus as chamberlains, [11]to bring Queen Vashti before the king with her royal crown, in order to show the peoples and the princes her beauty; for she was fair to behold. [12]But Queen Vashti refused to come at the king's command conveyed by the eunuchs. At this the king was enraged, and his anger burned within him.*

[13]*Then the king said to the wise men who knew the times—for this was the king's procedure toward all who were versed in law and judgment, [14]the men next to him being Carshena, Shethar, Admatha, Tarshish, Meres, Marsena, and Memucan, the seven princes of Persia and Media, who*

saw the king's face, and sat first in the kingdom—: [15]*"According to the law, what is to be done to Queen Vashti, because she has not performed the command of King Ahasu-erus conveyed by the eunuchs?"* [16]*Then Memucan said in presence of the king and the princes, "Not only to the king has Queen Vashti done wrong, but also to all the princes and all the peoples who are in all the provinces of King Ahasu-erus.* [17]*For this deed of the queen will be made known to all women, causing them to look with contempt upon their husbands, since they will say, 'King Ahasu-erus commanded Queen Vashti to be brought before him, and she did not come.'* [18]*This very day the ladies of Persia and Media who have heard of the queen's behavior will be telling it to all the king's princes, and there will be contempt and wrath in plenty.* [19]*If it please the king, let a royal order go forth from him, and let it be written among the laws of the Persians and the Medes so that it may not be altered, that Vashti is to come no more before King Ahasu-erus; and let the king give her royal position to another who is better than she.* [20]*So when the decree made by the king is proclaimed throughout all his kingdom, vast as it is, all women will give honor to their husbands, high and low."* [21]*This advice pleased the king and the princes, and the king did as Memucan proposed;* [22]*he sent letters to all the royal provinces, to every province in its own script and to every people in its own language, that every man be lord in his own house and speak according to the language of his people.*

OVERVIEW: Rabanus Maurus provides a reading of Esther through the eyes of the later Christian teachers and the earlier prophets. Queen Vashti symbolizes the Jewish people. The seventh day of the banquet prefigures the beauty of the age in which the incarnate Lord manifested with more abundant grace all the mysteries of the Law and the Prophets. The sentence passed against Queen Vashti foreshadows the sentence passed by Christ against the arrogance of the Jews in favor of the Gentiles (RABANUS MAURUS).

1:9 Queen Vashti Gave a Banquet for the Women

QUEEN VASHTI REPRESENTS THE JEWISH PEOPLE. RABANUS MAURUS: The person of Queen Vashti provides a clear expression of the Jewish people who themselves appeared to reign as queen when they were found to prevail over all the other nations in the worship of the one God. Therefore when she gave a banquet for the women where the king used to linger, this symbolized the Jewish people who demonstrated

their observance of the law in the worship they performed in Jerusalem where the temple and the Holy of Holies used to be. EXPLANATION ON THE BOOK OF ESTHER 2.[1]

1:10-12 On the Seventh Day

THE FULLNESS OF TIME. RABANUS MAURUS: The seventh day of the banquet signifies the beauty of the time in which the incarnate Lord manifested with more abundant grace all the mysteries of the law and the prophets on which the pious minds of the faithful had until then pastured. And writing about that fullness to the Galatians, the apostle Paul says, "But when the fullness of time had come, God sent his Son, born of a woman, born under the law, in order to redeem those who were under the law, so that we might receive adoption as children. And because you are children, God has sent the Spirit of his Son into our hearts, crying, 'Abba Father.'"[2]

---

[1]PL 109:642B. [2]Gal 4:4-6.

EXPLANATION ON THE BOOK OF ESTHER 2.[3]

1:13-22 *The King Consulted the Sages*

A FORESHADOWING OF THE CHURCH OF THE NATIONS. RABANUS MAURUS: The advice which King Ahasuerus asks of his seven sages who were, according to royal custom always by his side, concerning the insolent Vashti—as well as the sentence he orders them to pass concerning her— undoubtedly signifies the sentence our Savior passes against the arrogance of the Jewish people. He passes this sentence through his teachers who are always in his presence and full of the grace of the Holy Spirit in their orthodox faith and good works. The Jewish people themselves who incurred this judgment bear the responsibility for the punishment and condemnation they have received of being expelled from the royal bridal room,[4] that is, from the congregation of God for which they had been ordained and elected, so that another, better bride, namely, the church of the nations, may take their place with sincere faith and full devotion. EXPLANATION ON THE BOOK OF ESTHER 2.[5]

---

[3]PL 109:642C-D. [4]Here Rabanus is seeing again Vashti as an allegorical figure of the Jewish people; see above comments on 1:9. [5]PL 109:644B-C.

2:1-18 AHASUERUS MAKES ESTHER QUEEN

[1]*After these things, when the anger of King Ahasu-erus had abated, he remembered Vashti and what she had done and what had been decreed against her.* [2]*Then the king's servants who attended him said, "Let beautiful young virgins be sought out for the king.* [3]*And let the king appoint officers in all the provinces of his kingdom to gather all the beautiful young virgins to the harem in Susa the capital, under custody of Hegai the king's eunuch who is in charge of the women; let their ointments be given them.* [4]*And let the maiden who pleases the king be queen instead of Vashti." This pleased the king, and he did so.*

[5]*Now there was a Jew in Susa the capital whose name was Mordecai, the son of Jair, son of Shime-i, son of Kish, a Benjaminite,* [6]*who had been carried away from Jerusalem among the captives carried away with Jeconiah king of Judah, whom Nebuchadnezzar king of Babylon had carried away.* [7]*He had brought up Hadassah, that is Esther, the daughter of his uncle, for she had neither father nor mother; the maiden was beautiful and lovely, and when her father and her mother died, Mordecai adopted her as his own daughter.* [8]*So when the king's order and his edict were proclaimed, and when many maidens were gathered in Susa the capital in custody of Hegai, Esther also was taken into the king's palace and put in custody of Hegai who had charge of the women.* [9]*And the maiden pleased him and won his favor; and he quickly provided her with her ointments and her portion of food, and with seven chosen maids from the king's palace, and advanced her and her maids to the best place in the harem.* [10]*Esther had not made known her peo-*

ple or kindred, for Mordecai had charged her not to make it known. ¹¹And every day Mordecai walked in front of the court of the harem, to learn how Esther was and how she fared.

¹²Now when the turn came for each maiden to go in to King Ahasu-erus, after being twelve months under the regulations for the women, since this was the regular period of their beautifying, six months with oil of myrrh and six months with spices and ointments for women— ¹³when the maiden went in to the king in this way she was given whatever she desired to take with her from the harem to the king's palace. ¹⁴In the evening she went, and in the morning she came back to the second harem in custody of Sha-ashgaz the king's eunuch who was in charge of the concubines; she did not go in to the king again, unless the king delighted in her and she was summoned by name.

¹⁵When the turn came for Esther the daughter of Abihail the uncle of Mordecai, who had adopted her as his own daughter, to go in to the king, she asked for nothing except what Hegai the king's eunuch, who had charge of the women, advised. Now Esther found favor in the eyes of all who saw her. ¹⁶And when Esther was taken to King Ahasu-erus into his royal palace in the tenth month, which is the month of Tebeth, in the seventh year of his reign, ¹⁷the king loved Esther more than all the women, and she found grace and favor in his sight more than all the virgins, so that he set the royal crown on her head and made her queen instead of Vashti. ¹⁸Then the king gave a great banquet to all his princes and servants; it was Esther's banquet. He also granted a remission of taxes^c to the provinces, and gave gifts with royal liberality.

c Or a holiday

OVERVIEW: The seven princes of Persia subdue Ahasuerus's regret for Vashti by inducing him to love other maidens. The maidens represent the different nations gathered together through the doctrine of Christ. Esther symbolizes the holy church, while Mordecai foreshadows the teachers of the Gentiles who will convert the nations to the word of Christ. In not revealing her origin Esther represents the church of the Gentiles that did not want to disclose immediately the place of its homeland and people, because it was not able to bear the shame of its recently cleansed sin of impiety. The magnificent banquet for Esther's wedding, which was prepared for the princes and the people, represents the greatest bliss that is enjoyed by all human beings (RABANUS MAURUS).

2:1-4 Seeking a New Queen

THE PRINCIPLE FOLLOWED BY THE SEVEN SAGES. JEROME: The worldly philosophers drive out an old passion by instilling a new one; they hammer out one nail by hammering in another. It was on this principle that the seven princes of Persia acted toward Ahasuerus, for they subdued his regret for Vashti by inducing him to love other maidens. But whereas they cured one fault by another fault and one sin by another sin, we must overcome our faults by learning to love the opposite virtues. "Depart from evil," says the psalmist, "and do good; seek peace and pursue it." LETTER 125.14.[1]

THE NEW MARRIAGE WITH THE CHURCH. RABANUS MAURUS: After Judea[2] had been expelled from the royal marriage, different peoples and different individuals from each nation from different parts of the world were led to the royal

---

[1]NPNF 2 6:248. [2]Rabanus identifies Vashti with Judea; see above: 1:9; 1:10-22.

congregation by the holy preachers who were ministers of the evangelical word. They were given into the custody of Hegai,[3] whose name is interpreted as "celebration" or "solemnity." He was the superintendent of the royal women. In other words, they[4] were given to the care of the pastors and leaders of the church to whom the custody of the souls of the faithful was entrusted. EXPLANATION ON THE BOOK OF ESTHER 3.[5]

2:5-9 Mordecai Had Brought Up Esther

MORDECAI SIGNIFIES THE GENTILE CHURCH AND ITS TEACHERS. RABANUS MAURUS: It is evident that Esther signifies the gentile church. Her name is interpreted as "hiding place," and she also had the other name of Hadassah, that is, "mercy." The church is pleasing to God in the hiding place of his heart because of the chastity of her faith and before the eyes of God it finds a greater mercy and grace than the synagogue of the Jews which with good reason the prophet Hosea calls merciless because of its impiety. Therefore the spiritual Mordecai adopted [Esther] as his own daughter because she had lost both her parents. And what is signified by Mordecai but the future teachers of the Gentiles? This is especially true of the blessed apostle Paul who also descended from the stock of Jemin, that is, he testified to be from the tribe of Benjamin. After Paul was transformed from persecutor into apostle, the gentile church was entrusted to him. And he himself, after her mother and father had died—namely, the errors and superstitions of the Gentiles—made her his own daughter when he regenerated her through the grace of baptism and the word of the gospel, making her also a daughter of the almighty Father, saved for all eternity. Therefore Paul said to them, "For though you might have ten thousand guardians in Christ, you do not have many fathers. Indeed, in Christ Jesus I became your father through the gospel."[6] EXPLANATION ON THE BOOK OF ESTHER 3.[7]

2:10-11 Esther Did Not Reveal Her People

PRUDENCE OF THE CHURCH OF THE NATIONS. RABANUS MAURUS: Indeed the church of the nations, being instructed with the precepts of the holy teachers, did not want to disclose the place of its homeland and people, because, after being purified through baptism from any corruption of sin or defilement of idolatry, it is no longer able to bear the shame of its former impiety. And the Lord taught [the church] through the prophet by saying, "Hear, O daughter, consider and incline your ear; forget your people and your father's house, because the king desired your beauty, as he is also the Lord your God."[8] EXPLANATION ON THE BOOK OF ESTHER 3.[9]

2:15-18 The King Gave a Great Banquet

THE SPIRITUAL UNION OF CHRIST WITH THE CHURCH. RABANUS MAURUS: It is evident that the magnificent banquet for Esther's wedding, prepared for both the princes and the people, represents the greatest bliss that is enjoyed by the entire human race, both great and small, for the spiritual union of Christ with the church. In this banquet, in fact, no carnal foods are consumed by those who are worthy to participate in it. Instead they consume a spiritual diet of wisdom and virtue. In this banquet, all the faithful receive the holy mysteries of the body and blood of the Lord as a remedy for their salvation. Here the meal of eternal life resides. And our king gives peace to all the provinces, and bestows abundant gifts in freeing those who believe in him from the weight of sins, and rewarding them with spiritual gifts. Therefore he himself says in the gospel, "Come to me, all you who are weary and are carrying heavy burdens, and I will give you rest. Take my yoke upon you, and learn from me; for I am gentle and humble in heart, and you will find rest for your souls."[10] EXPLANATION ON THE BOOK OF ESTHER 4.[11]

---

[3]See Esth 2:3. [4]The royal women who symbolize the royal congregation. [5]PL 109:646 B-C. [6]1 Cor 4:15. [7]PL 109:646B-C. [8]Ps 45:10-11 (44:11-12 Vg). [9]PL 109:646-47. [10]Mt 11:28-29. [11]PL 109:649D-650A.

2:19-23 A PLOT THWARTED BY MORDECAI

^{19}*When the virgins were gathered together the second time, Mordecai was sitting at the king's gate.* ^{20}*Now Esther had not made known her kindred or her people, as Mordecai had charged her; for Esther obeyed Mordecai just as when she was brought up by him.* ^{21}*And in those days, as Mordecai was sitting at the king's gate, Bigthan and Teresh, two of the king's eunuchs, who guarded the threshold, became angry and sought to lay hands on King Ahasu-erus.* ^{22}*And this came to the knowledge of Mordecai, and he told it to Queen Esther, and Esther told the king in the name of Mordecai.* ^{23}*When the affair was investigated and found to be so, the men were both hanged on the gallows. And it was recorded in the Book of the Chronicles in the presence of the king.*

OVERVIEW: The two eunuchs who were the janitors of the royal house and conspired against Ahasuerus prefigure the Scribes and Pharisees (RABANUS MAURUS).

2:19-23 *Knowledge of a Plot Came to Mordecai*

A FIGURE OF THE SCRIBES AND THE PHARISEES. RABANUS MAURUS: There is no doubt that the Scribes and Pharisees of the Jews are signified by the two eunuchs who were the caretakers of the royal house and guarded the threshold of the palace. Indeed it was said that even though they had the key to knowledge, they did not enter and did not let others enter. They wanted to rebel against the king and kill him because they were jealous of the teaching and virtue of the Savior. They constantly put him in danger and conspired with the ministers of Roman power to find a way to kill him. Therefore it is written in the gospel, "Then the Pharisees went and plotted to entrap him in what he said. So they sent their disciples to him, along with the Herodians, saying, 'Teacher, we know that you are sincere, and teach the way of God in accordance with truth, and show deference to no one; for you do not regard people with partiality. Tell us, then, what you think. Is it lawful to pay taxes to Caesar, or not?'"[1] And in another passage it is read, "So the chief priests and the Pharisees called a meeting of the council, and said, 'What are we to do? This man is performing many signs. If we let him go on like this, everyone will believe in him, and the Romans will come and take our place and people.'"[2] And a bit further it is added, "So from that day on they planned to put him to death."[3] EXPLANATION ON THE BOOK OF ESTHER 5.[4]

---

[1]Mt 22:16-17. [2]Jn 11:47-48. [3]Jn 11:53. [4]PL 109:650D-651a.

3:1-15 HAMAN'S PLOT AGAINST THE JEWS

¹*After these things King Ahasu-erus promoted Haman the Agagite, the son of Hammedatha, and advanced him and set his seat above all the princes who were with him. ²And all the king's servants who were at the king's gate bowed down and did obeisance to Haman; for the king had so commanded concerning him. But Mordecai did not bow down or do obeisance. ³Then the king's servants who were at the king's gate said to Mordecai, "Why do you transgress the king's command?" ⁴And when they spoke to him day after day and he would not listen to them, they told Haman, in order to see whether Mordecai's words would avail; for he had told them that he was a Jew. ⁵And when Haman saw that Mordecai did not bow down or do obeisance to him, Haman was filled with fury. ⁶But he disdained to lay hands on Mordecai alone. So, as they had made known to him the people of Mordecai, Haman sought to destroy all the Jews, the people of Mordecai, throughout the whole kingdom of Ahasu-erus.*

⁷*In the first month, which is the month of Nisan, in the twelfth year of King Ahasu-erus, they cast Pur, that is the lot, before Haman day after day; and they cast it month after month till the twelfth month, which is the month of Adar. ⁸Then Haman said to King Ahasu-erus, "There is a certain people scattered abroad and dispersed among the peoples in all the provinces of your kingdom; their laws are different from those of every other people, and they do not keep the king's laws, so that it is not for the king's profit to tolerate them. ⁹If it please the king, let it be decreed that they be destroyed, and I will pay ten thousand talents of silver into the hands of those who have charge of the king's business, that they may put it into the king's treasuries." ¹⁰So the king took his signet ring from his hand and gave it to Haman the Agagite, the son of Hammedatha, the enemy of the Jews. ¹¹And the king said to Haman, "The money is given to you, the people also, to do with them as it seems good to you."*

¹²*Then the king's secretaries were summoned on the thirteenth day of the first month, and an edict, according to all that Haman commanded, was written to the king's satraps and to the governors over all the provinces and to the princes of all the peoples, to every province in its own script and every people in its own language; it was written in the name of King Ahasu-erus and sealed with the king's ring. ¹³Letters were sent by couriers to all the king's provinces, to destroy, to slay, and to annihilate all Jews, young and old, women and children, in one day, the thirteenth day of the twelfth month, which is the month of Adar, and to plunder their goods. ¹⁴A copy of the document was to be issued as a decree in every province by proclamation to all the peoples to be ready for that day. ¹⁵The couriers went in haste by order of the king, and the decree was issued in Susa the capital. And the king and Haman sat down to drink; but the city of Susa was perplexed.*

OVERVIEW: Haman symbolizes the arrogance of the powerful of this world, who take advantage of the benefits conceded to them by divine mercy. Haman's actions and his plan to destroy the Jews foreshadow the different phases of Christ's passion (RABANUS MAURUS).

3:1-6 Ahasuerus Promoted Haman

A Symbol of the Powerful of this World.

Rabanus Maurus: Nothing else is symbolized by the arrogant Haman than the opulence of the powerful of this world who take advantage of the benefits conceded to them by divine mercy. They despise allowing their neighbors, who are given to them as companions by nature, to have as sharers of such grace. Therefore they are guilty of striving to transfer to themselves the honor and reverence that are rightly due to God alone. And so they pursue with hatred all those who do not want to act according to such behavior or comply with it. They persecute them with afflictions and endeavor to put them to death. But the heavenly judge, "who regards the lowly, and perceives the haughty from far away, who knows the deceiver and he, who is deceived, makes the pain return upon the heads of the sinful, and their iniquity descends on their head. The sinful are caught in their own traps: the righteous will be freed from their anguish, the impious will be handed over in their stead."[1] Explanation on the Book of Esther 6.[2]

3:7-15 A Decree Issued for the Destruction of the Jews

Allegorical Interpretation of Haman's

Actions. Rabanus Maurus: The fact that the twelfth month, which is called Adar, was chosen for the destruction of Israel after casting lots is not with its own spiritual meaning. It is referring, in fact, to the grace of Christ which has been prepared for the faithful in the fullness of time when the faithful will undergo a fierce persecution in the world in the last days. And writing about this to Timothy, the teacher of the Gentiles says, "You must understand this, that in the last days distressing times will come. For people will be lovers of themselves, lovers of money, boasters, arrogant, abusive, disobedient to their parents, ungrateful, unholy, inhuman, implacable, slanderers, profligates, brutes, haters of good, treacherous, reckless, swollen with conceit, lovers of pleasure rather than lovers of God, holding the outward form of godliness but denying its power."[3] And the Lord himself says in the Gospel, "And this gospel of the kingdom will be proclaimed throughout the world, as a testimony to all the nations; and then the end will come."[4] And a bit further: "For at that time there will be great suffering, such as has not been from the beginning of the world until now, and never will be."[5] Explanation on the Book of Esther 6.[6]

---

[1]Ps 138:6 (137:6 Vg); Ps 7:15-16 (7:16-17 Vg). [2]PL 109:652B-C. [3]2 Tim 3:1-5. [4]Mt 24:14. [5]Mt 24:21. [6]PL 109:653A-D.

4:1-17 ESTHER AGREES TO ENTREAT THE KING

[1]*When Mordecai learned all that had been done, Mordecai rent his clothes and put on sackcloth and ashes, and went out into the midst of the city, wailing with a loud and bitter cry;* [2]*he went up to the entrance of the king's gate, for no one might enter the king's gate clothed with sackcloth.* [3]*And in every province, wherever the king's command and his decree came, there was great mourning among the Jews, with fasting and weeping and lamenting, and most of them lay in sackcloth and ashes.*

⁴*When Esther's maids and her eunuchs came and told her, the queen was deeply distressed; she sent garments to clothe Mordecai, so that he might take off his sackcloth, but he would not accept them. ⁵Then Esther called for Hathach, one of the king's eunuchs, who had been appointed to attend her, and ordered him to go to Mordecai to learn what this was and why it was. ⁶Hathach went out to Mordecai in the open square of the city in front of the king's gate, ⁷and Mordecai told him all that had happened to him, and the exact sum of money that Haman had promised to pay into the king's treasuries for the destruction of the Jews. ⁸Mordecai also gave him a copy of the written decree issued in Susa for their destruction, that he might show it to Esther and explain it to her and charge her to go to the king to make supplication to him and entreat him for her people. ⁹And Hathach went and told Esther what Mordecai had said. ¹⁰Then Esther spoke to Hathach and gave him a message for Mordecai, saying, ¹¹"All the king's servants and the people of the king's provinces know that if any man or woman goes to the king inside the inner court without being called, there is but one law; all alike are to be put to death, except the one to whom the king holds out the golden scepter that he may live. And I have not been called to come in to the king these thirty days." ¹²And they told Mordecai what Esther had said. ¹³Then Mordecai told them to return answer to Esther, "Think not that in the king's palace you will escape any more than all the other Jews. ¹⁴For if you keep silence at such a time as this, relief and deliverance will rise for the Jews from another quarter, but you and your father's house will perish. And who knows whether you have not come to the kingdom for such a time as this?" ¹⁵Then Esther told them to reply to Mordecai, ¹⁶"Go, gather all the Jews to be found in Susa, and hold a fast on my behalf, and neither eat nor drink for three days, night or day. I and my maids will also fast as you do. Then I will go to the king, though it is against the law; and if I perish, I perish." ¹⁷Mordecai then went away and did everything as Esther had ordered him.*

OVERVIEW: The persecutions that the Jews suffered because of Haman are a figure of the persecutions that the holy church will suffer because of the evil of the world (RABANUS MAURUS). Friendship must always be combined with virtue, so that we may never commit a fault in order to favor a friend (AMBROSE). When the people were about to be destroyed because of Haman's plot, salvation was obtained through the prayer that Mordecai and Esther offered with fasting (ORIGEN). Esther shows how many women, fortified by the grace of God, have accomplished heroic actions (CLEMENT OF ROME).

4:1-4 Mordecai Wore Sackcloth

A TYPE OF THE PERSECUTIONS AGAINST THE HOLY CHURCH. RABANUS MAURUS: When Mordecai heard about the destruction of the Jews which had been sanctioned with an imperial decree, he put on clothes for mourning and proceeded to the gates of the palace with bitterness in his soul and grief in his voice. In the same way, after the teachers of the church hear of the persecution which the princes of this world want to bring against the innocent servants of Christ, they come with their prayers and alms, with vigils and prayers, with tears and heavy hearts in view of what they know must happen. They give their all before the supreme judge, so that through the dignity and prayers of the true queen, namely, the holy church—which is still a stranger in this world even as it reigns in heaven together with the Lord—they might be heard by the king of the universe. If someone, then, should ask how it might be fitting to a most just king to inflict torments on the innocent, let him know that this is not the result of an evil decision, but of the command of a supreme will. Indeed divine wisdom— a wisdom which defeats every wickedness and leads things from beginning to end with its power, and perfectly arranges everything—does whatever it wants in heaven and on earth, in the sea, and in every abyss. The events that occur, occur fairly so that (God's) faithful servant may be given into the hands of their persecutors both for the expiation of sin, and the correction of their habits . . . as the prophet testifies, "the Lord is just in all his ways, and kind in all his doings. The Lord is near to all who call on him."[1] EXPLANATION ON THE BOOK OF ESTHER 7.[2]

4:5-17 Gather All the Jews and Fast

FRIENDSHIP MUST BE COMBINED WITH VIRTUE. AMBROSE: Why did Queen Esther expose herself to death and not fear the wrath of a fierce king? Was it not to save her people from death, an act both seemly and virtuous? The king of Persia himself also, though fierce and proud, yet thought it seemly to show honor to the man[3] who had given information about a plot that had been laid against himself,[4] to save a free people from slavery, to snatch them from death and not to spare him who had pressed on such unseemly plans. So finally he handed over to the gallows[5] the man who stood second to himself and whom he counted chief among all his friends, because he considered that he had dishonored him with his false counsels. For that commendable friendship that maintains virtue is to be preferred most certainly to wealth, or honors or power. It is not accustomed to be preferred to virtue indeed, but to follow after it. So it was with Jonathan, who for his affection's sake avoided not his father's displeasure or the danger to his own safety.[6] So, too, it was with Ahimelech, who, to preserve the duties of hospitality, though he must endure death rather than betray his friends when fleeing.[7] DUTIES OF THE CLERGY 3.21.123-24.[8]

THE POWER OF PRAYER. ORIGEN: But what use is there to recall all the examples of those who, because they prayed as they ought, received great favours from God? Everyone can choose for himself many examples from the Scriptures. Anna obtained the birth of Samuel, who was reckoned with Moses,[9] because when she was barren she prayed to the Lord with faith.[10] And Ezechias, being still childless and having learned from Isaias that he was about to die, prayed and was included in genealogy of the Saviour.[11] Again, when, as a result of a single order arising from the intrigues of Aman, the people were about to be destroyed, the prayer and fasting of Mardochai and Esther were heard, and hence there arose, in addition to the feasts ordained by Moses, the festival of Mardochai for the people.[12] ON PRAYER 13.2.[13]

ESTHER'S HEROISM. CLEMENT OF ROME: Many women, fortified by the grace of God, have accomplished many heroic actions. The blessed Judith,[14] when the city was besieged, asked permission of the elders to be allowed to go into the foreigners' camp. By exposing herself to danger she went out for love of her country and of the people who were besieged, and the Lord delivered Holophernes into the hand of a woman. To no less danger did Esther, who was perfect in faith, expose herself, in order to save the twelve tribes of Israel that were to be destroyed. For by fasting and humiliation she begged the all-seeing Master of the ages, and he, seeing the meekness of her soul, rescued the people for whose sake she had faced danger. 1 CLEMENT 55.3-6.[15]

---

[1]Ps 145:17-18 (144:17-18 Vg). [2]PL 109:654A-C. [3]See Esth 6:10. [4]Esth 2:19-23. [5]See Esth 7:9-10. [6]See 1 Sam 23:16-18. [7]See 1 Sam 22:17. [8]NPNF 2 10:87. [9]See Jer 15:1; Ps 99:6 (98:6 LXX). [10]1 Sam 1:9-18. [11]See 2 Kings 20:1-6; Is 38:1; Mt 1:9. [12]Esth 3; 4:16-17; 9:26-28. [13]ACW 19:48-49. [14]See Jdt 8. [15]FC 1:51.

5:1-14 ESTHER PREPARES A BANQUET FOR AHASUERUS AND HAMAN

¹On the third day Esther put on her royal robes and stood in the inner court of the king's palace, opposite the king's hall. The king was sitting on his royal throne inside the palace opposite the entrance to the palace; ²and when the king saw Queen Esther standing in the court, she found favor in his sight and he held out to Esther the golden scepter that was in his hand. Then Esther approached and touched the top of the scepter. ³And the king said to her, "What is it, Queen Esther? What is your request? It shall be given you, even to the half of my kingdom." ⁴And Esther said, "If it please the king, let the king and Haman come this day to a dinner that I have prepared for the king." ⁵Then said the king, "Bring Haman quickly, that we may do as Esther desires." So the king and Haman came to the dinner that Esther had prepared. ⁶And as they were drinking wine, the king said to Esther, "What is your petition? It shall be granted you. And what is your request? Even to the half of my kingdom, it shall be fulfilled." ⁷But Esther said, "My petition and my request is: ⁸If I have found favor in the sight of the king, and if it please the king to grant my petition and fulfil my request, let the king and Haman come tomorrow[d] to the dinner which I will prepare for them, and tomorrow I will do as the king has said."

⁹And Haman went out that day joyful and glad of heart. But when Haman saw Mordecai in the king's gate, that he neither rose nor trembled before him, he was filled with wrath against Mordecai. ¹⁰Nevertheless Haman restrained himself, and went home; and he sent and fetched his friends and his wife Zeresh. ¹¹And Haman recounted to them the splendor of his riches, the number of his sons, all the promotions with which the king had honored him, and how he had advanced him above the princes and the servants of the king. ¹²And Haman added, "Even Queen Esther let no one come with the king to the banquet she prepared but myself. And tomorrow also I am invited by her together with the king. ¹³Yet all this does me no good, so long as I see Mordecai the Jew sitting at the king's gate." ¹⁴Then his wife Zeresh and all his friends said to him, "Let a gallows fifty cubits high be made, and in the morning tell the king to have Mordecai hanged upon it; then go merrily with the king to the dinner." This counsel pleased Haman, and he had the gallows made.

d Gk: Heb lacks *tomorrow*

OVERVIEW: The Lord places more importance on beauty of soul than on that of the body, and the only woman we know of who used ornaments without blame is Esther (CLEMENT OF ALEXANDRIA). The fact that Esther put on all her royal robes on the third day signifies that the church of the nations, in the third time of the world, that is, after the incarnation, passion and resurrection of Christ, clothed itself with faith, hope and charity. The one who comes to the banquet of the Lord with an evil mind and, even though he has his heart defiled by hatred, is not ashamed to enter unworthily the banquet of the Lord will be condemned to the harshest punishment. Esther's postponement of the petition is not due to laziness but must be attributed to the virtue of patience, and this signifies that the reward of the righteous and the punishment of the sinners will be especially given in the future, that is, on judgment day (RABANUS MAURUS).

5:1-4 Esther Wore Her Royal Robes

ESTHER USES ORNAMENTS WITHOUT BLAME. CLEMENT OF ALEXANDRIA: If the Lord places more importance on beauty of soul than on that of the body, what must he think of artificial beautification when he abhors so thoroughly every sort of lie? "We walk by faith, not by sight."[1] As a matter of fact, it is the Lord who plainly teaches by the example of Abraham that one who obeys God will make small account of even father and relations and possessions and of his entire fortune. He made Abraham an exile, and then, because of that, gave him the name "friend," because he was so little attached to the things of his own home.[2] Yet, Abraham was of a noble family and had possessed a large fortune. A proof of this is that he overcame the four kings who had captured Lot, with 318 servants belonging to him.[3] As for women, the only one we know of who used ornaments without blame is Esther. Her action in making herself beautiful had a mystical significance, however, for, as the wife of her king, she obtained deliverance for her people by her beauty when they were being slaughtered. CHRIST THE EDUCATOR 3.2.12.[4]

CLOTHED WITH ALL VIRTUES. RABANUS MAURUS: The fact that Esther put on all her royal robes on the third day undoubtedly signifies that the church of the nations, in the third time of the world, that is, after the incarnation, passion and resurrection of Christ, clothed herself through the sacrament of baptism and the confession of the Holy Trinity with faith, hope and charity, and the ornament of every virtue so that she might become worthy of the royal marriage while the love of (the Lord) remained constantly fervent. She stood in the inner court of the royal palace, that is, in the pious actions of this life which look

at the future reward in heaven where the king himself sits on the supreme throne and fulfills the prayers of those who implore him piously. He, who held out to that queen the golden scepter that was in his hand, showed the power of his rule, that is, the cross of his passion through which he gained authority over heaven, earth and the underworld so that "at his name every knee shall bow in heaven, on earth and under the earth."[5] And (the church) lovingly kissed it, that is, worshiped it with all her devotion. And with regard to her petition, the king answered that he would listen to it, as it is said in the gospel as well, "Ask, and it will be given you; seek and you will find; knock, and the door will be opened for you."[6] And again: "Ask, and you will receive, that you joy may be full."[7] Indeed the full joy of the church is provided nowhere but in the perception of the heavenly kingdom where the queen will happily reign with the king Christ forever. But she, after choosing her petition, invited him to the banquet that she had prepared. This cannot be better interpreted than as the full and perfect devotion of her faith of which the supervisor and arbiter of all things himself nourishes in her. To that magnificent repast, that is, to the communion of wholesome faith, the church invites not only her friends but also her enemies and persecutors, namely the pagans, the Jews, and the heretics so that, after abandoning the wrong path of error, they may rejoice in the one house of universal confession for the common good. EXPLANATION ON THE BOOK OF ESTHER 8.[8]

5:5-6 The Banquet That Esther Prepared

NO UNWORTHY PERSON IS RECEIVED. RABANUS MAURUS: Notice how the will of the inviting queen and the order of the commanding king agree. But woe to the one who comes to the banquet of the Lord with an evil mind! Even

---

[1]2 Cor 5:7. [2]See Gen 12:1. [3]See Gen 14:14. [4]FC 23:208-9. [5]Phil 2:10. [6]Mt 7:7. [7]Jn 16:24. [8]PL 109:655C-656B.

though such a person has his heart defiled by hatred and a corrupt conscience, he is not ashamed to enter unworthily the banquet of the Lord. Even though he comes after being invited, he does not bask in the joy of the guests. But when the king comes and sees that he sits there without wearing a wedding robe, he will rebuke his temerity and will order him to be bound hand and foot and thrown into the outer darkness[9] where he will be forced to suffer the evil of his deception which he was wickedly preparing against the innocent, as Solomon says, "The wicked will be caught in his snares." EXPLANATION ON THE BOOK OF ESTHER 8.[10]

5:6-7 The King and Haman Invited to the Banquet

A FIGURE OF THE FINAL JUDGMENT. RABANUS MAURUS: This postponement of the petition is not due to a fault of laziness but must be attributed to the virtue of patience, clearly indicating that the reward of the righteous and the punishment of the sinners are reserved for the future. "Tomorrow," in fact, must be interpreted as "the future," as in that comforting sentence, "Do not worry about tomorrow."[11] And in Genesis Jacob says to Laban, "My justice will answer for me tomorrow."[12] And in Exodus, when the rules about the eating of the Passover lamb are given, it is added, "You shall let none of it remain until the morning."[13] Therefore when the day of future judgment comes and the entire human race, both righteous and sinners, is brought before the supreme Judge, then it will be revealed with which mind each person lived in this world. The righteous will be invited to reach the kingdom of the heavenly homeland through the sentence of this judge, and the sinners will be punished and expelled together with the devil into the torments of hell. EXPLANATION ON THE BOOK OF ESTHER 8.[14]

---

[9]Cf. Mt 22:11-14. [10]PL 109:656B. [11]Mt 6:34. [12]Gen 30:33. [13]Ex 12:10. [14]PL 109:656C-D.

6:1-13 MORDECAI RECEIVES THE HONOR HE DESERVES

[1]On that night the king could not sleep; and he gave orders to bring the book of memorable deeds, the chronicles, and they were read before the king. [2]And it was found written how Mordecai had told about Bigthana and Teresh, two of the king's eunuchs, who guarded the threshold, and who had sought to lay hands upon King Ahasu-erus. [3]And the king said, "What honor or dignity has been bestowed on Mordecai for this?" The king's servants who attended him said, "Nothing has been done for him." [4]And the king said, "Who is in the court?" Now Haman had just entered the outer court of the king's palace to speak to the king about having Mordecai hanged on the gallows that he had prepared for him. [5]So the king's servants told him, "Haman is there, standing in the court." And the king said, "Let him come in." [6]So Haman came in, and the king said to him, "What shall be done to the man whom the king delights to honor?" And Haman said to himself,

"Whom would the king delight to honor more than me?" [7]*And Haman said to the king, "For the man whom the king delights to honor,* [8]*let royal robes be brought, which the king has worn, and the horse which the king has ridden, and on whose head a royal crown is set;* [9]*and let the robes and the horse be handed over to one of the king's most noble princes; let him[e] array the man whom the king delights to honor, and let him[e] conduct the man on horseback through the open square of the city, proclaiming before him: 'Thus shall it be done to the man whom the king delights to honor.' "* [10]*Then the king said to Haman, "Make haste, take the robes and the horse, as you have said, and do so to Mordecai the Jew who sits at the king's gate. Leave out nothing that you have mentioned."* [11]*So Haman took the robes and the horse, and he arrayed Mordecai and made him ride through the open square of the city, proclaiming, "Thus shall it be done to the man whom the king delights to honor."*

[12]*Then Mordecai returned to the king's gate. But Haman hurried to his house, mourning and with his head covered.* [13]*And Haman told his wife Zeresh and all his friends everything that had befallen him. Then his wise men and his wife Zeresh said to him, "If Mordecai, before whom you have begun to fall, is of the Jewish people, you will not prevail against him but will surely fall before him."*

e Heb *them*

OVERVIEW: God removes sleep from the eyes of Ahasuerus, so that he might turn over the memoirs of his faithful ministers and come on Mordecai, by whose evidence he had been delivered from a conspiracy (JEROME). Ahasuerus's thoughts were inspired by the Lord, when he was moved to examine the annals and remember the good deeds of Mordecai (CASSIAN). Mordecai's persecution under Haman foreshadows the different phases of Christ's persecution (APHRAHAT). The change in Haman's behavior is caused by the right hand of the Highest, so that he, who had been arrogant toward everybody, might become viler and weaker than anybody else (RABANUS MAURUS).

6:1-3 The King Could Not Sleep

GOD PREVENTS AHASUERUS FROM SLEEPING.
JEROME: Sleep was removed from the eyes of Ahasuerus, whom the Seventy call Artaxerxes, that he might turn over the memoirs of his faithful ministers and come on Mordecai, by whose evidence he was delivered from a conspiracy; and

that thus Esther might be more acceptable and the whole people of the Jews escape imminent death. There is no doubt that the mighty sovereign to whom belonged the whole East, from India to the north and to Ethiopia, after feasting sumptuously on delicacies gathered from every part of the world would have desired to sleep, and to take his rest and to gratify his free choice of sleep, had not the Lord, the provider of all good things, hindered the course of nature, so that in defiance of nature the tyrant's cruelty might be overcome. If I were to attempt to produce all the instance of the holy Scripture, I should be tedious. All that the saints say is a prayer to God; their whole prayer and supplication is a strong wrestling for the pity of God, so that we, who by our own strength and zeal cannot be saved, may be preserved by his mercy. But when we are concerned with grace and mercy, free will is in part void; in part, I say, for so much as this depends on it, that we wish and desire and give assent to the course we choose. But it depends on God whether we have the power in his strength and with his help to perform what we desire and to bring to effect our toil and effort. AGAINST THE PELAGIANS 3.10.[1]

6:4-11 Let Haman Robe the Man

THOUGHTS INSPIRED BY GOD. JOHN CASSIAN: Above all we should know what the three sources of our thoughts are: They come from God, from the devil and from ourselves. They are from God when he deigns to visit us by the illumination of the Holy Spirit, which raises us up to a higher level of progress; and when we have made little gain or have acted lazily and been overcome and he chastens us with a most salutary compunction; and when he opens to us the heavenly sacraments and changes our chosen orientation to better acts and to a better will. This was the case when King Ahasuerus was chastised by the Lord and was moved to examine the annals, whereupon he remembered the good deeds of Mordecai, exalted him to the highest degree of honor and immediately recalled his exceedingly cruel sentence concerning the killing of the Jewish people. CONFERENCE 1.19.1.[2]

MORDECAI AS A FIGURE OF CHRIST THE SAVIOR. APHRAHAT: Mordecai was also persecuted as Jesus was persecuted. Mordecai was persecuted by the wicked Haman; and Jesus was persecuted by the rebellious people. Mordecai by his prayer delivered his people from the hands of Haman; and Jesus by his prayer delivered his people from the hands of Satan. Mordecai was delivered from the hands of his persecutor; and Jesus was rescued from the hands of his persecutors. Because Mordecai sat and clothed himself with sackcloth, he saved Esther and his people from the sword; and because Jesus clothed himself with a body and was illuminated, he saved the church and its children from death. Because of Mordecai, Esther was well pleasing to the king and went in and sat instead of Vashti, who did not do his will; and because of Jesus, the church is well pleasing to God and has gone in to the king, instead of the congregation that did not his will. Mordecai

admonished Esther that she should fast with her maidens, that she and her people might be delivered from the hands of Haman; and Jesus admonished the church and its children [to fast], that it and its children might be delivered from the wrath. Mordecai received the honor of Haman, his persecutor; and Jesus received great glory from his Father, instead of his persecutors who were of the foolish people. Mordecai trod on the neck of Haman, his persecutor; and as for Jesus, his enemies shall be put under his feet. Before Mordecai, Haman proclaimed, "Thus shall it be done to the man, in honoring whom the king is pleased"; as for Jesus, his preachers came out of the people who persecuted him, and they said, "This is Jesus the Son of God."[3] The blood of Mordecai was required at the hand of Haman and his sons;[4] and "the blood of Jesus," his persecutors took "on themselves and on their children."[5] DEMONSTRATIONS 21.20.[6]

6:12-13 Haman Hurried to His House

CHANGES CAUSED BY THE POWER OF THE LORD. RABANUS MAURUS: This is the change caused by the right hand of the Highest: the one who had just boasted about his power and was arrogant towards everyone else becomes viler and weaker than anyone else. When Mary the mother of our Lord considered the greatness of this divine ordering, she sang in her song of praise, "He has shown strength with his arm; he has scattered the proud in the thoughts of their hearts. He has brought down the powerful from their thrones, and lifted up the lowly; he has filled the hungry with good things and sent the rich away empty."[7] And through Isaiah it is said about this same power, "Shall not Lebanon be transformed into Carmel, and Carmel be regarded as a forest?"[8] EXPLANATION ON THE BOOK OF ESTHER 9.[9]

---

[1]NPNF 2 6:477. [2]ACW 57:57-58. [3]Mt 27:54. [4]See Esth 7:10; 9:10. [5]Mt 27:25. [6]NPNF 2 13:400. [7]Lk 1:51-53. [8]Is 29:17 (Vg). [9]PL 109:658C.

6:14–7:10 HAMAN IS CONDEMNED AND EXECUTED

¹⁴*While they were yet talking with him, the king's eunuchs arrived and brought Haman in haste to the banquet that Esther had prepared.*

7 *So the king and Haman went in to feast with Queen Esther.* ²*And on the second day, as they were drinking wine, the king again said to Esther, "What is your petition, Queen Esther? It shall be granted you. And what is your request? Even to the half of my kingdom, it shall be fulfilled."* ³*Then Queen Esther answered, "If I have found favor in your sight, O king, and if it please the king, let my life be given me at my petition, and my people at my request.* ⁴*For we are sold, I and my people, to be destroyed, to be slain, and to be annihilated. If we had been sold merely as slaves, men and women, I would have held my peace; for our affliction is not to be compared with the loss to the king."* ⁵*Then King Ahasu-erus said to Queen Esther, "Who is he, and where is he, that would presume to do this?"* ⁶*And Esther said, "A foe and enemy! This wicked Haman!" Then Haman was in terror before the king and the queen.* ⁷*And the king rose from the feast in wrath and went into the palace garden; but Haman stayed to beg his life from Queen Esther, for he saw that evil was determined against him by the king.* ⁸*And the king returned from the palace garden to the place where they were drinking wine, as Haman was falling on the couch where Esther was; and the king said, "Will he even assault the queen in my presence, in my own house?" As the words left the mouth of the king, they covered Haman's face.* ⁹*Then said Harbona, one of the eunuchs in attendance on the king, "Moreover, the gallow which Haman has prepared for Mordecai, whose word saved the king, is standing in Haman's house, fifty cubits high."* ¹⁰*And the king said, "Hang him on that." So they hanged Haman on the gallows* which he had prepared for Mordecai. Then the anger of the king abated.*

*Vg *wood*

OVERVIEW: Haman represents the spiritual enemy of the people of God, because he does not have the robe of charity and cannot be worthy of the royal banquet. He tries to entreat the queen for his salvation, but to no avail because he is not able to find the right time for that. Haman's appeal to Queen Esther is considered by King Ahasuerus to be an act of trickery (RABANUS MAURUS).

6:14–7:7 A Foe and an Enemy

HAMAN CANNOT BE FORGIVEN. RABANUS MAURUS: The second day of the banquet arrives to which Haman is invited like before. However, after Esther reveals her petition, he is condemned and brought to his place of execution. The gospel mentions this as a noonday meal in one passage and as an evening meal in another. For it designates the noonday meal of the present church but also the eternal supper and final banquet where only the righteous will rejoice before their creator after sinners have been separated out. Therefore Haman, the spiritual enemy of the people of God, realized that the king was angry because he did not have the robe of charity that would make him worthy of the royal banquet. And while he was hurrying to the palace gardens, that is, while he

---

invited his elect to the delights of paradise, he tried to entreat the queen for his salvation. It was to no avail, however, because he was not able to find the right time for this. It is already too late to ask for the remedies of salvation when revenge and punishment are near.

In the parable of the gospel concerning the coming bridegroom, the foolish virgins also ask the wise for oil to fill their lamps, but do not receive any. And after the bridegroom has entered the wedding banquet with the wise virgins, the door is closed. And because they are left outside, they ask to be admitted. They are no longer able to incur this favor, however, because the time for mercy which they neglected to ask for previously with their good works is now past.[1]

One who has no desire to hear what the Lord has commanded cannot receive from him what he asks for. And one who has neglected the time for appropriate repentance comes in vain to the door of the kingdom with his prayers. And indeed the Lord says through Solomon, "I called you and you refused. I stretched out my arms and no one heeded. And because you ignored all my counsel and would have none of my reproof, I also will laugh at your calamity; I will mock when panic strikes you like a storm, and your calamity comes like a whirlwind, when distress and anguish come upon you. Then they will call upon me, but I will not answer; they will seek me diligently, but will not find me."[2] EXPLANATION ON THE BOOK OF ESTHER 10.[3]

7:8 Haman's Face Covered

THE TIME OF RETRIBUTION. RABANUS MAURUS: Haman's appeal to Queen Esther was considered by King Ahasuerus to be an act of deceit. Indeed, when the day of judgment is about to come, the petition of the wicked is no longer a prayer but a source of irritation. This is what is written in the psalm: "When he is tried, let him be found guilty; let his prayer be counted as sin."[4] Therefore the request is made for the oppression of those who previously oppressed the humble because the time of retribution has come. Then, after they are condemned, they are covered with the shame of their sins, as is written, "The confusion of their face will cover them,"[5] when they are dragged to the darkness of hell to be rewarded with retribution suitable to their works. EXPLANATION ON THE BOOK OF ESTHER 10.[6]

7:9-10 Haman Hanged

THE JUDGMENT OF THE LAW. RABANUS MAURUS: It is written in the book of Proverbs: "Whoever digs a pit will fall into it, and a stone will come back on the one who starts it rolling."[7] So also Haman was forced to support the cross[8] that he had prepared for Mordecai. EXPLANATION ON THE BOOK OF ESTHER 10.[9]

---

[1]See Mt 25:1-13. [2]Prov 1:24-28. [3]PL 109:659B-D. [4]Ps 109:7 (108:7 Vg). [5]See Ezek 7:18. [6]PL 109:660A. [7]Prov 26:27. [8]The text of the Vulgate reads "wood," which is identified by Rabanus with the cross. [9]PL 109:660 B-D.

8:1-17 A NEW DECREE IN FAVOR OF THE JEWS

[1]*On that day King Ahasu-erus gave to Queen Esther the house of Haman, the enemy of the Jews. And Mordecai came before the king, for Esther had told what he was to her;* [2]*and the king*

took off his signet ring, which he had taken from Haman, and gave it to Mordecai. And Esther set Mordecai over the house of Haman.

³Then Esther spoke again to the king; she fell at his feet and besought him with tears to avert the evil design of Haman the Agagite and the plot which he had devised against the Jews. ⁴And the king held out the golden scepter to Esther, ⁵and Esther rose and stood before the king. And she said, "If it please the king, and if I have found favor in his sight, and if the thing seem right before the king, and I be pleasing in his eyes, let an order be written to revoke the letters devised by Haman the Agagite, the son of Hammedatha, which he wrote to destroy the Jews who are in all the provinces of the king. ⁶For how can I endure to see the calamity that is coming to my people? Or how can I endure to see the destruction of my kindred?" ⁷Then King Ahasu-erus said to Queen Esther and to Mordecai the Jew, "Behold, I have given Esther the house of Haman, and they have hanged him on the gallows, because he would lay hands on the Jews. ⁸And you may write as you please with regard to the Jews, in the name of the king, and seal it with the king's ring; for an edict written in the name of the king and sealed with the king's ring cannot be revoked."

⁹The king's secretaries were summoned at that time, in the third month, which is the month of Sivan, on the twenty-third day; and an edict was written according to all that Mordecai commanded concerning the Jews to the satraps and the governors and the princes of the provinces from India to Ethiopia, a hundred and twenty-seven provinces, to every province in its own script and to every people in its own language, and also to the Jews in their script and their language. ¹⁰The writing was in the name of King Ahasu-erus and sealed with the king's ring, and letters were sent by mounted couriers riding on swift horses that were used in the king's service, bred from the royal stud. ¹¹By these the king allowed the Jews who were in every city to gather and defend their lives, to destroy, to slay, and to annihilate any armed force of any people or province that might attack them, with their children and women, and to plunder their goods, ¹²upon one day throughout all the provinces of King Ahasu-erus, on the thirteenth day of the twelfth month, which is the month of Adar. ¹³A copy of what was written was to be issued as a decree in every province, and by proclamation to all peoples, and the Jews were to be ready on that day to avenge themselves upon their enemies. ¹⁴So the couriers, mounted on their swift horses that were used in the king's service, rode out in haste, urged by the king's command; and the decree was issued in Susa the capital.

¹⁵Then Mordecai went out from the presence of the king in royal robes of blue and white, with a great golden crown and a mantle of fine linen and purple, while the city of Susa shouted and rejoiced. ¹⁶The Jews had light and gladness and joy and honor. ¹⁷And in every province and in every city, wherever the king's command and his edict came, there was gladness and joy among the Jews, a feast and a holiday. And many from the peoples of the country declared themselves Jews, for the fear of the Jews had fallen upon them.

OVERVIEW: The fact that Ahasuerus gives Esther the house of Haman, the enemy of the Jews, signifies that our Lord would have transferred to the holy church the dignity and honor that the Jews derived from their knowledge of the Law, the Prophets and the worship of the true religion of God. As Esther falls at the feet of the king and entreats him for the salvation of the people, so the holy church humbly implores the almighty Lord every day for the rescue of its children through faith. The new letters written and sent by Ahasuerus foreshadow the word of Christ written in the holy Gospels. The king's permission given to the Jews to defend themselves symbolizes God's invitation to all Christians to defend their souls against all their enemies. The words "Many of the peoples of the country professed to be Jews" refer to the future conversion of the Gentiles (Rabanus Maurus).

8:1-2 Ahasuerus Gave the House of Haman to Esther

Honor and Glory Given to the Church.
Rabanus Maurus: The fact that King Ahasuerus gave Queen Esther the house of Haman, the enemy of the Jews, clearly signifies that the true king who is our Lord transferred to the holy church all the dignity and honor which the people previously possessed because of their knowledge of the law and the prophets and because of their holy and religious worship. This happened because they despised the advent in flesh of the Mediator between God and humanity and because they had no desire to receive his gospel. And so the church was able to possess all the spiritual riches and become the sincere guardian of all virtue. Therefore it is written in the book of Proverbs, "The sinner's wealth is laid up for the righteous."[1] And the Lord says to the Jews themselves in the gospel, "The kingdom of God will be taken away from you and given to a people that produces the fruits of the kingdom."[2] And again it is said through Solomon, "The good obtain favor from the Lord."[3] Explanation on the Book of Esther 11.[4]

8:3-8 Esther Fell at the Feet of Ahasuerus

The Church at the Feet of the Lord.
Rabanus Maurus: The fact that Esther falls at

the feet of the king and entreats him for the salvation of the people plainly symbolizes the holy church that humbly implores the almighty Lord every day for the rescue of her children through the faith and the mystery of the incarnation of the only begotten Son, so that the arrogance of her enemies may be restrained by the (Lord's) grace, and the innocence of the faithful may be freed from the clutches of the (wicked). The heavenly king holds out his golden scepter to the pleading queen because he abundantly bestows the clemency of his mercy upon her. She asks that the old decree of the most wicked Haman may be changed into a new decree. Indeed this is the interest of the true queen,[5] namely that any sect that is in error, any hostile plot which the ancient enemy prepares through his ministers for the extinction of the people of God, may be repelled and destroyed through the saving documents of the gospel. Explanation on the Book of Esther 11.[6]

8:9-10 An Edict Written

A Foreshadowing of the Gospel.
Rabanus Maurus: The month of Sivan, which is the third after Nisan among the Jews, and is called Thessari among the Greeks, is named June among Latin peoples. On the twenty-third day of this month new letters were written according to Mordecai's dictation in order to invalidate the old letters of Haman. And the meaning of this event is quite clear, because the doctrine of the gospel was founded by the writers of the New Testament through our Lord Jesus Christ so that the faith of the Holy Trinity might be contained in it in its fullest form, and the supreme perfection might be shown to lie in two principles of charity that encompass the entire Decalogue. And the Scripture itself, through mounted couriers, that is the holy preachers, was provided to the whole

---

[1]Prov 13:22. [2]Mt 21:43. [3]Prov 12:2. [4]PL 109:661A-B. [5]Here there is a plain and constant identification of Queen Esther with the Christian church. [6]PL 109:662B-C.

world, which is signified by the one hundred twenty provinces that constituted the kingdom of Ahasuerus. EXPLANATION ON THE BOOK OF ESTHER 11.[7]

8:11-14 The Jews Allowed to Defend Themselves

A FIGHT FOR OUR SOUL. RABANUS MAURUS: The fact that this earthly king sends his couriers to gather the Jews in each place and to assemble them in a single location so that they may fight for their lives and destroy all their enemies with their children and women and houses signifies that through his preachers our king, the absolute ruler of heaven and earth, orders the true Jews and his confessors among all the Gentiles, after they have gathered in the unity of society and peace, to fight for the salvation of their souls and to condemn their enemies both visible and invisible, namely the false Jews, who belong to the synagogue of Satan, and the unredeemed pagan and heretics, and the unclean spirits with all their impieties. EXPLANATION ON THE BOOK OF ESTHER 11.[8]

8:15-16 Mordecai Wore Royal Robes

THE GLORY OF THE HOLY TEACHERS. RABANUS MAURUS: The glory of the holy teachers is exalted because it is through their doctrine and exhortation that the faithful defeat the cru-

elty of their most evil enemy with the help and strength of their heavenly king. And their reward remains with them in the heavenly kingdom of eternal blessedness and perpetual splendor, which appears to be signified by the colors of blue and white and the brightness of gold. EXPLANATION ON THE BOOK OF ESTHER 12.[9]

8:17 Many People Professed to Be Jews

A REFERENCE TO THE CONVERSION OF THE GENTILES. RABANUS MAURUS: Thanks to the strength, wisdom and constancy of the holy martyrs—and to the virtue of Christ which shines among them—many among the Gentiles and the enemies of the church abandoned their idolatry and their pagan superstitions and were converted to the Christian faith because it does not hide the suffering of the saints and the triumphs of the martyrs from those it encounters. And therefore, through God's mercy, the number of the faithful increases daily and the flocks of the church are filled. The power of the Christian name causes terror among infidels and joy among believers the world over. The psalmist also wrote about this: "Let all the earth fear the Lord; let all inhabitants of the world stand in awe of him."[10] EXPLANATION ON THE BOOK OF ESTHER 12.[11]

---

[7]PL 109:662D–663A. [8]PL 109:663C-D. [9]PL 109:664C-D. [10]Ps 33:8 (32:8 Vg). [11]PL 109:665A-B.

9:1-32 THE FEAST OF PURIM

[1]*Now in the twelfth month, which is the month of Adar, on the thirteenth day of the same, when the king's command and edict were about to be executed, on the very day when the enemies of the Jews hoped to get the mastery over them, but which had been changed to a day when the Jews should get the mastery over their foes,* [2]*the Jews gathered in their cities throughout all the provinces*

of King Ahasu-erus to lay hands on such as sought their hurt. And no one could make a stand against them, for the fear of them had fallen upon all peoples. ³All the princes of the provinces and the satraps and the governors and the royal officials also helped the Jews, for the fear of Mordecai had fallen upon them. ⁴For Mordecai was great in the king's house, and his fame spread throughout all the provinces; for the man Mordecai grew more and more powerful. ⁵So the Jews smote all their enemies with the sword, slaughtering, and destroying them, and did as they pleased to those who hated them. ⁶In Susa the capital itself the Jews slew and destroyed five hundred men, ⁷and also slew Parshan-datha and Dalphon and Aspatha ⁸and Poratha and Adalia and Aridatha ⁹and Parmashta and Arisai and Aridai and Vaizatha, ¹⁰the ten sons of Haman the son of Hammedatha, the enemy of the Jews; but they laid no hand on the plunder.

¹¹That very day the number of those slain in Susa the capital was reported to the king. ¹²And the king said to Queen Esther, "In Susa the capital the Jews have slain five hundred men and also the ten sons of Haman. What then have they done in the rest of the king's provinces! Now what is your petition? It shall be granted you. And what further is your request? It shall be fulfilled." ¹³And Esther said, "If it please the king, let the Jews who are in Susa be allowed tomorrow also to do according to this day's edict. And let the ten sons of Haman be hanged on the gallows." ¹⁴So the king commanded this to be done; a decree was issued in Susa, and the ten sons of Haman were hanged. ¹⁵The Jews who were in Susa gathered also on the fourteenth day of the month of Adar and they slew three hundred men in Susa; but they laid no hands on the plunder.

¹⁶Now the other Jews who were in the king's provinces also gathered to defend their lives, and got relief from their enemies, and slew seventy-five thousand of those who hated them; but they laid no hands on the plunder. ¹⁷This was on the thirteenth day of the month of Adar, and on the fourteenth day they rested and made that a day of feasting and gladness. ¹⁸But the Jews who were in Susa gathered on the thirteenth day and on the fourteenth, and rested on the fifteenth day, making that a day of feasting and gladness. ¹⁹Therefore the Jews of the villages, who live in the open towns, hold the fourteenth day of the month of Adar as a day for gladness and feasting and holiday-making, and a day on which they send choice portions to one another.

²⁰And Mordecai recorded these things, and sent letters to all the Jews who were in all the provinces of King Ahasu-erus, both near and far, ²¹enjoining them that they should keep the fourteenth day of the month Adar and also the fifteenth day of the same, year by year, ²²as the days on which the Jews got relief from their enemies, and as the month that had been turned for them from sorrow into gladness and from mourning into a holiday; that they should make them days of feasting and gladness, days for sending choice portions to one another and gifts to the poor.

²³So the Jews undertook to do as they had begun, and as Mordecai had written to them. ²⁴For Haman the Agagite, the son of Hammedatha, the enemy of all the Jews, had plotted against the Jews to destroy them, and had cast Pur, that is the lot, to crush and destroy them; ²⁵but when Esther came before the king, he gave orders in writing that his wicked plot which he had devised against the Jews should come upon his own head, and that he and his sons should be hanged on the gallows. ²⁶Therefore they called these days Purim, after the term Pur. And therefore, because

of all that was written in this letter, and of what they had faced in this matter, and of what had befallen them, [27] *the Jews ordained and took it upon themselves and their descendants and all who joined them, that without fail they would keep these two days according to what was written and at the time appointed every year,* [28] *that these days should be remembered and kept throughout every generation, in every family, province, and city, and that these days of Purim should never fall into disuse among the Jews, nor should the commemoration of these days cease among their descendants.*

[29] *Then Queen Esther, the daughter of Abihail, and Mordecai the Jew gave full written authority, confirming this second letter about Purim.* [30] *Letters were sent to all the Jews, to the hundred and twenty-seven provinces of the kingdom of Ahasu-erus, in words of peace and truth,* [31] *that these days of Purim should be observed at their appointed seasons, as Mordecai the Jew and Queen Esther enjoined upon the Jews, and as they had laid down for themselves and for their descendants, with regard to their fasts and their lamenting.* [32] *The command of Queen Esther fixed these practices of Purim, and it was recorded in writing.*

OVERVIEW: In a mystical sense the thirteenth day proclaims the light of faith and good works that is produced by the preaching of the gospel in the church through the faithful. The honor given to the Jews foreshadows that given to the multitude of the faithful thanks to the holiness of their teachers. Esther's zeal against her enemies reveals the zeal of a true queen, namely, that of the holy church that constantly combats its enemies and fights to defeat them (RABANUS MAURUS). The Jews call a feast, thanking and praising the Lord because he had changed the situation for them. Our feast does not relate only to time, as the one celebrated at the time of Esther, but to eternity: we do not announce the victory on our enemy as a shadow or a picture or a type but as the real thing (ATHANASIUS). Haman, who prefigures the enemies of the church, had to suffer the death that he had prepared for Mordecai, because God can always overturn human schemes. While we are on this earth, the fateful days in which God gave us victory over our enemies, will not be forgotten and will be celebrated all over the world by each single generation (RABANUS MAURUS).

9:1-2 The Twelfth Month, the Thirteenth Day

A FIGURE OF THE VICTORY OF THE CHURCH.
RABANUS MAURUS: The twelfth month, as we have said above, signifies the last age of the world when our Redeemer became incarnate and the preaching of the gospel spread over the entire world. In a similar way, the thirteenth day proclaims the light of faith and good works which is produced by the preaching of the gospel in the church through the faithful. Indeed, in the twelfth month on the thirteenth day when the destruction of all the Jews was being prepared and their enemies longed for their blood, the Jews, on the contrary, began to triumph and started taking revenge on their adversaries because they [represent] the assembly of the faithful where the true confession of the right faith resides who are helped by the grace of God and comforted by the shield of faith and the weapons of justice in the face of the enemies and persecutors of the name of Christ who persecute and oppress them wherever they are. The assembly of the faithful is thus able to defeat its enemies and to gain the triumph of glory over them. EXPLANATION ON THE BOOK OF ESTHER 12.[1]

---

[1] PL 109:665C-D.

9:3-4 Officials and Governors Supported the Jews

THE HONOR OF THE TEACHERS OF FAITH.
RABANUS MAURUS: "All the officials of the provinces, the satraps and the governors, and the royal officials were supporting the Jews." Certainly the praiseworthy action of the holy teachers and the strength of their virtue have contributed great honor and respect to the multitude of the faithful. Therefore, in the Acts of the Apostles, in which we read how the first preachers of the gospel labored to teach the word of God and cared for it, it is written, "They devoted themselves to the apostles' teaching and fellowship, to the breaking of bread and prayer. Awe came upon everyone, because many wonders and signs were being done by the apostles."[2] EXPLANATION ON THE BOOK OF ESTHER 12.[3]

9:5-14 The Jews Defend Themselves

THE INTENTION OF A TRUE QUEEN. RABANUS MAURUS: Queen Esther's endeavor to successfully crush her enemies and root them out reveals the eagerness and zeal of a true queen, namely, of the holy church that constantly fights against her enemies and strives to defeat them completely and subdue them. And it is her voice the psalmist uses when he says, "I pursued my enemies and overtook them; and did not turn back until they were consumed. I struck them down so that they were unable to rise."[4] And when she first kills five hundred people in Susa, and then three hundred, she shows that eternal death awaits not only those who do not want to repent of their sins, but also those who neglect to adorn the faith of the Holy Trinity with good works. EXPLANATION ON THE BOOK OF ESTHER 12.[5]

9:15-23 A Day of Feasting

A FEAST FOR THE LORD. ATHANASIUS: In the face of all this, brothers and sisters, what should we do but give thanks to God, the king of all? Let us start by crying out the words of the psalm, "Blessed is the Lord, who has not let them eat us up."[6] Let us keep the feast in that way that he has established for our salvation—the holy day of Easter—so that we, along with the angels, may celebrate the heavenly feast. Remember that Israel, coming out of affliction to a state of rest, sang a song of praise for the victory as they kept the feast. And in the time of Esther the people kept a feast to the Lord because they had been delivered from a deadly decree. They called a feast, thanking and praising the Lord because he had changed the situation for them. Therefore, let us keep our promises to the Lord, confess our sins, and keep the feast to him—in behavior, moral conduct, and way of life. Let us keep it by praising the Lord, who has disciplined us so lightly but has never failed us nor forsaken us nor stopped speaking to us. FESTAL LETTERS 8.[7]

CELEBRATION OF THE VICTORY. ATHANASIUS: When the whole nation of Israel was about to perish, blessed Esther defeated the tyrant's anger simply by fasting and praying to God. By faith she changed the ruin of her people into safety.[8] Those days are feast days for Israel; they used to call a feast when an enemy was slain or a conspiracy against the people was broken up and Israel was delivered. That is why Moses established the Feast of the Passover: because Pharaoh was killed and the people were delivered from bondage. So then, especially when tyrants were slain, temporal feasts and holidays were established in Judea. Now, however, the devil, that tyrant against the whole world, is slain. Therefore, our feast does not relate only to time but to eternity. It is a heavenly feast! We do not announce it as a shadow or a picture or a type but as the real thing. FESTAL LETTERS 4.[9]

9:24-27 The Plot Overturned

---

[2]Acts 2:42-43. [3]PL 109:666A. [4]Ps 18:37-38 (17:37-38 Vg). [5]PL 109:666D–667A. [6]Ps 124:6 (123:6 Vg). [7]ARL 141. [8]See the commentary on Esth 4:16. [9]ARL 82.

The Evil Schemes Overturned. Rabanus Maurus: Very often people's evil schemes turn out differently than they had hoped and the trap they had placed to capture others ensnares them, as the Scripture confirms, "The wicked are ensnared in their traps. And whoever digs a pit will fall into it."[10] Therefore also Haman, who prefigures the enemies of the church, was obligated to suffer the death that he had prepared for Mordecai. The lot cast into the urn represents the machinations of the human mind; but the result of such machinations entirely depends on divine judgment. Therefore it is said through Solomon, "The lot is cast into the lap, but the decision is the Lord's alone."[11] Explanation on the Book of Esther 13.[12]

9:28-32 The Deliverance to Be Remembered

Celebrations Not to Be Forgotten. Rabanus Maurus: The fateful days in which God gives the victory over the enemies to his true confessors must never be forgotten but must be celebrated all over the world by every generation, because the remembrance of the future rest of souls and of the resurrection of the bodies on the day of judgment must be kept alive with firm hope among all the faithful. And no church of Christ in the whole world must be deprived of this religious celebration but, always remembering this truly saving rite, must be ready at any moment and make herself worthy of receiving future blessings so that what she now celebrates in this world with faith and hope she may possess there forever in true reality and eternal blessedness. In the meantime, while we journey as pilgrims, the zeal of the teachers and the admonishment of the church must lead us to follow the example of Esther and Mordecai in doctrine and zeal so that we may be always devout in observing this rite which is to be celebrated and performed. Explanation on the Book of Esther 13.[13]

---

[10]Prov 26:27 (Vg).   [11]Prov 16:33.   [12]PL 109:668D–669A.   [13]PL 109:669B-C.

10:1-3 THE POWER OF AHASUERUS AND MORDECAI

[1]*King Ahasu-erus laid tribute on the land and on the coastlands of the sea*. [2]And all the acts of his power and might, and the full account of the high honor of Mordecai, to which the king advanced him, are they not written in the Book of the Chronicles of the kings of Media and Persia? [3]For Mordecai the Jew was next in rank to King Ahasu-erus, and he was great among the Jews and popular with the multitude of his brethren, for he sought the welfare of his people and spoke peace to all his people.*

* Vg on every land and all the islands

OVERVIEW: The words "King Ahasuerus laid tribute on the land and on the islands of the sea" do not refer to the historical king of the Persians but to the true king and our Lord Jesus Christ (RABANUS MAURUS).

10:1-3 *Tribute on the Land and on the Islands*

A FORESHADOWING OF THE KINGDOM OF CHRIST. RABANUS MAURUS: What does the text mean when it says that King Ahasuerus made all lands and all islands of the sea subject to his tributes? Since the historical king of the Persians and Medes did not have all lands under his rule, nor was he able to make all the islands of the sea subject to his tributes since the fame of his name could not even reach some of those islands or parts of the world, this sentence more truly applies to our king and Lord Christ whose power is in heaven, on earth, over the sea and every abyss. And he called himself "door," because through him we have access to eternal life,

according to the testimony of the psalmist, "And the kings of the entire universe adore him. And all the kings of the earth serve him, the kings of Tharsis and the islands offer gifts, the kings of Arabia and Sheba bring gifts."[1] Therefore not only the voices and the writings of the Jewish people alone, but also those of all the nations testify how the power of this king, his authority, dignity and preeminence advanced the true Mordecai, that is, the assembly of the holy teachers and masters of the church who lead the Christian people. Those whom he made his elect at the beginning through the gift of grace, those whom he made glorious and honorable before all the nations are the ones who look out for the good of his people and speak the words which concern the peace of his seed, according to the prediction of Isaiah: "Listen! Your sentinels lift up their voices; together they sing your praises."[2] EXPLANATION ON THE BOOK OF ESTHER 14.[3]

---

[1]Ps 72:10 (71:10 Vg). [2]Is 52:8. [3]PL 109:670B-D.

Appendix

Early Christian Writers and the Documents Cited

The following table lists all the early Christian documents cited in this volume by author, if known, or by the title of the work. The English title used in this commentary is followed in parentheses with the Latin designation and, where available, the Thesaurus Linguae Graecae (=TLG) digital referenences or Cetedoc Clavis numbers. Printed sources of original language versions may be found in the bibliography of works in original languages.

Ambrose

Cain and Abel (De Cain et Abel)	Cetedoc 0125
Concerning Virgins (De virginibus)	Cetedoc 0145
Consolation on the Death of Emperor Valentinian (De obitu Valentiniani)	Cetedoc 0158
Duties of the Clergy (De officiis ministrorum)	Cetedoc 0144
Flight from the World (De fuga saeculi)	Cetedoc 0133
Jacob and the Happy Life (De Jacob et vita beata)	Cetedoc 0130
Letters (Epistulae)	Cetedoc 0160
On Elijah and Fasting (De Helia et jejunio)	Cetedoc 0137
On Naboth (De Nabuthae)	Cetedoc 0138
On Theodosius (De obitu Theodosii)	Cetedoc 0159
The Prayer of Job and David (De interpellatione Job et David)	Cetedoc 0134

Aphrahat

Demonstrations (Demonstrationes)	

Athanasius

Defense Before Constantius (Apologia ad Constantium imperatorem)	TLG 2035.011
Discourses Against the Arians (Orationes tres contra Arianos)	TLG 2035.042
Festal Letters (Epistulae festales)	
Life of St. Anthony (Vita sancti Antonii)	TLG 2035.047

Augustine

Admonition and Grace (De corruptione et gratia)	Cetedoc 0353

Against Julian (*Contra Julianum*)	Cetedoc 0351
Against Lying (*Contra mendacium*)	Cetedoc 0304
Against Two Letters of the Pelagians (*Contra duas epistulas Pelagianorum*)	Cetedoc 0346
The Care to Be Taken for the Dead (*De cura pro mortuis gerenda*)	Cetedoc 0307
Christian Instruction (*De doctrina Christiana*)	Cetedoc 0263
City of God (*De civitate Dei*)	Cetedoc 0313
Eight Questions of Dulcitius (*De octo Dulcitii quaestionibus*)	Cetedoc 0291
Expositions of the Psalms (*Enarrationes in Psalmos*)	Cetedoc 0283
Letters (*Epistulae*)	Cetedoc 0262
The Nature and Origin of the Soul (*De natura et origine animae*)	Cetedoc 0345
On Grace and Free Will (*De gratia et libero arbitrio*)	Cetedoc 0352
Predestination of the Saints (*De praedestinatione sanctorum*)	Cetedoc 0354
Sermons (*Sermones*)	Cetedoc 0284

Augustine (Caesarius of Arles)

Sermons (*Sermones Caesarii vel ex aliis fontibus hausti*)	Cetedoc 1008

Basil the Great

Homilies on the Psalms (*Homiliae super Psalmos*)	TLG 2040.018
Letters (*Epistulae*)	TLG 2040.004
On Humility (*De humilitate*)	TLG 2040.036

Bede

Commentary on the Acts of the Apostles (*Expositio actuum apostolorum*)	Cetedoc 1357
Homilies on the Gospels (*Homiliarum evangelii libri ii*)	Cetedoc 1367
On Ezra and Nehemiah (*In Ezram et Neemiam libri iii*)	Cetedoc 1349
On the Temple (*De templo libri ii*)	Cetedoc 1348

Caesarius of Arles

Sermons (*Sermones*)	Cetedoc 1008

Cassian, John

Conferences (*Collationes*)	Cetedoc 0512
Institutes (*De institutis coenobiorum et de octo principalium vitiorum remediis*)	Cetedoc 0513

Cassiodorus

Explanation of the Psalms (*Expositio psalmorum*)	Cetedoc 0900

Clement of Alexandria

Christ the Educator (*Paedagogus*)	TLG 0555.002
Fragments (*Fragmenta*)	TLG 0555.008
Stromateis (*Stromata*)	TLG 0555.004

Clement of Rome

1 Clement (*Epistula i ad Corinthios*)	TLG 1271.001

Constitutions of the Holy Apostles (*Constitutiones apostolorum*)   TLG 2894.001

Cyprian
Exhortation to Martyrdom (*Ad Fortunatum [De exhortatione martyrii]*)   Cetedoc 0045
Letters (*Epistulae*)   Cetedoc 0050
The Lord's Prayer (*De dominica oratione*)   Cetedoc 0043
The Unity of the Church (*De ecclesiae catholicae unitate*)   Cetedoc 0041

Cyril of Jerusalem
Catechetical Lectures (*Catecheses ad illuminandos*)   TLG 2110.003
Mystagogical Lectures (*Mystagogiae [sp.]*)   TLG 2110.002

Ephrem the Syrian
Commentary on Tatian's Diatessaron (*In Tatiani Diatessaron*)
Homily on the Solitaries
Hymns on Paradise (*Hymni de paradiso*)
Hymns on the Nativity (*Hymni de nativitate*)
On the First Book of Kings (*In Primum Librum Regnorum*)
On the Second Book of Kings (*In Secundum Librum Regnorum*)
The Pearl: Seven Hymns on the Faith (*Hymni de Fidei*)

Eusebius of Caesarea
Proof of the Gospel (*Demonstratio evangelica*)   TLG 2018.005

Fulgentius of Ruspe
Letter to Scarila (*Liber ad Scarilam de incarnatione filii dei et vilium animalium auctore*)   Cetedoc 0822

Gregory of Nazianzus
The Last Farewell, Oration 42 (*Supremum vale*)   TLG 2022.050
On the Holy Lights, Oration 39 (*In sancta lumina*)   TLG 2022.047
On Theology, Theological Oration 2(28) (*De theologia*)   TLG 2022.008

Gregory the Great
Dialogues (*Dialogorum libri iv libri duo*)   Cetedoc 1713
Letters (*Registrum epistularum*)   Cetedoc 1714
Morals on the Book of Job (*Moralia in Job*)   Cetedoc 1708

Hippolytus
Fragments on Proverbs (*Fragmenta in Proverbia [Sp.]*)   TLG 2115.015

Isaac of Nineveh
Mystical Treatise (*De perfectione religiosa*)

Isho'dad of Merv
Books of Sessions 1 Kings

Books of Sessions 2 Kings

Jerome
Against Jovinianus (*Adversus Jovinianum*) — Cetedoc 0610
Against the Pelagians (*Dialogi contra Pelagianos libri iii*) — Cetedoc 0615
Homilies on the Psalms (*Tractatus lix in psalmos*) — Cetedoc 0592
Letters (*Epistulae*) — Cetedoc 0620

John Chrysostom
Against the Anomoeans (*Contra Anomoeos*)
  1-5 (*Contra Anomoeos homiliae 1-5=De incomprehensibili dei natura*) — TLG 2062.012
Discourses Against Judaizing Christians (*Adversus Judaeos [orationes 1-8]*) — TLG 2062.021
Homilies on Genesis (*In Genesim [homiliae 1-67]*) — TLG 2062.112
Homilies on St. Ignatius and St. Babylas (*In sanctum Ignatium martyrem*) — TLG 2062.044
Homilies on the Gospel of John (*In Joannem [homiliae 1-88]*) — TLG 2062.153
Homilies on the Gospel of Matthew (*In Matthaeum [homiliae 1-90]*) — TLG 2062.152
Letter to the Fallen Theodore (*Ad Theodorum lapsum [lib. 1]*) — TLG 2062.002
On the Epistle to the Hebrews (*In epistulam ad Hebraeos*) — TLG 2062.168

John of Damascus
On Divine Images (*Orationes de imaginibus tres*) — TLG 2934.005

John the Monk
Canons for the Month of June (*Analecta Hymnica Graeca, Canones Junii*) — TLG 4354.010

Justin Martyr
Dialogue with Trypho (*Dialogus cum Tryphone*) — TLG 0645.003
First Apology (*Apologia*) — TLG 0645.001

Lactantius
Epitome of the Divine Institutes (*Epitome divinarum institutionum*) — Cetedoc 0086

Maximus of Turin
Sermons (*Collectio sermonum antiqua*) — Cetedoc 0219a

Methodius
Symposium *or* Banquet of the Ten Virgins
(*Symposium sive Convivium decem virginum*) — TLG 2959.001

Novatian
On the Trinity (*De Trinitate*) — Cetedoc 0071

Origen
Against Celsus (*Contra Celsum*) — TLG 2042.001
Commentary on the Gospel of John

(Commentarii in evangelium Joannis [lib. 1, 2, 4, 5, 6, 10, 13])	TLG 2042.005
(Commentarii in evangelium Joannis [lib. 19, 20, 28, 32])	TLG 2042.079
Commentary on the Gospel of Matthew	
(Commentarium in evangelium Matthaei [lib. 10-11])	TLG 2042.029
(Commentarium in evangelium Matthaei [lib. 12-17])	TLG 2042.030
Commentary on the Song of Songs (Commentarium in Canticum Canticorum)	Cetedoc 0198
	TLG 2042.026
Fragments on Jeremiah (Fragmenta in Jeremiam [in catenis])	TLG 2042.010
Homilies on Genesis (Homiliae in Genesim)	TLG 2042.022
Homilies on Jeremiah (In Jeremiam [homiliae 1-11])	TLG 2042.009
(In Jeremiam [homilae 12-20])	TLG 2042.021
Homilies on Leviticus (Homiliae in Leviticum)	TLG 2042.024
Homilies on the Gospel of Luke (Homiliae in Lucam)	TLG 2042.016
Letter to Julius Africanus (Epistula ad Africanum)	TLG 2042.045
On First Principles (De principiis)	TLG 2042.002
(Fragmenta de principiis)	TLG 2042.003
On Prayer (De oratione)	TLG 2042.008

Paulinus of Nola

Poems (Carmina)	Cetedoc 0203

Peter Chrysologus

Sermons (Collectio sermonum)	Cetedoc 0227+

Procopius of Gaza

Commentary on 1 Chronicles (In Librum Tertium Regum)

Prudentius

The Spiritual Combat (Psychomachia)	Cetedoc 1441

Pseudo-Dionysius

Letters (Epistulae)	TLG 2798.006-015

Pseudo-Tertullian

Five Books in Reply to Marcion (Carmen adversus Marcionem)	Cetedoc 0036

Rabanus Maurus

Commentary on the Third Book of Kings (Commentaria in Libros IV Regum)
Explanation on the Book of Esther (Expositio in Librum Esther)

Sahdona

Book of Perfection

Salvian the Presbyter

The Governance of God (De gubernatione Dei)	Cetedoc 0485

Tertullian

An Answer to the Jews (*Adversus Judaeos*)   Cetedoc 0033

On Fasting (*De jejunio adversus psychicos*)   Cetedoc 0029

Theodoret of Cyr

Commentary on the Song of Songs (*Explanatio in Canticum canticorum*)   TLG 4089.025

Questions on the Books of Kings and Chronicles

  (*De quaestionibus ambiguis in Libros Regnorum et Paralipomenon*)   TLG 4089.023

Walafridius Strabo

Glossa Ordinaria, Third Book of Kings (*Glossa Ordinaria-Liber Regnum Tertius et Quartus*)

BIOGRAPHICAL SKETCHES & SHORT DESCRIPTIONS OF SELECT ANONYMOUS WORKS

This listing is cumulative, including all the authors and works cited in this series to date.

Abraham of Nathpar (fl. sixth-seventh century). Monk of the Eastern Church who flourished during the monastic revival of the sixth to seventh century. Among his works is a treatise on prayer and silence that speaks of the importance of prayer becoming embodied through action in the one who prays. His work has also been associated with John of Apamea or Philoxenus of Mabbug.

Acacius of Beroea (c. 340-c. 436). Syrian monk known for his ascetic life. He became bishop of Beroea in 378, participated in the council of Constantinople in 381, and played an important role in mediating between Cyril of Alexandria and John of Antioch; however, he did not take part in the clash between Cyril and Nestorius.

Acacius of Caesarea (d. c. 365). Pro-Arian bishop of Caesarea in Palestine, disciple and biographer of Eusebius of Caesarea, the historian. He was a man of great learning and authored a treatise on Ecclesiastes.

Adamantius (early fourth century). Surname of Origen of Alexandria and the main character in the dialogue contained in *Concerning Right Faith in God*. Rufinus attributes this work to Origen. However, Trinitarian terminology, coupled with references to Methodius and allusions to the fourth-century Constantinian era bring this attri-

bution into question.

Adamnan (c. 624-704). Abbot of Iona, Ireland, and author of the life of St. Columba. He was influential in the process of assimilating the Celtic church into Roman liturgy and church order. He also wrote *On the Holy Sites*, which influenced Bede.

Alexander of Alexandria (fl. 312-328). Bishop of Alexandria and predecessor of Athanasius, on whom he exerted considerable theological influence during the rise of Arianism. Alexander excommunicated Arius, whom he had appointed to the parish of Baucalis, in 319. His teaching regarding the eternal generation and divine substantial union of the Son with the Father was eventually confirmed at the Council of Nicaea (325).

Ambrose of Milan (c. 333-397; fl. 374-397). Bishop of Milan and teacher of Augustine who defended the divinity of the Holy Spirit and the perpetual virginity of Mary.

Ambrosiaster (fl. c. 366-384). Name given by Erasmus to the author of a work once thought to have been composed by Ambrose.

Ammonas (fourth century). Student of Antony the Great and member of a colony of anchorite monks at Pispir in Egypt. He took over leadership of the colony upon Antony's death in 356.

He was consecrated by Athanasius as bishop of a small unknown see. He died by 396. Fourteen letters and eleven sayings in the *Apophthegmata Patrum* are attributed to him, although it is unlikely that all of the identified sayings are his.

Ammonius (c. fifth century). An Aristotelian commentator and teacher in Alexandria, where he was born and of whose school he became head. Also an exegete of Plato, he enjoyed fame among his contemporaries and successors, although modern critics accuse him of pedantry and banality.

Amphilochius of Iconium (b. c. 340-345, d.c. 398-404). An orator at Constantinople before becoming bishop of Iconium in 373. He was a cousin of Gregory of Nazianzus and active in debates against the Macedonians and Messalians.

Andreas (c. seventh century). Monk who collected commentary from earlier writers to form a catena on various biblical books.

Andrew of Caesarea (early sixth century). Bishop of Caesarea in Cappadocia. He produced one of the earliest Greek commentaries on Revelation and defended the divine inspiration of its author.

Andrew of Crete (c. 660-740). Bishop of Crete, known for his hymns, especially for his "canons," a genre which supplanted the *kontakia* and is believed to have originated with him. A significant number of his canons and sermons have survived and some are still in use in the Eastern Church. In the early Iconoclastic controversy he is also known for his defense of the veneration of icons.

Antony (or Anthony) the Great (c. 251-c. 356). An anchorite of the Egyptian desert and founder of Egyptian monasticism. Athanasius regarded him as the ideal of monastic life, and he has become a model for Christian hagiography.

Aphrahat (c. 270-350; fl. 337-345). "The Persian Sage" and first major Syriac writer whose work survives. He is also known by his Greek name Aphraates.

Apollinaris of Laodicea (310-c. 392). Bishop of Laodicea who was attacked by Gregory of Nazianzus, Gregory of Nyssa and Theodore for denying that Christ had a human mind.

Aponius/Apponius (fourth–fifth century). Author of a remarkable commentary on Song of Solomon (c. 405-415), an important work in the history of exegesis. The work, which was influenced by the commentaries of Origen and Pseudo-Hippolytus, is of theological significance, especially in the area of Christology.

Apostolic Constitutions (c. 381-394). Also known as *Constitutions of the Holy Apostles* and thought to be redacted by Julian of Neapolis. The work is divided into eight books, and is primarily a collection of and expansion on previous works such as the *Didache* (c. 140) and the *Apostolic Traditions*. Book 8 ends with eighty-five canons from various sources and is elsewhere known as the *Apostolic Canons*.

Apringius of Beja (middle sixth century). Iberian bishop and exegete. Heavily influenced by Tyconius, he wrote a commentary on Revelation in Latin, of which two large fragments survive.

Arethas of Caesarea (c. 860-940) Byzantine scholar and disciple of Photius. He was a deacon in Constantinople, then archbishop of Caesarea from 901.

Arius (fl. c. 320). Heretic condemned at the Council of Nicaea (325) for refusing to accept that the Son was not a creature but was God by nature like the Father.

Arnobius the Younger (fifth century). A participant in christological controversies of the fifth century. He composed *Conflictus cum Serapione*, an account of a debate with a monophysite monk in which he attempts to demonstrate harmony between Roman and Alexandrian theology. Some scholars attribute to him a few more works, such as *Commentaries on Psalms*.

Athanasius of Alexandria (c. 295-373; fl. 325-373). Bishop of Alexandria from 328, though often in exile. He wrote his classic polemics against the Arians while most of the eastern bishops were against him.

Athenagoras (fl. 176-180). Early Christian philosopher and apologist from Athens, whose only authenticated writing, *A Plea Regarding Christians*, is addressed to the emperors Marcus Aurelius and Commodius, and defends Christians from the common accusations of atheism, incest and cannibalism.

Augustine of Hippo (354-430). Bishop of Hippo and a voluminous writer on philosophical, exegetical, theological and ecclesiological topics. He formulated the Western doctrines of predestination and original sin in his writings against the Pelagians.

Babai (c. early sixth century). Author of the Letter to Cyriacus. He should not be confused with either Babai of Nisibis (d. 484), or Babai the Great (d. 628).

Babai the Great (d. 628). Syriac monk who founded a monastery and school in his region of Beth Zabday and later served as third superior at the Great Convent of Mount Izla during a period of crisis in the Nestorian church.

Basil of Seleucia (fl. 444-468). Bishop of Seleucia in Isauria and ecclesiastical writer. He took part in the Synod of Constantinople in 448 for the condemnation of the Eutychian errors and the deposition of their great champion, Dioscurus of Alexandria.

Basil the Great (b. c. 330; fl. 357-379). One of the Cappadocian fathers, bishop of Caesarea and champion of the teaching on the Trinity propounded at Nicaea in 325. He was a great administrator and founded a monastic rule.

Basilides (fl. second century). Alexandrian heretic of the early second century who is said to have believed that souls migrate from body to body and that we do not sin if we lie to protect the body from martyrdom.

Bede the Venerable (c. 672/673-735). Born in Northumbria, at the age of seven, he was put under the care of the Benedictine monks of Saints Peter and Paul at Jarrow and given a broad classical education in the monastic tradition. Considered one of the most learned men of his age, he is the author of *An Ecclesiastical History of the English People*.

Benedict of Nursia (c. 480-547). Considered the most important figure in the history of Western monasticism. Benedict founded many monasteries, the most notable found at Montecassino, but his lasting influence lay in his famous Rule. The Rule outlines the theological and inspirational foundation of the monastic ideal while also legislating the shape and organization of the cenobitic life.

Besa the Copt (5th century). Coptic monk, disciple of Shenoute, whom he succeeded as head of the monastery. He wrote numerous letters, monastic catecheses and a biography of Shenoute.

Book of Steps (c. 400). Written by an anonymous Syriac author, this work consists of thirty homilies or discourses which specifically deal with the more advanced stages of growth in the spiritual life.

Braulio of Saragossa (c. 585-651). Bishop of Saragossa (631-651) and noted writer of the Visigothic renaissance. His *Life* of St. Aemilianus is his crowning literary achievement.

Caesarius of Arles (c. 470-543). Bishop of Arles renowned for his attention to his pastoral duties. Among his surviving works the most important is a collection of some 238 sermons that display an ability to preach Christian doctrine to a variety of audiences.

Callistus of Rome (d. 222). Pope (217-222) who excommunicated Sabellius for heresy. It is very probable that he suffered martyrdom.

Cassia (b. c. 805, d. between 848 and 867). Nun, poet and hymnographer who founded a convent in Constantinople.

Cassian, John (360-432). Author of the *Institutes* and the *Conferences,* works purporting to relay the teachings of the Egyptian monastic fathers on the nature of the spiritual life which were highly influential in the development of Western monasticism.

Cassiodorus (c. 485-c. 580). Founder of the monastery of Vivarium, Calabria, where monks transcribed classic sacred and profane texts, Greek and Latin, preserving them for the Western tradition.

Chromatius (fl. 400). Bishop of Aquileia, friend of Rufinus and Jerome and author of tracts and sermons.

Clement of Alexandria (c. 150-215). A highly educated Christian convert from paganism, head of the catechetical school in Alexandria and pioneer of Christian scholarship. His major works, *Protrepticus, Paedagogus* and the *Stromata*, bring Christian doctrine face to face with the ideas and achievements of his time.

Clement of Rome (fl. c. 92-101). Pope whose *Epistle to the Corinthians* is one of the most important documents of subapostolic times.

Commodian (probably third or possibly fifth century). Latin poet of unknown origin (possibly Syrian?) whose two surviving works suggest chiliast and patripassionist tendencies.

Constitutions of the Holy Apostles. *See Apostolic Constitutions.*

Cosmas of Maiuma (c. 675-c.751). Adopted son of John of Damascus and educated by the monk Cosmas in the early eighth century. He entered the monastery of St. Sabas near Jerusalem and in 735 became bishop of Maiuma near Gaza. Cosmas in his capacity as Melodus ("Songwriter") is known for his canons composed in honor of Christian feasts. An alternate rendering of his name is Kosmas Melodos.

Cyprian of Carthage (fl. 248-258). Martyred bishop of Carthage who maintained that those baptized by schismatics and heretics had no share in the blessings of the church.

Cyril of Alexandria (375-444; fl. 412-444). Patriarch of Alexandria whose extensive exegesis, characterized especially by a strong espousal of the unity of Christ, led to the condemnation of Nestorius in 431.

Cyril of Jerusalem (c. 315-386; fl. c. 348). Bishop of Jerusalem after 350 and author of *Catechetical Homilies.*

Cyril of Scythopolis (b. c. 525; d. after 557). Palestinian monk and author of biographies of famous Palestinian monks. Because of him we have precise knowledge of monastic life in the fifth and sixth centuries and a description of the Origenist crisis and its suppression in the mid-sixth century.

Diadochus of Photice (c. 400-474). Antimonophysite bishop of Epirus Vetus whose work *Discourse on the Ascension of Our Lord Jesus Christ* exerted influence in both the East and West

through its Chalcedonian Christology. He is also the subject of the mystical *Vision of St. Diadochus Bishop of Photice in Epirus.*

Didache (c. 140). Of unknown authorship, this text intertwines Jewish ethics with Christian liturgical practice to form a whole discourse on the "way of life." It exerted an enormous amount of influence in the patristic period and was especially used in the training of catechumen.

Didascalia Apostolorum (Teaching of the Twelve Apostles and Holy Disciples of Our Savior) (early third century). A Church Order composed for a community of Christian converts from paganism in the northern part of Syria. This work forms the main source of the first six books of the *Apostolic Constitutions* and provides an important window to view what early liturgical practice may have looked like.

Didymus the Blind (c. 313-398). Alexandrian exegete who was much influenced by Origen and admired by Jerome.

Diodore of Tarsus (d. c. 394). Bishop of Tarsus and Antiochene theologian. He authored a great scope of exegetical, doctrinal and apologetic works, which come to us mostly in fragments because of his condemnation as the predecessor of Nestorianism. Diodore was a teacher of John Chrysostom and Theodore of Mopsuestia.

Dionysius of Alexandria (d. c. 264). Bishop of Alexandria and student of Origen. Dionysius actively engaged in the theological disputes of his day, opposed Sabellianism, defended himself against accusations of tritheism and wrote the earliest extant Christian refutation of Epicureanism. His writings have survived mainly in extracts preserved by other early Christian authors.

Dorotheus of Gaza (fl. c. 525-540). Member of Abbot Seridos's monastery and later leader of a monastery where he wrote *Spiritual Instructions.* He also wrote a work on traditions of Palestinian monasticism.

Ennodius (474-521). Bishop of Pavia, a prolific writer of various genre, including letters, poems and biographies. He sought reconciliation in the schism between Rome and Acacius of Constantinople, and also upheld papal autonomy in the face of challenges from secular authorities.

Ephrem the Syrian (b. c. 306; fl. 363-373). Syrian writer of commentaries and devotional hymns which are sometimes regarded as the greatest specimens of Christian poetry prior to Dante.

Epiphanius of Salamis (c. 315-403). Bishop of Salamis in Cyprus, author of a refutation of eighty heresies (the *Panarion*) and instrumental in the condemnation of Origen.

Epiphanius the Latin. Author of the late fifth-century or early sixth-century Latin text *Interpretation of the Gospels*, with constant references to early patristic commentators. He was possibly a bishop of Benevento or Seville.

Epistle of Barnabas. See Letter of Barnabas.

Eucherius of Lyons (fl. 420-449). Bishop of Lyons c. 435-449. Born into an aristocratic family, he, along with his wife and sons, joined the monastery at Lérins soon after its founding. He explained difficult Scripture passages by means of a threefold reading of the text: literal, moral and spiritual.

Eugippius (b. 460). Disciple of Severinus and third abbot of the monastic community at Castrum Lucullanum, which was made up of those fleeing from Noricum during the barbarian invasions.

Eunomius (d. 393). Bishop of Cyzicyus who was attacked by Basil and Gregory of Nyssa for maintaining that the Father and the Son were of different natures, one ingenerate, one generate.

Eusebius of Caesarea (c. 260/263-340). Bishop of Caesarea, partisan of the Emperor Constantine and first historian of the Christian church. He argued that the truth of the gospel had been foreshadowed in pagan writings but had to defend his own doctrine against suspicion of Arian sympathies.

Eusebius of Emesa (c. 300-c. 359). Bishop of Emesa from c. 339. A biblical exegete and writer on doctrinal subjects, he displays some semi-Arian tendencies of his mentor Eusebius of Caesarea.

Eusebius of Gaul, or Eusebius Gallicanus (c. fifth century). A conventional name for a collection of seventy-six sermons produced in Gaul and revised in the seventh century. It contains material from different patristic authors and focuses on ethical teaching in the context of the liturgical cycle (days of saints and other feasts).

Eusebius of Vercelli (fl. c. 360). Bishop of Vercelli who supported the trinitarian teaching of Nicaea (325) when it was being undermined by compromise in the West.

Eustathius of Antioch (fl. 325). First bishop of Beroea, then of Antioch, one of the leaders of the anti-Arians at the council of Nicaea. Later, he was banished from his seat and exiled to Thrace for his support of Nicene theology.

Euthymius (377-473). A native of Melitene and influential monk. He was educated by Bishop Otreius of Melitene, who ordained him priest and placed him in charge of all the monasteries in his diocese. When the Council of Chalcedon (451) condemned the errors of Eutyches, it was greatly due to the authority of Euthymius that most of the Eastern recluses accepted its decrees. The empress Eudoxia returned to Chalcedonian orthodoxy through his efforts.

Evagrius of Pontus (c. 345-399). Disciple and teacher of ascetic life who astutely absorbed and creatively transmitted the spirituality of Egyptian and Palestinian monasticism of the late fourth century. Although Origenist elements of his writings were formally condemned by the Fifth Ecumenical Council (Constantinople II, A.D. 553), his literary corpus continued to influence the tradition of the church.

Eznik of Kolb (early fifth century). A disciple of Mesrob who translated Greek Scriptures into Armenian, so as to become the model of the classical Armenian language. As bishop, he participated in the synod of Astisat (449).

Facundus of Hermiane (fl. 546-568). African bishop who opposed Emperor Justinian's *post mortem* condemnation of Theodore of Mopsuestia, Theodoret of Cyr and Ibas of Ebessa at the fifth ecumenical council. His written defense, known as "To Justinian" or "In Defense of the Three Chapters," avers that ancient theologians should not be blamed for errors that became obvious only upon later theological reflection. He continued in the tradition of Chalcedon, although his Christology was supplemented, according to Justinian's decisions, by the theopaschite formula *Unus ex Trinitate passus est* ("Only one of the three suffered").

Fastidius (c. fourth-fifth centuries). British author of *On the Christian Life*. He is believed to have written some works attributed to Pelagius.

Faustinus (fl. 380). A priest in Rome and supporter of Lucifer and author of a treatise on the Trinity.

Faustus of Riez (c. 400-490). A prestigious British monk at Lérins; abbot, then bishop of Riez from 457 to his death. His works include *On the Holy Spirit*, in which he argued against the Macedonians for the divinity of the Holy Spirit, and *On Grace*, in which he argued for a position on salvation that lay between more categorical views of free-will and predestination. Various letters and (pseudonymous) sermons are extant.

The Festal Menaion. Orthodox liturgical text containing the variable parts of the service, including hymns, for fixed days of celebration of the life of Jesus and Mary.

Filastrius (fl. 380). Bishop of Brescia and author of a compilation against all heresies.

Firmicus Maternus (fourth century). An anti-Pagan apologist. Before his conversion to Christianity he wrote a work on astrology (334-337). After his conversion, however, he criticized paganism in *On the Errors of the Profane Religion*.

Flavian of Chalon-sur-Saône (d. end of sixth century). Bishop of Chalon-sur-Saône in Burgundy, France. His hymn *Verses on the Mandate in the Lord's Supper* was recited in a number of the French monasteries after the washing of the feet on Maundy Thursday.

Fructuosus of Braga (d. c. 665). Son of a Gothic general and member of a noble military family. He became a monk at an early age, then abbot-bishop of Dumium before 650 and metropolitan of Braga in 656. He was influential in setting up monastic communities in Lusitania, Asturia,

Galicia and the island of Gades.

Fulgentius of Ruspe (c. 467-532). Bishop of Ruspe and author of many orthodox sermons and tracts under the influence of Augustine.

Gaudentius of Brescia (fl. 395). Successor of Filastrius as bishop of Brescia and author of twenty-one Eucharistic sermons.

Gennadius of Constantinople (d. 471). Patriarch of Constantinople, author of numerous commentaries and an opponent of the Christology of Cyril of Alexandria.

Gerontius (c. 395-c.480). Palestinian monk, later archimandrite of the cenobites of Palestine. He led the resistance to the council of Chalcedon.

Gnostics. Name now given generally to followers of Basilides, Marcion, Valentinus, Mani and others. The characteristic belief is that matter is a prison made for the spirit by an evil or ignorant creator, and that redemption depends on fate, not on free will.

Gregory of Elvira (fl. 359-385). Bishop of Elvira who wrote allegorical treatises in the style of Origen and defended the Nicene faith against the Arians.

Gregory of Nazianzus (b. 329/330; fl. 372-389). Cappadocian father, bishop of Constantinople, friend of Basil the Great and Gregory of Nyssa, and author of theological orations, sermons and poetry.

Gregory of Nyssa (c. 335-394). Bishop of Nyssa and brother of Basil the Great. A Cappadocian father and author of catechetical orations, he was a philosophical theologian of great originality.

Gregory Thaumaturgus (fl. c. 248-264). Bishop of Neocaesarea and a disciple of Origen. There are at least five legendary *Lives* that recount the events and miracles which led to his being called "the wonder worker." His most important work was the *Address of Thanks to Origen*, which is a rhetorically structured panegyric to Origen and an outline of his teaching.

Gregory the Great (c. 540-604). Pope from 590, the fourth and last of the Latin "Doctors of the Church." He was a prolific author and a powerful unifying force within the Latin Church, initiating the liturgical reform that brought about the Gregorian Sacramentary and Gregorian chant.

Heracleon (fl. c.145-180). Gnostic teacher and disciple of Valentinus. His commentary on John, which was perhaps the first commentary to exist on this or any Gospel, was so popular that Ambrose commissioned Origen to write his own commentary in response, providing a more orthodox approach to the Fourth Gospel.

Hesychius of Jerusalem (fl. 412-450). Presbyter and exegete, thought to have commented on the whole of Scripture.

Hilary of Arles (c. 401-449). Archbishop of Arles and leader of the Semi-Pelagian party. Hilary incurred the wrath of Pope Leo I when he removed a bishop from his see and appointed a new bishop. Leo demoted Arles from a metropolitan see to a bishopric to assert papal power over the church in Gaul.

Hilary of Poitiers (c. 315-367). Bishop of Poitiers and called the "Athanasius of the West" because of his defense (against the Arians) of the common nature of Father and Son.

Hippolytus (fl. 222-245). Recent scholarship places Hippolytus in a Palestinian context, personally familiar with Origen. Though he is known chiefly for *The Refutation of All Heresies,* he was primarily a commentator on Scripture (especially the Old Testament) employing typological exegesis.

Horsiesi (c. 305-c. 390). Pachomius's second successor, after Petronius, as a leader of cenobitic monasticism in Southern Egypt.

Ignatius of Antioch (c. 35-107/112). Bishop of Antioch who wrote several letters to local churches while being taken from Antioch to Rome to be martyred. In the letters, which warn against heresy, he stresses orthodox Christology, the centrality of the Eucharist and unique role of the bishop in preserving the unity of the church.

Irenaeus of Lyons (c. 135-c. 202). Bishop of Lyons who published the most famous and influential refutation of Gnostic thought.

Isaac of Nineveh (d. c. 700). Also known as Isaac the Syrian or Isaac Syrus, this monastic writer served for a short while as bishop of Nineveh before retiring to live a secluded monastic life. His writings on ascetic subjects survive in the form of numerous homilies.

Isaiah of Scete (late fourth century). Author of ascetical texts, collected after his death under the title of the *Ascetic Discourses.* This work was influential in the development of Eastern Christian asceticism and spirituality.

Isho'dad of Merv (fl. c. 850). Nestorian bishop of Hedatta. He wrote commentaries on parts of the Old Testament and all of the New Testament, frequently quoting Syriac fathers.

Isidore of Seville (c. 560-636). Youngest of a family of monks and clerics, including sister Florentina and brothers Leander and Fulgentius. He was an erudite author of comprehensive scale in matters both religious and sacred, including his encyclopedic *Etymologies.*

Jacob of Nisibis (d. 338). Bishop of Nisibis. He was present at the council of Nicaea in 325 and took an active part in the opposition to Arius.

Jacob of Sarug (c. 450-c. 520). Syriac ecclesiastical writer. Jacob received his education at Edessa. At the end of his life he was ordained bishop of Sarug. His principal writing was a long series of metrical homilies, earning him the title "The Flute of the Holy Spirit."

Jerome (c. 347-420). Gifted exegete and exponent of a classical Latin style, now best known as the translator of the Latin Vulgate. He defended the perpetual virginity of Mary, attacked Origen and Pelagius and supported extreme ascetic practices.

John Chrysostom (344/354-407; fl. 386-407). Bishop of Constantinople who was noted for his orthodoxy, his eloquence and his attacks on Christian laxity in high places.

John of Antioch (d. 441/42). Bishop of Antioch, commencing in 428. He received his education together with Nestorius and Theodore of Mopsuestia in a monastery near Antioch. A supporter of Nestorius, he condemned Cyril of Alexandria, but later reached a compromise with him.

John of Apamea (fifth century). Syriac author of the early church who wrote on various aspects of the spiritual life, also known as John the Solitary.

Some of his writings are in the form of dialogues. Other writings include letters, a treatise on baptism, and shorter works on prayer and silence.

John of Carpathus (c. seventh/eighth century). Perhaps John the bishop from the island of Carpathus, situated between Crete and Rhodes, who attended the Synod of 680/81. He wrote two "centuries" (a literary genre in Eastern spirituality consisting of 100 short sections, or chapters). These were entitled *Chapters of Encouragement to the Monks of India* and *Chapters on Theology and Knowledge* which are included in the *Philokalia*.

John of Damascus (c. 650-750). Arab monastic and theologian whose writings enjoyed great influence in both the Eastern and Western Churches. His most influential writing was the *Orthodox Faith*.

John the Elder (c. eighth century). A Syriac author also known as John of Dalyatha or John Saba ("the elder") who belonged to monastic circles of the Church of the East and lived in the region of Mount Qardu (northern Iraq). His most important writings are twenty-two homilies and a collection of fifty-one short letters in which he describes the mystical life as an anticipatory experience of the resurrection life, the fruit of the sacraments of baptism and the Eucharist.

John the Monk. Traditional name found in *The Festal Menaion*, believed to refer to John of Damascus. *See* John of Damascus.

Josephus, Flavius (c. 37-c. 101). Jewish historian from a distinguished priestly family. Acquainted with the Essenes and Sadducees, he himself became a Pharisee. He joined the great Jewish revolt that broke out in 66 and was chosen by the Sanhedrin at Jerusalem to be commander-in-chief in Galilee. Showing great shrewdness to ingratiate himself with Vespasian by foretelling his elevation and that of his son Titus to the imperial dignity, Josephus was restored his liberty after 69 when Vespasian became emperor.

Julian of Eclanum (c. 385-450). Bishop of Eclanum in 416/417 who was removed from office and exiled in 419 for not officially opposing Pelagianism. In exile, he was accepted by The-odore of Mopsuestia, whose Antiochene exegetical style he followed. Although he was never able to regain his ecclesiastical position, Julian taught in Sicily until his death. His works include commentaries on Job and parts of the Minor Prophets, a translation of Theodore of Mopsuestia's commentary on the Psalms, and various letters. Sympathetic to Pelagius, Julian applied his intellectual acumen and rhetorical training to argue against Augustine on matters such as free will, desire and the locus of evil.

Julian the Arian (c. fourth century) Antiochene, Arian author of *Commentary on Job*, and probably a follower of Aetius and Eunomius. The *85 Apostolic Canons*, once part of the *Apostolic Constitutions*, and the Pseudo-Ignatian writings are also attributed to him.

Justin Martyr (c. 100/110-165; fl. c. 148-161). Palestinian philosopher who was converted to Christianity, "the only sure and worthy philosophy." He traveled to Rome where he wrote several apologies against both pagans and Jews, combining Greek philosophy and Christian theology; he was eventually martyred.

Lactantius (c. 260-c. 330). Christian apologist removed from his post as teacher of rhetoric at Nicomedia upon his conversion to Christianity. He was tutor to the son of Constantine and author of *The Divine Institutes*.

Leander (c. 545-c. 600). Latin ecclesiastical writer, of whose works only two survive. He was instrumental in spreading Christianity among the Visigoths, gaining significant historical influence in Spain in his time.

Leo the Great (regn. 440-461). Bishop of Rome whose *Tome to Flavian* helped to strike a balance between Nestorian and Cyrilline positions at the Council of Chalcedon in 451.

Letter of Barnabas (c. 130). An allegorical and typological interpretation of the Old Testament with a decidedly anti-Jewish tone. It was included with other New Testament works as a "Catholic epistle" at least until Eusebius of Caesarea (c. 260/263-340) questioned its authenticity.

Letter to Diognetus (c. third century). A refutation of paganism and an exposition of the Christian life and faith. The author of this letter is unknown, and the exact identity of its recipient, Diognetus, continues to elude patristic scholars.

Lucifer (d. 370/371). Bishop of Cagliari and vigorous supporter of Athanasius and the Nicene Creed. In conflict with the emperor Constantius, he was banished to Palestine and later to Thebaid (Egypt).

Luculentius (fifth century). Unknown author of a group of short commentaries on the New Testament, especially Pauline passages. His exegesis is mainly literal and relies mostly on earlier authors such as Jerome and Augustine. The content of his writing may place it in the fifth century.

Macarius of Egypt (c. 300-c. 390). One of the Desert Fathers. Accused of supporting Athanasius, Macarius was exiled c. 374 to an island in the Nile by Lucius, the Arian successor of Athanasius. Macarius continued his teaching of monastic theology at Wadi Natrun.

Macrina the Younger (c. 327-379). The elder sister of Basil the Great and Gregory of Nyssa, she is known as "the Younger" to distinguish her from her paternal grandmother. She had a powerful influence on her younger brothers, especially on Gregory, who called her his teacher and relates her teaching in *On the Soul and the Resurrection*.

Manichaeans. A religious movement that originated circa 241 in Persia under the leadership of Mani but was apparently of complex Christian origin. It is said to have denied free will and the universal sovereignty of God, teaching that kingdoms of light and darkness are coeternal and that the redeemed are particles of a spiritual man of light held captive in the darkness of matter (*see* Gnostics).

Marcellus of Ancyra (d. c. 375). Wrote a refutation of Arianism. Later, he was accused of Sabellianism, especially by Eusebius of Caesarea. While the Western church declared him orthodox, the Eastern church excommunicated him. Some scholars have attributed to him certain works of Athanasius.

Marcion (fl. 144). Heretic of the mid-second century who rejected the Old Testament and much of the New Testament, claiming that the Father of Jesus Christ was other than the Old Testament God (*see* Gnostics).

Marius Victorinus (b. c. 280/285; fl. c. 355-363). Grammarian of African origin who taught rhetoric at Rome and translated works of Platonists. After his conversion (c. 355), he wrote against the Arians and commentaries on Paul's letters.

Mark the Hermit (c. sixth century). Monk who lived near Tarsus and produced works on ascetic practices as well as christological issues.

Martin of Braga (fl. c. 568-579). Anti-Arian metropolitan of Braga on the Iberian peninsula. He was highly educated and presided over the provincial council of Braga in 572.

Martyrius. *See* Sahdona.

Maximinus (the Arian) (b. c. 360-65). Bishop of an Arian community, perhaps in Illyricum. Of Roman descent, he debated publicly with Augustine at Hippo (427 or 428), ardently defending Arian doctrine. Besides the polemical works he wrote against the orthodox, such as his *Against the Heretics, Jews and Pagans*, he also wrote fifteen sermons that are considered much less polemical, having been previously attributed to Maximus of Turin. He is also known for his twenty-four *Explanations of Chapters of the Gospels*.

Maximus of Turin (d. 408/423). Bishop of Turin. Over one hundred of his sermons survive on Christian festivals, saints and martyrs.

Maximus the Confessor (c. 580-662). Palestinian-born theologian and ascetic writer. Fleeing the Arab invasion of Jerusalem in 614, he took refuge in Constantinople and later Africa. He died near the Black Sea after imprisonment and severe suffering, having his tongue cut off and his right hand mutilated. He taught total preference for God and detachment from all things.

Melito of Sardis (d. c. 190). Bishop of Sardis. According to Polycrates, he may have been Jewish by birth. Among his numerous works is a liturgical document known as *On Pascha* (ca. 160-177). As a Quartodeciman, and one involved intimately involved in that controversy, Melito celebrated Pascha on the fourteenth of Nisan in line with the custom handed down from Judaism.

Methodius of Olympus (d. 311). Bishop of Olympus who celebrated virginity in a *Symposium* partly modeled on Plato's dialogue of that name.

Minucius Felix (second or third century). Christian apologist who was an advocate in Rome. His *Octavius* agrees at numerous points with the *Apologeticum* of Tertullian. His birthplace is believed to be in Africa.

Montanist Oracles. Montanism was an apocalyptic and strictly ascetic movement begun in the latter half of the second century by a certain Montanus in Phrygia, who, along with certain of his followers, uttered oracles they claimed were inspired by the Holy Spirit. Little of the authentic oracles remains and most of what is known of Montanism comes from the authors who wrote against the movement. Montanism was formally condemned as a heresy before by Asiatic synods.

Nemesius of Emesa (fl. late fourth century). Bishop of Emesa in Syria whose most important work, *Of the Nature of Man*, draws on several theological and philosophical sources and is the first exposition of a Christian anthropology.

Nestorius (c. 381-c. 451). Patriarch of Constantinople (428-431) who founded the heresy which says that there are two persons, divine and human, rather than one person truly united in the incarnate Christ. He resisted the teaching of *theotokos*, causing Nestorian churches to separate from Constantinople.

Nicetas of Remesiana (fl. second half of fourth century). Bishop of Remesiana in Serbia, whose works affirm the consubstantiality of the Son and the deity of the Holy Spirit.

Nilus of Ancyra (d. c. 430). Prolific ascetic writer and disciple of John Chrysostom. Sometimes erroneously known as Nilus of Sinai, he was a native of Ancyra and studied at Constantinople.

Novatian of Rome (fl. 235-258). Roman theologian, otherwise orthodox, who formed a schismatic church after failing to become pope. His treatise on the Trinity states the classic western doctrine.

Oecumenius (sixth century). Called the Rhetor or the Philosopher, Oecumenius wrote the earliest extant Greek commentary on Revelation. Scholia by Oecumenius on some of John Chrysostom's commentaries on the Pauline Epistles are still extant.

Olympiodorus (early sixth century). Exegete and deacon of Alexandria, known for his commentaries that come to us mostly in catenae.

Origen of Alexandria (b. 185; fl. c. 200-254). Influential exegete and systematic theologian. He was condemned (perhaps unfairly) for maintaining the preexistence of souls while purportedly denying the resurrection of the body. His extensive works of exegesis focus on the spiritual meaning of the text.

Pachomius (c. 292-347). Founder of cenobitic monasticism. A gifted group leader and author of a set of rules, he was defended after his death by Athanasius of Alexandria.

Pacian of Barcelona (c. fourth century). Bishop of Barcelona whose writings polemicize against popular pagan festivals as well as Novatian schismatics.

Palladius of Helenopolis (c. 363/364-c. 431). Bishop of Helenopolis in Bithynia (400-417) and then Aspuna in Galatia. A disciple of Evagrius of Pontus and admirer of Origen, Palladius became a zealous adherent of John Chrysostom and shared his troubles in 403. His *Lausaic History* is the leading source for the history of early monasticism, stressing the spiritual value of the life of the desert.

Paschasius of Dumium (c. 515-c. 580). Translator of sentences of the Desert Fathers from Greek into Latin while a monk in Dumium.

Paterius (c. sixth-seventh century). Disciple of Gregory the Great who is primarily responsible for the transmission of Gregory's works to many later medieval authors.

Paulinus of Milan (late 4th-early 5th century). Personal secretary and biographer of Ambrose of Milan. He took part in the Pelagian controversy.

Paulinus of Nola (355-431). Roman senator and distinguished Latin poet whose frequent encounters with Ambrose of Milan (c. 333-397) led to his eventual conversion and baptism in 389. He eventually renounced his wealth and influential position and took up his pen to write poetry in service of Christ. He also wrote many letters to, among others, Augustine, Jerome and Rufinus.

Paulus Orosius (b. c. 380). An outspoken critic of Pelagius, mentored by Augustine. His *Seven Books of History Against the Pagans* was perhaps the first history of Christianity.

Pelagius (c. 354-c. 420). Contemporary of Augustine whose followers were condemned in 418 and 431 for maintaining that even before Christ there were people who lived wholly without sin and that salvation depended on free will.

Peter Chrysologus (c. 380-450). Latin archbishop of Ravenna whose teachings included arguments for adherence in matters of faith to the Roman see, and the relationship between grace and Christian living.

Peter of Alexandria (d. c. 311). Bishop of Alexandria. He marked (and very probably initiated) the reaction at Alexandria against extreme doctrines of Origen. During the persecution of Christians in Alexandria, Peter was arrested and beheaded by Roman officials. Eusebius of Caesarea described him as "a model bishop, remarkable for his virtuous life and his ardent study of the Scriptures."

Philip the Priest (d. 455/56) Acknowledged by Gennadius as a disciple of Jerome. In his *Commentary on the Book of Job*, Philip utilizes Jerome's Vulgate, providing an important witness to the transmission of that translation. A few of his letters are extant.

Philo of Alexandria (c. 20 B.C.-c. A.D. 50). Jewish-born exegete who greatly influenced Christian patristic interpretation of the Old Testament. Born to a rich family in Alexandria, Philo was a contemporary of Jesus and lived an ascetic and contemplative life that makes some believe he was a rabbi. His interpretation of Scripture based the spiritual sense on the literal. Although influenced by Hellenism, Philo's theology remains thoroughly Jewish.

Philoxenus of Mabbug (c. 440-523). Bishop of Mabbug (Hierapolis) and a leading thinker in the early Syrian Orthodox Church. His extensive writings in Syriac include a set of thirteen *Discourses on the Christian Life*, several works on the incarnation and a number of exegetical works.

Photius (c. 820-891). An important Byzantine churchman and university professor of philosophy, mathematics and theology. He was twice the patriarch of Constantinople. First he succeeded Ignatius in 858, but was deposed in 863 when Ignatius was reinstated. Again he followed Ignatius in 878 and remained the patriarch until 886, at which time he was removed by Leo VI. His most important theological work is *Address on the Mystagogy of the Holy Spirit*, in which he articulates his opposition to the Western filioque, i.e., the procession of the Holy Spirit from the Father and the Son. He is also known for his Amphilochia and Library (Bibliotheca).

Poemen (c. fifth century). One-seventh of the sayings in the *Sayings of the Desert Fathers* are attributed to Poemen, which is Greek for shepherd. Poemen was a common title among early Egyptian desert ascetics, and it is unknown whether all of the sayings come from one person.

Polycarp of Smyrna (c. 69-155). Bishop of Smyrna who vigorously fought heretics such as the Marcionites and Valentinians. He was the leading Christian figure in Roman Asia in the middle of the second century.

Possidius (late fourth-fifth century). A member of Augustine's monastic community at Hippo from 391, then bishop of Calama in Numidia sometime soon after 397. He fled back to Hippo when Vandals invaded Calama in 428 and cared for Augustine during his final illness. Returning to Calama after the death of Augustine (430), he was expelled by Genseric, Arian king of the Vandals, in 437. Nothing more is known of him after this date. Sometime between 432 and 437 he wrote *Vita Augustini*, to which he added *Indiculus*, a list of Augustine's books, sermons and letters.

Potamius of Lisbon (fl. c. 350-360). Bishop of Lisbon who joined the Arian party in 357, but later returned to the Catholic faith (c. 359?). His works from both periods are concerned with the larger Trinitarian debates of his time.

Primasius (fl. 550-560). Bishop of Hadrumetum in North Africa (modern Tunisia) and one of the few Africans to support the condemnation of the Three Chapters. Drawing on Augustine and Tyconius, he wrote a commentary on the Apocalypse, which in allegorizing fashion views the work as referring to the history of the church.

Proclus of Constantinople (c. 390-446). Patriarch of Constantinople (434-446). His patriarchate dealt with the Nestorian controversy, rebutting, in his *Tome to the Armenian Bishops*, Theodore of Mopsuestia's Christology where Theodore was thought to have overly separated the two natures of Christ. Proclus stressed the unity of Christ in his formula "One of the Trinity suffered," which was later taken up and spread by the Scythian monks of the sixth century, resulting in the theopaschite controversy. Proclus was known as a gifted preacher and church politician, extending and expanding Constantinople's influence while avoiding conflict with Antioch, Rome and Alexandria.

Procopius of Gaza (c. 465-c. 530). A Christian exegete educated in Alexandria. He wrote numerous theological works and commentaries on Scripture (particularly the Hebrew Bible), the latter marked by the allegorical exegesis for which the Alexandrian school was known.

Prosper of Aquitaine (c. 390-c. 463). Probably a lay monk and supporter of the theology of Augustine on grace and predestination. He collaborated closely with Pope Leo I in his doctrinal statements.

Prudentius (c. 348-c. 410). Latin poet and hymn-writer who devoted his later life to Christian writing. He wrote didactic poems on the theology of the incarnation, against the heretic Marcion and against the resurgence of paganism.

Pseudo-Clementines (third-fourth century). A series of apocryphal writings pertaining to a conjured life of Clement of Rome. Written in a form of popular legend, the stories from Clement's life, including his opposition to Simon Magus, illustrate and promote articles of Christian teaching. It is likely that the corpus is a derivative of a number of Gnostic and Judeo-Christian writings. Dating the corpus is a complicated issue.

Pseudo-Dionysius the Areopagite (fl. c. 500). Author who assumed the name of Dionysius the Areopagite mentioned in Acts 17:34, and who composed the works known as the *Corpus Areopagiticum* (or *Dionysiacum*). These writings were the foundation of the apophatic school of mysticism in their denial that anything can be truly predicated of God.

Pseudo-Macarius (fl. c. 390). An anonymous writer and ascetic (from Mesopotamia?) active in Antioch whose badly edited works were attributed to Macarius of Egypt. He had keen insight into human nature, prayer and the inner life. His work includes some one hundred discourses and homilies.

Quodvultdeus (fl. 430). Carthaginian bishop and friend of Augustine who endeavored to show at length how the New Testament fulfilled the Old Testament.

Rabanus (Hrabanus) Maurus (c. 780-856). Frankish monk, theologian and teacher, student of Alcuin of York, then Abbot of Fulda from 822 to 842 and Archbishop of Mainz from 848 until his death in 856. The author of poetry, homilies, treatises on education, grammar, and doctrine, and an encyclopedia titled *On the Nature of Things*, he also wrote commentaries on Scripture, including the books of Kings and Esther. Though he is technically an early medieval writer, his works are included as they reflect earlier thought.

Romanus Melodus (fl. c. 536-556). Born as a Jew in Emesa not far from Beirut where after his baptism later he later became deacon of the Church of the Resurrection. He later moved to Constantinople and may have seen the destruction of the Hagia Sophia and its rebuilding during the time he flourished there. As many as eighty metrical sermons (*kontakia*, sg. *kontakion*) that utilize dialogical poetry have come down to us under his name. These sermons were sung rather than preached during the liturgy, and frequently provide theological insights and Scriptural connections often unique to Romanus. His

Christology, closely associated with Justinian, reflects the struggles against the Monophysites of his day.

Rufinus of Aquileia (c. 345-411). Orthodox Christian thinker and historian who nonetheless translated and preserved the works of Origen, and defended him against the strictures of Jerome and Epiphanius. He lived the ascetic life in Rome, Egypt and Jerusalem (the Mount of Olives).

Sabellius (fl. 200). Allegedly the author of the heresy which maintains that the Father and Son are a single person. The patripassian variant of this heresy states that the Father suffered on the cross.

Sahdona (fl. 635-640). Known in Greek as Martyrius, this Syriac author was bishop of Beth Garmai. He studied in Nisibis and was exiled for his christological ideas. His most important work is the deeply scriptural *Book of Perfection* which ranks as one of the masterpieces of Syriac monastic literature.

Salvian the Presbyter of Marseilles (c. 400-c. 480). An important author for the history of his own time. He saw the fall of Roman civilization to the barbarians as a consequence of the reprehensible conduct of Roman Christians. In *The Governance of God* he developed the theme of divine providence.

Second Letter of Clement (c. 150). The so-called *Second Letter of Clement* is an early Christian sermon probably written by a Corinthian author, though some scholars have assigned it to a Roman or Alexandrian author.

Severian of Gabala (fl. c. 400). A contemporary of John Chrysostom, he was a highly regarded preacher in Constantinople, particularly at the imperial court, and ultimately sided with Chrysostom's accusers. He wrote homilies on Genesis.

Severus of Antioch (fl. 488-538). A monophysite theologian, consecrated bishop of Antioch in 522. Born in Pisidia, he studied in Alexandria and Beirut, taught in Constantinople and was exiled to Egypt.

Shenoute (c. 350-466). Abbot of Athribis in Egypt. His large monastic community was known for very strict rules. He accompanied

Cyril of Alexandria to the Council of Ephesus in 431, where he played an important role in deposing Nestorius. He knew Greek but wrote in Coptic, and his literary activity includes homilies, catecheses on monastic subjects, letters, and a couple of theological treatises.

Shepherd of Hermas (second century). Divided into five *Visions,* twelve *Mandates* and ten *Similitudes,* this Christian apocalypse was written by a former slave and named for the form of the second angel said to have granted him his visions. This work was highly esteemed for its moral value and was used as a textbook for catechumens in the early church.

Sulpicius Severus (c. 360-c. 420). An ecclesiastical writer from Bordeaux born of noble parents. Devoting himself to monastic retirement, he became a personal friend and enthusiastic disciple of St. Martin of Tours.

Symeon the New Theologian (c. 949-1022). Compassionate spiritual leader known for his strict rule. He believed that the divine light could be perceived and received through the practice of mental prayer.

Tertullian of Carthage (c. 155/160-225/250; fl. c. 197-222). Brilliant Carthaginian apologist and polemicist who laid the foundations of Christology and trinitarian orthodoxy in the West, though he himself was later estranged from the catholic tradition due to its laxity.

Theodore of Heraclea (d. c. 355). An anti-Nicene bishop of Thrace. He was part of a team seeking reconciliation between Eastern and Western Christianity. In 343 he was excommunicated at the council of Sardica. His writings focus on a literal interpretation of Scripture.

Theodore of Mopsuestia (c. 350-428). Bishop of Mopsuestia, founder of the Antiochene, or literalistic, school of exegesis. A great man in his day, he was later condemned as a precursor of Nestorius.

Theodore of Tabennesi (d. 368) Vice general of the Pachomian monasteries (c. 350-368) under Horsiesi. Several of his letters are known.

Theodoret of Cyr (c. 393-466). Bishop of Cyr (Cyrrhus), he was an opponent of Cyril who commented extensively on Old Testament texts as a lucid exponent of Antiochene exegesis.

Theodotus the Valentinian (second century). Likely a Montanist who may have been related to the Alexandrian school. Extracts of his work are known through writings of Clement of Alexandria.

Theophanes (775-845). Hymnographer and bishop of Nicaea (842-845). He was persecuted during the second iconoclastic period for his support of the Seventh Council (Second Council of Nicaea, 787). He wrote many hymns in the tradition of the monastery of Mar Sabbas that were used in the *Paraklitiki.*

Theophilus of Alexandria (d. 412). Patriarch of Alexandria (385-412) and the uncle of his successor, Cyril. His patriarchate was known for his opposition to paganism, having destroyed the Serapeion and its library in 391, but he also built many churches. He also was known for his political machinations against his theological enemies, especially John Chrysostom, whom he himself had previously consecrated as patriarch, ultimately getting John removed from his see and earning the intense dislike of Antioch Christians. He is, however, venerated among the Copts and Syrians, among whom many of his sermons have survived, although only a few are deemed authentically his. His *Homily on the Mystical Supper,* commenting on the Last Supper, is perhaps one of his most well known.

Theophilus of Antioch (late second century). Bishop of Antioch. His only surviving work is *Ad Autholycum,* where we find the first Christian commentary on Genesis and the first use of the term *Trinity.* Theophilus's apologetic literary heritage had influence on Irenaeus and possibly Tertullian.

Theophylact of Ohrid (c. 1050-c. 1108). Byzantine archbishop of Ohrid (or Achrida) in what is now Bulgaria. Drawing on earlier works, he wrote commentaries on several Old Testament books and all of the New Testament except for Revelation.

Tyconius (c. 330-390). A lay theologian and exegete of the Donatist church in North Africa who influenced Augustine. His *Book of Rules* is the first manual of scriptural interpretation in the Latin West. In 380 he was excommunicated by the Donatist council at Carthage.

Valentinus (fl. c. 140). Alexandrian heretic of the mid-second century who taught that the material world was created by the transgression of God's Wisdom, or Sophia (*see* Gnostics).

Valerian of Cimiez (fl. c. 422-439). Bishop of Cimiez. He participated in the councils of Riez (439) and Vaison (422) with a view to strengthening church discipline. He supported Hilary of Arles in quarrels with Pope Leo I.

Verecundus (d. 552). An African Christian writer, who took an active part in the christological controversies of the sixth century, especially in the debate on Three Chapters. He also wrote allegorical commentaries on the nine liturgical church canticles.

Victorinus of Petovium (d. c. 304). Latin biblical exegete. With multiple works attributed to him, his sole surviving work is the *Commentary on the Apocalypse* and perhaps some fragments from *Commentary on Matthew.* Victorinus expressed strong millenarianism in his writing, though his was less materialistic than the millenarianism of Papias or Irenaeus. In his allegorical approach he could be called a spiritual disciple of Origen. Victorinus died during the first year of Diocletian's persecution, probably in 304.

Vincent of Lérins (d. before 450). Monk who has exerted considerable influence through his writings on orthodox dogmatic theological method, as contrasted with the theological methodologies of the heresies.

Walafridius (Walahfrid) Strabo (808-849). Frankish monk, writer and student of Rabanus Maurus. Walafridius was made abbot of the monastery of Reichenau in 838 but was exiled in 840, when one of the sons of Emperor Louis the Pious—to whom Walafridius was loyal—invaded Reichenau. He was restored in 842 and died in 849. His writings include poetry, commentaries on scripture, lives of saints and a historical explanation of the liturgy. Though he is technically an early medieval writer, his works are included as they reflect earlier thought.

Timeline of Writers of the Patristic Period

Location / Period	British Isles	Gaul	Spain, Portugal	Rome* and Italy	Carthage and Northern Africa
2nd century				Clement of Rome, fl. c. 92-101 (Greek)	
				Shepherd of Hermas, c. 140 (Greek)	
				Justin Martyr (Ephesus, Rome), c. 100/110-165 (Greek)	
		Irenaeus of Lyons, c. 135-c. 202 (Greek)		Valentinus the Gnostic (Rome), fl. c. 140 (Greek)	
				Marcion (Rome), fl. 144 (Greek) Heracleon, 145-180 (Greek)	
3rd century				Callistus of Rome, regn. 217-222 (Latin)	Tertullian of Carthage, c. 155/160-c. 225 (Latin)
				Minucius Felix of Rome, fl. 218-235 (Latin)	
				Hippolytus (Rome, Palestine?), fl. 222-235/245 (Greek)	Cyprian of Carthage, fl. 248-258 (Latin)
				Novatian of Rome, fl. 235-258 (Latin)	
				Victorinus of Petovium, 230-304 (Latin)	

*One of the five ancient patriarchates

Alexandria* and Egypt	Constantinople* and Asia Minor, Greece	Antioch* and Syria	Mesopotamia, Persia	Jerusalem* and Palestine	Location Unknown
Philo of Alexandria, c. 20 B.C. – c. A.D. 50 (Greek)				Flavius Josephus (Rome), c. 37-c. 101 (Greek)	
Basilides (Alexandria), 2nd cent. (Greek)	Polycarp of Smyrna, c. 69-155 (Greek)	*Didache* (Egypt?), c. 100 (Greek)			
Letter of Barnabas (Syria?), c. 130 (Greek)		Ignatius of Antioch, c. 35–107/112 (Greek)			
Theodotus the Valentinian, 2nd cent. (Greek)	Athenagoras (Greece), fl. 176-180 (Greek)	Theophilus of Antioch, c. late 2nd cent. (Greek)			*Second Letter of Clement* (spurious; Corinth, Rome, Alexandria?) (Greek), c. 150
	Melito of Sardis, d.c. 190 (Greek)	*Didascalia Apostolorum*, early 3rd cent. (Syriac)			
Clement of Alexandria, c. 150-215 (Greek)	*Montanist Oracles*, late 2nd cent. (Greek)				
Sabellius (Egypt), 2nd–3rd cent. (Greek)					Pseudo-Clementines 3rd cent. (Greek)
			Mani (Manichaeans), c. 216-276		
Letter to Diognetus, 3rd cent. (Greek)	Gregory Thaumaturgus (Neocaesarea), fl. c. 248-264 (Greek)				
Origen (Alexandria, Caesarea of Palestine), 185-254 (Greek)					
Dionysius of Alexandria, d. 264/5 (Greek)					
	Methodius of Olympus (Lycia), d. c. 311 (Greek)				

Timeline of Writers of the Patristic Period

Location	British Isles	Gaul	Spain, Portugal	Rome* and Italy	Carthage and Northern Africa
Period					
4th century				Firmicus Maternus (Sicily), fl. c. 335 (Latin)	Isaiah of Scete, late 4th cent. (Greek)
		Lactantius, c. 260- 330 (Latin)		Marius Victorinus (Rome), fl. 355-363 (Latin)	
				Eusebius of Vercelli, fl. c. 360 (Latin)	
			Hosius of Cordova, d. 357 (Latin)	Lucifer of Cagliari (Sardinia), d. 370/371 (Latin)	
		Hilary of Poitiers, c. 315-367 (Latin)	Potamius of Lisbon, fl. c. 350-360 (Latin)	Faustinus (Rome), fl. 380 (Latin)	
				Filastrius of Brescia, fl. 380 (Latin)	
			Gregory of Elvira, fl. 359-385 (Latin)	Ambrosiaster (Italy?), fl. c. 366-384 (Latin)	
			Prudentius, c. 348-c. 410 (Latin)	Faustus of Riez, fl. c. 380 (Latin)	
			Pacian of Barcelona, 4th cent. (Latin)	Gaudentius of Brescia, fl. 395 (Latin)	Paulus Orosius, b. c. 380 (Latin)
				Ambrose of Milan, c. 333-397; fl. 374-397 (Latin)	
				Paulinus of Milan, late 4th-early 5th cent. (Latin)	
				Rufinus (Aquileia, Rome), c. 345-411 (Latin)	
5th century	Fastidius (Britain), c. 4th-5th cent. (Latin)	Sulpicius Severus (Bordeaux), c. 360-c. 420/425 (Latin)		Aponius, fl. 405-415 (Latin)	
				Chromatius (Aquileia), fl. 400 (Latin)	
		John Cassian (Palestine, Egypt, Constantinople, Rome, Marseilles), 360-432 (Latin)		Pelagius (Britain, Rome), c. 354-c. 420 (Greek)	Augustine of Hippo, 354-430 (Latin)
				Maximus of Turin, d. 408/423 (Latin)	Possidius, late 4th-5th cent. (Latin)
					Luculentius, 5th cent. (Latin)
		Vincent of Lérins, d. 435 (Latin)		Paulinus of Nola, 355-431 (Latin)	
		Valerian of Cimiez, fl. c. 422-449 (Latin)		Peter Chrysologus (Ravenna), c. 380-450 (Latin)	Quodvultdeus (Carthage), fl. 430 (Latin)
		Eucherius of Lyons, fl. 420-449 (Latin)		Julian of Eclanum, 386-454 (Latin)	

*One of the five ancient patriarchates

Alexandria* and Egypt	Constantinople* and Asia Minor, Greece	Antioch* and Syria	Mesopotamia, Persia	Jerusalem* and Palestine	Location Unknown
Antony, c. 251-355 (Coptic /Greek)	Theodore of Heraclea (Thrace), fl. c. 330-355 (Greek)	Eustathius of Antioch, fl. 325 (Greek)	Aphrahat (Persia) c. 270-350; fl. 337-345 (Syriac)	Eusebius of Caesarea (Palestine), c. 260/ 263-340 (Greek)	Commodius, c. 3rd or 5th cent. (Latin)
Peter of Alexandria, d. c. 311 (Greek)	Marcellus of Ancyra, d.c. 375 (Greek)	Eusebius of Emesa, c. 300-c. 359 (Greek)			
Arius (Alexandria), fl. c. 320 (Greek)	Epiphanius of Salamis (Cyprus), c. 315-403 (Greek)	Ephrem the Syrian, c. 306-373 (Syriac)	Jacob of Nisibis, fl. 308-325 (Syriac)		
Alexander of Alexandria, fl. 312-328 (Greek)	Basil (the Great) of Caesarea, b. c. 330; fl. 357-379 (Greek)	Julian the Arian (c. fourth century)			
Pachomius, c. 292-347 (Coptic/Greek?)	Macrina the Younger, c. 327-379 (Greek)				
Theodore of Tabennesi, d. 368 (Coptic/Greek)	Apollinaris of Laodicea, 310-c. 392 (Greek)				
Horsiesi, c. 305-390 (Coptic/Greek)	Gregory of Nazianzus, b. 329/330; fl. 372-389 (Greek)	Nemesius of Emesa (Syria), fl. late 4th cent. (Greek)			Maximinus, b.c. 360-365 (Latin)
Athanasius of Alexandria, c. 295-373; fl. 325-373 (Greek)	Gregory of Nyssa, c. 335-394 (Greek)	Diodore of Tarsus, d. c. 394 (Greek)		Acacius of Caesarea (Palestine), d. c. 365 (Greek)	
Macarius of Egypt, c. 300-c. 390 (Greek)	Amphilochius of Iconium, c. 340/345- c. 398/404 (Greek)	John Chrysostom (Constantinople), 344/354-407 (Greek)		Cyril of Jerusalem, c. 315-386 (Greek)	
Didymus (the Blind) of Alexandria, 313-398 (Greek)	Evagrius of Pontus, 345-399 (Greek)	Apostolic Constitutions, c. 375-400 (Greek)			
Tyconius, c. 330-390 (Latin)	Eunomius of Cyzicus, fl. 360-394 (Greek)	Didascalia, 4th cent. (Syriac) Theodore of Mopsuestia, c. 350-428 (Greek)			
Ammonas, 4th cent. (Syriac)	Pseudo-Macarius (Mesopotamia?), late 4th cent. (Greek)	Acacius of Beroea, c. 340-c. 436 (Greek)		Diodore of Tarsus, d. c. 394 (Greek)	
Theophilus of Alexandria, d. 412 (Greek)	Nicetas of Remesiana, d. c. 414 (Latin)			Jerome (Rome, Antioch, Bethlehem), c. 347-420 (Latin)	
Palladius of Helenopolis (Egypt), c. 365-425 (Greek)	Proclus of Constantinople, c. 390-446 (Greek) Nestorius (Constantinople), c. 381-c. 451 (Greek)	Book of Steps, c. 400 (Syriac) Severian of Gabala, fl. c. 400 (Greek)	Eznik of Kolb, fl. 430-450 (Armenian)		
Cyril of Alexandria, 375-444 (Greek)				Philip the Priest (d. 455/56)	
	Basil of Seleucia, fl. 440-468 (Greek)	Nilus of Ancyra, d.c. 430 (Greek)		Hesychius of Jerusalem, fl. 412-450 (Greek)	
	Diadochus of Photice (Macedonia), 400-474 (Greek)			Euthymius (Palestine), 377-473 (Greek)	

Timeline of Writers of the Patristic Period

Location Period	British Isles	Gaul	Spain, Portugal	Rome* and Italy	Carthage and Northern Africa
5th century (cont.)		Hilary of Arles, c. 401-449 (Latin) Eusebius of Gaul, 5th cent. (Latin) Prosper of Aquitaine, c. 390-c. 463 (Latin) Salvian the Presbyter of Marseilles, c. 400-c. 480 (Latin) Gennadius of Marseilles, d. after 496 (Latin)		Leo the Great (Rome), regn. 440-461 (Latin) Arnobius the Younger (Rome), fl. c. 450 (Latin) Ennodius (Arles, Milan, Pavia) c. 473-521 (Latin) Epiphanius the Latin, late 5th–early 6th cent. (Latin)	
6th century		Caesarius of Arles, c. 470-543 (Latin) Flavian of Chalon-sur-Saône, fl. 580-600 (Latin)	Paschasius of Dumium (Portugal), c. 515-c. 580 (Latin) Apringius of Beja, mid-6th cent. (Latin) Leander of Seville, c. 545-c. 600 (Latin) Martin of Braga, fl. 568-579 (Latin)	Eugippius, c. 460- c. 533 (Latin) Benedict of Nursia, c. 480-547 (Latin) Cassiodorus (Calabria), c. 485-c. 540 (Latin) Gregory the Great (Rome), c. 540-604 (Latin) Gregory of Agrigentium, d. 592 (Greek)	Fulgentius of Ruspe, c. 467-532 (Latin) Verecundus, d. 552 (Latin) Primasius, fl. 550-560 (Latin) Facundus of Hermiane, fl. 546-568 (Latin)
7th century	Adamnan, c. 624-704 (Latin)		Isidore of Seville, c. 560-636 (Latin) Braulio of Saragossa, c. 585-651 (Latin) Fructuosus of Braga, d.c. 665 (Latin)	Paterius, 6th/7th cent. (Latin)	
8th-12th century	Bede the Venerable, c. 672/673-735 (Latin)	Rabanus Maurus (Frankish), c. 780-856 (Latin) Walafridius Strabo (Frankish), 808-849 (Latin)			

*One of the five ancient patriarchates

Alexandria* and Egypt	Constantinople* and Asia Minor, Greece	Antioch* and Syria	Mesopotamia, Persia	Jerusalem* and Palestine	Location Unknown
Ammonius of Alexandria, c. 460 (Greek)	Gennadius of Constantinople, d. 471 (Greek)	John of Antioch, d. 441/2 (Greek)		Gerontius of Petra c. 395-c. 480 (Syriac)	
Poemen, 5th cent. (Greek)		Theodoret of Cyr, c. 393-466 (Greek)			
		Pseudo-Victor of Antioch, 5th cent. (Greek)			
Besa the Copt, 5th cent.					
Shenoute, c. 350-466 (Coptic)		John of Apamea, 5th cent. (Syriac)			
	Andrew of Caesarea (Cappadocia), early 6th cent. (Greek)				
Olympiodorus, early 6th cent.	Oecumenius (Isauria), 6th cent. (Greek)	Philoxenus of Mabbug (Syria), c. 440-523 (Syriac)	Jacob of Sarug, c. 450-520 (Syriac)	Procopius of Gaza (Palestine), c. 465-530 (Greek)	Pseudo-Dionysius the Areopagite, fl. c. 500 (Greek)
	Romanus Melodus, fl. c. 536-556 (Greek)	Severus of Antioch, c. 465-538 (Greek)	Abraham of Nathpar, fl. 6th-7th cent. (Syriac)	Dorotheus of Gaza, fl. 525-540 (Greek)	
		Mark the Hermit (Tarsus), c. 6th cent. (4th cent.?) (Greek)	Babai the Great, c. 550-628 (Syriac)	Cyril of Scythopolis, b. c. 525; d. after 557 (Greek)	
			Babai, early 6th cent. (Syriac)		
	Maximus the Confessor (Constantinople), c. 580-662 (Greek)	Sahdona/Martyrius, fl. 635-640 (Syriac)	Isaac of Nineveh, d. c. 700 (Syriac)		(Pseudo-) Constantius, before 7th cent.? (Greek)
	Andrew of Crete, c. 660-740 (Greek)			Cosmas Melodus, c. 675-751 (Greek)	Andreas, c. 7th cent. (Greek)
	John of Carpathus, 7th-8th cent. (Greek)	John of Damascus (John the Monk), c. 650-750 (Greek)	John the Elder of Qardu (north Iraq), 8th cent. (Syriac)		
	Theophanes (Nicaea), 775-845 (Greek)		Isho'dad of Merv, d. after 852 (Syriac)		
	Cassia (Constantinople), c. 805-c. 848/867 (Greek)				
	Arethas of Caesarea (Constantinople/Caesarea), c. 860-940 (Greek)				
	Photius (Constantinople), c. 820-891 (Greek)				
	Symeon the New Theologian (Constantinople), 949-1022 (Greek)				
	Theophylact of Ohrid (Bulgaria), 1050-1126 (Greek)				

This bibliography refers readers to original language sources and supplies Thesaurus Linguae Graecae (=TLG) or Cetedoc Clavis (=Cl.) numbers where available. The edition listed in this bibliography may in some cases differ from the edition found in TLG or Cetedoc databases.

Ambrose. "De Cain et Abel." In *Sancti Ambrosii opera*. Edited by Karl Schenkl. CSEL 32, pt. 1, pp. 337-409. Vienna, Austria: F. Tempsky; Leipzig, Germany: G. Freytag, 1897. Cl. 0125.

———. "De fuga saeculi." In *Sancti Ambrosii opera*. Edited by Karl Schenkl. CSEL 32, pt. 2, pp. 163-207. Vienna, Austria: F. Tempsky; Leipzig, Germany: G. Freytag, 1897. Cl. 0133.

———. "De Helia et jejunio." In *Sancti Ambrosii opera*. Edited by Karl Schenkl. CSEL 32, pt. 2, pp. 409-65. Vienna, Austria: F. Tempsky; Leipzig, Germany: G. Freytag, 1897. Cl. 0137.

———. "De interpellatione Job et David." In *Sancti Ambrosii opera*. Edited by Karl Schenkl. CSEL 32, pt. 2, pp. 211-96. Vienna, Austria: F. Tempsky; Leipzig, Germany: G. Freytag, 1897. Cl. 0134.

———. "De Jacob et vita beata." In *Sancti Ambrosii opera*. Edited by Karl Schenkl. CSEL 32, pt. 2, pp. 1-70. Vienna, Austria: F. Tempsky; Leipzig, Germany: G. Freytag, 1897. Cl. 0130.

———. "De Nabuthae." In *Sancti Ambrosii opera omnia*. Edited by J.-P. Migne. PL 14, cols. 765-792. Paris: Migne, 1882. Cl. 0138.

———. "De obitu Theodosii." In *Sancti Ambrosii opera*. Edited by Otto Faller. CSEL 73, pp. 371-401. Vienna, Austria: Hoelder-Pichler-Tempsky, 1955. Cl. 0159.

———. "De obitu Valentiniani." In *Sancti Ambrosii opera*. Edited by Otto Faller. CSEL 73, pp. 329-67. Vienna, Austria: Hoelder-Pichler-Tempsky, 1955. Cl. 0158.

———. "De officiis ministrorum." In *De officiis*. Edited by Maurice Testard. CCL 15. Turnhout, Belgium: Brepols, 2000. Cl. 0144.

———. "De virginitate." In *Opere II/2: Verginità e vedovanza*. Edited by F. Gori. Opera omnia di Sant'Ambrogio 14.2, pp. 16-106. Milan: Biblioteca Ambrosiana; Rome: Città nuova, 1989. Cl. 0147.

———. "Epistulae; Epistulae extra collectionem traditae." In *Sancti Ambrosii opera*. Edited by Otto Faller and Michaela Zelzer. CSEL 82. 4 vols. Vienna, Austria: F. Tempsky; Leipzig, Germany: G. Freytag, 1968-1990. Cl. 0160.

Analecta Hymnica Graeca, vol. 10: Canones Junii. Rome: Istituto di Studi Bizantini e Neoellenici, 1972. TLG 4354.010.

Aphrahat. "Demonstrationes (IV)." In *Opera omnia*. Edited by R. Graffin. PS 1, cols. 137-82. Paris: Firmin-Didor, 1910.

Athanasius. "Apologia ad Constantium imperatorem." In *Athanase d'Alexandrie: Apologie à l'empereur Constance. Apologie pour sa fuite*. Edited by J.-M. Szymusiak. SC 56, pp. 88-132. Paris: Cerf, 1958. TLG 2035.011.

———. "Epistulae festales." In *Opera omnia*. Edited by J.-P. Migne. PG 26, cols. 1351-1444. Paris: Migne, 1887. TLG 2035.014.

———. "Orationes tres contra Arianos." In *Opera omnia*. Edited by J.-P. Migne. PG 26, cols. 813-920.

Paris: Migne, 1887. TLG 2035.042.

▬▬▬. "Vita sancti Antonii." In *Opera omnia*. Edited by J.-P. Migne. PG 26, cols. 835-976. Paris: Migne, 1887. TLG 2035.047.

Augustine. "Contra duas epistulas pelagianorum." In *Sancti Aureli Augustini Opera*. Edited by Karl Franz Urba and Joseph Zycha. CSEL 60, pp. 423-570. Vienna, Austria: F. Tempsky; Leipzig, Germany: G. Freytag, 1913. Cl. 0346.

▬▬▬. "Contra Julianum." In *Augustini opera omnia*. Edited by J.-P. Migne. PL 44, cols. 641-874. Paris: Migne, 1845. Cl. 0351.

▬▬▬. "Contra mendacium." In *Sancti Aureli Augustini Opera*. Edited by J. Zycha. CSEL 41, pp. 469-528. Vienna, Austria: F. Tempsky, 1900. Cl. 0304.

▬▬▬. *De civitate Dei*. In *Aurelii Augustini Opera*. Edited by Bernhard Dombart and Alphons Kalb. CCL 47 and 48. Turnhout, Belgium: Brepols, 1955. Cl. 0313.

▬▬▬. "De corruptione et gratia." In *Augustini opera omnia*. Edited by J.-P. Migne. PL 44, cols. 915-46. Paris: Migne, 1845. Cl. 0353.

▬▬▬. "De cura pro moruis gerenda." In *Sancti Aureli Augustini Opera*. Edited by J. Zycha. CSEL 41, pp. 621-59. Vienna, Austria: F. Tempsky, 1900. Cl. 0307.

▬▬▬. "De doctrina christiana." In *Aurelii Augustini opera*. Edited by Joseph Martin. CCL 32, pp. 1-167. Turnhout, Belgium: Brepols, 1962. Cl. 0263.

▬▬▬. "De gratia et libero arbitrio." In *Augustini opera omnia*. Edited by J.-P. Migne. PL 44, cols. 881-912. Paris: Migne, 1845. Cl. 0352.

▬▬▬. "De natura et origene animae." In *Sancti Aureli Augustini Opera*. Edited by Karl Franz Urba and Joseph Zycha. CSEL 60, pp. 303-419. Vienna, Austria: F. Tempsky; Leipzig, Germany: G. Freytag, 1913. Cl. 0345.

▬▬▬. "De octo Dulcitii quaestionibus." In *Aurelii Augustini opera*. Edited by Almut Mutzenbecher. CCL 44A, pp. 253-97. Turnhout, Belgium: Brepols, 1975. Cl. 0291.

▬▬▬. "De praedestinatione sanctorum." In *Augustini opera omnia*. Edited by J.-P. Migne. PL 44, cols. 959-92. Paris: Migne, 1845. Cl. 0354.

▬▬▬. *Enarrationes in Psalmos*. In *Aurelii Augustini opera*. Edited by Eligius Dekkers and John Fraipont. CCL 38, 39 and 40. Turnhout, Belgium: Brepols, 1956. Cl. 0283.

▬▬▬. *Epistulae 31-123*. In *Sancti Aureli Augustini Opera*. Edited by A. Goldbacher. CSEL 34. Vienna, Austria: F. Tempsky; Leipzig, Germany: G. Freytag, 1898. Cl. 0262.

▬▬▬. *Epistulae 185-270*. In *Sancti Aureli Augustini Opera*. Edited by A. Goldbacher. CSEL 57. Vienna, Austria: F. Tempsky; Leipzig, Germany: G. Freytag, 1911. Cl. 0262.

▬▬▬. *Sermones*. In *Augustini opera omnia*. Edited by J.-P. Migne. PL 38 and 39. Paris: Migne, 1845. Cl. 0284.

Basil the Great. "De humilitate." In *Opera omnia*. Edited by J.-P. Migne. PG 31, cols. 525-40. Paris: Migne, 1885. TLG 2040.036.

▬▬▬. "Epistulae." *Saint Basile: Lettres*. Edited by Yves Courtonne. Vol. 1, pp. 3-219; Vol. 2, pp. 101-218; Vol. 3, pp. 1-229. Paris: Les Belles Lettres, 1957-1966. TLG 2040.004.

▬▬▬. "Homiliae super Psalmos." In *Opera omnia*. Edited by J.-P. Migne. PG 29, cols. 209-494. Paris: Migne, 1857. TLG 2040.018.

Bede. "De templo libri ii." In *Opera*. Edited by D. Hurst. CCL 119A, pp. 140-234. Turnhout, Belgium: Brepols, 1969. Cl. 1348.

▬▬▬. "Homiliarum evangelii." In *Opera*. Edited by D. Hurst. CCL 122, pp. 1-378. Turnhout, Belgium: Brepols, 1956. Cl. 1367.

▬▬▬. "In Esdram et Nehemiam Prophetas Allegorica Expositio." In *Opera*. Edited by D. Hurst. CCL

119A, pp. 235-392. Turnhout, Belgium: Brepols, 1969. Cl. 1349.

———. "Retractatio in Actus apostolorum." In *Opera*. Edited by M. L. W. Laistner and D. Hurst. CCL 121, pp. 103-63. Turnhout, Belgium: Brepols, 1983. Cl. 1358.

Caesarius of Arles. *Sermones Caesarii Arelatensis*. Edited by Germain Morin. CCL 103 and 104. Turnhout, Belgium: Brepols, 1953. Cl. 1008.

Cassian, John. *Collationes xxiv*. Edited by Michael Petschenig. CSEL 13. Vienna, Austria: F. Tempsky; Leipzig, Germany: G. Freytag, 1886. Cl. 0512.

———. "De institutis coenobiorum et de octo principalium vitiorum remediis." In *Johannis Cassiani*. Edited by Michael Petschenig. CSEL 17, pp. 1-231. Vienna, Austria: F. Tempsky; Leipzig, Germany: G. Freytag, 1888. Cl. 0513.

Cassiodorus. *Expositio psalmorum*. Edited by Mark Adriaen. CCL 97 and 98. Turnhout, Belgium: Brepols, 1958. Cl. 0900.

Clement of Alexandria. "Fragmenta." In *Clemens Alexandrinus*. Vol. 3, 2nd ed. Edited by Otto Stählin, Ludwig Früchtel and Ursula Treu. GCS 17, pp. 193-230. Berlin: Akademie-Verlag, 1970. TLG 0555.008.

———. "Paedagogus." In *Clement d'Alexandrie: Le pédagogue*. Edited by Mauguerite Harl, Chantel Matray and Claude Mondésert. Introduction and notes by Henri-Irénée Marrou. SC 70, pp. 108-294; SC 108, pp. 10-242; SC 158, pp. 12-190. Paris: Éditions du Cerf, 1960-1970. TLG 0555.002.

———. "Stromata." In *Clemens Alexandrinus*. Vol. 2, 3rd ed., and vol. 3, 2nd ed. Edited by Otto Stählin, Ludwig Früchtel and Ursula Treu. GCS 52, pp. 3-518, and GCS 17, pp. 1-102. Berlin: Akademie-Verlag, 1960-1970. TLG 0555.004.

Clement of Rome. "Epistula i ad Corinthios." In *Clément de Rome: Épître aux Corinthiens*. Edited by Annie Jaubert. SC 167. Paris: Éditions du Cerf, 1971. TLG 1271.001.

Constitutiones apostolorum. See *Les constitutions apostoliques*. Edited by Marcel Metzger. SC 320, 329 and 336. Paris: Éditions du Cerf, 1985-1987. TLG 2894.001.

Cyprian. "Ad Fortunatum." In *Sancti Cypriani episcopi opera*. Edited by R. Weber. CCL 3, pp. 183-216. Turnhout, Belgium: Brepols, 1972. Cl. 0045.

———. "De dominica oratione." In *Sancti Cypriani episcopi opera*. Edited by Claudio Moreschini. CCL 3A, pp. 87-113. Turnhout, Belgium: Brepols, 1976. Cl. 0043.

———. "De ecclesiae catholicae unitate." In *Sancti Cypriani episcopi opera*. Edited by Maurice Bévenot. CCL 3, pp. 249-68. Turnhout, Belgium: Brepols, 1972. Cl. 0041.

———. *Epistulae*. Edited by Gerardus Frederik Diercks. CCL 3B and 3C. Turnhout, Belgium: Brepols, 1994-1996. Cl. 0050.

Cyril of Jerusalem. "Catecheses ad illuminandos 1-18." In *Cyrilli Hierosolymorum archiepiscopi opera quae supersunt omnia*. Edited by W. C. Reischl and J. Rupp. Vol. 1, pp. 28-320; Vol. 2, pp. 2-342. Munich: Lentner, 1848 and 1860. Reprinted, Hildesheim: Olms, 1967. TLG 2110.003.

———. "Mystagogiae 1-5" [Sp.]. In *Cyrille de Jérusalem: Catéchèses, mystagogigues*. 2nd Edition. SC 126, pp. 82-174. Edited by Auguste Piédagnel. Paris: Éditions du Cerf, 1988. TLG 2110.002.

Ephrem the Syrian. "Homily on the Solitaries." In *Des Heiligen Ephraem des Syrers, Sermones 4*. Edited by E. Beck. CSCO 334, pp. 16-28. Leuven: Secrétariat du CSCO, 1973.

———. *Hymnen de fide*. Edited by Edmund Beck. CSCO 154 and 155. (Scriptores Syri 73-74). Leuven: Secrétariat du CSCO, 1955.

———. "Hymni de Paradiso." In *Des Heiligen Ephraem des Syrers Hymnen de Paradiso und Contra Julianum*. Edited by Edmund Beck. CSCO 174 (Scriptores Syri 78), pp. 1-66. Louvain: Imprimerie Orientaliste L. Durbecq, 1957.

———. "In Primum Librum Regnorum." In *Sancti patris nostri Ephraem Syri Opera omnia*, pp. 439-516. Edited by J. A. Assemani. Rome, 1737.

———. "In Secundum Librum Regnorum." In *Sancti patris nostri Ephraem Syri Opera omnia*, pp. 517-67. Edited by J. A. Assemani. Rome, 1737.

———. "In Tatiani Diatessaron." In *Saint Éphrem: Commentaire de l'Évangile Concordant—Text Syriaque (Ms Chester-Beatty 709)*. Vol. 2. Edited by Louis Leloir. Leuven and Paris: Peeters Press, 1990.

Eusebius of Caesarea. "Demonstratio evangelica." In *Eusebius Werke, Band 6: Die Demonstratio evangelica*. Edited by Ivar A. Heikel. GCS 23. Leipzig: Hinrichs, 1913. TLG 2018.005.

Fulgentius of Ruspe. "Liber ad Scarilam de incarnatione filii dei et vilium animalium autore." In *Sancti Fulgentii episcopi Ruspensis opera*. Edited by John Fraipont. CCL 91, pp. 312-56. Turnhout, Belgium: Brepols, 1968. Cl. 0822.

Gregory of Nazianzus. "De theologia (orat. 28)." In *Gregor von Nazianz: Die fünf theologischen Reden*, pp. 62-126. Edited by Joseph Barbel. Düsseldorf: Patmos-Verlag, 1963. TLG 2022.008.

———. "In sancta lumina (orat. 39)." In *Opera omnia*. Edited by J.-P. Migne. PG 36, cols. 336-60. Paris: Migne, 1858. TLG 2022.047.

———. "Supremum vale." In *Opera omnia*. Edited by J.-P. Migne. PG 36, cols. 457-92. Paris: Migne, 1858. TLG 2022.050.

Gregory the Great. "Dialogorum libri iv." In *Dialogues*. Edited by Paul Antin and Adalbert de Vogüé. SC 251, 260 and 265. Paris: Éditions du Cerf, 1978-1980. Cl. 1713.

———. *Moralia in Job*. Edited by Mark Adriaen. CCL 143, 143A and 143B. Turnhout, Belgium: Brepols, 1979-1985. Cl. 1708.

———. *Registrum epistularum*. Edited by Dag Norberg. CCL 140 and 140A. Turnhout, Belgium: Brepols, 1982. Cl. 1714.

Hippolytus. "Fragmenta in Proverbia." In *Hippolyt's kleinere exegetische und homiletische Schriften*. Edited by Hans Achelis. GCS 1, pp. 157-67, 176-78. Leipzig: Hinrichs, 1897. TLG 2115.013.

Isaac of Nineveh. "Discourses." In *Mar Isaacus Ninivita de Perfectione Religiosa*, pp. 1-99. Edited by P. Bedjan. Paris-Leipzig, 1909.

Isho'dad of Merv. "Books of Sessions." In *Commentaire d'IÜo'dad de Merv sur l'Ancien Testament. III. Livres de Sessions*. Edited by C. Van Den Eynde. CSCO 229 (ScriptoresSyri 96), pp. 97-151. Leuven: Sécretariat du CSCO, 1962.

Jerome. "Adversus Jovinianum." In *Opera omnia*. Edited by J.-P. Migne. PL 23, cols. 211-338. Paris: Migne, 1865. Cl. 0610.

———. *Dialogus adversus Pelagianos*. Edited by Claudio Moreschini. CCL 80. Turnhout, Belgium: Brepols, 1990. Cl. 0615.

———. *Epistulae*. Edited by I. Hilberg. CSEL 54, 55 and 56. Vienna, Austria: F. Tempsky; Leipzig, Germany: G. F. Freytag, 1910-1918. Cl. 0620.

———. "Tractatus lix in psalmos." In *S. Hieronymi presbyteri Opera*. Edited by Germain Morin. CCL 78, pp. 3-352. Turnhout, Belgium: Brepols, 1958. Cl. 0592.

———. "Tractatuum in psalmos series altera." In *S. Hieronymi presbyteri Opera*. Edited by Germain Morin. CCL 78, pp. 355-446. Turnhout, Belgium: Brepols, 1958. Cl. 0593.

John Chrysostom. "Ad Theodorum lapsum (lib. 1)." In *Jean Chrysostome: A Théodore*. Edited by J. Dumortier. SC 117, pp. 80-218. Paris: Éditions du Cerf, 1966. TLG 2062.002.

———. "Adversus Judaeos (orationes 1-8)." In *Opera omnia*. Edited by J.-P. Migne. PG 48, cols. 843-942. Paris: Migne, 1862. TLG 2062.021.

———. "De incomprehensibili dei natura (& Contra Anomoeos, homiliae 1-5)." In *Jean Chrysostome. Sur l'incompréhensibilité de Dieu*. Edited by A.-M. Malingrey. SC 28 bis., pp. 92-322. Paris: Éditions du Cerf, 1970. TLG 2062.012.

———. "In epistulam ad Hebraeos (homiliae 1-34)." In *Opera omnia*. Edited by J.-P. Migne. PG 63, cols. 9-236. Paris: Migne, 1862. TLG 2062.168.

———. "In Genesim (homiliae 1-67)." In *Opera omnia*. Edited by J.-P. Migne. PG 53; PG 54, cols. 385-580. Paris: Migne, 1859-1862. TLG 2062.112.

———. "In Joannem (homiliae 1-88)." In *Opera omnia*. Edited by J.-P. Migne. PG 59, cols. 23-482. Paris: Migne, 1862. TLG 2062.153.

———. "In Matthaeum (homiliae 1-90)." In *Opera omnia*. Edited by J.-P. Migne. PG 57, cols. 13-472; PG 58, cols. 471-794. Paris: Migne, 1862. TLG 2062.152.

———. "In sanctum Ignatium martyrem." In *Opera omnia*. Edited by J.-P. Migne. PG 50, cols. 587-96. Paris: Migne, 1862. TLG 2062.044.

John of Damascus. "Oratio apologetica adversus eos, qui sacras imagines abiciunt." In *Opera omnia*. Edited by J.-P. Migne. PG 94, cols. 1227-1420. Paris: Migne, 1862. TLG 2934.004.

John the Monk. See *Analecta Hymnica Graeca*.

Justin Martyr. "Apologia." In *Die ältesten Apologeten*, pp. 26-77. Edited by E. J. Goodspeed. Göttingen: Vandenhoeck & Ruprecht, 1915. TLG 0645.001.

———. "Dialogus cum Tryphone." In *Die ältesten Apologeten*, pp. 90-265. Edited by E. J. Goodspeed. Göttingen: Vandenhoeck & Ruprecht, 1915. TLG 0645.003.

Lactantius. "Divinae Institutiones." In *L. Caeli Firmiani Lactanti Opera omnia*. Edited by Samuel Brandt. CSEL 19, pp. 1-672. Vienna, Austria: F. Tempsky; Leipzig, Germany: G. Freytag, 1890. Cl. 0085.

Maximus of Turin. *Collectio sermonum antiqua*. Edited by Almut Mutzenbecher. CCL 23. Turnhout, Belgium: Brepols, 1962. Cl. 0219a.

Methodius. "Symposium *sive* Convivium decem virginum." In *Opera omnia*. Edited by J.-P. Migne. PG 18, cols. 27-220. Paris: Migne, 1857. TLG 2959.001.

Novatian. "De Trinitate." In *Opera*. Edited by Gerardus Frederik Diercks. CCL 4, pp. 11-78. Turnhout, Belgium: Brepols, 1972. Cl. 0071.

Origen. "Commentarium in Canticum Canticorum." In *Origenes Werke*. Vol. 8. Edited by William A. Baehrens. GCS 33, pp. 61-241. Leipzig: Teubner, 1925. Cl. 0198.

———. "Commentarii in evangelium Joannis (lib. 1, 2, 4, 5, 6, 10, 13)." In *Origene. Commentaire sur saint Jean*. Edited by Cécil Blanc. SC 120, 157 and 222. Paris: Éditions du Cerf, 1966-1975. TLG 2042.005.

———. "Commentarium in evangelium Matthaei (lib. 12-17)." In *Origenes Werke*. Vol. 10.1-10.2. Edited by E. Klostermann. GCS 40.1, pp. 69-304; GCS 40.2, pp. 305-703. Leipzig: Teubner, 1935, 1937. TLG 2042.030.

———. "Contra Celsum." In *Origène Contre Celse*. Edited by M. Borret. SC 132, pp. 64-476; SC 136, pp. 14-434; SC 147, pp. 14-382; SC 150, pp. 14-352. Paris: Éditions du Cerf, 1967-1969. TLG 2042.001.

———. "De oratione." In *Origenes Werke*. Vol. 2. Edited by Paul Koetschau. GCS 3, pp. 297-403. Leipzig: Hinrichs, 1899. TLG 2042.008.

———. "De principiis." In *Origenes Werke*. Vol. 5. Edited by Paul Koetschau. GCS 22. Leipzig: Hinrichs, 1913. Cl. 0198 E (A). TLG 2042.002.

———. "Epistula ad Africanum." In *Opera omnia*. Edited by J.-P. Migne. PG 11, cols. 48-85. Paris: Migne, 1857. TLG 2042.045.

———. "Fragmenta in Jeremiam (in catenis)." In *Origenes Werke*. Vol. 3. Edited by E. Klostermann. GCS 6, pp. 199-232. Leipzig: Hinrichs, 1901. TLG 2042.010.

———. "Homiliae in Genesim." In *Origenes Werke*. Vol. 6. Edited by W. A. Baehrens. GCS (CB) 29, pp. 23-30. Leipzig: Teubner, 1920. Cl. 0198 6 (A). TLG 2042.022.

———. "In Jeremiam (homiliae 1-11)." In *Origène: Homélies sur Jérémie*. Vol. 1. Edited by Pierre Nautin. SC 232, pp. 196-430. Paris: Éditions du Cerf, 1976. TLG 2042.009.

————. "In Jeremiam (homiliae 12-20)." In *Origenes Werke*. Vol. 3. Edited by E. Klostermann. GCS 6, pp. 85-194. Leipzig: Hinrichs, 1901. TLG 2042.021.

————. "In Jeremiam (homiliae 12-20 and *Homélies latines*)." In *Origène: Homélies sur Jérémie*. Vol. 2. Edited by Pierre Nautin. SC 238. Paris: Éditions du Cerf, 1977.

————. "Homiliae in Leviticum." In *Origenes Werke*. Vol. 6. Edited by W. A. Baehrens. GCS (CB) 29, pp. 280-507. Leipzig: Teubner, 1920. Cl. 0198 3 (A). TLG 2042.024.

————. "Homiliae in Lucam." In *Opera omnia*. Edited by J.-P. Migne. PG 13, cols. 1799-1902. Paris: Migne, 1862. TLG 2042.016.

Paulinus of Nola. "Carmina." In *Sancti Pontii Meropii Paulini Nolani Carmina*. Edited by W. Hartel. CSEL 30, pp. 1-3, 7-329. Vienna, Austria: F. Tempsky, 1894. Cl. 0203.

Peter Chrysologus. "Collectio sermonum." In *Opera omnia*. Edited by J.-P. Migne. PL 52, cols. 183-680. Paris: Migne, 1859. Cl. 0227+.

Procopius of Gaza. "Commentarii in Libros Paralipomenon." In *Procopii Gazaei*. Edited by J.-P. Migne. PG 87, cols. 1201-1220. Paris: Migne, 1860.

Prudentius. "Psychomachia." In *Aurelii Prudentii Clementis Carmina*. Edited by Mauricii P. Cunningham. CCL 126, pp. 149-81. Turnhout, Belgium: Brepols, 1966. Cl. 1441.

Pseudo-Dionysius. "Epistulae." In *Corpus Dionysiacum ii: Pseudo-Dionysius Areopagita. De coelesti hierarchia, de ecclesiastica hierarchia, de mystica theologia, epistulae*. Edited by G. Heil and A. M. Ritter. PTS 36, pp. 155-210. Berlin: De Gruyter, 1991. TLG 2798.006.

Pseudo-Tertullian. "Carmen Adversus Marcionem." In *Tertulliani opera*. Edited by R. Willems. CCL 2, pp. 1421-54. Turnhout, Belgium: Brepols, 1954. Cl. 0036.

Rabanus Maurus. "Commentaria in libros IV Regum." In *Opera omnia*. Edited by J.-P. Migne. PL 109, cols. 9-280. Paris: Migne, 1864.

————. "Expositio in librum Esther." In *Opera omnia*. Edited by J.-P. Migne. PL 109, cols. 635-70. Paris: Migne, 1864.

Sahdona. "Book of Perfection." In *Martyrius (Sahdona): Oeuvres spirituelles*, part 2. Edited by André de Halleux. CSCO 252 (Scriptores Syri 110). Leuven, Belgium: Secrétariat du CSCO, 1965.

Salvian the Presbyter. "De gubernatione Dei." In *Ouvres*. Vol. II. Edited by G. Lagarrigue. SC 220, pp. 95-527. Paris: Éditions du Cerf, 1975. Cl. 0485.

Tertullian. "Adversus Judaeos." In *Tertulliani opera*. Edited by E. Kroymann. CCL 2, pp. 1339-96. Turnhout, Belgium: Brepols, 1954. Cl. 0033.

————. "De jejunio adversus psychicos." In *Tertulliani opera*. Edited by A. Reifferscheid and G. Wissowa. CCL 2, pp. 1257-77. Turnhout, Belgium: Brepols, 1954. Cl. 0029.

Theodoret of Cyr. "Explanatio in Canticum canticorum." In *Opera omnia*. Edited by J.-P. Migne. PG 81, cols. 28-213. Paris: Migne, 1864. TLG 4089.025.

————. "De quaestionibus ambiguis in Libros Regnorum et Paralipomenon." In *Theodoreti Cyrensis episcopi Opera omnia*. Edited by J.-P. Migne. PG 80, cols. 527-858. Paris: Migne, 1860. TLG 4089.023.

Walafridius Strabo. "Glossa Ordinaria, Third Book of Kings." In *Walafridi Strabi Opera omnia*. Edited by J.-P. Migne. PL 113, cols. 581-610. Paris: Migne, 1852.

Bibliography of Works in English Translation

Ambrose. "Cain and Abel." In *Hexameron, Paradise, and Cain and Abel,* pp. 359-437. Translated by John J. Savage. FC 42. Washington, D.C.: The Catholic University of America Press, 1961.

———. "Concerning Virgins." In *Select Works and Letters,* pp. 363-87. Translated by H. De Romestin. NPNF 10. Series 2. Edited by Philip Schaff and Henry Wace. 14 vols. 1886-1900. Reprint, Peabody, Mass.: Hendrickson, 1994.

———. "Consolation on the Death of Emperor Valentinian." In *Funeral Orations by Saint Gregory Nazianzen and Saint Ambrose,* pp. 265-99. Translated by Roy J. Deferrari. FC 22. Washington, D.C.: The Catholic University of America Press, 1953.

———. "Duties of the Clergy." In *Select Works and Letters,* pp. 1-89. Translated by H. De Romestin. NPNF 10. Series 2. Edited by Philip Schaff and Henry Wace. 14 vols. 1886-1900. Reprint, Peabody, Mass.: Hendrickson, 1994.

———. "Flight from the World." In *Seven Exegetical Works,* pp. 281-323. Translated by Michael P. McHugh. FC 65. Washington, D.C.: The Catholic University of America Press, 1972.

———. "Jacob and the Happy Life." In *Seven Exegetical Works,* pp. 117-84. Translated by Michael P. McHugh. FC 65. Washington, D.C.: The Catholic University of America Press, 1972.

———. *Letters.* Translated by Mary Melchior Beyenka. FC 26. 1954. Reprint, Washington, D.C.: The Catholic University of America Press, 1987.

———. *On Elias [Elijah] and Fasting.* Translated by M. J. A. Buck. PSt 19. Washington D.C.: The Catholic University of America Press, 1929.

———. "On Theodosius." In *Funeral Orations by Saint Gregory Nazianzen and Saint Ambrose,* pp. 307-32. Translated by Roy J. Deferrari. FC 22. Washington, D.C.: The Catholic University of America Press, 1953.

———. "The Prayer of Job and David." In *Seven Exegetical Works,* pp. 329-420. Translated by Michael P. McHugh. FC 65. Washington, D.C.: The Catholic University of America Press, 1972.

———. *S. Ambrosii De Nabuthae [Saint Ambrose on Naboth].* Translated by M. McGuire. PSt 15. Washington D.C.: The Catholic University of America Press, 1927.

Aphrahat. "Demonstrations." In *Gregory the Great, Ephraim Syrus, Aphrahat,* pp. 345-412. Translated by James Barmby. NPNF 13. Series 2. Edited by Philip Schaff and Henry Wace. 14 vols. 1886-1900. Reprint, Peabody, Mass.: Hendrickson, 1994.

———. "Demonstration IV, on Prayer." In *The Syriac Fathers on Prayer and the Spiritual Life,* pp. 5-25. Translated by Sebastian Brock. CS 101. Kalamazoo, Mich.: Cistercian Publications, 1987.

Athanasius. "Defense Before Constantius." See "Apology to the Emperor." In *Selected Works and Letters,* pp. 238-53. Translated by M. Atkinson. Revised by Archibald Robertson. NPNF 4. Series 2. Edited by Philip Schaff and Henry Wace. 14 vols. 1886-1900. Reprint, Peabody, Mass.: Hendrickson, 1994.

———. "Discourses Against the Arians." In *Select Works and Letters,* pp. 306-447 [Fourth Oration Considered Spurious]. Translated by John Henry Newman. Revised by Archibald Robertson. NPNF 4. Series 2. Edited by Philip Schaff and Henry Wace. 14 vols. 1886-1900. Reprint, Peabody, Mass.: Hendrickson, 1994.

———. "Festal Letters." See *The Resurrection Letters.* Translated by Henry Burgess. Revised by Payne

Smith. Paraphrased and introduced by Jack N. Sparks. Nashville: Thomas Nelson, 1979.

———. "Life of St. Anthony." In *Early Christian Biographies*, pp. 133-216. Translated by Mary Emily Keenan. FC 15. Washington, D.C.: The Catholic University of America Press, 1952.

Augustine. "Admonition and Grace." In *Christian Instruction, Admonition and Grace, The Christian Combat, Faith Hope and Charity*, pp. 245-305. Translated by John Courtney Murray. FC 2. Washington, D.C.: The Catholic University of America Press, 1947.

———. *Against Julian*. Translated by Matthew A. Schumacher. FC 35. Washington, D.C.: The Catholic University of America Press, 1957.

———. "Against Lying." In *Treatises on Various Subjects*, pp. 125-79. Translated by Harold B. Jaffee. FC 16. Washington, D.C.: The Catholic University of America Press, 1952.

———. *Anti-Pelagian Writings*, pp. 377-434. Translated by Peter Holmes and Robert Ernest Wallis. Revised by Benjamin Warfield. NPNF 5. Series 1. Edited by Philip Schaff. 14 vols. 1886-1889. Reprint, Peabody, Mass.: Hendrickson, 1994.

———. "The Care to Be Taken for the Dead." In *Treatises on Marriage and Other Subjects*, pp. 351-84. Translated by John A. Lacy. FC 27. New York: Fathers of the Church, Inc., 1955.

———. "Christian Instruction." In *Christian Instruction, Admonition and Grace, The Christian Combat, Faith Hope and Charity*, pp. 27-235. Translated by John Courtney Murray. FC 2. Washington, D.C.: The Catholic University of America Press, 1947.

———. *City of God: Books 8-16* and *Books 17-22*. Translated by Gerald G. Walsh, Daniel J. Honan, and Grace Monahan. FC 14 and 24. Washington, D.C.: The Catholic University of America Press, 1952-1954.

———. "Eight Questions of Dulcitius." In *Treatises on Various Subjects*, pp. 427-66. Translated by Mary E. Deferrari. FC 16. Washington, D.C.: The Catholic University of America Press, 1952.

———. *Expositions of the Psalms*. Translated by Maria Boulding. WSA 15-19. Part 3. Edited by John E. Rotelle. New York: New City Press, 2000-2003.

———. *Expositions on the Book of Psalms*. Edited from the Oxford translation by A. Cleveland Coxe. NPNF 8. Series 1. Edited by Philip Schaff. 14 vols. 1886-1889. Reprint, Peabody, Mass.: Hendrickson, 1994.

———. *Letters*. 4 vols. Translated by Wilfred Parsons. FC 12, 18, 20 and 30. Washington, D.C.: The Catholic University of America Press, 1951-1955.

———. "The Nature and Origin of the Soul." In *Answer to the Pelagians*, pp. 473-561. Translated by Roland J. Teske. WSA 23. Part 1. Edited by John E. Rotelle. New York: New City Press, 1997.

———. "On Grace and Free Will." In *Anti-Pelagian Writings*, pp. 443-65. Translated by Peter Holmes and Robert Ernest Wallis. Revised by Benjamin Warfield. NPNF 5. Series 1. Edited by Philip Schaff. 14 vols. 1886-1889. Reprint, Peabody, Mass.: Hendrickson, 1994.

———. "On Grace and Free Will." In *The Teacher, The Free Choice of the Will, Grace and Free Will*, pp. 250-308. Translated by Robert P. Russell. FC 59. Washington, D.C.: The Catholic University of America Press, 1968.

———. "Predestination of the Saints." In *Four Anti-Pelagian Writings*, pp. 218-70. Translated by John A. Mourant and William J. Collinge. FC 86. Washington, D.C.: The Catholic University of America Press, 1992.

———. *Sermons*. Translated by Edmund Hill. WSA 1-11. Part 3. Edited by John E. Rotelle. New York: New City Press, 1990-1997.

———. "Sermons." In *Sermons on the Liturgical Seasons*. Translated by Mary Sarah Muldowney. FC 38. Washington, D.C.: The Catholic University of America Press, 1959.

Basil the Great. "Homilies on the Psalms." In *Exegetic Homilies*, pp. 151-359. Translated by Agnes Clare

Way. FC 46. Washington, D.C.: The Catholic University of America Press, 1963.

———. *Letters*. Translated by Agnes Clare Way. FC 28. Washington, D.C.: The Catholic University of America Press, 1955.

———. "On Humility." In *Ascetical Works*, pp. 475-86. Translated by M. Monica Wagner. FC 9. New York: Fathers of the Church, Inc., 1950.

Bede. *Commentary on the Acts of the Apostles*. Translated by Lawrence T. Martin. CS 117. Kalamazoo, Mich.: Cistercian Publications, 1989.

———. *Homilies on the Gospels*. Translated by Lawrence T. Martin and David Hurst. CS 110 and 111. Kalamazoo, Mich.: Cistercian Publications, 1991.

———. *On Ezra and Nehemiah*. Translated by Scott DeGregorio. TTH 47. Liverpool: Liverpool University Press, 2006.

———. *On the Temple*. Translated by Sean Connolly. TTH 21. Liverpool: Liverpool University Press, 1995.

Caesarius of Arles. *Sermons*. 3 vols. Translated by Mary Magdeleine Mueller. FC 31, 47 and 66. Washington, D.C.: The Catholic University of America Press, 1956-1973.

Cassian, John. *Conferences*. Translated and annotated by Boniface Ramsey. ACW 57. Mahwah, N.J.: Paulist Press, 1997.

———. "Institutes." In *Sulpitius Severus, Vincent of Lerins, John Cassian*, pp. 201-90. Translated by Edgar C. S. Gibson. NPNF 11. Series 2. Edited by Philip Schaff and Henry Wace. 14 vols. 1886-1900. Reprint, Peabody, Mass.: Hendrickson, 1994.

Cassiodorus. *Explanation of the Psalms*. 3 vols. Translated and annotated by P. G. Walsh. ACW 51, 52 and 53. Mahwah, N.J.: Paulist Press, 1990-1991.

Clement of Alexandria. *Christ the Educator*. Translated by Simon P. Wood. FC 23. Washington, D.C.: The Catholic University of America Press, 1954.

———. "Fragment 12." In *Fathers of the Second Century: Hermas, Tatian, Athenagoras, Theophilus, and Clement of Alexandria (Entire)*, pp. 584-87. Translated by William Wilson. ANF 2. Edited by Alexander Roberts and James Donaldson. 10 vols. 1885-1887. Reprint, Peabody, Mass.: Hendrickson, 1994.

———. *Stromateis*. Translated by John Ferguson. FC 85. Washington, D.C.: The Catholic University of America Press, 1991.

Clement of Rome. "The Letter of St. Clement of Rome to the Corinthians." In *The Apostolic Fathers*, pp. 9-58. Translated by Francis X. Glimm. FC 1. New York: Christian Heritage, Inc., 1947.

"Constitutions of the Holy Apostles." In *Lactantius, Venantius, Asterius, Victorinus, Dionysius, Apostolic Teaching and Constitutions, 2 Clement, Early Liturgies*, pp. 385-508. Translated by W. Whiston. Revised by Irah Chase. ANF 7. Edited by Alexander Roberts and James Donaldson. 10 vols. 1885-1887. Reprint, Peabody, Mass.: Hendrickson, 1994.

Cyprian. "Exhortation to Martyrdom." In *Treatises*, pp. 313-44. Translated by Roy J. Deferrari. FC 36. Washington, D.C.: The Catholic University of America Press, 1958.

———. *Letters 1-81*. Translated by Rose Bernard Donna. FC 51. Washington, D.C.: The Catholic University of America Press, 1964.

———. "The Lord's Prayer." In *Treatises*, pp. 127-59. Translated by Roy J. Deferrari. FC 36. Washington, D.C.: The Catholic University of America Press, 1958.

———. "The Unity of the Catholic Church." In *Early Latin Theology*, pp. 124-42. Translated by S. L. Greenslade. LCC 5. Philadelphia: The Westminster Press, 1956.

Cyril of Jerusalem. "Catechetical Lectures." In *The Works of Saint Cyril of Jerusalem, Volume 1*. Translated by Leo P. McCauley and Anthony A. Stephenson. FC 61. Washington, D.C.: The Catholic University of America Press, 1969.

————. "Mystagogical Lectures." In *The Works of Saint Cyril of Jerusalem, Volume 2*, pp. 153-203. Translated by Leo P. McCauley and Anthony A. Stephenson. FC 64. Washington, D.C.: The Catholic University of America Press, 1970.

Ephrem the Syrian. "A Homily on the Solitaries, Desert-dwellers and Monks, and on Those Who Dwell in the Mountains, Dens, Caves, and Clefts of the Earth, and on Those Who Have Stripped Themselves of All Things Earthly." In *The Ascetical Homilies of Saint Isaac the Syrian*, pp. 471-80. Boston, Mass.: Holy Transfiguration Monastery, 1984.

————. *Hymns on Paradise*. Translated by Sebastian Brock. Crestwood, N.Y.: St. Vladimir's Seminary Press, 1990.

————. "The Pearl: Seven Hymns on the Faith." In *Gregory the Great, Ephraim Syrus, Aphrahat*, pp. 293-301. Translated by J. B. Morris. NPNF 13. Series 2. Edited by Philip Schaff and Henry Wace. 14 vols. 1886-1900. Reprint, Peabody, Mass.: Hendrickson, 1994.

————. *Saint Ephrem's Commentary on Tatian's Diatessaron: An English Translation of Chester Beatty Syriac MS 709*. Translated by Carmel McCarthy. *Journal of Semitic Studies* Supplement 2. Oxford: Oxford University Press for the University of Manchester, 1993.

Eusebius of Caesarea. *Proof of the Gospel*. 2 vols. Translated by W. J. Ferrar. London: SPCK, 1920. Reprint, Grand Rapids, Mich.: Baker, 1981.

Fulgentius of Ruspe. "Letters." In *Selected Works*, pp. 280-565. Translated by Robert B. Eno. FC 95. Washington, D.C.: The Catholic University of America Press, 1997.

Gregory of Nazianzus. "The Last Farewell, Oration 42." In *Cyril of Jerusalem, Gregory Nazianzen*, pp. 385-95. Translated by Charles Gordon Browne and James Edward Swallow. NPNF 7. Series 2. Edited by Philip Schaff and Henry Wace. 14 vols. 1886-1900. Reprint, Peabody, Mass.: Hendrickson, 1994.

————. "On Theology, Theological Oration 2(28)." In *Cyril of Jerusalem, Gregory Nazianzen*, pp. 288-301. Translated by Charles Gordon Browne and James Edward Swallow. NPNF 7. Series 2. Edited by Philip Schaff and Henry Wace. 14 vols. 1886-1900. Reprint, Peabody, Mass.: Hendrickson, 1994.

————. "Oration 39." In *Cyril of Jerusalem, Gregory Nazianzen*, pp. 352-59. Translated by Charles Gordon Browne and James Edward Swallow. NPNF 7. Series 2. Edited by Philip Schaff and Henry Wace. 14 vols. 1886-1900. Reprint, Peabody, Mass.: Hendrickson, 1994.

————. "Orations." In *Cyril of Jerusalem, Gregory Nazianzen*, pp. 203-434. Translated by Charles Gordon Browne and James Edward Swallow. NPNF 7. Series 2. Edited by Philip Schaff and Henry Wace. 14 vols. 1886-1900. Reprint, Peabody, Mass.: Hendrickson, 1994.

Gregory the Great. *Dialogues*. Translated by Odo John Zimmerman. FC 39. Washington, D.C.: The Catholic University of America Press in association with Consortium Books, 1959.

————. "Letters." In *Gregory the Great, Ephraim Syrus, Aphrahat*, pp. 1-111. Translated by James Barmby. NPNF 13. Series 2. Edited by Philip Schaff and Henry Wace. 14 vols. 1886-1900. Reprint, Peabody, Mass.: Hendrickson, 1994.

————. *Morals on the Book of Job*. Translated by Members of the English Church. LF 18. Oxford: John Henry Parker, 1844.

Hippolytus. "Fragment on Proverbs." In *Hippolytus, Cyprian, Caius, Novatian*, pp. 172-76. Translated by S. D. F. Salmond. ANF 5. Edited by Alexander Roberts and James Donaldson. 10 vols. 1885-1887. Reprint, Peabody, Mass.: Hendrickson, 1994.

Isaac of Nineveh. "Discourses." In *The Syriac Fathers on Prayer and the Spiritual Life*, pp. 246-63. Translated by Sebastian Brock. CS 101. Kalamazoo, Mich.: Cistercian Publications, 1987.

Jerome. "Against Jovinianus." In *Letters and Selected Works*, pp. 346-416. Translated by W. H. Fremantle et al. NPNF 6. Series 2. Edited by Philip Schaff and Henry Wace. 14 vols. 1886-1900. Reprint, Peabody, Mass.: Hendrickson, 1994.

————. "Against the Pelagians." In *Dogmatic and Polemical Works*, pp. 230-378. Translated by John N. Hritzu. FC 53. Washington, D.C.: The Catholic University of America Press, 1965.

————. "Against the Pelagians." In *Letters and Selected Works*, pp. 448-83. Translated by W. H. Fremantle et al. NPNF 6. Series 2. Edited by Philip Schaff and Henry Wace. 14 vols. 1886-1900. Reprint, Peabody, Mass.: Hendrickson, 1994.

————. "Homilies on the Psalms." In *The Homilies of Saint Jerome*. Vol. 1. Translated by Marie Liguori Ewald. FC 48. Washington, D.C.: The Catholic University of America Press, 1964.

————. "Letters." In *Letters and Selected Works*, pp. 1-295. Translated by W. H. Fremantle et al. NPNF 6. Series 2. Edited by Philip Schaff and Henry Wace. 14 vols. 1886-1900. Reprint, Peabody, Mass.: Hendrickson, 1994.

John Chrysostom. "Against the Anomoeans." In *On the Incomprehensible Nature of God*, pp. 51-163. Translated by Paul W. Harkins. FC 72. Washington, D.C.: The Catholic University of America Press, 1984.

————. *Discourses Against Judaizing Christians*. Translated by Paul W. Harkins. FC 68. Washington, D.C.: The Catholic University of America Press, 1979.

————. *Homilies on Genesis, 18-45*. Translated by Robert C. Hill. FC 82. Washington, D.C.: The Catholic University of America Press, 1990.

————. "Homilies on the Gospel of John." In *Commentary on Saint John the Apostle and Evangelist, Homilies 1-47 and 48-88*. Translated by Thomas Aquinas Goggin. FC 33 and 41. Washington, D.C.: The Catholic University of America Press, 1957-1959.

————. *Homilies on the Gospel of Matthew*. Translated by George Prevost. Revised by M. B. Riddle. NPNF 10. Series 1. Edited by Philip Schaff. 14 vols. 1886-1889. Reprint, Peabody, Mass.: Hendrickson, 1994.

————. "Homilies on St. Ignatius and St. Babylas." In *On the Priesthood, Ascetic Treatises, Select Homilies and Letters, Homilies on the Statues*, pp. 135-43. Translated by T. P. Brandram. NPNF 9. Series 1. Edited by Philip Schaff. 14 vols. 1886-1889. Reprint, Peabody, Mass.: Hendrickson, 1994.

————. "Letters to the Fallen Theodore." In *On the Priesthood, Ascetic Treatises, Select Homilies and Letters, Homilies on the Statues*, pp. 91-116. Translated by W. R. W. Stephens. NPNF 9. Series 1. Edited by Philip Schaff. 14 vols. 1886-1889. Reprint, Peabody, Mass.: Hendrickson, 1994.

————. "On the Epistle to the Hebrews." In *Homilies on the Gospel of Saint John and the Epistle to the Hebrews*, pp. 363-522. Edited from the Oxford translation by Frederic Gardiner. NPNF 14. Series 1. Edited by Philip Schaff. 14 vols. 1886-1889. Reprint, Peabody, Mass.: Hendrickson, 1994.

John of Damascus. *On the Divine Images*. Translated by David Anderson. Crestwood, N.Y.: St. Vladimir's Seminary Press, 1980.

Justin Martyr. "Dialogue with Trypho." In *Writings of Saint Justin Martyr*, pp. 147-366. Translated by Thomas B. Falls. FC 6. New York: Christian Heritage, Inc., 1948.

————. "First Apology." In *Early Christian Fathers*, pp. 242-89. Translated by Cyril C. Richardson et al. LCC 1. Philadelphia: The Westminster Press, 1953.

Lactantius. "Epitome of the Divine Institutes." In *Lactantius, Venantius, Asterius, Victorinus, Dionysius, Apostolic Teaching and Constitutions, 2 Clement, Early Liturgies*, pp. 224-55. Translated by William Fletcher. ANF 7. Edited by Alexander Roberts and James Donaldson. 10 vols. 1885-1887. Reprint, Peabody, Mass.: Hendrickson, 1994.

Maximus of Turin. *The Sermons of St. Maximus of Turin*. Translated by Boniface Ramsey. ACW 50. Mahwah, N.J., 1989.

Methodius. "The Banquet of the Ten Virgins or Concerning Chastity." In *Gregory Thaumaturgus, Dionysius the Great, Julius Africanus, Anatolius and Minor Writers, Methodius Arnobius*, pp. 309-55. Translated by William R. Clark. ANF 6. Edited by Alexander Roberts and James Donaldson. 10 vols. 1885-1887. Reprint, Peabody, Mass.: Hendrickson, 1994.

Novatian. "On the Trinity." In *The Trinity, The Spectacles, Jewish Foods, In Praise of Purity, Letters*, pp. 23-111. Translated by Russell J. DeSimone. FC 67. Washington, D.C.: The Catholic University of America Press, 1974.

Origen. "Against Celsus." In *Tertullian, Part Fourth; Minucius Felix; Commodian; Origen, Parts First and Second*, pp. 395-669. Translated by Frederick Crombie. ANF 4. Edited by Alexander Roberts and James Donaldson. 10 vols. 1885-1887. Reprint, Peabody, Mass.: Hendrickson, 1994.

————. *Commentary on the Gospel According to John, Books 1-10* and *Books 13-32*. Translated by Ronald E. Heine. FC 80 and 89. Washington, D.C.: The Catholic University of America Press, 1989-1993.

————. "Commentary on the Gospel of Matthew." Translated by John Patrick. ANF 9. Edited by Alexander Roberts and James Donaldson. 10 vols. 1885-1887. Reprint, Peabody, Mass.: Hendrickson, 1994.

————. "Commentary on the Song of Songs." In *Origen: An Exhortation to Martyrdom, Prayer, and Selected Works*, pp. 217-44. Translated by Rowan A. Greer. New York: Paulist Press, 1979.

————. "Commentary on the Song of Songs." In *The Song of Songs: Commentary and Homilies*, pp. 21-263. Translated by R. P. Lawson. ACW 26. New York: Newman Press, 1957

————. "Fragments from the Catena on Jeremiah." In *Homilies on Jeremiah, Homily on 1 Kings 28*, pp. 280-316. Translated by John Clark Smith. FC 97. Washington, D.C.: The Catholic University of America Press, 1998.

————. "Homilies on Genesis." In *Homilies on Genesis and Exodus*, pp. 47-224. Translated by Ronald E. Heine. FC 71. Washington, D.C.: The Catholic University of America Press, 1982.

————. "Homilies on Jeremiah." In *Homilies on Jeremiah, Homily on 1 Kings 28*, pp. 3-273. Translated by John Clark Smith. FC 97. Washington, D.C.: The Catholic University of America Press, 1998.

————. *Homilies on Leviticus*. Translated by Gary Wayne Barkley. FC 83. Washington, D.C.: The Catholic University of America Press, 1990.

————. "Correspondence Between Julius Africanus and Origen." In *Biblical Interpretation*, pp. 118-36. Translated Joseph W. Trigg. MFC 9. Wilmington, Del.: Michael Glazier, 1988.

————. "Homilies on the Gospel of Luke." In *Homilies on Luke, Fragments on Luke*, pp. 5-162. Translated by Joseph T. Lienhard. FC 94. Washington, D.C.: The Catholic University of America Press, 1996.

————. "On First Principles." In *Origen: An Exhortation to Martyrdom, Prayer, and Selected Works*, pp. 171-216. Translated by Rowan A. Greer. New York: Paulist Press, 1979.

————. "On First Principles." See "Origen De Principiis." In *Fathers of the Third Century*, pp. 239-382. Translated by Frederick Crombie. ANF 4. Edited by Alexander Roberts and James Donaldson. 10 vols. 1885-1887. Reprint, Peabody, Mass.: Hendrickson, 1994.

————. "Prayer." In *Prayer, Exhortation to Martyrdom*, pp. 15-140. Translated by John J. O'Meara. Westminster, Md.: Newman Press, 1954.

Paulinus of Nola. *The Poems of St. Paulinus of Nola*. Translated by P. G. Walsh. ACW 40. New York: Newman Press, 1975.

Peter Chrysologus. "Sermons." In *Saint Peter Chrysologus: Selected Sermons and Saint Valerian: Homilies*, pp. 25-282. Translated by George E. Ganss. FC 17. New York: Fathers of the Church, 1953.

Prudentius. "The Spiritual Combat." In *The Poems of Prudentius: Apologetic and Didactic Poems*, pp. 79-110. Translated by M. Clement Eagan. FC 52. Washington, D.C.: The Catholic University of America Press, 1965.

Pseudo-Dionysius. "Letters." In *Pseudo-Dionysius: The Complete Works*, pp. 263-89. Translated by Colm Luibheid. Mahwah, N.J.: Paulist Press, 1987.

Pseudo-Tertullian. "Five Books in Reply to Marcion." In *Tertullian, Part Fourth; Minucius Felix; Commodian; Origen, Parts First and Second,* pp. 142-65. Translated by S. Thelwall. ANF 4. Edited by Alexander Roberts and James Donaldson. 10 vols. 1885-1887. Reprint, Peabody, Mass.: Hendrickson, 1994.

Sahdona. "Book of Perfection." In *The Syriac Fathers on Prayer and the Spiritual Life,* pp. 202-37. Translated by Sebastian Brock. CS 101. Kalamazoo, Mich.: Cistercian Publications, 1987.

Salvian the Presbyter. "The Governance of God." In *The Writings of Salvian, the Presbyter,* pp. 27-232. Translated by Jeremiah F. O'Sullivan. FC 3. Reprint, Washington, D.C.: The Catholic University of America Press, 1962.

Tertullian. "An Answer to the Jews." In *Latin Christianity: Its Founder, Tertullian,* pp. 151-73. Translated by S. Thelwall. ANF 3. Edited by Alexander Roberts and James Donaldson. 10 vols. 1885-1887. Reprint, Peabody, Mass.: Hendrickson, 1994.

———. "On Fasting." In *Tertullian, Part Fourth; Minucius Felix; Commodian; Origen, Parts First and Second,* pp. 102-14. Translated by S. Thelwall. ANF 4. Edited by Alexander Roberts and James Donaldson. 10 vols. 1885-1887. Reprint, Peabody, Mass.: Hendrickson, 1994.

Theodoret of Cyr. *Commentary on the Song of Songs.* Translated by Robert C. Hill. ECS 2. Brisbane: Center for Early Christian Studies, 2001.

Authors/Writings Index

Subject Index

Scripture Index